The Doctrine of Justification

THE DOCTRINE OF JUSTIFICATION

AN OUTLINE OF

ITS HISTORY IN THE CHURCH

AND OF

ITS EXPOSITION FROM SCRIPTURE

The Second Series of the "Cunningham Lectures"

BY

James Buchanan, D.D., LL.D.

Introduction by Roger Nicole

SOLID GROUND CHRISTIAN BOOKS
BIRMINGHAM, ALABAMA USA

Solid Ground Christian Books
PO Box 660132
Birmingham, AL 35266
205-443-0311
sgcb@charter.net
http://solid-ground-books.com

THE DOCTRINE OF JUSTIFICATION
An Outline of its History in the Church,
And of its Exposition from Scripture

James Buchanan (1804-1870)

Solid Ground Classic Reprints

First edition May 2006

Taken from 1970 edition by Baker Books, Grand Rapids, MI

Cover work by Borgo Design, Tuscaloosa, AL
Contact them at nelbrown@comcast.net

Cover image is Edinburgh Castle which was seen nearly everyday by the author as he labored for Christ at the New College.

1-59925-073-X

FOREWORD

The Value of
Buchanan's *Doctrine of Justification*
in Light of the Current Debate on Justification

Among the doctrines of grace, justification is the most susceptible to, and least tolerant of imprecision. A great illustration of this fact comes from the little-known Colloquy of Ratisbon in 1541. At this Colloquy six theologians attempted to come to a consensual statement on the doctrine of Justification. Eck, Gropper, and Pflug represented the Catholic side and Melancthon, Bucer, and Pistorius the Protestant side. In the end, the statement that was crafted proved satisfactory to neither side. Though the Catholics in the Colloquy had conceded significantly to the Protestants, yet one point remained ambiguous. This point concerned the nature of the faith that justifies. They all could agree to the statement that justification was by faith. However, as they conceived of the nature of the faith that justifies, they differed fundamentally. This point, then, made it impossible for the Protestants to subscribe to Ratisbon, and the Catholic side denounced it as well. Buchanan aptly summarized the outcome as follows: "It had too much of the Gospel in it to be palatable to the consistent adherents of Rome, and too much of disguised legalism to be acceptable to the Reformed" (p. 134).

The great lesson of Ratisbon, of course, is the danger of equivocating on any aspect of justification. In the words of James Buchanan, Ratisbon "shows the possibility of appearing to concede almost everything, while one point is reserved or wrapped up in ambiguous language, which is found afterwards sufficient to neutralize every concession, and to leave the parties as much at variance as before" (p. 136).

Though the lessons of Ratisbon and other Reformational and post-Reformational arguments are many, few today consult them. In the current controversy surrounding justification, prompted by the so-called "New Perspective on Paul," we would do well to review past controversies. I believe that we would find that the "New Perspective on Paul" is for the most part *not new*, just as the rejoinders to it are not new. A clear, concise, and compelling treatment of the doctrine, based on Scripture, and delineated against past controversies would prove immensely valuable. Buchanan's *Justification* affords such value.

The Current Controversy

Throughout the past centuries, there have been many and varied challenges to the Reformation understanding of justification. There was, of course, the Catholic challenge culminating in the Council of Trent (1545-1563). There was the Socinian challenge; the Neonomian challenge, the Hopkinsian challenge, and others as well. The latest challenge is known as "The New Perspective on Paul" (NPP). This is a common-place name for a variety of related views on what Paul teaches concerning law, covenant, church, and justification, that distinguishes itself from the old, Protestant Perspective.[1] At the heart of NPP is the contention that Paul's arguments regarding justification did not deal with the issue of whether or not individuals could earn salvation; rather they addressed the issue of whether Gentiles should be accepted into the church alongside of Jews apart from some of the ethnic and ceremonial boundary-markers, such as circumcision and the

---

[1] A good, overall guide to the NPP is Guy Prentiss Waters, *Justification and the New Perspectives on Paul: A Review and Response* (Phillipsburg, NJ: Presbyterian and Reformed, 2004). The term "New Perspective on Paul" was coined by James Dunn, himself an advocate of, and original thinker within the NPP (see J. D. G. Dunn, "The New Perspective on Paul" *Bulletin of the John Rylands University Library of Manchester* 65 [1983]: 95-122).

dietary laws. Instead of being primarily a soteriological doctrine, justification, according to the NPP, is primarily ecclesiological and social.

One of the driving forces behind the NPP is the charge that the Protestants have misconstrued first-century Judaism. This has been vigorously and systematically argued by E. P. Sanders in various works.[2] On the basis of a large-scale study of pre-Rabbinic sources, he concluded that first century Judaism was not legalistic, as the Reformers and their heirs suggested. Instead, he termed the regnant paradigm a "non-legalistic covenantal nomism." His oft-quoted definition runs as follows: "[C]ovenantal nomism is the view that one's place in God's plan is established on the basis of the covenant and that the covenant requires as the proper response of man his obedience to its commandments, while providing means of atonement for transgression." Thus "the intention and effort to be obedient constitute the *condition for remaining in the covenant*, but they do not *earn* it" (emphasis his).[3]

In his re-interpretation of Paul, Sanders sees little significance for the "forensic" or "judicial" in Paul's view of salvation. Instead, he considers the "participationistic" as the fundamental category in Paul. Paul only uses the forensic as another and inferior way to show that man needs Christ.[4] Sanders is famous for his contention that Paul's basic hermeneutical move is from "solution" (Christ) to "plight" (sin).[5]   The forensic emphasis thus only helped Paul rhetorically construe the plight of man, and is not a distinct emphasis alongside of his real center, namely participation in Christ. In fact, according to Sanders, Paul's judicial language is "defective, lacking a discussion of repentance, and forgiveness, and guilt."[6]

---

[2] See especially, E. P. Sanders, *Paul and Palestinian Judaism: A Comparison of Patterns of Religion* (Philadelphia: Fortress, 1977).
[3] Sanders, *Paul and Palestinian Judaism*, 75, 180.
[4] Sanders, *Paul and Palestinian Judaism*, 488-506.
[5] See especially E. P. Sanders, *Paul, the Law, and the Jewish People* (Philadelphia: Fortress, 1983).
[6] Sanders, *Paul and Palestinian Judaism*, 503.

Others have offered their own reconstructions of Paul, based on Sanders' work on Judaism, but differing from Sanders on Paul himself. Notably, James Dunn has written extensively on Paul's phrase "the works of the law."[7] He has persuaded many that Paul did not have in mind good works, which presumably would merit rewards, but rather "ethnic boundary markers" or "badges of membership." According to Dunn, Paul was arguing against a sense of distinctiveness and privilege of Israel because they possessed the Torah—especially circumcision, the Sabbath, and their dietary laws. Moreover, according to Dunn, we should understand righteousness as a relational concept. It involves meeting obligations laid upon a person as part of a framework of relationship. God's righteousness refers to his faithfulness in creating and sustaining his relationship with Israel and the world.[8] Israel's mistake, according to Dunn, was not that it was ignorant of God's righteousness in general; instead, it was that Israel conceived of its exhibition too narrowly, too exclusively, and tied its display to the maintenance of certain ethnic and ceremonial markers.[9]

The other main influential representative of the NPP is the prolific N. T. Wright.[10] Like Dunn, he argues that the problem with the Jews in Paul's day was their focus on a "truncated covenant status focused on zeal, flesh, and ethnocentric exclusivity."[11]

Thus, Paul's main concern, in Wright's words, is not: "How can individual sinners find salvation? But rather, Are Christian Jews bound, by the Jewish kosher laws, to eat

---

[7] See J. D. G. Dunn, "New Perspective on Paul"; and "Works of the Law and Curse of the Law (Galatians 3.10-14)," *New Testament Studies* 31 (1985): 523-43. Both of these articles have been reprinted in J. D. G. Dunn, *Jesus, Paul, and the Law: Studies in Mark and Galatians* (Louisville: Westminster John Knox, 1990). See also J. D. G. Dunn, *The Theology of Paul the Apostle* (Grand Rapids: Eerdmans, 1998).

[8] Dunn, *Theology of Paul*, 341-344.

[9] J. D. G. Dunn, *Romans*, Vol 2: *9-16* (Word Biblical Commentary; Waco: Word, 1988), 587.

[10] A condensed and accessible version of Wright's thought can be found in N. T. Wright, *What Saint Paul Really Said: Was Paul of Tarsus the Real Founder of Christianity?* (Grand Rapids: Eerdmans, 1997).

[11] I owe this phrase to Waters, *Justification and the New Perspective on Paul*, 148.

separately from Christian Gentiles, or are they bound by the gospel to eat at the same table with them?"[12]

In Galatians, for example, Wright sees Paul's main aim as persuading the Galatians to see themselves within the covenantal "narrative structure" of Israel. They are to regard themselves "as the children of Abraham, the heirs of the entire Jewish narrative."[13]

As a result, Wright conceives of the juristic emphasis as part and parcel of the participationist emphasis. He writes:

> The story of the new exodus in Christ, and the homeward journey of God's people led by the Spirit, provides the setting for incorporative and participationist language to have its full meaning and weight simultaneously with the juristic meaning of justification. Because of sin, and the distortion of Torah by the people to whom it was given, the fulfillment of the covenant cannot but come about as an apocalyptic event, declaring God's judgment on what has gone before and God's new creation of what is now beginning. But when the dust settles and God's renewed people look around them, they discover that this apocalyptic event is indeed the fulfillment of God's promises to Abraham. This is how God is faithful to the covenant.[14]

Thus justification, according to Wright,

> is not the general, abstract theological issue of, shall we say, how to go to heaven when one dies. It was not part of a theory of soteriology, understood in this way. It was the question of whether Christian Jews ought or ought not eat with Christian Gentiles. In other words, it addressed the question of the *identity and demarcation* of the people of God, now redefined in Jesus Christ—a question that is both

---

[12] N. T. Wright, "The Letter to the Galatians: Exegesis and Theology," in *Between Two Horizons: Spanning New Testament Studies and Systematic Theology,* Joel B. Green and Max Turner, eds., (Grand Rapids: Eerdmans, 2000), 209.
[13] Wright, "Galatians," 231.
[14] Wright, "Galatians," 233.

sociological, in the sense that it has to do with a
community and its behavior, which can itself be
understood by the proper application of sociological
methods, and theological, in the sense that this
community believes itself to be the people of God
who has drawn up quite clear conditions precisely
for its communal life.[15]

Stating it more succinctly, Wright contends that justification
"is the recognition and declaration by God that those who
are thus called and believing are in fact his people, the single
family promised to Abraham, that as the new covenant
people their sins are forgiven, and that since they have
already died and been raised with the Messiah they are
assured of final bodily resurrection at the last."[16]

Besides a present justification, there is also a "future
justification." In Wright's words, "Present justification
declares, on the basis of faith, what future justification will
affirm publicly on the basis of the entire life."[17]

In summary, then, the NPP offers a variety of nuanced
views on justification, faith, and covenant, which present
themselves in opposition to the classical view of the
Reformers. The nexus of these views is a revised
understanding of Judaism, and the thrust of these views
offers a vision of the gospel that essentially subordinates the
judicial to the transformative in the gospel and reformulates
other related doctrines, such as sin, atonement, and faith
accordingly.[18]

The Relevance of Buchanan's *Doctrine of Justification*

The relevance of Buchanan to the present day controversy on
justification is chiefly in four areas: biblical, historical,
theological, and experiential.

---

[15] Wright, "Galatians," 233,234.
[16] Wright, "Galatians," 235.
[17] Wright, *What Saint Paul Really Said*, 129.
[18] We cannot here deal with all the "cousins" of the NPP, including the Federal
Vision, Auburn Avenue Theology, and Norman Shepherd. I refer the reader to a
succinct but telling treatment in Guy Waters, *Justification and the New
Perspective on Paul*, 191-212.

Biblical

Buchanan treats the biblical foundation for the doctrine of justification in two steps: first, as it is found in the Old Testament, and secondly, as it was formulated during the age of the Apostles in the controversy with the Judaizers. Buchanan offers a lucid treatment of the controversy, which is rather relevant given the current debates. He traces the connection between the Judaizing controversy and the doctrine of justification.

Buchanan shows how this controversy was understandable given the times and the shift from the old, ceremonial economy to the new, spiritual economy. This controversy raised the important point whether obedience of any kind, both to the ceremonial and the moral law, can be part and parcel of a sinner's merit before God. It occasioned the apostles' clear delineation of justification without works of any kind, whether ceremonial or moral. Buchanan shows how this is clear not only from the explicit teaching of the apostles, but also from the insinuations of their detractors. Their charge, "Shall we continue in sin that grace may abound?" (Rom 6:1), shows, in the words of Buchanan, "that the Justification of which he [Paul] spoke was not understood on either side to be Sanctification, or to depend at all on Sanctification as its ground,—for there could be no room for the objection, if Paul was supposed to teach that men are justified by their infused or inherent righteousness" (pp.74-75). This and many similar points show us the abiding value of Buchanan's astute biblical analysis.

Historical

Extremely illuminating is Buchanan's treatment of the history of the doctrine of justification, specifically the corruption of the doctrine by Catholicism, Socinianism, Neo-nomianism, and other movements. Particularly since much of modern-day liberalism espouses a Socinianism *Revivus*, particularly on the person of Christ and the nature of his atonement, it is not surprising that the Socinian view of justification would prevail in our current setting. Buchanan defines the Socinian view of justification as "sinners obtain[ing] pardon and acceptance with God through His mere mercy, on the ground of their own repentance and reformation" (p. 162). It is notable that the Socinians would maintain speech such as "justification by faith," "by grace," etc., while in the meantime redefining each to include man's personal repentance and reformation.

Not only does Buchanan offer surveys of these views, but arguments against them as well. Therein lies a considerable portion of his current-day value. Since our age suffers from considerable historical amnesia, including and particularly in the area of theology, Buchanan's treatment of the history of theological controversy is refreshing and illuminating.

Theological

Undoubtedly, the most significant contribution of Buchanan's *Justification*, is his theological clarity, finesse, and comprehensiveness. His arguments are as relevant today in light of the NPP as they were in the 19th century. We saw above that the NPP has supplanted the forensic and judicial with the participationistic and transformative. Buchanan furnishes three arguments for why Scripture requires the forensic or judicial sense of the terms justification and righteousness. He calls these the antithetic, correlative, and equivalent arguments (pp. 229-233).

What is more, Buchanan shows the inextricability of the doctrine of justification to the doctrine of God, his holiness and justice, the spirituality and inflexibility of the moral law, the grand and crucial doctrine of Christ's satisfactory and propitiatory atonement, and the sovereignty of grace. Each one of these doctrines is worthy of careful treatment, and is connected to the other, and the doctrine of justification, so that if any falls, so do the others, especially, the doctrine of justification. Allow one quote from Buchanan to suffice:

> If they [the Reformers] held that God's justice requires the punishment of disobedience for the vindication of His law and the manifestation of His glory,—that men are universally chargeable with the guilt of original and actual sin,—that they are alike unwilling to be subject to God's law, and unable to yield perfect obedience to it,—that for them and their salvation, the Son of God became incarnate, and acted as Mediator between God and man,—that He executed the office of a Priest in offering Himself up as a sacrifice for sin,—that His sufferings were strictly penal, and properly vicarious,—and that they were both appointed and accepted by God as sufficient to render it consistent with His justice to extend mercy to the guilty, and to grant a full and free remission of their sins,—then, holding these views, they could hardly fail to believe that Christ's work is the meritorious procuring cause, and the only, but all-sufficient, ground of a sinner's justification (p. 164).

It is here that Buchanan shows the NPP for what it truly is. It requires a different view of God, a different view of the law, a different view of the atonement, and a different view of grace and faith. The interconnectedness of these Scriptural doctrines with the Reformed understanding of justification is so entire, that the smallest reformulation of justification entails a thoroughly altered view of religion.

Experiential

The final point of value in Buchanan's *Justification* is the thorough-going, experiential warmth that pervades the book. This is something the NPP and even some of its critics lack. Yet, it is precisely the personal and experiential relevance of the doctrine of justification that makes it so extremely precious to God's children. Their acceptance with God, their assuaged consciences, their hope of eternal life all depend on the proper construal of this doctrine. Buchanan simply excels in bringing this gloriously to the fore. Again, allow one quotation to represent thousands of instances through the book:

Some vague opinion in regard to His [God's] general mercy, or some undefined purpose to propitiate His favour by future repentance and amendment of life, before they are brought face to face with the awful realities of death, and judgment, and eternity, may suffice, in the meantime, as an answer to the accusing voice of conscience, and as an opiate to allay its forebodings and fears. But minds in this state never grapple with any of the real difficulties of the problem, and can scarcely be said to have the slightest apprehension of its true meaning. They overlook all the most momentous conditions which are involved in it, and on which its right solution depends. The Gospel of Christ alone has presented that problem in all its magnitude, and in its just proportions; and the Gospel of Christ alone has offered a solution of it, based on a full view of the Attributes of God,—of the unalterable requirements of His Law,—of the principles and ends of His Moral Government,—and of the state, character, and prospects of man, as a dying yet immortal being, chargeable with past guilt, and still depraved by inherent sin (p. 406).

Here and throughout the book, the godly will find justification not only a doctrine consonant with the Bible, vindicated throughout history, theologically integral, but also experientially vital.

Reformulations of the great doctrine of justification seem to require little ingenuity, whereas the defense of the doctrine obviously demands rigorous acumen. In Buchanan, we find such an excellent specimen of this rare acumen. May God use this magisterial treatment of this crucial doctrine to expose the NPP for what it is and settle the current controversy in its disfavor once and for all.

Dr. Gerald P. Bilkes
Puritan Reformed Theological Seminary
Grand Rapids, Michigan

PREFACE

THE Deed, by which the 'Cunningham Lectureship' was established in connection with the New College, requires that a certain number of Discourses shall be delivered, biennially, in the presence of the Principal, Professors, and Students; but provides also for the admission of non-professional hearers, should any such be disposed to attend. This provision seems to imply, that it was the wish of the liberal and enlightened Founder to make these Lectures useful beyond the College circle; and it may be held to indicate that they should be so constructed as to be suitable alike to an Academic and to a popular audience. It is necessary, therefore, to adapt the method of exposition to different classes, while the same truth in substance is proclaimed to all; and this may perhaps be best accomplished by presenting, in the body of the work, the substantial results of the inquiry, as one that is mainly directed to unfold the history, to explain the meaning, and to establish the truth, of a doctrine of Scripture; and reserving the processes by which these results have been attained, and the critical or controversial discussions by which they may be illustrated and defended, for Notes in an Appendix, containing such references to standard works, on each successive topic, as may serve to direct younger students to the best sources of information. The Notes are indicated by numerals inserted in the Text of each Lecture, which will be found to correspond with those in the Appendix. It has not been thought necessary to extend the Index beyond the body of the work, as the Notes in the Appendix are sufficiently indicated by the insertion of these numerals in the Text.

The topic for discussion in each series of the 'Cunningham Lectures' is left to be selected by the Author, subject to the consent of the Council. For the second series, the Doctrine of Justification by Grace through Faith has been chosen, after much serious reflection. In treating this important subject, it is proposed to offer, both an outline of its History in the Church, and an outline also of its Exposition from Scripture. There are various methods of teaching Theology, but the most important are the Historical and the Logical. They are both systematic, but they are founded on two different relations subsisting between the truths of Scripture; the first,

—on the relation of prior and posterior in respect to their chronological development,—the second, on the internal relation between them in respect to their doctrinal meaning, which arises from the fact that some truths necessarily presuppose certain other truths, and can neither be stated nor proved without reference to them. Each of these methods has some advantages which are peculiar to itself, and the combination of the two is necessary to any complete course of Theology. The one marks the successive unfoldings of divine truth, and the various controversies which have arisen in regard to it; the other, keeping in view the doctrinal results of that history, expounds the lessons of Scripture, in the light which has thus been shed upon them. Every great doctrine of Scripture might be treated in this way; and that of Justification having been selected, an outline of its History in the Church is given, as introductory to an outline of its Exposition from Scripture. The former only was delivered from the chair, as far as time permitted, and constitutes properly the second series of the 'Cunningham Lectures;' the latter is offered as a sequel to it, which, it is hoped, will not be deemed unseasonable in the present critical times. From the nature of this complex plan, it was unavoidable that the same topics should occur more than once; but if they are presented in new aspects and relations, and applied in different ways, any instances of this kind can scarcely be regarded as mere repetitions. Cross references are occasionally inserted where the same topic is lightly touched in one place, and more fully treated in another.

INTRODUCTION

JAMES BUCHANAN was born at Paisley, Scotland in 1804. After carrying classical studies at the University of Glasgow and theological studies in Edinburgh, he was ordained to the Gospel ministry in 1827 at Roslin near Edinburgh. In 1828 he accepted a call to North Leith where he remained until 1840, gaining there the reputation of being one of the most gifted and heart moving preachers of the Church of Scotland. In 1840 he went to the High Church, St. Giles in Edinburgh, where he remained until the disruption in 1843. After that he accepted the pastorate of St. Stephens Free Church where he stayed only two years, having been called to the chair of apologetics in New College, Edinburgh. After the death of Thomas Chalmers, he became professor of divinity and continued in this position until his retirement in 1868.

He left a number of volumes: *Comfort in Affliction*, 1837, of which more than 25 thousand copies have been sold; *Improvement of Affliction*, 1840; *Office and Work of The Holy Spirit*, 1842; *On the "Tracts for the Times"*, 1843; *Faith in God and Atheism Compared in their Essential Nature, Theoretic Grounds and Practical Influence*, 2 vols., 1855; *Modern Atheism under its Form of Pantheism, Materialism, Secularism, Development, and Natural Laws*, (extracts from the previous work), 1857; *The "Essays and Reviews" Examined*, 1861; *Analogy Considered as a Guide to Truth and Applied as an Aid to Faith*, 1864.

In 1866 he delivered the second series of Cunningham lectures on the *Doctrine of Justification; an Outline of its History in the Church and of its Exposition from Scripture*. This was published in 1867 and remains to this day one of the finest works on the subject, written at any time in any language. In it Buchanan showed a profound acquaintance with the history of the doctrine and a masterful grasp of its Scriptural foundations, as well as of its position in the system of Christian truth. This work may easily be viewed as the finest achievement from his pen. One of the most significant of the great Cunningham lectures, it is a worthy product of a period of the history of the church which was marked in the Free Church of Scotland by an unusual devotion to the cause of Christ and trust in Him on the part of the ministry, and by an extraordinary blessing of God, who raised in those days a galaxy of first rate men of theological insight, which it would be difficult to match anywhere else at any time. This work unfortunately had become quite scarce and it is a cause of thanksgiving for the upholder of the Protestant view of justification that such a classic exposition of this key doctrine can again be available.

Buchanan wrote a number of pamphlets, in addition to the works previously mentioned. He also contributed to the editing of the late William Cunningham's works, collaborating in this with his colleague, Dr. James Bannerman. He received an honorary doctorate of divinity from Princeton Seminary and a doctorate of laws from the University of Glasgow. He died in 1870.

— ROGER NICOLE

CONTENTS.

———◆———

THE DOCTRINE OF JUSTIFICATION.

PART I.

HISTORY OF THE DOCTRINE OF JUSTIFICATION.

PART II.

EXPOSITION OF THE DOCTRINE OF JUSTIFICATION.

CONTENTS.

THE DOCTRINE OF JUSTIFICATION.

INTRODUCTION.

IT may be thought by some that the subject of Justification is trite and exhausted; that, as one of the 'commonplaces' of Theology, it was conclusively determined and settled at the era of the Reformation; and that nothing new or interesting can now be introduced into the discussion of it. It is not necessary to say in reply to this, as some might be disposed to say, that 'what is new in Theology is not true, and what is true is not new;' for we believe, and are warranted by the whole history of the Church in believing, that Theology, like every other science, is progressive,—progressive, not in the sense of adding anything to the truth once for all revealed in the inspired Word, but in the way of eliciting and unfolding what has always been contained in it,—of bringing out one lesson after another, and placing each of them in a clearer and stronger light,—and discovering the connection, interdependency, and harmony, of all the constituent parts of the marvellous scheme of Revelation. In this sense, Science and Theology are both progressive, the one in the study of God's works, the other in the study of God's Word; and as human Science has not yet exhausted the volume of Nature, or reached the limit of possible discovery in regard to it, much less has human

Theology fathomed the depths of Scripture, or left nothing to reward further inquiry into 'the manifold wisdom of God.' There may be room, therefore, for something new, if not in the substance, yet in the treatment, even of the great doctrine of Justification,—in the exposition of its scriptural meaning, and in the method of adducing, arranging, and applying the array of its scriptural proofs.

But apart from this, and looking to the character of our current literature, may it not be said that, to a large class of minds in the present age, nothing could well be more *new* than the *old* Theology of the Reformation? The Gospel is older than Luther; but, to every succeeding generation, it is still new,—good news from God,—as fresh now as when it first sprung from the fountain of Inspiration. It was new to ourselves,—surprising, startling, and affecting us strangely, as if it were almost too good to be true,—when it first shone, like a beam of heaven's own light, into our dark and troubled spirits, and shed abroad 'a peace which passeth all understanding.' It will be equally new to our children, and our children's children, when they come to know that they have sins to be forgiven, and souls to be saved; and to the last sinner who is convinced and converted on the earth, it will still be as 'good tidings from a far country,' —as 'cold water to a thirsty soul.' It can never become old or obsolete, for this obvious reason, that while it is 'the everlasting Gospel,' and, as such, like its Author, unchangeable,—'the same yesterday, and to-day, and for ever,'—yet it comes into contact, in every succeeding age, with new minds, who are ignorant of it, but need it, and can find no peace without it; and when they receive it as 'a faithful saying, and worthy of all acceptation, that Christ came into the world to save sinners,' they will learn from their own experience that the old truth is still the germ of 'a new creation'—the spring of a new life, a new peace, a new hope, a new spiritual existence, to which they were utter strangers before.

There are many, even in Protestant communities, who have long been familiar with the sound of the Gospel, to whom this inward sense of it, in its application to their own souls, would be nothing less than a new spiritual revelation. The doctrine of Justification, by grace, through faith in Christ, is the old doctrine of the Reformation, and the still older doctrine of the Gospel; yet the vivid apprehension of its meaning, and the cordial reception of its truth, must be a new thing in the experience of every one, when he is first enabled to realize and to believe it. The free pardon of all sin, and a sure title to eternal life, conferred by the mere grace of God, and resting solely on the redemption and righteousness of the Lord Jesus Christ,—this, as the actual and immediate privilege of every sinner, on the instant when he begins to rely on Christ alone for salvation, as He is offered to *him* individually in the Gospel,—may come home, with all the freshness of new truth, even to many who bear the Christian name; and a realizing sense of them, in the conscious experience of their own souls, will be the best safeguard against the prevailing errors of the times, and the danger to which so many are at this moment exposed, of being 'tossed about with every wind of doctrine.'

If we take a calm survey of the state of religious sentiment in the present crisis,—for it is a crisis, and a very solemn one,—we can hardly fail to observe, that the minds of many are uneasy and unsettled; that there is a wide-spread feeling of unrest and dissatisfaction; and that this feeling manifests itself mainly in two apparently opposite tendencies, which have been so strikingly de-

veloped in the present age as to constitute its most
marked and characteristic features;—the one is the
tendency towards Rationalism, whose final goal is a
cheerless and dreary Scepticism ; the other, the tendency
towards Ritualism, which can only find its complete
realization in the Church of Rome.   We see one large
class of educated men relinquishing some of the most
fundamental articles of the Christian faith, as if they
had no need of them for their salvation, and contenting
themselves with such lessons as Reason can learn by the
mere light of Nature, or at least prove by rational arguments ; and we see another large class of educated men
betaking themselves to forms and ceremonies, to sacramental grace and ascetic practices, to auricular confession
and priestly absolution, as if they could not find, in the
simple Gospel of the grace of God in Christ, enough for
their soul's need, without borrowing some additions to
it from the inventions of men, and even from the corruptions of Popery.   Each of these tendencies is a symptom
of the same radical evil—the want of true peace, and
good hope through grace ; for those who have listened
to Christ's voice, and complied with His gracious call,
' Come unto me, and ye shall find rest unto your souls,'
have an anchor, both sure and stedfast, which keeps
them, amidst all the fluctuations of human opinion, from
drifting with the current ; and neither Scepticism nor
Superstition has any charms for them.   ' They have
drunk of the old wine, and have no desire for the new ;
for they say, The old is better.'   Those who yield to these
opposite tendencies differ in many respects from each
other ; but they agree in this : they have both abandoned
the old doctrine of Justification, as revealed in the Gospel,
and revived at the Reformation ; and that cardinal doctrine is the one truth which alone can neutralize their

respective errors, just as in the times of Luther it had power to overthrow alike the speculations of the Schools, and the superstitions of the Church. They differ in being more or less convinced of sin, more or less earnest in seeking salvation, more or less sincere in professing a reverential faith in God's Word,—for the hale-hearted Rationalist contrasts unfavourably in these respects with many an anxious-minded Ritualist,—but the Gospel doctrine of Justification, expounded in all its fulness, and exhibited in connection with the great scriptural principles which it involves or implies, is the most effective instrument at once for rousing the conscience of the Rationalist out of its false security, and for relieving the conscience of the Ritualist from its slavish anxieties and fears.

The false security of the Rationalist arises, not from the knowledge and belief of Christ's Gospel, but from ignorance or disbelief in regard to the demands and sanctions of God's Law; and the doctrine of Justification, as it is taught in Scripture, is fitted to break up that false security, and to awaken every thoughtful man to a sense of his real condition in the sight of God. For, in its negative aspect, it teaches us, first of all, how we cannot be justified,—it excludes the possibility of pardon and acceptance, in the case of man fallen, on the ground of his own obedience, and insists on the necessity of a satisfaction to divine justice, such as shall be at once an adequate expression of God's infinite abhorrence of sin, and an effectual means of securing all the ends of punishment under His moral government. What the Rationalist most needs at the outset is a work of the Law on his conscience, —a clearer and more impressive apprehension of the spirituality and extent of its preceptive requirements,—a deeper sense of sin—of the fact of sin, as undeniably chargeable against himself, and, especially, of the guilt of sin, as that which exposes him to imminent and awful danger, — a realizing conviction of those threatened penalties, which are expressive of God's holy hatred of it, and His inflexible determination to punish it,—and a close and faithful application of the whole Law to himself individually, as a sinner in the sight of God, standing before His awful tribunal, and awaiting His sentence, as a righteous Judge.   Without some such experience as this, he will feel little or no interest in the question of Justification, and will scarcely be able to understand what it means, or what principles are involved in it.   But that doctrine, when it is scripturally stated and explained in all its fulness, is related to the Law as well as to the Gospel; and for this reason it is admirably adapted to his case, just because it brings out, and places clearly before his conscience, the great fundamental principles of man's inexcusable guilt, and God's inflexible justice; and also because, when it proceeds to unfold a scheme of grace and redemption, it never loses sight of these principles, but exhibits them, all the more impressively, as exemplified and embodied in that scheme itself, which is a divine provision for the vindication of God's Law, with a view to the free exercise of His mercy towards the guilty.   Let this doctrine take effect, first of all, in its Legal aspect,— bringing the Law to bear on his conscience, convincing him of the guilt which he has incurred, and awakening a sense of the punishment which he has deserved, as a sinner in the sight of a holy and righteous God; and then, but not till then, he will be prepared to understand and appreciate it, in its Evangelical aspect, when it proclaims a free pardon, but a pardon founded on a divine propitiation,—a gracious remission, but a remission by means of a divine redemption,—a full salvation, but a salvation procured by a divine satisfaction to God's eternal justice.

The anxieties of the Ritualist, again, arise from some sense of sin, combined with a more or less earnest desire of salvation; but accompanied also with much remaining ignorance in regard to the fulness and freeness of the Gospel provision for his immediate pardon and acceptance with God, and a latent feeling that there is still something that remains to be done or suffered by himself, in the way of satisfying the justice, averting the wrath, and propitiating the favour, of his righteous Judge. He has 'a zeal for God,' but 'not according to knowledge;' and 'he goes about to establish,' at least in part, 'his own righteousness,' instead of 'submitting,' at once and altogether, 'to the righteousness of God.' Hence he has recourse to confession and penance, not merely for the mortification of sin, but for relief from a sense of unforgiven guilt; and hence, too, his zeal in almsgiving and good works, not as expressions of gratitude for grace received, but as a means of deprecating the wrath, and securing the favour, of God. There is much in his state of mind which contrasts favourably with the careless indifference of multitudes who are at ease in Zion,—who have never felt that they have sins to be forgiven, or souls to be saved,—and who are only lulled into deeper security, and case-hardened in impenitence and unbelief, by their partial knowledge even of the message of mercy in the Gospel. One must feel a deep and tender sympathy with every earnest soul, which is really convinced of its sin and danger, and struggling to obtain deliverance,—and many a Ritualist may be in this condition. What he needs is a deeper and more thorough conviction of his ruined and helpless condition as a sinner, utterly unable to expiate any of his past sins by his own sufferings, or to secure divine acceptance by anything that he either has done, or can yet do: and along with this, a clearer perception of the perfect all-sufficiency of the

finished work of Christ, to secure the immediate and full
justification of every sinner, on the instant when he receives
and rests on Him alone for salvation. The doctrine of
Justification, therefore, as it is stated and explained in
Scripture, is exactly suited to his case, just as it was to
that of the Jewish Ceremonialist in apostolic times, and
the Romish Ritualist at the era of the Reformation ; for
while, in its negative aspect, it excludes from the ground
of his acceptance all works, whether done after faith or
before it, and thus cuts up by the roots the principle of
self-righteousness in its most insidious and seductive form,
it proceeds, in its positive aspect, to bring in another
righteousness—emphatically called 'the righteousness of
God,' and to lay it down as 'a sure foundation in Zion ;'—
a righteousness already wrought out,—a righteousness
already accepted,—a righteousness proposed to him individually by God Himself, as the ground on which he is
warranted at once to rely for his present acceptance, and
his eternal welfare. As soon as he betakes himself to this
ground, and begins to rest upon it alone, he will find, in
his blessed experience, that it is adequate to sustain his
troubled soul,—to relieve it at once from all the anxieties
of unforgiven guilt,—to set it free from 'the spirit of
bondage which is unto fear,'—and to impart 'joy and
peace in believing;' even that 'peace which passeth all
understanding'—'the very peace of God reigning in the
conscience through Jesus Christ,' and that 'joy of the
Lord' which will be his 'strength' in duty, and his support
in trial, enabling him to 'run in the way of His commandments' when the Lord has thus 'enlarged his heart.'

It was by the doctrine of Justification by grace through
faith, as by a ray of light from heaven shining into their
hearts, that the Reformers, in whose souls the work
of the great spiritual revival was first wrought before it

took effect on the face of Europe, obtained relief from the bondage of legal fear, and entered into the liberty wherewith Christ makes His people free. (1) It was by the fearless proclamation of the same doctrine that they were enabled to impart immediate peace and comfort to many anxious inquirers, even in the cells and cloisters of the Church of Rome, who were prepared for its reception by those convictions of sin which the Law of God had power to awaken, but which all the Ritualism of Popery could not appease. And it was mainly to the influence of this one truth, carried home to the conscience ' in demonstration of the Spirit and with power,' that they ascribed their success, under God, in sweeping away the whole host of scholastic errors and superstitious practices, by which, in the course of many preceding centuries, men had corrupted the simpler faith and worship of the primitive Church. 'At the beginning of our preaching,' says Luther, ' the doctrine of Faith had a most happy course, and down fell the Pope's pardons, purgatory, vows, masses, and such like abominations, which drew with them the ruin of all Popery. . . . . And if all had continued, as they began, to teach and diligently urge the article of Justification —that is to say, that we are justified neither by the righteousness of the Law, nor by our own righteousness, but only by faith in Jesus Christ,—doubtless this one article, by little and little, had overthrown the whole Papacy.' (2)

If the doctrine of Justification by grace through faith be, as it unquestionably is, the only sovereign and effectual antidote to each of the two great tendencies of the age,— the tendency to Rationalism, on the one hand, and the tendency to Ritualism, on the other,—the re-exposition of it, in a form adapted to the more recent phases of these prevailing errors, might be, at least, a new and season-

able application of the old truth to the most urgent
wants of men's minds in the present day; and, as such,
it might be both interesting and useful, even if the
doctrine of the Reformation were universally acknowledged to be still the doctrine of the Protestant Church.
But an additional reason for a renewed exhibition of
that truth, which has heretofore been unanimously recognised as the distinctive principle of the Reformation,
may be found in the fact, that, of late years, and within
the ranks of Protestantism itself, it has been openly
assailed, as having no place either in the formularies of
the Church of England, or in the writings of the Christian
Fathers, or even in the Word of God itself.   When old
truths are attacked with new weapons, they must be vindicated by new defences, adapted to meet the most recent
forms of error; and this is pre-eminently the case, at the
present day, with the cardinal doctrine of Justification.
It is not denied by its recent assailants that it was the
doctrine of the leading Reformers, or that it was unanimously adopted and professed by all the churches which
they founded, whether Lutheran or Calvinistic, with one
singular exception only—the Church of England,—which,
it seems, is neither Lutheran nor Calvinistic, and, of course,
not Protestant,—and yet not Popish,—but purely Catholic
and Apostolical!   It is now alleged that the Reformed
doctrine is a ‘novelty,’ which was introduced for the
first time in the sixteenth century, and which, for fifteen
hundred years, had been unknown to Catholic Antiquity,
or the Church Universal; and that the Anglican Establishment, having always adhered to a complex rule of faith,
composed of the Scriptures as interpreted by the Fathers,
is unlike all other Protestant churches in this—that she
has never adopted or sanctioned this novelty as part of her
authorized creed.   What renders this ‘sign of the times’ all

the more significant and ominous is the additional fact, that all these assaults on the cardinal doctrine of the Reformation, from whatever quarter they have proceeded, whether from Rationalists or from Ritualists,—and they have proceeded from both,—have invariably had one and the same aim and direction—a return, in substance, if not in form, to the corrupt doctrine of the Church of Rome. The views on this important subject, which are now openly avowed in many influential quarters, are not only essentially the same with those which were exploded, we had hoped, for ever at the Reformation, but they are supported by the same arguments and the same interpretations of Scripture which were then current in the Popish Church, and which all the great divines of England—such as Davenant, and Downhame, and Barlow, and Prideaux, and Hooker—combated and demolished, especially in that marvellous age of sound theological learning, the seventeenth century. Yet now Protestants have been found willing to re-furbish the weapons of Bellarmine and Osorio, and to direct them anew against the very stronghold of our faith.

Within the last thirty years, several writers of unquestionable ability and learning, belonging at the time to the United Church of England and Ireland, have come prominently forward as uncompromising opponents of the Protestant, and zealous advocates or apologists for the essential principle of the Popish, doctrine on this subject. The first in order was a layman, but with a bishop as his coadjutor—Mr. Knox of Dublin,—at one time private secretary to Lord Castlereagh, then Viceroy of Ireland, and all along the friend and correspondent of Wilberforce, John Wesley, and Hannah More, whose 'Correspondence' during thirty years with Dr. Jebb, Bishop of Limerick, and also his 'Remains,' derive their chief interest from the zeal

with which he opposes the doctrine of a Forensic Justification, and seeks to substitute for it that of a Moral
Justification by our own inherent righteousness; a doctrine
which is identical, in its radical and distinctive principle,
with that of the Church of Rome. A seasonable antidote
to some of the errors, which were thus sought to be
revived in the Protestant Church, was supplied by Dr.
O'Brien, now Bishop of Ossory, in a work on 'The Nature
and Effects of Faith;' but it was directed, in the first
instance, against the doctrine of Bishop Bull, which made
our justification to rest on faith and works conjointly; and
it was only in the second edition, published with many
enlargements, after an interval of more than twenty years,
that the special views of Mr. Knox were fully examined
and criticised. Another valuable work appeared by George
Stanley Faber, partly prepared on his own spontaneous
motion, and partly called forth by a personal appeal
addressed to him by the Editor of the two concluding
volumes of Knox's 'Remains,' that he should throw the
shield of his authority over the new views, by bringing his
great learning to bear on the establishment of the historical
fact, asserted by Knox, that the doctrine of Forensic
Justification was a novelty introduced by the Reformation,
and that it had no place in the genuine remains of Catholic
Antiquity. The appeal was responded to, but in a style
which must have surprised and disappointed its too sanguine author; for Faber's answer is a thorough vindication
of the Protestant doctrine, and the conclusion at which
he arrives, in regard alike to the schemes of Bull, Knox,
and Trent, is, that 'not a vestige of any one of them can be
discovered in the writings of Ecclesiastical Antiquity,'—
a conclusion which is considerably stronger, as it appears
to me, than is either warranted by the facts of the case, or
necessary for the vindication of Protestant truth. His

statement of the Protestant doctrine, and his proof of its having been taught by *some* of the Fathers, are highly satisfactory; but his conclusion, as thus stated, is utterly untenable, and need not be adopted by any one who does not hold that the unanimous consent of the Fathers is necessary to verify any article of faith. Let any one read 'Ancient Christianity,' by Isaac Taylor, and he can scarcely fail to be convinced that much grievous error, affecting both the doctrine and the worship of the Church, had crept in before the close of the second century, and that it is to be found, mixed with many precious truths, in the writings of the most esteemed Fathers. Indeed, the germ of it existed even in the primitive Church.[1]

Dr. J. H. Newman, in his 'Lectures on Justification,' refers cursorily to the treatises of O'Brien and Faber, but offers no formal reply to them, otherwise than by expounding and attempting to establish his own theory, which is substantially the same, in its fundamental principle, with those of Bull, Knox, and Trent, although it is intended to be a middle way between the Protestant and the Popish doctrines. It was ably answered by Dr. James Bennett and others. Dr. Newman was then a minister of the Church of England, and is now a priest of the Church of Rome. This is of itself a significant indication of the tendency of the views which he had promulgated in the 'Tracts for the Times;' and it is deeply instructive to learn this additional fact, which is expressly stated in his recent 'Apology,' that in early life, and at what he still believes to have been the period of his conversion, he came under the influence of 'a definite creed,' and 'received impressions which have never been effaced or obscured,'—that he learned his first lessons in 'the school of Calvin,'—that the writer who made the deepest impression on his mind,

[1] 2 Thess. ii. 7 ; 1 John iv. 3.

and to whom, he says, ' (humanly speaking) I almost owe
my soul,' was Thomas Scott, the commentator,—that he
admired the writings of Romaine, and 'hung upon the
lips of Daniel Wilson;' yet all this Evangelical, and even
Calvinistic, teaching has resulted in his renouncing the
Protestant, and preferring the Romish, doctrine of a
sinner's acceptance in the sight of God. (3)

This is only one specimen, selected from among many
which might be mentioned, of a process which has been
going on extensively for years past, in certain circles of
society, and which, whether it results in avowed Romanism, or stops short at some intermediate stage, indicates,
with sufficient clearness, an uneasy restlessness of mind,
arising partly from some sense of sin, but also from superficial views of men's guilt and helplessness as sinners, and
partly from inadequate apprehensions of the nature, value,
and efficacy of the remedy which is provided for them in
the Gospel. Hence the necessity of expounding anew,
in these critical times, and that, too, for the benefit of
Evangelical Protestants themselves, the full meaning, and
the scriptural proofs, of the cardinal doctrine of the Gospel,—the doctrine of a full and free Justification, by grace,
through faith in Christ alone. It is true that the writings
to which I have referred, may be confined, in the first
instance, to the educated classes, and may not directly
affect the great body of the Protestant community; but,
not to speak of the inevitable influence which, in this age
of general literature, minds of high culture will ever exercise on popular opinion, it must never be forgotten that
there is a deeper and more fertile source of error on this
subject than false teaching from without,—it has an ally
and an accomplice within; for there is profound truth
in the memorable saying of Robert Trail: ' There is not
a minister that dealeth seriously with the souls of men,

but he finds an Arminian scheme of justification in every unrenewed heart.' (4)

That these Lectures may be adapted to the exigencies of the present times, it is necessary to keep steadily in view the theories and speculations which have recently appeared, and to suggest such considerations as may serve to neutralize or counteract their injurious influence. But they are designed to be didactic, rather than controversial. For it has long been my firm conviction, that the only effective refutation of error is the establishment of truth. Truth is one, error is multiform; and truth, once firmly established, overthrows all the errors that either have been, or may yet be, opposed to it. He who exposes and expels an error, does well; but it will only return in another form, unless the truth has been so lodged in the heart as to shut it out for ever. The great object, therefore, should be, to expound the doctrine of Justification in its full meaning, as it is revealed in Scripture,—to illustrate the great principles which are involved or implied in it,—to adduce and apply the scriptural proofs on which it rests,—and to contrast it with such other methods of obtaining pardon and acceptance with God as men have devised for themselves; and this, with a view to two practical results : first, to direct some, whose consciences have been awakened but not appeased, to a sure ground of immediate pardon and acceptance; and secondly, to direct believers, who are still burdened with doubts and fears, to such views of the nature, grounds, and evidences of this great Gospel privilege, as may serve, under the divine blessing, to raise them to a more comfortable enjoyment of it, by adding the 'assurance of faith' and 'hope' to 'the assurance of understanding.'

PART I.

HISTORY OF THE DOCTRINE OF JUSTIFICATION. (1)

———◆———

LECTURE I.

HISTORY OF THE DOCTRINE IN THE OLD TESTAMENT.

BY Justification we mean—man's acceptance with God, or his being regarded and treated as righteous in His sight—as the object of His favour, and not of His wrath; of His blessing, and not of His curse. This is the formal definition, or generic description of it, whether it be considered as an act on the part of God, or as a privilege on the part of man. Many have taken a partial and defective view of it, as if it consisted merely in the pardon of sin; but in the case of a moral and responsible agent, placed in a state of probation, with a view to reward or punishment, there might, and there would, have been justification, had there been no sin to be forgiven, as is evident from that of the angels who 'kept their first estate.'

When Justification is thus defined or described, it may seem to be possible only in the case of innocent and unfallen beings, and to be utterly beyond the reach of such as are guilty and depraved. And so it is on the footing of mere law, and on the ground of personal obedience to it. For that law is the rule of God's righteous judgment;

and, His judgment being ever according to truth, He cannot justify the wicked, any more than He can condemn
the righteous, when respect is had solely to their personal
character and conduct.   The law which proclaims the
punishment of sin can contain no provision for the pardon
of it ; and if it be the sole rule by which we are to be
justified or condemned, our justification is impossible ; for
' our own hearts condemn us, and God is greater than our
hearts, and knoweth all things.'   Had we been left, therefore, to the mere light of nature, and without a supernatural revelation of 'the will of God for our salvation,'
we could never have answered the question—' How shall
a man be just with God ?'

This is the great problem which the Gospel of Christ,
and that only, has undertaken to solve ; and it is the history of that problem, and of its divine solution, as contrasted
with the devices and inventions of men, which we propose
to trace through its successive stages, from the beginning
down to the present day.   But we cannot understand the
relation which subsists between the Law and the Gospel, in
so far as they bear respectively on the question at issue,
without some knowledge of the fundamental principles
which are common to both ; and, for this reason, we must
consider, in the first instance, the Justification of the
Righteous, and thereafter proceed, in the second, to the
Justification of Sinners.

I. The Justification of the Righteous comes first.
The doctrine of Justification had its origin in the
earliest revelations which were made to the first parents
of our race in primæval times.   It cannot be ranked
among the truths of, what is commonly called, Natural
Religion ; for, although there is a valid natural evidence for
the being and attributes of God, for His providential and

moral government, for the responsibility of man and the immortality of his soul, such as might suggest the idea of retribution, and awaken a foreboding of future judgment; yet the tenure on which life should be held, and the terms on which the favour of God should continue to be enjoyed, could only be determined by a free act, and announced by an authoritative revelation, of His sovereign will. Viewed in the mere light of reason and conscience, the punishment of sin is far more certain than the reward of obedience; for while it is evident that, under a scheme of moral government, sin deserves punishment, it is not so clear that any obedience which man might render could, strictly speaking, merit a reward, or constitute a claim in justice to anything more than exemption from penal suffering in a state of innocence. Yet this was a subject which could hardly fail to engage the thoughtful inquiry of a rational, responsible, and immortal being, and it deeply concerned him to know what was the will of God in regard to it.

We find, accordingly, that after God had revealed Himself, in the first instance, as the Creator of the world, and instituted the Sabbath as a weekly day of religious rest and worship, the next revelation which was addressed to the common father and representative of the race, was directed to this precise point, and made known the terms on which ' eternal life,'—not the continuance merely of a state of conscious personal existence, but the continuance of that holy and happy life which was enjoyed in a state of original righteousness, and which consisted essentially in the divine favour and image,—should be infallibly secured, to him, and to all his posterity, by the express promise, and the unchangeable faithfulness, of God. In that primæval revelation He made Himself known to our first parents, not only as their Creator and Benefactor, but

also as their Lawgiver, Governor, and Judge; and, founding upon that Moral Law which He had already written
on the fleshly tablets of their hearts, and which bound
them equally to believe whatever God might say, and to do
whatever God might command, He imposed upon them a
single positive precept as the test of their obedience,—connecting this precept, on the one hand, with the penalty
of death, and, on the other, with the promise of eternal
life. The precept, the penalty, and the promise, were associated with a visible sign or symbol in the tree of life,
which was the sacrament of this dispensation; and the
real import of each of these must be distinctly apprehended if we would form a correct conception of the
method of Justification which was thus revealed.

The *precept* required perfect obedience; for although
it was restricted to one duty in the shape of a positive
observance, that duty was enjoined as a test of man's submission to God's authority—of his faith in God's word,
and his obedience to God's will—of his love to God, and
his desire for the continued enjoyment of His favour and
fellowship; and such a test was evidently framed on the
principle that 'every sin deserves God's wrath and curse,'
and that 'whosoever shall keep the whole law, and yet
offend in one point, he is guilty of all.'[1]   The *penalty* denounced ' death ' as the wages or desert of sin; not, as
some have said, mere temporal death, or the dissolution of
the union between body and soul; nor the annihilation
of the soul, and the destruction of conscious existence,
at the close of the present life,—nor even the mere natural
effect of sin itself as it is a subjective evil, or as it is in its
essential nature, a loathsome and mortal disease of the
soul, which is destructive of spiritual life,—but the death
denounced was primarily, and principally, the loss of God's

[1] Jas. ii. 10.

' favour, which is life, and of His loving-kindness, which is better than life,' and the infliction of penal suffering, as at once the effect and the manifestation of God's 'wrath' and 'curse' on account of sin. (2) The *promise*,—which was implied in death being threatened only in the event of transgression, and which was visibly embodied and symbolized in the 'tree of life,'—secured, not merely the continuance of temporal life, nor even a state of immortal existence, but the perpetuity of that holy blessedness which consisted in the favour and fellowship of God; for the life, which was promised, was the counterpart of the death, which was threatened; and these are identified with God's *blessing*, and God's *curse:* ' Behold ! I set before you this day a blessing and a curse ; a blessing, if ye obey the commandments of the Lord your God, ... and a curse, if ye will not obey the commandments of the Lord your God.'[1]   God's 'blessing,' and God's 'curse,'—the one as comprehending all the good, and the other as comprehending all the evil, which flow from them respectively,—these were the sanctions of God's law. The benefits bestowed, and the penalties inflicted, are only effects or manifestations of God's favour, which is *life*, or of God's curse, which is *death*.

The Law, thus promulgated, became a divine covenant, in which God was pleased to bind Himself by His promise, and to become, as Boston says, ' debtor to His own faithfulness ' for its fulfilment,—while He bound the father of the human family, as the divinely appointed Representative and Federal Head of his posterity, by the obligation of the precept, on peril of penal condemnation in the event of disobedience.   There was much grace in this covenant ; for eternal life could never have been earned, or claimed as due, on the ground of merit at the hand of justice,

[1] Deut. xi. 26.

however perfect man's obedience might be to the precept
of the Law, while now, in virtue of the free and unchangeable promise, it might be claimed on the ground of
God's faithfulness and truth ; and further, the precept
itself, connected as it was with a solemn penalty, was
yet of a 'protective character;' for while it did not exclude
the possibility of sin, which seems to be necessarily involved in a state of probation and trial, it narrowed the
range of man's danger by summing up his duty in one
positive precept as the test of his obedience to the whole
Law, and making him invulnerable at all other points as
long as he remained stedfast in submitting to the only
restriction which had been imposed on his freedom. (3)
Yet while it had much grace in it, this Law is properly
called a Covenant of Works; for it established a certain
relation between obedience and reward, such as that which
subsists between work and wages.   Eternal life was promised on condition of obedience, and, on that condition
being fulfilled, the reward might have been claimed, not
as a 'reward of grace,' but 'of debt.'   Even then it could
not have been claimed on the ground of merit, as if it were
due in justice to our obedience, but it might have been
claimed on the plea of covenant faithfulness, and that, too,
on the ground of *personal* obedience. (4)

Such was the first method of Justification.   The Law,
in its covenant form, was 'ordained unto life ;' and its
terms were simply these, 'This do, and thou shalt live,'
but 'the soul that sinneth, it shall die.'   The Law provided
for the justification of the righteous, and of the righteous
only.   It was evidently adapted to the case of man while
he was yet, not only innocent and sinless, but possessed of
original righteousness, enjoying the 'favour of God, which
is life,' and retaining that divine 'image' in which he was
created.   But the favour of God was forfeited, and the death

of the soul incurred, by sin. There was something now
which 'the Law could not do,[1] in that it was weak,' not in
itself, but 'through the flesh,' or the fallen state of man :
it could no longer give life, simply because righteousness
could not come by a law which had been broken,—and
although it still remains in force, it is only as 'a ministration of death,' a 'ministration of condemnation.'[2]   For this
reason, no sooner had man transgressed the precept, than
he was solemnly debarred from the sacrament, of this
covenant ;—he was shut out from Eden, and God fenced it
round with 'cherubim, and a flaming sword which turned
every way, to keep the way of the tree of life.'[3]

The Law, as it was promulgated in a state of holy
innocence, while man still retained the 'image and likeness' of God, was adapted to his powers as an unfallen
being, and related only to the justification of the righteous.
It made no provision, and, from its very nature, it could
make none, for the acceptance of sinners.   It is a method of
justification by Law; and Law, as such, when it is applied
in judgment, must either justify or condemn.   But there
are many reasons why the Law, which justifies the righteous only, and condemns every sinner, should be carefully
studied, in the first instance, in order that we may be
prepared to understand and appreciate that other method
of justification which the Gospel reveals.   The Law and
the Gospel are so related, that the one presupposes the
other, and is founded upon it; and, by a marvellous
device of divine wisdom, the justification of sinners is
brought into intimate connection with that same Law,
by which they are convicted and condemned.   The Law
worketh 'wrath,' the Gospel proclaims 'reconciliation ;'
but the two are connected by means of a 'redemption,'

[1] Τὸ ἀδύνατον τοῦ νόμου.   Rom. viii. 3.
[2] 2 Cor. iii. 7, 9.   [3] Gen. iii. 24.

wrought out by One who 'redeemed us from the curse of the Law, by being made a curse for us.' The penalty of the Law takes effect, not on the sinner, but on a Divine Substitute; and the end of punishment being thus secured, pardon is proclaimed on the ground of a propitiation. But this method of justification for sinners, although it be 'without the Law,'[1] as being above and beyond what the mere Law could provide, is so closely related both to its preceptive and penal requirements, that we can form no scriptural views of the one without some suitable conception of the other. Hence the careful study of the Law, as a covenant of works, is necessary at all times to the right understanding of the Gospel, as a covenant of grace: and it is peculiarly seasonable in the present age, when the eternal Law of God is supposed, by some, to have been abrogated, and, by others, to have been modified or relaxed. We must believe that the Law of God, in all its spirituality and extent, is still binding, if we are to feel our need of the Gospel of Christ; and we must be brought to tremble under 'the revelation of wrath,' if we are ever to obtain relief and comfort from 'the revelation of righteousness.' (5)

II. The doctrine of the Justification of *Sinners* had its origin immediately after the Fall. Having broken the condition of the covenant, by an act of wilful transgression, our first parents had incurred the double guilt, of disbelieving God's word, and of disobeying God's will. They had thereby forfeited the promise of life, and incurred the penalty of death. They had listened to the tempter, first, when he suggested a doubt as to the divine prohibition, and again, when he denied the certain execution of the divine penalty; but now they were unde-

---

[1] χωρὶς νόμου.　Rom. iii. 21.

ceived by their own conscious experience; for, no sooner had they committed sin, than immediately conscience awoke as God's vicegerent in their own breasts, and they were self-convicted and self-condemned. That one act had changed their whole relation to God, and reversed, at the same time, all their feelings towards Him; they had forfeited His favour, and incurred His wrath; and instead of being, as He once was, the object of their supreme love and confidence, He had become the object of their jealousy, suspicion, and distrust. A sense of His displeasure produced, through fear, a feeling of enmity; and that enmity could never have been subdued, without some token of His continued interest in their welfare, and of His disposition to receive them again into His favour. So sudden and so great had been the change which sin had wrought in all their relations and feelings towards Him, that they were ashamed, and afraid, and would have hid themselves, if they could, 'from the presence of the Lord God.' They now dreaded the penalty, because they felt it to be deserved; and they dreaded it, not merely on account of the sufferings which it might entail, but also, and chiefly, as it was an expression of God's displeasure, and a manifestation of His wrath.

When they were summoned to appear before Him as their Judge, they must have been prepared to hear—what alone the Law could have led them to expect—a sentence of condemnation. But He was pleased to interpose at this critical moment for their immediate and effectual relief. He pronounced, in their hearing, a curse on 'the serpent and his seed,' and conveyed, in the very bosom of that curse, an intimation of His sovereign purpose of grace and mercy towards themselves. There was a profound significance in this brief and simple, but most comprehensive, statement of God's purpose, when viewed

in connection with the circumstances in which they were
then placed, and the convictions which had been already
awakened in their minds. It implied that God, instead
of appearing *against* them as their enemy, was to interpose *for* them as their friend; that He had formed a
purpose of grace and mercy towards them, and had
devised a plan for their relief and restoration. It implied
that, with a view to their ultimate deliverance, they were
to be spared, and placed under a dispensation of forbear-
ance, during which the execution of His penal sentence
should be suspended; for their 'seed' is distinctly mentioned, intimating that their lives were to be prolonged.
It implied that, in the exercise of His sovereignty, He
had taken their case entirely into His own hands, as if
He, and He only, had the right, and the power, to deal
with it: 'I WILL PUT enmity between thee and the
woman, and between thy seed and her seed;'—words
which clearly intimate that the whole plan of their deliverance originated in His sovereign purpose, and that
it was to be accomplished by His own agency. It implied
that His purpose of mercy towards them should be effected,
not immediately and directly, by a mere act of indemnity
as an expression of His sovereign will, or by the direct
exertion of His almighty power, but through the mediation of 'the Seed of the woman,' who should be born
into the world, and enter into conflict with Satan, so as
to be himself a sufferer, yet to come off victorious. It
implied that, through this human deliverer, God would
break up the unholy league which had been formed
betwixt them and that evil spirit,—emancipating them
from his usurped dominion, crushing his power, frustrating
his schemes, and destroying his works. It implied that
their salvation was secured by a purpose of grace which
was absolute, as it depended on the mere 'good pleasure

of His will,' and by a promise which was unconditional, since no terms are imposed, and no works required, and no mention made of any human agency, excepting only the sufferings and work of the 'woman's Seed.' It implied that the 'woman's Seed'—the promised deliverer— was now to be the Hope of the world, and the Head of a redeemed people, who should be rescued from the curse of the Law, and restored to the favour and friend- ship of God; for Adam, the head of the old covenant, is superseded under the new, by One who is predicted and promised as 'the Seed of the woman.' It implied an 'election according to grace,' for distinct mention is made of 'the woman's seed,' and 'the serpent's seed;' and the serpent's seed are left under the curse, while the woman's seed are delivered from it. And it points for- ward to a mysterious conflict between Satan and the promised Saviour, in which there should be mutual 'enmity' and 'bruising,'—opposition and suffering on both sides,—but resulting in victory over the Wicked One.

The announcement of God's purpose of mercy was made in general terms, and it gave no definite information on many points which are now more fully and clearly revealed; but it contained enough to lay a solid founda- tion for faith and hope towards God, and it was the first beam of Gospel light which dawned on our fallen world. For what is the Gospel, if it be not the revelation of God as 'the just God and the Saviour,'—reconciling sinners to Himself by a Redeemer,—not imputing their trespasses unto them, but accepting them as righteous, admitting them to His favour and fellowship, and giving them peace of conscience here, and the hope of eternal life hereafter, by faith in His gracious promise? God had already revealed Himself as the Lawgiver, Governor, and Judge; He now reveals Himself as the 'just God and the

Saviour;'—as the just God, for He pronounces a curse
on the serpent, and predicts the sufferings also of the
woman's Seed, thus manifesting His holy displeasure
against sin; and yet as 'the Saviour,' for He promises
a Deliverer, who should suffer indeed on account of sin,
but, by suffering, accomplish the salvation of sinners.
Looking to God in this character, our first parents might
believe, as Abraham afterwards believed, in 'Him that
justifieth the ungodly;' and looking to the promised
'Seed,' they might believe, as Abraham afterwards believed, that in this Seed should 'all the families of the
earth be blessed.' The object of faith in these primitive
times was, in substance, the same as now: God in His
revealed character as 'just, and the justifier of him that
believeth;'—with this difference, that the Saviour was
then promised as 'coming,' but is now proclaimed as
'having come.' (6)

Such are some of the truths which are expressed or
implied in the first promise of a Saviour, as it was conveyed in a curse pronounced against the serpent. They
were fitted to produce a feeling of reverence for the justice
of God, as the supreme Lawgiver, Governor, and Judge,
both of men and of higher orders of invisible beings;
and yet also a feeling of hope and trust in His mercy,
through that Saviour whom He had promised to raise
up for their deliverance. (7) And these mingled feelings
of fear and hope towards God were fitly expressed, and
could scarcely fail to be deepened and confirmed, by *the
rite of sacrifice*, which formed the most solemn part of
their religious worship. For that rite, as habitually
practised by them, was as significant as the first promise;
and its meaning was in manifest correspondence with the
truths which that promise revealed. Sacrifice was offered
to God in His revealed character as 'the just God,' and

yet the 'Saviour of sinners;' it consisted in the slaying
of an innocent animal, which was substituted in the
room of the sinner, and devoted to God as an atonement
for his soul, by the shedding of its blood; it implied
that his sin was laid upon the head of the victim, and
that his life, forfeited by sin, was redeemed by the
victim's death; it expressed, on the part of every sincere
worshipper, a confession of personal guilt, and a sense
of penal desert, but a hope also of divine forgiveness
and acceptance, for it was employed with a view to
deprecate and avert God's wrath, and to implore and
propitiate His favour; and the habitual observance of
this rite, as the most solemn act of religious worship,
had a tendency to strengthen all those feelings, both of
fear and hope, of reverence and trust, of repentance and
faith, which the revelation of God's justice in the curse,
and of His mercy in the promise, was fitted to produce.
It served also to familiarize the mind of every believer,
even in primitive times, with those great principles of
substitution, imputation, and vicarious satisfaction, which
were involved in the divine scheme of grace and redemption, and which were only to be more fully developed,
and more clearly exhibited, in connection with the person
and work of the promised Seed, in 'the fulness of times.'

It has been made a question, indeed, whether the rite
of sacrifice, in connection with religious worship, was an
invention of man, or an institution of God.   The only
pretext for raising such a question arises from there being
no statement in Scripture ascribing it, in express terms,
to divine appointment.   But apart from any categorical
announcement, there may be sufficient scriptural evidence
to prove that it could not have originated from the will
of man, and that it must be ascribed to the revealed will
of God.   It is highly improbable, on the one hand, that

the thought of propitiating God's favour by the slaying
of His innocent animals could have suggested itself, in
any circumstances, as an acceptable part of religious
worship; it is still more improbable that it could have
suggested itself at a time when man was not allowed to
use them even for food; and it is most improbable of all
that he would have ventured to introduce an act of mere
will-worship into the divine service, at a time when God
was revealing His mind and will, or that it would have
been accepted by Him, who acted then, as He acts now,
on the great principle declared in His Word,—' In vain
do ye worship me, teaching for doctrines the commandments of men.' It is certain, on the other hand, that
God accepted the animal sacrifice of Abel, and testified
His acceptance of it, probably by fire from heaven consuming the victim on the altar,—that He accepted it in
preference to the mere thank-offering of Cain, which
consisted in the fruits of the ground, and had no relation
to atonement by blood,—that when Cain was wroth
because God had no respect to his offering, the Lord said
to him, ' If thou doest well, shalt thou not be accepted?
and if thou doest not well, sin lieth,' or a sin-offering
coucheth, ' at the door,'[1]—that Abel is expressly said to
have offered his sacrifice ' in faith,'[2] and faith invariably
implies, according to Scripture, a divine testimony or a
divine authority as its ground and warrant; and that
the distinction between animals as clean and unclean,—
which could have reference at that time only to sacrifice,
not to food, and which depended entirely on divine
appointment,—existed in the earliest times, and is repeatedly referred to in the sacred narrative. These
arguments appear to me to be conclusive in favour of the
divine institution of animal sacrifice as a part of solemn

[1] Gen. iv. 4-7.   [2] Heb. xi. 4.

religious worship; but they derive additional strength from the manifest correspondence of that rite, in its spiritual significance, with the truths which had been previously revealed, and also with the method of redemption as it was subsequently more fully unfolded in the Ritual of Moses and the Gospel of Christ. For it was evidently fitted, by its radical meaning and the lessons which it taught, to be the sacrament and symbol of the first promise of a Saviour, and, as such, a type of 'the Lamb of God who should take away the sin of the world,' —a sacrament which then prefigured to the eye of faith that same sacrifice of the Cross which is now commemorated at the Lord's table. By offering that sacrifice 'in faith'—by believing the great truth which it symbolized and typified as it was revealed in the first Gospel promise, —the worshipper was justified then, as he is justified now: he obtained forgiveness and acceptance with God; and not only so, but he might enjoy the assurance of both, when, as in the case of Abel, he 'obtained *witness* that he was righteous, God testifying of his gifts.' (8)

The first promise of a Saviour, commemorated and illustrated by sacrificial observances as a permanent part of divine worship, was the primæval Gospel. Both were transmitted by tradition from one generation to another, at a time when, from the longevity of men during that early age, they might long be preserved in a state of purity. That they were sufficient, under the teaching of God's Spirit, to form the characters of true believers, and to embue them with an enlightened and exalted piety, appears from the case of Abel, the first martyr for the truth, of whom it is said, that 'by faith he offered a more excellent sacrifice than Cain, by which he obtained witness that he was righteous,'[1] or accepted as righteous

---

[1] Heb. xi. 4.

in the sight of God; from the case of Enoch, of whom we
read, that 'Enoch walked with God, and he was not, for
God took him,' and that before his translation 'he had
this testimony, that he pleased God,' or was accepted as a
justified man.[1] We have also the case of Noah, of whom
it is written, that 'he found grace in the eyes of the
Lord,'—that he was 'a just man, and perfect, or upright,
in his generation, and walked with God,'—that he was 'a
preacher of righteousness,'—and that 'he became heir of
the righteousness which is by faith.'[2] These cases are
only specimens of primæval believers, who were justified
freely by grace through faith in a promised Saviour, and
who testified their faith by worshipping God, as the Holy
One and the just, yet as the justifier of the ungodly,—
worshipping Him in the way of His own appointment, by
offering bloody sacrifices on His altar. How many they
may have been, or how few, we cannot tell; but if the
primæval Gospel was sufficient for the justification of all
believers who worshipped God in spirit and in truth, then
as long as God continued to be known in His revealed
character as the just God and the Saviour, and as long as
His promise—transmitted by tradition and symbolized
by sacrifice—was the object of faith and hope anywhere
among the children of Adam or his children's children,
so long might it be, then as it now is, the 'power of God
unto salvation.' For it was addressed to men universally,
while as yet there was no distinction between Jew and
Gentile, and no other difference betwixt man and man
except the radical and permanent one, which was recognised in the first promise itself, betwixt the 'woman's
seed' and 'the serpent's seed.' There was the same
limit to its efficacy then as there is still, but there was
no other;—all believers were justified, and none else.

---

[1] Gen. v. 24; Heb. xi. 5, 6.   [2] Gen. vi. 8, 9; 2 Pet. ii. 5; Heb. xi. 7.

Unbelief was early manifested in the mere will-worship of Cain, and it gradually spread so as to become all but universal ; and when ' God saw that the wickedness of man was great in the earth, and that every imagination of the thoughts of his heart was only evil continually,'[1] He resolved to manifest, by one stupendous act of supernatural power, at once the ' curse ' which He had pronounced against ' the serpent's seed,'—and the ' grace ' which He had promised through ' the Seed of the woman,'—by bringing in ' the flood on the world of the ungodly,'[2] and ' saving Noah and his family by a great deliverance,' that this small but precious remnant might transmit His promise, and maintain His worship, as they had received them from their believing fathers.

After the flood, the revelation of God's purpose of redeeming mercy was progressive, and became at once more copious, and more precise. In the first promise, the future Saviour had been revealed simply as ' the Seed of the woman' who should ' bruise the serpent's head;' but, as the Church advanced on her course, additional information was vouchsafed, in regard to the constitution of His person,—the line of His human descent,—the nature of the offices which He should sustain,—the work which He should accomplish,—the blessings which He should procure for His people,—and the time of His advent. That He was to be a Man, was implied in His being promised as ' the Seed of the woman ;' but He was afterwards revealed to Abraham as ' the mighty God,' and at a still later period to Moses as ' Jehovah ;' for it was the ' Angel of the Lord ' that appeared to Moses in the bush,—who revealed Himself as ' the God of Abraham, the God of Isaac, and the God of Jacob,'—and said, ' I appeared unto Abraham, and unto Isaac, and unto Jacob, by the name of God Almighty, but

[1] Gen. vi. 5.   [2] 2 Pet. ii. 5.

by my name Jehovah I was not known unto them:'
'Thus shalt thou say unto the children of Israel, I AM
hath sent me unto you.' (9)

In the Patriarchal age after the flood, the first and, in
many respects, the most memorable case of Justification,
is that of Abraham, who was to be 'the father of many
nations,' and the pattern or model of all true believers
till the end of time. It is frequently referred to in
Scripture, not as an isolated or singular instance, having
no resemblance to the justification of sinners now, but as
an example or specimen which exhibits the same principles,
and illustrates the same truths, that are only more clearly
and fully revealed in the Gospel of the New Testament.
For this reason, he is called ' the father of all them that
believe;' and all believers, Christian as well as Jewish,
are called 'the children of Abraham.' For the same
reason, the Apostles derived some of their strongest proofs
of the doctrine of Justification by grace, through faith,
from that part of Scripture which records God's gracious
dispensations towards him, and his experience as a sinner,
who had been freely forgiven, and accepted as righteous.
He was chosen and called by sovereign mercy while he
was yet an idolater in the land of Chaldea.[1]   God entered
into covenant with him, and called him His 'friend.'[2]
'The Gospel' was preached unto Abraham,—the same
Gospel in substance which is now preached unto us,—
even that ' in him and his seed should all the families of
the earth be blessed.'[3]   By faith in that Gospel he was
justified; for it is expressly recorded 'that he believed
in the Lord, and He counted it to him for righteousness.'[4]
He believed in God, not merely as a Lawgiver, Governor,

[1] Gen. xiii. 1 ; Acts vii. 2, 4; Neh. ix. 7.
[2] Isa. xli. 8; 2 Chron. xx. 7; Jas. ii. 23.   [3] Gal. iii. 8.
[4] Gen. xv. 6 ; Rom. iv. 3 ; Gal. iii. 6; Jas. ii. 23.

and Judge, but as 'Him who justifieth the ungodly;'[1] and he believed in Christ as the promised 'Seed in whom all the families of the earth should be blessed,'—for, says our Lord Himself, 'Your father Abraham rejoiced to see my day; and he saw it, and was glad.'[2]

The Apostles made use of the case of Abraham to prove all the most important points of the doctrine of Justification. They assume that it was a case of real justification before God, declared and attested by God Himself in His inspired Word; and that it was not singular, but similar, in all essential respects, to the justification of every other sinner. They apply it to prove especially, in opposition to the prevailing opinion of the Jews, these *five* positions: *First*, that he was justified, not by works, but by faith; for 'to him that worketh, is the reward reckoned, not of grace, but of debt; but to him that worketh not, but believeth in Him that justifieth the ungodly, his faith is counted for righteousness:'[3] *Secondly*, that having been justified by faith, he was consequently justified by grace; for 'therefore it is of faith, that it might be by grace;'[4]— neither faith itself, nor any of the fruits of faith, being the ground, or the meritorious cause, of his acceptance with God: *Thirdly*, that having been justified by grace through faith, justification came to him, not through the Law, but through the Promise; 'for if the inheritance be of the Law, it is no more of promise, but God gave it to Abraham by promise;' but 'if they which are of the Law be heirs, faith is made void, and the promise made of none effect:'[5] *Fourthly*, that having been justified by faith in God's free promise, he was not justified by circumcision or any other outward privilege: 'Cometh this blessedness, then, upon the circumcision only, or upon the uncircum-

---

[1] Rom. iv. 5.   [2] John viii. 56.   [3] Rom. iv. 4, 5.
[4] Rom. iv. 16.   [5] Gal. iii. 18; Rom. iv. 14.

cision also? for we say that faith was reckoned to Abraham
for righteousness.   How was it then reckoned ? when he
was in circumcision or in uncircumcision?   Not in circumcision, but in uncircumcision ; and he received the sign of
circumcision, a seal of the righteousness of the faith which
he had, yet being uncircumcised :'[1] and, *Fifthly*, that having
been justified by grace through faith in God's promise, he
had no ground of boasting, or of glorying, or of self-
righteous confidence ; for 'if Abraham were justified by
works, he hath whereof to glory, but (he had nothing
whereof to glory) before God.'   'Where is boasting, then ?
It is excluded.   By what law? of works?   Nay, but by
the law of faith.'[2]   These positions, deduced from the
scriptural account of Abraham, will be found to exclude
almost all the errors which prevailed among the Jews in
the apostolic age, or which have since arisen in the Christian Church, on the subject of Justification. (10)

The Patriarchs who succeeded Abraham had the same
promise renewed to them, and were also justified by faith.
They had peculiar privileges and hopes, as being in the
direct line of the promised Seed: but there were true
believers who did not belong to the family of Abraham,
such as Melchizedek, 'the priest of the most high God,'
and, as such, an eminent type of Christ ;[3] and 'just Lot,'
' a righteous man,' to whom 'the Lord was merciful ;'[4] and
Abimelech, to whom the Lord revealed Himself, and
acknowledged the 'integrity of his heart ;'[5] and Job, who
' was perfect and upright, one that feared God, and
eschewed evil,'—who ' offered burnt-offerings ' continually
for his children, saying, 'It may be my sons have sinned,
and cursed God in their hearts.'[6]   These were true be-

---

[1] Rom. iv. 9, 10, 11.   [2] Rom. iv. 2, iii. 27.
[3] Gen. xiv. 18 ; Heb. vii.; Ps. cx. 4 ; Heb. v. 6.
[4] Gen. xix. 16 ; 2 Pet. ii. 7, 8.   [5] Gen. xx. 6.   [6] Job i. 1, 5.

lievers, and, as such, accepted of God, although they were not of the seed of Abraham according to the flesh, nor directly interested in the peculiar promises of God's covenant with him; but they shared, in common with him, the first promise of a Saviour, and testified their faith in it by worshipping Jehovah in His revealed character, and offering sacrifices on His altar. Such believers were not disfranchised of their privileges or hopes by that new dispensation which first established the distinction betwixt Jews and Gentiles. (11)

The next great era in the History of Justification under the Old Testament was that of Moses, and the proclamation of the Law at Sinai. A new economy was now introduced, which differed in many respects from the Patriarchal system, and yet was designed and fitted, in various ways, to develop God's purpose of mercy, and to carry it on to its accomplishment in the fulness of times. That economy cannot be understood, as it is described and commented on in various parts of Scripture, unless it be contemplated in two distinct aspects : *first*, as a system of religion and government, designed for the immediate use of the Jews during the term of its continuance; and *secondly*, as a scheme of preparation for another and better economy, by which it was to be superseded when its temporary purpose had been fulfilled.

It was designed, in the first instance, for the instruction of the Jews, now formed into a nation, and about to be established in the land which the Lord had promised to give to Abraham and his seed; and, in the second instance, to prepare them, by a course of discipline and education, for the coming of Him 'in whom all the families of the earth should be blessed.' They were put 'under tutors and governors until the time appointed of the Father,'—

and 'the Law was their schoolmaster to bring them unto Christ, that they might be justified by faith.'[1] For this reason it had a mixed character,—the 'Law' which came by Moses being 'added' to the 'Promise' which had been given to Abraham. It was neither purely Evangelical, nor purely Legal; it contained the Gospel, but 'the Law was added to it because of transgressions, till the Seed should come to whom the Promise was made.'[2] The addition of the Law was not intended to alter either the ground, or the method, of a sinner's justification, by substituting obedience to the Law for faith in the Promise; for the Law which was originally 'ordained unto life' was now found, by reason of sin, 'to be unto death;' but it was now 'added,' and promulgated anew with awful sanctions amidst the thunderings and lightnings of Sinai, to impress the Jews, and through them the Church at large, with a sense of the holiness and justice of Him with whom they had to do,—of the spirituality and extent of that obedience which they owed to Him,—of the number and heinousness of their sins,—and of their utter inability to escape the wrath and curse of God, otherwise than by taking refuge in the free promise of His grace. Believers were justified, therefore, under the Law, not by works, but by faith : by faith, they were 'the children of Abraham,' and 'heirs with him of the same promise.' The Law—considered as a national covenant, by which their continued possession of the land of Canaan, and of all their privileges under the Theocracy, was left to depend on their external obedience to it,— might be called a national Covenant of Works, since their temporal welfare was suspended on the condition of their continued adherence to it; but, in that aspect of it, it had no relation to the spiritual salvation of individuals, other- wise than as this might be affected by their retaining, or

[1] Gal. iv. 2, iii. 24.   [2] Gal. iii. 19.

forfeiting, their outward privileges and means of grace. It may be considered, however, in another light, as a re-exhibition of the original Covenant of Works, for the instruction of individual Jews in the principles of divine truth ; for in some such light it is evidently presented in the writings of Paul. (12)   In this aspect, it was designed, not for the justification of sinners, but for the conviction of sin.   In that form, it was afterwards employed even by the Apostles of Christ, to prove the impossibility of justification by the deeds of the Law, and the necessity of another righteousness, the righteousness of faith ; and for the same end, it is still applied to the conscience by every faithful preacher of the Gospel.   Thus considered,—as a re-exhibition of the Covenant of Works,—it had a tendency to produce ' a spirit of bondage unto fear ;' and this would have been its only effect, had it not been associated with a revelation of God's purpose and promise of grace.   But when the Gospel, which had been preached beforehand to Abraham, was known and believed, so as to impart a lively apprehension of ' the forgiveness which is with God,' then conviction of sin might become genuine contrition,—remorse might be turned into repentance,—and the more thoroughly the Law had done its work in the conscience, the more gladly would the promise of a Saviour be received into the heart.

The economy of Moses, whatever prominence it gave to the Law, was unquestionably a dispensation of the Covenant of Grace.   So far from superseding the promise given to Abraham, or ' making it void ' and ' of none effect,' it was expressly founded upon it, and designed to carry it on to its accomplishment.   That economy gathered up into itself all prior revelations of divine truth.   It adopted also the Primæval and Patriarchal institutions—the Sabbath, Sacrifice, and Circumcision,—while it added to these a

multitude of ordinances which were peculiar to itself—
ceremonial and ritual observances, which were in themselves 'weak and beggarly elements,' and were felt to be
'a heavy yoke,'—yet they were all significant symbols, and
typical prefigurations, of spiritual blessings. The believer,
therefore, who could look beyond the sign to the thing
signified, and see in the shadow the figure of the substance,
might find Christ in every ordinance of the Old Testament
Church, and obtain through Him, as revealed in the promise, forgiveness and acceptance with God. The devout
Israelite, therefore, was justified by grace through faith,
not less than the Christian believer. The divine Law,
spiritually understood, awakened a deep conviction of
sin; the divine promises, embodied and exhibited in the
divine ordinances,—in those especially which related to the
expiation of sin and the removal of ceremonial defilement,
—pointed to a divine method of deliverance based on the
principles of substitution and atonement, and produced
trust in God's mercy and hope of His gracious acceptance;
while the prospective character of these ordinances, as
types of better things to come, and their utter insufficiency
in themselves to 'take away sin,' or 'to make the comers
thereunto perfect as pertaining to the conscience,' directed
their thoughts forward to the time when the work of
redemption should be actually accomplished by the promised Seed. (13)

Provision was made, also, under the Law, for a growing
knowledge of God's purpose and plan of redeeming mercy,
by a series of Prophets, who were raised up to instruct the
people in the Law, but especially to expound the promise
of a Saviour, and to explain the spiritual import of the
types by which He was then prefigured. Their successive
announcements gave greater definiteness and precision to
the meaning of both.

As Prophecy advanced, it became at once more full, and more definite, in its delineation of the person and work of the promised Saviour. It had a sudden and signal expansion in the age of David and Samuel, when the typical offices under the Law were fully established and brought into regular order. Then David began to speak of Him as 'the Christ,'[1]—the Anointed One,—in whose person the typical offices of Prophet, Priest, and King should be combined. Afterwards Isaiah described Him as ' a man of sorrows and acquainted with grief,'—who was ' wounded for our transgressions, and bruised for our iniquities,'—who should ' make His soul a sacrifice for sin,' for 'the Lord hath laid upon Him the iniquities of us all,'—and then, connecting His redeeming work with the justification of His people, he adds, 'By His knowledge shall my righteous Servant justify many, for He shall bear their iniquities ;' ' Surely, shall one say, In the Lord have I righteousness,'—'in the Lord shall all the house of Israel be justified and shall glory.'[2] Jeremiah spoke of Him, when he said, ' This is the name whereby He shall be called, The Lord our righteousness.'[3] Zechariah spoke of Him as ' the man whose name is the Branch '—the man who is ' Jehovah's fellow,'—the ' Shepherd,'—'a Priest upon His throne ;'[4] and Daniel spoke of Him as ' Messiah the Prince,' who should come when the time arrived to ' anoint the Most Holy,'—' to finish the transgressions, and to make an end of sins, and to bring in everlasting righteousness.'[5] Thus was the Gospel method of Justification 'witnessed by the Law and the Prophets,'[6] for ' the testimony of Jesus was the spirit of prophecy ;' and ' to Him gave all the prophets witness, that, through His name, whosoever

---

[1] Ps. xlv. 7, cx. 4.   [2] Isa. liii. 3, 5, 6, 10, 11, xlv. 24, 25.
[3] Jer. xxiii. 6.   [4] Zech. xiii. 7, vi. 12, 13.
[5] Dan. ix. 24.   [6] Rom. iii. 21.

believeth in Him shall receive remission of sins.'[1] When
He came, Moses, representing the Law, and Elijah, representing the Prophets, descended from heaven, and spake
with Him 'of the decease which He should accomplish
at Jerusalem;'[2] and after His resurrection, 'beginning at
Moses and all the prophets, He expounded in all the
Scriptures the things concerning Himself.'[3]

These truths, thus gradually revealed, were the life-
blood of faith and piety in the Jewish Church ; and after
the time of Moses and David, when they were more fully
unfolded, in connection with the office and work of the
promised Seed in His character as the Messiah or the
Christ, the Priesthood and the Sacrifices of the Law were
regarded by every believing Israelite as 'figures' and
'types' of Him 'who should come to put away sin by the
sacrifice of Himself.' (14)   But they did not relate only
to the future,—they supplied evangelical instruction to
every believing Israelite ; and how rich and precious that
instruction was, appears from the spiritual worship which
it maintained in the Church, and especially from that
most marvellous record of their experience,—the Book of
PSALMS.   It may be safely affirmed, that every point in the
Gospel doctrine of Justification is there brought out by
anticipation, and strikingly exhibited in connection with
the faith and worship of Old Testament believers.   There is
the same confession of sin : 'There is none righteous, no,
not one ;'[4]—there is the same conviction of guilt and demerit: 'If Thou, Lord, shouldest mark iniquity, O Lord,
who shall stand ?'[5]—there is the same fear of God's
righteous judgment : 'Visit me not in Thy wrath, chasten
me not in Thy hot displeasure ;'[6]—there is the same sense
of inevitable condemnation on the ground of God's Law :

[1] Rev. xix. 10 ; Acts x. 43.   [2] Luke ix. 31.   [3] Luke xxiv. 27.
[4] Ps. xiv. 1.   [5] Ps. cxxx. 4, 7. .   [6] Ps. vi. 1.

'Enter not into judgment with Thy servant, for in Thy sight shall no flesh living be justified;'[1]—there is the same earnest cry for undeserved mercy: ' Have mercy upon me, O Lord, according to Thy loving-kindness; according to the multitude of Thy tender mercies blot out my transgressions;'[2]—there is the same faith in His revealed character as the just God and the Saviour: ' Good and upright is the Lord; therefore will He teach sinners in the way;'[3]— there is the same hope of pardon, resting on a propitiation; for ' with the Lord there is mercy, and with Him is plenteous redemption;'[4]—there is the same pleading of God's *name*, or the glory of all His perfections: ' For Thy name's sake, O Lord, pardon mine iniquity, for it is great;'[5]—there is the same joy and peace in believing; for ' blessed is the people that know the joyful sound: they shall walk, O Lord, in the light of Thy countenance; in Thy name shall they rejoice all the day;'[6]—there is the same trust in God and the faithfulness of His promises: ' I will sing of the mercies of the Lord for ever; with my mouth will I make known Thy faithfulness to all generations; for mercy shall be built up for ever, Thy faithfulness shalt Thou establish in the very heavens;'[7]— there is the same trust in the Saviour of sinners: ' Kiss the Son, lest He be angry, and ye perish from the way: blessed are all they that put their trust in Him;'[8]—there is the same confidence in another righteousness than their own: ' Behold, O God, our shield, and look on the face of Thine Anointed;'[9]—there is the same patient, persevering, hopeful waiting upon God: 'My soul, wait thou only upon God, for my expectation is from Him; He only is my rock and my salvation: He is my defence; I shall not be moved.

[1] Ps. cxliii. 2. [2] Ps. li. 1. [3] Ps. xxv. 8.
[4] Ps. cxxx. 7. [5] Ps. xxv. 11. [6] Ps. lxxxix. 15, 16.
[7] Ps. lxxxix. 1, 2. [8] Ps. ii. 12. [9] Ps. lxxxiv. 9.

In God is my salvation and my glory: the rock of my strength, and my refuge, is in God. Trust in Him at all times; ye people, pour out your heart before Him: God is a refuge for us.'[1]

Every one must feel that the Old Testament, considered simply as a record of man's spiritual life and experience, stands ALONE among all the extant remains of ancient thought, and has no parallel with which it can even be compared. What is it but the Gospel, and faith in that Gospel, that gives it a character so unique, a spirit so unearthly and divine? What is it but the Gospel, pervading every page, and breathing in every utterance of contrition, or faith, or hope, that makes the book of Psalms a fit expression for the highest worship even of the Christian Church? And why, if not because the Gospel was known and believed in the Old Testament Church, and felt then, as it is felt now, to be 'the power of God unto salvation,' did the Apostles themselves seek to establish the doctrine of a free justification by grace, through faith, by making mention of the long roll of 'the elders who by faith obtained a good report,'[2] and why did they found so much of their teaching on the recorded experience of Abraham and of David?[3]

Provision was thus made for the justification of sinners, by grace, through faith in the promised Saviour, throughout the whole course of the Jewish dispensation; and at its very close we find some true believers who understood its spiritual meaning,—who looked for redemption 'in Jerusalem,'—and 'waited for the consolation of Israel.' Zacharias and Elisabeth, Mary the mother of Jesus, Simeon and Anna,[4] were ready to welcome their long-expected Saviour when He came, and gave joyful

[1] Ps. lxii. 5-8.   [2] Heb. xi.   [3] Rom. iv.
[4] Luke i. 5-24, 26-56, 67-80, ii. 25-36, 37, 38.

utterance to their faith in heartfelt songs of praise.   It
is remarkable, too, that they connected His advent with
God's covenant 'promise,' and with 'the oath which He
sware to their father Abraham ;' for Mary, in her sublime
' Magnificat,' exclaims, ' He hath holpen His servant
Israel in remembrance of His mercy, as He spake to our
fathers, to Abraham, and to his seed for ever :' and
Zacharias celebrates the Lord's faithfulness in fulfilling
His word, ' as He spake by the mouth of His holy prophets, which have been since the world began.'   These
songs of faith fall on our ears like a chorus of sweet
music, as the Jewish Church was ready to vanish away ;
and they give touching evidence of the living piety which
the Old Testament still nourished within her bosom, while
they form a fit introduction to the new and better dispensation of ' the fulness of times.'   The Spirit of Prophecy, withdrawn since the age of Malachi, is now
restored ; and the Jewish Church, like an organ long
silent, is once more touched by a divine hand, and its
last notes resound in honour of Christ the Lord.

LECTURE II.

HISTORY OF THE DOCTRINE IN THE APOSTOLIC AGE.

WE have seen that the privilege of Justification was enjoyed by all true believers, from the date of the first promise of a Saviour, till His advent in the 'fulness of time.' But the divine doctrine on this subject was in process of time sadly corrupted, both among Gentiles and Jews.

Our attention will now be directed to the state of opinion which prevailed in regard to it among the Gentiles, and also among the Jews, when the Gospel was first brought to them,—to the manner in which their respective errors were treated, by our Lord Himself during His personal ministry, and afterwards by His Apostles,—and to the controversies on the subject which arose, in that age, within the Christian Church itself, from the influence of Judaizing teachers, on the one hand, and the introduction of Gentile philosophy, on the other.

The state of opinion on the subject of Justification before God, which prevailed both among the Gentiles and the Jews, when the Gospel was proclaimed in 'the fulness of time,' is worthy of special consideration, as it serves to throw much light on the teaching of our Lord and His Apostles.

The divine doctrine of the Justification of sinners was associated, from the beginning, with the promise of a Saviour, and with the significant rite of Sacrifice; and these were universal, or common to the whole race of mankind, on two occasions,—first, when Adam, the father of the old world, and, secondly, when Noah, the father of the new world, were each admitted into covenant with God. (1) There was as yet no distinction,—no middle wall of partition,—between Gentiles and Jews; and God's revelation was available for all mankind. It was transmitted at first from sire to son, and from age to age, by oral tradition. How far the revealed promise of a Saviour, combined with the practical observance of sacrificial worship,—with the instinctive dictates of conscience which awakened a sense of guilt, and a foreboding of judgment,—and with the experience of God's dispensations in providence, as manifest proofs both of His justice and goodness, and as significant indications of their having been placed in a state of respite and reprieve, rather than of strict retribution,—may have led some to repent, and to 'seek after God, if haply they might find Him,' we cannot tell; but, for ought we know, the Spirit of God may have applied these elementary truths to the heart and conscience of many a sinner in that morning twilight of Revelation, so as to lead them to confess their sins with godly sorrow, and to trust and hope in the forgiving mercy of God through a promised Saviour. For, although there is only one method of Justification for sinners, there have been 'many diversities of administration' in applying it to the souls of men; and on every question respecting the extent of its efficacy, it is enough to say, that all who were pardoned and accepted of God in any age, or in any land, must have been chosen by His grace, redeemed by the blood of Christ, and renewed by His Holy Spirit.

It is manifest, however, that the first promise of a

Saviour, and the real significance of Sacrifice, as a part
of divine worship, were soon greatly obscured, or altogether forgotten, by those to whom no new revelation was
vouchsafed; and that, while the outward rite of sacrifice
continued to be universally observed, it was divorced, in
most cases, from all knowledge of Gospel truth, and became,
in process of time, the principal part of a gorgeous, but
gloomy, system of superstition.

We cannot doubt, indeed, that the great question in
regard to man's relation to God, and his prospects under
the divine government, must have exercised thoughtful
minds, in all nations, and in all ages. For Gentiles as
well as Jews—Greeks and barbarians—civilised and
savage races—have all observed some form of religious
worship, and must have had some idea, therefore, of their
relation to an unseen Power. Their religious opinions
and observances were no doubt inherited by tradition
from their fathers, but they must have been sustained,
also, and kept alive, by the instinctive promptings of
their own conscience, and the suggestive facts of their
own experience. Many a troubled spirit must have felt
its need of some means of allaying the fears of guilt,
and averting the tokens of judgment; and may have
anxiously cast about for some hope of relief, asking
in substance the same question with Balak—'Wherewith shall I come before the Lord, and bow myself before
the high God? Shall I come before Him with burnt-
offerings, with calves of a year old? Will the Lord be
pleased with thousands of rams, or with ten thousands of
rivers of oil? Shall I give my first-born for my transgression, the fruit of my body for the sin of my soul?'[1]
Some such anxious questionings as these may have been
suggested by conscience, burdened with a sense of guilt,

[1] Micah vi. 6.

to many a troubled spirit even in the Gentile world, and
they serve to account for a fact,—otherwise inexplicable,—
the permanent continuance of animal sacrifice, however it
may have been first introduced, among all the nations of
the earth.   When great crimes had been committed, or
signal calamities were supposed to be impending, they had
recourse to extraordinary means for averting the divine
displeasure : they betook themselves to public confession
and prayer,—to fasting, and sackcloth, and ashes,—to
solemn washings and lustrations,—to severe self-inflictions
and torture,—and to the most costly sacrifices, in which
they spared neither their flocks nor their families, but
devoted even their sons and their daughters to death.[1] (2)
There is much that is deeply impressive in the sad
earnestness, and almost savage fervour, of this heathen
worship ; and it is fraught with profound instruction,
since it shows that everywhere, and at all times, conscience was alive and active, even amongst the most
ignorant and degraded tribes,—that it was impressed,
more or less deeply, with the same solemn truths—the
fact of guilt, the displeasure of God, and the desert of
punishment,—and that in dealing with these truths,
it invariably pointed to some expiation of sin, some
satisfaction to justice, and some vicarious means of
securing pardon, or, at least, impunity.   It is probable,
indeed, that many might take part in sacrificial worship
merely as a traditional observance handed down by
their forefathers, and in conformity with the established
custom of their country, who had no real concern about
religion, and who were living a godless life in carnal
security ; and it is certain, that where there was little
knowledge of a holy and righteous God, and of a pure
and spiritual law, there could be no adequate conviction

[1] Jonah iii. 5, 6 ; 2 Kings iii. 28.

of sin, and no sure and satisfying answer to the question—
'How shall a man be just with God?'

Among the more cultivated classes, the popular
religion was generally despised, and even ridiculed, as
superstitious; yet always patronized, and occasionally
practised, by the wisest of their sages, in servile deference
to the laws and customs of their country. Every sect
of philosophy had its own favourite theory, and specu-
lated keenly on many questions of profound interest
and importance. They discussed the constitution of the
universe,—the origin of nature,—the doctrine of first
causes,—the nature of the gods,—the chief end or highest
good of man,—the nature and ground of moral distinctions,—the laws and conditions of happiness,—the
extent and limits of free-will,—the power of fate,—the
province of chance,—and the great problem of a life
beyond the grave. In that dim light of nature they
grappled with some of the most arduous problems which
can occupy the human mind, and they treated them with
a degree of intellectual power, and in a spirit of serious
earnestness, such as contrast favourably with the more
superficial, and less reverent, treatment which they have
sometimes received from philosophical inquirers in modern
times. (3) But some were Atheists,—others Pantheists,—
others Epicureans, who admitted the existence of God,
but denied His providential and moral government; while
those who held most of the truths of Natural Religion,
and discoursed sublimely on the principles of moral
virtue, had vague and doubtful conceptions of their relation to God, and their prospects under His government.
They had, properly speaking, no definite doctrine of Justification; and if they thought of pardon and acceptance
at all, they looked mainly to *three* grounds of hope: the
placability of God,—the efficacy of repentance,—and the

merit of personal rectitude.   The doctrine of the educated
Gentiles was, in these respects, substantially the same
with that of modern Socinians, while it contained also the
Pelagian element, so natural to the human mind, which
appeared especially in the proud self-sufficiency of the
Stoics, and represented the virtue of man as independent
of God Himself. (4)

In the Jewish Church, the doctrine of Justification
by grace, through faith, was never altogether extinguished, but was sadly obscured and corrupted in the
later ages of her history.

The reasoning of the Apostles with the Jews on the
subject of Justification relates chiefly to the doctrine
which was revealed in the Old Testament; and, apart from
its inspired authority, or considered simply as a process of
logical deduction from the facts which are there recorded,
it is one of the finest specimens of close, consecutive, conclusive reasoning to be found in the whole range of human
authorship.   It is founded, to a large extent, on the historical relation between the Promise (ἐπαγγελία), the Law
(νόμος), and the Gospel (εὐαγγέλιον).   In the case of man
unfallen, the Law came first, and then the Promise :—' Do
this' was the preceptive requirement, 'and thou shalt
live' was the promised blessing; but the Promise was
suspended on the condition of obedience to the precept,
and was forfeited in the event of transgression.   In the
case of man fallen and ruined, the Promise came first;
then after a long interval the Law was added; and in the
fulness of time, the Gospel was proclaimed, as the fulfilment *both* of the Promise and of the Law.   The Promise
came first to the parents of the human race in the shape
of a curse pronounced on their tempter: 'I will put
enmity between thee and the woman, and between thy
seed and her seed : he shall bruise thy head, and thou

shalt bruise his heel;' and this was associated, as we have seen, with the rite of sacrifice as its symbol and seal. It was afterwards renewed to Abraham in the gracious assurance, 'In thee and in thy seed shall all the families of the earth be blessed;' and in this form it was associated with the rite of circumcision as its sacramental sign and pledge. The Law was not given by Moses till four hundred and thirty years after the Promise had thus been sealed to Abraham; and the Apostle founds his argument for Justification by faith, without the works of the Law, on the historical relation between the Promise and the Law,—in other words, on the priority of the one to the other. His argument, as addressed to the Jews, was irresistible. They objected that the Gospel, as preached by him, annulled or set aside the Law, as given by Moses : Beware, he replied, lest you be chargeable with the very error which you impute to me, that of making one divine dispensation annul or set aside another which had gone before it,—that of making the Law of Moses to supersede the Promise made to Abraham : 'To Abraham and to his seed were the promises made. And this I say, that the covenant, which was confirmed *before* of God in Christ, the law, which was four hundred and thirty years *after*, cannot disannul, that it should make the promise of none effect. For if the inheritance be of the law, it is no more of promise : but God gave it to Abraham by promise.'[1] If it was 'by Promise,' then it was 'by faith,' for faith only receives the Promise; if it was by the Law, then it was by works, for works only fulfil the Law. True, the Law was afterwards added to the Promise, but not to disannul or to supersede it; on the contrary, it was itself a dispensation of the covenant of grace, for it was proclaimed in the name of the 'God of Abraham, and Isaac, and Jacob;' and if it

[1] Gal. iii. 16–18.

republished in all their rigour the original terms of the covenant of works, it was only 'because of transgressions, till the seed should come to whom the *Promise* was made.'[1] It was for conviction of sin, for 'the Law worketh wrath,' and is a 'ministration of death;' but, as such, it was 'our schoolmaster to bring us unto Christ, that we might be justified by faith.'[2] 'Is the *Law* then against the *Promises* of God? God forbid: for if there had been a law given which could have given life, verily righteousness should have been by the Law; but the Scripture hath concluded all under sin, that the promise by faith of Jesus Christ might be given to them that believe;'—'and we were kept under the Law, shut up unto the faith which should afterwards be revealed.' The Gospel, which reveals that faith, is the fulfilment both of the Promise and of the Law; for as the Promise made to Abraham was this Gospel anticipated, so the Gospel is the Promise fulfilled: and it is also the fulfilment of the Law,—for 'Christ is the end of the Law for righteousness to every one who believeth.'[3] And thus, 'what the Law could not do, in that it was weak through the flesh, God sending His own Son in the likeness of sinful flesh, and for sin, condemned sin in the flesh, that the righteousness of the Law might be fulfilled in us,'—and that 'we might be made the righteousness of God in Him.'[4]

The fact that the promise of grace was *prior* to the Law, and could not be annulled by it,—and that the Law itself was 'added' as a means of carrying out the Promise to its fulfilment in the Gospel, is the main ground of the Apostle's argument from the Old Testament; while a subordinate, but powerful, proof is derived from the additional fact, that Abraham was justified *before* he was even circumcised.[5]

[1] Gal. iii. 19.   [2] Gal. iii. 21, 22.   [3] Rom. viii. 3.
[4] 2 Cor. v. 21.   [5] Rom. iv.

The Jews trusted in the Law; they trusted also in Circumcision : and the Apostle cuts the sinews of their
confidence in the Law, by reminding them, first, that 'the
Promise was not to Abraham or to his seed, through the
Law, but through the righteousness of faith ;'[1] and that ' if
they which are of the Law be heirs, faith is made void, and
the Promise made of none effect :' and he equally cuts the
sinews of their confidence in Circumcision, by reminding
them, secondly, that Abraham, the father of the faithful,
was justified before he was circumcised.   ' Faith was
reckoned to Abraham for righteousness.   How was it then
reckoned ?   When he was in circumcision, or in uncircumcision ?   Not in circumcision, but in uncircumcision : and
he received the sign of circumcision, a seal of the righteousness of the faith *which he had, yet being uncircumcised.*'[2]

The Apostle thus proves the Gospel doctrine of Justification from the Old Testament Scriptures, because, while
it had not been so fully or so clearly revealed, it was
nevertheless ' witnessed by the Law and the Prophets,'[3] and
had been embraced by all true believers from the beginning,
as the method of their pardon and acceptance with God.
And in addressing this argument to the Jews, he does not
plead merely his authority as an inspired Apostle, but
appeals to the plain and obvious meaning of their own
Scriptures,—proving from undeniable facts the principles
which he lays down, and showing a marvellous insight
into the doctrinal importance of these facts, and their
logical bearing on the question at issue.

The errors which prevailed among the Jews, before,
and at the time when, the Gospel was first proclaimed,
have been classified and arranged according to their historical origin and development (5) ; but, in a mere outline,
we cannot enter into details, and must confine ourselves to

[1] Rom. iv. 13.   [2] Rom. iv. 9-11.   [3] Rom. i. 2, iii. 21.

the most prominent and characteristic features of corrupted Judaism.   The chief sources of information on the
subject are some incidental notices in the Scriptures of the
Old and New Testaments, and a fuller exposition of the
views of their more learned men in the writings of the
Talmud.   In the Old Testament, they are described as
resting in mere ceremonial observances, and sacrificial
offerings, while they neglected the weightier matters of
the Law.[1]   In the New Testament, our Lord speaks of the
Pharisees as men who 'trusted in themselves that they
were righteous, and despised others ;' and Paul ascribes
their rejection of the Gospel to their ' being ignorant of
God's righteousness, and going about to establish their own
righteousness.'[2]   Their grand error, therefore, consisted in
Self-righteousness,—and this error implied defective views
both of the spiritual requirements of the Law, by which
is ' the knowledge of sin,' and also of the free promise of
grace, by which is the knowledge of salvation.

But while this general statement sufficiently marks,
and brings into due prominence, the most characteristic
feature of their religious profession, their self-righteous
confidence rested on some peculiar opinions which were
inherited by tradition from their elders, and are expounded
and defended in the Talmudical writings.   From these
we learn that, such was their ignorance of the spiritual
meaning and extent of God's Law, which requires perfect
obedience, and holds him who ' offendeth in one point to
be guilty of all,' that their Rabbis were in the habit of
dividing men into three classes,—the righteous, whose
good works preponderated over the evil,—the wicked,
whose evil works preponderated over the good,—and a
third class who were neither righteous nor wicked, but
neutral, since their good and evil works exactly counter-

---

[1] Isa. i. 11-15, lviii. 2-7.   [2] Luke xviii.; Rom. x. 3.

balanced each other, and thus produced a perfect equili-
brium.   It was admitted that all the three classes needed
the pardon of sin,—the wicked most of all, for they had
more evil actions than good,—the neutral next, for they
had good and evil in equal proportions,—and the righteous
least of all; but still, to whatever extent they fell short of
perfection, they were guilty, and, as such, stood in need of
the divine forgiveness.   They held that such forgiveness
was attainable, but that it depended in every instance, not
on the free grace of God through the expiatory work of a
Divine Redeemer, but on the actions or the sufferings of
men themselves.   They thought little of the legal or judicial standing of moral agents, as being either simply
righteous or guilty in the sight of God; or even of their
radical spiritual character, as being either 'good trees,
bringing forth good fruit,' or 'evil trees, bringing forth
evil fruit:' they looked rather to particular actions, as
being in themselves either virtuous or vicious, according
to their mere external conformity, or want of conformity,
to the letter of the divine precepts; and they were thus
involved in two fundamental errors,—the error of overlooking the effect of any one sin in changing a man's whole
relation to God, by forfeiting His favour and incurring His
curse,—and the error of supposing that actions might be
morally good and acceptable to God, while the agents were
still chargeable with the guilt, and subject to the power,
of sin.   The one error lay at the root of their erroneous
views of Justification; the other prevented them from
feeling their need of Regeneration; and both proceeded
from a defective apprehension of the spirituality and
extent of God's Law.   This was their radical want; but
the peculiar feature of their doctrine consisted in their
looking to actions apart from the agent, and in their holding
that every good work is meritorious, just as every evil

work is deserving of punishment,—that no sin can ever extinguish the merit of any good work, and no good work extinguish the guilt of any sin,—and that, consequently, all sin must be expiated by suffering, while the sinner, nevertheless, may have a meritorious title to eternal life by reason of those good actions which he has done, and which all his sins have no power to cancel, or to deprive of their just reward. Nominal Christians sometimes think that their good works may be set over against their sins, as a sort of compensation for them ; but the self-righteous Jews, even in their blindest infatuation, never ventured to count on this. They held, indeed, that no good work is ever lost, and that its merit can never be extinguished by any amount of sin ; but they held, also, that sins and good works cannot neutralize each other,—that both must be dealt with according to their respective deserts,—and that all sin must invariably, and without any exception, be first punished in the person of the sinner, in order that his good works may then come in for their merited reward. Forgiveness of sin, therefore, could only be obtained by expiatory suffering, and eternal life secured by works of meritorious obedience.

In the way of obedience, they required such works as these : Repentance, or ' a turning to God,' which was supposed to have such an efficacy as to raise the penitent, in some respects, even above the innocent,—Prayer, which was supposed to be expiatory and meritorious, especially when it included confession of sin, and was accompanied with outward signs of grief and humiliation,—Almsgiving, for ' he that giveth to the poor lendeth unto the Lord,' and makes God his debtor,—the diligent use of ceremonial observances, such as the diverse washings and lustrations, prescribed in the Law,—the due celebration of sacrifice,— above all, the sacrament of Circumcision, which was held to have such sovereign virtue that no circumcised person could finally perish, since Abraham himself would secure his exemption from hell, and his admission into heaven. They ascribed a certain efficacy to the due observance of morning and evening sacrifice, and especially to the services of the great day of Atonement, but chiefly, it would seem, because they were offered in obedience to the divine Law, and were, on that account, acceptable to God. It was not the sacrifice that secured the acceptance of the worshipper, but rather the obedience of the worshipper that secured the acceptance of the sacrifice. Faith was required as one of the chief means of meriting eternal life, for they knew from their own Scriptures that 'the just shall live by faith;' but by faith they meant a meritorious virtue, which consisted in acknowledging the divine authority of the Law, and trusting in God, without reference to the promised Messiah, at least as a suffering and atoning Redeemer. The only Messiah whom they now expected, was a human and temporal deliverer,—not a divine and spiritual Saviour; and thus their whole salvation was left to depend on their observance of the Law of Moses, and their trust in the general mercy of God.

While the merit of good works formed an essential part of their doctrine of Justification, the indispensable necessity of some satisfaction for sin was also recognised. The satisfaction to which they looked, however, was not a vicarious one,—such as had been symbolized and typified from the beginning in the rite of sacrifice, and revealed in the writings of their own prophets; it was strictly personal, and consisted entirely in their own sufferings, whether these were inflicted by God as a punishment, or imposed on themselves as a penance, for sin. In both forms, penal satisfaction was expressly recognised. It was one of their fundamental principles, that every sin deserved punishment, and that no sin could pass with impunity ; and, as good works could not remove its guilt, it could only be expiated by the sufferings of the offender. These sufferings might be self-imposed,—by voluntary castigation,—by fasting,—by sitting in sackcloth and ashes ; or they might be divinely inflicted, in the shape of disease,—poverty,—bereavement,—and death itself, which were regarded, not as paternal chastisements, but as parts of the satisfaction due to divine justice on account of sin; and if at the hour of death its guilt had not been fully expiated, there was a Rabbinical purgatory, which was mercifully limited to twelve months of torment, at the end of which, all sin being fully expiated, the good works of every Israelite will come in for their due reward in heaven. Such was the Pharisaic doctrine of a sinner's Justification ; and its general prevalence among the Jews, at the time of our Lord's advent, affords a key to the explanation of many passages in the writings of the Evangelists and Apostles. (6)

The Gospel was addressed equally to Jews and to Gentiles; and we are now to consider how they were dealt with respectively, by our Lord Himself, during His personal ministry, and afterwards by His Apostles. The Gospel was designed to counteract the errors on this subject which then prevailed among both. These errors assumed different forms as they appeared, respectively, in the Gentile world, and in the Jewish Church; but some of them were, in substance, common to both, and sprung from the same prolific root,—the natural blindness and depravity of all men as fallen creatures; while others were peculiar to the Jews, and arose out of their traditional notions in regard to the nature and value of their special privileges, as a people in covenant with God.

The errors which were common to Jews and Gentiles alike, may be reduced to these two : *first*, to reliance on what they were, or had done, or might yet do ; and *secondly*, to reliance on mere rites and ceremonies in the formal observance of religious worship. These were the fundamental errors which then prevailed equally among both (7) ; and if we investigate the sources from which they flowed, or the grounds on which they were maintained, we shall find that they originated, in either instance, from the same causes, which can be specified with the utmost precision, and proved to have been in powerful operation, both among Jews and Gentiles. These causes were,—*First*, their overlooking the *guilt* of sin, or its immediate and inevitable effect in subjecting the sinner to a sentence of condemnation, whatever may have been his conduct in other respects, and exposing his person to the righteous displeasure of an offended Lawgiver and Judge. *Secondly*, their overlooking the spirituality of the Law in its preceptive requirements, as reaching to the state of the heart, not less than the actions of the life, and prescribing holy principles, as well as correct practice. *Thirdly*, their overlooking, or underrating, the penal sentence of the Law, as if it did not imply any serious danger, or such only as might easily be averted by repentance, reformation, and temporal sufferings, while it could, in no case, be supposed to endure for ever. And *fourthly*, their overlooking, or proudly denying, their inability, as sinners, to do anything that could effectually secure their deliverance either from the guilt or dominion of sin, and give them any well-grounded assurance of pardon and acceptance here, or of eternal life hereafter.

These deep-seated causes of error on the subject of a sinner's justification, were then in powerful operation both among Jews and Gentiles ; but there was another class of

errors which prevailed especially among the Jews, and
which arose partly from their misconception of the nature
and design of the privileges which undeniably belonged to
them, as a people in covenant with God,—and partly from
the mere human interpretations which they had received
from their fathers, and which served, in many cases, to
make 'the commandments of God of none effect by their
traditions.' They rested in their national privileges,—they
relied on their connection with Abraham as his children,—
they trusted in Moses, and 'made their boast of the law,'—
they gloried in circumcision, as the badge of their peculiar
relation to God,—they proudly contrasted their condition
with that of the Gentiles, 'who were aliens from the
commonwealth of Israel, and strangers to the covenants
of promise ;' for 'they were Israelites, to whom pertained
the adoption, and the glory, and the covenants, and the
giving of the law, and the service of God, and the promises.'

When we combine in one view the errors which were
thus peculiar to the Jews, with those which were common
to them with the Gentiles, we are able to understand, in
some measure, the views which then prevailed on the
subject of Justification, and are prepared to estimate the
wisdom and suitableness of the teaching of our Lord and
His Apostles, when, in dealing with both parties, they
sought to sweep away alike their common and their
peculiar prejudices, and to convey the Gospel to their
minds, as a divine message which proclaimed the free
pardon of all sin, and the sure hope of eternal life,
through faith alone.

We find our Lord, during His personal ministry,
insisting much on the supreme and unchangeable authority of God's Law ; expounding the spiritual meaning of
its precepts,—as requiring the homage of the heart, as
well as the obedience of the life,—setting forth its penal

sentence, as extending to everlasting punishment, where
' the worm dieth not, and the fire is not quenched,'—and
insisting on the depraved state of all men, as rendering
necessary something more than a mere outward reform,
even an inward regeneration of the soul, if they would
enter into the kingdom of God.[1] We find Him making
use of the Law, even in its covenant form, and saying, at
one time, ' If thou wilt enter into life, keep the commandments,' and at another, ' Thou hast answered right, This
do, and thou shalt live ;'[2] for He knew that a pure and
spiritual law, requiring perfect obedience as the condition
of life, was the most powerful instrument of conviction,
and that it could not be brought home to the conscience
without making every sinner feel that he is self-convicted
and self-condemned.   He thus sought to impress them, in
the first instance, with a sense of their guilt, and misery,
and danger, as sinners—to convince them of their need
of another method of Justification than that by works of
obedience to the Law, and of a far deeper, more inward
and radical, change of mind and heart, than they had
ever imagined to be either necessary or even possible :
and then He proclaimed, in all its richness and freeness,
the Gospel of the grace of God ; revealing Himself as the
Messiah who had been promised to their fathers ; announc-
ing the object of His coming, even to give ' His life a
ransom for many,' that His ' blood might be shed for the
remission of sins,' and proclaiming the doctrine of a free
Justification by grace through faith, in that summary
statement of the whole Gospel—' God so loved the world
as to give His only-begotten Son, that whosoever believeth
in Him might not perish, but might have eternal life.'[3]

[1] Matt. v.-vii. ; Mark ix. 44-48 ; John iii. 1-8.
[2] Matt. xix. 17 ; Luke x. 28.
[3] John iv. 26 ; Matt. xx. 28, xxvi. 28 ; John iii. 16.

He thus dealt with the deep-seated errors that were common to the Gentile and the Jew; and in dealing with those which were peculiar to the latter, He spoke of the humble publican as justified rather than the proud Pharisee,—of the wretched prodigal restored to his father's home and heart,—of there being 'more joy in heaven among the angels of God over one sinner that repenteth, than over ninety and nine just persons that need no repentance.'[1] Speaking of their peculiar privileges, as the seed of Abraham, and the disciples of Moses, He told them, 'If ye were the children of Abraham, ye would do the works of Abraham;' 'but ye are of your father the devil, and the lusts of your father ye will do.' 'There is one that accuseth you, even Moses, in whom ye trust. For had ye believed Moses, ye would have believed me: for he wrote of me.' 'I say unto you, That except your righteousness shall exceed the righteousness of the scribes and Pharisees, ye shall in no case enter into the kingdom of heaven.'[2]

The Apostles dealt in like manner with the errors which were common alike to Jews and Gentiles, and those which were peculiar to the former. They were brought into immediate contact and collision with both; and equally in their preaching and in their epistles, they first applied the doctrine of the Law, whether of Nature or of Revelation, for the conviction of sin, and then proclaimed the Gospel, for the justification of the sinner. Paul especially, in his Epistles to the Romans and Galatians, sets himself to prove that both Jew and Gentile were 'all under sin,'—that 'the wrath of God was revealed from heaven against all ungodliness and unrighteousness,'—that 'every mouth must be stopped, and all

[1] Luke xviii. 10-15, xv. 11-25, xv. 7-10.
[2] John viii. 39, 44, v. 45, 46 ; Matt. v. 20.

the world become guilty before God,'—and that 'by the
works of the Law shall no flesh be justified in His sight;
for by the law is the knowledge of sin.'[1] He thus seeks
to bring them to a sense of their need of another method
of pardon and acceptance than any that could be found
in their own righteousness, and then proclaims another
righteousness, even 'the righteousness of God, which is
by faith in Christ alone.'

The manner in which our Lord and His Apostles
dealt with the errors which then prevailed, both among
Jews and Gentiles, is still deeply instructive, and fitted
to throw much light both on the doctrine of Justification
which they taught, and on the nature and causes of the
opposition which it has encountered in all ages of the
Church. These errors assumed various forms, but they
had a common origin in the fallen nature of man, and
they exhibit some marked features of resemblance to
those which prevail at the present day. Nothing, indeed,
is more remarkable, and nothing can well be more instructive, than the fact that, on a comparison of all the
errors on this subject, whether ancient or modern,—the
Gentile, the Jewish, the Mohammedan, the Pelagian, the
Popish, the Socinian, the Arian, and the Neonomian,—
they are found to exhibit, amidst some circumstantial
differences, so much substantial sameness in their radical
principles, as to show that human invention in such
matters is extremely limited, and that all false religions,
which originated from men, have a certain family likeness, by which they stand opposed to the Religion which
is from God. It has been said that 'it would be difficult
to invent a new heresy' (8); and the reason is, that all
heresy has its roots in the depraved tendencies of nature,
while nature is radically the same in all ages and in all

---

[1] Rom. i. 18, iii. 19, 20 ; Gal. iii. 10.

nations.　The grand characteristic of all human systems, as distinguished from the divine method of Justification, is self-righteousness or self-sufficiency, in one or other of its manifold forms, which are all, more or less, opposed to dependence on the grace of God: and this radical error manifests itself universally amongst men,—either in reliance on the general goodness of their character and moral conduct,—or in their observance of religious forms and ceremonies, as a compensation for any short-coming in moral obedience,—or in their possession of peculiar privileges, viewed as special tokens of God's favour.　The two former grounds of false confidence appeared in Gentilism, the corruption of the Patriarchal religion,—and in Pharisaism, the corruption of the Jewish religion ; while in the latter, they were combined with a third delusion,—reliance on their peculiar privileges as a Church, in special covenant with God ; and all the three are equally manifest, in the corrupt forms, and mere nominal adherents, of Christianity itself.　The errors were the same, and their causes were the same,—slight views of the evil and demerit of sin, arising from ignorance of the spirituality and extent of the divine law, and from unbelief in regard to its penal sanctions ; and from the careful study of the manner in which they were dealt with by our Lord and His Apostles, we may best ascertain, both the true import of the doctrine which they taught, and the only effectual way of counteracting the same errors wherever they still prevail at the present day.

Besides the errors which prevailed, both among Jews and Gentiles, on the subject of a sinner's acceptance with God, before the Gospel was proclaimed, there arose afterwards certain questions within the Christian Church itself,

which had an important bearing on the doctrine of Justification, and which gave rise to new controversies, depending on different grounds from the former, and requiring,
therefore, distinct and separate consideration. These
questions arose partly from the influence of Judaizing
teachers, on the one hand, and partly from the introduction into the Church of Gentile philosophy, on the other.

The first great controversy in the Apostolic Church
was occasioned by the influence of Judaizing teachers, and
had reference to the continued obligation and observance
of the Mosaic Law. It was natural, and perhaps inevitable, that questions should arise on this subject at a time
when the Church was in a state of transition from one
divine dispensation to another, each of which was equally
supernatural, and equally sanctioned by the same supreme
authority. They were such as these: Whether the Jews
who believed in Christ should, and how far they might
lawfully, continue to attend the worship of the Jewish
Church, or observe the ordinances of the Mosaic Law,—
Whether the Gentile believers might be admitted into the
Christian Church without passing through the porch of
Judaism, and submitting to the rite of circumcision which
bound them to observe the Law of Moses ; and lastly,—a
more general question which arose out of these two, and
which had a most important bearing on the whole doctrine
of Justification,—Whether faith in Christ was, or was not,
sufficient for a sinner's pardon and acceptance with God,
without obedience to any law, whether Ceremonial or
Moral, as the reason or ground of his being justified. (9)

The last of these questions, as it was discussed by the
Apostles in opposition to certain false teachers who had
crept into the Church, is one, not only of deep historical
interest, but of permanent value, as having a decisive
bearing on the ground of a sinner's Justification in every

nation and in every age. It originated in, and was occasioned by, circumstances which were of a local and temporary nature, and the first questions which were suggested by these circumstances related chiefly to the mere observance of the Ceremonial Law: but these led on to a wider, and far more vital, question, which involved the radical principle of the whole Gospel, and included all obedience to law, whether Ceremonial or Moral, considered as the ground of a sinner's pardon and acceptance with God. The fact that the discussion arose at first in connection with the observance of the Ceremonial Law, has been made a pretext for saying that it related to that law only, and had no bearing on obedience to the Moral Law; and hence it has been inferred that when Paul excludes ' works' from the ground of Justification, he means only such works as were peculiar to the Mosaic, as distinguished from the Christian, economy, and not those works of moral obedience which are due to the law that was common to both. (10) But while the discussion related, in the first instance, to the observance of the Ceremonial Law, it involved from the beginning the special question, whether that observance, considered as an act of obedience, was necessary to a sinner's justification; and this led on to the more general question, whether obedience of whatever kind, Ceremonial or Moral, formed any part of the ground of his acceptance with God. The Apostle excludes all works without exception, Moral as well as Ceremonial, —and that, too, for the self-same reason,—namely, that they were works of law, and part of man's obedience to God. There was a difference between the two in some respects; but in the one only respect in which they had any bearing on the Justification of sinners, they were precisely the same; for while the Ceremonial Law consisted of positive precepts which were binding on the Jews only, the observance of these precepts was a moral duty by reason of the divine authority which enacted them, and became binding only by virtue of that Moral Law which was common alike to Jews and Gentiles. To admit, therefore, that the observance of the Ceremonial Law was necessary to the Justification of a sinner, would have been to admit that he was justified in part by his obedience; but so far from admitting this, the Apostle takes occasion to show that neither Jew nor Gentile could be justified by works of obedience to any law, whether peculiar to the one or common to both, and that the one, not less than the other, might be justified, fully and freely, by grace through faith.

The special question, as to the necessity of Circumcision in the case of the Gentiles, was thus the occasion of a much more general discussion, in regard to the relation which Justification, in the case of a sinner, bears to Grace and Faith, on the one hand, and to Law and Works, on the other: and in conducting that discussion, in opposition to Judaizing teachers who insisted on the necessity of Circumcision, the Apostle passes far beyond the observance of the Ceremonial Law, and grapples with the fundamental principle which lay at the root of their false doctrine,—namely, that obedience to God's Law, whether Ceremonial or Moral, was necessary as being the ground, in whole or in part, of a sinner's Justification in His sight. And so far from confining himself to the Ceremonial Law, —which was the mere occasion, and not the chief subject, of his great argument,—he merely refers to it, in his Epistle to the Galatians, as that part of the Law which was morally binding on the Jews, until it was repealed by the same divine authority which imposed it, and shows that neither that part of their obedience, nor any other, could secure their Justification before God. He excludes, therefore, all works of obedience of whatever kind, and, in his Epistle to the Romans, his whole argument is based on a law which was common both to Jew and Gentile, and which made it manifest that 'by the deeds of the law shall no flesh be justified in His sight.'

The more special questions which led to this general discussion of the method of Justification, were speedily determined by the unanimous judgment of the Apostles, which obtained the general acquiescence of the primitive Church.

The question,—whether the Jews who believed in Christ should, or might lawfully, continue in the observance of those Mosaic institutions to which they had been accustomed from their earliest years,—was not settled abruptly by any dogmatic decree, but left to the judgment of every worshipper, who was held free to act on his own responsibility in this matter, provided he neither looked to any of these observances for his own justification, nor sought to impose them on others, as if they were necessary to salvation. In one view, the Jewish Dispensation may be said to have come to an end, when the figures under the Law were superseded by the substance under the Gospel, or when 'the veil of the temple was rent from the top to the bottom;' and already the middle wall of partition between Jew and Gentile was taken down by the vision and revelation which the Lord vouchsafed to Peter; but, practically, the old economy was to continue, to some extent, until God should finally abolish it by the destruction of Jerusalem, and the dispersion of His ancient people. During that interval, while the Ceremonial Law was no longer binding even on the Jews, it might still be observed, at least in part, and treated with reverence, both on account of its divine origin, and in deference to the general estimation in which it was held. A difference of practice in this respect was not deemed of such moment as to occasion division among Christian believers, or to disturb the peace of the Church; and it was dealt with by the Apostles in a truly catholic spirit, and on the most enlightened principles of mutual toleration.[1] It was important, however, that the disciples should be gradually weaned from these observances; and the Epistle to the Hebrews was written on purpose to convince them—that they had now the substance instead of the shadow,—that the new dispensation was in every respect superior to the old,—that the type had now been realized in the antitype, —and that the services of the Law were 'merely shadows of good things to come, but that the body is of Christ.'

The question, again,—whether the Gentiles might continue to eat meats which had been offered in sacrifice to idols,—was dealt with on the same enlightened principles. They were left free 'to eat whatever might be set before them, asking no question for conscience sake;' but if they were told that this meat was offered in sacrifice to idols, they were not to eat, simply because, by partaking of that food, they might seem to encourage idolatry,—might embolden weaker brethren who had not the same faith to sin against their conscience,—and might thus 'put a stumbling-block, or an occasion to fall, in their brother's way.'[2]

The question, again,—whether the Gentiles who believed in Christ should be circumcised, and keep the Law,—was settled by God Himself, when He poured out the Holy Ghost, first on Cornelius and his company, and afterwards on the Gentiles at Antioch: and the decree of the Council of Jerusalem, which was founded on the concurrent testimony of Peter, Barnabas, and Paul,[3] and proposed by

[1] Rom. xiv. 1, 5, 6.   [2] Rom. xiv. 2, 3, 4, 14, 15; 1 Cor. x. 25-30.
[3] Acts xi. 1-18, xv. 5-31.

James of Jerusalem, was merely declarative of the divine decision, and was passed unanimously by all the Apostles and brethren then convened. It rejected the opinion of those Pharisaic believers who insisted on the circumcision of the Gentile converts, and it imposed no other restriction on the Gentiles than what was equally incumbent on their Jewish brethren,—namely, that they should abstain from whatever might give offence or scandal to others, whose welfare they were bound to regard in the exercise of their Christian freedom. Some have attempted to show that the Apostles were divided in opinion on this subject, and that while Peter and James and the Church at Jerusalem agreed with the Pharisaic believers in holding the necessity of circumcision in the case of the Gentile converts, Paul and the Gentile churches stood alone in rejecting and condemning their doctrine. But this is at direct variance with the sacred narrative, which bears that the decree of the Council was unanimous—that it was adopted on the proposal of James himself—and that it was founded on the narrative of Peter and Barnabas, not less than of Paul. This gross misrepresentation rests entirely on a statement of Paul himself,[1] to the effect that 'at Antioch he withstood Peter to the face, because he was to be blamed;' and the reason why 'he was to be blamed' is distinctly stated: it was,—not that he differed in doctrine from Paul, or that he affirmed, while Paul denied, the necessity of circumcision in the case of Gentile believers,— but simply that his conduct was inconsistent, on that occasion, both with his avowed principles and his previous practice; for, 'before certain persons came down from Jerusalem,' he associated freely with the Gentiles, and did eat with them, but after their arrival 'he withdrew and separated himself.' It was not doctrinal error, but

[1] Gal. iii. 11–16.

practical inconsistency, for which Paul 'withstood him to
the face;' and Paul did so all the more boldly, because
such conduct on the part of one who had learned at an
earlier period 'to call no man common or unclean' was
fitted, although not intended, to give offence to the Gentile
believers, and to confirm the Pharisaic professors in the
Jewish prejudices which still cleaved to them. When
some other Jews, and even Barnabas, Paul's chosen companion, 'dissembled likewise,' and 'walked not uprightly
according to the truth of the Gospel,' Paul, with that
straightforward integrity by which he was eminently
characterized, pointed out, in the first place, the inconsistency of Peter's personal conduct, saying 'to him before
them all, If thou, being a Jew, livest after the manner
of Gentiles, and not as do the Jews, why compellest thou
the Gentiles to live as do the Jews?' and then, including
Peter, and Barnabas, and all the Jews along with himself,
and giving expression to their common faith, he declared
that the Justification of Jew and Gentile alike rested on
the same ground, and that it did not depend, in the case
of either, on their observance of the Mosaic Law. He
strikes at the root of the evil by founding mainly on the
case of the Jews, and argues from the one to the other, *a
fortiori*. 'We who are Jews by nature, and not sinners
of the Gentiles, knowing that a man is not justified by the
works of the law, but by the faith of Jesus Christ, even
we have believed in Jesus Christ,—that we might be
justified by the faith of Christ, and not by the works of
the law: for by the works of the law shall no flesh be
justified.'[1] Both might be justified, the circumcised Jew,
and the uncircumcised Gentile; but both must be saved
in the same way, by the faith of Christ, and not by the
works of the law. For the great question which was

[1] Gal. ii. 15, 16.

ever present to his mind was one which related alike to
Jew and Gentile,—whether by any work of man, of whatever kind, or only by the mere grace of God, through the
righteousness of Christ, apprehended by a lively faith, any
one can attain the pardon of sins, and a right to eternal
salvation. (11)

Paul's views in regard to circumcision, in its relation
to the Jews, on the one hand, and to the Gentiles, on
the other, receive an instructive illustration from the
seemingly opposite course which he pursued in dealing
with the cases of Timothy and Titus. Timothy was the
son of a Jewess, Eunice, whose 'unfeigned faith' was
attested by the Apostle; him Paul 'took and circumcised,
because of the Jews which were in those quarters,'[1]—
thereby showing that, like the other Apostles, he tolerated
the continued observance of this part of the law among the
Jews, while the Church was yet in a state of transition
from the old to the new dispensation. On another occasion, also, he complied with the ceremonial requirements
of the law, when he purified himself with four men who
had a vow on them, and entered into the temple with
them, on express purpose to disarm the prejudices of Jewish
believers against him, as one who was supposed to teach
'that the Jews must forsake Moses, and cease to circum-
cise their children.'[2] But Titus was 'a Greek;' and when
certain 'false brethren' would have 'compelled him to be
circumcised,' as if this were necessary, in the case of
a Gentile believer, to his acceptance with God, 'Paul
gave place by subjection, no, not for an hour, that the
truth of the Gospel might continue' with the Gentile
Church.[3] In both cases, he acted on the same comprehensive principle, and in the same catholic spirit: 'I
made myself servant unto all, that I might gain the more.

---

[1] Acts xvi. 3; 2 Tim. i. 5.   [2] Acts xxi. 20, 26.   [3] Gal. ii. 3, 5.

And unto the Jews I became as a Jew, that I might gain
the Jews : to them that are under the law, as under the
law, that I might gain them that are under the law : to
them that are without law, as without law, that I might
gain them that are without law.'[1]   There was no dis-
sembling, and no time-serving here ; he openly avowed,
and fearlessly acted on his convictions, in regard alike to
the lawfulness of circumcision for a time among the Jews,
and the utter unlawfulness of imposing it on the Gentiles ;
and he maintained that, being unnecessary for the Justification of believing Gentles, it could form no part of
the ground of Justification even in the case of believing
Jews.

The questions, which have been briefly explained,
had an important bearing, more or less directly, on the
fundamental doctrine of a sinner's Justification ; and the
precise import of that doctrine, as it was taught by the
Apostles, may be best ascertained by a careful consideration of the discussions which were occasioned by them
in the primitive Church.   Not only the arguments of
the Apostles, but the objections of their opponents also,
serve to bring out, and to place very clearly before us,
the salient points of what the Apostles were understood
to have taught.   It was objected, for example, that ' they
made void the law through faith ;' the Apostle denies
the charge, but adds, ' Yea we establish the law,'—clearly
showing that he spoke not of the ceremonial, but of the
moral law.[2]   It was objected again, that if his doctrine
of Justification by grace without works were true, ' men
might continue in sin because grace abounds ;' the Apostle
rejects and refutes this false inference from his doctrine,
—but that inference, whether true or false, clearly shows

[1] 1 Cor. x. 19-21.   [2] Rom. iii. 31.

that the Justification of which he spoke was not understood on either side to be Sanctification, or to depend at
all on Sanctification as its ground,—for there could be no
room for the objection, if Paul was supposed to teach that
men are justified by their infused or inherent righteousness. And so in many other instances, the objections of
avowed unbelievers, or of Pharisaic professors, throw much
light on what was then understood to be the Apostle's
meaning, and go far to determine many modern questions
in regard to the Gospel doctrine of Justification. (12)

Another controversy, which arose at a later period in
the Apostolic Church, was occasioned by the introduction,
through some learned converts, of certain false principles
of Gentile philosophy. Paul took occasion to warn the
disciples of the danger that might arise from this source:
' Beware lest any man spoil you through philosophy and
vain deceit, after the tradition of men, after the rudiments
of the world, and not after Christ.'[1] But it was at a later
period that John referred more specifically to the heresy
which had begun to appear among some speculative members of the Church, and which threatened to undermine
their faith in all the peculiar doctrines of the Gospel.
It arose from a mere figment of philosophy, which
represented matter as being essentially evil, and it consisted in denying the reality of our Lord's body,—thereby
setting aside the doctrine of His incarnation, and consequently the doctrine of His human sufferings, and His
atoning death. Of course this heresy undermined the
very foundations of Christian faith, and left no ground for
a sinner's Justification in the shedding of the Saviour's
blood. For this reason, the aged Apostle condemned it
with the same energy and earnestness with which Paul

[1] Col. ii. 8.

had opposed the errors of Judaizing teachers: 'Beloved, believe not every spirit, but try the spirits whether they are of God; because many false prophets are gone out into the world. Hereby know ye the Spirit of God: every spirit that confesseth that Jesus Christ is come in the flesh is of God: and every spirit that confesseth not that Jesus Christ is come in the flesh is not of God: and this is that spirit of Antichrist, whereof ye have heard that it should come, and even now already it is in the world.'[1]

It had been well for the Christian Church, if this seasonable warning against 'philosophy, falsely so called,' had been remembered and applied in every stage of her subsequent history; for all the chief corruptions of her doctrine,—especially on the subject of a sinner's pardon and acceptance with God,—arose, in the East, from the admixture of the Platonic, and in the West, from the admixture of the Aristotelian, philosophy, with the articles of the Christian faith.

[1] 1 John iv. 1-3.

LECTURE III.

HISTORY OF THE DOCTRINE IN THE TIMES OF THE FATHERS AND SCHOLASTIC DIVINES.

THE Post-Apostolic history of the doctrine can only be derived from the writings of uninspired men : and there is a wide difference, therefore, between the Historical Theology of Scripture, and the Historical Theology of the Church.   These writings, whether of ancient or modern date, possess no divine authority in matters of *Faith*, and their teaching on these subjects has no claim on our belief, except in so far as it can be proved to be in conformity with the unerring standard of God's Word.   Yet, in regard to matters of *Fact*, they may be unexceptionable witnesses, and they are the only authorities to which we can appeal, in attempting to ascertain what was the belief of the Church on any particular doctrine in the successive ages of her history. We possess an unbroken series of writings,—commencing with a few published by the companions and fellow-labourers of the Apostles, and extending down to those of the present times,—which constitute a vast library of Christian literature, and an inexhaustible storehouse of materials, for illustrating the Historical Theology of the Church.

Before adducing the evidence which may be derived from this source, it is necessary, in the first instance, to settle the exact state of the question,—for this will determine the conditions of the argument. The question is not,—Whether all the Fathers taught invariably the same doctrine of Justification,—nor even whether any one of the Fathers ever taught it in a state of perfect purity, without exhibiting in his writings any confusion of thought, or exposing himself to the charge of occasional self-contradiction? Such imperfections might be expected to occur in the writings of men uninspired; and to become more frequent and more glaring, in proportion as the teachers receded farther from the apostolic age. For the Antichristian leaven, which existed in the primitive Church, gradually spread and fermented in after times, and had become almost universal, when the Roman power, which had obstructed its earlier development, was taken out of the way, and the predicted 'Apostasy' had free course, so as at length to culminate in the 'Man of Sin,'—sitting 'in the temple of God,'—as 'the lawless one' (ὁ ἄνομος), the visible embodiment of the 'mystery of iniquity,'[1] or lawlessness (ἀνομίας). (1) We cannot expect that during the progress of this predicted Apostasy, the truth of the Gospel should continue to retain all its original purity; and we find, accordingly, that while it continued to be taught with comparative simplicity during the times of persecution and martyrdom, yet from the end of the second century it began to be corrupted by many erroneous doctrines and superstitious practices, which grew up under the fostering hand of the most eminent Fathers, both in the Eastern and the Western Church. (2) The question, therefore, is not,—Whether all the Fathers taught the doctrine of Justification in its original purity, nor even whether any one of the Fathers was entirely exempt from the corruptions which were gradually growing up in the Church; but simply, whether

[1] 2 Thess. ii. 3-8.

the doctrine of Justification by grace, through faith in
the merits of Christ, may not be traced in the writings
of some witnesses for the truth, along the whole line of
the Church's history; and whether some true believers
were not nourished and refreshed by it, even in the
darkest and most degenerate times? We answer this
question in the affirmative, by adducing testimonies from
the Fathers of every succeeding age; and in doing so,
we refer to them, not as authorities in matters of faith,
but simply as witnesses to a matter of fact. We do not
add their writings to the inspired Scriptures, so as to
frame a complex rule of faith, or even to find in them
an authoritative,—still less, an infallible,—guide in the
interpretation of the sacred writings; for man's word
can never possess co-ordinate authority with the Word
of God, and the interpretation of Scripture must never
be placed under the intolerable servitude of the 'consent
of the Fathers.' We use the writings of Augustine and
Chrysostom, just as we use the writings of Luther and
Calvin, as helps to the correct interpretation of Scripture;
and in doing so, we exercise the sacred right of private
judgment, subject only to the authority of God speaking
in His Word.

The authority of the Fathers has often been pled
in opposition to the Protestant principle of private judgment; and this might be expected on the part of Popish
and Tractarian divines; but it is passing strange, that
one so wise and learned as Stanley Faber (3) should be
found railing against it, as 'that polymorphic idol of
modern Ultra-Protestantism,' as if it had never occurred
to him, that by adding a hundred folio volumes of the
Fathers to the Old and New Testaments, as a constituent
part of a complex rule of Faith, or even as a mere rule
of Interpretation, so far from dispensing with private

judgment, we are only extending its range; for, whatever may be said of inspired Scripture, there can be no interpretation, at least, of the Patristic writings, without the free exercise of our intellectual powers, unless, indeed, we are to submit, in this department also, to the teaching of an infallible Church. (4)

It is of special importance that the precise object and reason of any appeal to the writings of the Fathers on the subject of Justification should be distinctly understood. It is simply to prove a matter of FACT, in opposition to an erroneous assertion,—the fact, namely, that the Protestant doctrine of Justification was not a 'novelty' introduced for the first time by Luther and Calvin,—that it was held and taught, more or less explicitly, by some writers in every successive age,—and that there is no truth in the allegation that it had been unknown for fourteen hundred years before the Reformation. It is only as affording evidence on this matter of fact that we appeal to the Fathers at all; and for the establishment of that fact it is not necessary that we should prove, either that it was universally taught by all the Fathers, or that any one of them taught it in its purity, with uniform consistency, and without any admixture of human error,—for that must be the hopeless task of those who still adhere to Vincent's rule of 'common consent' as the test of Catholic doctrine; but holding, with Vincent and Tertullian (5), the far sounder principle, that no power on earth has a right to introduce new articles of faith, and feeling that this principle is applicable to the Protestant, not less than to the Popish Church, we adduce extracts from the writings of the Fathers merely to neutralize what might be justly regarded as a 'legitimate presumption' against the Protestant doctrine, could it be shown that it was altogether unknown to the Church before the Reforma-

tion. Beyond this, we make no use of testimonies of the
Fathers ; but for this limited purpose, they are absolutely
conclusive.

With these preliminary remarks, we proceed to consider the doctrine of the Fathers on the subject of Justification. The first, in the order of time, and in respect also
of the interest which is felt to belong to them, are the
writings of the Apostolical Fathers, or those who lived and
laboured while some of the Apostles were still spared to
the Church. (6) Perhaps, the first impression which is left
on one's mind by the perusal of these early remains, is
that of their great inferiority to the writings of the Apostles,
—a fact with which every one must have been impressed
on passing from the study of the one to the study of the
other. It is sufficiently accounted for by the presence of
Inspiration in the Apóstles, and the absence of it in their
immediate successors. But there is another fact which
is equally evident—the striking contrast which subsists
between the writings even of the Apostolic Fathers,—
inferior as they are to the canonical Scriptures,—and
the whole contemporaneous literature of Greece, and
Rome, and Judea. We find there the lively expression of a faith such as was a new thing in the Roman
world—the faith of men who could rise above the sceptic's
question, 'What is truth?' by feeling assured that they
had found it,—so assured, that they were ready to die for
it ; the lively expression also of a zeal which was kindled
by the fire of love, and embraced the whole family of man,
—of a hope which sustained them in every trial,—a peace
and a joy which sweetened persecution itself,—and a new
spiritual life, such as had heretofore been unknown amongst
men : nay more than this, we find all these—the faith, the
love, the hope, the peace, the joy, the new spiritual life—
having their living root, and their bond of union, in the

Person and work of One, who died, and rose again, and whom they worshipped, and trusted in, as a Divine Redeemer. This is their peculiar character, and these are their distinctive features ; and in passing from the pages which give expression to their simple, but sublime, piety, to those of the most accomplished and eloquent writers of the same age, we can hardly fail to mark the immeasurable distance which separates the two, or to feel that, inferior as the first Fathers might be to many of their classical contemporaries in point of genius and learning, they had inherited from their teachers, and transmitted to their disciples, a GOSPEL, such as none of the princes of this world's wisdom had ever conceived. (7)

The doctrine of the forgiveness of sins, and of eternal life, by faith in a crucified, but risen and exalted Redeemer, pervades every part of their writings, and is evidently assumed and implied, where it is not formally or explicitly affirmed.   Their whole scheme of thought presupposes and rests upon the facts which are recorded, and the doctrines which are taught, in the New Testament.   It has been said, indeed, that the faith of the primitive Church was extremely simple,—that it was 'a life rather than a creed,'—that few, if any, of the doctrines of Scripture had as yet been developed and defined, —and that Theology had not then assumed a systematic form.   This statement is true, so far as it is meant merely to affirm, that the articles of faith were less rigorously reasoned out, and often more vaguely stated, before they were subjected to the ordeal of controversial discussion; for this holds good of every age; but it is not true, if it be understood to imply, either that the primitive Church did not believe, in substance, the self-same doctrines which were afterwards defined, or that her members were incapable of giving a sufficient reason for the hope that was in them.   The primitive Church was instructed by the ministry of the Apostles, and continued to be nourished by the Gospels and Epistles; she was the aggregate of all those individual churches,—at Rome, at Ephesus, at Corinth, at Philippi, at Colosse, at Thessalonica,—to whom Paul addressed his profound arguments, in the confident persuasion that they would be understood by those to whom he wrote; and the controversies with false teachers, which were expounded in his writings, were surely sufficient to give them clear and definite views of the doctrines of Grace.   The doctrine of Justification, in particular, was so thoroughly discussed in the writings of the Apostles, and that, too, in the way of controversy both with Jews and Gentiles, that their immediate successors had no occasion to treat it as an undecided question;— they found it an established and unquestioned article of the common faith, and they assumed and applied it in all their writings, without thinking it necessary to enter into any formal explanation or proof of it.   They were soon assailed, however, by the Gnostic and Ebionite heretics, who denied the Incarnation and Atonement of Christ; and in opposing them, they insisted chiefly on the great facts of the Gospel history, and stated, in substance, the evangelical doctrine of the real sufferings of a Divine Redeemer,—of their judicial character as a satisfaction to divine justice,—and of their expiatory purpose, as a sacrifice for 'the remission of sins.' (8)   A few specimens only can be given.

Clement of Rome, the first of the Fathers, and a fellow-labourer with Paul,[1] says in his Epistle to the Corinthians, ' Let us stedfastly look unto the blood of Christ, and let us see how precious unto God is His blood; which being shed on account of our salvation, has brought to the,

[1] Phil. iv. 3.

whole world the grace of repentance.' And again, ' All the
ancient fathers descended from Abraham, both before the
Law and under the Law, were glorified and magnified, not
through themselves, nor through their works of righteousness which they had done, but through His (God's) will.
Therefore we, also, being called through His will in Christ
Jesus, are not justified through ourselves, neither through
our own wisdom, or understanding, or piety, or works which
we have done in holiness of heart, but through faith,—
that faith through which the Almighty God hath justified
all that ever lived ; to whom be glory for ever, Amen !'
This testimony is equally full and explicit. It connects
' our salvation ' with ' the blood of Christ,'—it represents
that blood as the object of faith, and the procuring cause
of the ' grace of repentance,'—it ascribes the justification
of Abraham and all the Old Testament believers, both
before, and under, the Law, to the gracious will of God,—
it places the justification of New Testament believers
on the same ground—it excludes their own ' works ' from
having any share in their justification, even such works as
were done ' in holiness of heart,' or after their saving conversion to God,—and it speaks of Justification through
faith—the same faith by which all His people were
justified from the beginning. (9)

' To me,' says Ignatius, the disciple of John, ' Christ is
in the place of all ancient muniments. For His Cross,
and His death, and His resurrection, and the faith which
is through Him, are my unpolluted muniments ; and in
these, through your prayers, I am willing to have been
justified.' Polycarp, also a disciple of John, writing to the
Philippians, speaks of ' the Lord Jesus Christ, who endured
to submit unto death for our sins ; whom God raised up,
having loosed the pains of hell ; in whom ye believe, not
having seen Him, but believing ye rejoice with joy un-

speakable and full of glory, . . . knowing that through grace ye are saved, not of works, but by the will of God, through Jesus Christ.'

The earliest Apologist, Justin Martyr, says: 'No longer by the blood of goats and of sheep, or by the ashes of a heifer . . . are sins purged; but by faith, through the blood of Christ and His death, who died on this very account.' And again, 'Abraham was testified of God to be righteous, not on account of Circumcision, but on account of Faith; for, before he was circumcised, it was said of him, "Abraham believed in God, and it was imputed unto him for righteousness."'

Nothing can be more explicit than the testimony of the author of the Epistle to Diognetus: 'God gave His own Son the ransom for us: the holy, for the transgressors; the good, for the evil; the just, for the unjust; the incorruptible, for the corruptible; the immortal, for the mortal. For what, save His righteousness, could cover our sins? In whom was it possible that we, transgressors and ungodly as we were, could be justified, save in the Son of God alone? O sweet interchange! O unsearchable operation! O unexpected benefit! that the transgression of many should be hidden in One Righteous Person, and that the righteousness of One should justify many transgressors.' (10)

The Church of the Catacombs speedily became the Church of the Empire; and the faith, which had only been brightened and purified by the fires of persecution, began to wane and wax dim, in the season of outward safety, and worldly prosperity. All danger being removed, it was no longer in the prospect of martyrdom that men professed to be Christians, and multitudes assumed that profession who were Christians only in name. A declining sense of sin, accompanied with a growing indifference and formality in the Church, weakened their attachment to the peculiar doctrines of the Gospel, and gradually opened the door for the admission of flagrant heresy in regard to some of the most fundamental articles of faith. In the absence of any deep conviction of sin, and of its infinite demerit in the sight of God, men did not feel their need of a Divine Redeemer, and fell an easy prey to Arius, and his followers, when they denied the divinity of Christ, and spoke of Him merely as the highest of created beings. By the mere fact that they *denied*, and attempted to *disprove*, His supreme divinity, the Arians afford convincing evidence that it had hitherto been the faith of the Church. It was not His divinity, but His humanity, that was first assailed by the Docetæ and the Marcionites; and even now it was not His mere humanity, but His super-angelic dignity, which was affirmed by the Arians; but in both cases alike, although for different reasons, the doctrine of the Atonement was superseded,—the Gnostics denying the humanity of Christ, on which its reality depended; and the Arians His supreme divinity, without which its sufficiency, as a satisfaction to Divine Justice, could not be established. The doctrine of His atoning sacrifice being thus brought into doubt, of course the method of Justification by grace, 'through faith in His blood,' was also obscured, and another way of acceptance with God through the repentance and reformation of sinners was substituted in its stead. For all the peculiar doctrines of Scripture are so indissolubly connected, that an error on one point generates error on every other; and thus defective views of the guilt and demerit of sin prevented some nominal Christians from feeling their need of a Divine Redeemer; and from this point they were led on to deny the divinity of Christ,—to reject His atoning sacrifice,—and to forsake the old method of Justification by faith in His blood.

The first great heresies—the Gnostic, Ebionite, and Arian—related to the doctrine concerning God (Theology proper),—the Trinity in Unity,—the Incarnation of the Son, and each of His two natures, the human and divine : the second class of heresies—the Manichean, Pelagian, and Semi-pelagian—related to the doctrine concerning Man (Anthropology),—his natural character and actual condition as a sinner,—the freedom or bondage of his will,—his power or his impotency to raise and restore himself: and both had a most important bearing on the whole doctrine of salvation (Soteriology), but especially on the method and grounds of a sinner's justification with God.   The doctrine concerning God, and then the doctrine concerning Man, were thoroughly discussed and defined by the Church,— the one under the guidance of Athanasius,—the other under that of Augustine; and these illustrious defenders of the faith, by establishing, first, the real incarnation and the supreme divinity of the Son of God, and secondly, the total depravity of man, and the freeness and efficacy of divine grace, contributed largely to strengthen the foundations of a sound doctrine of Justification by grace through faith. This doctrine was always held in substance by true believers; but it seems to have been reserved, for its fuller development, and more precise definition, till the great controversy which arose between the Romish and the Reformed Churches in the sixteenth century.

The Patristic doctrine of Justification, as it may be gathered from the extant remains of a long series of writers who succeeded the companions and fellow-labourers of the Apostles, has always been, for obvious reasons, a subject of controversy between Romanists and Protestants ; but in recent times some Protestants have been found, who, professing to reject certain corruptions of that doctrine which they conceive to be peculiar to the Church of Rome, and proclaiming at the same time their unbounded deference to the consent of Catholic Antiquity, have affirmed, that the doctrine of a forensic Justification, as taught by Luther and Calvin, was 'a novelty' which first obtained a place in Theology at the era of the Reformation,—that it was unknown to the Church for fourteen hundred years after the Apostolic age,—and that it was at direct variance with the uniform and unanimous teaching of the Fathers, both of the Greek and Latin Church. (11)

Augustine, as the great Doctor of Grace, has been singled out, and exhibited with marked prominence, as the advocate of 'moral,' and the opponent of 'forensic,' Justification, chiefly because his views, on other subjects, were known to be in accordance with those of the Reformers. For this reason, his authority was supposed to afford a conclusive proof of the novelty of the Protestant doctrine : and, certainly, it would be strange, if it were true, that he who did so much to establish the doctrine of free grace, in opposition to free-will, in the matter of our Sanctification, should have said anything to undermine the doctrine of free grace, in opposition to self-righteousness, in the matter of our Justification. But before we adopt so improbable a conclusion, we must carefully consider the occasion and nature of the controversy in which he was then engaged. It was materially different from the subsequent controversy between Rome and the Reformation. (12) The Pelagians, with whom he was called to contend, admitted the doctrine of Grace in the free remission of sins, while they denied the necessity of efficacious grace for the conversion of the sinner. Their heresy, therefore, did not *directly* raise the question of a sinner's Justification in the sight of God, although it involved principles which had an important bearing upon it.   They believed, that 'there is forgiveness with God;' but they believed also, that man is able of himself 'to repent and turn to God.'   Augustine defended the doctrine of Grace on the side on which it was then assailed; and, in doing so, he established certain great principles which were sufficient to counteract the tendency, inherent in the Pelagian doctrine, towards a self-righteous scheme of Justification.   These two fundamental principles, in particular, were clearly taught by Augustine,—first, that works done before faith are not good, but evil, (*splendida peccata*); secondly, that works done after faith, although good, as being the fruits of grace in the believer, are so imperfect in themselves, and so defiled by remaining sin, that they need to be sprinkled with the blood of Christ, and can only be accepted through His merits: and these two principles, when combined with his more general doctrine of free, sovereign, efficacious grace, involve the substance of the Protestant doctrine.   He affirmed the free grace of God in opposition to the free-will of man, as the spring and fountainhead of a sinner's whole salvation.   That salvation comprehended both his Justification and his Sanctification,— the remission of his sins and the renovation of his nature, —and it was ascribed by Augustine, in each of its constituent parts, to the free and unmerited grace of God alone.   By establishing this fundamental truth, he laid a firm foundation for the more special doctrine of a free Justification by grace through faith in Christ; and his writings contributed largely to the illustration of that great truth at a later period, when it became the subject of formal controversy between Rome and the Reformers. In this way, and to this extent, Augustine prepared the

way for Luther and Calvin, by excluding the merit of
man, and exalting the grace of God.

It has been alleged, not only that Augustine knew
nothing of a ' forensic' Justification by faith, but that
he taught the opposite doctrine of a 'moral' Justification,
by infused or inherent righteousness.   This allegation
rests mainly on two grounds,—first, the use which he
made of the term ' Merits' when he spoke of good works ;
and secondly, the sense in which he used the term
' Justification,' when he spoke of the benefit bestowed
by the Gospel.

In regard to the first, it has been conclusively proved
by most of our great writers in their controversy with
the Romish Church, that Augustine, in common with all
the Latin Fathers, used the term ' Merits,' not to denote
legal, or even moral desert, properly so called, but to
signify, either simply a means of obtaining some blessing,
—or, at the most, an action that is rewardable, not ' of
debt, but of grace.'   It was at a later period, and chiefly
through the Scholastic Theology, that the doctrine of
Merit, properly so called, was constructed ; but, as used
by the Fathers, the term had no such offensive meaning
as was afterwards attached to it, and denoted merely that
by which benefit was obtained.   In this general sense, as
denoting the obtaining or procuring of something, it was
said that we might merit Christ, or merit the Spirit, or
merit eternal life ; not that we could deserve any one of
these inestimable gifts, or that they could ever become
due to us in justice,—for this is inconceivable,—but
simply that they might thus be procured and enjoyed.
In this sense, the verb occurs even in the Protestant
Confession of Augsburg ; but now, when the meaning of
the term has been entirely changed, it is not safe to speak
of Merits at all, excepting only the Merits of Christ. (13)

In regard, again, to the sense of the term Justification, as it was used by Augustine, there can be no doubt
that he often employed it to denote the whole of that
change which is wrought both on the *state* and *character*
of a sinner,—on his relation to God, and also on the
spirit of his mind,—at the time of his conversion. According to its etymology, the term is sufficiently comprehensive to admit of this application of it; and in this
wide sense, it has sometimes been employed even by
Protestant writers;—for instance, by John Forbes (of
Corse), who defines the term, taken in its largest acceptation, as denoting all that righteousness by which we
become righteous; and then adds, that this righteousness
is twofold—the one being the righteousness of Christ,
imputed by God, and received by faith, which is the
righteousness of Justification; and the other the personal
righteousness of the believer, which is inherent in him,
as having been infused by the Holy Spirit, and which is
the righteousness of Sanctification. (14)   In the same
comprehensive sense, the term was used by Augustine.
But while he included under it the renovation of the
sinner, as well as his forgiveness and acceptance with
God, there is no evidence to prove, either that he confounded these two blessings of God's grace, or that he
made the one the ground or reason of the other.   This
is the only important point in the question which has
been raised, if we are to ascertain, not the sense merely
in which he uses a particular term, but what was the
real substance of his doctrine.   His was not a mind that
could confound things so different as the guilt of sin and
its defilement,—the remission of sin and the renewal of
the sinner,—a man's external relation to God, and his
inherent spiritual character.   And as he could not confound the two, or treat them otherwise than as distinct,

though inseparable, blessings, so there is no evidence to
show that he made a sinner's forgiveness and acceptance
with God to rest on his own inherent righteousness, as
its procuring cause, either before or after his conversion ;
—not before, since the whole of Augustine's doctrine was
directed to prove that man, in his unrenewed state, has
no righteousness whatever, but must be indebted to God's
sovereign grace, not only for the forgiveness of sin, but
also for the gift of faith to receive it ; and not after, since
Augustine's doctrine recognised the remains of indwelling
sin even in the regenerate,—sin, which was not deleted
by baptism, nor destroyed by regeneration itself,—sin,
which needed daily pardon, and vitiated even the best
works of the believer.   The whole tenor of his teaching
shows, that he would have responded, with heart and
soul, to the memorable saying of Bernard, ' So far from
being able to answer for my sins, I cannot answer even
for my righteousness.' (15)

If the sense of these two terms, ' Merit,' and ' Justification,' as they were used by Augustine and many of the
Fathers, be correctly understood, the question whether
they held the doctrine of a ' forensic,' or of a ' moral,'
Justification, admits of being easily determined.   It is a
matter of fact, and can only be ascertained by an appeal
to their writings.   That appeal has been made, in former
times by Downham, Davenant, Usher, and others, and
more recently by O'Brien, Faber, and Bennett; and uniformly with the same result, the adduction of a mass of
testimonies, extending from Apostolic times down to
Bernard, the last of the Fathers, abundantly sufficient to
prove that the doctrine of Justification by grace through
faith alone had some faithful witnesses in every succeeding age of the Church.   It was never universally received,
any more than it is at the present day ; it was always

opposed by the spirit of self-righteousness,—often corrupted by human inventions,—sometimes perverted and
abused by Antinomian licence; but it was then, as it is
now, the doctrine of many true believers, and the very
'joy and rejoicing of their hearts.' So far from its being
true, that for fourteen hundred years it was lost to the
Church, it was at all times the refuge of awakened sinners,
and the relief of humble penitents. Divines have collected
testimonies to this effect from the writings of the Fathers,
and presented them in regular historical order; and these
testimonies,—considered simply as evidences in proof of a
fact, and not as authorities in proof of a doctrine,—are
more than sufficient to decide the only question now at
issue. Faber adduces quotations from *sixteen* of the Fathers
who wrote before the middle of the fifth century, and
refers to *twelve* more as having been adduced by Archbishop Usher, making together *twenty-eight* Fathers, and
showing that every century down to the twelfth furnishes
one or more witnesses to the truth. (16)   They prove not
merely the fact that the doctrine of a forensic Justification
by grace through faith was held by these Fathers, but
that it was held in connection with the cognate truths on
which it depends;—that Justification was ascribed to the
free grace and favour of God, as its source,—to the redeeming blood and meritorious righteousness of Christ, as
its ground,—to the reciprocal imputation of our sins to
Him, and of His righteousness to us, as its true scriptural
explanation,—and to faith alone, as the instrumental
means, by which it is appropriated and made ours, when
it is applied by the grace of the Holy Spirit.

A few extracts may be offered, simply as specimens of
these Patristic testimonies :—

' As through the disobedience of one man,' says Irenæus, the disciple of
Polycarp, ' many were made sinners, and forfeited life, so it behoved also,

that through the obedience of one man who first was born from the Virgin, many should be justified, and receive salvation.' 'The Apostle Paul says in his Epistle to the Romans—"But now, without the Law, the righteousness of God is manifested, being witnessed by the Law and the Prophets;" for "the just shall live by faith." But, that "the just shall live by faith," had been foretold by the Prophets.'

'What person,' says Cyprian, 'was more a Priest of the Most High God than our Lord Jesus Christ, who offered a sacrifice unto God the Father? . . . If Abraham "believed in God, and it was imputed unto him for righteousness," then each one, who believes in God, and lives by faith, is found to be a righteous person, and long since, in faithful Abraham, is shown to be blessed and justified.'

'Not by these,' i.e. by works, says Athanasius, 'but by faith, a man is justified as was Abraham.' . . . 'In no other manner can there be redemption and grace to Israel and to the Gentiles, except the original sin, which through Adam passed unto all, be loosed. But this, says he (the Apostle), can be blotted out through no other than through the Son of God.' . . . 'It is necessary, therefore, to believe the holy Scriptures,— to confess Him who is the First-fruit of us, . . . to be struck with wonder at the great dispensation,—to fear not the curse which is from the Law, for "Christ hath redeemed us from the curse of the Law." Hence the full accomplishment of the Law, which was made through the First-fruit, is imputed to the whole mass.'

'This is the true and perfect glorying in God,' says Basil, 'when a man is not lifted up on account of his own righteousness, but has known himself to be wanting in true righteousness, and to be justified by faith alone in Christ. And Paul glories, in that he despises his own righteousness, and seeks the righteousness which is through Christ, even the righteousness which is from God by faith. . . . Thou hast not known God through righteousness on thy part, but God hath known thee on account of His goodness; thou hast not apprehended Christ through thy virtue, but Christ hath apprehended thee through His coming.'

'Without the works of the Law,' says Ambrose, 'to an ungodly man, that is to say, a Gentile, believing in Christ, his "faith is imputed for righteousness," as also it was to Abraham. How, then, can the Jews imagine, that through the works of the Law they are justified with the justification of Abraham, when they see that Abraham was justified, not by the works of the Law, but by faith alone? There is no need, therefore, of the Law, since through faith alone, an ungodly man is justified with God.'

'Through faith, without the works of the Law,' says Origen, 'the thief was justified; because, for that purpose, the Lord inquired not what he had previously wrought, nor yet waited for his performance of some work after he should have believed; but, when about to enter into Paradise, He took him unto Himself for a companion, justified through his confession alone.'

'When an ungodly man is converted,' says Jerome, ' God justifies him through faith alone, not on account of good works, which he possessed not; otherwise, on account of his ungodly deeds, he ought to have been punished. . . . Christ, who " knew no sin," the Father "made sin for us," that, as a victim offered for sin was in the Law called " sin," so likewise Christ, being offered for our sins, received the name of " sin," that " we might be made the righteousness of God in Him"—not our righteousness, nor in ourselves.'

'The Apostle,' says Chrysostom, 'hath accused the Gentiles, hath accused the Jews; his next step, in regular order, was to speak of the " righteousness which is by faith." For, if neither the Law of nature profited anything, nor the written Law was of greater avail; if both alike only oppressed those who made a wrong use of them, and showed them to be worthy of greater punishment, henceforth salvation through grace became necessary. . . . What, then, did God do? . . . "He made," says the Apostle, " a righteous person to be a sinner, in order that He might make sinners righteous," . . . not simply that we might be made righteousness, but that we might be made the very " righteousness of God." For, certainly, it is the righteousness of God, when we are justified, not by works (for, in that case, it were needful that no stain should be found), but by grace, where all sin is made to vanish away.'

'Behold,' says Augustine, ' Christ came for this very purpose, that He might redeem those who were under the Law, in order that we might no longer be " under the Law, but under Grace." " All who are justified through Christ, are righteous, not in themselves, but in Him." . . . What grace have we first received? Faith. When we walk in Faith, we walk in Grace. Whence, then, have we merited (or obtained) this? By which of our precedent merits? Let no one here flatter himself. Let him rather return to his conscience,—let him explore the secret hiding-places of his thoughts,—let him return to the series of his actions. Let him not consider what he now is, if indeed he be anything; but what he was, that he might be somewhat; and he will find that he was worthy of nothing but punishment. If, then, thou wert worthy of punishment, and if He came whose office was not to punish sins, but to pardon them,

Grace is given unto thee, not wages paid to thee. Why, indeed, is it called Grace? Because it is given gratuitously. For by no precedent merits didst thou buy what thou hast received. The sinner, therefore, received this grace first, that his sins should be forgiven him. . . . Good works follow after a justified person, they do not go before, in order that he may be justified. . . . We are "His workmanship, created in Christ Jesus unto good works," for man can work no righteousness, unless he be first justified. The Apostle saith, "Believing in Him who justifieth the ungodly." He begins from Faith, in order to make it clear that, not good works, preceding Justification, show what man hath merited, but that good works, following after Justification, show what man hath received.'

In a direction for the visitation of the sick by Anselm, whose views on the Atonement and Justification were thoroughly Protestant (17), we find these precious words :—

'Dost thou believe that thou canst not be saved but by the death of Christ? Go to, then, and, whilst thy soul abideth in thee, put all thy confidence in this death alone—place thy trust in no other thing,—commit thyself wholly to this death,—cover thyself wholly with this alone,—cast thyself wholly on this death,—wrap thyself wholly in this death. And if God would judge you, say, "Lord! I place the death of our Lord Jesus Christ between me and Thy judgment: otherwise I will not contend, or enter into judgment, with Thee." And if He shall say unto thee, that thou art a sinner, say unto Him, "I place the death of our Lord Jesus Christ between me and my sins." If He shall say unto thee, that thou hast deserved damnation, say, "Lord! I put the death of our Lord Jesus Christ between Thee and all my sins; I offer His merits for my own, which I should have, and have not." If He say, that He is angry with thee, say, "Lord! I place the death of our Lord Jesus Christ between me and Thy anger."'

We close with a few words from Bernard, the latest of the Fathers :—

'What can all our righteousness be before God? Shall it not, according to the prophet, be viewed as "a filthy rag;" and if it is strictly judged, shall not all our righteousness turn out to be mere unrighteousness and deficiency? What, then, shall it be concerning our sins, when not even our righteousness can answer for itself? Wherefore, exclaiming vehemently with the Prophet, "Enter not into judgment with Thy servant, O Lord!" let us flee, with all humility, to Mercy, which alone can save our souls. . . . Whosoever, feeling compunction for his sins, hungers and thirsts after righteousness, let him believe in Thee, who "justifiest the ungodly;" and thus, being justified by faith alone, he shall have peace with God. . . . Thy Passion is the last refuge, the alone remedy.   When wisdom fails, when righteousness is insufficient, when the merits of holiness succumb, it succours us.   For who, either from his own wisdom, or from his own righteousness, or from his own holiness, shall presume on a sufficiency for salvation?'   'Oh, he alone is truly blessed to whom the Lord imputes not sin; for there is no one who has not sin.   "All have sinned, and come short of the glory of God."   Yet "who shall lay anything to the charge of God's elect?"   To me, it is sufficient, only to have Him propitiated, against whom only I have sinned. . . . The Apostle says, "If one died for all, then were all dead," meaning thereby to intimate, that the satisfaction made by One should be imputed to all, even as One conversely bore the sins of all.' (18)

The result of this appeal to the writings of the Fathers may be stated in a few words:—It proves, beyond all controversy, the fact that the Protestant doctrine of Justification by grace through faith, was not a novelty introduced into the Church by Luther and Calvin,—that it was held and taught by some of the greatest writers in every successive age,—and that there is no truth in the allegation that it had been unknown for fourteen hundred years before the Reformation.

There exists, however, in the extant remains of Patristic literature, abundant evidence to show, that the doctrine of a free Justification by grace, through faith in Christ alone, was obscured and corrupted at a very early period in the history of the Church.   Human additions to divine truth, and human inventions in the worship of God, crept in gradually and insensibly, and existed at least in germ even in the Apostolic age.   They infected, to some extent, the theology of the earliest

Fathers, although their writings are still sufficient to prove that they continued for a time to hold the truth in substance, and in a state of comparative purity, as contrasted with its subsequent corruption. But towards the close of the Patristic period, and notwithstanding the sound doctrinal teaching of such men as Anselm and Bernard, there arose a new method of Theology, which has been called, from the date of its appearance, the Mediæval, and, from the source in which it originated, the Scholastic, System. It forms the connecting link between the Patristic Theology, on the one hand, and the fully developed doctrine of Rome, on the other ; and it exercised an important influence in moulding the form, and corrupting the substance, of the Church's creed, as it existed at the dawn of the Reformation.

The Scholastic Theology may be described, in general terms, as a system which attempted to explain the doctrine of the Church by the philosophy of the Schools. It differed essentially from the traditionary method which had previously prevailed, and which consisted in collecting the ' sentences' of Fathers, Popes, and Councils, as sufficient to determine any article of faith. It sought to substitute Philosophy for Tradition, as the basis of Christian doctrine, and to bring every revealed truth to the test of some intellectual or ethical principle. (19) The prevailing philosophy was that of Aristotle, not in its original integrity, but as it had been commented on, and corrupted by, his Arabian expounders; and as the heathen sage knew nothing of any righteousness except such as was human and personal, the application of his doctrines to the system of revealed truth led to the substitution of the inherent righteousness of man, for the imputed righteousness of Christ, as the ground of Justification before God. This was the radical error of Scholasticism, and it was the prolific root of several kindred errors which naturally sprung from it. It produced, in particular, *three* doctrines which were directly opposed to the truth of Scripture ;— *first*, the doctrine that justifying grace consists, not in the free favour and blessing of God, as these are opposed in Scripture to His wrath and penal sentence, but in subjective grace,—or a gracious quality infused, such as is opposed in Scripture, not to the guilt, but to the power of sin ; *secondly*, the doctrine that good works are meritorious, in the proper sense of the term, as being the conditions of pardon and acceptance with God,—the effectual means of satisfying His justice, averting His displeasure, and securing His favour now, and eternal life hereafter ; and *thirdly*, the doctrine, that there is a difference between the precepts of the divine Law which are binding on all men, and certain 'Counsels of Perfection' which some may voluntarily undertake to fulfil, and by the fulfilment of which they may not only secure eternal life for themselves, but acquire a surplusage of merit, which may be imputed to others for their Justification—a merit arising from 'works of supererogation,' which even the mild Melancthon characterized as 'that irony of the devil.' The substitution of the inherent righteousness of man for the imputed righteousness of Christ, as the ground of a sinner's Justification, naturally led on to these kindred errors ; and the doctrine of Merit, which was elaborated by the Scholastic theologians, lay at the foundation of all the superstitions and corruptions of the Papal system. (20) Scholasticism contained the germs of Popery, and Popery was just Scholasticism developed and full-blown ; while all the corruptions of the Church and all the speculations of the Schools coalesced, and found their point of union, in that crowning abomination,—the sale of Indulgences.

LECTURE IV.

HISTORY OF THE DOCTRINE AT THE ERA OF THE REFORMATION.

THE revival of the Gospel doctrine of Justification
was the chief means of effecting the Reformation of
religion in Europe in the sixteenth century. That we
may form some adequate estimate of the urgent necessity,
the real nature, and the practical results of that great
revival, it is necessary to consider—the corrupt practices
in the Church of Rome which were the immediate occasion of exciting inquiry and discussion on the subject of
a sinner's pardon and acceptance with God,—and the
doctrine of the Reformers, as contrasted with that on
which these practices depended for their support.

The immediate occasion which led to inquiry and
discussion at this time on the subject of a sinner's pardon
and acceptance with God, was the prevalence of gross
practical abuses in the Church of Rome. The Scholastic
theory of Merit had reached its culminating point in the
proclamation of Indulgences. The public sale of Papal
pardons gave rise to a thorough discussion of the whole
subject of a sinner's justification before God ; it was the
spark which ignited all the combustible matter that had
been accumulating for ages, and produced an explosion
which rent the Church to her foundation. It might seem,
at first sight, as if it were rather one of the many practical
abuses, or corrupt usages, which had sprung up in a dark
and superstitious age, than a heretical doctrine, which
threatened to subvert the divine method of Justification ;

and it has sometimes been said that, at the first, there was no serious difference between the two parties in point of doctrine, but that the Reformers lifted their voice only against a practice, which must have been peculiarly offensive to enlightened and generous minds, by reason of its sordid and mercenary character, and might almost prompt them to say indignantly to the Priesthood, as the Apostle said of old to Simon Magus, 'Thy money perish with thee, because thou hast thought that the gift of God may be purchased with money.' But it was more than a practical abuse; it was the visible embodiment of a whole system of false doctrine, which subverted or undermined all the scriptural grounds of faith and hope towards God. Luther, like every other noble and unselfish spirit, must have recoiled from the unholy traffic, as alike dishonouring to God, and disgraceful to the Church; but, not content with denouncing corrupt practices, as some of his precursors had been, he had the sagacity to see that they had their root in false doctrine, and that he must strike at the root, if the Church was to be really reformed. Deeply exercised in his own mind on the subject of sin and salvation, he had felt the burden of guilt on his conscience, and had been all but overwhelmed by despair of mercy. He had the charge, too, of many penitents who came to him as their pastor, and poured into his ear in the confessional the expression of their sorrows and fears; and when the Pope's pardons were promulgated and offered for sale among the members of his own flock,—when they were actually presented to him, and pled as a reason for neglecting the penance which he prescribed,—and when he observed their effect in deadening the sense of sin, and acting as an opiate on the conscience of the sinner,—his soul was stirred within him; for he felt that it was God's pardon, and not man's, that he needed for himself,—that it was

God's pardon, and not man's, that was equally needed by every one of his penitents. He was thus led to compare the Bull of Indulgences with the Gospel of Christ,—and he saw, with the vividness of intuition, that they rested respectively on two doctrines of Justification, which were not only different, but diametrically opposed;—the one revealed by God, the other invented by the Church,—the one a doctrine of Grace, the other a doctrine of Merit,— the one founded on the finished work of Christ, the other depending on the imperfect works of sinful men. Seeing this striking contrast between the two, and knowing that both could not be true, unless light could have fellowship with darkness, he rejected the doctrine of man, and adhered to the doctrine of God; and from that day forth, in the whole exercise of his ministry, whether by word or writing, he set himself to disprove the one, in the only effectual way, by explaining and establishing the other. Convinced that truth alone can expel error, just as light alone can expel darkness, he sought to bring home to the hearts and consciences of his people the simple but sublime truth, that 'there is forgiveness with God' through faith in the blood of Christ; and to make them feel that they had no need of any of those human inventions by which that truth had been obscured and corrupted in the Church of Rome. He did not protest merely against Popish errors, he proclaimed the Gospel method of Justification, as that which, if it were once clearly understood and cordially believed, was sufficient to exclude them all; and his teaching, if it was necessarily to a large extent controversial, was far from being on that account either negative or destructive; it was mainly directed to the establishment of positive truth, and the building up of the Church on the only sure foundation, 'the faith which was once delivered to the saints.'

That we may see what doctrinal importance belonged at that time to the selling and buying of Indulgences, and how naturally Luther was led, by his horror for that monstrous corruption, to discuss the whole subject of a sinner's justification with God, it is necessary to trace them to their origin in those false views, which had long prevailed in the Church, and to exhibit a brief outline of the Romish doctrine on the subject.

The invention of Indulgences was the result of several distinct doctrines, which followed each other in consecutive order, and ultimately formed a compact and self-consistent system, opposed at every point to the doctrine of the Gospel. In delineating that system, we shall begin with the first error in the series, and then show how, by successive additions to it, all resting on that false principle, although not logically deducible from it, it was gradually matured till it reached its state of full development. In attempting to trace the idea of Indulgences to its origin, we connect it, in the first instance, with the Romish doctrine concerning the pardon of sin. This alone, and without the additions which were subsequently made to it, will not afford an adequate explanation of its origin,—for several distinct causes contributed to the result. But the Romish doctrine of pardon was the fundamental error, on which all subsequent additions were built. That doctrine divides itself into two parts—the pardon of sin contracted before, and the pardon of sin contracted after, baptism. All sin contracted before baptism, such as original sin in the case of infants, and both original and actual sin in the case of adults possessing certain previous dispositions, were said to be pardoned in Baptism,—but pardoned, not in the sense of being blotted out as criminal offences, which implied a charge of guilt and a sentence of condemnation for what was past, but in the sense of being 'deleted' in the

heart of the baptized person,—deleted by an infused principle of grace which 'renewed him in the spirit of his
mind.' All sins, again, contracted after baptism, were
held to be pardoned, not by an act of God's grace, freely
forgiving them through faith in Christ, and for His sake,
—nor even in the way of the whole of that penalty, which
these sins had deserved, being remitted at once and for
ever,—but only in the sense of eternal punishment being
taken away, while temporal punishment remained to be
endured : and hence the pardon of these sins was left to
be secured by the confession of the penitent, and the absolution of the priest,—by the sacrament of Penance in this
life, and, if that was not sufficient, by the sufferings of
Purgatory in the life to come.   These personal sufferings,
both temporal and purgatorial, were regarded as penal
inflictions on account of sin, and as an indispensable part
of the satisfaction which was due to divine justice.   Here
apparently there is pardon for all sin, whether contracted
before or after baptism ; but, in point of fact, it may be
justly said, that, in the Protestant sense of the term, there
is, in the Popish doctrine, no pardon for sin at all;—it is the
deletion of sin rather than its forgiveness; and it does not
restore the sinner immediately to the favour and friendship of God,—it leaves him still exposed to penal infliction,
in the shape of temporal, and even of purgatorial, suffering,
and bound to submit to self-mortification and penance,
in the vain hope of meeting the claims of that awful
justice, which the blood of Christ had not fully satisfied,
and of deserving that divine mercy which the merits of
Christ had not fully secured !

The Romish doctrine of Pardon proceeded on two distinctions, which, in the sense then attached to them, had
no foundation in Scripture.   The Scholastic theologians
distinguished between the guilt of sin and the guilt of

punishment (*Reatus culpæ, Reatus pœnæ*),—meaning by the
one, the personal ill-desert of the sinner, and by the other,
the legal obligation to punishment,—and contending that
the former is removed by pardon bestowed in baptism,
while the latter remains, and can only be removed by
penance or purgatory; whereas, according to Scripture,
the sinner's guilt is entirely taken away, and along with
it his obligation to punishment, while the *fact* of his ill-
desert as a sinner can never be undone, but must continue
to be confessed and acknowledged as an everlasting reason
for repentance and humiliation before God.   They distinguished also between Mortal and Venial Sins—the
former deserving eternal death, the latter deserving only
temporal punishments,—whereas, according to the Scriptures, 'every sin deserves God's wrath and curse, both in
this life and that which is to come;' and whatever difference there may be between one sin and another, as being
more or less heinous, and between the sins of believers and
those of unbelievers, that difference does not arise from
any sin being in its own nature venial, or undeserving of
punishment, and still less from one class of sins being
pardonable, and another not ; for the Law declares that
all sins are mortal, while the Gospel proclaims that all
sins, short of the sin against the Holy Ghost, are pardonable, by the free grace of God, through the infinite merits
of Christ.   The Romish doctrine of Pardon, therefore, considered in its essential nature, and in connection with the
two Scholastic distinctions to which we have referred, lay
at the foundation of that system of satisfaction by Penance,
and Purgatory, which obscured the whole doctrine of Justification, and paved the way for other corruptions, which
gradually grew into the sale of Indulgences.

But the Romish doctrine of Pardon was only the first
step in the process.   That doctrine related merely to the

penalty of the divine Law, and another was necessary to
dispose of its precept.   If the penalty denounced death as
'the wages of sin,' the precept required obedience as a
title to life.   As the former had been met by the doctrine
of personal satisfaction and penance, so the latter was
met, in the first instance, by that of personal righteousness
and merit.   By the infusion of a principle of grace into
his heart at baptism, the sinner was supposed to be made
inherently righteous, so as to be entitled to claim eternal
life on that ground, and enabled also to do good works
which were properly meritorious.   The works done before
this infusion of grace, and in the mere strength of nature,
might constitute a claim only in equity (*meritum ex con-
gruo*),—but the works done after this infusion, constituted
a claim in strict justice (*meritum ex condigno*), on the favour
and acceptance of God.   They might go about, therefore,
'to establish their own righteousness,' by the diligent
observance of all religious and relative duties, and still
more by aspiring to a higher degree of sanctity than was
supposed to be required by God's Law itself, through the
voluntary assumption of monastic vows, and submission to
ascetic rules.   It was held, theoretically, that such obedience might be, although few, if any, could venture to say
that it actually is, perfect, in the present life (1); but still,
being meritorious, it might be sufficient to meet the demands of a law, which was itself so imperfect as to leave
room for 'Counsels of Perfection.'   The doctrine of personal merit, or of meritorious obedience on the part of
every individual for himself, was, next to the doctrine
of pardon by personal satisfaction and penance, another
step in the process which led on to the invention of
Indulgences.

But the hope of divine acceptance, on the ground of
personal merit, must have been sadly troubled by the

irrepressible consciousness of much remaining imperfection and sin ; and while some might look to the merits of Christ as sufficient to supplement the defects of their own righteousness, others were led to lay hold of a new and most surprising invention—the doctrine of Supererogation, and to look for relief to the surplus merits of the saints. They had been taught to believe that holy men and women had been enabled, by assuming the vows of poverty, celibacy, and humility, or observing the 'Counsels of Perfection,' not only to acquire a sufficiency of merit for their own salvation, but to lay up a large fund of redundant merit, which was available for the benefit of others,—that this merit was transferable to all who, sensible of their own imperfection, might wish to participate in it,—and that it had power with God to procure for them the remission of their sins, and their final admission into heaven.   The doctrine of the transference of human merits, or of the imputation of what saints and martyrs had merited, for the benefit of those to whom they might be applied, was a third step in the process which led on to the invention of Indulgences.

But another step was still indispensable.   This fund of human merit, which had been accumulating in the Church for ages, must be placed under the guardianship and control of some competent authority, if it was to be administered and applied for the benefit of the faithful,— and what authority could be more unquestionable than that of the Supreme Pontiff, the reigning head of the Church, the vicegerent and representative of Christ Himself?   To him had been committed the power of ' the keys ;' it belonged to him ' to bind and to loose ;' and what more natural than that he should assume the entire administration of this fund of merits, and delegate subordinate agents to distribute them in his name ?   Hence the Bulls of Indulgence which were issued from the Roman

See, and hence the certificates of Papal pardons which were showered, like snowflakes, at intervals over the whole face of Europe, and which gave the assurance of pardon, in the sense of exemption from temporal and purgatorial punishment, for a longer or shorter term of years, in proportion to the liberality of the Pope in dispensing them, or rather, perhaps, to the price which the faithful might be induced to pay for them. (2)

It was the publication of the Pope's Bull, and the open sale of Indulgences by Tetzel in the immediate neighbourhood of Wittemberg, which first roused the spirit of Luther, and led him on, step by step, to the discussion of the whole question of a sinner's Justification with God. Burdened himself with a sense of sin, and meeting many in the confessional whose consciences were ill at ease, could he accept the Pope's pardon for the relief of his own soul, or suffer them to rest upon it without being unfaithful to his solemn trust? This was the practical shape in which the question was first presented to his mind; but the more he considered it, the more he was convinced that the invention of Indulgences had grown out of certain false doctrines which had long prevailed in the Church, on the subject of a sinner's Justification. It was a solemn and critical moment when this conviction first flashed on his spirit; and he resolved, in the strength of God and His Word, to lay the axe to the root of the tree, and to strike home at those corruptions in doctrine which alone could account for such an enormous abuse. In doing so, he was led on gradually to assail all the fundamental errors of the Church of Rome, and above all, the doctrine of the Mass, from which, with his profound and almost superstitious reverence for the Sacraments, he was disposed at first to shrink, and to let it alone. He soon found, however, that it was the very stronghold of Popery.   For while the doctrine of human merits was gradually advancing, there grew up alongside of it another doctrine which may seem, at first sight, to maintain and do homage to the merits of Christ, but which in reality implied a denial of their sufficiency, and a disparagement of their value, as the only ground of a sinner's acceptance with God,—the doctrine, namely, of a human priesthood, properly so called,—and of a priestly sacrifice and oblation offered on God's altar.   Whatever might be said of a man's own merits, or of the merits of the saints, it would evidently be a great object to get the merits of Christ's passion and death added to them, and thrown into the same common fund for Indulgences, which would thus appeal more strongly to the hearts of the faithful, and become at the same time altogether inexhaustible.   This object was to be accomplished by means of a sacrificing priesthood in the Church.   The priesthood which now came into prominence was not that of the only High Priest, 'the one Mediator between God and men, the man Christ Jesus,'—nor was it the universal priesthood of all true believers, 'offering up spiritual sacrifices, holy and acceptable unto God ;' it was a priestly caste, like the Levitical priesthood under the Law,—a distinct order of men, 'ordained for men in things pertaining to God, to make reconciliation for the sins of the people :' and the sacrifice which they offered, was not a mere sacramental commemoration of the one all-sufficient sacrifice for sin, nor even a eucharistic feast upon that sacrifice ; but a repetition of it, in which Christ, in His divine and human natures, was laid once more upon the altar, and offered by human hands as 'a sacrifice and oblation of a sweet-smelling savour unto God.'   A human priesthood assumed the functions of the great High Priest, and the sacrifice of the Altar was added to the sacrifice of the Cross.   It may

seem that Christ, and the merits of His death and passion,
were thus solemnly recognised, and perpetually presented
to the faith of the Church ; but the perfection of Christ's
priesthood, and the all-sufficiency of His one sacrifice, were
virtually denied, when human priests were acknowledged
as acting officially ' for men towards God,' and when it
was supposed that His sacrifice could be, or needed to be,
repeated, for the forgiveness of their sins.   The imperfection which belonged to the sacrifices that were offered
under the Law was thus transferred to the sacrifice of
Christ ; for the Apostle contrasts the two by insisting on
the repetition of the one, and the non-repetition of the
other.   ' In those sacrifices there is a remembrance again
made of sins every year, for it is not possible that the
blood of bulls and of goats should take away sin;' but ' we
are sanctified through the offering of the blood of Jesus
Christ once for all'[1] (ἐφάπαξ): ' Now *once* in the end of the
world hath He appeared to put away sin by the sacrifice
of Himself;'—' Christ was *once* offered to bear the sins of
many ;' and ' after He had offered *one* sacrifice for sin, He
sat down for ever on the right hand of God;'—' He is
exalted as a Prince and a Saviour, to give repentance
and remission of sins ;'—now, ' where remission of these
is, there is no more offering for sin ;'[2]—He came ' to finish
transgression, and to make an end of sin, and to make
reconciliation for iniquity, and to bring in everlasting
righteousness.'[3]

The sacrifice of the Altar, as representing the passion,
and recognising, to some extent, the merits, of Christ,
took a far stronger hold on the hearts of the devout
adherents of Rome, than the mere doctrine of Indulgences
could ever acquire; and it, too, was converted into a
source of priestly gain, by the invention of private masses,

[1] Heb. x. 3, 4, 10, 12, ix. 26.   [2] Heb. x. 18.   [3] Dan. ix. 24.

repeated for the souls of the living and the dead,—but especially of departed friends,—while their efficacy was supposed to depend on the intention of the priest; and hence Luther said, 'This article (of the Mass) will be made a main point with the Council (at Trent): though they should allow us all the rest, they will not yield a hair's-breadth here. Campeggio said at Augsburg, that he would be torn limb from limb, rather than consent to abolish the Mass. And I would rather be burned to ashes, than put an administrator of the Mass, with the service which he performs, on a footing with Christ, by making his offering "a sacrifice for the sins of the living and the dead."' (3)

It is evident from what has been said, that the doctrine of Indulgences, as it was generally understood at the era of the Reformation, rested for its support on several flagrant corruptions of divine truth. It is not wonderful, therefore, that the controversy which arose from the 'Theses' of Luther on that subject, should have embraced the whole subject of Justification, and touched, at every point, the great question as to the ground and means of a sinner's forgiveness and acceptance with God. Considering the protracted course of the discussion,—the wide and public arena on which it took place,—the number and variety of the points of mutual attack and defence, —the important interests which it involved,—the great ability and learning which were brought to bear upon it on either side,—and the momentous consequences which flowed from it;—no controversy which has ever agitated society, or the Church, could possibly possess a deeper historical interest; and such is its value, in a theological point of view, that, even at the present day, a thorough course of reading on the discussions which then took place, between the respective advocates of Romish error

and Protestant truth, may justly be said to be the best
method of studying the whole doctrine of Justification.
For the details of these discussions, recourse must be had
to the standard authorities on the subject (4) ; while we
can only attempt to sketch a general outline of the two
antagonistic systems, as they came into direct collision
with each other, at the era of the Reformation.

In framing that outline we are not necessarily confined to the materials which are supplied by the Canons,
Decrees, and Catechism of the Council at Trent, for this
simple reason, that they were not published till nearly
half a century after the commencement of the Reformation.   There is reason to believe, that the Fathers who
assembled there had already come, to some extent, under
the influence of the spirit of the age,—and were afraid,
or ashamed, to avow all the doctrines which had been
previously maintained and allowed.   There were men in
the Council itself who held views at variance with these
doctrines,—some from their strong attachment to the
theology of Augustine and Anselm,—others from their
having imbibed the lessons of such precursors of the
Reformers, as Wesel and Contarenus, Wickliffe and Huss ;
and others still, who, like Cajetan himself, had acquired
clearer views of the Gospel scheme even from the writings of their opponents. (5)   Their decisions, therefore,
were not pronounced till after protracted discussion, and
are often couched in vague and general terms, as if they
wished to avoid an articulate deliverance on some controverted points.   Besides, the doctrines of the Romish
Church are not to be gathered only from the Trentine
Decrees ; for they were followed by a long series of decisions on the doctrine of Baius, of Quesnel, and of the
Jansenists, which, although not pronounced by a Council,
are equally sanctioned by her supreme head, with the

most recent addition to her creed—the immaculate conception of the Virgin. (6) It thus appears that the Canons and Decrees of the Council of Trent on the subject of Justification, although important documents with reference to the views which then prevailed, do not afford a full account of the faith of the Church either before, or after, their promulgation; and more particularly, that in treating of the controversy at the time when Luther appeared, we are entitled to take into account whatever other evidence exists to show,—what was the doctrine on the subject of Justification, which was then publicly taught by the priesthood,—generally received by the people,—and maintained in the writings of Catholic divines.   Did we confine ourselves to the Canons of Trent alone, we might bring out the substance of that doctrine,—for it is there, expressed, however, in less explicit, and less offensive, terms, than those which are known to have been in use in every part of Christendom before the Reformation,—but we should not be able to prove such an express recognition of the scholastic doctrine of Merit in each of its two forms, or such a manifest rejection of the righteousness of Christ in the matter of a sinner's justification, as is so frequently obtruded on our notice in the controversial writings of the times in which Luther began his work.

Looking, then, at the doctrine as it was generally taught in the Church, and discussed in controversy by eminent Romish writers, at the era of the Reformation, it exhibits a striking contrast to the teaching of the Reformers on *four* points, which may be justly held to include whatever is essential and fundamental in the question of Justification.   These four points are,—The nature of Justification, or what that is which is denoted by the term in Scripture; the ground of Justification,

or what that is to which God has regard as the reason on
account of which He 'justifies the ungodly,'—in other
words, what that is to which the believer should look as
the foundation of his acceptance ; the means of Justification, or what that is through which God bestows, and man
receives, forgiveness of sin, and a title to eternal life ; and
the effect of Justification, or what consequences must
ensue from this change in a man's relation to God, as
regards alike his condition now, and his future prospects,
in time and eternity.   Under one or other of these topics
every question of any real importance on the subject of
Justification may be conveniently ranked ; and they were
all involved in the great controversy between the first
Reformers and the Church of Rome.

In regard to the Nature of Justification, or what that
is which is denoted by the term in Scripture, the fundamental error of the Church of Rome consisted in confounding it with Sanctification.   It is not enough to say,
that they employ the term Justification to denote the
whole of that great change which is wrought on the soul
of a sinner at the time of his conversion, and which
includes both the remission of his sins, and the renovation
of his nature,—for in this comprehensive sense it was
sometimes used by Augustine, and occasionally even by
some Protestant writers; but it is further affirmed that,
while Augustine distinguished these two effects of divine
grace, as bearing respectively on a sinner's relation to
God, and on his spiritual character, Popish writers confounded, and virtually identified, them ; and thereby
introduced confusion and obscurity into the whole scheme
of divine truth.   For if Justification were either altogether the same with Sanctification; or if,—not being
entirely the same, but in some respects distinguishable
from it,—it was founded and dependent on Sanctifica-

tion, so as that a sinner is only justified, when, and because, and in so far as, he is sanctified; then it would follow,—that Justification, considered as an act of God, is the mere infusion, in the first instance, and the mere recognition, in the second, of a righteousness inherent in the sinner himself; and not an act of God's grace, acquitting him of guilt, delivering him from condemnation, and receiving him into His favour and friendship. It would not be a forensic or judicial proceeding terminating on man as its object, and rectifying his relation to God; but the exertion of a spiritual energy, of which man is the subject, and by which he is renewed in the spirit of his mind. Considered, again, as the privilege of believers, it would not consist in the free forgiveness of sins, and a sure title to eternal life; but in the possession of an inward personal righteousness, which is always imperfect, and often stained with sin,—which can never, therefore, amount to a full justification in the present life, as the actual privilege of any believer.

In opposition to these and similar errors on this point, the Reformers held and taught that Justification is 'an act of God's free grace, whereby He pardoneth all our sins, and accepteth us as righteous in His sight;'—that it is an act of God external to the sinner, of which he is the object, —not an inward work, of which he is the subject;—that it is a forensic and judicial change in his relation to God, such as takes place in the condition of a person accused, when he is acquitted,—or of a person condemned, when he is pardoned,—or of a person in a state of enmity, when he is reconciled and received as a friend,—not a change in his moral and spiritual character, although this must always accompany or flow from it; and that it is the present privilege of every believer, however weak his faith, and however imperfect his holiness,—for 'being justified by

faith, we *have* peace with God through our Lord Jesus
Christ;' and 'in Him we *have* redemption through His
blood, even the remission of sins, according to the riches
of His grace.' Thus widely did the two parties differ in
regard to the *nature* of Justification.

In regard, again, to the Ground of Justification, or
what that is to which God has regard as the reason on
account of which He 'justifies the ungodly,' and to which
the believer also should look as the foundation of his hope,
—the fundamental error of the Church of Rome consisted
in substituting the inherent righteousness of the regenerate, for the imputed righteousness of the Redeemer.
There might seem to be no room, in their system, for any
question in regard to the ground of Justification, as something distinct from Justification itself; for if Justification
be the same with Sanctification, and if Sanctification consists in righteousness, infused and inherent, then this
righteousness is the matter and substance of both, rather
than the ground of either. But when, instead of confounding, they made a distinction between, the two, they
were in the habit of representing the infused righteousness
which makes us acceptable to God, as the ground or reason
of His acceptance of our persons, which is consequent upon
it,—while they utterly rejected the imputed righteousness
of Christ. It is true, they spoke of the merits of Christ,
and ascribed some influence to His sufferings and death in
connection with our justification; but they denied that
His righteousness is imputed to us, so as to become the
immediate ground of our acceptance with God, or the
sole reason on account of which He pardons our sins, and
accepts us as righteous in His sight. The merits of Christ
were rather, according to their doctrine, the procuring
cause of that regenerating grace by which we are made
righteous; while the inherent personal righteousness,

which is thus produced, is the real proximate ground of our justification.   At the best, they only admitted Christ's righteousness to a partnership with our own, in the hope that whatever was defective in ours might be made up, and supplemented, by the perfection of His.   But that His righteousness imputed is the sole and all-sufficient ground of our justification, which neither requires nor admits of any addition being made to it in the shape either of suffering or obedience, and which is effectual, for that end, without the aid of any other righteousness, infused and inherent,—they strenuously denied.   This fundamental error in regard to the ground of a sinner's justification, explains and accounts for many collateral or subordinate errors,—such as, their doctrine of a first and second Justification: a first Justification, by the original infusion of righteousness; and a second Justification, by that same righteousness remaining inherent and become actual;— their doctrine that works done before faith are excluded by the Apostles, but not works done after faith;—and their doctrine that Paul and James can only be harmonized on the supposition that Paul speaks of the one, and James of the other.   All these doctrines rested on the same fundamental principle, namely, that the ground of our justification is a righteousness personal and inherent,—procured, it may be, by the merits of Christ, and infused into us by the regenerating grace of His Spirit, but becoming really and properly our own, just as any other attribute of character is our own, and securing our forgiveness and acceptance with God by its intrinsic worth.

In opposition to these and similar errors on this point, the Reformers held and taught, that we were justified ' only for the righteousness of Christ imputed to us,' or put down to our account; and they based their doctrine on such considerations as these,—that a righteousness of some

kind is indispensable, if God is to accept us as righteous,
—that it must be such a righteousness as is adequate to
meet and satisfy all the requirements of that perfect Law,
which is God's rule in judgment,—that its requirements,
both penal and preceptive, were fulfilled by the obedience,
passive and active, of the Lord Jesus Christ,—that He
thus became 'the end of the Law for righteousness to
every one that believeth in His name,'—that our inherent
personal righteousness, even were it perfect, could not
cancel the guilt of our past sins, or offer any satisfaction
to divine justice on account of them,—that so far from
being perfect, even in the regenerate, it is defiled by indwelling sin, and impaired by actual transgression,—and
that the work of the Spirit in us, indispensable and precious as it is for other ends, was not designed to secure
our justification in any other way than by applying to
us the righteousness of Christ, and enabling us to receive
and rest upon it by faith. Thus widely did the two parties
differ in regard to the ground of Justification.

In regard, again, to the Means of Justification,—or
what that is through which God bestows, and man receives, forgiveness of sin, and a title to eternal life,—the
fundamental error of the Church of Rome consisted in
denying that we are justified by that faith which 'receives
and rests on Christ alone for salvation, as He is freely
offered to us in the Gospel.' They affirmed that we are
justified, not simply by faith in Christ, for faith might exist
where there is no justification, but by faith informed with
charity, or love, which is the germ of new obedience ;—
that this faith is first infused by baptism, so as to delete
all past sin,—original sin, in the case of infants, and both
original and actual sin in the case of adults, duly prepared
to receive it,—while it is restored or renewed, in the event
of post-baptismal sin, by confession and absolution, which

effectually deliver the sinner from all punishment, except such as is endured in penance, or in purgatory. This general statement embraces their whole doctrine on this part of the subject, and comprehends under it several distinct positions, each of which became the occasion of intricate and protracted discussion. The main questions related to—the nature of saving faith,—the reason of its efficacy as a means of Justification,—and the respective uses or functions of faith and the sacraments. The real bearing of these questions, as to the nature and effects of Faith, on the general doctrine of Justification, will not be discerned or appreciated aright, unless we bear in mind, that they were all connected with, and directed to the establishment of, the fundamental principle of the Romish system respecting the ground of our forgiveness and acceptance with God, as being a righteousness inherent in man, and not the righteousness of Christ imputed. This being the grand leading doctrine, every other must be brought into accordance with it, and so explained as to contribute to its support. Accordingly faith, to which so much efficacy and importance are everywhere ascribed in Scripture, was, first of all, defined as a mere intellectual belief, or assent to revealed truth, such as an unrenewed mind might acquire in the exercise of its natural faculties, without the aid of divine grace, and described as having, in itself, no necessary connection with salvation, but as being only one of seven antecedent dispositions or qualifications, which always precede, in the case of adults, but are not invariably followed by, Justification. This faith, in order to be effectual and saving, must be ' informed with charity or love ;' and forthwith that which was barren before becomes fruitful, and, being fruitful, it justifies, not because it rests on the righteousness of Christ, but because it is itself our inherent personal righteousness, the product of a new birth, and the germ of a new creation.   It was regarded as the seminal principle of holiness in heart and life, and, *as such,* the ground of our justification.   Some admitted that it was procured for us by the merits of Christ, and is infused into us by the grace of His Spirit; but they held that it exists as a subjective principle in our own hearts, and secures by its own intrinsic worth, without any righteousness imputed, the forgiveness of our sins, and the acceptance of our persons and services.   The 'faith informed by charity,' which constitutes our righteousness, cannot, of course, be a means of receiving Justification, since it is itself the substance of that Gospel blessing; and accordingly Justification was said to be conveyed on God's part, and received on man's, through the medium, not of faith, but of the sacraments.   The sinner, being regenerated by baptism, and purified, from time to time, by confession and penance, was held to be justified,—not by faith in Christ, as the means, or by the righteousness of Christ, as the ground, of his forgiveness and acceptance, —but by inherent righteousness, sacramentally infused and nourished, with or without the exercise of an explicit faith in Christ and His finished work.

   In opposition to these and similar errors on this point, the Reformers held and taught, that we are 'justified by faith alone,' simply because faith receives and rests upon Christ alone for salvation, and apprehends and appropriates His righteousness as the ground of acceptance.   They admitted the existence of a mere historical faith, such as men might acquire in the exercise of their natural faculties; for this is recognised in Scripture; but they affirmed that there is a faith,—clearly distinguishable from it by sure scriptural tests,—which is immediately and invariably effectual in securing the pardon of a sinner and his accep-tance with God,—a faith, which does not consist in the bare assent of the understanding, but involves the cordial consent of the whole mind,—which not only apprehends, but appropriates, Christ and all His benefits,—receiving and resting upon Him alone for salvation,—and looking to His righteousness as its only prevailing plea; which, wherever it exists, and in whatever degree, though it were small even as a grain of mustard-seed, has an immediate and certain efficacy, simply because it unites the believer to Christ, and makes him a partaker of His righteousness; and which, when it has once been implanted in the soul, will never be suffered to die out, but will spring up unto life eternal. They held this faith to be necessary to salvation; but they held it also to be immediately, invariably, and infallibly effectual for salvation, insomuch that he in whom it exists may be fully assured that 'he has passed from death unto life, and that he will never come into condemnation.' They did not deny, on the contrary they affirmed, that this faith 'worketh by love,' and through love, as the main spring of new obedience, produces all 'the peaceable fruits of righteousness;' but its justifying efficacy they ascribed, not, as the Church of Rome did, to its 'enclosing charity, as a ring encloses a diamond,' which enhances its intrinsic worth, but to its 'enclosing Christ, the pearl of great price,' whose righteousness alone makes it of any avail. (7) They joyfully acknowledged it to be a spiritual grace, a gift of God, and one of the fruits of His Spirit, which is in its own nature acceptable and pleasing to Him; but they regarded the infusion of this living faith as the means by which God applies to men individually the redemption which was purchased by Christ; and as a means admirably adapted to this end, just because it directs the sinner to look out of himself to Christ alone as his Saviour,—to relinquish all self-righteous confidence in anything that he has done,

or can do,—and to cast himself entirely on the free grace
of God and the finished work of the Redeemer.   They
rejected the whole doctrine of sacramental Justification,
because they learned from Scripture that, as Abraham
was justified, under the Old Dispensation, before he was
circumcised, and received circumcision only as ' a sign and
seal of the righteousness of the faith which he had yet
being uncircumcised,'[1] so, under the New Dispensation,
Justification is inseparably connected with faith, and not
with baptism, insomuch that every believer is justified
before, and even without, being baptized, while many are
baptized who are neither regenerated, nor justified, nor
saved.   Thus widely did the two parties differ in regard
to the means of Justification.

In regard, finally, to the Effect of Justification,—or
the consequences which must ensue from it in respect
alike to the present condition of the justified man and his
future prospects, in time and eternity,—the fundamental
error of the Church of Rome consisted in holding, that it
was neither so complete in its own nature, nor so infallibly
secured, as to exempt him from the necessity of making
some further satisfaction for sin, or to warrant the certain
hope of eternal life.   In some of its aspects, the Romish
doctrine may seem to have ascribed a greater effect to
that infusion of inherent righteousness, which they confound with Justification, than the Protestant doctrine
did; for its immediate and invariable effect was said to
be the deletion of all sin,—whether original or actual,—
which restores the sinner to a condition of pristine innocence, similar to that of Adam before the fall; and if
natural concupiscence, such as may become an occasion
of temptation, still remained, it was not sinful in itself,
nor peculiar to the fallen state of man, since it equally

[1] Rom. iv. 11.

existed in our first parent when he was created in the image of God, and was only bridled and kept in check, then as it is now, by the gift of supernatural grace. In addition to this, they held that the effect of Justification, in their sense of the term, was such as to render it possible for the Christian to rise to a state of perfection in the present life, and even to merit rewards both for himself and for others. In these respects, they ascribed a greater effect to Justification than the Reformers did; for the latter spoke, not of natural concupiscence merely, but of indwelling sin, as still cleaving to the believer, and of his best services being imperfect and defiled. But in some of its other aspects, the Romish doctrine ascribed far less effect to Justification than the Protestant; for, according to their favourite principle, that Justification is the same with Sanctification, or, at the least, necessarily dependent upon it, it is manifest that there is no one point at which a sinner can believe himself to be actually justified, unless he has already attained to a state of Christian perfection,—that with him Justification cannot be a present privilege, but can only be an object of desire and hope,—that it is left to depend on his final perseverance, but does not ensure it,—and that it still leaves him liable at least to temporal punishment, as a satisfaction which is due for post-baptismal sins. No wonder, therefore, that the Reformers spoke of 'the uncertain and doubtsome faith' of the Romish Church, and contrasted it with the comfortable assurance which might be derived from the direct act of faith in Christ, as He is exhibited in the offers and promises of the Gospel, and which might be confirmed by its reflex exercise on their own spiritual experience, as compared with the marks and evidences of a justified state which are revealed in the infallible Word.

In opposition to these and similar errors on this point,

the Reformers held and taught, that, as Justification properly consists in the free pardon of sin and a sure title to eternal life, so it is the present privilege of every believer from the instant when he receives and rests on Christ alone for salvation,—that it is a complete, final, and irreversible act of divine grace, by which he is translated, at once and for ever, from a state of wrath and condemnation, into a state of favour and acceptance ; and that it is either accompanied or followed in the present life by 'the assurance of God's love, peace of conscience, joy in the Holy Ghost, increase of grace, and perseverance therein to the end,'—while it is indissolubly connected with 'glory, honour, and immortality' in the world to come.   'For whom He did predestinate, them He also called ; and whom He called, them He also justified ; and whom He justified, them He also glorified.'   So wide was the difference between the two parties in regard to the effect of Justification.

On a review of the whole controversy at the era of the Reformation, the two antagonist systems, considered generally,—as each unfolding a method of Justification for sinners,—may be briefly characterized.   The Romish doctrine was one which engrafted a method invented by man, on a method revealed by God,—retaining some part of divine truth, but mixing it with much human error, and thereby obscuring and corrupting it.   In so far as it was of human invention, its whole tendency was to exalt man, and everything of human attainment, instead of glorifying God, and the riches, freeness, and efficacy of His grace.   In so far as it recognised the grace of God, it made the exercise of it dependent on man's free-will, by speaking of predisposing qualifications in the sinner which fitted, and in equity entitled him, to receive it, and of his subsequent co-operation with grace, by which he might even merit eternal life. In so far as it recognised the merits of Christ, they were exhibited, not as the immediate and all-sufficient ground of a sinner's justification, but only as the remote procuring cause of that infused personal righteousness which was the real reason of his being accepted as righteous in the sight of God. It thus fluctuated between the free grace of God and the free-will of man,—between the merits of Christ and the merits of His people ; and attempted to combine these heterogeneous elements in one system, as if Justification depended partly on grace, and partly on works—partly on the perfect righteousness of Christ, and partly on the imperfect righteousness of man. But it went beyond this, and had characteristics which were distinctive and peculiar to itself. It did not recognise One only Mediator, and One only sacrifice for sin : it taught the merits and mediation of saints,—the repetition of the one sacrifice on the Cross by the sacrifice on the Altar,—and additional satisfactions for sin in the austerities of penance, and the pains of purgatory. It made the pardon of sin dependent on the confession of the penitent and the absolution of the priest,—thereby placing the Church in the room of Christ, and interposing the priest between the sinner and God : and when absolution was granted on condition of penance, or some other work of mere external obedience, it led men to look to something which they could themselves do or suffer, instead of relying by faith simply and solely on Christ and His finished work.

Such were the general characteristics of the Romish doctrine at the era of the Reformation ; and that of the Reformers offered a striking contrast to them all. It proclaimed at once the glorious truth, that every sinner to whom the Gospel comes has direct and free access to God,

through the sole mediation of the Lord Jesus Christ; that
he is independent of all priestly absolution, since ' none can
forgive sins but God only ;' that he is independent of all
other merits and mediation than those of Christ, the ' one
Mediator between God and man ;' that a full pardon of all
sin, and a sure title to eternal life, are freely offered to
him, in Christ's name, and may be immediately appropriated and enjoyed by faith ; that he is warranted, and
even bound, guilty and condemned as he is, to receive and
rest upon Christ at once as his Saviour; that nothing
which he ever did, or may yet do, is necessary to constitute any part of the ground of his present acceptance
or of his eternal hope ; and that, being united to Christ
by faith, he will be made partaker in due time of all the
blessings of a complete and everlasting salvation.   Such,
in substance, was the doctrine of the Reformers ; and it
imparted immediate relief and comfort to many anxious
and distressed consciences, which all the masses and indulgences of Rome had failed to pacify ; it passed through
Europe, like an electric current, and proved, at many a
homely hearth, and in many a monastic cell,—in some,
even, of the palaces of princes,—that it was still, as of old,
' the power of God unto salvation.'   It reformed a large
part of the Church, and constituted it anew after the
model of primitive times ; and it is yet destined to overthrow the whole fabric of Popery, and to be hailed as
God's Gospel in every part of a regenerated world. (8)

LECTURE V.

HISTORY OF THE DOCTRINE IN THE ROMISH CHURCH AFTER THE REFORMATION.

THE controversy between Rome and the Reformation was carried on, with much keenness and with great ability on both sides, long after Protestantism had acquired a firm footing in Europe, and assumed a distinct and permanent form, as an ecclesiastical organization. The history of that protracted struggle is replete with interest and instruction;—and no part of it is more important than that which relates to the doctrine of a sinner's Justification in the sight of God. The more salient points of this part of the history may be sufficiently illustrated by considering—the original charge of the Romanists against the Protestant doctrine of Justification, as contrasted with their subsequent treatment of it; and the persistent attempts which were made by some men on both sides to effect a reconciliation and compromise between the two antagonist systems, and even to harmonize the symbolical books in which they were respectively embodied, by leaving out of view, or explaining away, whatever was peculiar or distinctive either in the Protestant, or in the Popish, doctrine.

The original charge of the Romanists against the Protestant doctrine of Justification should be carefully considered, in the first instance, and then compared with their subsequent treatment of it.

The light in which the Protestant doctrine was universally regarded at first by the adherents of the Church
of Rome,—by the Pope and his legates, by the Emperor
and his princes, by the Bishops and their clergy, and,
generally, by both the civil and ecclesiastical partisans of
the Papal See,—is sufficiently shown by the treatment
which they bestowed on the 'Confession,' which was presented at the Diet of Augsburg, and afterwards on the
'Apology' for it, which was prepared in reply to their
objections.   Both the 'Confession' and the 'Apology'
were carefully composed by the learned, prudent, and
conciliatory Melancthon, but were revised and cordially
approved by Luther and the Elector of Saxony ; and they
contained, in substance, a faithful exhibition of the doctrine which was then held by the whole body of the
Reformers. (1) . The method of Justification by the free
grace of God, through faith alone in the sole merits of
Christ, as the only Saviour of sinners, was there stated in
the most moderate, and least offensive, terms ; yet the
Romish divines—Faber and Eckius—who undertook to
answer the 'Confession,' rejected the Protestant doctrine
on that subject entirely, and, on their report, it was rejected also in the Edict of the Diet. (2)   The chief ground
of their opposition to it, at that time, was its alleged
'novelty,' as a method of teaching which was now introduced for the first time, and which was at direct variance
with that which had long prevailed in the Romish Church.
It was this doctrine, more than any other, that excited
the hostility both of the Papal See, and of the Imperial
Diet ; and the Reformers were made to feel that, unless
they could consent to abandon, or at least to modify it,
they must expose themselves and their cause to imminent
danger.   'It cannot be denied,' says Melancthon, 'that
we are brought into trouble, and exposed to danger, for

this *one only reason*, that we believe the favour of God to be procured for us, not by our observances, but for the sake of Christ alone.' . . . ' If the exclusive term, *only*, is disliked, let them erase the Apostle's corresponding terms, *freely*, and *without* works.' In reply to the charge of novelty, they admitted that the doctrine might be new to many in the Church of Rome, since it had long been obscured and corrupted by the false teaching and superstitious practices which generally prevailed,—but affirmed, that it was as old as the Gospel of Christ and His Apostles, to which they fearlessly appealed. ' I, Dr. Martin Luther, the un-worthy evangelist of the Lord Jesus Christ, thus think and thus affirm :—That this article,—namely, that faith alone, without works, justifies us before God,—can never be over-thrown, for . . . Christ alone, the Son of God, died for our sins ; but if He alone takes away our sins, then men, with all their works, are to be excluded from all concurrence in procuring the pardon of sin and justification. Nor can I embrace Christ otherwise than by faith *alone;* He cannot be apprehended by works. But if faith, before works follow, apprehends the Redeemer, it is undoubtedly true, that faith *alone*, before works, and without works, appro-priates the benefit of redemption, which is no other than justification,. or deliverance from sin. This is our doc-trine ; so the Holy Spirit teaches, and the whole Christian Church. In this, by the grace of God, will we stand fast, Amen !' (3)

Such was the original charge of the Romish Church against the Protestant doctrine of Justification, and such the firm reply which the Reformers made to it, when they appealed from the corrupt traditions of later times to the ancient faith of the Apostolic age. But between the Diet of Augsburg in 1530, and that of Ratisbon in 1541, a marked and striking change occurred in the

policy of the Romish party.   Instead of denouncing the
Protestant doctrine of Justification, as a dangerous
novelty, directly opposed to the teaching of the Romish
Church, they were now prepared ostensibly to adopt it
as their own,—to claim it, even, as a part of that truth
which they had always held and taught,—and to make
it appear, that there was no real, or, at least, no radical,
difference between the two parties, but only such as might
be easily adjusted by mutual explanation and concession.
Hence originated a long series of conferences, appointed
by the Emperor, and attended by the Reformers, with
the avowed object, on the part of their powerful promoters, of effecting a settlement by means of conciliation
and compromise.   The way had been prepared for some
such attempt by the work of Erasmus, ' On Concord in
Religion,' in 1533, which aimed at the reconciliation of
the two parties, and ascribed almost as much to grace
and faith as the Reformers could desire, while it adhered
to the Popish idea of Justification, as ' a purifying work
on the heart,' and to the Popish doctrine also of reward
and ' merit.' (4)   But the book which was the immediate
occasion of the negotiations that followed, was compiled
by Gropper, one of the Canons of Cologne, whose Archbishop, the pious Hermann, had attempted to reform his
diocese by means of a Provincial Council in 1536.   That
Council drew up a number of articles, which were afterwards digested and published by Gropper, and which
were mainly directed ' to palliate the Popish doctrines,
and to colour them with new interpretations.'   This
worthless book, which Luther had seen before, and characterized as ' crafty and ambiguous,' and of which the
mild Melancthon had said, ' There is nothing so monstrous, that it may not be made to appear plausible by
dexterous management, and the magic touch of a skilful

sophister,' came into the hands of the Emperor. It pleased
him as a politician, because it recommended concessions,
sometimes on one side, and sometimes on the other; and
he presented it to the Diet at Ratisbon as a basis of
agreement, naming three divines on each side—Eckius,
Gropper, and Pflug, for the Romanists,—and Melancthon,
Bucer, and Pistorius, for the Protestants,—to examine
it, and report.   Strange as it may seem, an article on
Justification was agreed upon in the conference of divines,
—subject, however, to the approbation of the Diet,—an
article which was afterwards found to be satisfactory to
neither party, but offensive to both; and as it throws an
instructive light on the new policy which began to be
adopted at that time by the adherents of Rome, and
which has been pursued, more or less consistently, ever
since, we may mark, *first*, the large concessions which
were now made in favour of the Protestant doctrine of
Justification; and, *secondly*, the careful reservation of one
point, and only one, which was so ambiguously expressed
as to be susceptible of different interpretations, while,
according to the sense in which it was understood, it
involved the whole difference between the Popish, and
the Protestant, method of acceptance with God,—between Justification by imputed, and Justification by
infused or inherent, righteousness.

The concessions which were made to the Protestants
were apparently large and liberal; for the article, as preserved by Du Pin, expressly bears,—that 'since the fall
of Adam, all men are born enemies of God, and children
of wrath by sin,'—that 'they cannot be reconciled to God,
or redeemed from the bondage of sin, but by Jesus Christ,
our *only* Mediator,'—that 'their mind is raised up to God,
by faith in the promises made to them, that their sins are
freely forgiven them, and that God will adopt those for

His children who believe in Jesus Christ,'—that 'faith justifies not, but as it leads us to mercy and righteousness, which is *imputed* to us through Jesus Christ and His merits, and not by any perfection of righteousness which is *inherent* in us, as communicated to us by Jesus Christ,'—and that ' we are not just, or accepted by God, on account of our own works or righteousness, but we are *reputed just on account of the merits of Jesus Christ only.*' (5)   That these statements contain the substance of the Protestant doctrine is undeniable ; and had they stood alone, they might have justified the fond belief which Melancthon once expressed when he said, ' The times have much softened down the controversy respecting Justification ; for the learned are now agreed on many points, concerning which there were at first fierce disputes.' (6)   But amidst all these concessions, one point was carefully reserved, or expressed in ambiguous terms, which was of such vital and fundamental importance that, according to the sense in which it was understood, it would determine the whole character of the article, as a deliverance in favour, either of the Popish, or the Protestant, doctrine of Justification.

That point was—the *faith* by which we are justified,— or rather the precise function which belongs to it, and the ground or reason of the efficacy which is ascribed to it. According to the Protestant doctrine, it is the means of Justification, simply because it receives and rests upon Christ alone,—because it apprehends and appropriates His righteousness as its only plea,—because it implies an absolute renunciation of all self-dependence, and consists in an entire and cordial reliance on Christ as ' the Lamb of God which taketh away the sin of the world,'—as ' the propitiation for our sins through faith in His blood,'—and as ' the end of the law for righteousness to every one that believeth in His name.'   But according to the Popish doctrine, faith justifies, not by uniting the sinner to Christ, and making him a partaker of Christ's righteousness,—but by 'working' in him, and 'sanctifying' him,—by being, in its own essential nature as one of the 'fruits of the Spirit,' and by producing, in its actual operation as a vital principle which 'worketh by love,' a real inherent righteousness, which is, on its own account, acceptable to God, and which constitutes the immediate ground of his acceptance ;—in short, by *making him righteous*, subjectively, so that thereby, and on that account, he may be *reputed* righteous, and obtain at once the pardon of sin, and a title to eternal life.   This cardinal point, which may be justly said to be the hinge on which the whole question turned, was carefully reserved, or wrapt up in ambiguous terms, at Ratisbon ;—and these were only the more insidious, because they contained a truth respecting the nature and effects of justifying faith, which the Reformers held as strongly as their opponents.   The article declared, that 'sinners are justified by a living and effectual faith, which is a motion of the Holy Spirit, whereby, repenting of their lives past, they are raised to God, and made real partakers of the mercy which Jesus Christ hath promised,' . . . 'which no man attains but at the same time love is shed abroad in his heart, and he begins to fulfil the law;' and that 'this is not to hinder us from exhorting the people to increase this faith and this charity by outward and inward works; so that, though the people be taught that *faith alone justifieth*, yet repentance, the fear of God and of His judgments, and the practice of good works, ought to be preached unto them.'   All this is true, but it is not relevant to the question at issue.   It relates to faith, not as it justifies, but as it sanctifies, a sinner.   It diverts the mind from the external object of justifying faith, which is Christ alone, and His perfect righteousness ; and directs

it to the inward effect of faith, in changing the character
and conduct of the sinner, and producing an inherent, but
imperfect, righteousness of his own.   The doctrine is sound
and wholesome in its own place, and in its proper connection ; but it becomes unsound and dangerous, when it is
mixed up with the truth which relates to the ground and
reason of a sinner's pardon and acceptance with God.   It
virtually substitutes the work of the Spirit *in us,* in the
place of the work of Christ *for us ;* or, at least, it does
not represent the work of the Spirit as the mere application of the redemption and righteousness of Christ, already
wrought out by Him, and sufficient of itself for the immediate justification of every believer, but as being, either in
whole or in part, the ground or reason on account of
which God bestows His forgiveness and favour.   And
thus, by introducing the sanctifying effects of faith into
their definition of it, as it is the means of Justification, the
Popish divines made provision for falling back on their
favourite doctrine of an inherent, as opposed to an imputed, righteousness ; and for ultimately setting aside all
the concessions which they had apparently made.

The article thus carefully concocted, and couched in
ambiguous terms, was satisfactory to neither party, and
was openly denounced by both.   It had too much of the
Gospel in it to be palatable to the consistent adherents of
Rome, and too much of disguised legalism to be acceptable
to the Reformed.   On the one side, the Legate, Cardinal
Contarini, was charged by Cardinal Caraffa, who afterwards became Pope as Paul IV., with having betrayed
the cause of the Church, especially on the question of
Justification.   On the other side, the Elector of Saxony
objected strongly to the article, and complained that 'the
doctrine of Justification *by faith alone,* was well nigh
buried beneath appendages and explanations.' (7)

From this narrative we may derive several important lessons. It shows that, between the Diet of Augsburg and that of Ratisbon,—or in the course of little more than ten years,—the same doctrine of Justification which had been openly rejected as a 'novelty,' at direct variance with the teaching of the Church, came to be regarded in an entirely different light, and even to be claimed as a truth which had always been taught by the priests and bishops of Rome. Luther, marking this sudden change, could hardly restrain his indignant sarcasm, and exclaimed, 'Popish writers pretend that they have always taught, what we now teach, concerning faith and good works, and that they are unjustly accused of the contrary: thus the wolf puts on the sheep's skin till he gains admission into the fold.' That their original charge against the Protestant doctrine as a 'novelty,' and their subsequent claim to it as the 'old doctrine' of the Church, could not both be true, is evident, for they are manifestly contradictory; and it might seem incredible that they could have been adopted by the same parties in good faith. In the minds of some, there might have grown up a clearer perception of the Protestant doctrine and of its scriptural evidence than they had before the Reformation,—as in the·case of Bishop Vergerio, who was converted in attempting to refute it,—of Cardinal Cajetan, whose commentary on the Epistle to the Romans bears traces of his having learned something from his conferences with Luther,—and even of the Emperor himself, of whom it has been said that, 'as he drew near his end, and was more deeply impressed with the awful thought of appearing before the divine tribunal, he approximated more and more to some of the leading doctrines of Luther, and particularly that of Justification by faith.' (8)   In the case of others, there might be a change of policy and

profession, where there was no corresponding conviction
of the truth ; and this seems to be the true explanation
of the conduct which was pursued by the chief Popish
agents at Ratisbon ; for Melancthon, speaking of Eckius,
complained of his 'sophisms and juggling tricks,' and
said, ' He sports with terms of the most serious import,—
continually conceals his real meaning, and only aims
to embarrass an adversary. There is great danger in
encountering sycophants of this kind.' And Bucer,
speaking of Gropper, who afterwards wrote against the
very doctrine which he had professed to receive, and
actively promoted the deposition of the venerable re-
forming Archbishop of Cologne, affirmed that ' Gropper
either sincerely assented to the Evangelical doctrine, or
with solemn asseverations protested it.' (9) Whether it
proceeded from conviction or from policy, there was a
striking change at this date in the treatment which
the Romish Church bestowed on the Protestant doctrine
of Justification ; a change so great as to warrant the
distinction, which still exists, between OLD and NEW
Popery.

    We learn another lesson from what occurred at the
Diet of Ratisbon. It shows the possibility of appearing
to concede almost everything, while one point is reserved,
or wrapped up in ambiguous language, which is found
afterwards sufficient to neutralize every concession, and
to leave the parties as much at variance as before. It has
been justly said that, in controversies of faith, the difference between antagonist systems is often reduced to a line
sharp as a razor's edge, yet on one side of that line there
is God's truth, and on the other a departure from it. (10)
At Ratisbon, the difference between the Popish and Protestant doctrines of Justification seemed to resolve itself
into one point, and even on that point both parties held

some views in common.   It might seem, then, that there was no radical or irreconcilable difference between the two; and yet, when they came to explain their respective views, it was found that they were contending for two opposite methods of Justification,—the one by an inherent, the other by an imputed, righteousness,—the one by the personal obedience of the believer, the other by the vicarious obedience of Christ,—the one by the inchoate and imperfect work of the Spirit *in* men, the other by the finished work of Christ *for* them, when 'He became obedient unto death, even the death of the cross.'   This fact shows the utter folly of every attempt to reconcile two systems, which are radically opposed, by means of a compromise between them; and the great danger of engaging in private conferences with a view to that end. In the open field of controversy, truth, so far from being endangered, is ventilated, cleared, and defined; in the secret conclaves of divines, and the cabinets of princes, it is often smothered, or silenced.   It has far less to fear from discussion, than from diplomacy.   There can be no honest compromise between the Popish and the Protestant doctrine of Justification,—the one is at direct variance with the other, not in respect of verbal expression merely, but in respect of their fundamental principles,—and any settlement, on the basis of mutual concession, could only be made by means of ambiguous expressions, and could amount to nothing more than a hollow truce, liable to be broken by either party as soon as the subject was brought again into serious discussion.   This was the abortive result of the apparent agreement at Ratisbon; it settled no question,—it satisfied no party,—and it led afterwards to much misunderstanding and mutual recrimination.   'Let them go on,' said Luther, referring to the schemes of those who thought that the differences between Roman Catholics

and Protestants might be made up by such conferences,
' we shall not envy the success of their labours : they will
be the first who could ever convert the devil and reconcile
him to Christ. . . . The sceptre of the Lord admits of no
bending and joining; but must remain straight and unchanged, the rule of faith and practice.'

The double policy of the Romish Church, so strikingly
exhibited at Ratisbon,—in first rejecting the Protestant
doctrine of Justification as an unauthorized and dangerous
' novelty,' and afterwards claiming it, in their own sense,
as a truth which they had always held and taught,—was
pursued in several successive diets of the Empire.   At
length, finding it impossible either to convince or to concuss
the Reformers, the Emperor published his scheme, known
as the 'Interim,' which was so called because it was to
remain in force only till the convocation of a general
council, and was designed, at least ostensibly, to preserve,
till then, the *status quo* between the contending parties.
It contained a statement of doctrine, framed on the model
of Gropper's book, and in accordance generally with the
creed of the Romish Church; but expressed 'in the softest
words, or in scriptural phrases, or in terms of studied
ambiguity.'   Bucer refused to subscribe it at the peril of
his life; and Melancthon was so decidedly opposed to it,
that the Emperor ordered his person to be seized, and he
escaped only through the protection of the Elector.   It
proved a signal failure, like every other attempt at compromise between systems which were essentially opposed;
and at length, the Council which had been demanded, not
less by the princes of the Empire, for the reformation of
the Church, than by the Protestants, for the discussion
of doctrine, was reluctantly summoned by the Pope to
assemble at Trent.

The Council first met in 1545, and was continued,

with frequent, and often long, adjournments, till 1563—
a period of eighteen years ; but its actual sessions occupied only four years ; and of these no less than seven
months were devoted to the question of Justification.
Their deliberations on this subject were held in their
sixth session, 1547, and resulted in *sixteen* decrees, setting
forth the doctrine of the Church, and *thirty-three* canons,
denouncing the errors which are opposed to it. (11)   The
latter are much more explicit and decided than the
former ; and the anathemas, which are launched against
what were supposed to be Protestant doctrines, are much
more vigorous than the statements, which are made in
support of their own.   They seem, indeed, to have been
much perplexed in dealing with the subject.   It was felt
to be singularly important, as all the errors of Luther
resolved themselves into his doctrine concerning it ; and
also singularly difficult, since Justification by faith was
regarded by many as a doctrine which had never been
thought of by any School-writer, and therefore never
discussed or confuted before. (12)   But while some treated
it as a 'novelty,' there were others even in the Council
of Trent who were not prepared to reject it on that
ground.   Hence the decrees, which are devoted to the
exposition of the Catholic faith on this important subject,
were purposely, and perhaps unavoidably, expressed in
vague and ambiguous terms ; for they were prepared at
a time when scriptural views had been widely dissemi-
nated in all the countries of Europe, and in the presence
also of many members of the Council itself, who had
either been impressed by these views, or had inherited
doctrines of a similar import from the founders of the
Religious Orders to which they respectively belonged.
Different opinions were openly avowed by the Domini-
cans, Franciscans, and Augustinians.   Soto insisted on

the difference between faith and works,—or the Gospel
and the Law,—showing that these terms denoted, not
a difference of dispensation merely under the Old and
New Testament, but a more fundamental difference between two methods of acceptance with God ; Marinarus
held the forensic sense of the term Justification, and
objected to the Popish doctrine of ' faith informed with
charity ;' Pighius and Vega admitted the imputed righteousness of Christ ; and the Bishop of Cava was favourable
to the doctrine of Justification by faith only.   Amidst
such a diversity of opinion within the Council itself, it
was necessary, if the concurrence of all parties was to
be secured, to draw up the decrees, which embodied a
statement of their own doctrine, in vague and somewhat
ambiguous terms, which every one might interpret in
favour of his own views ; and accordingly, no sooner had
they been published, than Soto, a Dominican, and Vega,
a Franciscan, produced in 1548 contradictory comments
on their real meaning.   But besides being a vague and
ambiguous statement of the opinions of those who sat
in the Council, they were very far from being an accurate
representation of the doctrine which was then generally
taught by the priests, and as generally believed by the
members, of the Romish Church.   They did not contain
a full and frank exposition, or profess to offer an honest
and manly defence, of many opinions and practices which
were known to prevail universally, except where they
had been checked and counteracted by the Reformers ;
and which had a most important bearing on the great
question of a sinner's justification in the sight of God.
It has been admitted even by those who take a favourable
view of the Church of Rome, that her practical system
is in many respects much worse than the decrees of the
Council of Trent. (13)

But vague and ambiguous as is the language of some
of these decrees, they are sufficiently explicit to show
that, while their framers professed to acknowledge the
grace of God, and the merits of Christ, as necessarily
implied in the doctrine of Justification, they still adhered
to the radical principles of the Popish system, by which
it has always been distinguished from that of the Reformers. These principles are not presented, indeed, so
obtrusively, or expressed in such offensive language, as
they have often been in the writings of Romish contro-
versialists; but they are there, although coloured and
disguised by some evangelical expressions. Both Calvin,
in his 'Antidote,' and Chemnitz, in his 'Examination,'
have noticed some statements in these Decrees which
make a near approach to the true doctrine of Justification; but have also shown that these seeming concessions
to the force of truth are effectually neutralized by other
erroneous principles, and that the resulting product is
an amalgam of some truth mixed with much error, such
as is fitted to be deeply injurious to the souls of men.
The earlier Decrees speak much of the grace of God, and
the merits of Christ; but as they advance, they ascribe
as much to man and his free-will, and end in ascribing
justification partly to grace, and partly to works. They
come very near to a scriptural statement of Justification,
when they speak of it as a change in man's relation to
God, by which he who was a child of wrath is forgiven
and accepted, through the redemption which is in Christ
Jesus; but they immediately confound it with the renovation of his nature, and make it to depend upon an
infused and inherent habit of grace as its immediate
and proper ground. (14)

It is the more important to bear these remarks in
mind, because some recent writers, founding on the

cautious and guarded statements of the Council on the subject of Merit, and their references to the sufferings and death of Christ as the ultimate procuring cause of salvation, have endeavoured to show that the authorized doctrine of the Romish Church has been misunderstood or misrepresented by Protestants, and that there is much less difference than is usually supposed between the canons of Trent and the creeds of the Reformed. It is thus made to assume, at least in Protestant countries, a very plausible and harmless aspect; while the radical error, which lies at the foundation of the whole Popish doctrine, and which is incorporated with the decrees of the Council, is carefully covered up and kept out of view. The last of the sixteen chapters, which are devoted to the subject of Justification, contains a summary statement of that doctrine, which amounts in substance to this,—that the righteousness, by which we are justified, is a righteousness infused and inherent; that it is called our own righteousness, because it is inherent in us,— and that it is also called the righteousness of God, because it is infused by Him. This is the radical error; for the whole question between the Popish and Protestant Churches lies here: Are we justified by our own righteousness, or by the righteousness of Christ? by a righteousness infused and inherent, or by a righteousness imputed, which is not in us, but in Him?

In this sense, their doctrine was understood and defended by their ablest controversial writers,—such as Andradius, Bellarmine, Vasquez, and Osorio. These writers adhered to the old doctrine of the Church. Andradius was answered by Chemnitz, Bellarmine by Amesius, Bishop Downham, Bishop Davenant and many more; Vasquez's extreme views on the subject of Merit are exposed by Archbishop Wake in his 'Exposition' and

'Defence;' and Osorio was ably met by John Foxe, the Martyrologist. But another class of writers advocated a diluted and disguised doctrine, which may be called New Popery, as distinguished from the Old, and which had its origin after the Reformation. For the double policy of Rome, in alternately denouncing the Protestant doctrine as a dangerous novelty, and claiming it, in her own sense of it, as a truth which she had always taught, continued to be pursued by two classes of writers within her pale,— the one representing Old Popery, such as it was before the Reformation,—the other New Popery, or Popery transformed, if not reformed, and appearing now as if it were an angel of light. 'Let any one compare,' says Bishop Atterbury, 'Bellarmine's bold truths with the softenings of the Bishop of Condom, . . . and it will appear that Old Popery and New Popery agree no more than the two Styles.' (15) Old Popery was still taught in Roman Catholic countries, such as Spain, Italy, Austria, and Mexico; while the New was specially intended for Catholics living in Protestant communities, such as those in France, England, Germany, and America, where the Bible was generally read and valued. But it is a still more instructive fact, that even in Protestant countries, the priesthood have made use of two distinct sets of books,—the one containing Old Popery undiluted, and consisting of catechisms and books of devotion,—such as 'The Sacred Heart of Jesus,' or 'The Angelical Exercise,' designed for the edification of the ruder part of their flocks;—the other intended for the better educated class of their own communion, but still more, perhaps, for their Protestant neighbours, in which all the grosser features of Popery are concealed, or softened down, or coloured over, and all its distinctive doctrines kept in the background, or explained away. (16) At a much earlier period, they were so ready to disclaim both the old doctrines and the old practices of their Church, that Luther found it expedient to publish an account of the 'Conformities of St. Francis,' that 'it might not be forgotten what things had really been taught under the Papacy;' and more recently, our acute brethren the Protestants in America have reprinted, at their own expense, the Rhemish New Testament, as a necessary means of self-defence, against the plausible pretences of modern Catholicism. (17)

In pursuance of the same policy, attempts were made, by writers on both sides, to harmonize even the symbolical books of the two Churches, and to show that there is no real, or at least no radical, difference between them on the momentous subject of a sinner's justification before God. We find Soto and Vega, who were both active members of the Council of Trent, explaining the Decrees, the one in favour of the Dominican, the other in favour of the Franciscan doctrine ; but this was a question between two orders within the bosom of the Church itself. Afterwards we find Dezius, a Jesuit of Strasburg, publishing a work on express purpose to prove that there was little or no difference between the Decrees of Trent and the Confession of Augsburg ; and this with a view to the reunion of the Protestants at Strasburg with the Church of Rome. (18) Many others, who are mentioned by Mosheim, made a similar attempt; but the most influential were Bossuet, in France, and Davenport, or Francis à Sancta Clara, in England. Bossuet attempted to bring back the Protestants of France to the pale of the Romish Church by his 'History of the Variations of the Protestant Churches,' and his 'Exposition of Catholic Doctrine,' in which he made it his object to show, that the Protestants differed as widely from one another as they did from the Popish creed; and this he could only do by explaining away all

that was peculiar and distinctive in the doctrine of Trent,
as compared with that of the catechisms and confessions
of the Reformed. (19)   Notwithstanding the array of
official 'approbations' which were prefixed to it, his 'Exposition' never commanded the confidence of the more
honest members of his own Church; it has been much
more lauded by ill-informed Protestants than by stanch
Romanists; and it was characterized by the divines of
Louvaine as 'scandalous and pernicious.'   Dr. Davenport, or Francis à Sancta, who was himself an English
convert to Romanism, and confessor to the queen of
Charles I., published a work containing an elaborate
attempt to show that the Articles of the Church of
England might be interpreted in a sense which would
bring them into entire accordance with the doctrine of
Rome, and that in that sense they might be subscribed by
men holding the Popish faith. (20)   To this work further
reference will be made in connection with the history of
the doctrine in the Church of England.

The work which has exercised, perhaps, the strongest
influence, in modern times, on the minds of educated men,
both on the continent and in this country, in disposing
them to think more favourably of Popish doctrine than
the Reformers did, is the plausible and elaborate treatise
of Moehler on 'Symbolism.'   He has been justly described
as 'the most skilful and accomplished defender of Popery
in the present century,' and his work exhibits, as its title
imports, a comparative view of the symbolical books of
the Romish and Protestant Churches, in which their respective doctrines on most of the leading topics in Theology
are stated and discussed.   In the earlier editions of it, he
proceeded on the assumption that the Decrees and Canons
of the Council of Trent are the only authoritative standards
of the Romish Church; but afterwards admitted that there

were other decisions which were equally binding, and more
explicit on some points of faith, such as the Bulls by which
the Popes condemned the doctrines of Baius, of Jansenius,
and of Quesnel.   These Bulls are important, as authoritative decisions on some points which are more vaguely set
forth by the Fathers of Trent.   His leading design was to
explain 'the doctrinal differences between Catholics and
Protestants,' and to set them in such a light as should be
most favourable to the doctrines of his own Church.   On
the subject of Justification he enlarges at considerable
length, but connects it throughout with what may be regarded as his fundamental doctrine,—that of original
righteousness as a supernatural gift, and of original sin
as the forfeiture of that gift, with the consequences which
such forfeiture naturally produced, and necessarily entailed.
Setting out from this starting-point, he assumes that the
nature of the remedy must be adapted to, and may be
determined by, the nature of the evil that is to be redressed
by it ; and as that evil, in his view of it, was a subjective
one—a defect or a disorder in man's moral nature—it
could only be remedied by a subjective moral change,—
in other words, by the restoration through grace of that
original righteousness which was bestowed on man as a
supernatural gift after his creation, but which was forfeited and withdrawn at his fall ; and thus he reaches his
goal, and concludes in favour of a 'moral,' as distinguished
from a 'forensic,' Justification.   The radical error of his
doctrine, both on the subject of sin and of salvation, may
be said to be essentially the same, and to proceed from one
and the same cause : it consists,—on the subject of sin,—
in regarding it simply as a subjective moral evil, vitiating
the character and destroying the happiness of men, without taking duly into account its guilt and demerit as an
offence against God, which provoked His wrath and in-

curred His condemnation; and,—on the subject of salvation,—it consists, in like manner, in regarding it simply as
a subjective moral remedy, renewing the character, and
thereby restoring the happiness, of men, without taking
duly into account the provision which was necessary for
the pardon and acceptance of a guilty and condemned
sinner as righteous in the sight of God.   In the one case,
the consideration of man's guilt gives place to that of his
depravity; in the other, the consideration of his pardon
and acceptance gives place to that of his renovation; and
in both cases alike, the error proceeds from overlooking,
or making little account of, *man's judicial relation to
God.* (21)

Moehler's 'Symbolism' was claimed by Dr. Newman
as an authority in favour of the principle, which he announced in his 'Essay on the Development of Christian
Doctrine.' That essay was an elaborate attempt to account
for the 'Variations' which history shows to have occurred
both in the doctrines, and practices, of the Romish Church.
He shows that, in order to meet the Protestant allegation,
that corruptions had gradually crept in after the Apostolic
age, the defenders of that Church had successively depended on the 'common consent' of the first three or four
centuries, proceeding on Vincent's rule ('quod semper,
quod ubique, et quod ab omnibus') as a sufficient test of
Catholicity,—and when that failed, or was found difficult
in its application, on the 'doctrine of reserve' (the 'dis-
ciplina arcani'), which implied that there existed from the
beginning an esoteric, as well as an exoteric, doctrine in
the Church.   He sets aside these old defences, as being
untenable in themselves, as well as insufficient to account
for the facts which modern history has established; and
he betakes himself to this third ground—of a developing
power always existing in the Church.   His theory was

broached immediately before his admission into the Church
of Rome, but has found little favour with her authorities.
It was openly rejected by many, and merely tolerated by
others.   The older defences are still held to be sufficient,
and the novel theory is regarded with doubt and distrust. (22)   The old doctrine of the Church is still taught,
in substance, in her Theological Colleges,—and embodied
in those works which have been specially prepared for the
education of the priesthood. (23)

Many attempts have been made to show that the
difference between the Romish and the Reformed Churches,
on the subject of Justification, is not vital or fundamental;
and that it is of so little importance as to present no
insuperable obstacle to their reunion, were certain other
corruptions in the Popish system removed.   It has been
thought that intelligent men, selected from either side,
might find, by means of mutual explanation, and, perhaps,
of mutual concession, a common ground of agreement.
Le Blanc, in a former age, did what he could to reduce
the difference between them to its minimum (24); and
several sanguine men have, at various times, entered into
correspondence and negotiation with a view to effect an
adjustment, while others, in the present age, are earnestly
labouring for the same end.   But all such attempts have
signally failed.   Wake's correspondence with Du Pin,
and the negotiations of Leibnitz and Grotius, proved
equally abortive.   Even within the Church of Rome
itself, the history of Baius, Jansenius, Quesnel, Martin
Boos, and many more, is sufficient to show that the
doctrine of free efficacious Grace, although taught by
Augustine and others, can scarcely be tolerated, when
it is openly proclaimed, and faithfully applied; for they
were all persecuted, and their doctrines suppressed. (25)
No one who thoroughly understands and firmly ad-

heres either to the Romish or the Reformed doctrine, can honestly propose a compromise between the two. Such a proposal can only be made or entertained by those who have a very inadequate sense of the difference which separates the one from the other. That difference is radical and fundamental, and involves, on some impor-tant points, a direct contradiction. It is not a difference of degree, as if the same doctrine were only more or less clearly stated, or exhibited in different shades of colour; it is a difference of kind, which becomes only the more marked in proportion as each of them is placed in a clearer and stronger light. It is true that the Church of Rome has always held some important doctrines of Scripture, and that these, applied by the Spirit of God, may have produced in some within her pale saving con-version to God; but it is equally true, that the whole subject of the method and ground of a sinner's justifica-tion has been so obscured and corrupted by her teaching, that in proportion as men became thoroughly imbued with her peculiar lessons, they were just so much the less likely to have recourse to Christ alone for salva-tion. (26)

Do we then deny the possibility of pardon and accep-tance with God within the Church of Rome? God forbid! What we deny is, that any sinner was ever justified, there or elsewhere, by his own righteousness; and we reject the Romish doctrine of Justification, as having a tendency to lead men to rely on their own good works, rather than on the finished work of Christ. We rejoice to know and believe, that some members of that Church may, like Martin Boos, renounce their own right-eousness, and take refuge in Christ alone. This was the declared belief of Luther himself; for as our Lord said to the Scribes and Pharisees of old, 'Verily I say unto

you, that the publicans and harlots go into the kingdom
of God before you,' so Luther said to the Religious
Orders of his times : ' If no flesh be justified by the
works of the law of God, much less shall any be justified
by the rule of Benedict, Francis, or Augustine, in the
which there is not one jot of true faith in Christ. . . . .
But some there were whom God called by the text of the
Gospel and by baptism.   These walked in simplicity, and
humbleness of heart, thinking the monks and friars, and
such only as were anointed of the bishops, to be religious
and holy, and themselves to be profane and secular, and
not worthy to be compared to them.   Wherefore, they
finding in themselves no good works, to set against the
wrath and judgment of God, did fly to the death and
passion of Christ, and were *saved in this simplicity*.'[1]

[1] Luther on the Galatians, Eng. Tr., p. 107.

LECTURE VI.

HISTORY OF THE DOCTRINE AS A SUBJECT OF CONTROVERSY AMONG PROTESTANTS.

FEW things in the history of the Church are more remarkable than the entire unanimity of the Reformers on the subject of a sinner's Justification before God. When it is considered that the doctrine of Scripture on that subject is one of the peculiar truths of Revelation,—that it is closely connected with a supernatural scheme of Grace and Redemption,—that it runs counter to some of the strongest tendencies of the unrenewed mind,—that it had long been obscured and perverted by the speculative errors of the Schools, and the practical corruptions of the Church,—that all the Reformers had been bred and trained from their earliest years in a system which had a tendency to foster a spirit of self-righteousness,—that they had been educated in false doctrine, and accustomed to the devout observance of confession, absolution, and penance,—that the theological literature, and even the devotional manuals, of their age were imbued and saturated with principles at variance with the free grace of the Gospel,—that even when they had recourse to the writings of the Fathers, they could only find, here and there, a distinct testimony to the truth, 'like a light shining in a dark place,' but obscured, and well nigh extinguished, by the shadows of those errors and superstitions which surrounded it on every side; and yet that, on the dawn of the Reformation, this feeble spark was everywhere kindled into a flame, dispersing the darkness which had been gathering around it for centuries, and consuming the 'wood, hay, and stubble' by which it had been overlaid,—that no sooner was the doctrine of a free and full Justification by grace through faith vividly apprehended by the awakened soul of Luther, and by him proclaimed, in accents clear and strong as a trumpet call, to the nations of Europe, than immediately it arrested the attention, and commanded the enthusiastic belief, of multitudes in every land, who had long laboured under the spirit of bondage, seeking rest for their souls, but finding none,—that it henceforth became the watchword and the badge of the Reformation, the rallying-point and bond of union among all believers, still more than their battle-cry in their conflict with Rome,—and that, differ as they might in other respects, they never differed in this, but gave forth a united testimony to the glad tidings of a free salvation by faith in an all-sufficient Saviour,—when these facts are duly considered, the entire unanimity of the Reformers in regard to the substance of the truth which they held and taught, is one of the most remarkable facts in history, and can only be accounted for by ascribing it to a copious effusion of the Holy Spirit, awakening everywhere deep convictions of sin, and enlightening men's minds in the knowledge of Christ as an all-sufficient Saviour. (1)

Their harmonious concurrence, in all that concerned the substance of the doctrine of Justification, is proved by a comparison of the writings of all the leading Reformers, and of the public confessions, catechisms, and articles of all the Reformed Churches. It is attested also by the assaults of their opponents, who never failed to select this doctrine as the special object of attack, and thereby showed that they regarded it as one which was common to the whole body of the Reformers, and which was justly held to be the very citadel and stronghold of their cause. Doubtless there may be found in the writings of the Reformers, and even in the confessions of the Reformed Churches, as there will always be found in the compositions of men who think for themselves, some diversities of opinion on minor points, and, still more frequently, diverse modes of stating or expressing the same truths; but due allowance being made for these shades of difference, there can be no reasonable doubt, that there was a far more 'unanimous consent' among the Reformers on the subject of Justification, than any that has ever been proved to exist among the Fathers on any article of faith whatever. (2)

While unanimity prevailed, among the Reformers and their immediate successors, in regard to the substance of the Gospel doctrine of Justification, Luther knew human nature too well to suppose that the truth could be preserved in its purity without a constant conflict with error; and he predicted more than once the gradual declension even of the Protestant Churches from this fundamental article of faith. He knew that men would invariably grow indifferent to it, in proportion as they became less impressed with a sense of sin, and less alive to the claims of the Law and Justice of God. He was soon taught by observation of what was passing around him, as well as by his own inward experience, that there are, in the heart of every fallen man, two great tendencies,—pointing apparently in opposite directions, but equally at variance with the doctrine which he taught,—the one, a tendency to Legalism, or self-righteous confidence; the other, a tendency to Licence, and Antinomian error. Between these two extreme tendencies, the true doctrine of Justification has often been, as Tertullian said, 'like Christ crucified between two thieves:' and all the errors which have arisen on that subject in the Church, may be ascribed to the one or the other, more or less fully developed.

The History of the doctrine of Justification in the Protestant Churches after the Reformation, is of a chequered character, and exhibits a series of successive declensions and revivals. Serious errors in regard to it soon sprung up in many quarters, and have been transmitted to our own times. It may be useful to examine with some care the various forms which the great question has successively assumed; and I propose to offer a brief sketch of the different controversies on this subject which have arisen in the Protestant Churches, during the three centuries which have elapsed since the establishment of the Reformation.

Many real, and very grave, differences of opinion on the subject speedily arose among the multitudes who bore the common name of Protestant,—a fact which we need neither shrink from avowing, nor attempt to disguise, from any idle fear of Bossuet's argument founded on the alleged 'Variations of Protestantism.' For that argument might be retorted with powerful effect, since the 'Variations of Popery' are notorious, whether regard be had to the different sects which have always existed at the same time within the pale of the Roman Catholic Church, or to the additions which have been made to her public doctrine, discipline, and worship, at different times in the course of her history. So far from denying the fact of differences amongst Protestants, on the subject of Justification, we avow it, as one that is attested by the best historical evidence, and that might be expected to occur wherever the pure truth of the Gospel was brought into close contact with unrenewed minds. But these heresies were not adopted,—they were abjured, by the Protestant Churches; and the sects which maintained them were not formed into so many 'religious orders' holding communion with one another, as belonging to the same fold; but were left to take their own course in a state of separation, as tolerated, without being either sanctioned, or persecuted, by the Churches which continued to adhere to the genuine doctrines of the Reformation.

Some of the different opinions, on the subject of Justification, which arose among Protestants in the sixteenth century, were held only by a few individuals in opposition to the prevailing doctrine of the Churches; while others were embraced by large parties who formed themselves into distinct sects, under some sort of ecclesiastical organization. These errors appeared in several distinct forms.

Among the peculiar opinions of individuals, which gave rise to controversy on this subject during the lifetime of the Reformers, the first place is due to that of A. OSIANDER, both because it indicated a tendency to revive the essential principle of the Romish doctrine, and also because it has been recently reproduced by Dr. Newman. It consisted in affirming, that the righteousness by which we are justified is the eternal righteousness of God the Father, which is imparted to us, or infused, through His Son Jesus Christ;—that it is not the meritorious work, or vicarious righteousness, of the Redeemer imputed to us, but an internal principle implanted. This is the radical principle of the doctrine of Trent; and, as such, it was at once denounced and rejected both by Calvin and Melancthon. (3)

Another divine, LAUTERWALD, of Upper Hungary, broached an opinion different, in some respects, from that of Osiander, but agreeing with it in so far, as it represented our personal, inherent righteousness as the ground of our

pardon and acceptance with God.   He conceived that our
repentance, love, and new obedience, are all included in
the faith by which we are justified, and are thus, conjointly with it, the means of obtaining the benefit of
Christ's redemption.   The University of Wittemberg pronounced, in 1554, a judgment upon it which was prepared
by Melancthon: 'Though true faith, or reliance on the
Saviour, cannot exist in those who go on securely in their
sins, and are destitute of contrition, yet contrition and
new obedience are not, as Lauterwald would make them,
the means of applying the promise of grace. . . . The
promise is embraced and applied only by faith, or affiance
in the Mediator, and not on account of our contrition, or
the virtues which follow after.   Faith relies only on the
Mediator, or on the mercies promised for His sake; in
which the heart rests, knowing that the promises are sure
in Him. . . . Lauterwald's corruption of the doctrine does
not differ from the *Synecdoche* of the monks, who say, that
faith justifies us, as being the originating principle of love
and of good works.   But the fact is this, nothing but faith
lays hold on the promise.   In this, faith differs from all
other works, that it embraces the promise, and receives
the blessing as unmerited.' (4)

STANCARI differed from the Reformers, not so much on
the subject of Justification, as on that of the Mediatorial
character and work of Christ; but the two topics are so
closely related, that any serious error in regard to the one
must affect our views in regard to the other.   He held in
substance that Christ's mediation was discharged by His
human nature only, whereas Melancthon showed that it
was discharged by His One Person, as did afterwards
Calvin and Turretin.   The question is important in
many respects, but chiefly as the right solution of it
is necessary to a correct estimate of the value and

efficacy of His vicarious satisfaction, and meritorious obedience. (5)

PISCATOR, also, held some peculiar views on the subject of Justification; but as they form the connecting link between the doctrinal discussions of the sixteenth and seventeenth centuries, and exerted a powerful influence on the New Methodists in France, and through them on the Neonomians in England, they will be stated in connection with the history of these movements.

The opinions to which we have hitherto referred were held by individuals only, who professed them within the Churches to which they respectively belonged. But far graver differences on the subject of Justification speedily arose, amongst bodies of men bearing the name of Protestants, who constituted themselves into distinct sects, and stood opposed to the confessions of all the Reformed Churches. These sects were formed under the influence of one or other of two great natural tendencies,—the tendency to Licence, on the one hand, and the tendency to Legalism, on the other. In the sixteenth century, these tendencies were developed, respectively, in two great systems of opinion, which were strongly contrasted with each other, as lying at opposite extremes, while both were, although in widely different respects, at direct variance with the doctrine of the Reformation. The one was the ANTINOMIAN, the other the SOCINIAN, system. Both sprung up during the lifetime of the Reformers, and occasioned them much sorrow; while both survived the vigorous efforts which Luther, Melancthon, and Calvin severally put forth to arrest their progress. They may be said to have appeared simultaneously, as reactions, in opposite directions, against the truth of the Gospel as taught by the Reformers. We shall first notice the Antinomian doctrine,—and thereafter the Socinian system, because the

latter was closely connected with the Arminian and Neonomian schemes, in the order of their historical development in the seventeenth century.

The ANTINOMIAN doctrine of Justification, which sprung
up among the Anabaptists in Germany, obtained a footing
among some sectaries in our own country, and spread
to some extent in New England.   Its origin has been
ascribed, most unjustly, to the teaching of Luther, because
he seemed to speak occasionally against the Law, as if
believers should regard and treat it as an enemy; but
it might with equal justice be ascribed to the teaching
of Paul, for he also said, and in the same sense, that ' the
strength of sin is the Law,' and that ' we are not under
the Law, but under Grace.'   If any one will candidly
examine the writings of Luther, with an honest desire to
ascertain his real meaning, he will find—that, while he
uses, like Paul, some strong expressions, which a more
timid, or, as some might say, a more prudent, man would
have avoided, he excludes the Law only as ' a covenant of
works,' and never as ' a rule of life,'—that he denounces
it as the ground of a sinner's Justification, but never as
the guide of a believer's conduct,—that he will not have
it to reign in the Conscience, for the 'Law worketh wrath,'
and the Gospel only can bring ' peace,'—but that he leaves
it all its rightful authority, first, over the unbelieving
sinner as a message of guilt and condemnation,—and,
secondly, over the justified believer, as a law which is
' holy, and just, and good.' (6)

The Antinomian doctrine of Justification was directly
opposed to that of the Reformers, and could not, therefore,
be its natural fruit, or its legitimate development.   The
two came into direct collision at many points; and a few
of the most important may be briefly specified, with the
view of laying bare the radical principles which were

involved in Antinomianism, when, instead of being a mere lawless impulse, it came to be propounded and defended as a doctrinal theory. The advocates of that theory differed from the Reformers, *first*, in regard to the nature and effects of imputation,—for they were in the habit of speaking, as if the imputation of our sins to Christ had made Him personally a sinner, and even the greatest sinner that ever was; and as if the imputation of His righteousness to us made us personally righteous,—so per- fectly, that God can see no sin in believers, or visit them with any token of His fatherly displeasure: *secondly*, in regard to the nature and effects of our union to Christ,— for they often spoke as if believers were in *all* respects one with Him, forgetting the wide difference between 'a union of representation' and a 'union of identity :' *thirdly*, in re- gard to the time and manner of a sinner's Justification— confounding it sometimes with the eternal purpose of election,—sometimes connecting it with the death, or with the resurrection, of Christ,—as if there were no difference between a divine purpose in eternity, and its execution in time, or between the work of Christ in procuring, and that of the Holy Spirit in applying, the blessings of redemption: *fourthly*, in regard to the use of the Law under the Gospel, —whether regarded as a covenant of works, or as a rule of life : *fifthly*, in regard to the existence and ill-desert of sin in believers, and the duty of praying for the pardon of it, and cherishing a 'broken and contrite spirit' on account of it: and, *lastly*, in regard to the nature and function of faith, which was represented, not as the means of obtaining pardon and acceptance with God, but rather as the evidence or declaration, merely, of our Justification, by which we obtain the assurance of it; as if it was equally true, but only not so manifest, before we believed. These are the most prominent points of difference between the

doctrine of the Antinomians, and that of the Reformers, on
the subject of Justification; and they are deserving of careful study, not only because they threatened at first to create
a permanent division in the Protestant Church, and even
to shipwreck the Reformation altogether, by exciting
general prejudice against it, but also because they serve
to define the precise doctrine of the Reformers by placing
it in contrast with its antagonist errors. The difference
between the two is all the more important, because they
must severally exercise an opposite influence on the minds
of those who embrace them. They relate, not to purely
speculative distinctions, but to points of faith which
possess a deep practical importance. It may be safely
affirmed that the whole spiritual character and experience
of a believer who receives the doctrine of the Reformers,
will differ from that of a man who is imbued with Antinomian opinions. The former is fitted to produce and
sustain—a profound reverence for the divine law,—a deep
and abiding sense of sin,—a broken and a contrite spirit,
—a godly sorrow, which worketh repentance unto salvation,—an habitual dependence on Christ for pardon,—a
holy fear of offending God, and incurring His fatherly
chastisement—such as cannot be expected to flow from
Antinomian opinions, in so far as they are opposed to the
generally received creed of the Protestant Church.

It may be thought that the Antinomian doctrine is
obsolete,—that it never acquired a permanent footing in
Germany, Britain, or New England, but only appeared for
a time among a few sectaries,—and that no danger can
arise from this source in these more enlightened times.
But when we find that the Apostles themselves were careful to guard against it,—that it sprung up and spread in
the wake of the Reformation,—and that it has generally
reappeared in connection with any signal revival of reli-

gion, it becomes us to remember, that the Antinomian Theory is one thing, and the Antinomian Tendency another,—that the one may be comparatively rare, while the other is alike natural and inveterate,—and that the danger of practical, if not of speculative, Antinomianism, must always exist, as long as the doctrines of Grace are presented to minds which are either entirely carnal, or as yet imperfectly sanctified. The prevailing power of sin in an unrenewed heart, or even the remains of indwelling sin in the believer himself, will ever tend towards an Antinomian perversion of the Gospel; and the last day only will declare how much practical Antinomianism has prevailed even in Evangelical congregations, which theoretically disowned it; and to how many the Gospel itself has thus proved 'the savour of death unto death.' (7)

The SOCINIAN doctrine of Justification had its origin in another natural tendency,—the tendency to self-righteousness. It was founded on the peculiar views which its advocates entertained in regard to many other parts of divine truth. They sought to undermine, and, in that way, to overthrow, the doctrine of the Reformers on the subject of Justification, by assailing, and attempting to disprove, some one or more of those truths which are presupposed in it, and which are necessary to its establishment. Hence the controversy with the Socinians turned, not so much on the main question—'How shall man be just with God?'—as on various other questions, which, however important in themselves, were merely preliminary, and ought to have been conclusively disposed of, before the precise doctrine as to the nature, method, and ground of a sinner's justification was entertained as a subject for discussion at all. The Socinian doctrine of Justification might, doubtless, have been disproved by express testimonies of Scripture bearing on that precise point,—but the doctrine of the Reformers could not have been established in opposition to it, without the aid of those peculiar truths of Revelation on which it depended; and these truths were either denied, or explained away, by Socinians, so as to impose on their antagonists the arduous task of defending revealed truth at every point along the whole line of theological inquiry. For the Socinian system is inadequately apprehended, when it is supposed to relate merely, or chiefly, to the doctrine of the Trinity, and the Divinity of Christ—or to consist only of a series of negative conclusions without any positive creed;—it embraced every question in the whole range of Theology, and exhibited a comprehensive scheme of thought, whose constituent parts were all fitly adjusted to each other, and firmly concatenated like links in a chain; and so far from being merely negative, it substituted in the room of every doctrine, which it rejected, a dogmatic deliverance, which it offered to establish by proof, as being either contained in Scripture, or, at the least, not at variance with its real meaning. Its authors dealt largely in destructive criticism, but they aimed also at being constructive; and their doctrines were so closely connected and interdependent, in point of logical sequence, that not one of them could be discussed without reference to all the rest, or detached from the series of which it formed an indispensable part.

The Socinian doctrine of Justification may be stated, in general terms, as amounting, in substance, to this— that sinners obtain pardon and acceptance with God, through His mere mercy, on the ground of their own repentance and reformation. When reduced to its ultimate principle, and stated in its simplest form, it teaches us to rely, not on anything that Christ has done for us, but only on the unchangeable placability of the divine nature, and on that which Christ has taught us to do for ourselves. It is not His work, but our faith, our repentance, our amendment of life, that constitutes the ground and reason of our justification. The radical difference between the Socinian doctrine and that of the Reformers turned on this hinge, and consisted mainly in the opposite answers which they respectively returned to the question,—whether we are justified by a personal, or a vicarious, righteousness? But it is necessary to add, that while they held the ground of a sinner's justification to be his own personal repentance and reformation, they taught, nevertheless, that, in their own sense of the terms, he is 'justified freely by grace,'—that he is 'justified by faith,'—that he is justified by means 'of the death of Christ,'—and that his faith, repentance, and obedience are not the meritorious or procuring causes of his pardon and acceptance, but simply the conditions on which his enjoyment of these blessings depends. They made large use of all these scriptural expressions, and had no scruple, even, in applying to the death of Christ the sacrificial terms, which the sacred writers employ to describe its expiatory nature, as a satisfaction for sin; but they attached their own meaning to every one of them, and that meaning was entirely different from the sense in which the same terms were understood by the Reformers, and led, of course, to an entirely opposite conclusion. The Socinian doctrine of Justification flows as a corollary from their peculiar views—of God's justice as a modification of His benevolence,—of man's relation to God as the universal Father,—of sin as a moral disease or disorder, rather than as a crime involving guilt and demerit,—of the nature and end of punishment as corrective, rather than penal or exemplary,—of the Person of Christ and His mere humanity,—

of His mediatorial office and work, as a Prophet, King, and Pattern only, but not as a Priest, at least before His ascension,—of His death as a martyrdom, but not an expiation—as a divine infliction, but not as a proper satisfaction for sin. If these preliminary views were admitted, there could be no room for the justification of any sinner except through the mere mercy of God in pardoning his sin, and accepting him on the ground of his personal repentance and reformation. In like manner, the doctrine of the Reformers, besides being expressly taught in Scripture, flowed as a corollary from the opposite views which they entertained on all these subjects; for if they held that God's justice requires the punishment of disobedience for the vindication of His law and the manifestation of His glory,—that men are universally chargeable with the guilt of original and actual sin,—that they are alike unwilling to be subject to God's law, and unable to yield perfect obedience to it,—that for them and their salvation, the Son of God became incarnate, and acted as Mediator between God and man,—that He executed the office of a Priest in offering Himself up as a sacrifice for sin,—that His sufferings were strictly penal, and properly vicarious,—and that they were both appointed and accepted by God as sufficient to render it consistent with His justice to extend mercy to the guilty, and to grant a full and free remission of their sins,—then, holding these views, they could hardly fail to believe that Christ's work is the meritorious procuring cause, and the only, but all-sufficient, ground of a sinner's justification. (8)

The Socinian doctrine, originally confined to Italy and Poland, soon spread over the continent, thence made its way into England, and, at a later period, into America. It has since undergone several changes, and has exhibited a tendency to advance in two opposite directions. The

Socinianism of Priestley and Belsham was very different from that of Channing and Ellis; and this again from its more recent development by Martineau and Blanco White. It has tended, in one direction, towards Deism and Antisupernaturalism,—a scheme of thought more remote from Christianity than even the meagre doctrine of Socinus; and, in another direction, towards Arianism, which admitted the pre-existence, superhuman dignity, and incarnation of the Saviour, while it denied His supreme divinity; and aimed at a somewhat more spiritual religion, than was generally prevalent among Socinians in former times. In the one case, Socinianism was either Deistic, and then it had no other doctrine of Justification than that of pardon on repentance and reformation; or it was Pantheistic, and then it had no room even for pardon or repentance, since it had no knowledge of sin, except perhaps as a disease, and none of punishment, properly so called, although it admitted suffering as the natural consequence of certain dispositions and habits. But in the other case, where the pre-existence and incarnation of the Saviour were acknowledged, and also His design to save sinners, and to save them, in some way, by means of what He did and suffered, there arose at once the possibility, and the necessity, of a modification of the old Socinian doctrine on the subject of Justification. Hence the new theory of the Arians. (9)

The ARIAN doctrine of Justification was offered as a ' via media '—a scheme intermediate between that of the Socinians and the Reformers. It has been confounded with the Neonomian theory, but should be distinguished from it; for while all Arians were Neonomians, all Neonomians were not Arians; and their respective doctrines were made to rest on different grounds.

Holding their peculiar views of the person of Christ, as the highest of created beings, incarnate, the Arians thought, that they could assign a sufficient reason for His interposition in the affairs of men, and give a Scriptural account of the work which He accomplished on their behalf, without admitting the doctrine of His vicarious satisfaction and righteousness, and yet without adopting the meagre and strained interpretation, by which Socinians explain away all that is revealed concerning the design and effects of His death.   Their leading idea was, that, although God was free to forgive sin, as Socinians affirm, without any satisfaction to His justice,—and would probably do so on the repentance of a sinner, since He delights in mercy, and has no pleasure in the infliction of punishment,—yet it might be expedient, if not necessary, for the good of the sinner himself, as well as for the general interests of God's moral government, to make a distinction between *innocent beings* and *penitent sinners,* in His mode of manifesting His love toward them; that while those, who had kept their first estate, were accepted and blessed on their own account, as members of His holy and happy family, His prodigal sons, who had forsaken their Father's house, but never forfeited their Father's love, should be restored to it by the good offices of a Mediator, so as to mark the difference between them and those who had never been defiled by sin; that, for this end, the highest of created beings consented to become man,—'a man of sorrows and acquainted with grief,'—that He conversed with men on the earth, instructing the ignorant, healing the diseased, and comforting the wretched, as a teacher and pattern of celestial virtue,—that He devoted Himself even to death for the accomplishment of His sublime mission,—that God accepted His generous interposition, and rewarded it, by

giving Him power to save men from sin and all its consequences,—that this reward, being personal to Himself,
implied that they were indebted to Him for salvation ; so
that, in this sense, 'by His obedience many were made
righteous,'—and that, in this way, they would be for
ever reminded of their own sinfulness, and of their deep
obligation to His generous, self-sacrificing love. (10)

Such is a brief account of the 'middle system,'—
intermediate between the Socinian doctrine and that of
the Reformers,—which was broached by some Arian
writers in England in the eighteenth century.   It relates
chiefly to the nature of the remedy which God provided
for the evils of our fallen state, and has a direct bearing,
therefore, on the doctrine of Justification.   It admits
that men are benefited by the incarnation, sufferings, and
obedience of Christ, as well as indebted to His generous
love, and powerful intercession ; but it excludes His
substitution in their room,—His bearing the burden
of their imputed guilt,—His enduring the punishment
which their sins deserved,—His offering up of Himself
as a sacrifice to satisfy divine justice,—His interceding
for them as an High Priest who has already made atonement for sin,—His obeying the law as their representative,
so as to work out a righteousness which might be imputed
to them,—and, generally, His saving them in any other
sense than as He is their friend and benefactor ; or in
any other way, than by the exercise of that authority and
power which He acquired, to bestow the forgiveness of
sins, on condition of repentance and amendment of life.
It ascribes a certain work to Christ, and represents men
as being indebted to it : but it is not a work of expiation
and redemption, undertaken for the satisfaction of divine
justice, and the vindication of the divine law ; it is merely
a work of voluntary self-abasement and self-sacrificing

love, undertaken with a view to the moral benefit of men,—it is the work of a friend and benefactor, not of a vicarious Redeemer, or atoning High Priest. And the benefit which accrues to men from His interposition, is not Justification, on the ground of His satisfaction and obedience, but the assurance merely that they may be justified by their own repentance and amendment,—a privilege for which they are, to some extent, indebted to Him, since His mission was designed to mark the difference betwixt innocent and fallen beings, and to remind them of their sinfulness, while it assured them of God's unchangeable love,—but which did not consist either in their deliverance from His wrath, or their admission into His favour, on account of what He suffered and did for them.

The SOCIETY OF FRIENDS exhibited a marked difference from the common doctrine of the Protestant Churches, and a near approximation to that of Rome, on the subject of Justification. They were the first to introduce into this country an idea,—which had been broached by some Popish writers as well as by Osiander, and which has been recently revived in the Lectures of Dr. Newman,— that we are justified by the indwelling presence of Christ, and the inward operation of His Spirit. But they went beyond this, for they seemed to identify Christ and His Spirit with 'the Light within,' which is common to all men, whether they be Christians or heathens; and which can scarcely be distinguished from natural conscience. Founding on the fact that Christ is said to be 'the true Light, which lighteth every man that cometh into the world,' and that Christ is 'formed in us, the hope of glory,' they inferred, that Christ dwells in all men, and that His indwelling presence needs only to be felt and recognised to become the source of spiritual and eternal life. They were thus the precursors of another recent school,—very different from that of Dr. Newman,—the school of modern Spiritualists, whose doctrine is much less original than it is commonly supposed to be, and has never been more ably expounded than in the 'Theses' and 'Apology' of Robert Barclay.

It is not easy to state their doctrine in precise terms, for it is blended, in the writings of Fox, Penn, and Barclay, with much mystical speculation; but in substance it amounts to this,—that all men have the 'Light within,' —that in those who receive, and do not resist, the illumination of that Light, it 'becomes a holy, pure, and spiritual birth,'—that this holy birth is 'Christ formed within,' whose presence sanctifies, and, by sanctifying, justifies us in the sight of God. Justification is made to depend, therefore, on the subjective work of Christ *in* us, not on the Mediatorial work of Christ *for* us; and to consist, not in the sinner's pardon and acceptance with God, but in the renovation of his nature, and his consequent blessedness as a new creature. 'The Light,' or 'the Christ within,' is not the historical Christ of the Gospels, the Son of God incarnate, who came in the flesh 'to put away sin by the sacrifice of Himself,' and to accomplish, by His own personal sufferings and obedience, 'the work which the Father had given Him to do;' it is rather the reason or conscience which belongs to all men, and which would have existed equally if Christ had never appeared on the earth; it is an attribute of human nature, baptized only with the name of Christ. The Justification of a sinner is made to rest on an internal moral change in himself, not on the atoning sacrifice and meritorious obedience of Christ. His satisfaction to divine justice, and the imputation of His righteousness

to the believer, are explicitly denied.   The forensic sense
of Justification is rejected, and the moral sense of that
term is substituted for it ; the sinner is made holy, and
therefore accounted righteous, according to the teaching
of the Popish Church. (11)

The ARMINIAN scheme of doctrine, in its earlier form,
did not directly affect the subject of Justification.   It
was not one of the ' five points.'   The sentiments of
Arminius himself on that subject,—as compared with
those of his immediate successors, Episcopius, Curcellæus,
Limborch, and Grotius,—were, on the whole, but with
some important qualifications, sound and scriptural, and
in harmony with the faith of the Reformed Churches.
He says expressly, ' I believe that sinners are accounted
righteous solely by the obedience of Christ ; and that the
righteousness of Christ is the only meritorious cause on
account of which God pardons the sins of believers, and
reckons them as righteous as if they had perfectly fulfilled
the law.'   He adds, ' I am not conscious to myself of
having taught or entertained any other sentiments concerning the justification of men before God, than those
which are held unanimously by the Reformed and Protestant Churches.' . . . ' None of our divines blames
Calvin, or considers him to be heterodox on this point ;
yet my opinion is not so widely different from his, as to
prevent me from employing the signature of my own
hand, in subscribing to those things which he has delivered on this subject in the Third Book of his "Institutes ;" this I am prepared to do at any time, and to
give them my full approval.'
Still there were some points on which he differed from
the Reformers ; and these may be said to have opened
the door, if they did not pave the way, for the admission

of those errors which were afterwards introduced under
his name.   Referring to the question, whether the active,
as well as the passive, obedience of Christ is imputed
for Justification, he declines, in one place, to decide upon
it, and says, in another, 'I do not enter into the question
of the active and the passive righteousness of Christ, or
that of His death and of His life.   On this subject, I
walk at liberty; I say, "Christ hath been made of God
unto me righteousness;" "He has been made sin for
me, that, through faith, I may be the righteousness of
God in Him."'   But the chief point on which he differed
from most of the Reformers—although his statements in
regard to it might, perhaps, be explained in a sense not
opposed to theirs—was the proper meaning of the Apostle's
words, that 'faith was counted for righteousness'—whether
the term ' faith' is to be understood as having been used,
figuratively (by metonymy), for the object of faith, or
properly, for the grace or act of faith itself.   He held
that faith was imputed as an act or state of mind, as
Bishop O'Brien also does ; but that this was to be understood as comprehensive, not as exclusive, of Christ and
His righteousness ; for, referring to the charge that, according to his doctrine, ' Christ and His righteousness
are excluded from Justification, and that it is thus attributed to the worthiness of our faith,' he rejects the
inference as not deducible from his sentiments, and adds,
' I do not deny that the obedience of Christ is imputed
to us ; i.e. that it is accounted or reckoned for us, and
for our benefit ; because this very thing—that God
reckons the righteousness of Christ to have been performed for us and for our benefit—is the cause why God
imputes to us for righteousness our faith, which has
Christ and His righteousness for its object and foundation, and why He justifies us by faith, from faith, or

through faith.' But overlooking or disregarding this explanation of his meaning, his followers insisted on the statement that faith,—considered as a grace or act,—is counted for righteousness ; and then, by making faith to be a compendious expression for all the other graces which are associated with it, or spring out of it, they made way for the doctrine that our whole obedience is imputed to us for our justification, although Arminius had attempted to guard against this application of his statement, by saying, that ' faith, and faith only (though there is no faith alone without works), is imputed for righteousness.'

But it was not so much any of his statements on the subject of Justification, as some of the principles which were involved in the 'five points' of Arminianism, which led subsequently to the corruption of his doctrine in regard to it. These points had, apparently, no direct or imme- diate bearing on that subject; but erroneous views in regard to them led inevitably to conclusions, which were incompatible with the doctrine of a free Justification by grace through faith alone. The sentiments of Arminius on these collateral questions exerted, in process of time, an injurious influence on men's views of Justification, chiefly because they were fitted to obscure the great doc- trines of Sin and Grace. A Pelagian or Semi-Pelagian germ was involved in the Arminian doctrine on the five points—an element which might be latent for a time, but which came to be developed when they were defended in controversy ; for they could not be maintained without some modification of the scriptural doctrine of Sin, or without making the free grace of God dependent on the free-will of man. Accordingly the Pelagian tendency of the doctrine became more manifest in the immediate suc- cessors of Arminius,—Episcopius, Curcellæus, Limborch, and Grotius ; and if some who embraced them continued to adhere to Scriptural views, both of the depravity of man, and the satisfaction of Christ, it was not because they had imbibed Arminian principles on the five points, or because they were more consistent than others in maintaining them, but because, under the teaching of God's Spirit, they had learned from another source, and felt in their own experience, that, as sinners, they were utterly ruined and unable to save themselves, and that they could have no hope of mercy except through a divine Redeemer, and the shedding of His blood as an expiation for sin. In consequence of this real and important difference in the results which followed from the adoption of Arminian views on the five points, it is necessary to divide the adherents of that system into two distinct classes,—the Pelagian or Semi-Socinian Arminians, who still admitted the divinity of Christ and His official character as the Saviour, but denied the penal and expiatory nature of His death, as a satisfaction to divine justice for the sins of men,—and the Evangelical Arminians, who affirmed the reality of His atoning sacrifice, and trusted in it alone for the pardon of their sins; but were disposed to doubt, if not to deny, the doctrine of imputed righteousness, in so far as it related to Christ's active obedience in fulfilling the precept of the divine law. (12)

The NEW METHODISTS, of the French Protestant Church, were not Arminians, but they adopted *one* of the Arminian points—the doctrine of universal redemption; and it led to a great change in their Theology. In them, and their followers, was the pithy remark of ROBERT TRAILL verified, that 'such men as are for "middle ways" in point of doctrine, have usually a greater kindness for that extreme they go half-way *to*, than for that which they go half-way *from*.' That Church was originally Calvinistic; and their

Confession was drawn up by Calvin. The French Protestants were not represented, indeed, at the Synod of Dort; but Molinæus (Du Moulin) assisted in preparing the Canons, and they were afterwards received without objection by the Church which he adorned. But a gradual change in the doctrinal sentiments, first of a few, and afterwards of a larger number, was effected by the introduction among them of the writings of Piscator and Tilenus. At a time when some illustrious Scotchmen,—such as Andrew Melville, Boyd of Trochrig, and John Welsh, the son-in-law of Knox,—had taken refuge among them, and when their Church could number more than two thousand congregations, their Synods began to be agitated by the discussion of the new views. Piscator's doctrine was, that Christ's passive obedience is the only ground of Justification. At the third National Synod of Rochelle, his views were considered, and an Act passed in regard to them of the following tenor: 'Whereas Dr. John Piscator, Professor in the University of Herborn (Nassau), by his letters of answer to those sent him from the Synod of Gap, doth give us an account of his doctrine on the point of Justification,—as that it is only wrought out by Christ's death and passion, and not by His life and active obedience; this Synod, in no wise approving the dividing of causes so nearly conjoined in this great effect of divine grace, and judging those arguments produced by him for the defence of his cause weak and invalid, doth order that all the pastors in the respective churches of this kingdom do wholly conform themselves in their teaching to that " form of sound words" which hath been hitherto taught amongst us, and is contained in the Holy Scriptures; to wit, that the *whole* obedience of Christ, both in His life and death, is imputed to us, for the full remission of our sins, and acceptance unto eternal life: and, in short, that this being but one and the self-same obedience, is our entire and perfect justification.'

The doctrine of Piscator, although condemned by several Synods, was adopted by D. TILENUS, Professor at Sedan, who introduced also the views of Arminius on some of the five points. These new views were refined upon by CAMERO, AMYRALDUS, and others, and Calvinism gradually lost its hold on the Reformed Church of France. John Welsh, who was present at the Synod of Rochelle, gives his opinion in a letter to Robert Boyd of Trochrig in 1613, in which, after stating some difficulties which he felt in signing the formula of the Synod, he says, ' I cannot agree with those who confound *remission* with *imputation,* since imputation is the *cause* of remission, and the cause is always distinct from the effect.' (13)

The doctrine of Piscator has an important bearing on the ground of a sinner's Justification before God ; for while it ascribed the remission of sins to the passive obedience, or the sufferings and death of Christ, it excluded the imputation of His active obedience, or righteousness, as the believer's title to eternal life ; and thus left a door open for the introduction of his own personal obedience, as the only ground of his future hope, after he had obtained the remission of his past sins.

There were thus brought to bear on the Theology of England, nearly about the same time, two adverse influences, proceeding apparently from opposite sources,—the one from Arminianism, as developed by the Remonstrants in Holland,—the other from New Methodism, as promulgated in the Calvinistic Church of France. Each of the two systems of opinion had its own partisans in this country, both within, and beyond, the pale of the Establishment. There were some who were avowed Arminians, such as John Goodwin, the friend of Milton ;

there were others who refused to be called Arminians, but preferred the system of the New Methodists, such as Richard Baxter.   But the two streams, although they sprang apparently from opposite sources, were flowing, if not in the same channel, yet in the same direction; and they found their confluence, or point of junction, first in the Neonomian theory, which was the ultimate terminus of both, and afterwards in Wesleyan Methodism, which had a direct and most important bearing on the doctrine of a sinner's Justification.

NEONOMIANISM gave rise to a public and protracted controversy between its advocates and opponents, who were agreed on some of the fundamental truths of Christianity, but differed widely from each other in regard to the method and ground of a sinner's Justification.   It has often been said that the publication of Dr. Crisp's writings gave rise to the Neonomian Controversy; and there can be no doubt that some of his statements entered largely into the subsequent discussion of it, and served to protract its duration, as well as to increase the vehemence with which it was conducted on both sides.   But the real cause of the controversy, was the introduction into England, first of the Arminian, and secondly of the New Methodist, doctrines,—which involved in substance, although not precisely in the same form, the Neonomian theory; since they equally maintained that the immediate ground of a sinner's Justification was his own personal obedience,— and that this was accepted, although imperfect, if it were only sincere, instead of that sinless righteousness which the Law of God originally required.   These doctrines were equally opposed to that of Justification on the ground of Christ's imputed righteousness; and those who adhered to it were stigmatized, by a strange misnomer, as Antinomians,—whereas, in rejecting the ' new law ' of grace, they were really contending for the unchangeable authority of the 'old law' of works, as one which could not be modified, but must be fulfilled.   Under this odious name, they were assailed both by Arminians and New Methodists; while, so far from deserving this treatment, their most strenuous efforts were directed, to vindicate the integrity of God's Law, and enforce its claims to perfect obedience,— either personal or vicarious,—in opposition to those who sought to accommodate its requirements to man's fallen state ; and the special ground on which they opposed the new doctrine was its irreconcilable variance with the original law of righteousness.   So far as this law was concerned, the real Antinomians were those who sought to relax and modify it, so as to substitute an imperfect, for a perfect, righteousness, as the ground of a sinner's acceptance with God ; and those who affirmed the unalterable claims of the original rule of righteousness, while they rejected the new law of grace, simply because it departed from that rule, should have been called, in common fairness, not Anti-Nomians, but ANTI-NEONOMIANS,—since that name would have marked the distinctive difference between the two parties, who severally contended,—the one for the old law which required perfect obedience, such as Christ only could render,—the other for the new law which every man, with the assistance of divine grace, could fulfil for himself. (14)

The Neonomian doctrine of Justification amounts in substance to this—That Christ, by His death, made full satisfaction to divine justice for the sins of all mankind, so as to remove every obstacle to their pardon and acceptance, and to bring them into a salvable state, or to make their salvation possible ;—that having satisfied the claims of the old law on their behalf, He procured for them ' a new law,' called the law of grace, to distinguish it from

the law of works,—a new law, which prescribes easier
terms of salvation, and instead of requiring a perfect
righteousness as the ground of a sinner's justification, is
satisfied with sincere, though imperfect, obedience ;—that
the work of Christ, by which these easier terms of acceptance were procured for us, may be called our Legal
righteousness, since we are entitled to plead it against
the demand of the old law for perfect obedience ; but that
our Evangelical righteousness consists in our personal
obedience to the new law, which we are entitled to plead as
sufficient to satisfy the only conditions which it prescribes ;
—and that the immediate ground of our justification is,
not the imputed righteousness of Christ, but the inherent,
personal righteousness of the believer himself, which
begins with faith, grows with sanctification, and is completed and made sure only by final perseverance.

This general outline or summary represents the sentiments both of the Arminians and the New Methodists in
England in the seventeenth century ; for while they differed on some minor points, and especially in their mode
of stating their respective views, there was a substantial
agreement between them on the subject of Justification.
They were equally opposed to the doctrine of Justification
by the imputed righteousness of Christ,—they equally
maintained the doctrine of Justification by the personal,
though imperfect, obedience of the believer,—and in
opposing the one, and maintaining the other, they proceeded on the same principles, and made use of the same
arguments. (15)

The WESLEYAN METHODISTS were a favourable specimen of the Evangelical Arminians, who stood opposed,
both to the Pelagians on the subject of man's depravity,
and to the Socinians on the subject of Christ's satisfaction ;

and yet they differed from the followers of Whitfield, and
other evangelical Christians, on the subject of Justification; for while they ascribed the pardon of sin to the merit
of Christ's expiatory death, they did not ascribe the acceptance of the sinner to the imputation of Christ's active
obedience, or vicarious fulfilment of the precept of the
divine Law.   They agreed generally with Arminius on
most of the five points,—but they agreed with him also
in maintaining the Priesthood,—the vicarious sufferings,—
and the atoning sacrifice, of Christ; and we cannot doubt
that, holding so much evangelical truth, many among
them have been so humbled under a sense of sin, and
so impressed by the justice and mercy of God manifested
in the Cross, as to 'flee for refuge to the hope that
was set before them,' and 'to receive and rest upon
Christ alone for salvation,' although from some confused
or mistaken apprehension of its meaning, they might
still hesitate to adopt, in its full sense, the doctrine of
imputed righteousness.   The germ of that doctrine is
really involved in what they believe, — for they held
the substitution of Christ in the room of sinners,—the
imputation of their sins to Him,—and His bearing the
punishment which these sins deserved; they further held,
that what He did and suffered on the Cross is imputed to
believers for their justification,—not what He suffered
merely, but what He did, when He became 'obedient unto
death.'   Obedience was involved in His sufferings,—and
if this was believed to be imputed to us for the pardon of
our sins, as constituting, along with His sufferings, the
satisfaction which He rendered to the law and justice of
God, then they admitted the principle of His vicarious
righteousness, which needs only to be extended so as to
include His active obedience in fulfilling the precept, as
well as the penalty, of the divine Law.

Wesley's sentiments on this point seem to have been influenced, to some extent, by his fear that the doctrine of imputed righteousness might be perverted into Antinomian error.   In his letters to Hervey, he admits the doctrine, but demurs to the phraseology in which it has often been taught; and urges many of the usual objections to it.   Yet no Calvinist could desire a clearer or fuller statement of it than is to be found in one of his 'Hymns and Spiritual Songs.'

> ' Join, earth and heav'n, to bless
>   The Lord our Righteousness.
> The mystery of Redemption this,
>   This the Saviour's strange design ;
> Man's offence was counted His,
>   Ours His righteousness divine.
>
> In Him complete we shine ;
>   His death, His life, is mine ;
> Fully am I justified,
>   Free from sin, and more than free,
> Guiltless, since for me He died ;
>   Righteous, since He lived for me.'

In these lines, the active and passive obedience of Christ —that of His life and that of His death—are distinctly recognised; and both are represented as concurring to a full justification.   The extreme dread of Antinomianism which was felt by Wesley and Fletcher, and which was justified, they said, by its prevalence among many of their professed converts, should have led them,—not to suspect the doctrine of Christ's imputed righteousness, which they did not teach,—but rather to inquire whether there might not be something else in their own opinions,—such as the views which they held of the nature of Justification itself, —of the object of justifying faith,—and the immediate enjoyment of personal assurance,—which might better account for the declension of some, and the apostasy of

others, than either the doctrine of imputed righteousness,
or that of final perseverance, in which their disciples had
never been taught to believe. (16)

The MORAVIAN BRETHREN were brought into close connection, for some time, with Mr. Wesley and his Societies.
A century before the Reformation, a strong reaction had
been excited in Bohemia and Moravia, against some of the
corrupt practices and doctrines of the Church of Rome, by
the devoted zeal of JOHN HUSS, and the impetuous eloquence of JEROME of Prague. The truth, proclaimed by
them, continued to work, like new leaven, in the minds of
their countrymen, long after they had sealed their testimony with their blood; and when Luther appeared, the
Reformation was joyfully welcomed by the Bohemian
Brethren, as well as by the still older Church of the Wal-
denses.   But what is now known as the Moravian Church,
or the 'Unitas Fratrum,' was organized by Count Zinzendorf at Herrnhutt in the eighteenth century, almost con-
temporaneously with the rise of Methodism under Wesley;
and their theology has been expounded by Spangenberg.
From some of their peculiar doctrines they have often been
classed among Antinomians, although men of all parties
have united in pronouncing the highest eulogiums on
the personal worth of many of the Brethren, and on the
organization and working of their co-operative settlements.
Wesley visited Herrnhutt, and held personal converse
with its founder and many of his associates; and there
can be no doubt that he derived from them many ideas
which he afterwards turned to good account in framing
the rules of the Methodist Societies.   The two bodies were
brought into close connection in England; but they soon
differed, and separated from each other, chiefly on account
of diversity of opinion on the subject of Justification, and

of Wesley's strong objection to their views, as having, in his opinion, an Antinomian tendency.

The Moravians seem to have differed among themselves in the statement of their doctrine of Justification. Some of the Brethren have stated it in terms which will be cordially assented to by all who hold, that the sole ground of a sinner's pardon and acceptance is the imputed righteousness of Christ; while others made use of expressions which implied, not only that His meritorious righteousness was imputed, but that His personal holiness also was transfused into the believer, and that sinners became partakers of it so as to become absolutely perfect, simply by believing that they were pardoned, and freed from all sin. (17)

The MARROW controversy in Scotland was a protest against alleged Antinomianism, on the one side, and a reaction against real Neonomianism, on the other. It was occasioned by the republication in this country of a work entitled 'The Marrow of Modern Divinity,' which had been written by Edward Fisher, an Independent, and published in 1647 with the approbation of Caryl, Burroughs, and Strong. It was assailed by Principal Hadow, of St. Andrews, in a work entitled 'The Antinomianism of the Marrow Detected:' and Mr. Hog, of Carnock, with the brethren who concurred with him in recommending the book, were cited to appear before the Church Courts, and ultimately forbidden to teach the doctrines contained in it. This Act of Assembly gave rise to a keen and protracted controversy, and ultimately led, in concurrence with other causes, to the secession of some of the ablest and best ministers of the Church. The discussion involved many important points of doctrine, but it mainly turned on a question of fact,—the one party affirming, and the other denying, that certain Antinomian errors were contained in Fisher's work,—while these errors were equally rejected by both.   In so far as it related merely to that fact, the controversy could have no permanent importance; and it would have resembled that which was waged between the Jansenists and the Jesuits, whether certain propositions, which were equally disclaimed by both parties, were contained in Jansen's 'Augustinus,'—or that between the Neonomians and their opponents in England, whether certain doctrines, which were disclaimed by both parties, were taught in the writings of Dr. Crisp.   In regard to this question of fact, in the case of the 'Marrow,' we shall only say, that a book which is held even by its admirers to require explanatory or apologetic notes, may be fairly presumed to contain some unguarded expressions, which might be understood in a sense dangerous to some part of the scheme of divine truth; and that this remark applies equally to Fisher's 'Marrow of Modern Divinity,' which was annotated by Thomas Boston, and to Dr. Crisp's 'Sermons,' which were annotated by Dr. Gill.

But we should take a very superficial view of the 'Marrow' controversy in Scotland, did we say, either that it related only to the right interpretation of Fisher's work, or that it originated entirely in its being reprinted by Mr. Hog.   Its republication in this country was the occasion, rather than the cause, of the discussion which ensued upon it; and other influences were in operation of a much more powerful kind.   The discussion on the 'Marrow' was closely connected with the Neonomian controversy in England during the previous century. That scheme of doctrine soon became known in Scotland; and the different views which were held in regard to it were the real, although not the ostensible, cause of the 'Marrow' controversy.

We are not warranted, indeed, to say that Principal
Hadow, and those who concurred with him in opposing
the 'Marrow,' had themselves adopted the Neonomian
doctrine; for unquestionably their views, as explained
in an elaborate statement at the commencement of
Hadow's work, were, on the whole, sound and scriptural,
—much more so than the opinions which became prevalent at a somewhat later period, when patronage began
again to be enforced with a high hand, and the piety of
Scotland withered under the blight of a meagre Arminian
or semi-Socinian theology.   But we are warranted in
saying that, in their opposition to the 'Marrow,' they
manifested a leaning towards some of the Neonomian
views, and that, in assailing its alleged Antinomianism,
they did not sufficiently bear in mind the important
distinction between Antinomianism, properly so called,
and another very different system, which was branded
with that name in England, but which ought, as we
have said, to have been called Anti-Neonomianism.

The doctrine of Justification was not directly involved
in the 'Marrow' controversy, for both parties professed
adherence to that of the Westminster Confession; but
some points closely connected with it were brought into
discussion.   The adherents of the 'Marrow' were charged
with holding that assurance is of the essence of faith,
and with contradicting, in that respect, the doctrine of
the Westminster Confession, which expressly teaches,
that while assurance of salvation is attainable, yet 'it
doth not so belong to the essence of faith, but that a
true believer may wait long, and conflict with many
difficulties, before he be partaker of it.'   But the Confession relates to a complex assurance, resting on several
distinct grounds, and capable of existing in different
degrees; for it speaks, first, of 'an infallible assurance

of faith, founded upon the divine truth of the promises
of salvation;' and thereafter of that which is founded
on 'the inward evidence of those graces unto which
these promises are made, the testimony of the Spirit of
adoption witnessing with our spirits that we are the
children of God.' It is of this complex or full assurance,
that the Confession says, that 'it doth not so belong to
the essence of faith, but that a true believer may be
without it for a time;' and this was never denied by the
'Marrow' divines. They meant merely to bring out the
full meaning of the statement, that the assurance of faith
is founded, in the first instance, upon 'the divine truth
of the *promises* of salvation,' and to give due prominence
to the fact, that faith, resting upon a divine testimony,
must necessarily involve an assurance of the infallible
certainty of whatever God has been pleased to reveal.
The assurance of which they spoke was that which is
implied in THE DIRECT act of faith, when the sinner first
'receives and rests upon Christ for salvation as He is
freely offered in the Gospel,'—as distinct from, but
necessarily presupposed in, that which springs from the
REFLEX exercise of faith, when the believer finds in his
own experience 'the inward evidence of those graces,'
which are the scriptural marks of a saving change. The
former may not amount to the 'full assurance' of which
the Confession speaks; but assuredly the latter cannot
exist,—cannot even commence,—without it; and it may
continue, in the absence of sensible evidence, and in the
midst of much darkness and doubt; since it is, in the
words of the Confession, that 'seed of God, and life of
faith,' by which believers, while they 'walk in darkness,
and have no light,' are, 'in the meantime, supported from
utter despair.' Many reasons might be stated for insisting, in the first instance, on that assurance which is

involved in the direct exercise of faith in Christ. Not
only is it necessarily presupposed in every other degree
of assurance, but it is the ultimate ground of that which
springs from the inward evidence of the believer's experience itself; for this would be mere presumption, did it
not rest, from first to last, on the infallible testimony of
God. It is of the utmost importance that men should
be taught from the beginning that there is a ground of
assured faith and hope, even for the chief of sinners, in
the Gospel of Christ, and that they are divinely warranted
to rest upon it at once for their own salvation. It is of
equal importance that professing Christians should be
reminded of the same truth ; for there is reason to fear
that the want of assurance, of which many complain,
often arises from a latent doubt in regard to some of
the truths of the Gospel,—that they have never
thoroughly believed Jesus to be the Christ, the divinely
anointed Saviour of sinners,—that they have never
actually received and rested upon Him for salvation,—
that they have never realized to themselves the fact, that
they are individually warranted, and even commanded, to
embrace Him as God's ordinance for their salvation,—and
that, consequently, they have not yet commenced that
direct exercise of faith on Christ, in the absence of which
there can be no spiritual experience, and no inward
evidence, to confirm their hope. True believers themselves may need to be reminded of the direct exercise of
faith on Christ, as an indispensable duty, which can never
be superseded by any amount of inward evidence, and as
an unfailing source of relief and comfort even in their
darkest hours ; for at such a time, they will find little to
reassure them by 'looking within,'—they must 'look
out' to Christ the Sun of righteousness, shining still,
unchanged and unchangeable, in all His glory, behind

the cloud which has cast its transient shadow on their souls. The adherents of the 'Marrow' were further charged with holding the doctrine of universal redemption, and insisting that every believer must be able to say, 'Christ died for me.' The charge of holding the doctrine of universal redemption, is inconsistent with that of the assurance of personal salvation being of the essence of faith ; for, according to the confession of all parties, universal redemption can give only the assurance of salvability, unless it be combined with the additional doctrine of universal salvation ; and this they were never supposed to teach. They held that Christ's death was effectual in procuring salvation for all who were given to Him in the everlasting covenant, and who should hereafter believe in His name. They did not embrace the doctrine of universal redemption ; although one of them, —Mr. Fraser of Brea,—had so far adopted the views of Amyrald as to speak of a double reference—special and general—of Christ's death, while he disowned Amyrald's doctrine of 'conditional redemption.' With this partial exception, if it be one, all the 'Marrow' divines adhered to the usual method of stating the design and extent of the death of Christ. They were charged, however, with insisting that every believer should be able to say, 'Christ died for me.' If this expression was used by them, it should be understood in a sense that will bring it into accordance with their other views. Their main object was to establish the warrant of every sinner to whom the Gospel comes to receive and rest upon Christ as his Saviour. This warrant they found, not in the unrevealed, but in the revealed, will of God,—not in His eternal decree, but in His inspired Word,—not in His secret purpose, but in His public proclamation, of grace. They knew that the unrevealed will of God forms no part of

the rule either of faith or of duty; that His eternal
purpose, whatever it may be, and however it may
regulate His own dispensations towards His creatures,
can, in no way, affect their duty to believe the Gospel,
any more than it affects their duty to obey the Law;
and that it cannot possibly run counter to His revealed
will, since, in common with it, it is determined by all
His adorable perfections, and must therefore be infinitely
'holy, and just, and good.' (18)

The SANDEMANIAN system was an extreme reaction
against the 'Neonomian,' and also against the 'Marrow,'
doctrine, which arose during last century, almost simultaneously in Ireland and Scotland, and which continues
to exist, within a limited circle, in the present age,
among the followers of Sandeman and Glass, while it
has tinged the writings of many who did not, in all
respects, embrace their opinions. It was a recoil from
the 'Neonomian' doctrine which had prevailed in the
preceding age, but it went to the opposite extreme,
and was equally at variance with that of the 'Marrow'
divines, for it denied that faith is an act of the mind
at all,—or at least an act of the renewed mind, and
affirmed that if it were an act of obedience, we must
be justified by a 'work.' The writings of Sandemanians
contain some important truths, and are fitted to correct
several prevalent errors; but not content with vindicating
the one, and exposing the other, they have gone much
further, and have virtually claimed for themselves a
monopoly of the only sound view of free Justification by
grace, on grounds which bring them into direct collision
with the doctrine of the Reformed Churches.

The difference between the two is one of a much
more fundamental nature than is generally supposed.

It is often regarded as a mere difference of opinion on a metaphysical question respecting the nature and definition of faith ; but on deeper inquiry into the grounds on which the Sandemanian doctrine rests, and the arguments by which it is maintained, it will be found to resolve itself into one of the most important questions which ever engaged the attention of the Church.   For that question, considered in its widest extent, and reduced to its ultimate analysis, amounts to this,—Whether the work of the Holy Spirit in applying to men individually the redemption purchased by Christ, and producing faith and repentance in them in order to their Justification, be, or be not, inconsistent with a free Justification by the imputed righteousness of Christ ?   Sandemanians are anxious to reduce faith to a mere intellectual assent, and to exclude from it trust, affiance, and assurance, with everything that is spiritual or holy, or that can be regarded as a moral duty,—for this express reason, that were it considered as including any of these fruits of the Spirit, or as being an act of moral obedience, we must be held to be justified by 'a work.'   But this reason involves the tacit assumption that faith is itself the righteousness by which we are justified,—for if it be not that righteousness, but merely the means by which we receive and rest on the righteousness of Christ, it may be, as the Protestant Church teaches, a fruit of the Spirit, a holy principle, and even a moral duty, without implying the slightest departure from the doctrine of a free Justification.   Let faith itself be excluded, as well as every other grace, from forming any part of the ground of our acceptance, and the work of Christ *for* us will still remain the only righteousness by which we are justified, while the work of the Spirit *in* us may be acknowledged in all its fulness and efficacy, as that by which alone we can be so united to Christ as to become partakers of His righteousness.   Instead of an intellectual, we may have a spiritual, apprehension of divine truth, and instead of a cold assent, a cordial consent, to the Gospel, without impairing in the slightest degree our reliance on Christ alone.   The relation of the work of the Spirit in us to the work of Christ for us is one of the most important subjects in Theology. (19)

The HOPKINSIAN Theology, which sprung up in America early in last century, had an important bearing on the doctrine of Justification, because it rejected the imputation both of sin and of righteousness : and traces of its influence may be discerned in the writings of many transatlantic divines, such as Prof. M. Stuart and Mr. Albert Barnes.   If the fundamental principles of representation,— substitution,—imputation,—and satisfaction, be discarded or tampered with, the ground, on which alone the scriptural doctrine of pardon and acceptance with God can be maintained, is undermined ; and the Newhaven Theology would present but a feeble barrier to the inroads of Socinianism. But America has furnished a sufficient antidote to these errors in the writings of many distinguished theologians, especially in those of the venerable Dr. Hodge, and his associates in the ‘ Princeton Theological Review ’ and ‘ Essays.’   The subject of Imputation will come under our notice in the sequel. (20)

The enumeration of so many diversities of opinion is apt to create, in some minds, a feeling of perplexity, instead of conveying useful instruction.   But that feeling may be mitigated, by considering *first*, that whatever may be the fluctuations of human opinion, ‘ the word of the Lord ’— the only rule of faith—is, like its Author, unchangeable

—'the same yesterday, and to-day, and for ever,' and that 'this is His word which by the Gospel is preached unto us;' while the subordinate standards of all the great Protestant Churches have continued all along to bear their united testimony to the truth which was established at the Reformation ; *secondly*, that the Scriptures teach us to expect differences of opinion, amounting even to heresies and divisions in the visible Church, and not only so, but to believe that they are wisely permitted, and will be over-ruled for good, by Him who can bring order out of confusion ; for 'there must be heresies among you, that they which are approved may be made manifest;'[1] *thirdly*, that in point of fact, controversy has been the great means of defining the truth in all ages of the Church, and a powerful corrective of partial and one-sided views of it; and *lastly*, that, after all the discussion which it has undergone, the question of Justification may be reduced to *two* simple alternatives—since our pardon and acceptance must depend either on the free grace of God, or the free-will of man,— and rest either on the imputed righteousness of Christ, or on an inherent righteousness of our own.   These are the ultimate alternatives on the subject of Justification, and no one need feel much difficulty in deciding between them, if the opposite errors of Legalism and Antinomianism be both excluded by affirming the equal necessity, and the inseparable connection, of the work of Christ *for* us, and the work of His Spirit *in* us, for our actual salvation.

[1] 1 Cor. xi. 19.

LECTURE VII.

HISTORY OF THE DOCTRINE IN THE CHURCH OF ENGLAND.

THE Church of England has often been described as
'the great bulwark of the Reformation,' and in
some important respects the statement is true. The
strongest Nonconformists have cheerfully acknowledged
their obligations to the learning, ability, and sound piety
of many of her divines. Their writings are a precious
legacy to the universal Church of Christ,—an armoury
richly furnished with all needful weapons in defence of
the common faith,—and a storehouse of spiritual instruction for minds of the highest culture. They did signal
service at an early period to the cause of the Reformation; and Protestantism is indebted to them for some
of the ablest refutations of the errors of Rome. 'The
Church of England,' says one who was thoroughly versed
in the Popish controversy, 'contained then' (in the
reign of Charles II.), 'as it had always done, men of
great talent and consummate learning, ready and willing
to contend for the cause of truth; and the works then
produced by the divines of the Church of England not
only constitute a very important part of the Popish controversy, but form one of the noblest monuments of talent
and learning which any Church has ever erected in any one
generation of its history. Besides many large treatises,
in which particular subjects in the controversy between
Protestants and Papists were elaborately discussed, an

immense number of smaller discourses were published, in which every topic bearing upon the points in dispute was illustrated with great success.   Most of them were afterwards collected together by Dr. Gibson, Bishop of London, and published in three folio volumes under the title of " A Preservative against Popery," which is a complete storehouse of valuable materials upon every department of the controversy.' (1)

Such was the well-earned character of the Church of England in her earliest and best times.   But, if we are to believe some of her modern divines, she never was distinctively Protestant, and was always fully more in accord with the Church of Rome, than with the Churches of the Reformation.   In saying so, they refer not merely to her having retained the Episcopal form of government, and some of the litanies, ceremonies, and ·vestments of the Church of Rome, but also to her having rejected, or at least refused explicitly to sanction, the peculiar views of the Reformers on some important points of doctrine, and especially on the doctrine of Justification. They affirm that the ' Articles of Religion,' and even the ' Homilies,' do not contain that doctrine, as it was taught by the Reformers, but another, which is clearly distinguishable from it, and which they hold to be the only one that is truly Catholic and Apostolic.   They have not attempted to prove that the German and Swiss Reformers, as a body, did not hold the commonly received doctrine of a free Justification by grace, through faith in Christ,— for they might well feel that any such attempt must be utterly hopeless ; but they have endeavoured to raise a doubt, in the first instance, whether the same doctrine had been received by the framers of the Articles and Homilies, and then ventured more boldly to affirm that she differed from the first, and that she differs still, from

all the other Churches of the Reformation on this fundamental point,—that she never taught, and does not now
teach, in any of her authorized formularies, the doctrine
of a 'forensic' Justification, as it was held by Luther,
and Zuingle, and Calvin; but speaks only of a 'moral'
Justification, consisting in pardon and renovation, or
depending, at least, on repentance and obedience,—and
that this doctrine of a 'moral' Justification is opposed
to that of the Reformers, on the one hand,—and yet not
identical, in all respects, with that of the Council of Trent,
on the other; while it is in entire accordance with the
teaching of the Fathers, and the consent of Catholic
antiquity.   Some of her own sons have thus been found
willing to place the Church of England in a state of
solitary isolation from all the Reformed Churches in
Europe; and not only so, but to represent her as occu-
pying a position of antagonism with them, on the most
fundamental article of the Christian faith. (2)

In undertaking the defence of the Church of England
and her Reformers on this point, we must advert, in the
first instance, to the peculiar line of argument which the
writers referred to have adopted, and the specific grounds
on which their conclusion is made to rest.   They have
had recourse,—not to a simple interpretation of the
Articles, or an impartial comparison of their statements
with the Decrees and Canons of Trent, on the one hand,
and the Catechisms and Confessions of the Reformed
Churches, on the other—although this would seem to be
the most direct method of procedure in a question of such
a kind,—but to certain matters of history, which are supposed to throw some light on the sentiments of their
compilers, and the sense in which their statements were
intended to be understood.   They have referred especially
to the alleged influence of the more moderate Reformers,

such as Bucer and Melancthon, in guiding the leading
agents in the English Reformation, and preserving, through
them, the Catholicity of the Anglican doctrine.   The first
remark, which is suggested by such a line of argument, is
that, even were the historical facts on which it is founded
more undeniably certain than they are, they could only
afford, at the best, a mere adminicle of evidence, amounting to a slight presumption, in support of other more
direct and cogent proofs; and that the main strength of
the evidence must ever lie in the deliberate statements
of the English Reformers, whether published by them
individually in their respective writings, or embodied by
them collectively in the Articles and Homilies which they
compiled.   The first question here is an exegetical one—
What is the natural and obvious meaning of these statements? while the history of their compilation, and of the
influences, whether native or foreign, which affected the
sentiments of the compilers, can afford no more than an
indirect means of arriving at any conclusion in regard to it.
Historical facts may afford a slight presumption, on either
side of such a question, but can never warrant any attempt
to put a forced construction on the Articles, or to explain
them in a non-natural sense.   The duty of an interpreter,
like that of a translator, is simply to render the true
meaning of any document, whether he agrees with it or
not; and in the present case, as Bishop Kaye has said,
to compare the doctrine of the Decrees of Trent with that
of the Articles of England, simply as *a matter of fact*, irrespective altogether of the question—Which is true? (3)
Were it possible to prove that, of all the foreign Reformers,
Melancthon and Bucer exercised the greatest influence on
Cranmer and Ridley; and further, that Melancthon and
Bucer differed essentially from Luther and Calvin on the
subject of Justification, it would still remain to be proved

that the language of the Articles and Homilies admits of
being interpreted,—on sound exegetical principles, and
without any forced construction, or jesuitical evasion,—
in a sense which is opposed to the general doctrine of the
Reformers.

But, further, the historical presumption derived from
the alleged influence of Bucer and Melancthon on the
minds of the English Reformers, which has been applied
to give an aspect of verisimilitude to the Anglo-Catholic
interpretation of the Articles, is effectually neutralized by
two undeniable facts,—first, that Bucer and Melancthon
really exercised no exclusive or peculiar influence over
Cranmer and Ridley, such as was not equally exercised
by Luther and Calvin, by Peter Martyr and John Knox;
—and secondly, that, even if they did exercise such an
influence, their sentiments on the subject of Justification
were in entire accordance with those of the other Reformers.   There is no reason to believe that Bucer or
Melancthon were more implicitly followed by the English
Reformers than Luther or Calvin.   It is certain that
Calvin was an esteemed correspondent of Cranmer, and
that Peter Martyr and John Knox were his zealous fellow-
labourers.   In fact, for a long time after the Reformation,
—down, indeed, to the times of Laud,—the prevailing
theology of the most eminent divines of England was the
same in substance with that which was then generally
received on the continent of Europe. (4)   It is not alleged,
either that they received it implicitly from Calvin, or
Luther, or Zuingle, or that on minor points there might
not be different shades of opinion between them; for they
were a noble brotherhood of free inquirers, united only in
the bonds of the Gospel; and while they gave and received
mutual aid in the exposition of the truth, they all alike
drew their doctrine mainly from the earnest study of God's

inspired Word.   It is true that Bucer and Melancthon differed on some points from Luther, and on others from Calvin; but their sentiments on the subject of Justification were, and always continued to be, in entire accordance with theirs.   The only pretext for ascribing to them any laxity of opinion in regard to it, is founded on their having agreed at Ratisbon, for the sake of peace, to concur with the Canons of Cologne in adopting an ambiguous statement of it.   But there is ample proof that, as soon as they were made aware of the erroneous construction which might be put upon it, they expressed their deep regret that they should even have appeared to make light of the difference between the Popish and Protestant doctrine,— that they often reiterated, in the most solemn way, and in the most affecting terms, their decided opposition to the one, and their devoted attachment to the other,— and that among all the changes which were introduced into the successive editions of Melancthon's 'Common Places,' there is no trace of any change of opinion on the subject of Justification; while in a paper which he intended as his last will, he declared his adherence to the Protestant doctrine as the life and nourishment of his own soul, and warned his descendants against any concession or compromise in regard to it.   For his mature views on this subject, he refers to one of his earliest works, the 'Prolegomena on Justification' prefixed to his 'Commentary on the Epistle to the Romans,' and to all the editions of his 'Common Places,' as maintaining the same doctrine, but only more fully explained and established; and on comparing these works with the 'Treatise on Justification' by Peter Martyr, his fellow-labourer in England, who was a strict adherent to the doctrine of the Reformers, they will be found to teach in substance the same truth, and to make use of the same scriptural proofs. (5)

But, apart from these historical questions, an appeal may
be made at once to the authorized Articles and Homilies of
the Church of England ; for it seems a needlessly circuitous
and roundabout process to make the doctrine which she
teaches a matter of mere inference or conjecture, from the
influence supposed to have been exercised on her own Reformers by any class of continental divines.   When we turn
to the Articles, this one fact should be conclusive ;—all the
Protestant Churches, at home or abroad, Lutheran and Calvinistic, whether they be the adherents of the Augsburg, or
the French, or the Belgic, or the Westminster Confessions,
will cheerfully accept the 11th Article, and the 'Homily
of Salvation,' as being in substance a sound and correct
expression of their faith on the subject of Justification,
—provided only they be allowed to understand them in
their plain and obvious meaning.   The other Protestant
Churches may prefer their respective Confessions, as being
either more comprehensive, or more explicit, than the
11th Article, in the statement of some points involved in
the general doctrine (6) ; but, so far as it goes, they will
unanimously acknowledge that it contains the substance
of what is taught in Scripture on the subject, and that it
is in entire accordance with the Protestant, as opposed to
the Popish, doctrine.   Both before and after the dates at
which the Articles of Religion were framed and repeatedly
revised, the Protestant doctrine of Justification had taken
a firm hold on the convictions of Englishmen ; and it has
seldom been better explained, or more ably defended, at
any later period, than it was in the earlier stages of the
controversy by John Foxe, the Martyrologist, in reply to
Osorio.   At the era of the Reformation, therefore, the
Church of England formed no exception to the unanimity
which then prevailed in regard to the ground and method
of a sinner's acceptance with God ; and if the light of the

Gospel, which dawned upon her at first so brightly, has often since then suffered a partial eclipse, she has always preserved her Articles and Homilies as the authorized exponents of her creed; and there have never been awanting, in any age of her history, some faithful and stedfast witnesses to the truth, such as Davenant and Downham, Barlow and Beveridge, Andrewes, and even the 'judicious' Hooker,—who continued to shine 'like lights in a dark place,' and transmitted a noble testimony to the generation following. (7)

There has long been, and there still is, in the Church of England, a widespread and growing defection from the old Theology of the Reformation ; and it is of the last importance that we should form a right estimate of the various influences which have been operating in this country, and especially in the Church of England, since the Reformation, to produce a declension from the faith of the Reformers, and to predispose many to the adoption of views more akin to the Popish, than to the Protestant, doctrine of Justification. These influences proceeded from several distinct sources, and were fitted, when combined, to operate powerfully on the Theology of England ; while the remarkable changes which it has undergone can scarcely be accounted for, if any of these causes be left out of view.

The *first* was the influence of some works, characterized by great ability and learning, which appeared in defence of the Romish doctrine, as it had been defined and declared by the Council of Trent,—such as Bellarmine's 'Disputations' in earlier, and Möhler's 'Symbolism' in more recent, times. (8)

The *second* was the influence of several works, proceeding both from Popish and Protestant writers, which

were designed to prove, either that there was no real difference between the Romish and the Reformed doctrine
on the subject of Justification, or that, if there was any
difference, it was one of little practical importance. Of
this class of works we have a specimen in Bossuet's 'Exposition' on the Popish side, and in Le Blanc's 'Theses'
on the Protestant,—while the jesuitical work of Davenport,
or Francis à Sancta Clara, attempted to obliterate the
difference between the English Articles and the Trentine
Canons and Decrees. The influence which these, and
similar treatises, exercised on the views of many leading
divines in the Church of England, is evident from the
statements of such men as Atterbury, Wake, Burnet, Barrow, and Laurence, who may be said to represent so many
different parties within her pale. (9)

The *third* influence which acted powerfully on many
English divines, in the way of predisposing them to embrace a doctrine on the subject of Justification more akin
to that of the Romish, than of the Reformed, Churches,
was the leaven of Arminian and Pelagian error, which was
introduced soon after the Synod of Dort, and imbibed by
many who continued to adhere to the Thirty-nine Articles.
For a time, the Protestant doctrine of Justification was
universally professed ; but some eminent divines began
to question, in the first instance, the truth of what had
hitherto been taught respecting the divine decrees, and the
final perseverance of believers ; and this gradually led on
to a thorough change of view in regard to the ground and
method of a sinner's acceptance with God. BARRETT and
BARO first raised these questions in the days of Queen
Elizabeth, and were proceeded against by the authorities at
Cambridge. Subsequently Bishop Montagu avowed their
opinions in his ' Appeal to Cæsar ;' and he was answered by
Bishop Carleton, who says expressly that—' the Church of

England was reformed by the help of our reverend and learned bishops,' . . . 'who held consent in doctrine with Peter Martyr and Martin Bucer;' and—that 'it was then the open confession both of the bishops and of the Puritans, that both parts embraced a mutual consent in doctrine, —only the difference was in matter of non-conformity.; hitherto there was no Puritan doctrine known.' Bishop Montagu's book was denounced by the House of Commons as an 'encouragement to Popery;' and they further issued a remonstrance in 1628, in which they 'profess and avow for truth, that sense of the Articles of Religion, which by the public acts of the Church of England, and by the general and current exposition of the writers of our Church, has been delivered unto us; and do reject the sense of the Jesuits and Arminians, and all others wherein they differ from us.' (10)   But the leaven continued to spread, in opposition alike to ecclesiastical and parliamentary authority, and the prevailing doctrine on the subject of Justification was seriously affected by it.   The result was the general prevalence of views in regard to it widely different from those of the Reformers, and akin in their radical principle to the Popish idea of Justification by infused and inherent righteousness.   This was the doctrine of Bull, of Cave, and of Hoadley. (11)

A *fourth* cause which had considerable influence on many divines in England, in exciting prejudice against the Protestant doctrine of Justification, and predisposing them to adopt views on that subject scarcely distinguishable from those of the Romish Church, may be found in the extreme opinions of the Antinomian party, which first appeared in Munster, and led to great excesses there, and were afterwards imported into England in the troubled times of the Commonwealth.   No dispassionate judge could possibly identify these opinions with the doctrine of

the Reformers, or even affect to believe that they flowed
from it as its legitimate fruits;—for they were not only
disclaimed, but denounced and disproved, both by Luther
and Calvin, as being at direct variance with their teaching.
Still the fact, that they were openly avowed by sectaries
who bore the name of Protestants, and that they had been
productive of much moral and social evil wherever they
were embraced, had a tendency to revive and strengthen
the prejudice which had been felt of old even against the
Apostles' doctrine, as if Justification by grace without
works were either naturally fitted to encourage, or might,
at least, be easily perverted so as to excuse, the continued
indulgence of sin.   This prejudice diminished their zeal for
the fundamental article of the Reformation, if it did not
entirely destroy their belief in it; and while they were subject to its influence, they were presented with a plausible
and seductive modification of the old Protestant doctrine,
which led to a nearer approximation to that of Rome.

A *fifth* cause which operated in the same direction was
the introduction of the doctrine propounded by the New
Methodists in France, and adopted by the Neonomians in
England.   This new method of stating the doctrine of
Justification consisted mainly in substituting the personal
righteousness of the believer, for the imputed righteousness of Christ, as that which is the immediate or proximate ground of his acceptance.   In this respect, it is
substantially the same with the doctrine of the Romish
Church; but its Evangelical character was supposed to
be sufficiently preserved by ascribing to Christ the whole
merit of procuring—not the pardon and acceptance of any
sinner—but a 'new law of Grace,' whose conditions he
might fulfil for himself so as to secure his own justification; a law so relaxed and modified that it does not, like
the old law, require perfect obedience, but accepts and

rewards any kind or amount of obedience, however imperfect, if only it be sincere.   This Neonomian scheme was set up in the seventeenth century in opposition to what was then called the Antinomian doctrine, but really in opposition to the old Protestant doctrine of Justification by faith only ; for the real Antinomians were those who imagined that it could either be abrogated or relaxed, so as to admit of a sinner being justified, while it was not 'fulfilled' either by himself or his Substitute.   Thus the fear of gross Antinomianism, on the one hand, and the subtle influence of Neonomian theories, on the other, accelerated the declension of many English divines from the old doctrine of the Reformers, and led them on till they approached indefinitely near to that of the Church of Rome. (12)

Such were the chief sources of doctrinal declension in the Church of England.   But when we speak of the external causes or influences which produced a general defection from the doctrine of the Reformers, and a gradual approximation to that of the Romish Church, we must not forget the operation of another, of a more intimate and permanent kind,—the indigenous tendency to self-righteousness,—which has been aptly termed 'the natural Popery of the human heart.'   This tendency is alike universal and constant.   None are more self-righteous, or more ready to trust in the safety of their own condition, than those who are most habitually ungodly and sinful.   If they cannot speak of their good works, they are confident, at least, of their good motives, and good intentions ; while others who are moral and reputable in their conduct, trust in their temperate habits, or just dealings, or liberal alms, or religious observances, without inquiring whether these outward actions spring from such principles as a spiritual law imperatively re-

quires. Believers themselves are conscious of this tendency, even after they have been convinced of sin, and
renounced all dependence on their own righteousness.
'I have myself taught,' says Luther, 'this doctrine (*i. e.*
"of faith, by which, embracing the merits of Christ, we
stand accepted before the tribunal of God") for twenty
years, both in my preaching and my writings; and yet
the old and tenacious mire clings to me, so that I find
myself wanting to come to God, bringing something in
my hand, for which He should bestow His grace upon
me. I cannot attain to casting myself on pure and simple
grace only, and yet this is highly necessary.' (13) That
the same tendencies which produced the corruptions of
Popery are deeply rooted in our common nature, and
exist in the Protestant as well as the Romish Church, is
the leading principle of Archbishop Whately's work on
'The Errors of Romanism;' but there is a radical defect
in his statement, in so far as he overlooks the fact that the
Protestant doctrine is designed and fitted to counteract
that tendency; whereas both the teaching and the practices of the Church of Rome can only serve to foster and
increase it. (14) It is fitly called, therefore, 'the Popery
of the human heart,' while it is often heard 'speaking
out under a Protestant profession:' and this was one of
the most powerful causes which led many English divines
to recoil from the old doctrine of the Reformers, and to
approximate to that of the Church of Rome.

The present century has witnessed a still more rapid
and signal development of the same tendencies. The rise
of the Tractarian School at Oxford,—the appearance of
Tract No. xc.,—the recent republication of that tract with
a preface by Dr. Pusey,—and the reproduction of Sancta
Clara's jesuitical 'Exposition of the Articles of the Angli-

can Church,' can hardly fail to be regarded as ominous signs of what may yet be in reserve for the Church of England. (15)   But in addition to these, there have been several recent attacks on the Protestant doctrine of Justification, in elaborate treatises on that special subject, proceeding from different schools in the Church of England and Ireland, but all concurring in the same attempt to set aside the old Theology of the Reformation.

First, some disciples of the Alexandrian, or Neo-Platonic School, have virtually superseded the Mediatorial work of Christ,—in so far as regards His vicarious satisfaction and meritorious obedience,—by substituting for it the mere fact of His incarnation, as the ground of our hope towards God ; and by representing His Incarnation, rather than His Work, as the means—not of effecting our reconciliation, for on their principles no reconciliation, at least on God's part, was necessary, or even possible,— but of manifesting merely His unchangeable favour, which was independent alike of our obedience and disobedience, our belief or our unbelief, and which needed only to be attested by Christ's mission and message, and then realized in our own personal convictions, to remove all distrust of God, and restore us to the conscious enjoyment of His fatherly love.   This is the doctrine of Kingsley, Maurice, Stanley, and Robertson. *Secondly,* some writers have advocated the doctrine of what they call ' a moral ' Justification on the ground of a righteousness infused and inherent, in opposition to that of a ' forensic ' Justification on the ground of a righteousness vicarious and imputed.   This doctrine is essentially the same with that of the Church of Rome, and has been zealously advocated by Mr. Knox and Bishop Jebb. *Thirdly,* some writers have attempted to discover ' a via media ' between the Popish and Protestant doctrine of Justification, or rather to obliterate the difference between the two; such as Dr. Newman and Dr. Pusey,—the former advocating the notion of Osiander in a former age, that we are justified by 'Christ formed within us,' or by the indwelling presence by His Spirit, and that His benefits are conveyed through the sacraments, not through faith; while the latter denies that there is any real difference between the doctrine of Rome and that of the Church of England on this article of faith, and no obstacle therefore, on this ground, to their reunion. And, *lastly*, some writers have reproduced the old, and less refined, doctrine of Justification by works,—holding that, while the redemption of Christ is the ultimate cause of a sinner's acceptance, its proximate cause can only be his personal obedience to God's law. This seems to be the conclusion at which Dr. Ryder arrives, in his Donnellan Lectures for 1865, on 'The Scripture Doctrine of Acceptance with God.'

There is nothing that can appear formidable in these recent speculations to those who are well versed in the great controversies of the three preceding centuries; for they rest on assumptions, which were thoroughly discussed and disproved, by the able and learned men who were successively raised up to defend Protestant truth, against Popery, on the one hand, and Socinianism, on the other. But as they are the most recent forms of error on the subject in this country, and may be regarded as indications of a state of feeling in regard to it, which often prevails where it finds no definite expression, it may be useful to advert, however briefly, to some of the principles which are involved in them, and the reasons on which they respectively depend.

Those writers who supersede the Mediatorial work of Christ as a satisfaction to divine justice, and substitute for it the mere fact of His Incarnation as a manifestation of divine love, found their whole doctrine on a philosophical speculation, in regard to the natural relation which subsists between God and all His intelligent creatures. Their system is, in fact, a Philosophy, rather than a Theology; and, whether it can be traced to the Neo-Platonic School of Alexandria as its source, or may be sufficiently accounted for by ascribing it to the operation of those causes which produced the errors of Socinians and Universalists in more recent times, it depends, as little as either of these systems did, on the authority of Revelation, while it makes free use of scriptural terms in an unscriptural sense.

Leaving out of view the philosophical grounds of their doctrine, and looking merely to its bearing on the method of a sinner's justification, its first error lies in representing the natural relation which subsists between God and His intelligent creatures as being exclusively that of a Father to His children, and either ignoring or denying another relation, which is at least equally natural, while it is most expressly revealed,—the relation between God as a righteous and offended Lawgiver, Governor, and Judge, and man as being, in his present condition, fallen, guilty, and depraved. They insist much on the relation of paternity and sonship, and hold it to be necessarily involved in that of Creator and creature, in the case of all such living beings as were made 'in His image and likeness;' and, consequently, to be as indestructible and unchangeable as the fact of their creation unquestionably is. Their theory, when carried out to the full length of its legitimate application, extends equally to men and angels, since both were created in the 'image of God;' and it implies that neither devils, nor fallen men, have ceased to be 'sons' or 'children' of God, simply because they have not ceased, and never can cease, to be His creatures. That this doctrine enters largely into their teaching, they will readily acknowledge. Taken by itself, and viewed apart from the mystic speculations with which it has been associated, it is the most intelligible part of their system, and one that will be readily accepted by many who care little for the Neo-Platonic or any other philosophy, but who are anxious to be assured that there is not,—never has been,—and never can be,—anything seriously wrong in their relation to God. To such men the following assurances will be most welcome : ' All may call upon God as a reconciled Father. . . . . Their faith is to be grounded on a foregone conclusion ; their acts are to be the fruits of *a state they already possess.*' ' Christ revealed the fact that all men are God's children. He proclaimed a new name of God—" the Father ;" and a new name of man or humanity—" the Son." . . . . There is a difference, however, between being God's child by right, and God's child in fact. All who are born into the world are God's children by right. They are not so in 'fact, until they recognise it, and believe it, and live as such. To believe, and live it, is to be regenerate.' (16)

In answering these statements, it is not necessary— either to deny that the original relation between God as the Creator, and man as a creature made in His ' image and likeness,' might be fitly represented, analogically, by that which subsists between a human father and his children,—or to affirm that, in point of fact, it is not so represented in any part of Scripture. It is only necessary to discriminate aright between that original relation, in which man stood to God while he retained the ' image' in which he was created, and two other relations which are widely different from it—the actual relation of men to God in their present state, as being by nature fallen and sinful creatures ; and the new relation of sonship, which is constituted by the 'adoption of grace.' The original relation in which man stood to God is widely different from that which supervened after his fall, whether he be considered as a subject or as a son ; for the relation of subjection and of sonship might equally be affected by sin. If, being fallible, he should fall into transgression, and thereby lose both the image and favour of God, the whole nature of his relation to Him would be changed ; and while he might still retain some natural resemblance to Him, as being a spirit, endowed with intelligence and will, he must have lost that spiritual resemblance to Him, which consisted 'in knowledge, righteousness, and true holiness.' He never ceased to be a creature, but he is now a fallen creature ; he never ceased to be a subject, but he is now a rebellious subject; he never ceased to be a son,—in so far as he still possesses a natural resemblance to God, as a spirit, endowed with intelligence and will,—but he is now destitute of His spiritual image, and is one of 'the children of disobedience,' and 'the children of wrath.'[1] A man does not cease to be a subject, when he becomes a rebel ; and no more does he cease to be, in some respects, a son, when he becomes a prodigal.—But the original relation in which man stood to God in his state of pristine innocence, must also be distinguished from that new relation which God sustains to His people as His 'sons and daughters by the adoption of grace.' There is an important difference between the two. Were it proved that man, as he was created, stood in such a relation to God as may be fitly denoted by the term son-ship, the mere fact, that he was immediately placed in a state of probation, and subjected to a law as the test of his obedience, implies that the continued possession

_____
[1] Eph. ii. 2, 3, v. 6 ; Col. iii. 6.

of his rights and privileges, whether as a subject or a son, was conditional, and that he was not so *confirmed*, either in the one capacity or in the other, as all believers, under the New Covenant, are, by their union with Christ, and their adoption in Him as ' sons,' and ' heirs.'

But we have not yet reached the root of the doctrine. It consists in a theory of Creation, by which its advocates seek to connect the natural sonship of man with the necessary filiation of the eternal Word, by identifying the ' image' in which man was created with Him who is declared to be ' the brightness of the Father's glory, and the express image of His person.' They seem to have felt, that the sonship of a creature,—derived, dependent, and fallible,—could not be held to be unchangeable in itself, and that it must be based on the eternal sonship of One who was not a creature, or subject to the conditions of a creature. They attempted, therefore, to establish an indissoluble connection between the sonship of man and that of the Son of God,—such as might warrant them in saying that, ' by the law of creation, Christ is in every man, and every man in Christ.' They affirmed, that we were created in Him, and not in Adam, since Adam himself had the root of his being in the eternal Son,—that the Logos is the Archetype of the human race,—that by the constitution of their nature, He is in every man, and every man in Him,—that His indwelling presence is unchangeable, and can never cease to be true,—that it may be hidden or obscured, forgotten or not duly realized, in consequence of the darkness and disorder occasioned by sin, but that it needs only to be discerned and believed to regenerate the soul, and restore it to a conscious enjoyment of God's unchangeable love, —and that all men, even in their worst state, are, and have always been, and must ever continue to be, the objects of that love, simply because He sees His Son in them, and looks on them as existing in Him. (17)

This doctrine bears a striking resemblance to that of the founders of the Society of Friends, and it might be supposed to have been borrowed from them, if it had not been connected by some of its advocates with the Neo-Platonic Theosophy of Alexandria. (18) The chief difficulty in answering it arises from the extreme difficulty of ascertaining its real import. We were created *by* the eternal Word, and *for* Him;[1] but how can it be said, that we were created *in* Him? WAS HE CREATED? or must there not have been, as Athanasius argued against the Arians, an eternal Son, if there was an eternal Father? (19) And if His divine filiation was necessary and eternal, how can His peculiar, unparalleled, and incommunicable Sonship be shared by any creature, either by 'the law of creation,' or even by 'the grace of adoption?' Besides, it is not as the eternal Word, but as the Word incarnate, —it is not by the Logos, but by the Loganthropos,—and it is not by the mere fact of His incarnation, but by His Mediatorial work, or what He did and suffered, when He became 'obedient unto death, even the death of the cross,' that Christ is the Redeemer of His people ; and any doctrine which connects our salvation with His mere Sonship in a state of pre-existence, or even with His Sonship as manifested in time by His incarnation, may be justly said to evacuate the whole Gospel, and to explain away all that is most essential in the scheme and work of human Redemption.

'Better,' says Mr. Knox, 'continue systematic Calvinists, than become amphibious nondescripts in Divinity.' That he was not himself a systematic Calvinist, is certain;

[1] Col. i. 16, 17.

it is not quite so clear to what other class he belonged.
We can only conceive of him as an Eclectic, selecting
much, and rejecting more, from every recognised creed in
Christendom.   There can be no doubt, however, in regard
to his doctrine of Justification; for he zealously contends
for the 'moral' and 'efficient,' in opposition to the 'forensic' or 'judicial' sense of that term, and so far adopts,
in substance, the Popish, as distinguished from the Protestant, Theology.   He objects, indeed, to the Romish
divines on one point,—namely, that they have not been
sufficiently careful to give due prominence to what he
calls the 'reputative idea' which is involved in the term;
but this is very far from being the idea of imputed righteousness, which he entirely rejects; it means merely that,
in justifying a sinner, God first makes him righteous
inherently by grace infused, and then reputes him so to
be.   Bellarmine and Vasquez would not have objected to
such a doctrine; and he seems to have been aware that
it was more nearly akin to that of the Popish, than to that
of the Protestant, Church, since he expressly rejects the
latter as a 'novelty' which made its first appearance at
the Reformation, and says: 'I doubt really whether, on
the point of Justification, the Romish doctrine is not much
more scriptural and rational; as it involves in that term,
not the mere *accounting*, but also the *making*, righteous'
(*i.e.* by infused, not by imputed, righteousness), 'which,
when ascribed solely to divine grace, is so far from being,
in my mind, an erroneous idea, that I think the scriptural
meaning of Justification strictly requires it.'

But the radical error of his theology consists in defective views of the *guilt*, as distinguished from the power, of
sin,—of the curse and condemnation of a broken law,—of
the nature and design of Christ's atoning sacrifice, and
meritorious obedience,—of the efficacy of His death, as

procuring salvability for all, and securing salvation for
none,—and of the extent of that change which a sinner
undergoes when he is renewed in the spirit of his mind,
as if it implied spiritual perfection in the present life, and
excluded all indwelling sin. 'Of appeasing divine wrath,'
he says, 'I own I have no idea :'—here is the radical defect; for the 'revelation of wrath' comes first by the Law,
and then the 'revelation of the righteousness of God' by
the Gospel; and ignorance or unbelief in regard to the
law and justice of God must necessarily disqualify us for
judging aright of the nature and effects of the redeeming
work of Christ,—while any error in regard to the latter,
is fatal to sound views of Justification. (20)

The attempt to construct a 'via media' between the
Popish and Protestant doctrines of Justification, which
was made by Dr. Newman while he was yet a clergyman
of the Church of England, resulted only in his laying down,
not a third line of rails that should run parallel with the
other two, but a crossing merely, by which he, and many
of his followers, might effect a passage from the one to the
other. He seemed, indeed, to object, on many points,
both to the Romish and the Reformed Theology on this
subject; but it is remarkable that he invariably represented the one as being merely defective, while he charged
the other with being unsound and erroneous ; and as defective truth is better than positive falsehood, while it is
easier to supply a defect than to neutralize a heresy, he
seems to have concluded that it was safer, on the whole,
to accept the Popish, than to adhere to the Protestant,
doctrine. How striking the contrast, in this respect, between Dr. Newman and Cardinal Bellarmine! The Romish
cardinal contended with great ability and zeal, as a first
rate controversialist, against the Protestant doctrine, but

ended by making his memorable confession—'It is the
safest course,—by reason of the uncertainty of our
own righteousness, and the danger of vainglory,—to
repose our whole trust in the mercy and lovingkindness
of God alone;' the English clergyman contended, with
the utmost activity of a very subtle intellect, for a 'via
media' of his own, but ended by abandoning the doctrine
of the Reformers, and uniting himself to the Church of
Rome. (21)

Following out his leading idea, that the Popish doctrine of Justification is defective merely, while the Protestant is positively erroneous, he seeks to supply the
defect, in the one case, and to correct the error, in the
other, by instituting a comparison between them in
respect to each of the leading points on which they
differ, and by suggesting his own modifications and
amendments on both.   For example, he says that 'Justification by faith,' and 'Justification by obedience,' are
often said to be 'opposite doctrines;' but he denies this,
and affirms that they are 'separate, but not opposite,'—
that 'they are not at all inconsistent with each other,'
but 'so compatible in themselves, that they may be held
both at once, or indifferently, either the one or the other,'
as being 'but two modes of stating the same truth.'
Again, he says that 'Justification by faith,' and 'Justification by baptism,' need not be opposed to one another,
for 'baptism may be considered the instrument on God's
part, faith on ours,' as 'faith may receive what baptism
conveys.'   And again, in respect to the nature of Justification itself, he says that 'the change in God's sight is
Justification,—the change within is Regeneration; and
faith is the appointed means of both;' and further, that
'Justification, with reference to the past, is remission of
sins only,' but 'with reference to the present and the

future, it is renovation also.' These are only a few specimens of his ' intermediate doctrine,' but they are significant enough to show that it has throughout a far greater
affinity to Popish error, than to Protestant truth.

Many other points in the theory of Dr. Newman might
have claimed our attention, but those which have been
specified are sufficient to illustrate its general character.
The difficulty which one feels in dealing with it, arises not
so much from the strength of his arguments, as from the
subtle and intricate terms in which they are expressed,—
from the frequent occurrence of paradoxical, or contradictory, statements,—and what Lord Jeffrey called a sort of
' wriggling lubricity,' which makes them elude our grasp,
the more firmly we attempt to hold them.   ' The *least* evil
of Mr. Newman's system,' says Mr. Faber, ' is, that it is a
tissue of contradictions and inconsistencies;' and he specifies some of them, such as the following : ' We are justified
by faith ; we are justified by obedience ; we are justified by
baptism ; we are justified conjointly by the two sacraments
of baptism and the Lord's Supper.   Our Justification precedes our faith, and our faith precedes our Justification.
The word Justification cannot bear two meanings, yet it
clearly does bear two meanings, to wit, the *accounting* righteous, and the *making* righteous.   There is but one act of
Justification, nevertheless there are ten thousand Justifica-
tions.'   But these are not its *worst* features; it is an elaborate
attempt to overthrow the Protestant doctrine of Justification, and to undermine the only ground of a sinner's
acceptance with God.   As such it has been characterized
in strong terms by Dr. Bennett, when he says that, since
the Council of Trent, ' perhaps there never has been a book
published, at least among Protestants, more full of insidious, but determined, opposition to the Lord Jesus Christ
as our righteousness.   Contradiction, obscurity, mystifica-

tion, . . . monkish gloom, and schismatic profession of
dissent from Protestants and from Romanists,—all are
brought into the field, to bear against the only righteousness in which a sinner can stand before God.' (22)

The extent to which some Protestants have departed
from the doctrine of the Reformers, on the subject of Justification, could scarcely be placed in a more striking light,
than by simply comparing the Disputation of Bishop
Davenant with the Lectures of Dr. Newman in England,
and the Treatise of Bishop Downham with the Lectures
of Dr. Ryder in Ireland, on 'The Scripture Doctrine of
Acceptance with God.' The two bishops were substantially
agreed,—they taught the same doctrine, and defended it
by the same scriptural arguments ; the two modern divines
differ widely from each other, but not more widely than
both differ from the Reformers.

The title of the Donnellan Lectures is far from being a
correct index to their actual contents. It naturally leads
us to expect an exposition of the scriptural doctrine of Justification,—of the meaning of the term according to the
usage of the sacred writers,—of the nature of that which
is denoted by it, whether as it is an act of God, or a privilege of His people,—of the divine provision by which pardon
and acceptance were procured for the guilty, and the provision, equally divine, by which these blessings are effectually applied. But instead of this, the author presents us,
in the first instance, with an elaborate metaphysical discussion of the theory of modern Pantheism ; and, in the second
place, with a singularly meagre proof of his own doctrine of
' acceptance with God,' consisting, not of those passages of
Scripture which expressly treat of Justification, but of some
inferences merely from the historical record of the early
diffusion of the Gospel, and the admission of the first con-

verts into the Christian Church. 'The views I have maintained throughout,' says Dr. Ryder, 'upon the scriptural doctrine of acceptance with God, will run counter, I fear, to those of many faithful servants of Christ:' and assuredly this fear is not groundless, for these views are directly opposed to those of all the Reformers, and not less to' the Articles of the United Church of England and Ireland. He distinguishes between what he calls, 'for convenience sake, the *ultimate* and *proximate* causes of man's acceptance with God,' and says, that the ultimate cause 'is, of course, the redemption of the finite being,—the atonement for all sin, original and actual,—the satisfaction for all imperfection, —the "gifts for all men, yea, even for His enemies,"— effected by the objective sacrifice of the Saviour of the world;' while the proximate cause is variously described, as 'man's finite free-will,'—'the exercise of an independent power of cultivating or neglecting' his opportunities,— 'his wilful obedience or disobedience.' His theory recognises the eternal and essential reality of both causes— 'two distinctly co-existent and real agencies, the one absolute and ultimate, the other proximate and relative;' —but what connection subsists between them, has not been 'revealed,' and cannot, therefore, be 'explained.' (23)

Such are some of the most recent attacks on the great Protestant doctrine of Justification by faith. (24)

It has been said, that 'a period of about seventy years, or two generations, seems generally sufficient to complete a thorough and entire change in the prevailing system of Theology; that in 1560, under Archbishop Parker, the Church of England was Calvinistic and thoroughly Protestant; . . . that in 1630,—seventy years after,— under Archbishop Laud, the same Church had become Arminian, and scarcely, or very faintly, Protestant;'

and that if we 'once more pass over seventy years,
and come down to the year 1700, a third, and totally
different, school from either of the former meets our
view, for the Tillotsons and Burnets are neither of the
school of Parker, nor yet do they resemble Laud.' (25)
It may be added to this striking statement, that in
two generations more—or about 1770,—the Church of
England had reached its lowest point of declension in
doctrine and life, and was wrapped in spiritual slumber,
from which she was to be partially awakened by the
ministry of Whitfield and Wesley, and the volcanic
eruption of the French revolution ; and that in two
generations more, or about 1840, there had sprung up
the rival schools at Oxford—the one represented by the
'Tracts for the Times,' and tending towards Romanism,—
the other by the 'Essays and Reviews,' and strongly
tinctured with Rationalism.   Looking at the progress
which these systems have already made, and the actual
state of religious opinion in this country at the present
day, who will venture to say, what will be the prevailing
Theology of our grandchildren when .the current cycle
reaches its close ?   God may be pleased once more to
pour out His Spirit on the Churches, and to raise up, perhaps from the poorest of His people, a band of humble, but
devoted, believers,—men of faith and prayer, as 'living
epistles of Christ known and read of all men,' the noblest
witnesses for Christ in the land.   What we most need is
a great spiritual revival, which, commencing in the hearts
of our congregations, will work from within outwards, and
from beneath upwards, destroying 'the wisdom of the wise,
and bringing to nought the understanding of the prudent,'
and making it manifest to all that the Gospel is still
' mighty through God to the pulling down of strongholds.'
Our immediate prospects are dark and threatening ; and

'men's hearts are beginning to fail them for fear, and for looking after those things which are coming on the earth.' What course events may take, it is impossible to foretell; but, looking to mere human probabilities, of two schemes, one or other is likely to be attempted, or perhaps each of them in succession;—either the Established Churches will be stript of a definite creed, if not by a legislative act, by the more insidious method of judge-made law; and made so comprehensive as to include men of all shades of opinion, from semi-Popery, through the various grades of Pelagian, Arian, and Socinian error, down to ill-disguised infidelity; or, if the moral sense of the community revolts from the indiscriminate support of truth and error, then, the entire disestablishment of the Church in these islands, perhaps till the time when 'all the kingdoms of this world shall become the kingdoms of our God, and of His Christ.' Of the Church of Christ there is no fear: she is 'founded on a rock, and the gates of hell shall not prevail against her.' Somewhere in the earth she will find an asylum, should it only be as 'the woman flying into the wilderness:' but for any particular church, or any particular country, there is no absolute security, that her 'candlestick will not be removed out of its place, except she repents.' Let us pray that 'when the enemy is coming in like a flood, the Spirit of the Lord may lift up a standard against him;' and that those young men, who are about to enter on the ministry 'in troublous times,' may have a banner given to them, 'that it may be displayed because of the truth'—a banner bearing this inspired inscription: 'I AM NOT ASHAMED OF THE GOSPEL OF CHRIST; FOR IT IS THE POWER OF GOD UNTO SALVATION TO EVERY ONE THAT BELIEVETH; FOR THEREIN IS THE RIGHTEOUSNESS OF GOD REVEALED FROM FAITH TO FAITH, AS IT IS WRITTEN, THE JUST SHALL LIVE BY FAITH.'

PART II.

EXPOSITION OF THE DOCTRINE OF JUSTIFICATION.

————◆————

INTRODUCTION.

THE History of the Doctrine, as it has been discussed between various parties in successive ages of the Church, should serve to shorten and simplify the Exposition of it, as it is taught in Scripture. A comprehensive survey of the various controversies which arose in regard to it during the times that are past, and which are still renewed in the present day, enables us to bring out into clear and distinct prominence, all the leading principles which are involved in it, and to determine the precise points on which we should endeavour to concentrate the scattered rays of Scripture light, when we endeavour to illustrate and establish this part of revealed truth. The conflicting opinions of men must now give place to the authoritative testimonies of God; and these must be treated on sound exegetical principles, with the view of ascertaining their real meaning, apart from the controversies which have arisen in regard to them, except in so far as previous discussions may have served to define the language of Scripture, and to supply the defects, or correct the errors, of a partial or perverse interpretation. The substance of the doctrine will be stated in a short series of propositions, relating to each of the leading topics involved in it; and the proofs on which they severally depend will be briefly indicated, although they cannot be fully discussed in a mere outline. This unavoidable defect may be, in some measure, supplied by appending such references to Scripture, and the writings of approved divines, as will guide the reader in studying the subject for himself.

The best preparation for the study of this doctrine is—neither great intellectual ability, nor much scholastic learning,—but a conscience impressed with a sense of our actual condition as sinners in the sight of God. A deep conviction of sin is the one thing needful in such an inquiry,—a conviction of the fact of sin, as an awful reality in our own personal experience,—of the power of sin, as an inveterate evil cleaving to us continually, and having its roots deep in the innermost recesses of our hearts,— and of the guilt of sin, past as well as present, as an offence against God, which, once committed, can never cease to be true of us individually, and which, however He may be pleased to deal with it, has deserved His wrath and righteous condemnation. Without some such conviction of sin, we may speculate on this, as on any other, part of divine truth, and bring all the resources of our intellect and learning to bear upon it, but can have no suitable sense of our actual danger, and no serious desire for deliverance from it. To study the subject with advantage, we must have a heartfelt interest in it, as one that bears directly on the salvation of our own souls; and this interest can only be felt in proportion as we realize our guilt, and misery, and danger, as transgressors of God's Law. The Law is still, as it was to the Jewish Church, 'a schoolmaster to bring us to Christ, that we may be justified by faith;' and the Law must be applied to the conscience, so as to quicken and arouse it, before we can feel our need of salvation, or make any serious effort to attain it. It is the convinced, and not the careless, sinner, who alone will lay to heart, with some sense of its real meaning and momentous importance, the solemn question —'How shall a man be just with God?'

But more than this. As, without some heartfelt conviction of sin, we could have no feeling of personal interest in the doctrine of Justification, such as is necessary to command our serious attention in the study of it, so we should be scarcely capable of understanding, in their full scriptural meaning, the terms in which it is proposed to us, or the testimonies by which alone it can be established. The doctrine of Salvation, which is taught by the Gospel, presupposes the doctrine of Sin, which is taught by the Law; and the two together constitute the sum and substance of God's revealed truth. They are distinct, and even different, from each other; but they are so related that, while there may be some knowledge of sin without any knowledge of salvation, there can be no knowledge of salvation without some knowledge of sin. As this is true of the general doctrine of Salvation, which includes deliverance from the power, as well as from the punishment, of sin, so it is equally true of each of its constituent parts,—the special doctrines of Justification and Sanctification,—with this only difference, that, in the one case, we must have some knowledge of sin, in its legal aspect, as guilt already incurred, in the other, of sin, in its spiritual aspect, as an inveterate inherent depravity.

It might be shown, both from the general history of the Church and from the personal experience of individuals, that, in both cases alike, partial and defective views of sin have always been associated with partial and defective views of salvation. The whole history of

Christian Doctrine, with all its vicissitudes and fluctuations, from the Apostolic age down to the present times,
teaches this great lesson, that, invariably, among all
parties, in all lands, and in all ages, the views which
men held of the evils in their condition and character
which required to be redressed, affected their views of
the nature, necessity, and value of the remedy proposed
to them in the Gospel; that their estimate of the guilt
and power of sin determined their estimate of the freeness and efficacy of divine grace; and this in regard
alike to their Regeneration by the agency of the Spirit,
and their Justification by the Mediatorial work of Christ.
A Pelagian or semi-Pelagian Anthropology has been the
latent, but prolific, root underground of all the heresies
respecting both, which have sprung up in those ages of
declension, when conscience slumbered, and a sense of
sin decayed; and every revival of sound evangelical
doctrine has been accompanied, or preceded, by a work
of conviction, produced by a closer application of the
Law to the conscience. Such has been the experience
of the Church as a collective body; and such also has
been the personal experience of individuals. Their views
of the nature, necessity, freeness, and efficacy of divine
grace, have uniformly varied with their more or less
vivid apprehensions of the evil and malignity of sin. No
change is more striking or more instructive than that
which is often produced instantaneously on all a man's
views of the method of salvation, when from being a
careless, he becomes a convinced, sinner. As a careless
sinner, he presumed on mercy; as a convinced sinner, he
can scarcely dare to hope for it : once he reckoned on
pardon, or rather on impunity; now 'his own heart condemns him,' and he knows that 'God is greater than his
heart :' formerly he imagined that reformation of life

would be sufficient to secure his welfare; now he feels that a radical heart-change is necessary, such as he is altogether unable to work in himself,—and immediately on this change of his views in regard to sin, there follows a change in all his views of salvation, and those very doctrines of free and efficacious grace, which he once despised or rejected as 'foolishness,' are found to be the 'wisdom of God.' (1)

LECTURE VIII.

JUSTIFICATION ; THE SCRIPTURAL MEANING OF THE TERM.

PROPOSITION I.   Justification is a legal, or forensic, term, and is used in Scripture to denote the acceptance of any one as righteous in the sight of God.

As God has been pleased to employ this term, and its cognates, in revealing His will in regard to the method of our acceptance with Him, it is our first duty to ascertain their precise import, and it cannot be a matter of slight importance to determine it aright.   Erroneous or confused views of the scriptural meaning of these terms, must exert an injurious influence on our conception of the doctrine which they are designed to teach; while the right interpretation of many passages of Scripture can only be satisfactorily established by a careful inductive inquiry into the ' usus loquendi ' of the sacred writers ; and it is far from being a mere verbal discussion, since it has an important bearing on the substance and evidence of the truth itself.

The scriptural meaning of these terms is to be determined, neither by their mere etymology, nor by the sense which they bear in classical literature, but by the usage of the Hebrew and Greek Scriptures, including the Septuagint version of the Old Testament.   So far as etymology is concerned, the verb to 'justify' might possibly mean to make righteous inherently, just as the verb to ' sanctify ' often means to ' make holy ' in that way ; but this can in no case be determined by the mere derivation or com-

position of the term,—as is manifest from the fact, that to
'glorify God' does not mean to *make* God glorious, and to
'sanctify the Lord God in our hearts,' does not mean to
make Him holy, but only to account and declare Him to
be glorious, in the one case, and holy, in the other.   In
this sense, God is said to be 'justified,' and Christ also,—
not that they were, or could be, made righteous,—but that
they were respectively declared to be righteous,—the one
by His judgments, the other by His resurrection from the
dead.   The mere etymology of the term cannot determine,
therefore, the question in regard to its scriptural meaning;
and this can only be ascertained from the usage of the
sacred writers. (1)

In order to determine its scriptural meaning, it is not
necessary to undertake the burden of proving, either that
it might not be used, or that, in point of fact, it has never
been used, in the sense of making one righteous; for,
although Popish divines and their followers have generally
attempted to show that, in some passages, it is used in an
'efficient, moral' sense, and some Protestant writers have
maintained, in opposition to them, that these passages do
not necessarily require that construction, it is enough to
establish the only point which is of essential importance
in the argument,—namely, that, wherever it is used with
reference to our acceptance with God, it can only be
understood in a judicial or forensic sense. (2)

Some recent writers, in assailing the Protestant doctrine, have proceeded on the supposition that, if the term
could be proved to bear in some instances, or even to be
capable of bearing, an 'efficient, moral sense,' Justification
could no longer be regarded as 'forensic.'   But it is an
egregious error, to imagine that the 'forensic,' or 'judicial,'
nature of Justification is at all affected by the ground on
which it is supposed to rest.   It would bear that character,

and could only be correctly described by these terms, in
the case even of a perfectly righteous man ; and were it
possible for a sinner to be justified on the ground of an infused and inherent, but imperfect, righteousness, his acceptance as righteous on that ground would still be a forensic
and judicial sentence, recognising his righteousness and
reputing him accordingly.   This is virtually admitted when
the ' reputative' idea is said to be involved in the meaning
of the term Justification: and yet, with singular inconsistency, the doctrine of a 'forensic,' is contrasted with
that of a 'moral,' Justification, as if the two epithets—
' forensic' and 'moral'—related to the same point, and
did not refer—the one to the nature of Justification,—the
other to the ground on which it is supposed to rest.   The
real question at issue is,—not whether Justification be
judicial or moral,—for it must be judicial even when it
rests on moral grounds,—but whether a sinner is accepted
on the ground of a righteousness vicarious and imputed, or
of a righteousness infused and inherent ?   It may be added,
that this being the point on which the discussion really
turns, the question is not fully stated when it is asked
whether the term signifies to 'make righteous' or to
' account righteous ;' for all parties must be held to admit
that, when a sinner is justified, he is, in some sense, both
made and accounted righteous ; and the real difference
between them becomes apparent only when they proceed
to explain in what way he is made righteous, and adjudged
so to be.   When the question is thus stated, Justification
must be regarded as involving a forensic or judicial sentence, on whatever ground it may be supposed to rest ;
and the two distinct alternatives are clearly presented to
us,—Justification by Christ's vicarious righteousness imputed, or by man's personal righteousness infused.   Which
of these alternatives is the true scriptural doctrine must

be determined by a careful consideration of the evidence bearing on that precise point. At present we are only adjusting the state of the question in regard to the meaning of the term, and extricating it from some collateral questions which must be determined afterwards, each on its proper merits.

The forensic or judicial sense of the term may be established by *three* distinct proofs, arising from the antithetic—correlative—and equivalent, expressions which also occur in Scripture.

We place the antithetic expressions *first*, because the true meaning of any term is often best ascertained from that of those which are placed in opposition to it. The Hebrew and Greek verbs which are employed by the sacred writers to denote 'justification,' are invariably set over against such as denote 'condemnation.' They are applied to the judgments of men, and also to the judgments of God; and the analogy between these two is the ground of its common application to both. With reference to the judgments of men, *justification* is always opposed to *condemnation*. ' If there be a controversy between men, and they come unto judgment, that the judge may judge them ; then they shall justify the righteous, and condemn the wicked.' ' He that justifieth the wicked, and he that condemneth the just, even they both are abomination to the Lord.' ' Woe unto them . . . which justify the wicked for reward, and take away the righteousness of the righteous from him.'[1] In these passages, and many more, two judicial sentences are mentioned which are directly the reverse of each other; and they are so stated, with reference both to the righteous and to the wicked, as to imply that the justification of the one no more signifies the infusion of righteousness,

[1] Deut. xxv. 1; Prov. xvii. 15; Isa. v. 23. See also 2 Chron. xviii. 6, 7.

than the condemnation of the other signifies the infusion of wickedness. With reference, again, to the judgments of God, the same terms—'justification' and 'condemnation'—are frequently employed to denote judicial sentences which are directly opposite to each other. 'It is God that justifieth: who is he that condemneth?' 'By thy words thou shalt be justified, and by thy words thou shalt be condemned.' 'The judgment was by one to condemnation, but the free gift is of many offences unto justification.'[1] If Justification is thus proved to be the opposite of condemnation, it can only be, like the latter, a forensic and judicial term; and the one can no more signify to sanctify or to make righteous inherently, than the other to deprave or deteriorate the moral character of one who is convicted of crime. (3)

A *second* proof of the forensic or judicial sense of the term may be derived from the fact, that all the correlative terms, with which it is associated, bear that character, and designate one or other of the various circumstances which are implied in a process of judgment. In strict connection with it, we read of a judgment: 'Enter not into judgment with Thy servant: for in Thy sight shall no man living be justified;'—of a Judge: 'Shall not the Judge of all the earth do right?' 'We are sure that the judgment of God is according to truth;'—of a tribunal: 'We shall all stand before the judgment-seat of Christ;' —of an accuser: 'Who shall lay anything to the charge of God's elect? It is God that justifieth;'—of an indictment: 'Forgiving you all trespasses, and blotting out the handwriting of ordinances which was against us, which was contrary to us;'—of a witness: 'Their conscience also bearing witness, and their thoughts accusing or else excusing one another;'—of an Advocate: 'If any man

[1] Rom. viii. 33, 34; Matt. xii. 37; Rom. v. 16.

sin, we have an advocate with the Father, Jesus Christ
the righteous ;'—and of a sentence of absolution : ' Blessed
is he whose transgression is forgiven, whose sin is covered.
Blessed is the man to whom the Lord imputeth not iniquity.'[1]   All these expressions imply a judicial process,
and they are correlative to the term Justification.

A *third* proof of the forensic or judicial sense of the
term ' Justification' is supplied by those equivalent expressions, which are sometimes substituted for it, and
which serve to explain it.   If these expressions cannot
imply infusion of righteousness, but denote merely either
the forgiveness of sin, or the acceptance of the sinner,
they show that Justification denotes a change in his
judicial relation to God, and not a change in his moral
or spiritual character.   It is expressly described as the
' imputation of righteousness :' ' Abraham believed God,
and it was counted unto him for righteousness. . . . David
also describeth the blessedness of the man unto whom
God imputeth righteousness without works ;'—it is inclu-
sive of the non-imputation,—the covering,—the forgiveness of sin : ' Blessed are they whose iniquities are
forgiven, whose sins are covered ; blessed is the man to
whom the Lord will not impute sin ;'—it is equivalent to
reconciliation : ' For God was in Christ, reconciling the
world unto Himself, not imputing their trespasses unto
them ;'—and it amounts to making us ' the righteousness
of God :' ' For He hath made Him to be sin for us, who
knew no sin, that we might be made the righteousness
of God in Him.'[2]   If these phrases are the scriptural
equivalents of Justification, they serve to explain the
import of that term, and to show that it can mean nothing

[1] Ps. cxliii. 2 ; Gen. xviii. 25 ; Rom. ii. 2, xiv. 10, viii. 33 ; Col. ii. 14 ;
Rom. ii. 15 ; 1 John ii. 1 ; Ps. xxxii. 1.
[2] Rom. iv. 3, 6-8 ; 2 Cor. v. 19, 21.

else than the acceptance of a sinner as righteous in the sight of God. (4)

There are thus three distinct classes of expressions,— the *antithetic, correlative,* and *equivalent* terms,—which are used in Scripture, and which afford abundant materials for determining the sense in which the sacred writers speak of Justification. Every one of them furnishes some contribution to the evidence of its scriptural meaning; and when they are all combined, they have the weight and force of a cumulative proof. It is necessary to add on this point, with reference to some recent cavils, that the meaning of the term may be strictly forensic, although the method of Justification by grace should differ, in many respects, from that of Justification by Law, and should have no exact analogue in the proceedings of human courts;—for the former may contain a provision for the fulfilment of the Law, and may only substitute a vicarious, for a personal, righteousness as the ground of our acceptance with God; while Justification itself is still a judicial sentence, and God is declared to be 'just' while He is 'the justifier of the ungodly.' Were it a mere act of indemnity, securing impunity for past sin, and were it proclaimed irrespective of any satisfaction to God's justice, or any vindication of His righteous Law, it might be regarded as a sovereign exercise of mercy,—above, and even against, the principles of His moral government; and, in that case, its judicial and forensic character must be merged and lost in the virtual abolition of any legal rule, whether of justification or of condemnation. But if, instead of being abolished, the Law is to be fulfilled,—and if a righteousness is still to be the ground of our acceptance with God, then Justification, as being related to, and founded upon, that righteousness, which is both provided and wrought out for

us, must still retain its forensic and judicial character, even
while it is also an act of grace. For this reason Protestant
divines have been careful to combine, in their definitions or
descriptions of it, both its judicial and its gracious aspect,
and to show that, according to the scheme of the Gospel,
' He is faithful and just,' while He is also 'merciful and
gracious' 'to forgive us our sins, and to cleanse us from all
unrighteousness.' ' Justification,' says Bishop Downhame,
' is a most gracious and righteous act of God, whereby
He, imputing the righteousness of Christ to a believing
sinner, absolveth him from his sins, and accepteth of him
as righteous in Christ, and as an heir of eternal life, to
the praise and glory of His own Mercy and Justice.'

PROP. II. While ' Justification' is a forensic or judicial
term, it is used in Scripture to denote, sometimes the
acceptance of a sinner as righteous in the sight of God,—
sometimes the manifestation or proof of his acceptance,
by which it is attested and made sure : and this variety
in the application of it is the ground of an important
theological distinction,—the distinction between ACTUAL
and DECLARATIVE Justification.

This distinction does not imply, either that there is
more than one Justification before God, as Romish
writers have alleged, or that the sense of the term is
ambiguous ; for that term relates invariably to one and
the same Justification, when it denotes a change in man's
relation to God ; but this change may be considered in
two distinct aspects,—either as being actually accomplished when he is accepted as righteous,—or as being
declared and attested, so as to give him the comfortable
assurance of it ; and the same term may be applied to it
in each of these aspects, without making its meaning
ambiguous, since the context will enable us to determine

in which of the two it is contemplated by the sacred writer. The Protestant doctrine affirms that a sinner is made or constituted righteous by having Christ's righteousness imputed to him; and that, being thus justified actually, he is also justified declaratively, when his acceptance is proved or attested, so as to be made manifest to his own conscience, or to his fellow-men. In both cases it is one and the same Justification that is spoken of,—his acceptance as righteous in the sight of God; but, in the one, it is considered simply as a fact, in the other, as a fact that is attested and proved. Actual Justification comes first, and is necessarily presupposed in that which is declarative; and hence, if any one is declared to have been justified, we conclude that he was actually justified, or accepted as righteous in the sight of God. While there is a real analogy, there is also an important difference, between the divine act of Justification, and the judicial procedure of human courts. The sentence of a human judge is merely *declarative*; it does not constitute a man either innocent or guilty, it only pronounces him to be so in the eye of the law: it may even be erroneous, and may pronounce one to be innocent who is really guilty, and another to be guilty who is really innocent; whereas in justifying a sinner, God does what no human judge can do,—He first constitutes him righteous, who was not righteous before, and then declares him to be righteous, in His infallible judgment, which is ever according to truth. It is chiefly in its *declarative* aspect that the divine act of Justification is analogous to the sentence of a human judge; and the difference between the two cases consists in the one having respect to a vicarious, the other to a personal, righteousness; while both are forensic or judicial, as being pronounced with reference to a law or rule of righteousness, which is applicable to each of them respectively.

The distinction between ACTUAL and DECLARATIVE Justification is illustrated by many passages of Scripture.

The term must necessarily bear a declarative sense only, when it is applied to God,—' All the people justified God;'[1] or to Christ,—' God manifest in the flesh, justified in the Spirit;'[2] or to Wisdom,—' Wisdom is justified of her children.'[3] In the same sense it must be understood when it is used to denote self-justification from a charge of guilt, true or false. The lawyer is described as ' willing to justify himself;'[4] and the Pharisees as ' they who justify themselves before men.'[5] In these and similar cases, the purely declarative sense of the term is self-evident, since every other is necessarily excluded.

We have a beautiful example of ACTUAL, followed by DECLARATIVE, justification, in the case of one, who is simply described as ' a woman in the city which was a sinner.'[6] She came into the presence of Jesus in the house of a Pharisee, and manifested her devoted love to Him; for ' she brought an alabaster box of ointment, and stood at His feet behind Him weeping, and began to wash His feet with tears, and did wipe them with the hairs of her head, and kissed His feet, and anointed them with the ointment.' The Pharisee, offended by such a sinner being permitted to approach one who professed to be a prophet sent from God, began to reason within himself against Christ's claims to that character, on the ground that He must be ignorant what manner of woman she was; but his unuttered thought was answered by our Lord, when He pointed to the tokens of her love to Him as a proof that if she had sinned, she had also been forgiven; and then proceeded to add His own assurance of her forgiveness, addressed to herself. It is manifest that she was

---

[1] Luke vii. 29.   [2] 1 Tim. iii. 16.   [3] Matt. xi. 19.
[4] Luke x. 29.   [5] Luke xvi. 15.   [6] Luke vii. 37–50.

actually justified before she came into His presence; for her love was the evidence and the effect,—not the cause or ground,—of her forgiveness: it was love which constrained her to follow Him,—it was love that prompted her to bring an alabaster box of ointment,—it was love that burned in her heart while she stood behind Him weeping: and 'she loved much,' because 'much had been forgiven her;' but she was now justified declaratively, so as to obtain, perhaps for the first time, an assurance of her personal acceptance,—for not only did her Lord acknowledge her 'great love' as being in itself a practical proof of her forgiveness, but He further attested it, first by His words to the Pharisee—'Wherefore, *I say unto thee*, her sins which are many are forgiven;' and then by His words to herself, when 'He said unto her, Thy sins are forgiven;' 'Thy faith hath saved thee, go in peace.' This case brings out very clearly both the distinction between actual and declarative Justification, and also the *two* distinct methods in which the justification of a believer may be manifested and proved. The woman was forgiven before, but she now obtained the assurance of her forgiveness; and that assurance was conveyed to her mind in two ways—first by means of an experimental evidence of her having that 'faith which worketh by love;' and secondly, in addition to this experimental evidence, by means of an authoritative testimony from the lips of her Lord Himself.

The distinction between ACTUAL and DECLARATIVE Justification, in the sense already explained, may be further illustrated by what is said of the Old Testament believers in the 11th chapter of the Epistle to the Hebrews. The Apostle refers to them as been actually justified by faith; but his expressions show that he speaks also, and very specially, of their declarative justification. By faith,

he says, 'the elders obtained *a good report*' (ἐμαρτυρήθησαν),[1]
—they were not only justified, but attested or declared so
to be. Of Abel it is said, that 'by faith he offered unto
God a more excellent sacrifice than Cain, by which *he
obtained witness that he was righteous, God testifying of his
gifts*' (ἐμαρτυρήθη εἶναι δίκαιος, μαρτυροῦντος ἐπὶ τοῖς δώροις αὐτοῦ
τοῦ Θεοῦ);[2] the prominent idea being not merely the fact,
that Abel and his offering were accepted of God, but that
God testified His acceptance of both, or bore witness to
him that 'he was righteous.' Of Enoch it is said, that
'before his translation *he had this testimony*, that he pleased
God' (μεμαρτύρηται εὐηρεστηκέναι τῷ Θεῷ).[3] And of many
more it is said, 'These all having obtained a good report
through faith' (μαρτυρηθέντες διὰ τῆς πίστεως).[4] Their ACTUAL
Justification is presupposed, but their DECLARATIVE Justification is specially referred to; and this is represented
as depending partly on the practical fruits of faith, by
which it was proved to be alive and active, and partly on
the divine testimony bearing witness to their acceptance.

The distinction between actual and declarative Justification may be still further illustrated by what is said in
Scripture of the final judgment at the last day. No one
will be actually justified then, who was not justified
before : but every believer will be justified *declaratively*,
when he is openly acknowledged and acquitted by the
sentence of the Judge. No one will then be forgiven or
accepted for the first time; for as there is no repentance,
so there is no pardon in the grave; the day of salvation
terminates at the close of life; and over every deathbed
this solemn inscription might be written, 'He that is
unjust, let him be unjust still; and he that is filthy, let
him be filthy still; and he that is righteous, let him be
righteous still; and he that is holy, let him be holy

---

[1] Heb. xi. 2.　　　[2] Heb. xi. 4.　　　[3] Heb. xi. 5.　　　[4] Heb. xi. 39.

still.'[1] But the righteous and holy, who have been already justified and sanctified on earth, will be publicly declared to be 'blessed' in that day which is emphatically called 'the day of the Apocalypse, or revelation, of the sons of God.' And on that solemn occasion, just as in the case of the woman that was a sinner, the acquittal and acceptance of the believer will not only be authoritatively declared by the sentence of the Judge, but that sentence will refer to the fruits of his faith, and especially to his love to Christ, as manifested by love to His afflicted people : 'Inasmuch as ye did it to one of these my brethren, ye did it unto me.' Justification, considered as the pardon of a sinner and his acceptance as righteous in the sight of God, is by faith ; but judgment is according to works ; and it is not a second Justification,—as if there might be two—the one by faith, the other by works —it is one and the same Justification, which is actually bestowed in the present life, and authoritatively declared and attested at the judgment-seat. Some have imagined that the doctrine of a free Justification now by grace, through faith alone, is inconsistent with that of a future judgment according to works ; and for this reason they have attempted to show, either that Justification and Judgment are precisely the same, or that we must modify the doctrine of Justification by faith alone so as to bring it into accordance with that of a judgment according to works. (5)   But there is no real inconsistency between the two doctrines. They relate to different parts of the divine procedure ; and are equally necessary,—the one for the immediate relief of the sinner's conscience,—the other for the regulation of the believer's conduct. 'I would have every preacher,' said Dr. Chalmers to the author, 'insist strenuously on these two doctrines—a pre-

[1] Rev. xxii. 11.

sent Justification by grace, through faith alone—and a future Judgment according to works;' and all faithful ministers have made use of both, that they might guard equally against the peril of self-righteous legalism, on the one hand, and of practical Antinomianism, on the other. But we refer to the future judgment only as it affords an additional proof of the distinction between actual and declarative Justification.

PROP. III. The distinction between actual and declarative Justification,—viewed in connection with the difference between a living and a dead faith,—affords a sufficient explanation of the apparent discrepancy between the teaching of Paul and James.

'Therefore we conclude,' says Paul, 'that a man is justified by faith without the deeds of the Law.'

'Ye see, then,' says James, 'how that by works a man is justified, and not by faith only.'[1]

That these statements might be understood in a sense in which they would be at direct variance with each other, is evident, both from a simple comparison of the terms in which they are expressed, and from the history of their actual interpretation. It is equally evident, that there can be no real contradiction between the two, since both Apostles wrote under the inspiration of the same Spirit of Truth ; and it is the first duty, therefore, of all parties to ascertain their real meaning, by a careful collation of their respective lines of thought, as these are developed in the context, and illustrated by other passages of Scripture ; and thereafter to show that, when thus interpreted, they are in perfect accordance with each other, and with the general ' analogy of faith.'

From the age of Augustine downwards, the most

[1] Rom. iii. 28 ; Jas. ii. 24.

various and conflicting interpretations have been proposed. Recourse has been had to each of the principal
terms in succession,—Justification,—Faith,—Works,—
with the view of finding, in one or other of them, a
means of harmonizing the teaching of the two Apostles.
Some have founded their theory on the first of these
terms, and have contended for a first and second, or an
initial and final, Justification,—not in the sense of the
one being actual, and the other declarative merely,—but in
the sense of both being actual, while the one is by faith,
and the other by works.   Others have founded on the
second term, and have attempted to show that, if every
believer is actually justified in the present life, it can
only be because faith is considered as the germ of
personal holiness, and as comprehensive of all the other
graces, and acts of new obedience, which spring from it.
Others still have founded on the third term, and have
endeavoured to show, that the works which are excluded
from the ground of our Justification, are—either mere
ceremonial observances such as were enjoined in that part
of the Mosaic law which is now abolished,—or moral
duties such as the heathen practised, which were done
in the unaided strength of nature, without grace, and
before faith in Christ,—or perfect obedience to the
divine law, such as no man in his own strength can
possibly accomplish, but not that sincere, though imperfect, obedience which every Christian is enabled by
the grace of the Spirit to render to its requirements.
For a full discussion of these various theories, recourse
must be had to the writings of their respective advocates
or opponents; it is sufficient for the establishment of the
proposition which is now before us, if it can be shown, by
a correct exposition of the language of both Apostles, that
Paul is treating of actual, and James of declarative, Justi-

fication; and that, when their respective statements are
thus understood, there is not even the shadow of a discrepancy between them.

Paul, in his Epistles to the Romans and Galatians,
treats at great length, and with much earnestness, the
question of a sinner's actual Justification, or acceptance
in the sight of God. He states the conclusion of his
whole argument, when he says, 'Therefore by the deeds
of the law shall no flesh be justified in His sight: for by
the law is the knowledge of sin;' and again, 'Therefore
we conclude that a man is justified by faith, without the
deeds of the law.'[1] To lay a deep and firm foundation for
this conclusion in each of its constituent parts, he had *first*
taken a comprehensive survey of the state and character
of all men,—whether Gentiles or Jews,—considered as
subjects of the divine Law; of the Gentiles, as being
subjects of a moral law inscribed on their own hearts,
by which 'they were a law to themselves;' and of the
Jews, as being subjects both of that natural law in
common with the Gentiles, and also of a revealed law,
which was peculiar to them: and the result of his
survey is declared in these sweeping terms—'What
things soever the law saith, it saith to them that are
under the law, that every mouth may be stopped, and
all the world may become guilty before God;' for 'there
is no difference; for all have sinned, and come short of
the glory of God.'[2] This result of his comprehensive
survey is the ground of the *first* part of his conclusion,
'Therefore by the deeds of the law shall no flesh be
justified in His sight, for by the law is the knowledge of
sin;' and this conclusion shuts out all Justification by the
law in the case of sinners, whether it be the purely moral
law of Conscience, or the partly moral and partly positive

[1] Rom. iii. 20, 28.   [2] Rom. iii. 19, 23.

law of the Mosaic Revelation. But at this point he
advances a step further, and, having excluded the
righteousness of man altogether from the ground of his
justification, he brings into view another righteousness,
emphatically called 'the righteousness of God,' because
God claims a special propriety in it, as being peculiarly
His own—devised, provided, wrought out, and revealed
by Himself alone; he speaks of this righteousness as
being now clearly manifested, and fully revealed; and
he describes it as 'a righteousness without the law,'—as
a righteousness, since it has some relation to the law; for
if it be true that 'where there is no law, there is no transgression,' it is equally true, that where there is no law,
there is no 'righteousness;'—and yet a 'righteousness
without the law,' as being above and beyond the law,
—neither contained in it, nor provided by it;—as a
'righteousness' which is, nevertheless, 'witnessed by the
law and the prophets,' having been indicated, although
not fully revealed—predicted, prefigured, and promised,
when mention was made of Him who 'should be called
the Lord our Righteousness,' and 'the Lord in whom all
the seed of Israel shall be justified;'[1]—as a 'righteousness which is by faith,' and 'upon all them that believe,'
so that 'they are justified freely by His grace;' and 'if
by grace, then is it no more of works; otherwise grace is
no more grace : and if it be of works, then is it no more
grace; otherwise work is no more work;' 'for to him
that worketh is the reward not reckoned of grace, but of
debt;'[2]—and, finally, as a righteousness which is 'through
the redemption that is in Christ Jesus;' and which was
wrought out for us when 'God set Him forth to be a
propitiation through faith in His blood, to declare His

---

[1] Jer. xxiii. 6; Isa. xlv. 25; also, xlv. 24, xlvi. 12, 13.
[2] Rom. xi. 6, iv. 4.

righteousness; . . .   that He might be just, and the
justifier of him that believeth in Jesus.' This result,
again, of the revealed method of grace and redemption
is the ground of the *second* part of his conclusion;—
'Therefore we conclude that a man is justified by faith,
without the deeds of the law.' So that man's righteousness arising from his works of obedience to the divine
Law, is excluded from the ground of his Justification on
two distinct grounds,—first, on the ground of God's
Law, which convicts and condemns every sinner;—and
secondly, on the ground of God's method of redeeming
mercy, which brings in another righteousness altogether,
—the righteousness of Him who 'became obedient unto
death, even the death of the Cross.' It is manifest from
the whole course of his argument, that Paul's design was
to explain the method and ground, and even, to some
extent, the *rationale*, of the actual justification of a sinner
in the sight of God,—to show how, and why, he may be
forgiven and accepted as righteous,—and to set forth this
as the immediate privilege of every believer, as soon as
he renounces all confidence in his own righteousness, and
submits 'to the righteousness of God.'

It is equally clear, that the Apostle James, while he
refers incidentally, or by necessary implication, to the
actual justification of sinners in the sight of God, is not
engaged in expounding either the nature, or grounds, of
that great Gospel privilege, but rather in illustrating the
declarative justification of believers, or the practical evidence by which their actual justification is attested and
proved. He refers to the same justification of a sinner
in the sight of God, which is more fully expounded by
Paul; for he speaks, like Paul, of the justification of
Abraham, which was evidently, in the first instance, that
of a sinner before God; and for this reason, it is a de-

fective statement to say that he speaks only of justification before men.   But actual justification is necessarily
presupposed in that which is declarative ; for the latter
is the mere evidence, manifestation, or proof of the former;
and the Apostle proves the actual justification of Abraham, *first*, from the testimony of God Himself, as it is
recorded in Scripture, ‘which saith, Abraham believed
in God, and it was imputed unto him for righteousness :
and he was called the Friend of God ;’[1] and *secondly*,
from the practical fruits or manifestations of his faith in
works of holy obedience : ‘ For was not Abraham our
father justified by works, when he had offered Isaac his
son upon the altar ?’[2]

Here Abraham is said to have been ‘ justified by
works,’ and the special work of obedience which is mentioned is that marvellous proof of his faith,—his offering
up his son Isaac on the altar.   But the history of Abraham shows that he was actually justified, in the sense of
being forgiven and accepted of God, long before his faith
was subjected to that severe trial.   He was a believer,
and, as such, a justified sinner, many years before Isaac
was born : and the first notice of his justification makes
mention only of God’s promise, and of Abraham’s faith ;
for ‘ he believed in the Lord, and He counted it to him
for righteousness.’[3]   But his justification, which was real
and saving as soon as he believed, was attested and made
sure at a later period, when ‘ the Lord called unto him
out of heaven, and said, Now I know that thou fearest
God, seeing thou hast not withheld thy son, thine only
son, from me. . . . And again the second time, By myself have I sworn, saith the Lord, because thou hast done
this thing, and hast not withheld thy son, thine only son,
that in blessing I will bless thee, . . . and in thy seed

[1] Jas. ii. 23.   [2] Jas. ii. 21.   [3] Gen. xv. 6.

shall all the nations of the earth be blessed; because thou hast obeyed my voice."[1] He was ACTUALLY justified before; but there was here a divine DECLARATION of his acceptance, which expressly referred to his obedience, as the fruit and manifestation of his faith. The fact that he was accepted at an earlier, and declared to be accepted at a later, period, while in both cases he is spoken of as 'justified,' has an important application to our present argument; for it shows conclusively that the same term is used to denote both his *actual* and his *declarative* justification. But in addition to this, the priority of his actual justification by faith to his declarative justification by works, affords ground for an argument precisely analogous to that which the Apostle founds on the date of his justification as compared with that of his circumcision. 'We say that faith was reckoned to Abraham for righteousness. How was it then reckoned? *When* he was in circumcision or in uncircumcision? Not in circumcision, but in uncircumcision. And he received the sign of circumcision, a seal of the righteousness of the faith *which he had yet being uncircumcised.*' Following this apostolic precedent, and proceeding exactly on the same principle, we might say, 'Faith was reckoned to Abraham for righteousness. How was it then reckoned? When he had manifested his faith by offering up his son Isaac upon the altar, and when both his faith and obedience were declared to be accepted by an audible voice from heaven? No, but long before; and he obtained that declarative justification, just as he received circumcision, as a sign and seal of the righteousness of the faith which he had before.'

But the distinction between actual and declarative Justification must be viewed in connection with the

[1] Gen. xxii. 12, 16, 18.

difference between a LIVING and a DEAD FAITH, in order
to afford a full explanation of the apparent discrepancy
between the teaching of the two Apostles. When Paul
and James speak of the faith of Abraham, they both
regard it as a genuine, vital, operative principle ; for
Paul, not less strongly than James, describes it as 'working by love,' and bringing forth the fruits of new obedience ; for 'by faith Abraham, when he was called to go
out into a place which he should afterward receive for an
inheritance, *obeyed ;*' and so, 'by faith Abraham, when
he was tried, offered up Isaac : and he that had received
the promises offered up his only-begotten son.'[1] He acted
by faith on both occasions ; so that faith was prior to
his obedience ; and if every believer is justified, he was
actually pardoned and accepted before he manifested his
faith in these signal acts of obedience.   But while James
refers, as Paul also does, to the living faith of Abraham
and its practical fruits, he speaks of another thing under
the name of faith, which is described,—partly as a mere
profession, where there was no real principle,—and partly
as a mere doctrinal belief, which had no spiritual life in
it.   He speaks, in the first instance, of a mere profession,
where there was no real principle : 'What doth it profit
though a man SAY he hath faith, and have not works ?
Can faith (evidently such a faith as is here meant) save
him ?' The case supposed is that of a faith professed
merely, and not productive of obedience—and the question
raised is, Whether that be saving faith ?   He compares
it to a mere profession of charity, which leads to no deeds
of active beneficence, and concludes that the one is as
worthless as the other.   'Even so,' says he, 'faith, if it
hath not works, is dead, being alone :' 'for as the body
without the spirit is dead, so faith without works is dead

[1] Heb. xi. 8, 17.

also.'[1] We read in Scripture both of a 'dead faith' and
of 'dead works ;'[2]—faith is dead when it is without works,
and works are dead when they are without faith ;—and
hence we are called equally, in the exercise of self-exami-
nation, to test our faith by our works, and to test our
works by the principle from which they spring. The
purely evidential or declarative use of works in their
relation to faith is very clearly brought out, when he
adds, ' Yea, a man may say, Thou hast faith, and I have
works : SHOW ME thy faith without thy works, and I
will SHOW THEE my faith by my works.' But suppose
that there is something more than mere profession,—
that there is a belief in some of the elementary truths
of religion, such as the devils have, who 'believe and
tremble,'—but that still it is productive of no fruits of
holy obedience ; it is still a ' dead faith,' and altogether
different from the faith of Abraham. ' For was not
Abraham our father justified by works, when he had
offered Isaac his son upon the altar ? Seest thou how
faith wrought with his works, and by works was faith
made perfect ? And the scripture was fulfilled which
saith, Abraham believed God, and it was imputed unto
him for righteousness : and he was called the Friend of
God.'[3] If we understand the words, ' Abraham was justified by works,' in a declarative sense, as importing that
he was then, and on account of his obedience, attested as
a true believer and a justified man, the whole passage
will be seen to be self-consistent, as well as in perfect
harmony with the doctrine of Paul ; but if we understand
them as referring to the ground and reason of his actual
justification, not only must one Apostle be held to con-
tradict another, but no consistent explanation can be
given of the statement of James himself.

[1] Jas. ii. 17, 26.   [2] Heb. ix. 14.   [3] Jas. ii. 21-23.

From this brief review of the teaching of Paul and James, it appears that the distinction between *actual* and *declarative* Justification, which can be established, as we have seen, from many other passages of Scripture, is sufficient, especially when viewed in connection with the difference between a *living* and a *dead* faith, to afford a sufficient explanation of the apparent discrepancy of their teaching on the subject of Justification. (6) It may be right to add, that the same practical doctrine which is taught by James, is frequently taught in substance, although in different terms, by Paul himself; and that, so far from regarding it as being either a contradiction or a correction of his own teaching, he would have cordially concurred with his fellow-Apostle in striving to guard against every perversion of the doctrine of grace. In treating the whole question of a sinner's justification, he does not overlook, but anticipates and answers, the false inferences which carnal minds might draw from it. ' Do we then make void the law through faith ? God forbid ! yea, we establish the law.'   ' What shall we say then ?   Shall we continue in sin, that grace may abound? God forbid !'   ' Our old man is crucified with Christ, that the body of sin might be destroyed, that henceforth we should not serve sin.'   ' But now, being made free from sin, and become servants to God, ye have your fruit unto holiness, and the end everlasting life.'[1] He declares that ' the grace of God which bringeth salvation' is designed to teach us that, ' denying ungodliness and worldly lusts, we should live soberly, righteously, and godly in the world ;' and that the grand end of Christ ' in giving Himself for us,' was that ' He might redeem us from all iniquity, and purify us to Himself, a peculiar people zealous (not jealous) of good works.'[2] He exhorts be-

[1] Rom. iii. 31, vi. 1, 15, 6, 22.   [2] Tit. ii. 11, 12, 14.

lievers to 'make their calling and election sure,' and, for
this end, to 'examine themselves whether they be in the
faith;'[1] and he furnishes them with a criterion or touch-
stone of their real condition in the sight of God, by speci-
fying in detail both 'the works of the flesh' and 'the
fruits of the Spirit.'[2]

The two Apostles were combating two opposite errors,
and sought to check two opposite tendencies. Paul contended against Legalism, and the self-righteous tendency
which leads men 'to go about to establish their own righteousness,' and to seek Justification by the works of the
Law. James contends against Libertinism, or the Antinomian tendency which leads men to pervert the Gospel
itself, and to 'turn the grace of God into licentiousness.'
Both tendencies still exist, alike in the world and in the
Church: for however Legalism and Libertinism may be
disowned in theory, the tendency towards the one exists
wherever there remains the slightest feeling of self-con-
fidence,—and the tendency towards the other, wherever
there is one lust unsubdued, or the smouldering fire of indwelling sin. And for this reason, every faithful minister
finds it necessary to make use, alternately, of the teaching
of Paul and of James. (7)

---

[1] 2 Cor. xiii. 5.   [2] Gal. v. 19 ; Eph. iv. 22.

LECTURE IX.

JUSTIFICATION ; THE PROPER NATURE OF THE BLESSING.

THE meaning of the term, as ascertained from the usage of the sacred writers, indicates generally the nature of the blessing which is denoted by it; but the consideration of that blessing, as it is described or exemplified in Scripture, will serve at once to define our views of its nature, and to shed a reflected light on the meaning of the term.

PROP. IV. The term 'Justification' denotes, either an act of God, or a privilege of His people ; and, in both cases, that which is denoted by it includes absolution and acceptance,—the full pardon of sin, admission into God's favour, and a title to eternal life.

It denotes an act of God; for 'it is God which justifieth :' 'He is near that justifieth me ;'[1]—and it denotes a privilege of His people ; for 'being justified by faith, we have peace with God through our Lord Jesus Christ, by whom also we have access by faith into this grace wherein we stand, and rejoice in hope of the glory of God.'[2]   In each of these aspects, some important truths have been revealed concerning it.

Considered as an act of God, who 'justifies the ungodly,' it is not a subjective operation producing a moral change in our personal character, although it is invariably

---

[1] Rom. viii. 33 ; Isa. l. 8.   [2] Rom. v. 1.

accompanied by renewing and sanctifying grace; but an
act which is external to us, and which effects an immediate and permanent change in our relation to God,—just
such as is consequent on the sentence of a judge, by which
any one is absolved from a charge of guilt,—or the act of
adoption, by which any one is invested with the privileges
of legal sonship. It is an act, too, which is completed at
once, and not a work which is gradually accomplished by
successive acts; for although we read of the continuance,
as well as the commencement, of Justification, considered
as the privilege of believers, and of the renewed exercise
of forgiving mercy as often as they contract fresh sin, yet
there is no second Justification, properly so called, but a
decisive and unalterable change in our relation to God,
which commences with our union to Christ, and is continued by our remaining in Him; an abiding state of
Justification, which is the effect of that indissoluble union.
'There is now no condemnation to them that are in Christ
Jesus.'[1] 'He that believeth . . . hath everlasting life,
and shall never come into condemnation; but is passed
from death unto life.'[2] The *act* of Justification introduces
believers into a state of Justification, which is stable and
enduring, and which is described as 'this grace wherein we
stand,' and as 'a new life:' for Christ is 'our life.'[3] Justification, considered in the same aspect, is, still further, an
act of God in time,—not His eternal purpose merely, as
some Antinomians have held,—nor is it a mere revealing
of what was always true, and is now only made known
and believed; it is a real efficacious act of grace, by which
God constitutes the sinner legally righteous, and accepts
him as such, although till that hour he was not righteous,
but guilty and condemned. It is an act of God with
reference to individuals, and it takes place at a definite

---

[1] Rom. viii. 1.   [2] John v. 24 ; Col. iii. 4.   [3] Rom. v. 2 ; Ps. xxx. 5.

period in the life of each,—for as long as any one remains
without Christ, and in a state of unbelief, he is charged
with guilt, and exposed to wrath; but as soon as he believes and is united to Christ, his state in this respect is
entirely changed. All who are justified were once 'dead
in trespasses and sins;'[1] and they continued in that state,
till the decisive moment when, by an act of divine grace,
they were taken out of it, and placed in a state of pardon
and peace. 'For as many as are of the works of the law,
are under the curse: for it is written, Cursed is every one
that continueth not in all things which are written in the
book of the law to do them.'[2] 'He that believeth on
Christ is not condemned; but he that believeth not is
condemned already, because he hath not believed in the
name of the only-begotten Son of God.' 'He that believeth on the Son hath everlasting life: and he that
believeth not the Son shall not see life; but the wrath
of God abideth on him.'[3] This act of God takes instant
effect, and produces an immediate and complete change in
the sinner's whole relation to Him; it bestows the full and
free pardon of sin, and translates him at once from a state
of condemnation into a state of favour and peace. His
person is first justified, and then his services are accepted:
and should he afterwards incur fresh guilt, he is not suffered
to fall again into condemnation, but, as an adopted child, he
'is chastened of the Lord, that he should not be condemned
with the world.' 'For whom the Lord loveth He chasten-
eth, and scourgeth every son whom He receiveth.'[4] (1)

Considered, again, as the privilege of a believer, it
includes absolution and acceptance—the full pardon of
sin, admission into God's favour now, and a title to eternal
life hereafter. We are not concerned at present with some

---

[1] Eph. ii. 1.   [2] Gal. iii. 10.
[3] John iii. 18, 36.   [4] 1 Cor. xi. 32; Heb. xii. 6.

questions, which will meet us at a later stage, in regard
to those requirements of the divine Law which render
these two parts of Justification equally necessary,—or to
the method by which they were procured by the mediatorial work of Christ,—or to the grounds on which they
are respectively bestowed; we are as yet only explaining
the nature of that which is denoted by the term, and
establishing the fact, that, according to the clear testimony of Scripture, it consists in an entire change in the
sinner's relation to God, and in this only; while it includes the pardon of sin, which delivers him from wrath
and condemnation, and also the privilege of acceptance,
which invests him with a title to eternal life.

The fact that the Gospel proposes to every sinner, and
promises to every believer, both the free pardon of sin,
and the privilege of immediate acceptance with God,
including the gift of eternal life, is so evident from innumerable testimonies of Scripture, that it is seldom, if
ever, denied in express terms. Both are included in the
most general statement of the Gospel message: 'God so
loved the world, that He gave His only-begotten Son,
that whosoever believeth in Him should not perish, but
have everlasting life.'[1] The free, and full, pardon of sin
is one of the most precious promises both of the Old and
the New Testament. 'Let the wicked forsake his way,
and the unrighteous man his thoughts: and let him return
unto the Lord, and He will have mercy upon him; and to
our God, for He will abundantly pardon.'[2] 'Come now,
and let us reason together, saith the Lord: though your
sins be as scarlet, they shall be as white as snow; though
they be red like crimson, they shall be as wool.'[3] 'I, even
I, am He that blotteth out thy transgressions for mine
own sake, and will not remember thy sins.'[4] 'I have

---

[1] John iii. 16.   [2] Isa. lv. 7.   [3] Isa. i. 18.   [4] Isa. xliii. 25.

blotted out, as a thick cloud, thy transgressions, and, as a cloud, thy sins : return unto me ; for I have redeemed thee.'[1] ' If Thou, Lord, shouldest mark iniquities, O Lord, who shall stand ? But there is forgiveness with Thee.'[2] ' To Him give all the prophets witness, that through His name whosoever believeth in Him shall receive remission of sins.'[3] ' In whom we have redemption through His blood, even the forgiveness of sins.'[4] But the believer is not merely forgiven, so as to be delivered from wrath and condemnation, he is also ' accepted in the Beloved,'[5] and ' made the righteousness of God in Him,'[6]—he is admitted into God's favour, ' which is life,'—he has the privilege of access into His presence,—he is restored to His fellowship, —and obtains the gift of an eternal inheritance.[7] For ' this is the record, that God hath given to us eternal life, and this life is in His Son.' In short, the full and free pardon of sin, delivering him from ' condemnation' now, and also from ' the wrath to come,'—and the acceptance, first of his person, and then of his services, together with the free gift of eternal life,—these are blessings which belong to every believer, and they are included in his Justifica-tion, which relates entirely to his judicial relation to God, here and hereafter.

Protestants have generally held that Justification de-notes a change in our judicial relation to God, and that only ; and that this change includes the pardon of sin, and the acceptance of the sinner. On what ground we are pardoned, on the one hand, and accepted, on the other, is not the present question, but simply the fact that these two blessings belong to every believer, and that they are included in his Justification. This fact is affirmed by all our greatest divines, and they have established their

[1] Isa. xliv. 22.   [2] Ps. cxxx. 3.   [3] Acts x. 43.   [4] Col. i. 20.
[5] Eph. i. 6.   [6] 2 Cor. v. 21.   [7] Eph. iii. 18, 12.

doctrine by a vast array of Scripture proofs and solid
arguments in their great controversy with the Romish
Church. (2)   But as some errors on this point,—distinct
from those which relate to the ground of Justification,
although closely connected with them,—have always prevailed in the Church of Rome, and have recently been
revived among certain parties belonging to the Protestant
body, it may be useful to advert to them briefly, not in
the way of controversy, but with the view of bringing out
clearly and definitely, the nature of Justification, and each
of its constituent parts.

That Justification, in the scriptural sense of the term,
denotes the acceptance of a sinner as righteous in the
sight of God, and that this acceptance must necessarily
include, or imply, the pardon of his sins, is the most
general and comprehensive statement of the doctrine of
Scripture on this point.   The truth of that statement is
seldom denied in express terms; for, however men may
differ in regard to the reason or ground of Justification,
they usually hold that, in some way or other, it secures
the forgiveness of sin, the enjoyment of the divine favour,
and the gift of eternal life.   Yet under this seeming agreement, there is a real and radical discordance, of opinion
between them in regard to the nature of these blessings ;
and that discordance becomes strikingly apparent as soon
as they severally state their views in distinct and definite
terms.

In regard to the pardon or forgiveness of sin, many
Popish writers have held that it consists in the deletion or
extinction of innate depravity,—this being a part of their
more general doctrine, that the Justification of a sinner
denotes his being made righteous inherently, with a view
to his final acceptance on the ground of his own personal
obedience (3); while some Protestants have recently ap-

proximated to this view, by maintaining that pardon consists in deliverance from the dominion of sin, as the only possible means of freedom from its natural consequences, which are, in their view, its entire punishment,—and that there neither is, nor can be, pardon in any other sense. We have seen that the doctrine of Pardon was corrupted at a very early period. The Rabbinical Jews, and many of the Gnostics, held that no sin is ever forgiven, or its punishment remitted, but that in every case, the sinner must expiate it, here or hereafter, by his own personal suffering. (4) The Popish doctrine has a close resemblance to theirs; for while it makes Justification to include remission and renovation, as if they were distinct blessings, it describes remission as consisting in the deletion of sin, which is a part of sanctification, and as securing only exemption from eternal punishment, while temporal punishment is still exacted, and that too as a satisfaction to divine justice, either in penance here, or in purgatory hereafter; so that in the Protestant sense of the term, the Romish Church may be said to have no doctrine of Pardon at all. It is said, indeed, by some that Justification is pardon 'relatively to the past,' and that 'nothing else it can be;' but that it is only a part of one gift, which includes renovation also with respect to the present and the future: and this admission is fatal to their doctrine, unless it can be shown, either that the pardon of past sin is not a change in a sinner's judicial relation to God, or that personal sanctification can of itself cancel guilt already contracted, and punishment already due. (5) Some Protestant writers have recently perverted, or rather denied, the doctrine of Pardon, in any other sense than that of deliverance from sin, and its natural consequences; and have affirmed that it cancels no curse,—that it removes no condemnation,—that it consists in deliverance from the power and pollution of sin, as the only means of freeing us from its inevitable consequences,—and that any other supposition is blasphemous. We are even told that the pardon of sin is impossible, since its punishment consists only in its natural consequences,—that these can never be removed by any act of God,—and that even the Socinian doctrine, which teaches the pardon of sin on repentance, is 'a pernicious fallacy.' (6)

All these errors in regard to the doctrine of Pardon sprung from the same source,—ignorance or unbelief in regard to the guilt and demerit of sin,—the wrath of God which is revealed from heaven against it,—and the nature of punishment, as that is declared in the curse, or condemning sentence, of His law. Those who can bring themselves to believe, either that there is no evil in sin, except as it is a subjective disorder or defilement of the soul,—or that it is not the object of God's righteous abhorrence and indignation, — or that there is no penal threatening or sentence to be executed against it by direct divine infliction, may feel as if there could be no need, and even no possibility, of pardon; but their false security springs from unbelief of God's Law, and is widely different from that true peace which springs from faith in Christ's Gospel. It is not 'the very peace of God, reigning in the conscience, through Christ Jesus;' it is rather the atheistic security of those of whom the Psalmist speaks—'Wherefore doth the wicked contemn God? He hath said in his heart, Thou wilt not require it.'[1] This state of mind is liable to be suddenly disturbed by the awakening of conscience, when God's holy law is carried home to it in power, or when any one is brought face to face with death and an eternal world; for then 'the revelation of wrath' calls forth a response from within,

[1] Ps. x. 13.

and all must feel, that if 'our own hearts condemn us, God is greater than our hearts, and knoweth all things.'

The revealed doctrine of Pardon cannot be understood, unless we distinguish the guilt and demerit of sin, from its dominion and defilement. The guilt of sin remains after the act of sin is past and gone ; and it is 'marked' or 'retained' against us, until it is 'blotted out,' or 're-mitted.' The fact of sin remains a fact for ever, and can never be undone ; it will be true to all eternity that we contracted guilt, and deserved punishment. Pardon pre-supposes both its reality, and its demerit, and frees us from the charge of guilt, and the sentence of condemnation, without impairing our sense of either : on the contrary, as it proceeds from the Cross of Christ, and is proclaimed in His Gospel, it deepens our deepest convictions of sin, so that 'we can never open our mouths any more on account of our shame, when God is pacified towards us for all that we have done.'[1] And it is only by pardon that guilt can be cancelled : it cannot be extinguished by repentance, or even by regeneration ; for while these may improve or renew our character, a divine sentence of condemnation can only be reversed by a divine act of remission. This act, like that sentence, affects only a sinner's relation to God ; and that it properly belongs to his Justification, as being included in it, is evident from the Apostle's statement, 'Be it known unto you, men and brethren, that through this Man is preached unto you the forgiveness of sins ; and by Him all that believe are justi-fied from all things, from which ye could not be justified by the law of Moses.'[2] (7)

The pardon of sin is an indispensable and important part of a sinner's justification, but is not an adequate or complete description of that privilege. It includes also

[1] Ezek. xvi. 63.   [2] Acts xiii. 38, 39.

his 'acceptance as righteous in the sight of God;' his admission to the divine favour, and possession of the gift of eternal life. His person, although he is still unworthy in himself, and also his services, although they are still imperfect and defiled by sin, 'are acceptable to God through Jesus Christ,' both being sprinkled with His blood, and perfumed with the incense of His intercession. Some have been anxious to show that Justification consists in pardon only, and that, when all sin has been forgiven, there is either no need of the distinct privilege of acceptance, or, if there be, that this is not secured by the righteousness of Christ, but is left to depend on the personal obedience of the believer. We are not considering at present the ground on which it rests, or what that righteousness is on account of which the believer is accepted of God, and obtains the gift of eternal life; but, that question being left open for future inquiry, the fact that Justification includes acceptance with God as well as the forgiveness of sin, should be distinctly apprehended, if we would form any adequate estimate of the nature and value of this great Gospel privilege. It has been alleged that some of the leading Reformers represented Justification as consisting in pardon only; but it can be conclusively proved from the writings of Luther and Calvin that when they made use of the expressions on which this allegation has been founded, they were arguing,— not against the doctrine which teaches that Justification includes acceptance with God as well as the forgiveness of sin,—but against the Popish doctrine, which made it to consist in remission and renovation. They excluded infused, but did not exclude imputed, righteousness; and this is admitted by Bellarmine himself. (8) Some Protestants, however, such as Piscator, Wendelinus, and Tillotson, have held that it consists in pardon only,—either because they thought, as Wesley did, that forgiveness necessarily implies our acceptance with God,—or because it seemed to them to be implied in the Apostle's argument when he adduces the words of David, which refer to forgiveness only, in proof of the doctrine that 'God imputeth righteousness without works.'[1] But the mere forgiveness of a sinner is evidently a distinct idea from that of his acceptance to God's favour and eternal life; and although, in the actual constitution of the scheme of grace, the one may be said to imply the other, since they are never separated, and every sinner who is forgiven is also accepted at the same time, yet, in their own nature, there is no necessary connection between the two; for it is conceivable that a sinner might be pardoned, and yet left to work out his own acceptance, as he best might, by his personal obedience. But the question is, whether this be God's method of justifying the ungodly, as that is revealed in Scripture? If it could be shown that any believer is there said to have been either accepted without being pardoned, or pardoned without being accepted to eternal life, we might conclude that there is, not only no necessary, but no actual and indissoluble, connection between the two; but if no such instances can be adduced, we are warranted by the fact of their inseparable union to argue, as the Apostle does, from the one to the other, and to prove the more comprehensive doctrine that 'God imputes righteousness without works' from that essential part of it which consists in the 'forgiveness of sins.' The generic idea of Justification is the imputation of 'righteousness;' and this includes under it the pardon of sin, and the acceptance of the sinner, as benefits which flow from it immediately in the case of every believer.

It has been said, indeed, that the pardon of sin restores

[1] Rom. iv. 6, 7, 8.

us to a state of innocence, and that nothing more is necessary to raise us to acceptance with God. But there are
several distinct considerations which should be seriously
weighed before we adopt this opinion. The *first* is, that
Adam before his fall was innocent,—*i.e.* not guilty, and
even personally holy; but while he continued in a state
of probation, he was not righteous, in the sense of having
a title to eternal life, which was promised only on condition of perfect obedience. The *second* is, that the precept
of the divine law, not only forbids sin, but requires righteousness; and that the mere remission of sin does not
necessarily imply such a righteousness as is required.
The *third* is, that while remission absolves us at once from
guilt and condemnation, neither remission, nor even regeneration itself, restores us to such a state of holiness
as that in which our first parents were created; we have
still within us the remains of indwelling sin, and the flesh
is ever lusting against the spirit; and our acceptance, as
righteous in the sight of God, can only be ascribed, therefore, to the merits of Christ. (9)

It has been said, again, that our acceptance with
God, were it supposed to be distinct from the pardon of
sin, may form no part of our Justification, but should
rather be connected with the grace of Adoption. The
privilege of Adoption is clearly revealed in Scripture.
The term is derived from the Roman law, and is purely
forensic : it denotes a change of relation, and not a change
of character. The privilege of Adoption is one thing;
the spirit of Adoption is another. In the case of legal
adoption amongst men, these two might be separated,—
the adopted son might have the rights and privileges of
sonship, although he continued to be destitute of filial
affection, or filial obedience. But in the case of divine
adoption, they are invariably combined; for no one is

adopted legally, who is not also regenerated, or born from above. Still Adoption, which implies only a change of relation, is distinct from the spirit of adoption, which implies a change of character; and the former is also distinct, in some respects, from Justification. For although both denote a change of relation, it may be affirmed that, according to the Scriptures, pardon, acceptance, and adoption, are distinct privileges, the one rising above the other in the order in which they have been stated; —that if it be conceivable that a sinner might have been pardoned, without being accepted to eternal life, it is equally conceivable that he might have been both pardoned and accepted, without being adopted as a son;— and that, while the two first properly belong to his justification, as being both founded on the same relation,— that of a Ruler and Subject,—the third is radically distinct from them, as being founded on a nearer, more tender, and more endearing relation,—that between a Father and his Son. The difference between these two relations is self-evident in the light of human experience; and it is distinctly recognised in Scripture. There is a manifest difference between the position of a servant and a friend,—and also between that of a servant and a son. Both are mentioned, and both affirmed in regard to God and His people, when it is said, ' A son honoureth his father, and a servant his master: if then I be a father, where is mine honour? and if I be a master, where is my fear?'[1]   A closer and dearer intimacy than that of a master and servant is said to subsist between Christ and His people: ' Henceforth I call you not servants; for the servant knoweth not what his lord doeth: but I have called you friends;'[2]—and a still closer and dearer relation is said to exist in consequence of adoption; for

[1] Mal. i. 6.   [2] John xv. 15.

'Thou art no more a servant, but a son, and an heir of God through Christ.'[1] The privilege of adoption presupposes pardon and acceptance, but is higher than either; for, 'To as many as received Him, to them gave He power,'—not inward strength, but authority, right, or privilege—'to become the sons of God, even to them that believe on His name.'[2] This is a higher privilege than that of Justification, as being founded on a closer and more endearing relation—'Behold! what manner of love the Father hath bestowed on us, that we should be called the sons of God.'[3] There is room for such an adoption, even if man, as originally created in the image and likeness of God, had been called,—by reason of this natural relation,—one of 'the sons of God;' for by sin, he became one of the 'seed of the serpent,' of 'the children of the wicked one,' and now he is restored to the same, or rather brought into a higher and more permanent, relation of sonship through the mediation of Christ. And just as there is an actual, and a declarative, Justification, so there is also an actual, and a declarative, Adoption; for we read both of our 'receiving the adoption of sons,' and also of our being declared to be sons,—now by the spirit of adoption, 'which witnesseth with our spirits that we are the children of God;' and hereafter there will be an 'Apocalypse,' or manifestation, of His sons.

This closer and more endearing relation to God, which is constituted by Adoption, is necessary, in addition to that which is included in our Justification, to complete the view of our Christian privileges, and to enhance our enjoyment of them, by raising us above 'the spirit of bondage, which is unto fear,' and cherishing 'the spirit of adoption, whereby we cry, Abba, Father.' It is necessary, also, to explain how the sins of believers are not

---

[1] Gal. iv. 7.   [2] John i. 12.   [3] 1 John iii. 1.

visited with penal inflictions properly so called, but are
nevertheless treated in the way of fatherly chastisement;
and, still further, to show that the kingdom of heaven
hereafter will not be bestowed as wages for work done,
but as an 'inheritance,' freely bestowed on those, and
those only, who are 'joint-heirs with Christ.'[1] (10)

Prop. V. Justification, although inseparably connected
with, is yet essentially different from, Sanctification; and
the former is not founded on the latter, as its procuring
or meritorious cause.

Justification and Sanctification have been confounded
by two opposite parties,—by Popish writers, who have
held that to justify is to make righteous inherently, by
the infusion of personal holiness; and by Antinomian
writers, who have spoken as if the righteousness of
Sanctification, as well as that of Justification, were imputed, and not infused or inherent. The former have
made, indeed, a verbal distinction between the two;
since they have described Justification as consisting in
remission and renovation : but, in their sense, the remission of sin is the deletion or extinction of it; and, as
such, is nothing more than the negative part of Sanctification, while the positive part of it is the infusion of
personal holiness. (11)   The latter, again, have spoken
as if the believer, to whom Christ's righteousness is imputed, were not only perfectly justified, but perfectly
sanctified also,—as if Christ, who is made unto him
'righteousness,' were, in the same sense, and in the same
way, made unto him 'sanctification;'—and as if, being
perfectly freed from guilt and condemnation, he must
also be perfectly delivered from indwelling sin, so as to
be no longer called to repent, or exposed even to fatherly

---

[1] Ps. lxxxix. ; Heb. xii.

chastisement, on account of it. (12) The doctrine of the
Reformation stands directly opposed to each of .these
errors. It admits the invariable and indissoluble connection between Justification and Sanctification, but
maintains that they are not only distinguishable in idea,
but different in nature,—that they depend on different
agencies, and are bestowed in different ways,—and that
many of the worst consequences, both of Popish and
Antinomian doctrine, may be ascribed to the one being
identified with the other, as if both consisted in the
infusion of righteousness.

The difference between them has been elaborately
stated, in many distinct particulars, by Protestant
writers (13) ; but the substance of their statements is
admirably summed up by the Westminster divines, in
answer to the question, 'Wherein do Justification and
Sanctification differ?' 'Although Sanctification be inseparably joined with Justification, yet they differ,—in
that God in Justification imputeth the righteousness of
Christ, in Sanctification His Spirit infuseth grace, and
enableth to the exercise thereof;—in the former, sin is
pardoned, in the other, it is subdued;—the one doth
equally free all believers from the avenging wrath of
God, and that perfectly in this life, that they never fall
into condemnation ; the other is neither equal in all, nor
in this life perfect in any, but growing up to perfection.'

The propositions which have been laid down are sufficient to explain the scriptural meaning of the term, and
the nature of that which is denoted by it. For a fuller
illustration of them, recourse should be had to the works
which have been referred to in connection with each successive topic. The first and most indispensable part of
the whole inquiry on the subject of Justification, is to

ascertain—What it is? and what it is not? and in order
to form distinct and definite ideas on this point, it is useful
to acquire some knowledge both of the several distinct
errors which have arisen in regard to it, and also of the
different methods in which these errors have been maintained. There are three leading errors on this point : the
first represents the term Justification as having an efficient
and not a forensic sense, and the privilege which is denoted
by it as consisting, not in the acquittal and acceptance of
a sinner, but in making him righteous by the infusion of
inherent personal holiness ; the *second* confounds Justification with the final sentence of the Judge at the last day,
as if it were not the present privilege of every believer ;
the *third* restricts Justification to pardon only, and leaves
acceptance and eternal life to depend on the personal
holiness and obedience of the believer. And there are
also several different methods in which the Protestant doctrine has been assailed,—namely, by attempting to show
that each of the leading terms,—'Justification,' 'Grace,'
'Faith,' 'Works,'—is susceptible of a different sense from
that which they severally bear in the theology of the
Reformation,—that Justification means sanctification, or
making righteous by a righteousness infused and inherent,
—that 'Grace' means, not the free favour of God, but the
inward operation and renewing power of His Spirit,—that
'Faith' is comprehensive of all the graces of the new
creature,—and that the 'Works' which are excluded from
Justification are either ceremonial observances merely, or
such as were done without grace, and before faith. The true
doctrine must be mainly determined by the import of these
terms as they are used by the sacred writers, and by their
explicit statements in regard to the nature, ground, and
method of a sinner's Justification ; while a strong collateral
proof may be derived from the demands of the law, which

is the rule of righteousness,—from the nature of Justification by works under the first covenant of life,—from the
change in his relation to God which must take place when
a condemned sinner is pardoned and accepted of Him,—
and from the connection which is revealed in Scripture
as subsisting between the Justification of sinners and the
redeeming work of Christ.   All these topics will demand
our consideration, each in its own order, as we advance,
step by step, to our ultimate conclusion.

LECTURE X.

JUSTIFICATION; ITS RELATION TO THE LAW AND JUSTICE OF GOD.

IT may be safely affirmed that almost all the errors, which have prevailed on the subject of Justification, may be traced ultimately to erroneous, or defective, views of the Law and Justice of God. His Law has either been supposed to be mutable and variable, so as to admit of being relaxed and modified,—as if its preceptive and penal requirements had no necessary connection with the demands of His eternal Justice; or, it has been set aside altogether, as if its claims might be superseded by the divine prerogative of mercy, and as if a sinner could be pardoned and accepted without any provision being made for its fulfilment. It is the more necessary to consider Justification in its relation to the Law and Justice of God, because erroneous or defective views on this point, have been the chief source, not only of many speculative errors, but also of that practical unconcern,—that false peace and carnal security,—which prevails so extensively both in the Church and the world ; and which springs, not from faith in the Gospel message, but from unbelief in the divine Law. For this reason, as well as from its close connection with the work of Christ, in fulfilling the Law, and satisfying the Justice of God, this topic is one of fundamental importance.

PROP. VI. As Justification is a forensic, legal, or

judicial term, so that which is denoted by it must necessarily have some relation to the Law and Justice of God.

The truth of this proposition, in so far as it relates to
the Justification of innocent and holy beings in a state of
probation and trial, can scarcely be denied by any one who
believes in a righteous moral government. The Law of
God, in whatever way it was made known to them, was
the rule of His moral government, and consequently the
ground of His judicial sentence in regard to them; and
His Law being a revelation of His essential and eternal
character as a righteous Governor and Judge, His Justice
can neither condemn any who are not guilty, nor accept
any who are not righteous. To be accepted as righteous
in His sight, every subject of that law must have a righteousness answerable to its requirements; for, if it be true
that where 'there is no law there is no transgression,' it
is equally true that where there is no law, there is no
'righteousness;' and if 'sin is not imputed, where there is
no law,' neither can righteousness be imputed without
reference to its requirements. The rule in both cases is
the same,—and righteousness is nothing else than conformity to the Law, while sin is any want of conformity
to it. That Law, considered as the rule of His moral
government, requires perfect obedience; and as partial
compliance with it is inadmissible, so it is impossible, from
its very nature, that there can be any neutral character,—
which is neither godly nor ungodly,—neither righteous
nor wicked,—neither innocent nor guilty,—neither justified nor condemned.

Such being the nature of God's Law,—and that Law
being an expression of His Justice,—it follows, that Justification must necessarily have some relation to both. In
the case of the innocent, Justification would have consisted
in the recognition and acceptance of a righteousness, per-

sonal and inherent, and amounting to a perfect conformity
to the divine Law ; in the case of the sinful, Justification,
—if it be possible at all,—must still have some relation to
the Law and Justice of God ; since it includes the pardon
of sin, which reverses the sentence of condemnation ; and
the acceptance of the sinner as righteous, which implies
some standard of righteousness as the rule of the divine
procedure.   What that righteousness is, or can be, in the
case of the guilty, is the great problem which is solved
only by the Gospel of Christ. (1)

PROP. VII. The rule of Justification, as revealed to
man in his state of original righteousness, was the Law of
God in the form of a divine covenant of life.

There is a difference between the Moral Law, or the
Law of Nature, considered simply as such, and the first
revealed covenant of life : for although this covenant presupposed that law, and was founded upon it, the one cannot be identified, in all respects, with the other.   The
Moral Law, considered simply as the law of man's nature,
was a rule of duty, which prohibited all sin, and required
perfect obedience ; and, considered as the instrument of
God's righteous government, it necessarily implied the
sanctions of reward and punishment, for these are the
indispensable conditions of all government, and without
them any rule of obedience would have been a mere exhortation or advice, rather than a formal law.   But a
Moral Law, however perfect, and although armed with
the sanctions of reward and punishment, is not necessarily
a covenant of life.   It could only denounce punishment
in the event of disobedience, and secure entire exemption
from punishment, with such blessings as might be connected with obedience, while man continued in a state of
holy innocence ; but, considered simply as a law, or an

instrument of government, it could give no assurance, either that he would continue in that state, or that, by continuing in it, he would ever become a confirmed heir of eternal life. Man might be naturally immortal, as a being destined,—not by the necessity of his nature, but by the sovereign appointment of God,—to an eternal existence; and yet as a subject of His government, the law under which he was placed could give him no assurance, that he would persevere in obedience, either in time or in eternity, so as to be exempt from its penalties, and entitled to an everlasting reward. The tenure by which life should be held, and the conditions of a holy and happy immortality, could not be discovered by the mere light of nature, even in a state of pristine innocence; and could only be made known by a revelation of God's sovereign will.

We find, accordingly, that this precise point was one of the earliest subjects of divine revelation. God is said to have promulgated a positive command, as the test of man's obedience; and to have annexed to it the threatening of death, in the event of transgression, with the promise of eternal life, which was signified and sealed by its sacramental symbol—'the tree of life'—in the event of his continued obedience during the term of his probation. The threatening, in the one case, included the whole penalty of sin; and the promise, in the other, the whole reward of obedience : and both had reference to the same life which Adam then possessed, as having been created 'in the image and likeness' of God. The penalty might contain many distinct privations and sufferings; but the worst part of it, and that which embittered every other, was the curse of God,—the instant forfeiture of His favour, and the inevitable subjection to His wrath. The promise might comprehend many distinct benefits, temporal, spi-

ritual, and eternal; but the best part of it, and that which
sweetened every other, was the blessing of God,—the
enjoyment of 'His favour, which is life, and of His loving-
kindness, which is better than life.'

By the addition of a positive appointment as a test
of man's obedience to God as the supreme Lawgiver,
Governor, and Judge, whose will man was bound to obey
by the law of his moral nature, that law was converted
into a divine covenant of life.   It was not, like many covenants between man and man, a mutual agreement between
equal and independent parties,—for this had been at variance with the rightful supremacy of God, and the dutiful
subjection of the creature; it was a constitution authoritatively imposed, as a test of man's obedience: for 'the
Lord God commanded the man, saying, Of every tree of
the garden thou mayest freely eat'—including 'the tree
of life in the midst of the garden,' which was the symbol
and sacrament of His covenant promise,—' but of the tree
of the knowledge of good and evil, thou shalt not eat of
it: for in the day thou eatest thereof thou shalt surely
die.'   And yet it was more than a mere law; it was a law
in the form of a covenant.   In the words of Bishop Hopkins, 'If God had only said, "Do this," without adding,
"Thou shalt live," this had not been a covenant, but a
law; and if He had only said, "Thou shalt live," without
commanding, "Do this," it had not been a covenant, but
a promise.   Remove the condition, and you make it a
simple promise; remove the promise, and you make it
an absolute law: but, both these being found in it, it is
both a law and a covenant.'   In this form, the law continued to be binding on man by its precept, but God
condescended, also, to bind Himself by His promise, and
became, in the expressive words of Boston, 'debtor to
His own faithfulness' to make that promise good.   A

new element was thus introduced into man's relation to God : he was still a creature dependent on the power, and subject to the law, of his Creator; but he was now advanced to be a 'confederate' with Him, and, as long as he continued to obey, could look to Him as his covenant God.

But there is a wider difference still between the Moral Law, considered simply as the law of man's nature, and the law in its positive form, as a divine covenant of life. The law, as it was originally inscribed on the moral nature of man, was a PERSONAL rule of duty,—it laid an obligation on each individual singly,—and held him responsible only for himself; but the law, as it was subsequently promulgated in the form of a divine covenant, was a GENERIC constitution, imposed by supreme authority on the first father of the human race, as the representative of his posterity,—and extending far beyond his individual interests, so as to affect the character and condition even of his remotest descendant.   He was constituted, by divine appointment, the trustee for the whole race which should spring from him; and was placed in the deeply responsible position of their covenant head, and legal representative.   He was a party to the covenant, not simply as a private individual, acting for himself alone, but as a public person, invested with an official character, and acting also for others.   He could not have assumed this office, or acted in this capacity, of his own will; he must have been constituted the legal representative of his posterity by the same supreme will, which enacted the law under which he was placed.

The fact of this federal arrangement is revealed,—the reason of it must be resolved ultimately into the sovereign will, and supreme wisdom, of the Most High.   His absolute supremacy, as the Creator and Lawgiver of the universe, is necessarily implied in His 'eternal power and

Godhead ;' and, while we may rest assured that it will
ever be exercised in accordance with His holiness, justice,
goodness, and truth, we are utterly incompetent to determine what methods might be adopted by His omniscient
wisdom, either for the creation, or for the government of
His subjects, in the different parts of His universal
empire. His sovereignty was displayed in the work of
Creation. He constituted different orders of being,—
inanimate, living, sentient, animal, intellectual, moral
and responsible,—and endowed them with their several
properties and powers. But besides this, He brought
them into being in different ways ; and the constitution,
under which they were respectively placed, was adapted
to the method of their creation. Several classes, for
example, of intellectual, self-conscious, moral, and responsible, creatures were brought into being, such as
angels and men. But all angels were brought into
being individually, as our first parent was, by the
direct exercise of creative power ; there was, in their
case, no birth, no hereditary descent, no paternal or
filial relation, for 'they neither marry, nor are given
in marriage ;' whereas, in the creation of man, God
called into being a single pair, and made them the
natural root of the race which should spring from
them ; He placed them under a family constitution, and
called their descendants into being mediately through
them. There was a radical difference, therefore, between
the angelic hosts, and the human race, in respect to the
position in which individuals, belonging to each of them,
were severally placed, and the relations which they
sustained to one another : in the one, every individual
was directly created,—connected with others by a common nature, and placed in social relations with them,
—but not derived from any created being, and not

dependent on any, as a child must be on his parents;
—in the other, every individual is created mediately,—
brought into being in a state of helpless infancy,—committed in trust for years to parental care,—dependent for
his life, and health, and comfort on domestic aid,—
endowed with faculties which are slowly developed,
under the influence of instruction and example,—and
liable, therefore, to be largely influenced, for good or
evil, by the condition and character of those with whom
he is so necessarily and closely related. Such was the
radical difference between angels and men in respect to
the natural constitution under which they were severally
placed,—and there was a corresponding difference between
them in respect to the law which was imposed upon them,
as moral and responsible beings. The law, as prescribed
to angels, was personal, and recognised only individual
responsibility; for however they might be connected
by social relations, or even subordinated, one rank to
another, as ' principalities and powers,' in a hierarchical
government,—and however they might be liable, in consequence, to the influence of each other's example,—they
were so far independent that each stood or fell for himself
according to his own conduct; and both those who 'kept,'
and those who ' left,' their first estate, did so by their own
voluntary act, and not by the act of any legal representative. Such a law was suitable to the condition of moral
and responsible beings, created directly each by himself,
and probably, like our first parent, in the full maturity
of his powers. But the law, as prescribed to man, was
generic, and recognised representative, as well as individual, responsibility: for while, as it was the law of
man's moral nature, it required—and must always continue to require—personal obedience, on the part of every
individual as soon as he is capable of moral agency,—yet

as a revealed covenant of life, it was imposed on Adam as the representative of his race, and made them dependent, for good or evil, on his conduct as their federal head.

Thoughtful men, considering the actual condition of the human race,—the universal and constant prevalence of moral and physical evil,—the certainty that every child born into the world will sin as soon as he is capable of sinning,—the sufferings which are entailed upon him by his birth,—and above all, the inevitable doom of death, have felt that it is difficult, if not impossible, to account for these facts occurring under the moral government of God, by referring them to any mere personal law, such as implies only individual responsibility; and that their minds were relieved, rather than oppressed, by being told of a generic law, which was imposed on the father of the human race as the legal representative of his posterity, and which warrants them in regarding all their hereditary evils as judicial penalties on account of his actual sin, and not as capricious or arbitrary inflictions proceeding from mere sovereignty. So strongly has this been felt, that some, who have rejected the doctrine of federal representation and imputed guilt, have been compelled to acknowledge that the actual state of men, under the moral government of God, cannot be satisfactorily accounted for except on the supposition of 'a forfeiture prior to birth,' and to take refuge, as the only way of evading that doctrine, in the theory of a state of pre-existence, in which every man sinned and fell by his own personal disobedience. But if there be no scriptural evidence for this theory, the actual condition of the race can only be accounted for,—either by their relation to Adam as their natural root,—or by their relation to him also as their legal representative,—or to both these relations combined; for the latter is not exclusive, but comprehensive, of the former. Had Adam been created merely as the natural root of his posterity, and not constituted also their legal representative, many evils might, or rather must, have flowed from his sin, to all his descendants, in the way of mere natural consequence, by reason of their hereditary connection with him; for his immediate offspring were dependent on him, and their children again on them, both for instruction and example; but some of the consequences of his fall cannot be accounted for at all,—such as the universal and irrevocable sentence of death,—and none of them can be accounted for so satisfactorily,—except on the supposition that, besides being their natural root, he was also their federal head. And this supposition is in evident accordance with the *analogy* of the constitution of nature: for if God manifested His sovereignty in creating angels individually 'without father, without mother, without descent,' and placing them under a personal law, adapted to this constitution, and recognising only individual responsibility; and if He also manifested His sovereignty in creating Adam as the root of a race which should spring from him, and placing him, as their representative, under a generic law, adapted to the family constitution, and recognising representative as well as individual agency,—in either case, the legal is adapted to the natural constitution; and there is such an analogy between the two, as serves to make the former credible, by reason of the undeniable certainty of the latter. (2)

Prop. VIII. The breach of the Law in its covenant form by the sin of our first parents, rendered it for ever impossible that either they, or any of their descendants, should be justified on the ground of their personal righteousness.

If Adam was the legal representative and federal
head of the race, then all its members 'sinned in him,'
as such, 'and fell with him in his first transgression ;'
and they were involved along with him in the guilt which
he had incurred, and the condemnation which he had
deserved.   This is necessarily implied in the fact, that, by
sovereign divine appointment, he acted *for* them, and was
dealt with as *one* with them, so that, according to his
obedience or disobedience, they, as well as he, should be
accepted, or rejected, of God.   The direct imputation of the
guilt of his first sin to all his descendants is necessarily
involved in the public character which he sustained as
their representative ; and it is confirmed by the consideration that the penal consequences of his transgression have
been entailed on every generation of his race.   It does
not imply that they committed the sin, or that they were
personally accessory to it ; for the transgression, considered as an actual sin, was his, and his only ; but it
was committed by him as their legal representative, and
the guilt of it is theirs simply as they were represented by
him.   If representative, as distinct from personal, agency,
be admissible at all under the divine government,—if it
was expressly recognised in the first covenant of life,—
and if it be also recognised in the new and better
covenant, the covenant of grace,—then we reach the
great general principle, that both righteousness, and guilt,
may be imputed to others on account of the obedience,
or disobedience, of those by whom they were severally
represented.   But the principle does not imply, in either
case, that the obedience was personally rendered, or the
sin actually committed, by those to whom they are
respectively imputed ; for this were to overlook the fundamental difference between personal, and representative,
action.

The direct imputation of the guilt of Adam's first sin to his descendants is not necessarily exclusive of their personal guilt, as individuals. The doctrine of mediate imputation, as taught by Placæus and Stapfer, is erroneous in its negative, rather than its positive part,—in what it denies, rather than in what it affirms. It denies the direct imputation of the guilt of Adam's first sin, and thus virtually sets aside his representative character; for if he acted as their representative, his conduct must directly affect the condition of all who were related to him, as such, under the covenant: but it affirms the imputation of personal guilt, arising from inherent depravity or actual transgression, and in this respect it teaches a solemn and momentous truth. For the direct imputation of the guilt of Adam's first sin is not exclusive of the additional charge of personal guilt in the case of every individual of his race; and it is of the utmost practical consequence that this fact should be distinctly realized. For the doctrine which affirms that 'God visits the iniquities of the fathers upon their children' has often been perverted and abused, and even applied as an opiate to soothe the conscience into a deep slumber, which may prove to be the sleep of death. We find, for example, two of the prophets expostulating with the Jews at Babylon on account of their sinful perversion of that doctrine: 'What mean ye, that ye use this proverb concerning the land of Israel, saying, The fathers have eaten sour grapes, and the children's teeth are set on edge? As I live, saith the Lord God, ye shall not have occasion any more to use this proverb in Israel. Behold, all souls are mine; as the soul of the father, so also the soul of the son, is mine: the soul that sinneth, it shall die.' This, and the corresponding statement of Jeremiah,[1] have often been urged as a

[1] Ezek. xviii. 1 ; Jer. xxx. 29.

scriptural argument against the doctrine of original sin; for
although there is an important difference between the relation which Adam sustained to his posterity as their legal
representative or covenant head, and that which other
parents bear to their children, yet the general principle
of individual responsibility which is so clearly announced
when it is said, 'The soul that sinneth, it shall die,' is
equally applicable, it has been said, to both cases, and is
sufficient to set aside the whole doctrine of hereditary
guilt, and inherited suffering.   But neither of the prophets meant to deny that the Jews in their capacity
suffered in consequence, and on account, of the sins of
their fathers; what they meant to teach was, that they
did not suffer on account *only* of their fathers' sins,—that
if their captivity was brought on them, as they knew it
had been, by the guilt of their rulers and people in the
land of Israel, it was prolonged by their own continued
impenitence and rebellion in Babylon,—and that as soon
as they repented and returned to the Lord with their
whole heart, He would remember no more against them
either their fathers' sins or their own, but 'receive them
graciously, and love them freely.'   It is expressly said
that they did suffer partly on account of their fathers'
sins;[1] and in the Decalogue itself, God had revealed Himself as 'a jealous God, visiting the iniquity of the fathers
upon the children unto the third and fourth generation of
them that *hate me.*'[2]   But they had not duly considered
these last words; they imagined that they suffered *only*
because of their fathers' sins, and were unmindful of their
own; and the prophets were sent to remind them of both,
that by godly repentance they might be graciously restored.   And it is deeply interesting to mark that both

[1] 2 Kings xxi. 9, 16, xxiii. 26; Jer. xv. 4; 2 Chron. xxxiii. 9.
[2] Ex. xx. 5.

are included in the confessions and prayers of those among
them who were suitably impressed and affected by the
prophet's message: 'Our fathers have sinned and are not,
and we have borne *their* iniquities.' 'The crown is fallen
from *our* head: woe unto us, that *we* have sinned.' 'Turn
thou us unto Thee, O Lord! and we shall be turned;
renew our days as of old.'[1]　A similar perversion may be,
and has been, made of the doctrine of original sin, as if
we suffered only on account of Adam's guilt, and not also
on account of our personal depravity and disobedience;
and it is the more important to counteract this fatal error,
because it is chiefly by the consciousness of his own inherent depravity, and the conviction of his actual transgressions, that a sinner is first impressed, as by that which
is nearest to him, with a sense of his fallen and ruined
condition, and is thereafter led up, like David, to the consideration of his birth-sin, saying first, 'I acknowledge
my transgressions, and my sin is ever before me; against
Thee, Thee only, have I sinned, and done this evil in Thy
sight;' and then, but scarcely till then, 'Behold, I was
shapen in iniquity; and in sin did my mother conceive
me.'[2]

There can scarcely be a greater or more dangerous
error than to suppose that the guilt of Adam's first sin is
the only guilt with which we are chargeable, or that it is
exclusive of the personal guilt of individuals. Such an
idea could only be entertained on one, or other, of these
two suppositions,—either, that there is no law to which
man is now subject,—or, that there is no want of conformity to that law, and no transgression of it. But the
doctrine of Scripture, while it affirms the direct imputation of the guilt of Adam's *first* transgression to his posterity,—and of that *only*, for he was their representative

_____
[1] Lam. v. 7, 16, 21.　　　　　[2] Ps. li. 3-5.

with reference merely to the one precept of the covenant,
—affirms also the transmission of hereditary depravity,
arising from his loss of original righteousness, and the
corruption of his whole nature by sin.   It follows that, as
sinners, neither Adam, nor any of his descendants, could
ever be justified on the ground of their personal obedience.
This is self-evident so far as their Justification depended
on the Law in its covenant form ; for by breaking its
precept, Adam forfeited its promise, and incurred its
penalty for himself, and for all whom he represented ;
and this conclusion is so inevitable, that it can only be
evaded by denying, as some have been bold enough to
deny, his representative character altogether.   It is equally
certain that, in so far as their Justification might be supposed to depend on the Law as a permanent rule of duty,
which continued to be binding on him and all his descendants after the fall, they could not be justified on the
ground of their personal obedience to it ; for, besides
being already subject to the penalty of the broken covenant, the corruption of their nature which immediately
ensued, made it certain that they would individually contract fresh guilt, and be for ever incapable of fulfilling the
righteousness which the Law required.   It is the nature
of the tree that determines the quality of its fruit,
although the quality of its fruit may be an evidence ot
the nature of the tree.   But if all men are born in the
image of their fallen parent,—if 'that which is born of
the flesh is flesh,' and if 'he that is in the flesh cannot
please God,'—it follows that 'no man since the fall can
perfectly keep the commandments of God, but doth daily
break them in thought, word, and deed ;' and consequently
that no man can be justified by his personal obedience
to that law, simply because 'the law is weak through
the flesh,' or fallen state of man,—and although it was

originally 'ordained unto life,' is now 'found to be unto death.'   There is something that ' the law cannot do ' (τὸ ἀδύνατον τοῦ νομοῦ)—*it cannot justify a sinner;* 'it condemns sin in the flesh,'[1] and is no longer 'the ministration of righteousness,' but has become, through sin, 'the ministration of condemnation.'   It thus appears that, whether the Law be considered as the original covenant of life, or as a permanent rule of duty, the breach of it rendered it for ever impossible that any man should ever be justified on the ground of his personal righteousness.

This conclusion can only be evaded on one, or other, of these two suppositions,—either that the law of God has been abrogated altogether, so as to be no longer binding, —or that it has been so modified and relaxed, as no longer to require perfect obedience, but to admit of our being justified on easier terms.   There is a third supposition, indeed, but it is so untenable that no man with a conscience in his breast can entertain or defend it,—namely, that the law is still binding as a rule of perfect obedience, and that men are able to fulfil it.   To those, if there be any, who are willing to take this ground, the Lord Himself has said, 'This do, and thou shalt live.'   But He also said, 'The whole have no need of a physician, but they that are sick;' and that 'He came to call, not the righteous, but sinners to repentance.'   If there were any 'just men who need no repentance,' they would be beyond the range of His commission, for 'He was not sent but to the lost sheep of the house of Israel.'   But discarding this supposition as unworthy of a moment's notice in a world of universal ungodliness and sin,—and looking only to the other alternatives, shall we say that the law of God has been abrogated?   Then all duty has been abolished along with it,—our duty to God, our duty to men, our duty to

[1] 2 Cor. iii. 7.

ourselves; sin has disappeared, and even the possibility of
sin has been annihilated,—for 'where there is no law,
there is no transgression;' we are no longer the subjects
of a moral government,—for where there is no law, there
can be no reward or punishment; and even the voice of
conscience, to which every man is compelled to listen, and
by which he is made to feel that 'he is a law to himself,'
is a mere chimera or illusion. Better far to be condemned
by a righteous law, which, like God Himself, is 'holy, and
just, and good,' than to live in a lawless world, or in universal anarchy!

But if the law of God has not been, and never can be,
entirely abrogated, may it not be, and has it not been,
modified and relaxed? This question has been answered
in the affirmative by two distinct parties,—*first*, by some
who hold that in the case of men who are unable, either
from their natural infirmity, or the corruption of their
nature by sin, to fulfil it, it must necessarily be accommo-
dated to their weakness, and cannot reasonably require
perfect obedience; and *secondly*, by others, who affirm
that one object for which Christ came into the world was
to procure for us a new law, or easier terms of acceptance
with God, so as to supersede the perfect obedience which
the original law required, and to substitute for it imperfect obedience, if it be only sincere, as the immediate
ground of our Justification. These are distinct positions,
and they rest, in some respects, on different grounds.

Those who speak of the law of God being modified or
relaxed, in accommodation to the present infirm and depraved state of human nature, must be held to proceed on
a general principle, applicable to all orders of moral and
responsible creatures, angels as well as men, and amounting, in substance, to this,—that wherever, and from whatever cause, they have become depraved, their inability or

unwillingness to render due obedience, must relieve them, in proportion to the extent in which they prevail, from the obligations of duty, and deprive God Himself of the right to require it. From such a principle it would follow, that His law can no longer be regarded as a fixed rule of righteousness, or an invariable test of sin, but only as a sliding scale of duty, whose requirements would become less in proportion as wickedness increased; and that while holy angels, and the spirits of just men made perfect, are 'not without law to God,' but bound to love and obey Him 'with their whole hearts,' evil spirits and wicked men, whose minds are filled with 'enmity against God,' would be relieved, by that very enmity which makes them unable or unwilling to serve Him, from all obligation to do so. That principle, consistently carried out to the full extent of its legitimate application, leads inevitably to this conclusion,—that the more wicked any creature becomes, the more must the law be relaxed in accommodation to his inability to comply with it, until he reaches a point at which he ceases to be a moral and responsible agent at all. The law of God is not thus dependent on the will of the creature, nor can its requirements be relaxed by the increasing power of sin.

Some, however, speak of the law of God as having been relaxed and modified in consequence of the incarnation, sufferings, and death, of Christ, so as no longer to require perfect obedience, but to accept such as is imperfect, provided it be sincere. But here several questions arise, to which distinct and definite answers may be reasonably expected from those who make our eternal welfare to depend on our obedience to this relaxed law. Where is it revealed in Scripture that Christ became incarnate, suffered, and died upon the Cross,—not to fulfil the law, but to alter it,—not to 'magnify the law and make it honourable,' but to modify its demands, and supersede it by a new law with easier conditions? Besides, what is that new law? What does it require? What does it forbid? What are its sanctions? Is it possible, in the nature of things, that any law can require less than perfect obedience, at least, to itself? Why, then, is the obedience which is required said to be imperfect? Is it imperfect with reference to the old law only, or also to the new? If it be imperfect with reference to the former, is there no sin in that imperfection? If it be imperfect with reference even to the latter, how can it justify according to the rule of that law? What is the sincerity which is connected with this imperfect obedience? Is it more perfect than the obedience which springs from it? Does the new law require any definite amount of obedience? And if not, what is the graduated scale of duty, and what is its *minimum?* If the original law required perfect obedience, could it be abrogated, or even relaxed, otherwise than by God's authority? If it was not abrogated, but republished, at Sinai, was it relaxed by Christ, when He repeated it, saying, ' Thou shalt love the Lord thy God with all thine heart, and thou shalt love thy neighbour as thyself,—for on these two commandments hang all the law and the prophets,' or when He expounded its spiritual meaning in His sermon on the mount? Did He come to abrogate, or relax, that eternal rule of righteousness, of which He said,—' I am not come to destroy the law and the prophets, but to fulfil,'— ' Heaven and earth shall pass away, but one jot or one tittle shall in no wise pass from the law till all be fulfilled?' Or did His Apostles exceed their commission when they said, ' Do we then make void the law through faith? God forbid! yea, we establish the law?' (3)

It is true that the graces and duties of believers,

although imperfect, are 'acceptable to God,' but only
'*through Jesus Christ;*' they are the fruits of His Holy
Spirit, but they are not in themselves, during the present
life, an adequate fulfilment of any law, whether old or
new; and they fall so far short of perfection, while they
are so defiled by remaining sin, that they are but as
'filthy rags' when compared with the righteousness which
the law requires.   They cannot, therefore, constitute a
justifying righteousness, and must themselves be accepted
through the atoning sacrifice and perfect obedience of
Christ.   So far from relying on them as the ground of
their acceptance, believers renounce them altogether, and
repair continually 'to the fountain which has been opened
for sin and for uncleanness;' and it is a sense of the
imperfection of their obedience, arising from the constant
presence and remaining power of indwelling sin, that
imbues them, more and more as they advance in the
divine life, with a 'broken and a contrite spirit,' and
deepens their consciousness of personal unworthiness.
For believing the divine law in all its perfection to be
still binding on them as a rule of duty, even when they
have been delivered from it as a covenant of works, and
comparing its pure and spiritual requirements with all the
obedience which they have ever been able to render, they
are more and more deeply convinced of their own sinfulness, and their absolute dependence on the grace of God,
and the righteousness of Christ.   For, in the words of
Archdeacon Hare, 'they who have ever had a deep
spiritual conviction of sin, and of their own sinfulness,
retain that conviction to the end.   Their growth in holiness does not stifle it, but on the contrary renders it
livelier and more piercing; and thus, ascending step by
step, we come to that singular phenomenon, that the
holiest men would be the most oppressed by the convic-

tion of their sinfulness, were it not for their conviction of
Christ's righteousness, of which they become partakers
through faith, incorporating them as living members in
His body; and through which, being "clothed upon" by
it, they may humbly hope to stand in the presence of
God.' (4)   This gracious frame of mind,—this 'broken and
contrite spirit,'—this growing humility and self-abasement,
is one of the most characteristic marks of a true believer,
and it is fostered by an abiding sense of the spirituality
and perfection of the divine law; but could it exist, or
would it not be supplanted by a very different feeling,
were that law supposed to be so relaxed and modified, as
to admit of our personal obedience to it being the ground
of our Justification in the sight of God?

PROP. IX.   The law of God, which is the rule of
man's duty, is also a revelation of God's eternal Justice
and Holiness.

Men talk lightly of His law being abrogated, modified,
or relaxed, not considering that, besides being an authoritative expression of His supreme will, it is also a revelation
of His essential nature, as the Holy One and the Just,
and the rule of His universal empire, as the Governor
and Judge of all.   It is not the mere product of what
Cudworth called 'arbitrary will omnipotent;' His will is
determined by the infinite perfections of His character,
and His character is the real ultimate standard of 'eternal
and immutable morality.'   His positive precepts may be
resolved into the sovereignty of His will, regulated in its
exercise by His omniscient wisdom; and these may be
imposed, abrogated, or modified, according to His mere
good pleasure; but His moral law, while it is an expression of His will, is also the image and reflection of His own
moral perfection.   God is 'holy, and just, and good;' and

therefore His law also 'is holy, and the commandment
holy, and just, and good.' 'Be ye holy,'—this is the voice
of His law, the expression of His supreme will : 'for I
am holy,'[1]—this is the ground or reason of that law, and
it is derived from His essential and unchangeable nature.
'The Lord is righteous in all His ways, and holy in all
His works ;' and, therefore, 'the righteous Lord loveth
righteousness,' but 'He is of purer eyes than to behold
evil, and cannot look on iniquity.'[2]   God is holy, and the
law of the universe is 'holiness to the Lord ;' God is just,
and the law of the universe is 'justice ;' God is true, and
the law of the universe is 'truth ;' God is love, and the
law of the universe is 'love.'   It reveals what He is, and
what His creatures *ought* to be.   Its precept requires obedience as a *duty*, or as what is *due* to Him, and its threatening declares punishment to be the *desert*, or the 'wages,'
of sin.   His law can never require more or less, either of
obedience or of punishment, than is just and right ; for 'a
God of truth, and without iniquity, just and right is He.'[3]
To suppose that it ever required more than was due, or
threatened more than could be justly inflicted, would be
derogatory to all His attributes—His wisdom, His holiness, His justice, His goodness, and His truth.   It cannot,
therefore, be modified or relaxed, since these perfections
are unchangeable ; and it cannot be abrogated, unless His
moral government is to be abolished altogether.

The Moral Law,—considered as the rule of His government, and also as a revelation of His character,—must, still
further, be viewed in connection with what is declared to
be His great ultimate end in all His works,—the manifestation of His own glory by the actual exercise of all
His perfections.   He reveals His character in the Law ;

---

[1] 1 Pet. i. 15, 16 ; also, Lev. xix. 2, xx. 7, xxi. 8.
[2] Ps. cxlv. 17, xi. 7 ; Hab. i. 13.   [3] Deut. xxxii. 4.

but it is the constant administration of that Law in His providence,—the application of it even to the works of Grace and Redemption,—and the final execution of it in the work of Judgment,—by which He will be most signally glorified. He has made Himself known by a series of divine revelations ; but these are to be followed up by a series of divine works, in which the unchangeable perfections of His nature, on which His Law is founded, will be manifested in their actual exercise, according to the tenor of that Law. The fulfilment of His promises, and the execution of His threatenings, seem to be equally necessary for this end. The non-fulfilment of the one, or the non-execution of the other, would be derogatory to the honour of His Law, and to the glory of His perfections, which it was designed to reveal. In the exercise of His sovereignty, He may form a purpose of mercy towards the guilty ; but in carrying that purpose into effect, some provision is necessary, such as His own omniscient wisdom alone could devise, and His own infinite love suggest, for vindicating the majesty of His Law, and securing the ends of His moral government. If punishment was justly due to sin, and if it was ordained as a manifestation of His eternal justice and holiness, it must either be inflicted on every sinner with a view to that end, or the same end must be equally, or better, accomplished in some other way.

It thus appears that the Law, besides being an authoritative expression of God's will, is also a revelation of His eternal justice and holiness,—that it is the unchange-able rule of His moral government,—and that, however it may consist with a sovereign purpose of mercy towards sinners, it can never be abrogated, modified, or relaxed, but must be executed or fulfilled, in such a way as shall manifest, in their actual exercise, the same divine per-

fections which it was designed to reveal, and secure the
end of punishment itself—the glory of His great Name. (5)

PROP. X. The doctrine of the Law is presupposed in
that of the Gospel, and the justifying righteousness which
is required in the one, is revealed in the other.

That the doctrine of the Law is presupposed in that
of the Gospel, has been already shown; and that the
justifying righteousness which the Law requires has been
revealed in the Gospel, will be proved hereafter, in dis-
cussing the questions which still remain to be determined,
—namely, What that righteousness is, which is revealed
as 'the righteousness of God?' How, and by whom, it
was wrought out? Why it is available for our Justification? By what means we become partakers of it? And
by what agency it is effectually applied? In the meantime, the proposition is merely stated for the purpose of
indicating, in the first place, the indissoluble connection,
and yet the radical difference also, between the Law and
the Gospel; and, in the second place, the indispensable
necessity of a careful study of the one, in order to a right
apprehension of the other.

LECTURE XI.

JUSTIFICATION; ITS RELATION TO THE MEDIATORIAL WORK OF CHRIST.

THAT the Mediatorial work of Christ has some relation to the Law of God,—and that our Justification has, also, some relation to the work of Christ,—are truths so evident from every part of Scripture, that they are universally admitted by those who acknowledge its authority in matters of faith. Popish, Pelagian, Arian, Socinian, Arminian, Neonomian, and Antinomian, writers are all agreed in affirming that Christ's work was a work of obedience to God's Law; and that our Justification is, in some way or other, founded upon it, or connected with it. But they differ from one another, as soon as they proceed to explain the sense in which these truths are understood by them respectively. It is not sufficient, therefore, to lay down the general statement,—that the Mediatorial work of Christ had some relation to the Law of God—that our Justification is, in some sense, dependent on His work—and that, through His work, it is connected, in some way, with the original rule of righteousness; for that statement, although true, so far as it goes, does not bring out the whole truth which is clearly revealed in Scripture; and the nature of the relation which subsists between Christ's work and the Law, on the one hand, and between our Justification and His work, on the other, must be explained in several distinct propositions, and established by scriptural proofs.

PROP. XI.   It was God's eternal purpose to overrule
the fall of man for His own glory, by a signal manifestation of all His moral perfections, in justifying 'the ungodly,' through Christ as Mediator.

We read in Scripture of 'the eternal purpose which
He purposed in Christ Jesus our Lord,' of 'the mystery of
His will, according to His good pleasure, which He hath
purposed in Himself,' and of 'the purpose of Him, who
worketh all things after the counsel of His own will.'[1]
That purpose, and the whole plan of salvation which
flowed from it, had its origin in 'the riches of His
grace,' and its end in 'the praise of the glory of His
grace,' 'wherein He hath abounded towards us in all
wisdom and prudence.' It was not a mere purpose of
mercy; it was a purpose of mercy 'in Christ Jesus;'
and through Him it was to be carried into effect.   It was
formed in the eternal councils of the Godhead before the
world was; and the fall itself, which was foreseen, was
permitted to occur, that it might be overruled for the
accomplishment of this great design.   Each of the three
Persons in the Godhead,—the Father, the Son, and the
Holy Ghost,—concurred in it; and they are represented
as severally assuming distinct offices, and undertaking
different parts of the work, by which it was to be carried
into effect.

That work was to be a signal and unparalleled revelation of God, in two distinct respects; *first*, as it should be
the highest manifestation of His moral attributes, each in
its utmost perfection, and all acting in perfect harmony,
such as could not have been equally afforded, either by
the mere reward of the righteous, or the mere punishment of the wicked (1); and, *secondly*, as it should be
an effectual means of making Him known in His essential

[1] Eph. iii. 11, i. 9.

nature as the Triune Jehovah, through the medium of the
distinct operations which should be accomplished by the
three Divine Persons respectively. (2)

We further read, in various parts of Scripture, of an
eternal covenant between the Father and the Son. The
Father, representing the majesty, and exercising the pre-
rogatives, of the undivided Godhead, invested the Son with
the office of Mediator,—commissioned and consecrated
Him for His work,—sent Him forth as His Son, and
yet as His servant,—gave Him a people to be redeemed
and saved,—prescribed the conditions which He should
fulfil for that end,—and promised Him that 'He should
see of the travail of His soul, and be satisfied.' The Son
accepted the office of Mediator,—consented to act in
official subordination to the Father's will,—voluntarily
engaged to 'empty Himself,' and to veil His glory, 'the
glory which He had with the Father before the world
was,'—and undertook to become incarnate, to suffer, to
obey, and to die, for the accomplishment of His work.
Express mention is made of mutual stipulations,—of
precepts, and promises, addressed by the Father to the
Son, and of the Son's acquiescence in the one, and His
acceptance of the other; while these stipulations were the
terms of 'an everlasting covenant, ordered in all things and
sure,' of which Christ is expressly said to be the Mediator
($\mu\epsilon\sigma\acute{\iota}\tau\eta\varsigma$) and the surety ($\check{\epsilon}\gamma\gamma\nu o\varsigma$).[1] (3)

The terms of this eternal covenant, whatever they
were, determined the whole plan of man's salvation, and
regulated every one of its provisions. It contemplated
the end which was to be accomplished, and prescribed the
agency and the means by which it was to be carried into
effect. It provided for the incarnation, the sufferings,

---

[1] Heb. vii. 22, xii. 24 ; Gal. iii. 17 ; John vi. 38, xii. 49 ; Ps. lxxxix. 27, 28, 34 ;
Isa. liii. 10, 11 ; Ps. xl. 7, 8 ; John xiii. 4, 5, 24.

the death, the resurrection, and the exaltation of Christ; it equally provided for the saving efficacy of His work by the effectual application of His Holy Spirit; and every part of the plan, from first to last, must be traced up to the sovereign Will, and the free Grace, of God, as its original source.   That covenant was the spontaneous expression of the ' good pleasure of His goodness;' and much evil has arisen from confused or incorrect conceptions of it, as if the provision which it made for man's salvation, instead of being the fruit and manifestation, had been the procuring cause, of His love; whereas the covenant of Grace, and every provision which it contains, had its spring and fountainhead in His spontaneous loving-kindness and tender mercy.   'God so loved the world as to give His Son ;' and 'herein truly is love, not that we loved God, but that God loved us.'[1]   It was not the Mediatorial work of Christ that prompted the love of the Father, or that procured the covenant of redemption; it was the free sovereign purpose of God which originated the whole plan of man's salvation,—which ordained the end, and provided also the means for its accomplishment.   He appointed His own Son to the office of Mediator, and His people ' were chosen in Him before the foundation of the world ;'[2] they were 'given to Him' to be redeemed, renewed, sanctified, and saved; but neither His election, nor theirs, was procured by His sufferings and obedience; for it was prior to both in the order of nature, although it was not irrespective of them as the means, by which His eternal purpose should be fulfilled in time.   His purpose of grace could not be irrespective of the work of Christ, for it comprehended the means, not less than the end; but it was not originated by that work,—it was a free, spontaneous movement of mercy in

[1] John iii. 16 ; 1 John iv. 10.   [2] Eph. i. 4.

the divine mind, and His omniscient wisdom provided the way in which it should take effect, so as to illustrate all the perfections of His nature, and overrule the fall itself for the vindication and establishment of His righteous government.

Some deprive themselves of all the comfort which such a manifestation of divine love might be expected to impart, by entertaining a confused notion of the real relation which subsists between the work of Christ and the love of God, as if the one were the procuring cause, and not, as it really is, the fruit and manifestation of the other; while many more, going to the opposite extreme, are ready to conclude, that if God could form a purpose of grace towards sinners, and if He could give the highest expression and proof of His love in the gift of His own Son, there could be no necessity, and no room even, for any expiation of human guilt, or any satisfaction to divine justice. Both extremes are equally dangerous; the one derogates from the free grace of God, the other from the claims of His justice : and the grand design of the whole plan of salvation is to combine the two,—to manifest them in their actual exercise, and harmonious co-operation, for the accomplishment of the same end,—and so to ' declare the righteousness' of God, as that He may be seen to be both ' merciful and just to forgive us our sins, and to cleanse us from all unrighteousness.' Men are ever prone to take partial, one-sided views of the character of God, and to deduce erroneous conclusions from them. They imagine,—either that there can be no real love in the divine mind, if there be any *law-wrath*, or judicial displeasure, against sin ; or that there can be no serious wrath, and no strict adherence to justice, when love exists. The experience of every parent and magistrate on earth might be sufficient to dispel these gross delusions ; for the one, in dealing with a prodigal son, and the other, with a convicted criminal, may be conscious of a yearning love,—a tender compassion,—such as he finds it difficult to restrain; and yet feels, notwithstanding, that justice has its claims, and government its laws, which he must not disregard,—that the rights of authority ought to be maintained, even by the infliction of punishment, and at whatever sacrifice of personal feeling.   In such cases every one may see that justice is never more solemn, or more sure, than when it is purified from every feeling of personal malice or vindictiveness, and when its sentence is pronounced by an affectionate father, or by a benevolent and compassionate judge.   But what are all these human analogies, when compared with the union of love and justice in God's treatment of His 'only-begotten,' and 'well-beloved,' Son?   Christ was the object of His supreme complacency and delight, and never more than when He became 'obedient unto death, even the death of the cross;' for 'therefore doth my Father love me, because I lay down my life;'[1] and yet even such love did not supersede the claims of justice and law, for when He stood charged, not with personal, but imputed guilt, 'it pleased the Father to bruise Him;' 'He spared not His own Son;' 'He set him forth to be a propitiation;' 'He made His soul an offering for sin;' and this, too, when once and again the Saviour knelt down and prayed, saying, 'O my Father! if it be possible, let this cup pass from me.'[2]   Never was the union of infinite love with inflexible justice more signally displayed, and never was the nature, as well as the reality, of both more strikingly illustrated, than in the Cross of Christ. (4)

Such a marvellous combination of mercy and justice in the salvation of sinners, is peculiar to the scheme which

---

[1] John x. 17.   [2] Isa. liii. 10; Rom. viii. 32, iii. 25; Matt. xxvi. 39.

is revealed in the Gospel.   It had no place in the Justification of the righteous, such as the 'angels who kept
their first estate;' for they were accepted and confirmed
in everlasting holiness, according to the terms of that
law which they had obeyed : it had no place in the condemnation of fallen spirits; for they were dealt with
according to the rule of strict retributive justice.   But in
the case of every sinner who is saved from among men,
'mercy and truth are met together; righteousness and
peace have kissed each other.'[1]   The manifestation of all
the moral perfections of God in the work of man's salvation, attracts the astonishment and attention of the
heavenly host, for 'into these things the angels desire
to look.'[2]   It was designed for their instruction in some
of the highest lessons of heavenly wisdom, as well as for
the saving benefit of men; for 'God created all things
by Jesus Christ, to the intent that now, unto the principalities and powers in heavenly places, might be known
by the church the manifold wisdom of God, according to
the eternal purpose which He purposed in Christ Jesus
our Lord.'[3]   And the whole plan of salvation, which is
revealed in the Gospel, is simply the unfolding and the
execution of God's eternal purpose to overrule the fall of
man for His own glory, by a signal manifestation of all
His perfections, in the salvation of sinners through the
mediatorial work of Christ.

PROP. XII. Christ, as Mediator, was 'made under
law' as the substitute, representative, and surety, of His
people.

A scheme of mediation does not necessarily imply in
all cases the substitution of the Mediator in the room and
stead of either of the two parties between whom he inter-

---

[1] Ps. lxxxv. 10.   [2] 1 Pet. i. 12.   [3] Eph. iii. 10, 11.

poses. Had Christ been a mere prophet, sent from God
to instruct men in the knowledge of divine truth,—or
had He even received a divine commission to exercise
royal powers, to establish a spiritual kingdom in the
earth, and to rule over it as His delegated dominion,—
He might have fulfilled His mission as the representative
of God, without becoming also the substitute of men :
and it is in some such sense that Socinians speak of His
mediation. But it is not in this one-sided and partial
sense that He is said to be ' Mediator of the new covenant' in Scripture ; for He is not only a prophet sent
from God to instruct them, or a king commissioned by
God to rule over them, in His name,—He is also their
' high priest *in things pertaining to God ;*' and what He
did for them, Godwards, was the fundamental part of
His mediatorial work. There may be other methods of
mediation, more or less partial, in many conceivable cases ;
but He identified Himself with His people, and acted
towards God as their substitute and representative. His
legal liability on their account depended on His taking
their law-place, and becoming answerable for them at
the bar of divine justice : and as this is involved in the
kind of mediation which is ascribed to Him in Scripture,
so it is fully expressed when He is called ' the surety' or
' the sponsor' of the covenant ; for just as a cautioner
becomes the legal substitute of a debtor, and is liable for
the payment of whatever he undertakes to discharge,
Christ became surety for the debts of His people, when
they were bankrupt, and ' had nothing to pay.'

But, it has been asked, can there be any real substitution of one for another under a system of moral
government ? Does not the Law require personal obedience, and threaten personal punishment ? and must it
not, therefore, be exclusive of vicarious agency, whether

in the shape of obedience, or of suffering ? We answer, that the Law of God, in its covenant form, recognised from the first the principle of representation, by constituting Adam the federal head of his race ; and that it is only the transference of the same principle to a new relation, when the Gospel reveals the fact that Christ, as Mediator, was constituted the legal representative and surety of His people. The 'first Adam' gives place to the 'second Adam, the Lord from heaven ;' and, in either instance, the welfare of others is made to depend on them. For 'as by one man's disobedience many were made sinners ; so by the obedience of one shall many be made righteous.'[1] For as Adam was 'made under law,' the representative of his posterity ; so Christ was 'made under law,' the substitute of His people. 'God sent forth His Son, made of a woman, made under the law.'[2]

If the question be raised, Under what law ? the Apostle teaches us that it was the same which was binding on men,—the Moral Law as a covenant of works ; for He was 'made under the law, to redeem them that were under the law,'—and He 'hath redeemed us from the curse of the law, being made a curse for us.'[3] The law to which He became subject, was evidently the same with that under which His people had been previously placed. Some have attempted to evade the force of this evidence, by having recourse to a distinction between the Moral Law, which was incumbent on men, and the Mediatorial Law, which was imposed upon Christ ; and they have contended that He was subject only to the conditions or terms of the covenant of grace, but not to the requirements, whether preceptive or penal, of the covenant of works. This theory is subversive of the

[1] Rom. v. 19.   [2] Gal. iv. 4.   [3] Gal. iii. 13.

doctrine of His legal substitution, for He could only be their substitute by standing in their room, and coming under the same law with them; it is equally subversive of His vicarious expiation and obedience, for His sufferings were not vicarious unless they were inflicted as the curse which rested on His people; nor was His obedience vicarious if it was not rendered to the precepts which they were bound to observe.   Moreover, it leaves the Law of God, as a covenant of works, for ever unfulfilled; for, on this theory, no provision has been made for its fulfilment, either vicariously or personally.   The Mediatorial Law, which was imposed on Christ, may be distinguishable, in some respects, from the Moral Law, to which His people were subject; but there is no such difference between them as makes it possible to separate the one from the other, or. to warrant us in affirming that Christ was not made under the same law which had been broken, and must be fulfilled.   The only important questions on this point are these two : *first*, Did not the law of mediation, supposing it to be distinguishable in some respects from the law of works, comprehend and include under it the fulfilment, by His vicarious sufferings and obedience, of that law, by which His people were bound ? and *secondly*, —if this question must be answered in the affirmative,— Was there any other difference between the Mediatorial and the Moral Law, except what consisted in the fact of His substitution in the room of His people, or what is necessarily involved in the distinction which must always subsist between a representative, and those who are represented by him ? (5)

PROP. XIII. The Mediatorial work of Christ on earth properly consisted in His humiliation, sufferings, and obedience ; or, as it is stated by the Apostle, ' He humbled

Himself, and became obedient unto death, even the death of the Cross.'[1]

His voluntary state of humiliation, including His assumption of human nature,—His being born in a low condition,—His taking the form of a servant,—and His being 'made under law,'—may be regarded partly as the commencement of His Mediatorial work, and partly as an indispensable preparation for His enduring those penal sufferings, and rendering that vicarious obedience, on which the redemption of His people mainly depended. His Incarnation is a fact of fundamental importance, not only as being in itself an amazing manifestation of His condescension and love, but also as it fitted Him for the discharge of every one of His offices, and the accomplishment of every part of His work. The union of the divine and human natures in His one Person, as 'God manifest in the flesh,' lies at the foundation of the whole system of Christian doctrine, and none of its peculiar lessons can be understood in their true meaning, or duly realized and felt, without constant reference to it. The Person of Christ is the 'great mystery of godliness;' and by the reception or rejection of the truth which has been revealed concerning it, every other doctrine will be brightened or obscured. The union of the divine and human natures in the constitution of His person was necessary to qualify Him, in various respects, for the execution of all His offices, even such of them as He was to exercise towards men; but especially for the work of His priesthood, in which He was to transact for men with God. He was to be both the Priest and the Victim; HE was to 'offer up HIMSELF as a sacrifice and an offering to God of a sweet-smelling savour;' and whether we regard Him as Priest or Victim, the union of the divine and human

[1] Phil. ii. 8.

natures in His Person, was that which served alike to make such an offering possible, and to impart to it, when presented, an infinite moral value, as a satisfaction to the Law and Justice of God. For, in the words of Sir M. Hale, 'the unsearchable wisdom of God is manifested in this—that He provided such a Mediator as was fit for so great a work. Had all the world consulted that God must suffer, it had been impossible; and had all the world contributed, that any man, or all the men in the world, should have been a satisfactory sacrifice for any one sin, it had been deficient. Here is, then, the wonderful counsel of the Most High God: the sacrifice that is appointed shall be so ordered, that God and man shall be conjoined in one Person, that so, as Man, He might become a sacrifice for sin, and as God, He might give a value to the sacrifice. And this is the great "mystery of godliness—God manifest in the flesh."' (6)

But the Incarnation of Christ, so far from being, as some recent writers seem to suppose, the whole of His Mediatorial work, was only a preparation for it, or, at the most, its mere commencement; for that 'work which the Father had given Him to do,' and on which the redemption of His people depended, was to be carried on during His whole life on earth, and to be completed only when He could say on the cross, 'It is finished.' All the other parts of His humiliation had a similar relation to that work; but the two which, more than any other,—more than His incarnation, more than His lowly birth, more than His early privations,—furnish a key to the nature and design of His whole undertaking, are these: *first*, the fact that 'He took upon Him the form of a servant,'— placing Himself voluntarily in a state of official subordination to the Father's will; and *secondly*, the fact that, in order to the accomplishment of that will, 'He was made under the law, to redeem them that were under the law.'[1] These expressions show that,—as He was the servant of God, and the subject of His law, so He was also the substitute and representative of His people,—that He came to 'redeem them who were under the law,' by being Himself 'made under the law' for them,—that He took their law-place, as their substitute and representative,—and that He engaged to fulfil all its requirements, whether preceptive or penal, for their redemption and deliverance.

Such being the relation of Christ, as Mediator, to His people and their sins, on the one hand, and to God and His Law, on the other, the nature of His redeeming work is necessarily determined by it. If all that He did and suffered, was done and endured by Him as the substitute of His people, and with a view to their salvation,—and if, moreover, all that He did and suffered, was done and endured by Him as His Father's 'servant,' and with a view to the fulfilment of His 'Law,' it follows, that His whole work is correctly described, when it is said to have been strictly Vicarious, with respect to those for whom it was accomplished, and, also, to have been a true and proper Propitiation for sin, with respect to God and His righteous government.

The general nature of His mediatorial work may thus be deduced from the fact of His subjection to law, as the substitute and representative of His people. But wherein that work properly consisted,—what were its constituent parts,—and how they severally contributed to the accomplishment of His great design, may be ascertained from many express testimonies of Scripture. His redeeming work included both His sufferings and His obedience, and is briefly but comprehensively stated, when it is said that 'He became obedient unto death, even the death of

[1] Gal. iv. 4.

the cross.' But the causes of His death, and the reasons of His obedience, which are also revealed, must be connected with that general statement, so as to explain its full meaning. His death is ascribed to various causes, according to the different aspects and relations in which it may be viewed. It is ascribed to 'the determinate counsel and foreknowledge of God,'[1]—to the justice of God the Father, who 'set Him forth to be a propitiation'[2] for sin, —to the love of God, 'who gave His only-begotten Son,'[3] and 'delivered Him up for us all ;'[4]—it is ascribed to the free, unconstrained will of Christ : 'I lay down my life, . . . I lay it down of myself ;'[5] and to His self-sacrificing love, for 'Christ loved the Church, and gave Himself for it ;'[6] and 'Christ loved us, and hath given Himself for us an offering and a sacrifice to God ;'[7]—it is ascribed, instrumentally, to the agency of evil spirits and of wicked men : 'This is your hour, and the power of darkness,'[8]—'Him ye have taken, and by wicked hands have crucified and slain ;'[9]—it is ascribed to the sins of those for whom He died, for 'He was wounded for our transgressions, He was bruised for our iniquities.'[10] We thus find, as we might have expected in such a case, various causes concurring to bring about His death ; but if we seek to ascertain the reasons which rendered it necessary, rather than the causes which contributed merely to the result, we are taught by Scripture to ascribe it to the sins of men,—and the justice of God,—viewed in connection with His purpose of saving sinners, in a way consistent with the honour of His law, and the interests of His righteous government, through a Divine Redeemer.

If this be a correct view of the reason of His death—

---

[1] Acts ii. 23.   [2] Rom. iii. 25.   [3] John iii. 16.   [4] John viii. 32.
[5] John x. 17, 18.   [6] Eph. v. 25.   [7] Eph. v. 2.   [8] Luke xxii. 53.
[9] Acts v. 23.   [10] Isa. liii. 5.

the reason which rendered it necessary, with a view to
the highest ends of the divine government,—the reason
for which it was ordained and inflicted by the Father,—
and the reason also for which it was voluntarily endured
by His incarnate Son,—then we cannot fail to regard
all the sufferings, which constituted so important a part
of Christ's Mediatorial work, as strictly penal. They
were the punishment, not of personal, but of imputed,
guilt. They were inflicted on Him as the Substitute of
sinners. He was 'made a curse' for them, but only
because He had been 'made sin for them.' In this view,
His sufferings were penal, because they were judicially
imposed on Him as the legal representative of those who
had come under 'the curse,' according to the rule of that
law which proclaimed that 'the wages of sin is death,'
and that ' the soul which sinneth it shall die.'

If His sufferings were penal, His obedience must also
have been vicarious; for, however easy it may be to
distinguish between two things so manifestly different as
suffering and obedience are, yet it is impossible, in this
case, to separate the one from the other, for He obeyed in
suffering, and He suffered in obeying: 'He became obedient unto death, even the death of the cross.' His mere
sufferings, apart from the moral element of obedience
which pervaded them, would not have been a sufficient
vindication of the divine Law, nor would they have been
acceptable to God, without the exercise of those lovely
graces of His character, which were 'the sweet spices'
that perfumed His sacrifice, and made it 'an offering of a
sweet-smelling savour.' His obedience, too, was not rendered in His personal and private character, but in His
official capacity as Mediator,—as the federal Head and
Representative of His people ; so that whatever He did in
the way of obedience, as well as whatever He endured

in the way of suffering, was done in their stead, and on their behalf.

Divines have generally made a distinction between what is called the active, and passive, obedience of Christ; and this distinction is both legitimate and useful, when it is correctly understood, and judiciously applied. It is not to be interpreted as if it meant, that His passive obedience consisted in mere suffering, or that His active obedience consisted in mere service ; for it implies obedience in both, and excludes suffering from neither: nor is it to be interpreted as if it meant, that the two might be so separated from each other, as to admit of His mere sufferings being imputed to us, without any part of His obedience ; for if His death be reckoned to us at all, it must necessarily include both the pains which He endured, and the obedience which he rendered, in dying. But the distinction may be understood in a sense which serves to discriminate, merely, one part of His work from another, without destroying their indissoluble union ; and to exhibit them in the relation which they severally bear to the penal and preceptive requirements of the divine Law. That Law required the punishment of sin, and in the sufferings and death of Christ we see its penalty fulfilled ; it required also perfect righteousness, and in the life-long obedience of Christ,—but especially in His death as the crowning act of His obedience,—we see its precept fulfilled ; and by thus connecting His penal sufferings with the evil desert of sin, and His vicarious obedience with the righteousness which the Law requires, we are enabled to apprehend more clearly our need of both, and also the suitableness and fulness of the provision which has thus been made for our acceptance with God. (7)

Prop. XIV.   The Mediatorial work of Christ, including

both His sufferings and His obedience, constituted a complete and effectual satisfaction to the Law and justice of God.

The term SATISFACTION is often restricted to His sufferings and death, as if it had an exclusive reference to the penalty of the Law which had been violated and dishonoured by sin. But as it must be held, even when employed with special reference to the death of Christ, to include, not only the pains which He endured, but also the obedience which He rendered, in dying,—so it may comprehend the whole of that work, by which ' He magnified the law and made it honourable.' The precept, not less than the penalty, of the Law must be fulfilled ; and His fulfilment of both is the complete satisfaction which He rendered to the Law and Justice of God. (8)

Using the term in this comprehensive sense, as including the whole homage which He paid to the divine Law both in His life and in His death, His satisfaction is said to be complete, because it was commensurate with all the righteous requirements of that Law, whether preceptive or penal ; and it is said to be effectual, because it actually secured the salvation of His people, and laid a sure and solid ground of immediate acceptance with God for all that should ever believe in His name.

Both the completeness, and the efficacy, of this satisfaction have been doubted or denied. So far from regarding it as complete, and resting upon it as the one foundation which God has laid in Zion, many have imagined that the merits of Christ's death must be supplemented by their own austerities, and penances, and satisfactions for sin ; and that the merits of Christ's obedience can only be made available by their own personal holiness, and diligence in good works. And so

far from regarding it as effectual, in actually securing the
redemption of His people, many have spoken of it as if
its only effect were to provide mere salvability for all,
without entitling any to salvation.   These views are as
injurious to the souls of men, as they are dishonouring to
the work of Christ.   They prevent many from 'receiving
and resting on Christ,' *at once* and *alone*, 'for salvation, as
He is freely offered *to them* in the Gospel;' and even when
there is a yearning of heart towards Him, and, perhaps,
an incipient trust in Him, they prevent all 'joy and peace
in believing,' by spreading a veil over the eye of faith
itself, and generating 'the spirit of bondage unto fear.'
These obstacles to a simple, childlike, cordial, confiding
reception of the Gospel as 'glad tidings of great joy,' can
only be removed by a right scriptural apprehension of the
completeness, and the efficacy, of that satisfaction, which
Christ has already made to the Law and Justice of God.
But what reason can there be, why we should doubt either
the completeness, or the efficacy, of His satisfaction?   If
it was sufficient for the acquittal and acceptance of Him
who 'was made sin for us,'—who 'bare our sins in His
own body on the tree,'—and on whom 'the Lord laid the
iniquities of us all,'—if it could expiate the accumulated
guilt of 'a great multitude whom no man can number, out
of every country, and nation, and people, and tongue,'—and
if it was rewarded, in His Person, with an everlasting and
universal dominion, in the exercise of which He has 'all
power in heaven and in earth,' to bestow the forgiveness
of sin, and the gift of eternal life, why should it be inadequate for the immediate Justification of any sinner who
believes in His name?   Or what need can there be of any
other satisfaction, to save us from 'the wrath to come,'
—of any other merit, to ensure our acceptance with
God,—of any other title to the inheritance of eternal

life, if Christ, as our Redeemer, has already 'finished the transgressions, and made an end of sins, and made reconciliation for iniquity, and brought in everlasting righteousness ?'[1]

PROP. XV. The Justification of sinners is directly connected in Scripture with the Mediatorial work of Christ, as a satisfaction rendered to the Law and Justice of God.

The reason why ' God set Him forth to be a propitiation through faith in His blood,' is explained by the Apostle, when he says that ' it was to declare His righteousness for the remission of sins ;'[2] and his statement evidently implies, both that there is a declaration of' righteousness, as well as of mercy, in this method of justifying sinners, and, also, that God could either not have been just in superseding the punishment of sin by an act of mere pardon, or that He could not have been so evidently declared to be just without a propitiation.

Accordingly, we find that, in Scripture, the punishment of sin, which is the penalty of the Law,—and the pardon of sin, which is the privilege of the Gospel,—are brought together and harmonized in a propitiation, in which justice and mercy are equally displayed. We further find that the Justification of sinners is directly connected with that propitiation, and described, in every variety of expression, as having been effectually procured by it, and as being entirely founded upon it. It is connected with the death of Christ : ' When we were enemies, we were reconciled unto God by the death of His Son ;'[3] ' You that were sometime alienated, and enemies in your mind by wicked works, yet now hath He reconciled, in the body of His flesh through death.[4] It is connected with the blood of Christ : ' In whom we

<hr>

[1] Dan. ix. 24.   [2] Rom. iii. 25.   [3] Rom. v. 10.   [4] Col. i. 21, 22.

have redemption through His blood, the forgiveness of sins, according to the riches of His grace;[1] 'This is my blood of the new testament which is shed for many for the remission of sins;'[2] 'Being now justified by His blood, we shall be saved from wrath through Him.'[3] It is connected with the obedience of Christ: 'By the obedience of one shall many be made righteous;'[4] 'Though He were a Son, yet learned He obedience by the things which He suffered; and being made perfect, He became the author of eternal salvation unto all them that obey Him.'[5] It is connected with the righteousness of Christ: 'Surely shall one say, In the Lord have I righteousness . . . In the Lord shall all the seed of Israel be justified;'[6] 'For He hath made Him to be sin for us, who knew no sin, that we might be made the righteousness of God in Him;'[7] 'I have suffered the loss of all things, and do count them but dung, that I may win Christ, and be found in Him, not having mine own righteousness which is of the law, but the righteousness which is through the faith of Christ, the righteousness which is of God by faith.'[8] It is connected with the name of Christ: 'Ye are justified in the name of the Lord Jesus;'[9] 'That repentance and remission of sins should be preached in His name among all nations;'[10] 'To Him give all the prophets witness, that, through His name, whosoever believeth in Him shall receive the remission of sins.'[11] It is connected with the knowledge of Christ: 'By His knowledge shall my righteous servant justify many, for He shall bear their iniquities;'[12] 'This is life eternal, that they might know Thee, the only true God, and Jesus Christ whom Thou hast

---

[1] Eph. i. 7.

[2] Matt. xxvi. 28.

[3] Rom. v. 9.

[4] Rom. v. 19.

[5] Heb. v. 8.

[6] Isa. xlv. 24, 25.

[7] 2 Cor. v. 21.

[8] Phil. iii. 8, 9.

[9] 1 Cor. vi. 11.

[10] Luke xxiv. 47.

[11] Acts x. 43.

[12] Isa. liii. 11.

sent. I have glorified Thee on the earth, I have finished the work which Thou gavest me to do.'[1] In short, in every form of expression, and in every part of Scripture, the Justification of sinners is connected directly with Christ, and His Mediatorial work : and His people are so absolutely dependent on what He did and suffered for their pardon and acceptance with God, that He is said to be their Life,—their Peace,—their Righteousness,—their Hope,—their Joy,—as if 'all their springs were in Him,' and 'Christ were all in all.' No marvel, that to them who believe 'He is precious.'[2]

The fact that the Justification of sinners is thus directly connected with the Mediatorial work of Christ, serves to connect it also with what is declared to be God's chief end in the whole administration of His righteous government—the glory of His great Name. For that work was designed to manifest, in their actual exercise, the moral perfections of His nature, and to make Him known as 'the Just God, and the Saviour,'—the righteous Ruler, and yet the gracious Redeemer,—of sinful men. By means of that work, He may be glorified in their salvation, glorified in His justice, and glorified, also, in His mercy and grace. What unspeakable peace may dawn upon the soul, when it first discerns 'the light of this knowledge of the glory of God in the face of Jesus Christ,'—when it is enabled to see that the same justice, which might have been glorified in the punishment of the sinner, may now be still more glorified in His pardon,— that the same love which prompted the gift of His Son will be glorified in the salvation of every one of His people,—and that all the attributes of God, which were

[1] John xvii. 3, 4.
[2] Gal. ii. 20 ; Eph. ii. 14 ; Jer. xxiii. 6 ; Col. i. 27 ; John xv. 11 ; 1 Pet. i. 8 ; Col. iii. 11.

formerly arrayed against us, are now in Christ, the firmest grounds of our confidence and hope,—that the flaming sword of justice itself, which once menaced us, has been converted into a shield and buckler for our protection and defence! What a comfort to know, that through Christ's redeeming work, our Justification is connected indissolubly with the glory of God,—that all His attributes will be more fully made manifest than they could have been, either in the mere justification of the righteous, or in the mere punishment of the wicked,—that the majesty of His Law, so far from being impaired, will be magnified and made honourable, and all the highest ends of His righteous government most effectually secured, by the very means which have opened up a way for the freest exercise of mercy even to the chief of sinners! But how insecure must be the hope, or rather how fatal the presumption, of those who look for pardoning mercy, without any regard either to the honour of His law, or the claims of His justice, or the glory His great Name!

LECTURE XII.

JUSTIFICATION ; ITS IMMEDIATE AND ONLY GROUND,—THE IMPUTED RIGHTEOUSNESS OF CHRIST.

MANY have admitted that the Justification of sinners is connected with the Mediatorial work of Christ, as its meritorious cause ; while they have denied that it rests on His righteousness as its immediate and only ground. They have not ventured to set aside His merits altogether, or to say that His redeeming work had no influence in procuring our pardon and acceptance with God ; on the contrary, they have professed to do signal homage to the merits of Christ, by acknowledging both their indispensable necessity, and their certain efficacy, but only as a means of procuring for us those terms of salvation, and that measure of grace, which render it possible for us to be justified by our personal obedience ; while they have utterly rejected the idea that His right- eousness is, or can be, imputed to us. Others, again, have admitted a real and important, but partial and imperfect, imputation of His righteousness ; and have restricted it to the merits of His passive, as distinguished from that of His active, obedience,—thereby leaving our Justification to rest, partly on His atoning sacrifice, and partly on our personal holiness in heart and life. It is necessary, there- fore, to show that His righteousness,—considered as the entire merit of His whole Mediatorial work,—is not only the meritorious cause, but also the immediate ground, of our Justification; and for this end, to inquire—What that righteousness is by which alone we can be justified,—why it is said to be the righteousness of God, or the merit of Christ,—and how it becomes ours, so as to be available for our Justification?

PROP. XVI. The righteousness, which is the ground of a sinner's Justification, is denoted or described by various terms in Scripture, so that its nature may be determined by simply comparing these terms with one another; and then ascertaining whether there be any righteousness to which they are all equally applicable, and in which they all coincide, in the fulness of their combined meaning.

That righteousness is called in Scripture,—'the righteousness of God,'—'the righteousness of Christ,'—the 'righteousness of One,'—'the obedience of One,'—the 'free gift unto justification of life,'—'the righteousness which is of,' or 'by,' or 'through, faith,'—'the righteousness of God without the law,'—and 'the righteousness which God imputes without works.'

It will be found that, while these various expressions are descriptive of its different aspects and relations, they are all employed with reference to the SAME RIGHTEOUSNESS,—that there is one righteousness, in which they all find their common centre, as so many distinct rays converging towards the same focus, while each retains its distinctive meaning,—and that there is no other righteousness to which they can all be applied, or in which they can find their adequate explanation.

It is called, pre-eminently and emphatically, 'The righteousness of God.' By this name it is distinguished from the righteousness of man, and even contrasted with it, as a ground of Justification. It is brought in as a divine righteousness, only when all human righteousness has been shut out. The Apostle first proves that 'by the deeds of the law there shall no flesh be justified in His sight, for by the law is the knowledge of sin;' and then introduces another righteousness altogether, 'But now the righteousness of God without the law is manifest, . . . even the righteousness of God which is by faith of Jesus Christ.'[1] He contrasts the two great revelations—the revelation of wrath, which is by the Law, and the revelation of righteousness, which is by the Gospel: 'For the wrath of God is revealed from heaven against all ungodliness and unrighteousness of men:' but 'the Gospel of Christ is the power of God unto salvation to every one that believeth, . . . *for* therein is the righteousness of God revealed.'[2] And, in his own case, he renounces his own personal righteousness altogether, as the ground of his acceptance and hope: 'That I may win Christ, and be found in Him, not having mine own righteousness, which is of the law, but that which is through the faith of Christ, the righteousness which is of God by faith.'[3] The two righteousnesses are not only distinct, but different; and not only different, but directly opposed, and mutually exclusive, considered as grounds of Justification; insomuch that he who is justified by the one, cannot possibly be justified by the other. If the righteousness of man be sufficient, the righteousness of God is superfluous; if the righteousness of God be necessary, the righteousness of man can have no place. Nor can any conciliation or compromise be effected between them, so as to admit of their being combined in one complex ground of acceptance; for they represent two methods of Justification which are irreconcilably opposed,—the one by grace, the other by works: 'For to him that worketh is the reward not reckoned of grace, but of debt; but to

---

[1] Rom. iii. 20, 22.   [2] Rom. i. 16, 18.   [3] Phil. iii. 8.

him that worketh not, but believeth on Him that justifieth
the ungodly, his faith is counted for righteousness.'[1] 'And
if by grace, then is it no more of works, otherwise grace
is no more grace: but if it be of works, then is it no more
grace, otherwise work is no more work.'[2]

But why is it called 'the righteousness of God?'
Some have interpreted the expression in a singularly
vague and indefinite sense, which amounts to a virtual
evasion of its true meaning. Instead of the clear and
precise words of the Apostle—'the righteousness of God,'
they would substitute their own loose paraphrase,—'God's
method of justifying sinners.' (1) His expression is much
more specific; it defines the RIGHTEOUSNESS which is
revealed for our Justification. 'God's method of justifying sinners' is described in the context, when it is said
that we are 'justified fully by His grace, through the
redemption which is in Christ Jesus, whom God hath set
forth to be a propitiation through faith in His blood;' but
the expression—'the righteousness of God'—stands connected with the reason which is assigned for the whole
work of redemption,—viz., 'to declare His righteousness
for the remission of sins, . . . that He might be just, and
the justifier of him which believeth in Jesus.' It points
specifically to the righteousness on which our Justification
depends. The right way to test the explanation of any
phrase, is to apply it to all the cases in which that phrase
occurs. It may possibly be found applicable to some of
these without any apparent straining; but if it cannot be
applied to some others without manifest incongruity, we
have reason to conclude that it is either not sufficiently
comprehensive, or not sufficiently precise. Suppose that
'the righteousness of God' might mean 'God's method of
justifying sinners' when it is said 'to be manifested,

[1] Rom. iv. 4.   [2] Rom. xi. 6.

being witnessed by the law and the prophets,' can it possibly be understood in that vague sense, when Christ is said to be 'made of God righteousness to us,' or when we are said to be 'made the righteousness of God in Him?' It means a righteousness by which, and not merely a method in which, we are justified.

If we would understand the reason why it is called 'the righteousness of God,' we must bear in mind that there was a twofold manifestation of righteousness in the Cross of Christ: there was *first* a manifestation of the righteousness of God the Father, in requiring a satisfaction to His justice,—and inflicting the punishment that was due to sin; and to this the Apostle refers when he says, that 'God set forth Christ to be a propitiation'— 'to declare His righteousness, that He might be just, and the Justifier of him that believeth in Jesus;' there was, *secondly*, a work of righteousness by God the Son,—His vicarious righteousness as the Redeemer of His people, when He 'became obedient unto death, even the death of the Cross,' and thus became 'the end of the law for righteousness to every one that believeth.' But these two—God's righteousness which was declared, and Christ's righteousness which was wrought out, on the Cross—although they may be distinguished, cannot be separated, from one another; for they were indissolubly united in one and the same propitiation; and while the righteousness which is revealed for our Justification may be called 'the righteousness of God' with some reference to both, it properly consists in the merit of Christ's atoning sacrifice and perfect obedience, for these were offered by Him as our substitute and representative.

The same righteousness which is called 'the righteousness of God,' is also called 'the righteousness of Christ.' We obtain 'precious faith through the righteousness of

God and our Saviour Jesus Christ,' or, as it might be rendered, 'through the righteousness of our God and Saviour Jesus Christ;'[1] 'This is the name whereby He shall be called, The Lord our Righteousness.'[2] He is so called on account of the righteousness which He wrought out by His obedience unto death; for this righteousness is expressly connected with His Mediatorial work. 'The Lord is well pleased for His righteousness' sake; He will magnify the law and make it honourable.'[3] By His vicarious sufferings and obedience, He fulfilled the Law both in its precept and its penalty; and is now said to be 'the end of the law for righteousness to every one that believeth,'[4] while His righteousness is identified with 'the righteousness of God,' to which the unbelieving Jews refused to 'submit themselves,' and contrasted with 'their own righteousness' which they 'went about to establish,' 'as it were by the works of the law.'

In like manner, this righteousness is called 'the righteousness of One,' and 'the obedience of One;'[5]—expressions which serve at once to connect it with the work of Christ, and to exclude from it the personal obedience of the many who are justified. It is called 'the free gift unto justification of life,' and 'the gift of righteousness,'[6] to show that it is bestowed gratuitously by divine grace, and not acquired by our own obedience. It is called 'the righteousness which is of faith,' or 'the righteousness which is by faith,' both to distinguish it from faith itself, and also to contrast it with another righteousness which is not received by faith, but 'sought for as it were by the works of the law.'[7] It is called 'the righteousness of God *without the law*,'[8] to intimate that, while it was 'wit-

---

[1] 2 Pet. i. 1.   [2] Jer. xxiii. 6.   [3] Isa. xlii. 21.
[4] Rom. x. 3, 4.   [5] Rom. v. 18, 19.   [6] Rom. v. 17, 18.
[7] Rom. iii. 30.   [8] Rom. ix. 32.

nessed by the law and the prophets,'[1] and while, as 'a righteousness,' it must have some relation to the unchangeable rule of rectitude, it was above and beyond what the law could provide, since it depends, not on personal, but on vicarious obedience. And it is called the righteousness 'which God imputes without works,' to show that it is 'reckoned of grace,' and not 'of debt,'—that 'God justifies the ungodly'[2] by placing this righteousness to their account,—and that He makes it theirs, because it was wrought out for them by Him, 'who was delivered for their offences, and rose again for their Justification.' All these expressions relate to one and the same righteousness—the only righteousness which God has revealed for the Justification of sinners,—they are all applicable to the vicarious righteousness of Christ,—and they serve, by their very diversity, to exhibit it in all its various aspects and relations, and to exclude every other righteousness from the ground of our pardon and acceptance, since there is no other to which all these terms can possibly be applied.

PROP. XVII. This righteousness,—being the merit of a work, and not a mere quality of character,—may become ours by being imputed to us, but cannot be communicated by being infused; and must ever continue to belong primarily and, in one important respect, exclusively to Him by whom alone that work was accomplished.

This statement consists of three distinct affirmations, which are directed against as many different errors, springing from a prevalent confusion of thought, in regard to the whole doctrine of Imputation; and it may be useful to consider each of them successively, in connection with the proofs on which they severally depend.

[1] Rom. iii. 21.   [2] Rom. iv. 6, 11, iv. 4, 5.

It is affirmed, *first*, that the righteousness which is the ground of Justification, being the merit of a work, undertaken and accomplished by Christ on behalf of His people, *may* become theirs by being imputed to them, or reckoned to their account.   This statement could scarcely be denied, if the merit of His work, done and finished 'once for all' (ἐφάπαξ), were duly distinguished from an inherent and abiding quality of His personal character ; and if that work were really regarded as having been undertaken and accomplished, on the behalf of others, by one acting as their substitute and surety.   For the merit of one can never, in any case, become available for the benefit of others, except when it is imputed to them ; it cannot, from the very nature of the case, become theirs by infusion.   The merit of one may be reckoned, or put down to the account of another ; but how can the merit of any work be infused, as a personal property, as holiness may unquestionably be ?   But when we affirm that the righteousness of Christ, or the merit of His Mediatorial work, may become ours by being imputed to us, we are met with a counter-statement to the effect,— not that there was no merit in His work, or that His work was not accomplished on behalf of others, which are the only important elements in the case,—but that biblical criticism forbids the use of the term 'impute,' except when it is applied to personal properties and acts. 'There is not in all the Scriptures,' says one, 'an instance in which one man's sin or righteousness is said to be imputed to another. . . . There is not in all the Bible one assertion that Adam's sin, or Christ's righteousness, is imputed to us ; nor one declaration that any man's sin is ever imputed by God or man to another man. . . . . Having followed (the Hebrew and Greek verbs) through the concordances, I hesitate not to challenge a single example which is fairly of this nature in all the Bible.' (2)

These are bold statements, and may seem to imply a denial of the doctrine, as well as a criticism on the term, by which it has been usually expressed; but we refer at present only to the latter. Every reader of his English Bible, without the aid of critical scholarship, may discover,—and it has never been denied, so far as we know, by any competent divine,—that the verbs in question are applicable to cases, in which that which is imputed to any one was personally his own beforehand,— that one man, for instance, who is righteous, is reckoned and treated as righteous; and that another man who is wicked, is reckoned and treated as wicked. But the question is, Whether the same verbs may not be equally applicable to other cases, in which that which is imputed to him was not personally his own, and did not previously belong to him, but became his only by its being put down to his account? The debt due, and the wrong done, by Onesimus to Philemon, were not chargeable against Paul personally or previously, but he became chargeable with them simply by their being imputed to him: 'If he hath wronged thee, or oweth thee ought, put that on mine account,' or 'impute that to me;' 'I will repay it.'[1] In like manner, 'He, who knew no sin, was made sin for us,' and 'bore our sins in His own body on the tree,'— not that our sins were chargeable against Him personally or previously, but they became His by imputation on God's part, and voluntary susception on His own. If it be said, that the mere word 'impute' is not employed in this case, it may be asked, whether there be any other which could more accurately express the fact, if it be a fact; and whether the word itself is not used in a parallel

[1] Philem. 18.

case, when God is said ' to impute righteousness without works,' as often as ' He justifieth the ungodly?'[1]   Indeed, Justification consists partly in the ' non-imputation' of sin, which did belong personally to the sinner, and partly in the ' imputation' of righteousness, of which he was utterly destitute before; and the meaning of the one may be ascertained from the meaning of the other, while both are necessary to express the full meaning of Justification. We conclude, therefore, that the righteousness of Christ, —being the merit of a work done and finished,—may be imputed for the Justification of His people, but cannot possibly be infused.

It is affirmed, *secondly*, that the righteousness of Christ, to be available for the benefit of His people, *must* become theirs by imputation, and not by infusion.   Most of the leading errors on the subject of Justification may be traced to obscure or defective views in regard to the nature or import of imputation, and have arisen from supposing—either that it consists in the infusion of moral qualities, in which case Justification is confounded with Sanctification—or that, in so far as imputation may be distinguished from such infusion, it is founded, at least, on the moral qualities which thus become inherent, in which case Justification has for its immediate ground a personal, and not a vicarious, righteousness.   The only effectual way of striking at the root of these prevailing and pernicious errors, is by forming distinct and definite conceptions of what is really meant by the general doctrine of Imputation, whether in regard to sin or to righteous- ness ; and the likeliest means of doing so seems to be,— to take the three cases of Imputation which have been affirmed by divines to have the express sanction of Scrip- ture,—namely, that of the guilt of Adam's first sin to his

---

[1] Rom. iv. 5, 6.

posterity,—that of the guilt of our sins to Christ as our
substitute,—and that of His righteousness to us as the
immediate ground of our Justification ;—to compare them
with one another,—to eliminate whatever is peculiar to
each of them,—and to frame our general idea of imputation by including in it only what is common to them all ;
for as each of the three is a specific example of the same
generic class, we may hope, by means of this process of
comparison and abstraction, to arrive at a correct result,
and to retain whatever is essential to the nature of imputation, while we exclude only what is peculiar to each
of its special exemplifications.   It may thus be made
manifest that imputation, whether it be of sin or of
righteousness, neither consists in the infusion of moral
qualities, nor is, in all cases, necessarily connected with it.

Take the three cases of Imputation which have been
specified, and compare them with one another.   We
find, that in two out of the three, a change of moral
character is the invariable concomitant or consequent
of imputation; for the imputation of Adam's guilt to
his posterity, was connected with their loss of original
righteousness and the corruption of their whole nature ;
and the imputation of Christ's righteousness to His people
is connected, in like manner, with their renewal and
sanctification; but we also find that, in the third case,
—which is as real and as complete an instance of imputation as either of the other two,—the imputation of our sins
to Christ was not connected with any change in His holy
character, or with the infusion of any, even the slightest,
taint of moral evil; whence we infer that imputation, so
far from consisting in, is not even invariably connected
with, the infusion of moral qualities.   We find again,
that in two out of the three cases, representative, and
personal, agency are so clearly distinguished as to make it

manifest, that the party to whom anything is imputed is
not supposed to have had any active participation in the
doing of it : for our sins were really, and in the full sense
of the term, imputed to Christ as our substitute, yet
He had no share in the commission of them ; and His
righteousness is, in like manner, imputed to us for our
Justification, yet we had no share with Him in ' finishing
the work which the Father had given Him to do.'—
Whence we infer that, in the third case,—that of the imputation of Adam's guilt to his posterity,—it is so far from
being necessary to suppose our personal participation in
his act, that such a supposition would go far to destroy
the doctrine of Imputation altogether, by setting aside the
fundamental distinction between the agency of the representative, and that of those who were represented by him.
We find, again, that in all the three cases, imputation,
whether of sin or of righteousness, is founded on a federal
relation subsisting between one and many,—for Adam
was constituted the head and representative of his race,
and Christ the substitute and surety of His people ; and
that this relation may be fitly described as amounting to
a union between them, in virtue of which they are regarded and treated as being, in some respects, one ; but
that this union is not such as to destroy the distinction
between their respective personalities, or to confound
their several acts : for it is still true, that the representative was personally different from those whom he represented, and that his obedience, or disobedience, was his
own act, and not theirs, although it is imputed to them ;
for ' a union of representation is not a union of identity.'
' No imputation of this kind,' says Dr. Owen, speaking
of the imputation of anything that was not ours ante-
cedently, but that becomes ours simply by being imputed,
—' is to account them, unto whom anything is imputed,

to have done the things themselves which are imputed
unto them. . . . This is contrary unto the nature of imputation, which proceeds on no such judgment, but on the
contrary, (implies) that we ourselves have done nothing of
what is imputed unto us, nor Christ anything of what is
imputed unto Him.' (3)

These few specimens may suffice to illustrate the
general doctrine of Imputation, and the best way of
acquiring a distinct conception of its true meaning.
They show that, while the righteousness of Christ, considered as the merit of His Mediatorial work, may
become ours by being imputed to us, it is not communicated as an inherent habit or quality might be;
and that our Justification, in so far as it depends on
that righteousness, neither consists in the infusion of
moral qualities, nor rests on these qualities, when they
have been infused, as its proper ground.

It is affirmed, *thirdly*, that the righteousness of Christ,
considered as the merit of His Mediatorial work, must
ever continue, even when it is imputed to us, to belong
primarily, and, in one important respect, exclusively, to
Him by whom alone that work was accomplished. It is
His righteousness in a sense in which it never can be
ours: it is His, as having been wrought out by Him;
and it is ours, only as it is imputed to us. It is His, as
it was the merit of His personal obedience; and it is ours,
only as it is derived to us from Him. He claims a special
propriety in it even when He makes it over to His people.
'I have trodden the wine-press alone, and of the people
there was none with me . . . I that speak in righteousness, mighty to save;' 'Hearken, ye stout-hearted, that
are far from righteousness, I bring near MY righteousness.'[1]
It is still His, and, moreover, it is only to be found 'in

[1] Isa. lxiii. 1, 3, xlvi. 13.

Him.' 'Surely shall one say, In the Lord have I righteousness,' and 'In the Lord shall all the seed of Israel be
justified, and shall glory.' 'We are made the righteousness of God,' but only 'in Him;' and if we would have
'the righteousness which is of God by faith,' we 'must win
Christ, and be found in Him;' for this righteousness is
part of that 'fulness which dwells in Him,'[1] and which is
'treasured up for us in Him.' The whole merit is His,—
the gracious imputation of it only is ours.

Had this simple, but important, truth been duly
considered, it would have served, both to obviate some
plausible objections which have been urged against the
doctrine of imputed righteousness; and also to prevent
or correct some dangerous perversions of it, on which
these objections have been mainly founded. It has
been said, for instance, that if Christ's righteousness be
imputed to us, then we must be as righteous as Christ
Himself was,—that we can no longer need the pardon of
sin; that in Him we may be said to have redeemed ourselves ; and that eternal life must come to us rather as a
reward of debt, than as a gift of grace. These, and many
other, rash and extravagant expressions, occur in the
writings of some avowed Antinomians, and have been
quoted by many Popish and Socinian writers, as if they
were a correct statement of the Protestant doctrine, with
the view of founding upon them various plausible objections against it. (4) But in the only sense in which they
could be made available for that purpose, they are explicitly disavowed by all sound divines; for Protestants have
always maintained that there is an essential difference,—
not between the righteousness which Christ wrought out,
and that which is imputed to His people, for this they
hold to be one and the same,—but between Christ as the

[1] Isa. xlv. 24, 25 ; 2 Cor. v. 21 ; Phil. iii. 9 ; Col. i. 19.

' author and finisher' of that righteousness, and those who
were represented by Him,—who were 'redeemed to God
by His blood,'—'reconciled to God by His death,'—and
' made the righteousness of God IN HIM.' In one important sense, His righteousness was peculiar to Himself,
for it was His, and His alone, considered personally; in
another important sense, it is common to Him with His
people, for it was wrought out, not for Himself only,
but for them, also, and considered as vicarious, it becomes
theirs by a gracious imputation.

PROP. XVIII. The imputation of Christ's righteousness
to His people, as the immediate ground of their pardon
and acceptance with God, may be proved, deductively,
from the character in which He acted, as their representative ; and from the vicarious nature of the work which
He undertook to accomplish.

When we speak of the imputation of His righteousness
as being the immediate ground of their Justification, we
do not intend to represent their Justification as the instantaneous effect of the completion of His Mediatorial work.
The term 'immediate' has no reference to time at all, and
may admit of a long interval between the accomplishment
of His vicarious obedience, and the actual application of
it to individuals, as also the instrumental use of many
means for that end.   The whole work of the Spirit intervenes between the redemption of Christ and the personal
Justification of His people.   But what the employment of
this term is intended to exclude, is the introduction of
any other righteousness between that which was wrought
out by His vicarious sufferings and obedience, and the
effectual Justification of all who receive and rest upon it
by faith—the introduction of any other righteousness as
being, either in whole or in part, the ground of our accep-

tance with God. For a theory of 'mediate,' has been
opposed to the doctrine of 'direct,' imputation,—a theory
which makes the Justification of believers to depend immediately upon their own inherent righteousness, and
only remotely, if at all, on the imputed righteousness of
Christ.   The same theory has been applied to explain, or
rather to explain away, the doctrine of our condemnation
in Adam, and the doctrine of our Justification in Christ.
It is alleged, that the guilt of Adam's first sin is not
directly imputed to his posterity, but only mediately,
through their own entailed and inherent depravity ; and in
like manner, as well as for similar reasons, that the righteousness of Christ is not directly imputed to His people,
but only mediately, through their own infused and inherent
holiness.   The immediate ground of condemnation, in
the one case, and of Justification, in the other, is made
to be our own personal character.   In opposition to this
theory, in so far as it relates to the righteousness of Christ,
we affirm that the merit of His suffering and obedience is
imputed directly to His people, as the immediate and only
ground of their Justification ; and that the truth of this
statement may be proved, deductively, from the character
in which He acted as their representative, and from the
vicarious nature of the work which He undertook to
accomplish. (5)

Socinians, and others,—who deny the substitution of
Christ in the room of the guilty, the imputation of their
sins to Him, and the vicarious nature of His sufferings
and obedience, as a satisfaction to the law and justice of
God,—are the only parties who can consistently reject
the imputation of His righteousness as the ground of their
pardon and acceptance ; indeed, they must do so, for they
sweep away the whole ground on which the doctrine of
Imputation is based.   But those who admit these funda-

mental truths, cannot consistently refuse this unavoidable inference from them, that what He did, as their substitute and representative, was done for them; and that, to be available for their benefit, it must be, in some way, made over to them, or put down to their account. To this extent, they must all admit the fact of imputation. If they ascribe any efficacy to the work of Christ at all, —considered as a vicarious work accomplished by Him on behalf of His people, which merited or procured anything for them,—His merit must be reckoned to them, if they are to derive any real benefit from it. Suppose, with some, that the only efficacy which belonged to it was, that it procured ' salvability for all, but not salvation for any,' or that it procured ' a new law of grace ' by which we might be saved on easier terms, and accepted on the ground of sincere, but imperfect, obedience,—still it must be imputed to us *to that effect*,—it must be reckoned to our account, if it was undertaken and accomplished for such an end; and it must be made available for our relief, if not from the guilt of sin and the wrath of God, yet from the law of perfect obedience. Suppose, with others, that the only efficacy which belonged to it was, that it procured the pardon of sin, while it left us to work out for ourselves a title to eternal life,—still it must be imputed to us to *that effect*, if pardon is bestowed solely on account of His sufferings and death. In both cases alike, too, it is the direct and immediate cause of *the effect which is ascribed to it*; for no other righteousness is interposed between the work of Christ and the relaxation of the Law, in the one case, or between that work and the pardon of sin, in the other. The latter is not a case of mediate, but only of partial, imputation; and the former, while it is a case of mediate imputation, so far as our Justification is concerned, is nevertheless a case of direct and immediate imputation, with reference to the only effect which is ascribed to the Mediatorial work of Christ. The merit of that work must be directly imputed to them to the effect of relieving them from a Law which requires perfect obedience, if they are to derive any benefit from it,—for it is not even alleged that there is any other righteousness which intervenes between Christ's work, and this supposed result ; and if the personal righteousness of the believer is interposed, at a subsequent stage, so as to be made the immediate ground of Justification, while Christ's work is still recognised as its remote, but meritorious, cause, we shall only have two distinct imputations,—the one direct, and the other mediate—the direct imputation of Christ's work, to the effect of relaxing the requirements of God's Law, and then the mediate imputation of His work, to the effect of sustaining our own personal righteousness, or our sincere, but imperfect obedience, as the proximate ground of our pardon and acceptance with God.

But if it can be clearly proved from Scripture, that the Mediatorial work of Christ was undertaken and executed for the purpose, not of relaxing the Law, but of fulfilling it, on behalf of His people ; and if it can be further shown that their Justification is directly connected with the efficacy of His work for that end, then any objection that is raised against the doctrine of His imputed righteousness, cannot be founded on the mere idea of imputation,—for that is really involved in every other doctrine which ascribes any efficacy to His work in connection with our Justification, —but must rest entirely on the proof of this precise point, —that, while the work of Christ was directly imputed to the effect of relaxing the divine Law, and relieving us from the requirement of perfect obedience, it is not directly imputed for our Justification, but becomes available with reference to this end only mediately,—through our own personal righteousness, or through our sincere, but imperfect, obedience. On any view that can be taken of the relation which subsists between Christ's work and our Justification, a direct imputation of His merit, at one point or another, must be admitted by all who ascribe any efficacy to it whatever; for it is necessarily involved in the representative character which He sustained, and the vicarious nature of His undertaking: it must come in, without the intervention of any other righteousness, at the point where the Law is supposed to be relaxed in consequence of what He did and suffered; or, if the Law was never relaxed, then at the point where the Law was fulfilled, and where Christ Himself became the 'end of the Law for righteousness to every one who believeth.'

That there may be such a direct imputation of Christ's righteousness as is not founded, either in whole or in part, on any change in the moral character of believers, although it is inseparably connected with it, is evident from the fact, that our sins were really, and in the full sense of the term, imputed to Christ, while the imputation was not even accompanied with the infusion of personal sin, and could not, therefore, be founded upon it. In the case of believers, the imputation of righteousness is invariably contemporaneous with the infusion of holiness; but that this infused and inherent personal holiness is not the ground of that imputation, is proved conclusively by the fact that we are called, like Abraham, to 'believe in Him who justifieth the ungodly,' and 'who imputeth righteousness without works.' (6)

PROP. XIX. The righteousness of Christ, considered as the merit of His Mediatorial work, is, not partially, but entirely imputed; and is effectual for the complete Justification of all who believe in His name.

Some have contended for a partial, in opposition to a plenary, imputation of His merits. They have acknowledged His sufferings and death as the immediate ground of a sinner's pardon, but have objected to His active obedience being imputed to the believer as his title to acceptance with God, and the inheritance of eternal life. But 'Christ is not divided,' nor is His righteousness capable of being separated into parts, so as that one part should be imputed, while the other is not imputed; nor is Justification ever bestowed except as a complete blessing, which includes the sinner's deliverance from wrath, and also his acceptance as righteous in the sight of God. It is perfectly legitimate, and, for some purposes, it may be useful, to distinguish between the active and passive obedience of Christ, as constituting together His one entire righteousness, and also between the pardon and the acceptance of the sinner, as constituting together the one entire privilege of Justification;—we are naturally led, even, to make use of such distinctions, in order to illustrate the relation which the constituent elements of Christ's righteousness, and also those of our own Justification, bear respectively to the penal and preceptive requirements of the divine Law; but we should ever remember, that two things which are distinguishable in idea, may be inseparable in fact. It will be found impossible to separate His atoning death from His holy obedience, so as to admit of the one being imputed without the other; for His death was the crowning act of His obedience— 'He became obedient unto death, even the death of the cross.' And if the obedience which was involved in His 'enduring the cross' may be imputed to us, why may not every other act of His obedience, by which 'He magnified the law, and made it honourable?' It will also be found impossible to defend the imputation of His passive obedience, and to reject that of His whole righteousness, without exposing those who make the attempt to an unanswerable retort from the opponents of both. Indeed, most of the objections which have been urged against the doctrine of imputed righteousness, by those who admit a vicarious satisfaction for sin, have been derived from Popish or Socinian sources, and bear a striking resemblance to those which Bellarmine and Crellius employed in a former age. (7)

PROP. XX. The imputation of sin and righteousness is not, in any bad sense of the expression, a 'legal fiction,' as it has been offensively called; nor is it a theory, invented by man, but a fact, revealed by God.

Instead of disproving the doctrine by a dispassionate appeal to Scripture, some recent writers have attempted to discredit it; and have characterized it sometimes as ' a fiction,' and sometimes as ' a theory.' This is a short and easy method of controversy, fitted to excite prejudice, while it dispenses with proof. But intelligent men, who know how often whatever is true and good among men has been caricatured and traduced by affixing to it some offensive epithet, will require something more than an assertion to convince them, that the faith of the Christian Church has rested from the beginning on nothing more solid than a fanciful figment, or an ingenious speculation.

The imputation of sin and righteousness is not ' a legal fiction,' if by that expression be meant anything that is unreal or untrue. We make this statement with a limitation, because there are some ' legal fictions,' so called, which are very far from being unreal. It is ' a legal fiction' to say, that ' the king can do no wrong;' for unquestionably in his private and personal capacity

he can commit sin, and may even be guilty of crime;
but in his public and official capacity, as the head of the
State, he is held in the law of this country to be irre-
sponsible; and the errors or crimes of the government
are imputed to his constitutional advisers, who are regarded and treated, by reason of their official position,
as alone answerable for them.   It is a 'legal fiction' to
say that 'the king never dies;' for as an individual he
cannot escape the doom of the meanest of his subjects,—
but royalty survives the person of the monarch, and the
throne is filled as soon as it becomes vacant, by the
immediate succession in law of the heir-apparent, even
should he be an infant in the arms of his nurse.   It is a
'legal fiction' to say that the Commons of England are
assembled in Parliament; for they are there only in the
persons of their representatives; and yet the whole nation
is bound by their acts, and subject to be governed, taxed,
fined, imprisoned, or even put to death, according to their
laws.   It is a 'legal fiction,' and far from being a seemly
one, to speak of the omnipotence of Parliament; yet under
an irreverent form of expression, the statement contains
the important truth, that the supreme power, which must
exist in every form of government, and from whose judgment there lies no appeal, is vested in the legislative
and executive authorities of the State.   Is constitutional
government, therefore, a 'legal fiction,' in the sense of
being either unreal, or unconnected with grave responsibilities?   Or was adoption, according to the Romish
Jurisprudence, which regarded and treated one as the
son of another in law who was not his son by birth, a
'legal fiction,' or a privilege of no real worth, when it
constituted a new relation between those who were not
related before, and conveyed a legal right of inheritance?
Or is the rule that the wife is one in law with her husband

an unreal thing, when it invests him with a right to her property, and makes him liable for her debts ?   These examples may serve to dispel the prejudice which is excited against the imputation of sin and righteousness, when it is described as a mere ' legal fiction ;' since they show that even amongst men, and in the common affairs of life, there are ' legal fictions' which embody and express important truths. (8)

Suppose that it were justly described as a ' legal fiction,' it might still represent an important truth, under the scheme of God's moral government.   It would only be the statement of a fact in that legal constitution under which He has been pleased to place us.   If we have reason to believe, as we have endeavoured to prove, that He promulgated His Law in a covenant form, as a law for the race at large, and imposed it on the first Adam as their representative, then that constitution may, or rather must, be productive of results in which they, as well as he, will be found to participate ; and yet these consequences, so far from being mere ' legal fictions,' are assuredly very solemn realities ;—the curse pronounced on the ground,—the doom of universal death,—the loss of God's image,—the forfeiture of His favour,—the depravity of human nature,—and all the evils and sufferings which have followed in the train of sin,—all these are brought upon us under the operation of that law, and every one of them is as real, as it is dreadful.   In like manner, if we have reason to believe, as we have endeavoured to prove, that He has promulgated a scheme of Redeeming Mercy, and this, too, in a covenant form, through the second Adam as the representative of His people,—imposing on Him the fulfilment of its conditions, and securing to them the benefits of His work on their behalf,—then this constitution also may, or rather must, be productive of results, in which they as well as He will be found to participate; and yet these results, so far from being mere 'legal fictions,' are substantial blessings of the highest and most permanent kind;—the pardon of sin,—the restoration of God's favour,—the renewal of His image,—the assurance of His love,—the privilege of adoption,—and the gift of eternal life,—all these are brought upon us under the operation of that scheme, and every one of them is as real, as it is desirable. When we are brought face to face with such realities as these, it is vain to talk of 'legal fictions,' whether under the Law or under the Gospel; for while condemnation, on the one hand, and justification, on the other, are strictly forensic or judicial acts, and must necessarily have some relation to the Law and Justice of God,—and while the representative character both of the first and second Adam, and the consequent imputation of their guilt and righteousness to those whom they respectively represented, can only be ascribed to the sovereign will and appointment of God,—yet the results are in their own nature real and true, and not, in any sense, fictitious or imaginary.

If it be said, again, that while the results are real and important, the doctrine of Imputation is a mere human attempt to offer some explanation of them, and that the results may be admitted, while the explanation is refused, we answer, that it is not a Theory, invented by man, but a Fact, revealed by God. (9)   A similar prejudice exists against all the peculiar revelations of Scripture, as if they were matters of speculative interest, rather than of practical importance.   Yet nothing is more remarkable in the doctrines of Christianity than this,—that every one of them is simply the statement of a FACT,—and that they all relate either to substantive Beings—God, angels, and

men,—or to real events, past, present, or future. What
is the doctrine of God, but the revelation of His existence,
and of the Perfections which really belong to Him, as
Jehovah, the Creator, Lawgiver, Governor, and Judge of
the world? What is the doctrine of the Trinity, but the
statement of a fact respecting the existence of distinct
Hypostases in His one undivided Godhead? What is the
doctrine of the divine Decrees, but the statement of a fact
respecting the eternal purposes of the Divine Mind?
What is the doctrine of Providence, but the statement of
a fact respecting His constant agency in sustaining and
governing the world? What is the doctrine of the Incarnation, but the statement of a fact respecting the union
of the divine and human natures in the person of our
Lord? And, in like manner, what is the doctrine of
Imputation, whether of sin or of righteousness, but the
statement of a fact respecting the relation in which we
stand to the first and second Adam, and the consequences
which result to us from the disobedience of the one, and
the obedience of the other? No doubt, when these facts
are revealed, and become the subjects of human thought,
they may occasion much speculation, and speculation may
give birth to many theories, which are all the more likely
to be wild and visionary when speculation is unrestrained
by faith; but let the Facts themselves be believed on the
testimony of the Revealer, let them be duly realised in
their full scriptural meaning, and in their application to
our own souls,—and we may safely discard every theory
about them which is the mere invention of men, and
adhere only to the truth as it has been taught by God.

LECTURE XIII.

JUSTIFICATION; ITS RELATION TO GRACE, AND WORKS.

THE great cardinal question on the subject of Justification,—and that on the right settlement of which
the determination of every other mainly depends,—relates
to its immediate ground; and amounts in substance to
this,—What is the righteousness, on account of which a
sinner is forgiven and accepted as righteous, in the sight
of God? or, What is the righteousness to which God has
regard in bestowing, and on which the sinner should
rely for obtaining, the forgiveness of his sins, and a title
to eternal life? or in yet another form,—Whether the
righteousness which is revealed as the ground of our
Justification be the vicarious righteousness of Christ imputed, or our own personal righteousness, infused and
inherent?   This is the real ultimate question; but the
fact that our Justification is, in Scripture, connected, in
various ways, with the source from which it is derived,—
the manner in which it is bestowed,—the means by which
it is appropriated and enjoyed,—the effects which flow
from it,—and the evidence by which it is attested and
proved, renders it necessary to consider some subordinate
questions which have been raised concerning it.

Pʀᴏᴘ. XXI. When God forgives sinners, and accepts
them as righteous in His sight, they are 'justified freely
by His grace, through the redemption which is in Christ
Jesus.'

Some have imagined that these two—Grace and Redemption—are necessarily incompatible with each other,
or mutually exclusive; and have held that, if Justification
be 'by grace,' it cannot be 'through a redemption,' or,
conversely, that if it be 'through a redemption,' it cannot
be 'by grace.' That the Apostle felt no difficulty in combining them, and no need to harmonize or reconcile the
one with the other, is sufficiently evident from the fact,
that he speaks of both in the same sentence, and invariably represents our Justification as depending equally,
although in different respects, on each of them. 'Being
justified freely,' says he, "by His grace, through the redemption that is in Christ Jesus."[1]   His language is peculiarly strong; he affirms, not only that we are 'justified by
His grace,' but that we are 'justified *freely* by His grace'
($\delta\omega\rho\epsilon\grave{\alpha}\nu$ $\tau\hat{\eta}$ $\alpha\grave{v}\tauo\hat{v}$ $\chi\acute{\alpha}\rho\iota\tau\iota$).   Nor is this a solitary instance of
the same combination; for he says elsewhere, 'He hath
made us accepted in the Beloved; in whom we have
redemption through His blood, the forgiveness of sins,
according to the riches of His grace, wherein He hath
abounded toward us :'[2] both the 'redemption through His
blood,' and 'the forgiveness of sin' which was procured
by it, are here said to be, not only 'by grace,' but 'according to the riches of His grace, wherein He hath abounded
toward us.' So that, according to the Apostle, the 'forgiveness of sins' is the fruit both of 'grace' and 'redemption.'   In other passages, he speaks of 'the righteousness
of Christ,' just as he here speaks of 'redemption through
His blood,' in immediate connection with the riches and
freeness of God's grace.   He speaks of those 'who receive
abundance of grace, and of the gift of righteousness ;' and
even of 'grace reigning through righteousness unto eternal
life by Jesus Christ our Lord.'[3]   The reason is clear.   The

---

[1] Rom. iii. 24.   [2] Eph. i. 7 ; also Col. i. 14.   [3] Rom. v. 17, 21.

grace of God was manifested, not only, nor even chiefly, in the forgiveness and acceptance of sinners, but also, and far more signally, in the divine provision for that end,—in the Father's gift of His only-begotten Son,—in His 'setting Him forth to be a propitiation,'—in His providing the satisfaction which His justice demanded,—and in His thus making 'mercy and truth to meet together, righteousness and peace to kiss each other.' For 'herein is love, not that we loved God, but that God loved us, and sent His Son to be the propitiation for our sins.'[1] Our sense of the riches and the freeness of His grace, so far from being impaired, is immeasurably enhanced, by the consideration of the costly sacrifice by which our justification was secured; and it is only when that consideration is kept in view, that we feel the full force of the Apostle's argument, when, founding upon it, he infers that there is no other blessing which the same grace will not bestow, when it delivered up His own Son to die for us. For 'God commendeth His love toward us, in that, while we were yet sinners, Christ died for us;' and 'if, while we were enemies, we were reconciled to God by the death of His Son, much more, being reconciled, we shall be saved by His life.'[2] It may be safely affirmed, that all our highest views of the riches and freeness of God's grace are derived from the work of redemption; and that those who seek to separate the pardon of sin from a sacrifice of propitiation have comparatively very slight impressions, both of the justice of God in punishing, and of the mercy of God in forgiving, the transgressors of His law. (1)

It is when we take into account both the privilege of Justification, and the divine provision which was made for its being bestowed, that we are enabled to form, not only a right estimate of the riches and freeness, but also a

[1] Ps. lxxxv. 10 ; 1 John iv. 10.   [2] Rom. v. 8, 10.

scriptural conception of the *nature*, of God's grace. The
meaning of the term is fixed by the manner in which His
grace has been manifested.   Its scriptural import has
been misunderstood and perverted, in a way which would
have been impossible, had this obvious remark been duly
attended to.   It has been held to denote, not the free love
and favour of God, from which every good and perfect
gift proceeds, but merely one of these gifts as bestowed on
men,—not the grace which resides in the Divine Mind,
and is the fountainhead of every blessing whatever, but
the grace which is infused into the mind of man, and
becomes subjectively inherent there,—not the mercy which
pardons and accepts the sinner, but the divine energy
which renews and sanctifies him.   That we may neutralize
or correct this pernicious error, it is not necessary to deny
that the term grace may be legitimately used to denote
every one of the gifts which grace bestows,—for, by an easy
figure of speech, that which properly belongs to the cause
is often applied derivatively to the effect; and we may
speak of the grace of pardon, or the grace of adoption, or
the grace of sanctification, or the graces of faith, hope, and
charity, merely for the purpose of indicating the source
from which they flow.   But it is a dangerous error, to
confound these effects with their common cause,—and
still more to restrict the grace of God, which is revealed
in the Gospel, as if it meant only the grace which is
infused into, and inherently subjective in, the soul of
man.   It is an attribute essential to the divine nature, and
acting freely according to the counsel of the divine will.
Some even of the blessings which it bestows on man,—
such as the free pardon of sin, and the gracious acceptance,
and adoption, of the sinner,—are not, in their own nature,
infused habits or inherent graces, but a change merely in
his relation to God ;—a change which is always connected

with a renewal of his moral character, but should never be confounded with it, or supposed to rest upon it, as its ground and reason,—and which implies only an act of God's grace, of which he is the object through the redemption which is in Christ Jesus. But the crowning proof that this is the scriptural meaning of the term is supplied by the fact, that His grace had its first and highest manifestation in the gift of His Son, and in the scheme of redemption through Him,—a manifestation in which there was nothing else than a free, unprompted, unsolicited expression of His sovereign love, and which consisted in a gift bestowed,—not in a grace infused,—yet such a gift as included in it every other fruit of His ' good-will to men.' (2)

PROP. XXII. Justification ' by grace ' is identified, in Scripture, with Justification ' by faith,' and opposed to Justification ' by works.'

Its gracious character, so far from being obscured, is only made the more manifest, by its being connected with faith ;—' Therefore it is of faith, that it might be by grace ;'[1] and the two expressions, ' by grace,' and ' by faith,' are used indifferently to express the same truth. There can be no reasonable doubt, therefore, that if we are justified ' by grace,' we are justified also ' by faith;' and, conversely, that, if we are justified ' by faith,' we are justified also ' by grace.' It is the more necessary to mark the convertible use of these two expressions, as being substantially equivalent to each other, because the Apostle often uses them interchangeably, and sometimes makes use of the first where we should have expected him to employ the second. When he is reasoning, for example, from the justification of Abraham to that of

[1] Rom. iv. 16.

other believers, he says : 'Abraham believed God, and
it was counted to him for righteousness. Now to him
that worketh is the reward not reckoned of grace, but of
debt; but to him that worketh not, but believeth on Him
that justifieth the ungodly, his faith is counted for righteousness.' We should have expected him to complete the
statement, by preserving the exact antithesis, and saying,
' The reward is reckoned not of debt, but of grace:' and
when, instead of this, he says, ' his faith is counted for
righteousness,' it is evident that Justification ' by faith '
was, in his sense of the expression, equivalent to Justification ' by grace ;' and that it was so because free grace
is necessarily implied in the object of faith as it is here
described, namely, ' Him that justifieth the ungodly.'

While Justification ' by grace ' is thus identified with
Justification ' by faith,' both are frequently opposed to
Justification ' by works.' ' Israel, which followed after
the law of righteousness, hath not attained to the law of
righteousness.   Wherefore ?   Because they sought it not
by faith, but as it were by the works of the law.' [1] ' Knowing that a man is not justified by the works of the law, but
by the faith of Jesus Christ, we have believed in Jesus
Christ, that we might be justified by the faith of Christ,
and not by the works of the law ; for by the works of the
law shall no flesh be justified.' [2] ' By grace are ye saved,
through faith, . . . not of works, lest any man should
boast.' [3] ' Who hath saved us, and called us with a holy
calling, not according to our works, but according to His
own purpose and grace.' [4] ' After that the kindness and
love of God our Saviour toward men appeared,—not by
works of righteousness which we have done, but according
to His mercy He saved us, . . . that being justified by His

---

[1] Rom. ix. 31, 32 ; also x. 3–13.   [2] Gal. ii. 16.
[3] Eph. ii. 8, 9.   [4] 2 Tim. i. 9.

grace, we should be made heirs according to the hope of eternal life.'[1]　As it is certain, therefore, that Justification 'by grace' is identified in Scripture with Justification 'by faith,' it is equally certain from these testimonies, that both are placed in contrast and opposition to Justification 'by works.'　What relation subsists between Justification and 'works,' on the one hand, and between Justification and 'faith,' on the other, will fall to be considered in separate propositions; in the meantime, we speak only of its relation to 'grace.'

PROP. XXIII. Justification by the 'works of the law' is expressly excluded in the case of every sinner; while Justification by a righteousness not his own, is as expressly revealed.

That a sinner cannot be justified by his own works, might be inferred from the mere fact of his guilt, viewed in connection with the essential nature of law; for law, considered as the rule at once of man's duty, and of God's judgment, can only justify the righteous, and condemn the wicked.　But this conclusion is declared in the most explicit terms, and with the utmost solemnity, in many passages of Scripture :—' For as many as are of the works of the law are under the curse; for it is written, Cursed is every one that continueth not in all things which are written in the book of the law to do them.'[2]　'Whosoever shall keep the whole law, and yet offend in one point, he is guilty of all.　For He that said, Do not commit adultery, said also, Do not kill.　Now if thou commit no adultery, yet if thou kill, thou art become a transgressor of the law.'[3]　'The wrath of God is revealed from heaven against all ungodliness and unrighteousness of men.'[4]　'What things soever the law saith, it saith to them who

[1] Tit. iii. 4, 5, 7.　　[2] Gal. iii. 10.　　[3] Jas. ii. 10, 11.　　[4] Rom. i. 18.

are under the law, that every mouth may be stopped, and all the world may become guilty before God. Therefore by the deeds of the law there shall no flesh be justified in His sight; for by the law is the knowledge of sin.'[1] 'If there had been a law given which could have given life, verily righteousness should have been by the law. But the Scripture hath concluded all under sin.'[2]

These testimonies are conclusive on *three* points : *first*, that wherever sin exists, there can be no Justification by works ; *secondly*, that sin exists wherever there is not perfect obedience to God's law ; and *thirdly*, that there is no perfect obedience among men, for 'all have sinned and come short of the glory of God.'

But this conclusion has been evaded in various ways, even by those who cannot altogether affirm their innocence, or deny their guilt. They have had recourse sometimes to a distinction between different kinds of 'works,'—such as works done in the strength of nature, or by the aid of grace,—works done before, or after, faith,—works of cere- monial observance, or of moral duty,—works of legal, or of evangelical, obedience,—works consisting in mere ex- ternal conformity, or springing from an inward principle of holiness,—works of human invention, or of divine obligation,—works of perfect, or of imperfect, but sin- cere, obedience. They have also had recourse to a difference between one class of laws and another; and have imposed a limited and partial sense on the 'law' of which the Apostle speaks,—as if he referred only to the Ceremonial, and not to the Moral, Law. But by far the most frequent, and most dangerous, error, is that of those who practically overlook the spirituality and extent of the divine requirements, and seek to palliate the guilt and demerit of sin by plausible excuses or

[1] Rom. iii. 19, 20.   [2] Gal. iii. 21.

extenuations. Some of these evasions have been applied
chiefly to the question as to the justification of *believers*,—
whether it may not be ascribed, in whole or in part, to
their infused and inherent holiness, and the works of
new obedience which spring from it,—a question which
depends, in some respects, on different considerations from
those which are applicable to the justification of *sinners*,
considered simply as such ; and which will be considered
afterwards on its own peculiar merits. In the meantime,
as all men are sinners before they become believers, we
restrict ourselves to the question, whether, *as sinners*, they
can be justified by works ?

Looking to the explicit statements of the Apostle, it
might well be thought that no one would venture to
answer this question in the affirmative; for the law
which condemns a man on account of his sin, can
scarcely be supposed to justify him on account of his
righteousness. And probably many of those who speak
most confidently of Justification by their works of obedience, have a tacit reference, in their own minds, to some
moral change, which has been, or may yet be, effected in
their character, sufficient, in their opinion, to alter their
whole relation to God,—to exempt them from the curse
of His law,—and to raise them to the enjoyment of His
favour. They think of Justification as the certain effect,
if not also as the just reward, of such a change ; and do
not seem even to entertain the question—how a sinner,
simply as such, may obtain forgiveness and acceptance
with God. If they could be brought to believe, as Abraham did, in 'Him which justifieth the ungodly,' they
might also see, that He can only do so by 'imputing
righteousness without works ;' for as yet, at least, whatever may be said of their obedience afterwards, they have
no works of their own, except such as are evil and sinful.

But here again, at this precise point, they have recourse
to a very subtle and plausible evasion; they take refuge
from the statement which describes God 'as Him that
justifieth the ungodly' (τὸν δικαιοῦντα τὸν ἀσεβῆ),[1] in another
statement of the same Apostle, which describes Him as
' the justifier of him which believeth in Jesus' (τὸν δικαιοῦντα τὸν ἐκ πίστεως 'Ιησοῦ) ;[2] and, as if these two statements were, or could be, at variance with each other,
they argue—that God does not justify any man simply as
a sinner, but only as a believer,—that if those who are
justified were previously 'ungodly,' they cease to be 'ungodly ' as soon as they 'believe,'—and that this change
in their moral and spiritual character, is the ground of
their pardon and acceptance, rather than any other righteousness, imputed to them, and received by faith.   There
is much that is true in this representation, and yet much,
also, that is false and dangerous.   It is true, that God
never justifies a sinner till he believes in Christ; it is
equally true, that the 'ungodly' do not continue to be
'ungodly' after they believe in Him : but it is not true,—
either that there is any contrariety between the two statements, which describe Him as justifying the ungodly and
justifying true believers,—or that the spiritual change
which is effected on the views and dispositions of a sinner,
when he is brought to believe in Christ, is the ground of
his pardon and acceptance with God.   That change is
effected by the grace of the Holy Spirit, but His grace
comes to us through the channel of Christ's mediatorial
work, and is dispensed by Christ Himself as the administrator of the covenant, with a view,—not to supersede
His own work, or even to supplement it, as if it were insufficient for the end for which it was accomplished,—but
simply to apply it, for the saving benefit of His people, by

[1] Rom. iv. 5.   [2] Rom. iii. 26.

making them willing to receive and rest upon it for their salvation.

The question has been raised—What are the ' works' which the Apostle meant to exclude from having any part in our Justification ? and what is the 'Law' to which he specially refers as being weak and unprofitable for that end ?   To this question,—for it is substantially one and the same in different forms,—some have replied,—that he meant to exclude only formal outward observances,—and that the law of which he speaks was only the ceremonial law of the Jews, not the moral law, which is of universal and permanent obligation ; whence they have inferred, that his statements cannot be applied to the virtuous actions of any class of men, and, still less, to the graces of the Christian character, or the good works of the Christian life. (3) But a conclusive refutation of this reply is supplied by the text, or the context, of every passage in which we are said to be justified ' without works,' or 'without the law.'

Take, first, the Apostle's discourse in the earlier part of the Epistle to the Romans, where he treats expressly of the two opposite methods of Justification, by works, and by grace, and which may be regarded as the *locus classicus* on the subject.[1] The question being—what is the law of which he speaks, and what works are excluded from Justification ?—we are supplied with ample materials for a decisive deliverance upon it.   It is manifest that he does not speak exclusively, or even specially, of the ceremonial law of the Jews ; but that he speaks of law in general, including what was peculiar to the Jews, but also what was common to them with the Gentiles ; or of that moral law which possesses universal and unchangeable authority.   This appears, *first*, from the scope

[1] Rom. i. 18–iii. 20.

of his whole argument, which is founded on the principle
that 'where there is no law, there is no transgression,' or
  that sin is not imputed where there is no law,' and
directed to prove that both Jews and Gentiles were under
law,—the Jews under the law of Moses in addition to
the light of nature,—and the Gentiles, who had not that
law, under the original, connatural, and indestructible
law, by which 'they were a law to themselves;'—*secondly*,
from the sweeping universality of his conclusion: 'Now
we know what things soever the law saith, it saith to
them that are under the law, that *every mouth* may be
stopped, and *all the world* may become guilty before God;'
'for there is no difference, for all have sinned, and come
short of the glory of God.'   'We have before proved both
Jews and Gentiles, that they are all under sin: for there
is none righteous, no, not one.'   'Therefore, by the deeds
of the law shall *no flesh* be justified in His sight, for by the
law is the knowledge of sin;'—*thirdly*, from his enumeration of the sins which were violations of the law to which
he refers,[1]—every one of which is a transgression of the
moral law,—such as ungodliness, violence, deceit, falsehood and evil-speaking, cursing and bitterness,—while no
mention whatever is made of any breach of ceremonial
precepts;—*fourthly*, from his answer to the question, 'Do
we then make void the law through faith? God forbid,
yea, we establish the law;' for this cannot be the ceremonial law, which was fulfilled, and abrogated, but the
moral law, which was fulfilled, and confirmed, by Christ;
—and, *lastly*, from his reference to the cases of Abraham
and David; for Abraham was justified when 'God imputed to him righteousness without works,' before the
ceremonial law was introduced, and before even the rite
of circumcision, for 'he received the sign of circumcision,

[1] Rom. iii. 10–18.

a seal of the righteousness of the faith which he had
yet being uncircumcised;' and David cannot be supposed
to have referred only to ceremonial defilements, if he
thought of them at all, when he described 'the blessedness of the man to whom God imputeth righteousness
without works, saying, Blessed are they whose iniquities
are forgiven, and whose sins are covered; blessed is the
man to whom the Lord will not impute sin.' (4)

Such being 'the law,' and such 'the works,' of which
the Apostle speaks, it is necessary to consider the design
and object of his argument. It can scarcely be supposed
—that he intended to prove, that men cannot be justified
by works which are evil and sinful; for this is self-evident, and could scarcely need to be proved;—nor can it
be supposed he intended to prove, that men cannot be
justified by works which are good and perfect; for that
is untrue, and could scarcely be affirmed in opposition to
the terms of the first covenant of life, or to our Lord's
own reference to these terms, when He said to the
Pharisee, 'Thou hast answered right: this do, and thou
shalt live.' His argument was mainly directed, not to
prove either of these doctrines, or to establish any position of a purely speculative kind, but to establish the
fact of universal guilt and depravity,—to carry home to
the conscience, both of Jew and Gentile, the conviction
of their demerit, and danger, as sinners,—to show them
that, while God's law was 'spiritual,' they were 'carnal,'
—that while 'the law was holy, and the commandment
holy, and just, and good,' they were themselves unholy,
and their works unholy, and unrighteous, and evil,—that,
in 'the judgment of God, they which commit such things
are *worthy* of death,'—and that 'the judgment of God is
ever according to truth.'[1] His object, in short, was a

[1] Rom. i. 32, ii. 2.

practical one,—to establish the fact of their guilt and
condemnation, in order that they might feel their need
of such a salvation as the Gospel proclaims ; and if that
fact, when established, is applied to prove that 'by the
deeds of the law shall no flesh be justified,' this inevitable
inference from it is designed to drive them out of those
'false confidences,' or 'refuges of lies,' which men are
so prone to construct for themselves, and to direct them,
as convicted and condemned sinners, to 'flee for refuge
to the hope which is set before them.'

This is the great desideratum still.   All error on the
subject of Justification springs from the defective views
which prevail almost universally among men of the
spiritual requirements of God's Law ; for these are invariably connected with a slight sense of sin, and a false
or exaggerated estimate of the virtues of their personal
character.   Many speak of 'good works,' without considering what is required to make any 'work' really
'good,' according to the rule of God's Law.   A 'work,'
to be really 'good,' must be itself in conformity to the
precept of His law,—it must be done in obedience to
His will,—it must spring from a right motive,—it must
be an expression of love, supreme towards God, disinterested towards men,—it must be directed to God's glory
as its end.   If any work be a violation of the precept of
His law, it cannot be a 'good work,' whatever may be
the motive from which it springs, for the motive cannot
consecrate a sin, nor can the end justify the means : if it
be not done in obedience to His will, it may be in conformity with the letter of His law, but is utterly destitute
of its spirit ; for a godless morality, which places conscience on the throne of God, and creates an autonomy
within, independent of Him who is the supreme Lawgiver, Governor, and Judge, may indicate some sense of

duty, or at least of prudence, while those who practise it have ' no fear of God before their eyes,' and may never have yielded, in any one action of their lives, a dutiful submission to His authority ;—if it be not done from a right motive, the work may be materially good, and yet morally evil ; for prayer to God, almsgiving to the poor, and fasting for the mortification of sin, are actions which are good in their own nature, and yet if they be done ' to be seen of men,'[1] they are utterly desecrated by that corrupt motive, and become examples of abominable hypocrisy ;—if it be not an expression of real heartfelt love, supreme towards God, and disinterested toward men, it has no right to a place among the duties of either table of God's Law ; for ' the first and great commandment is, Thou shalt love the Lord thy God with all thy heart ;' and the second is like unto it, ' Thou shalt love thy neighbour as thyself ;'[2]—and if it be done with no regard to God's glory, it is a dereliction of our chief end ; for in our most virtuous actions we may ' come short of the glory of God.'[3] If men could only be brought to understand and believe, that these are really the requirements of God's Law, and if they would then apply them seriously as tests of their conduct and springs of action, their own conscience would 'bear witness' against them, and no other argument would be needed to prove that, as sinners, they cannot be justified by Works.

Prop. XXIV. Justification by ' works,' such as are really ' good ' and ' acceptable to God,' is also excluded in the case of believers, excepting only as it may be manifested or declared by them.

This statement includes or implies several distinct truths of great practical interest and importance, which

[1] Matt. vi. 1-6, 16-18.   [2] Matt. xxii. 37, 39, 40.   [3] Rom. iii. 23.

cannot be understood in their true scriptural meaning, or
perceived in their right order of relation to one another,
without first placing them singly before our minds in the
light which Scripture sheds upon them respectively, and
then combining them in one general and comprehensive
view.   They must be considered in the exercise of careful
and correct discrimination, and then adjusted to each
other, as constituent parts of one self-consistent and
harmonious system of doctrine.

The *first* of these is the reality and necessity of Good
Works in the case of every true believer.   In Scripture,
they are not only required of all believers, but recognised
also as being truly acceptable to God, and even rewarded
by Him.   They are acceptable to Him for three distinct
reasons : *first*, because they are acts of dutiful obedience,
on the part of those who have been 'accepted in the Beloved,' and whom He has adopted as His own children ;
secondly, because they are agreeable to His revealed will ;
and *thirdly*, because they are the 'fruits of His Spirit,' and,
as such, very precious in themselves, and very pleasing to
Him.   No one with the Bible in his hands can possibly
believe, that faith is not more acceptable to Him than
unbelief,—or 'a broken and a contrite spirit' than 'a
hard and impenitent heart,'—or integrity and truth than
fraud and falsehood,—or purity in thought, word, and
deed, than a prurient fancy and a profligate life,—or that
infused and inherent holiness which, however imperfect,
is the incipient restoration of His own image, than that
habitual sinfulness, which is the image of the wicked one.
For both the graces and the good works of believers are
expressly declared to be acceptable to Him.   'The ornament of a meek and quiet spirit' is said to be 'in the
sight of God of great price;'[1]—believers are commanded,

[1] 1 Pet. iii. 4.

not only to 'offer the sacrifice of praise to God continually,' but also 'to do good and to communicate; for with
such sacrifices God is well pleased;'[1] their 'prayers and
their alms' are said 'to come up for a memorial before
God;'[2] their contributions to the cause of Christ are described as 'an odour of a sweet smell, a sacrifice acceptable,
well pleasing to God;'[3]—all believers are represented 'as
a spiritual house, an holy priesthood, to offer up spiritual
sacrifices, acceptable to God by Jesus Christ,'[4]—and they
are exhorted 'by the mercies of God, that they present
their bodies a living sacrifice, holy, acceptable unto God,
which is their reasonable service.' Their good works are
even said to be *rewarded*, and that, too, in a measure pro-
portioned to their number and excellence. 'For God is
not unrighteous, to forget your work and labour of love,
which ye have showed toward His name, in that ye have
ministered to the saints.' 'He that receiveth a prophet
in the name of a prophet, shall receive a prophet's reward;
and he that receiveth a righteous man in the name of a
righteous man, shall receive a righteous man's reward.
And whosoever shall give to drink unto one of these little
ones a cup of cold water only in the name of a disciple,
verily I say unto you, he shall in no wise lose his reward.'
'Whatsoever a man soweth, that shall he also reap. . . .
And let us not be weary in well-doing: for in due season
we shall reap, if we faint not.' 'But he which soweth
sparingly, shall reap also sparingly; and he which soweth
bountifully, shall reap also bountifully.' 'And every man
shall receive his own reward, according to his own labour.'
'The fire shall try every man's work of what sort it is. If
any man's work abide which he hath built thereupon' (the
only 'foundation that is laid, which is Jesus Christ'), 'he
shall receive a reward. If any man's work shall be burned,

[1] Heb. xiii. 15, 16.   [2] Acts x. 4.   [3] Phil. iv. 18.   [4] 1 Pet. ii. 5.

he shall suffer loss ; but he himself shall be saved, yet so as by fire.'[1]

From these testimonies it clearly appears,—that 'good works' hold an important place in the scheme of Grace and Redemption,—that they are, in their own nature, intrinsically good, as contradistinguished from those which are morally evil,—that they are acceptable to God, both as being in accordance with His revealed will, and also as being the fruits of His Spirit,—and that they are connected with the promise of a divine reward. These truths are so clearly revealed, that could they be proved to be necessarily exclusive of Justification by grace through faith alone, we should be obliged either to abandon that doctrine altogether, or to modify it, so as to bring it into accordance with the express teaching of Scripture on the subject of good works. But there will be no difficulty in reconciling the two doctrines if we take a sufficiently comprehensive view of the whole 'revealed counsel of God.' Let us bear in mind,—that the 'good works,' which are said to be acceptable, and even rewarded, are those of true believers, who have already been justified and 'accepted in the Beloved,'—that while believers are not now 'under the law' as a covenant of works, because it has been fulfilled by Christ as their substitute and surety, they are still 'under the law to Christ' as a rule of life,—that they are, and ever must be, the subjects of a moral government, even after they have been brought into His kingdom,— that while He promises to reward their obedience, and to relieve them entirely from the punishment due to them on account of sin, He still says even to His redeemed people, 'As many as I love, I rebuke and chasten : be zealous, therefore, and repent,'—that the 'rewards of

[1] Heb. vi. 10 ; Matt. x. 41, 42 ; Gal. vi. 7, 8 ; 2 Cor. ix. 6 ; 1 Cor. iii. 8, 13–15.

grace,' which are peculiar to the Gospel, are expressly contrasted with the 'rewards of debt,' which belong only to the Law,—and that the same afflictions which, in the case of the unbelieving and impenitent, are properly penal inflictions, embittered by the wrath of God, are converted, in the case of His children, into paternal chastisements, and even classed among their chartered privileges, while they are sweetened by a Father's love ;—let us give due weight to these considerations, and we shall see at once, that their free Justification by grace through faith only is not inconsistent, either with their being governed now according to law, or with their being judged hereafter according to works. (5)

This will become more evident if we further consider, how Good Works stand related to Faith, and to Justification, respectively. They are the effects of faith, and, as such, the evidences both of faith, and of justification. That they are the effects of faith is clear ; for 'whatsoever is not of faith is sin ;' and 'without faith it is impossible to please God ;' and 'the end of the commandment is charity, out of a pure heart, and of a good conscience, and of faith unfeigned.'[1] It is equally clear that, being the effects, they are also the evidences, of a true and living faith ; for 'a man may say, Thou hast faith, and I have works : show me thy faith without thy works, and I will show thee my faith by my works ;' and all the good works, which are ascribed to believers under the Old Testament, are traced to the operation of faith.[2] But if, besides being the effects and evidences of faith, they are also, *as such*, the evidences of Justification, it will follow that Justification is connected inseparably with faith, so as to be the privilege of every one as soon as he believes, and simply

[1] Rom. xiv. 23 ; Heb. xi. 6 ; 1 Tim. i. 5.
[2] Jas. ii. 18 ; Heb. xi. 4, 7, 8, 17, 23, 32.

because he believes, in Christ,—otherwise good works might prove the existence of faith, without proving the possession of that privilege; whereas they are applied in Scripture as evidences of both.   For example, the good work of the poor woman who anointed the Lord with ointment is adduced first as an evidence of her love to Him,—then her love is adduced as an evidence of her faith in Him,—and then all the three are applied as an evidence of her justification.   But if her good work, and her great love, were both the effects and evidences of her faith, and if, as such, they were also the evidence of her Justification, then her justification must have been connected immediately and directly with her faith in Christ, and not with her love and obedience ; for these are spoken of, not as its ground and reason, but as its manifestation and proof.   For this reason we have said, that ' Justification by good works is excluded in the case of believers,' —but with this limitation, ' excepting only as it may be manifested or declared by them;' for in this purely declarative sense, the term is unquestionably used by the Apostle James, when he says, ' Was not our father Abraham justified by works, when he had offered Isaac his son upon the altar ?'[1]

Good works being the effects and evidences of faith, and, as such, the signs or tokens of Justification, they cannot form any part of the ground on which faith relies, or on which Justification depends.   Nor can they come in, as an intervening cause or condition, between faith and justification, for they follow after faith, whereas every believer is justified as soon as he is united to Christ. They are the works of believing and justified men ; and no work can be acceptable to God while men remain in a state of unbelief and enmity.

[1] Jas. ii. 21.

There is another important question in relation to the
'good works' of believers : Are they perfect, or imperfect ?   Are they pure and spotless, or are they defiled
and polluted by sin ?   In answer to this question, those
who have contended, either in the Popish or Protestant
Churches, for Justification on the ground of good works,
or of the infused and inherent righteousness of the believer, have generally contended also for the doctrine of
Christian perfection, and denied, or modified, the doctrine
of indwelling sin.   In answer to the same question, those
who have contended for Justification on the ground of
the Mediatorial work of Christ, and His righteousness
imputed to the believer, have maintained the imperfection of his best works, and their defilement by much
remaining sin.   On this point, it may be affirmed with
undeniable certainty, that the good works of believers,
although they are so far in conformity with God's revealed
will, as to be more pleasing to Him than the evil works
of the wicked, cannot be more perfect than are the inward
principles or graces from which they spring ; and that
neither the faith, nor the repentance, nor the love, nor
the holiness, nor the new obedience, of the most mature
believer, is such as to fulfil the spiritual requirements
of the divine Law ; while, imperfect as they all are
in themselves, they are invariably soiled and contami-
nated by some 'spots of the flesh,' and defiled by the
constant presence, and frequent pollutions, of indwelling
sin.[1] (6)

The testimony of Scripture on this point has been
abundantly confirmed by the experience of all believers
in every age of the Church.   They have ever been ' a
chosen generation, a royal priesthood, an holy nation, a
peculiar people,' and they have ' shown forth' by their

[1] Rom. vii. 14-25 ; Gal. v. 17.

lives, as well as by their lips, 'the praises of Him who
called them out of darkness into His marvellous light;'
and yet one of their most striking and peculiar characteristics has ever been, an abiding sense of sin, and 'a
broken and contrite spirit' on account of it.   Read the
biographies, or examine the diaries, of the most eminent
saints, and you will discern no more marked feature of a
family likeness between them all, in every country and
in every age, than their frequent confessions of unworthiness, and their ceaseless conflicts with the evil which was
in their own hearts.   Day by day continually they have
prayed for 'mercy' to pardon, as well as for 'grace to
help them;' and day by day continually they have had
recourse anew to the 'fountain which has been opened
for sin and for uncleanness.'   Some of them may have
lived outwardly in the regular discharge of all religious
and relative duties, without being chargeable with any
signal act of overt transgression, like Zacharias and Elisabeth, who were, in this sense, 'righteous before God,
walking in all the ordinances and commandments of the
Lord blameless;'[1] others may have fallen,—like Noah,
David, and Peter,—into gross and scandalous offences,
which, when 'they were renewed again. to repentance,'
they could never remember without 'weeping bitterly,'
as Peter did, and confessing their sin, as David did in
that Psalm[2] which every penitent believer has made his
own in all ages and in all lands.   So far from regarding
their sins as mere 'infirmities' or 'imperfections,' because
they were committed by the children of God, they would
have felt them to be, in some respects, more highly aggra-
vated than those of the children of this world, and to
deserve what, but for God's pardoning mercy, they would
infallibly incur, 'everlasting destruction from the presence

[1] Luke i. 6.   [2] Ps. li.

of the Lord, and from the glory of His power.' If such
has been the uniform experience of all true believers, how
can the presence and power of indwelling sin be denied,
while the continued authority of a spiritual and perfect
law is still affirmed? or how can either their inherent
holiness, or their 'good works,' form any part of the
ground of their pardon and acceptance with God? How
scriptural, and how true to Christian experience, is the
saying of Bernard : ' So far from answering for my sins,
I cannot be answerable even for my own righteousnesses ;'
and that of Augustine : ' Your sins belong to yourselves ;
leave your righteousness to God !'

The most inconsistent and contradictory charges have
been brought against the Reformers and their successors,
in regard to their teaching upon the subject of ' Good
Works.' Sometimes they have been assailed, especially
by Popish writers, as denying either the reality of good
works in the believer altogether, or at least their necessity
to his salvation ; at other times they have been assailed,
especially by Antinomians, as subverting or impairing
the doctrine of Justification as a gift of free grace, by
insisting on good works as the fruits of faith and the
evidences of a justified state. It would seem as if, at the
present day, not less than in primitive times, the teachers
of ' the whole counsel of God' must lay their account
with the most contradictory objections. ' Whereunto,'
said our Lord, ' shall I liken this generation ? It is like
unto children sitting in the markets, and calling unto their
fellows, and saying, We have piped unto you, but ye have
not danced ; we have mourned unto you, but ye have not
lamented. For John came neither eating nor drinking,
and they say, He hath a devil. The Son of man came
eating and drinking, and they say, Behold a man gluttonous
and a wine-bibber, a friend of publicans and sinners : but

Wisdom is justified of her children.'[1]   The charge against
those who maintain the doctrine of a free Justification by
grace through faith only, that they deny either the reality
of good works, or their necessity to salvation, is a mere
calumny; for while the Reformers rejected many works
which were considered 'good' in the Romish Church,—
such as works of supererogation,—works done in fulfilment of counsels of perfection or monastic vows,—works
of penance and self-mortification for the pardon of sin;
and while, moreover, they denied the *merit* of all works,
whether performed in obedience to the commandments
of men, or even to the Law of God itself,—they never
denied the intrinsic excellence either of those inherent
graces which are 'the fruits of the Spirit,' or of those
external actions which flowed from them in conformity
with the requirements of God's Law; and so far from
teaching that they were not necessary to salvation,—in
the case of all who are capable, and have opportunity,
of manifesting their faith by its proper fruits,—they
represented the sanctification of the believer as an indispensable, a constituent, element of his salvation,—since
Christ came to deliver His people, not only from the
punishment, but also from the power, of sin,—and to
'present them to Himself a glorious church, not having
spot, or wrinkle, or any such thing, but that they should
be holy, and without blemish.'   It may be safely affirmed
that those who have most strenuously defended the doctrine of a free Justification by grace through faith only,
have also been the most earnest, and the most successful,
teachers of the doctrine which affirms that 'except a
man be born again, he cannot enter into the kingdom
of heaven;' and that 'without holiness no man shall see
the Lord.'

[1] Matt. xi. 16.

When the doctrine of the Reformers began to be abused by the Antinomians, the Puritans were raised up, in the good providence of God, to give the same prominence to Sanctification as Luther had given to Justification ; to insist as strenuously on the work of the Spirit in applying salvation as he had done on the work of Christ in procuring it : for although both doctrines were taught at an earlier period, and represented as constituent and co-ordinate branches of the same scheme of grace, it was reserved for their successors, when controversy arose, to expound them more fully in their necessary connection and mutual relations.   Such writers as Owen, and Goodwin, and Charnock, and Howe, and Trail adhered firmly to the doctrine of Justification as proclaimed by Luther and Calvin, while they checked every tendency to Antinomian licence by the firm assertion of the indispensable necessity of personal holiness as one of the essential parts of the great salvation, and by the full and masterly exposition which they were honoured to give of the office and work of the Holy Spirit. (7)   These great and good men taught that the good works of believers were really acceptable to God and agreeable to the divine will, while yet, being imperfect and defiled by much remaining sin, they could form no part of the ground of Justification, but were themselves accepted through the only merit of Christ.   When it is said that the same works cannot be consistently described both as ' an odour of a sweet smell, holy and acceptable to God,' and yet as ' dung,' or as ' filthy rags,' it seems to be forgotten, that these are the words of Scripture itself, and that there need be no contradiction in the case, unless they are applied (*eodem respectu*) with reference to the same uses and ends.   Considered as fruits of our sanctification, and as evidences of our 'MEETNESS for the inheritance of the saints in light,' they cannot be too highly

commended ; but considered as the ground of our Justification, or as forming any part of our TITLE to that
inheritance, they are to be utterly rejected, and treated
as 'dung' and 'filthy rags' *with reference to that end ;* for
they cannot be regarded as such, without dishonour to
the redeeming work of Christ ; and for this reason the
Apostle, speaking of himself as having been, ' as touching
the righteousness which is in the law, blameless,' declares
that he had renounced all dependence upon it, and upon
everything else but Christ alone. ' For what things were
gain to me, those I counted loss for Christ. Yea, doubtless, and I count all things but loss for the excellency of
the knowledge of Christ Jesus my Lord : for whom I have
suffered the loss of all things, and do count them but
dung, that I may win Christ, and be found in Him, not
having mine own righteousness, which is of the law, but
that which is through the faith of Christ, the righteousness which is of God by faith.''[1] (8)

[1] Phil. iii. 7-9.

LECTURE XIV.

JUSTIFICATION; THE NATURE AND REASON OF ITS CONNECTION WITH FAITH.

WHEN the doctrine of Justification by Works has been abandoned as untenable, and that of Justification by Grace has been admitted, the fact that Faith, which is an infused and inherent grace, and the germ of holiness in heart and life, is indispensably required for our pardon and acceptance with God, has been made the plea or pretext for holding, that we are still justified by it as our evangelical righteousness, and that it bears the same relation to our Justification under the New Covenant, as that which subsisted between works and wages under the Old. It is not regarded as being the means of receiving and resting on the righteousness of Christ, but as being itself the righteousness which is the immediate ground of our acceptance ; while the Grace of God which implants this faith in us, and the meritorious work of Christ, which procured for us the privilege of acceptance on this ground, are still, to some extent, acknowledged. For this reason, it is necessary to consider what relation subsists, according to Scripture, between Justification and Faith ; and, for the full discussion of it, to review several distinct questions which have been raised respecting it. They are chiefly these—Whether Faith itself, and not the imputed righteousness of Christ, be the immediate ground of our acceptance ? What is the nature of saving Faith, or what

is, the most correct and comprehensive definition of it?
What is the kind of influence or efficacy which is ascribed
to Faith in connection with our Justification, and whether
it be best expressed by calling it a means, or an instrument, or a condition, of that privilege ?   What is the
warrant of Faith, or what that is which entitles any one
to receive and rest on Christ for his own personal salvation ?   And what is the distinctive peculiarity of Faith
which renders it the sole and exclusive means of Justification, or, in what sense, and for what reason, it may be
said that we are justified ' by Faith only ?'   In reply to
these questions, we lay down the following propositions.

PROP. XXV. We are justified by Faith, and Faith is
counted, or imputed to us, for righteousness ; but Faith is
not itself the righteousness on account of which we are
justified.

When Justification by works, whether legal or evangelical, has been excluded, both in the case of sinners and
believers, a large class of writers have shown a disposition
to fall back on Faith, as if it might be represented as the
ground of our pardon and acceptance with God ; and they
have argued that, as it is the distinguishing difference
between one class of sinners and another, so it may be
regarded as the real reason why some are accepted, while
others, remaining in unbelief, are condemned.   They have
also adduced what they conceive to be express scriptural
authority for their doctrine in the statement which is
repeatedly made, and that, too, both by Paul and James,
when, quoting the Old Testament, they say : ' Abraham
believed God, and it was counted to him for righteousness.'[1]
There is reason to believe that this line of argument has
been adopted,—not with the view of showing that we are

[1] Rom. iv. 3 ; Jas. ii. 23.

justified by Faith only, considered simply as belief in God's promise, or reliance on Him in whom that promise was fulfilled,—but as a covert way of reintroducing the doctrine of Justification on the ground of an inherent personal righteousness, and rejecting that of the imputed righteousness of Christ.   For the writers who have had recourse to it, have generally represented Faith as a compendious expression for the ' new creature ;' as the germ or seminal principle of holiness, and as virtually containing in itself all the fruits which are subsequently produced by it. This seems to be implied in their speaking of it as ' the distinguishing difference ' between those who are justified, and those who still remain in a state of condemnation ; for that difference does not consist in any one grace, considered singly and apart from others, but in the whole of that gracious change which is wrought upon the mind and heart of a sinner, when he ' passes from death unto life.' It falls to be considered, therefore, in connection with the relation which Justification bears to the work of the Holy Spirit ; and it should be reserved till that important topic comes under discussion.   But whatever may be the sense in which they speak of Faith,—whether it be that of simple belief and trust, or that of a more complex grace, including contrition, charity, and hope,—their peculiar doctrine concerning it—in so far as it relates, not to the means, but to the ground or reason, of Justification—will be sufficiently disposed of, if it can be shown, that faith is expressly distinguished in Scripture from the righteousness by which we are justified,—and that, when it is said to be ' counted for right eousness,' the words are not intended to be exclusive, but comprehensive, of the imputed righteousness of Christ. (1)

No one truth, on this subject, can be established by clearer or more conclusive evidence than this—that the Faith and the Righteousness, which are both spoken of

in connection with Justification, are distinct and different
from each other,—that they are not one and the same in
their nature,—and, consequently, that the relation which
they severally bear to Justification cannot be one and the
same.   By identifying the faith with the righteousness,
each of which is equally indispensable, many clear passages of Scripture will become utterly unintelligible.   The
righteousness is said to be 'of faith' (ἐκ πίστεως), and
'to faith' (εἰς πίστιν), 'by faith' (ἐπὶ τῇ πίστει), 'through
faith' (διὰ πίστεως) :[1] it is connected, therefore, with faith ;
but if it be identical with it, what meaning can there be
in these various prepositions?   Suppose, even, that the
righteousness intended were an inherent, and not an imputed,—a personal, and not a vicarious, righteousness,—
it would still be distinct and different from the faith with
which it is said to be thus connected.   But still further
to mark the difference between them, the faith itself is
said to be 'through the righteousness of our God and
Saviour Jesus Christ ;'[2] it is bestowed upon us as the free
gift of divine grace, but also as the fruit of Christ's mediatorial work.   'It is given to us, on the behalf of Christ,
to believe in His name.'[3]   So that faith is doubly related
to this righteousness : *first*, as it is procured by it, and
bestowed on account of it ; and *secondly*, as it is the means
of apprehending and appropriating it,—the hand which
receives it,—the reliance which rests upon it.   The faith,
therefore, and the righteousness, which are both connected,
although in different ways, with Justification, are distinct
and different from each other; and the relation which
they bear, respectively, to that privilege must be different
also,—the one being the means, merely, by which it is
received and enjoyed, and the other the ground or reason
on which it depends.

[1] Rom. i. 17, iii. 30 ; Gal. ii. 16 ; Phil. iii. 9.   [2] 2 Pet. i. 1.   [3] Phil. i. 29.

Many Popish writers, not content with identifying the *two*, have spoken of Grace,—Faith,—Righteousness,—and Justification, as if all the *four* were one and the same ;— for they have confounded Grace with Faith, when they have made Grace to be an infused subjective habit, and not the free mercy or favour of God; they have confounded Faith with Righteousness, when they have made Faith to be an inherent quality, on account of which we are accepted of God ; and they have confounded Righteousness with Justification, when they have made Justification the same with Sanctification, and obliterated the difference between righteousness imputed, and righteousness infused.   Some Protestant writers have also held that faith is the righteousness by which we are justified, but have refused to admit that they are justly chargeable with overlooking the distinction between the two, since they only affirm that the one is substituted for the other, and that, under the new law of grace, faith and its fruits, or faith and sincere, but imperfect, obedience, are accepted instead of the complete righteousness which the law required.   But, even according to this statement of the case, they must be held to identify faith and its fruits,— not, indeed, with the perfect righteousness which the original law required, for that would be a manifest contradiction as long as there is a difference between what is perfect and what is imperfect,—but with the righteousness by which we are justified.   They do not say that our faith and obedience amount to a perfect righteousness, but they do say, that they are accepted as *if they* were perfect, and that, in God's estimation, they are a sufficient fulfilment of the only conditions on which their salvation now depends.   But God's 'judgment is ever according to truth :' He cannot accept that faith as perfect, which is really imperfect,—nor that obedience as complete, which is really

partial and intermittent; the one and the other must be
sufficient to fulfil,—if not the law which requires a perfect
righteousness,—yet that other law, whatever it may be,
which is satisfied with less, but still requires a personal
compliance with its easier terms.   And if so, then what
constant doubt and anxiety must be the portion of every
one who looks to his own inherent or actual righteousness
as the ground of his pardon and acceptance with God?
and how can he ever experience that 'joy and peace in
believing' which springs from the blessed persuasion that
' Christ is the end of the law for righteousness to every
one who believeth,' and that as 'He who knew no sin,
was made sin for us,' so we, who had no righteousness,
are 'made the righteousness of God in Him?'

But those who affirm that faith is substituted for the
righteousness which the original law required, allege
express scriptural authority for their doctrine; and the
passages on which they mainly insist, are those in which
'faith' is said to be 'counted' or 'imputed' for righteousness.   If it can be shown that these words are intended
to be, not exclusive, but comprehensive, of Christ and His
righteousness, their doctrine will be deprived of its chief
support.   As these passages have given rise to much discussion in all ages of the Church, and as they have occasioned difficulty to many sincere and honest inquirers after
truth, it may be useful to bestow upon them our most
careful consideration. (2)

Two distinct interpretations have been proposed.   That
which has been most generally received, amounts in substance to this,—that the term 'faith' is used in these
passages, tropically, to denote the object of faith,—that
is, Christ as revealed in the Promise, under the Old Testament,—and Christ as more fully revealed in the Gospel,
under the New.   It is clear that it does not always mean

either the grace, or the act, of faith, but is often employed
to signify the truth believed, as in the following examples:
' The faith which was once delivered to the saints,'—' thou
holdest fast my name, and hast not denied my faith,'—
' striving together for the faith of the Gospel,'—' he
preached the faith which once he destroyed,'—' he hath
denied the faith,'—' some have erred from the faith.'[1]   It
is used to denote ' the word of faith,' as well as ' the
spirit of faith;'[2] and may thus stand for Christ, of whom
the Apostle said, ' We preach Christ crucified.'[3]   The efficacy, too, which is ascribed to it is derived entirely from
its object; although that efficacy is connected in Scripture,
sometimes with faith, and sometimes with Christ.   ' His
name, through faith in His name, hath made this man
strong; yea, the faith which is by Him hath given him
this perfect soundness.'   The names of several other
graces are also used, tropically, to denote their object;
for example, Christ is expressly called ' our hope;'[4] and
future blessings are also called by that name, for ' we are
saved by hope, but that which is seen is not hope.'   It
was in this sense that ' faith' was understood by Luther,
when it is said to be ' imputed for righteousness;' and in
opposition to the Popish divines, who held that it justified
because, like a golden ring, it enclosed ' charity,' he
strenuously contended that it justified because it enclosed
' Christ,'—' the pearl of great price.'

But some Protestant writers, who have held the
doctrine of Justification on the ground of Christ's imputed righteousness, have not accepted this interpretation
of the term; and have preferred another, which they
think the words would more naturally suggest, while it

---

[1] Jude 3 ; Rev. ii. 17 ; Phil. i. 27 ; Gal. i. 23 ; 1 Tim. v. 8, vi. 10 ; also, Gal.
iii. 23, 25 ; Heb. vi. 7 ; Rom. i. 5, xvi. 26.
[2] Rom. x. 8 ; 2 Cor. iv. 12.   [3] 1 Cor. i. 23.   [4] 1 Tim. i. 1 ; Col. i. 27.

is equally consistent, in their opinion, with the truth of
that doctrine.   They have regarded it as denoting 'a
state of mind,' and as descriptive either of the grace, or
of the exercise, of faith.   That this interpretation may be
understood in a sense, in which it neither identifies faith
with the righteousness by which we are justified, nor
excludes the imputation of the merits of Christ to
the believer, is argued from the twofold use which is
made in Scripture of the verbs signifying to 'impute.'
We are reminded that these verbs sometimes mean to
reckon that to any one which did not belong to him
personally, and was not previously his own, but became
his only by its being imputed, or set down to his
account,—as when God is said to 'impute righteousness
without works,' or when the debt of Onesimus was set
down to Paul's account;—but that they sometimes mean,
also, to reckon that to any one which was really his
before, whether it be by the recognition of personal sin, or
of personal righteousness.   If faith be said to be imputed
in the latter sense, then all that is meant by the passages
in question amounts to this,—that God recognises true
saving faith wherever it exists,—not as the ground on
which any one is justified, for it can never supersede or
supplant the vicarious righteousness of Christ,—but as a
grace really existing in the believer, which is the effectual
means, and the certain proof, of his Justification.   It is
thus stated as an alternative interpretation by President
Dickinson.   'Let it be even supposed, that Faith is here
taken subjectively, and that it was Abraham's faith itself,
considered as an act of his own, that was imputed to him.
It may, notwithstanding, be set in such a view, as will
secure the truth of the doctrine I am pleading for.
" His faith was imputed *unto* righteousness " (εἰς δικαιο-
σύνην); that is, as he was reckoned, judged, or esteemed

of God to be a sound believer, so the faith, which was imputed or reckoned to him, was *unto righteousness,*—was instrumental to his attaining of righteousness,—was the means that "by the righteousness of One the free gift came upon him unto justification of life ;" in other words, was the means of his interest in that righteousness of Christ by which he was justified.   In this sense, the imputation respects his faith; and intends an approbation and acknowledgment of it, as true and sincere, and effectual for its proper purposes.   He was approved of God as having a true and sound faith,—a faith effectual, as an applying means "unto righteousness," and thereby "unto Justification."' (3)

Neither of these interpretations is exclusive of the imputed righteousness of Christ ; for whether faith be considered as used, in a tropical sense, to denote Christ as its object,—or, in a subjective sense, to denote the grace, or the act, by which a believer receives and rests upon Him alone, it is only through His righteousness that it is effectual for Justification.   The faith, and the righteousness, are not identified, nor is the one substituted for the other; while all the other expressions which are descriptive of their mutual relations are preserved inviolate.

PROP. XXVI. The Faith, by which we are justified, is a spiritual grace,—as being the gift of God, and one of the fruits of His Spirit,—and, as such, is acceptable and well-pleasing to Him ' through Jesus Christ.'

It is expressly declared to be the ' gift of God :' ' By grace are ye saved through faith ; and that not of yourselves, it is the gift of God.'   ' It is *given* to us on the behalf of Christ to believe in His name.'[1]   It is enumerated among the ' fruits of the Spirit :' ' The fruit of the Spirit is in faith.'[2]   And it is directly connected with the work

[1] Eph. ii. 5 ; Phil. i. 29.   [2] Gal. v. 19.

of Christ; for it is not only said to be 'given to us on His behalf,' but also to be 'obtained through the righteousness of God and our Saviour Jesus Christ.'[1]

The question which has been raised in regard to the nature of saving Faith, when stated in its most general form, may be said to be—Whether it is a simple, or, in a greater or less degree, a complex, state of mind? and this question falls under our present consideration, only in so far as the answer, which is given to it, may be supposed to affect the method, or the ground, of our Justification. Some have held, that it is a mere intellectual belief, involving no gracious affection of any kind,—an opinion which has been maintained on different grounds, and applied to different purposes, by two parties standing apparently at opposite extremes on the subject of Justification,—by Popish writers, with the view of showing that faith is only a preparatory disposition, and has no value or efficacy until it is 'informed by charity;' and by Sandemanian writers, with the view of excluding from it everything else but ' the truth believed,'—lest by conceiving it to include trust, or reliance, or gratitude, or love, we should thereby make Justification to depend on some other ground than the finished work of Christ. So far these parties, although placed at opposite extremes, have met, and occupied common ground; but beyond this point, they differ materially from each other; since the former have maintained that the faith of which they speak, and which is evidently nothing more than the ' dead faith' which James rejects, is not necessarily productive of love, or effectual for justification without it; while the latter have held that a true scriptural faith, although it consists only in the truth believed, is directly connected with, and inseparable from, Justification,—as

1 2 Pet. i. 1.

also, that it is invariably productive of trust, gratitude, and love, as its immediate effects, and through them of universal holiness in heart and life.   In opposition to both, Protestant divines have generally held, that faith itself is a spiritual grace, and that every act of faith is an act of obedience; since it is one of the fruits of the Spirit, which can only be implanted along with a spiritual apprehension of the truth, and a cordial approbation of it, while every exercise of faith is in conformity with the requirements of God's revealed will; and yet they have denied that its being such is at variance with the doctrine of a free justification by the vicarious satisfaction and righteousness of Christ, simply because they exclude FAITH ITSELF, as well as all its fruits,—whether more or less immediate,—from forming any part of the ground of our acceptance with God.   If it be once proved, by clear testimonies of Scripture, that faith is not itself the righteousness by which we are justified, but only the channel through which we receive another righteousness,—not personal, but imputed, —we need have little solicitude about the question how much, or how little, is included in it, and no jealousy of its being represented as invariably accompanied, or immediately followed, by other graces of the Spirit.   To ascertain wherein it properly consists,—we must have recourse to the various descriptions and exemplifications of it which are given in Scripture; for it is in this way, rather than by any formal definition of its nature, that the Holy Spirit has taught us to conceive of it.

It is there described, sometimes as the belief of the Truth,—sometimes as trust in a Person,—sometimes as 'looking unto Jesus,' like the wounded Israelite when he looked to the brazen serpent,—sometimes as 'fleeing for refuge to the hope that is set before us,'—sometimes as 'coming to Christ' that we may 'find rest to our souls,'

—sometimes as 'receiving Christ,'—sometimes as 'resting on Him' as the sure foundation,—sometimes as 'committing' our souls to Him, as One who is 'able to keep them until the great day.' By all these various expressions, and many more, which are for the most part figurative, and, for that reason, better fitted than any formal definition to convey to our minds a vivid conception of its nature, and to preserve us from partial or one-sided views of it, the Holy Spirit has set forth the gracious principle, and actings, of saving faith; while He has recorded many instructive exemplifications of it in the life of Abraham and the Patriarchs under the Old Testament, and in the cases of 'the woman that was a sinner,'—the Syrophenician,—the malefactor on the cross,—the gaoler at Philippi, and many more, under the New Testament, 'whose faith' we are called 'to follow, considering the end of their conversation, Jesus Christ, the same yesterday, and to-day, and for ever.' These figurative descriptions, and practical exemplifications, of Faith, seem to have been multiplied on purpose, to guard us against the danger of resting in defective views of it, and to impress our minds with the conviction that, while all true faith is saving, all faith is not true,—that there is 'a dead' as well as a 'living' faith,—and that it nearly concerns our everlasting salvation, to discriminate aright between the two, and still more to test our own faith by its fruits. (4)

Another question which has been much discussed in connection with the nature of Faith, is, whether the assurance of our own personal salvation is necessarily involved in it? Here, again, Popish writers have generally occupied one extreme, while a few Protestant writers have tended towards another. The former have maintained, not only that faith, in their sense of that term, does not include any sure hope of salvation, but that, even where vital religion exists in the heart as 'faith informed with charity,' assurance of salvation is unattainable in the case of the maturest believer, by reason of the uncertainty of his final perseverance ; and that, so far from being necessary, it is not even desirable, since it might operate, as they conceive, injuriously on his character, by relieving him from the pressure of those doubts and fears, which are supposed to be a salutary restraint on evil passions, and a better safe-guard against sin, than 'faith working by love,' or 'joy and peace in believing.'   Some Protestants, recoiling from what the National Covenant of Scotland called the 'desperate and uncertain repentance'—the 'general and doubtsome faith,' of the Church of Rome, have gone to the opposite extreme, and have maintained that the assurance of personal salvation is of the essence of saving faith ; and so inseparable from it, even in its earliest beginnings, that no man is a believer, or can be justified, until he has attained it.   In opposition to the one extreme, Protestant divines have generally held, that the assurance of personal salvation is attainable in the present life,—that, so far from being injurious to holiness, it is eminently conducive, not only to the believer's comfort, but to his advancement in the divine life,—to his cheerful discharge of every duty, and patient endurance of every trial,—that the actual attainment of it should be earnestly desired, since he is required 'to give diligence to make his calling and election sure,' and 'to show the same diligence to the full assurance of hope unto the end,'[1]—and that it is perfectly consistent with deep humility of heart, and a spirit of entire depend-ence on God, since it is founded, not on any presumptuous confidence in the strength of his own resolution, or his own ability to persevere, but on the faithfulness of God's promise, and the unchangeableness of Christ's love.[2]   In

---

[1] 2 Pet. i. 10 ; Heb. vi. 11.   [2] Rom. viii. 38, 39 ; Isa. liv. 10; Phil. i. 6.

opposition to the other extreme, they have generally
distinguished between two kinds or measures of assurance,—the one arising from the reflex,—the other from
the direct, exercise of faith ; and have held, that the
former, which rests on the fruits or effects of faith, as
evidences of its reality and genuineness, cannot be included
in its essential nature, but can only spring from its actual
exercise where it already exists,—that many true believers
have been long destitute of it, and that some have even
lived and died without it,—and that faith does not consist
in believing,—either that we have been elected to eternal
salvation,—or that our names are written in the Lamb's
book of life,—or that all our sins are already pardoned,—
for these things are nowhere revealed concerning any
particular persons in Scripture, although we may come to
be assured of them all in the progress of our Christian
experience ; but they have also held, that some measure of
assurance is involved in the direct exercise of faith, when
it first believes the promise, and begins to rely on Christ
for salvation,—that assurance which is implied in saying
from the heart, 'We believe, and *are sure*, that Thou art
the Christ, the Son of the living God ;' for, receiving it as
' a faithful saying and worthy of all acceptation that Christ
came into the world to save sinners,' and that 'He is able
to save to the uttermost all that come unto God by Him ;'
—believing, moreover, that ' to us is the word of this salvation sent,' and that it is addressed to us individually as
sinners, accompanied with the assurance that ' whosoever
believeth shall not perish, but shall have everlasting life,'
—how can any one take that word as a sufficient warrant
for his faith, and actually begin to rely on Christ, or trust
in Him, for salvation, without having some measure of
confidence, such as—whether it be called hope or assurance—will serve, at least, to sustain and comfort him,

while he waits for clearer and fuller evidence of his personal salvation? It is the more necessary to insist on that measure of assurance which arises from the direct exercise of faith, because there is reason to believe, that many suppose their doubts and fears to arise only from the want of clear experimental evidence of their faith, when they may really have a much deeper source, in the want of a thorough realising conviction that 'Jesus is the Christ, the Son of God, and the Saviour of sinners,'—of a clear apprehension of the perfect freeness of His Gospel,— and an honest and cordial surrender of themselves into His hands to be saved by Him, and by Him alone, in life and in death, in time and through all eternity. And even when faith in His Gospel is confirmed by the strongest experimental evidence of a saving change in ourselves, assurance will still continue to rest on Christ;—for the fact that 'we have believed' is not of itself, or apart from Him, any ground of confidence at all,—it is only important as it is an evidence, that we are united to Christ,—and therefore the Apostle's confidence was still grounded on Him and His all-sufficiency: 'I know WHOM I have believed, and am persuaded that HE is able to save, what I have committed to HIM until the great day.' (5)

PROP. XXVII. A real influence or efficacy is ascribed to Faith in connection with our Justification, but it is such only as belongs to a divinely appointed means of receiving and appropriating a free gift.

In regard to the influence or efficacy which is ascribed to Faith in connection with our Justification, the question, whether it may be best described as a means,—or as an instrument,—or as a condition, is of little importance, so far as it relates merely to the use of these terms,—for every one of them might be applied to it in a sound sense (6) ;

but it becomes important when faith, or faith combined
with charity, is represented, either as a meritorious means
of procuring pardon and acceptance with God, or as a
legal condition by the fulfilment of which we obtain for
ourselves the enjoyment of these privileges. Protestant
divines have generally held, that it is simply an instrumental means,—like the hand which a beggar stretches
out to receive alms,—by which we apprehend Christ, and
appropriate to ourselves the benefits of His salvation,—
these benefits being at once the fruits of His purchase,
and the free gifts of His grace ; and while they have
sometimes used the term ' condition,'—as in the Larger
Catechism of the Westminster divines,—they have been
careful to explain the two senses in which it may be
understood—as denoting either a legal condition, on the
fulfilment of which eternal life becomes due, as wages are
due for work done, in which sense it is rejected,—or as
denoting an indispensable means merely in the order of
the divine appointment for the attainment of an end, just
as breathing is necessary for the support of life, while it
is the air which really sustains it ; or as eating is necessary for the nourishment of the body, while it is the food
which really ministers to its health and strength ; in which
sense the term may be admitted, although, from its ambiguity, it is more expedient to employ another, that will
be less liable to be misunderstood or misapplied. (7)

PROP. XXVIII. The only warrant of Faith is the
Word of God, and that Word is sufficient, not only to
entitle every sinner to receive and rest upon Christ for
his personal salvation, but to make it his duty to do so
without delay.

The question in regard to the warrant of Faith,—or
what that is which entitles us to receive and rest upon

Christ as our own Saviour,—may be answered, in general terms, by saying that it is the truth revealed. It does not relate to the ground of belief in the Scriptures as the Word of God, or the evidence by which their divine authority is established ; that is a previous question, and it is one of primary importance ; but it relates, more specially, to the right, or rather the duty, of every one to whom the Gospel is sent, to receive and rest upon Christ for his own salvation. (8) His doing so will depend, of course, on his views of the claims of Scripture to be regarded as a revelation of God's mind and will ; and it is to be feared that some remaining doubt on this point lies at the root of that diffidence and distrust which many feel in regard to their warrant to ' believe and live ;' —but even after that point has been established, and when it is clearly understood that Faith, considered as the belief of divine truth on divine authority, can have its ground and reason only in the Word of God, not a few of the hearers of the Gospel are found to have confused or erroneous ideas as to what that is which entitles them, at once and without any delay, to receive and rest upon Christ as their own Saviour. This generally arises from one or other of two distinct causes ;—either from some miserable perversion of the doctrine of Election, which leads them to suppose that, since none but the elect will be saved, they are not entitled to rely on Christ for salvation, until they know that they belong to the number of His people ;—or from some equally injurious misapplication of the truth in regard to the great spiritual change which is involved in saving conversion, as if it implied the necessity of certain moral qualifications in the sinner, before he is warranted to receive Christ as his own Saviour. Whereas the doctrine of Election,—although it is revealed in Scripture, and should, therefore, be submissively be-

lieved, as a truth contained in God's Word,—has no
relation whatever to the warrant of faith, simply because
it makes known nothing more than the fact that there is
'an election according to grace,' but gives no information
in regard to the individuals who belong to it ; while 'the
word of the truth of the Gospel' is addressed, not to any
one class of men, but to sinners, as such, and to all sinners
without exception, to whom it is sent as the 'word of
salvation.' That word imposes on every one an immediate and imperative obligation to receive Christ, and to
rely upon Him for his own salvation,—an obligation which
does not depend in the least on his knowing 'the secret
things which belong to the Lord our God,' but only and
entirely on his knowing 'the things which are revealed,
and which belong to us, and to our children.' So far as
the doctrine of Election is concerned, we have the same
warrant of faith on which any one ever believed to the
saving of his soul ; for, without an immediate personal
revelation, such as was vouchsafed to Abraham and to
Paul,[1] with special reference to their peculiar vocation to
the prophetic or apostolic office, no one needed to know
his individual election before he believed, although he
might afterwards come to be assured of it,—and, therefore,
it was not the secret purpose of God, but the promise of His
word, that was regarded as the sole warrant of faith in all
ages of the Church. With regard, again, to the spiritual
change which is involved in saving conversion, it is not
denied,—either that such a change is indispensably necessary,—or that it may not be preceded by a preparatory
work of the Spirit in convincing men of sin, and bringing
them to feel their need of a Saviour ; but it is denied
that either the one, or the other, is the warrant of faith ;
for all are warranted to believe, and, for that reason, all

[1] Gen. xv. 1 ; Acts ix. 15.

are responsible for unbelief, to whom the Gospel comes ; and while it is true that none will actually believe, until they are convinced of sin, so as to feel their need of salvation, and are effectually enabled and persuaded to receive and rest on Christ for it, yet it is the free call, and express command, of the Gospel,—and not anything in themselves, even though it be wrought by the Spirit of God,—which entitles, and even obliges, them to rely at once on Christ, as He is freely offered to them in the inspired Word.

It is not necessary, nor would it be consistent with fact, to deny, that some of the calls and invitations of the Gospel are specially addressed to those who have been convinced of their sin and misery, and have begun to feel their need of a Saviour ; for there is a peculiar propriety in their being singled out for special encouragement, since they are apt, under deep convictions of sin, to 'write bitter things against themselves,' and to fall into dejection or despair.   Accordingly, some of the most precious passages of Scripture relate to them,—such as these : ' Come unto me, all ye that are weary and heavy laden ;' —and ' whosoever is athirst, let him come unto me and drink.'   But while this specialty is still preserved, the call is nevertheless addressed to sinners universally,—as when it is said, ' Let the wicked man forsake his way, and the unrighteous man his thoughts, and let him return unto the Lord, and He will have mercy upon him ;' and when ' the Spirit and the Bride say, Come,'—with a certain specification, in the first instance—' whosoever is athirst, let him come,' but more universally, in the second —and ' whosoever will, let him take of the water of life freely.'   The Gospel offer is made to all sinners without any exception ; the Gospel promise is made absolutely to ' all them that believe.'   If their faith may be said to be a condition in order to their final salvation, it is not a

condition in order to their warrant to receive and rest
upon Christ for salvation ; for that warrant consists in the
free calls,—the gracious invitations,—and the express
commands, of the Gospel, which speaks to sinners, as
such, and to every sinner individually, saying, as Paul
said to the Philippian gaoler, ' Believe in the Lord Jesus
Christ, and THOU SHALT be saved.'

PROP. XXIX. We are justified by faith only, simply
because it is by faith, and by no other grace, that we believe the truth concerning Christ, and rely on Him alone
for salvation as He is freely offered to us in the Gospel.

The exclusive instrumentality, and peculiar prerogative, which is ascribed to faith, in connection with our
justification, when it is said that we are justified 'by faith
only,' is sufficiently explained and established by proving,
first, that the only ground of our acceptance with God is
the finished work, or vicarious righteousness, of Christ ;
and *secondly*, that the only grace by which we rely or rest
on that ground, as it is revealed in Scripture, is faith,
considered as a cordial belief of the truth concerning
Christ, and a confiding trust in Him for' our personal
salvation.   If it were acknowledged, that we are justified
by the work of Christ only, and that this must be the sole
and immediate ground of our faith and hope, there would
be little need of any nice metaphysical distinctions respecting the nature of faith, in order to prove that we are
justified 'by faith only;' for that faith, whatever it be,
by which we receive and rest on Christ alone for our
acceptance with God, would be seen to be the only means
of our Justification.   It may involve a spiritual apprehension, and a cordial approbation, of the truth, as well as a
mere intellectual belief of it ; and it may be associated
from the first with some measure of desire, trust, grati-

tude, love, and hope, as well as immediately followed by these kindred graces, without affecting the truth of the statement, that we are justified 'by faith only;' for that statement relates,—not to the simple or complex nature of faith,—but to its sole instrumentality as the means of justification; and if neither faith itself, nor any of the other graces by which it is accompanied or followed, forms any part of our justifying righteousness, we have only to ascertain what that is, which unites us to Christ, and makes us partakers of His righteousness.   There can be no doubt that, in Scripture, a special connection is established between Justification and Faith, such as does not subsist between Justification and any other grace; and the reason of this is obvious, if that privilege is immediately apprehended and appropriated when a sinner so believes the truth concerning Christ as to rely on His righteousness only for salvation. (9)

It is true that 'forgiveness of sins,' which is included in Justification, is frequently connected, in Scripture, with repentance as well as with faith; as when we read of John preaching the 'baptism of repentance for the remission of sins,' and of 'repentance and remission of sins being preached in Christ's name among all nations.' 'Except ye repent,' said our Lord, 'ye shall all likewise perish;' 'Repent ye, therefore, and be converted,' said Peter, 'that your sins may be blotted out.'   But the repentance which is meant is not mere remorse of conscience, or sorrow on account of sin; it is a thorough change of mind and heart, and it includes faith, or 'a lively apprehension of the mercy of God in Christ.'   Repentance, in this sense, is necessary to salvation; but it is the faith which is included in it that unites us to Christ, and makes us partakers of His justifying righteousness. This is the special and peculiar function of faith only.

But the fact that it is connected in Scripture with repentance, and that both are declared to be necessary to salvation, is sufficient to show that they are constituent
elements of that great spiritual change which is described
as 'a second birth,' and 'a new creation;' and as this
change must be effected in the case of every sinner who
is pardoned and accepted of God, our inquiry would be
incomplete, did we not rise, from the consideration of the
special function and office of faith in justifying, to that of
the more general and comprehensive question, respecting
the connection which subsists between Justification and
the Work of the Holy Spirit.

LECTURE XV.

JUSTIFICATION ; ITS RELATION TO THE WORK OF THE HOLY SPIRIT.

THERE is, perhaps, no more subtle or plausible error, on the subject of Justification, than that which makes it to rest on the indwelling presence, and the gracious work, of the Holy Spirit in the heart. It is a singularly refined form of opposition to the doctrine of Justification by the imputed righteousness of Christ, for it merely substitutes the work of one divine Person for that of another ; and it is plausible, because it seems to do homage to the doctrine of Grace, by ascribing to the presence and operation of the Holy Spirit the production of faith, and all the effects which are ascribed to it, whether these belong to our Justification or to our Sanctification. It is the more difficult to expose and refute error, when it presents itself in this apparently spiritual form, than when it comes before us in its grosser and more common shape, as a doctrine of justification by works, because it involves some great truths which are held as firmly by those who advocate, as by those who abjure, the Protestant doctrine of Justification. Yet, subtle and plausible as it is, and difficult as it may be to disentangle the error from the partial truth which is involved in it, nothing can be more unscriptural in itself, or more pernicious to the souls of men, than the substitution of the gracious work of the Spirit *in* us, for the vicarious work

of Christ *for* us, as the ground of our pardon and acceptance with God ; for if we are justified solely on account
of what Christ did and suffered for us, while He was yet
on the earth, we may rest, with entire confidence, on a
work which has been already 'finished'—on a righteousness which has been already wrought out, and already
accepted of God on behalf of all who believe in His name,
—and we may immediately receive, on the sure warrant
of His word, the privilege of Justification as a free gift of
God's grace through Christ, and as the present privilege
of every believer, so as at once to have 'joy and peace in
believing.' Whereas, if we are justified on the ground of
the work of the Holy Spirit *in* us, we are called to rest on
a work, which, so far from being finished and accepted, is
not even begun in the case of any unrenewed sinner ; and
which, when it is begun in the case of a believer, is incipient only,—often interrupted in its progress by declension and backsliding,—marred and defiled by remaining
sin,—obscured and enveloped in doubt by clouds and
thick darkness,—and never perfected in this life, even
according to the low standard of a relaxed law, if that law
is supposed to require any definite amount of personal
holiness in heart and life. For these reasons, it is of the
utmost practical importance, to conceive aright, both of
the Mediatorial work of Christ, and of the internal work
of His Spirit, in the relation which they bear to each
other, under the scheme of Grace and Redemption : and
with the view of aiding the serious inquirer in doing so,
we lay down the following propositions.

PROP. XXXI. The Father, the Son, and the Holy
Spirit are revealed as concurring together in the whole
purpose and plan of man's redemption ; but as sustaining,
each of them, a distinct office, and undertaking a different

part of the work, in carrying that purpose and plan into effect.

Their common purpose of saving sinners, and their harmonious co-operation in its accomplishment, might be inferred from the unity of the divine nature, which necessarily implies unity in the counsels of the divine will; but the personal distinctions of the Godhead could never have been so clearly revealed in any other way than by the distinct offices and operations, which are ascribed to them in connection with the work of salvation. It is to mark at once their harmony of purpose, and also their several agencies, in this work, that every believer is required to be baptized,—not simply into the name of God,—but 'into the name of the Father, and of the Son, and of the Holy Ghost;'[1] and that each of the three is distinctly invoked in the Apostolic form of benediction: 'The grace of the Lord Jesus Christ, and the love of God, and the communion of the Holy Ghost, be with you all.'[2] The preparatory baptism of John, which is described as 'the baptism of repentance for the remission of sins,'— and which was administered to the people who attended his ministry,[3] that they might be taught to 'believe on Him who should come after him,' and 'baptize them with the Holy Ghost,'—was imperfect, as compared with Christian baptism, because it did not distinctly specify the Father, and the Son, and the Holy Ghost; and accordingly it was superseded on the establishment of the Christian Church. (1)

Each of the three Persons in the Godhead sustains a distinct office, and undertakes a work which is ascribed peculiarly to Him, in connection with the divine method of saving sinners.

The Father is revealed as representing the majesty,—

---

[1] Matt. xxviii. 19.   [2] 2 Cor. xiii. 14.   [3] Acts xix. 2-6.

exercising the sovereignty,—and maintaining the preroga-
tives, of the Godhead.   It is said of Him that 'He loved
us,'—that 'He blessed us with all spiritual blessings in
Christ,'—that ' He chose us in Him before the foundation
of the world,'—that 'He predestinated us to the adoption
of children by Jesus Christ, according to the good pleasure
of His will, to the praise of the glory of His grace, wherein He hath made us accepted in the Beloved,'—that 'He
gave His only-begotten Son,'—that ' He sent His Son to
be the Saviour of the world,'—that 'He made Him to be
sin for us,'—that ' He set Him forth to be a propitiation
through faith in His blood,'—that ' He spared not His
own Son, but delivered Him up to the death for us all,'—
that ' He commendeth His love towards us, in that, while
we were yet sinners, Christ died for us,'—that 'it pleased
the Lord to bruise Him,'—that ' He raised Him up from
the dead, and gave Him glory, that our faith and hope
might be in God,'—that He ' crowned Him with honour
and glory, and did set Him over the works of His hands,'
—and that 'God hath exalted Him with His right hand
to be a Prince and a Saviour, to give repentance, and
remission of sins.'[1]

The Son is revealed as acting in official subordination
to the Father,—as 'sent,'—as 'given,'—as 'coming to do
His will,'—as 'making Himself of no reputation,'—as
' taking upon Him the form of a servant, and appearing
in the likeness of man,'—as 'humbling Himself, and
becoming obedient unto death, even the death of the
cross,'—as being ' made under law,'—as being 'made sin
for us,'—as being 'made a curse for us,'—as ' wounded
for our transgressions, and bruised for our iniquities,'—
as bearing 'our sins in His own body on the tree,'—as

---

[1] John iii. 16; Eph. i. 3, 4, 5 ; 1 John iv. 14 ; 2 Cor. v. 21 ; Rom. iii. 25,
viii. 32 ; Isa. liii. 10 ; 1 Pet. i. 21 ; Heb. ii. 7; Acts v. 31.

'giving Himself for us an offering and a sacrifice to God
for a sweet-smelling savour,'—as 'crucified in weakness,
but raised in power,'—as ascending up into heaven, and
sitting down 'for ever on the right hand of God, from
henceforth expecting till His enemies be made His foot-
stool,'—as 'highly exalted, and having a name given to
Him which is above every name; that at the name of
Jesus every knee should bow, and every tongue confess
that He is Lord, to the glory of God the Father.'[1]

The Holy Spirit is revealed as 'proceeding from the
Father,'—as 'sent by the Son from the Father,'—as
'testifying' of Christ,—as 'glorifying Christ,'—as 'bearing witness' of Him,—as 'convincing the world of sin,
because they believe not on Him,'—as 'shining into the
hearts of men, and giving them the light of the knowledge of the glory of God in the face of Jesus Christ,'—
as 'renewing them in the spirit of their minds,'—as
'quickening them' into spiritual life,—as 'the Spirit of
wisdom and of revelation in the knowledge of Christ,'
—as 'the Spirit that dwelleth in us'—that 'worketh in
us'—that 'guideth us into all truth'—that 'helpeth our
infirmities'—that 'witnesseth with our spirits that we
are the children of God,'—as 'the Holy Spirit of promise,
which is the earnest of our inheritance.'[2]

These testimonies are sufficient to show,—*first*, that
there is a real distinction between the Father, the Son,
and the Holy Spirit, since many things are revealed concerning each of them which cannot be affirmed of the
other two;—and *secondly*, that they sustain different offices
under the same scheme of grace, and execute different
parts of the same work of redemption. If these fundamental truths are clearly revealed, it follows that we can

[1] Phil. ii. 7 ; Gal. iii. 13; Isa. liii. ; Eph. v. 2 ; Heb. x. 12 ; Phil. ii. 9, 10.
[2] John xv. 26, xvi. 14 ; 1 John v. 6 ; John xv. 8, 9 ; Eph. i. 17, 14.

only involve ourselves in inextricable confusion by overlooking the fact that such distinctions exist, and by
ascribing that to the Father which Scripture ascribes to
the Son,—or that to the Son which Scripture ascribes to
the Spirit,—or, conversely, that to the Spirit which the
Scripture ascribes to the Son.   Yet this is the very error
with which those are justly chargeable who substitute the
work of the Spirit *in* us, for the work of Christ *for* us, as
the ground of our Justification. (2)

PROP. XXXII. The work of the Holy Spirit is as
necessary for our Justification as the work of Christ Himself; but it is not necessary for the same reasons, nor is
it effectual for the same ends.

That the work of the Holy Spirit *in* us is as necessary,
in some respects, for our actual Justification, as the work
of Christ *for* us, has never been denied by sound Protestant divines; and the fact is proved by those passages
of Scripture in which the two are expressly connected
with each other.   For example, the Apostle says to believers, ' Ye are washed, ye are sanctified, ye are justified,
in the name of the Lord Jesus, and by the Spirit of our
God;'[1]—words which clearly imply, that there is a distinction between our being ' sanctified' and our being ' justified;' but that both blessings are connected, although it
may be in different ways, with the work of Christ, and
also with the work of His Spirit,—for we are ' sanctified,'
as well as ' justified,' ' in the name of the Lord Jesus,'
and also ' by the Spirit of our God.'   Again, the Apostle
says, ' After that the kindness and love of God our
Saviour toward man appeared,—not by works of righteousness which we have done, but according to His mercy
He saved us, by the washing of regeneration, and renew-

[1] 1 Cor. vi. 11.

ing of the Holy Ghost, which He shed on us abundantly
through Jesus Christ our Saviour; that, being justified by
His grace, we should be made heirs according to the hope
of eternal life;'[1]—words which clearly imply that our
whole salvation, — including regeneration, justification,
adoption, and eternal life,—depends equally on the 'kindness,' 'love,' and 'grace' of God,—on the work of 'Jesus
Christ our Saviour,'—and on 'the renewing of the Holy
Ghost.' The same truth is clearly taught in those passages
of Scripture which affirm, that not one saving privilege can
be enjoyed without the gracious work of the Holy Spirit,
and that every Gospel blessing is conferred through His
agency on the souls of men. Without the effectual work
of the Spirit there is no salvation. This is set forth in the
strongest way, negatively, and positively. First negatively:
'Verily I say unto thee, except a man be born again,' or
'from above' (ἄνωθεν, supernè, which is explained as 'born
of the Spirit'), 'he cannot see the kingdom of God;'—'If
any man have not the Spirit of Christ, he is none of His;'
—and 'no man can say that Jesus is the Lord, but by
the Holy Ghost.'[2] Then positively,—through His agency,
we are united to Christ, and are made, at one and the
same time, partakers of all the blessings of His redemption; for,—'Of Him are ye in Christ Jesus, who is made
of God unto us wisdom, and righteousness, and sanctification, and redemption.'[3] From these explicit testimonies
it is clear, that no man is a partaker of any of the blessings of salvation, until he is renewed by the Spirit of God;
and that every man is made a partaker of them all, as
soon as, by the Spirit's agency, he is united to Christ, and
enabled to believe on His name. Any doctrine, therefore,
which excludes the gracious operation of the Holy Spirit
in order to our Justification,—either by representing faith

[1] Tit. iii. 4–7.   [2] John iii. 3, 5, 6; Rom. viii. 9; 1 Cor. xii. 3.   [3] 1 Cor. i. 30.

as a mere intellectual belief, and ascribing it to the natural exercise of our faculties on the truth and its evidence,— or by describing it as the product of man's free-will, acting spontaneously and without the effectual influence of divine grace,—is at variance with the express teaching of Scripture, and should be rejected, as it was by Augustine, because it does not sufficiently recognise, either the natural depravity of man, or the efficacy of divine grace.

But, while the work of the Holy Spirit *in* us is as necessary for our Justification as the work of Christ *for* us, it is not necessary for the same reasons, nor is it effectual for the same ends.   There were two great evils in our natural condition, each of which must be redressed and removed, by means appropriate to itself, if we were to be thoroughly reconciled to God.   The first was the guilt of sin, the second was the dominion of sin.   By the one, we were exposed to the wrath of God, and to the curse of His law; by the other, we were slaves to our own evil passions, and subject to that carnal mind which is 'enmity against God.'   Both evils must be redressed, if there was to be a thorough reconciliation between God and man; His displeasure, on account of sin, must be averted, and man's enmity, on account of His holiness, must be subdued; and Christ undertook, as Mediator, to accomplish each of these ends, but in different ways. He undertook to do and suffer all that was necessary to procure,—not Justification only, and far less mere salvability,—but a complete salvation, for His people; to expiate their guilt,—to avert from them God's wrath and curse,—to earn for them a title to eternal life,—and to obtain for them, as the reward of His own work, the grace of the Holy Spirit, which was 'the promise of the Father' to Him.   He further undertook, as Mediator and Administrator of the covenant, to dispense the gift of the

Holy Spirit for the benefit of His people,—that they might thereby be enabled to believe on Him for their entire salvation, and to look to Him for their Sanctification, as well as for their Justification.   He contemplated, therefore, both evils, and provided a remedy for both ; but His own work, in so far as it is distinct from that of the Holy Spirit, consisted in the vicarious fulfilment of the divine law, both in its precept and penalty,—so as to lay a solid foundation, in the first instance, for their pardon and acceptance with God ; and also to procure for them, that He might freely bestow, the gift of the Holy Spirit, by which they might be made 'a willing people in the day of His power.'   But the work of the Spirit was to be entirely distinct from that of the Son, and was neither designed to supersede, or to supplement, it, for its own special and peculiar ends ; on the contrary, it was to consist mainly in persuading men effectually to 'receive and rest upon Christ alone for salvation, as He is freely offered in the Gospel.'   Christ was 'exalted as a Prince and a Saviour, to give repentance' as well as 'the remission of sins ;' and we must be indebted to Him for both ; for 'being by the right hand of God exalted, and having received of the Father the promise of the Holy Ghost, He shed forth' the Spirit on the day of Pentecost, and has continued to dispense it, as the fruit of His purchase, and the gift of His grace, in all ages of the Church down to the present day.

The Mediatorial work of Christ is thus clearly distinguished from the internal work of the Spirit.   By the former, all the blessings of salvation were procured ; by the latter, all these blessings are effectually applied.   The work of the Spirit is not the cause, but the consequent, of our redemption ; and it forms no part of the ground, although it is the evidence, of our Justification.   That blessing, like every other which is included in salvation, depends entirely on the sacerdotal work of Christ, by which He fulfilled the conditions of the Covenant; and it is dispensed by Him in the exercise of His prophetical and regal offices, as Administrator of the Covenant. The Holy Spirit is His Agent in the exercise of these offices, and by His grace and power men are enabled and per- suaded to rely on Him for salvation ; but in fulfilling the conditions which were imposed on Christ as Mediator, or in accomplishing 'the work which the Father had given Him to do,' the Spirit had no part, except in so far as He was 'given to Him without measure,' and sustained His holy human soul in obeying and suffering, when 'through the eternal Spirit He offered Himself without spot unto God.' Apart from such concurrence,—which might be equally affirmed of the Father Himself,—the Holy Spirit did no part of the work by which our redemption was secured ; and it is Christ's work alone, therefore, which is the ground of our Justification. That is said of Christ and His work, in this respect, which is never said of the Spirit and His work. It is said of the Son,—but never of the Spirit,—that He became incarnate, and 'took upon Him the form of a servant, and appeared in the likeness of men,'—that 'He was made under law,'—that He was 'made sin for us,'—that 'He was made a curse for us,'—that 'He bore our sins in His own body on the tree,'—that 'He died for us, the just for the unjust,'— that 'He redeemed us to God by His blood,'—that 'He is the end of the law for righteousness to every one that believeth on His name,'—that 'He obtained eternal re- demption for us,'—that 'now once in the end of the world hath He appeared to put away sin by the sacrifice of Himself,'—and that 'this is the record, that God hath given to us eternal life, and this life is in His Son.' From

these testimonies it is manifest that a peculiar work is
ascribed to Christ which is nowhere ascribed, in whole or
in part, to the Holy Spirit ; a work which was 'finished'
on the Cross, and is different even from that which He is
still carrying on in the Church by the agency of His
Spirit, and the instrumentality of His Word,—a work
which had a direct reference to the expiation of human
guilt, and the satisfaction of the law and justice of God,
—and a work which constitutes the only, but all-sufficient,
ground of our Justification. If that work accomplished
the end for which it was designed, no other ground of
acceptance is either necessary, or possible ; and the work
of the Spirit Himself cannot be supposed to supersede, or
even to supplement, it, without dishonour to the efficacy
of that 'precious blood,' and the merits of that perfect
righteousness, by which Christ satisfied the Law and
Justice of God. But this important truth will become
still more evident, if from the peculiar work which is
ascribed to Christ, we proceed to consider that other
work, equally peculiar, which is ascribed to the Holy
Spirit. (3)

PROP. XXXIII. The work of the Spirit consists in
'bearing witness to Christ,' and applying to men the
redemption which He obtained for them, so as to make it
effectual for their complete and everlasting salvation.
    'It is the Spirit which beareth witness, because the
Spirit is truth;'[1] and the great subject of His testimony
is Christ—Christ crucified, and Christ exalted:—' He shall
testify of Me ;'—' He shall glorify Me : for He shall receive
of mine, and shall show it unto you.   All things that the
Father hath are mine : therefore said I, that He shall
take of mine, and shall show it unto you.'[2] The testimony

[1] 1 John v. 6.   [2] John xv. 26, xvi. 14, 15.

of the Spirit relates to Christ as the only Saviour of sinners ; and He bears witness to Him both in the Word,
which was written by His inspiration, and in the hearts of
His people, when He is given unto them 'as the Spirit of
wisdom and revelation in the knowledge of Him,'[1] by
which they obtain 'the light of the knowledge of the
glory of God in the face of Jesus Christ.'[2]   Accordingly,
so far from leading us to rest on His own work *in* us, as
the ground of our acceptance with God, that work itself
mainly consists in applying to us the redemption which
was procured by Christ,—by convincing us of our need of
it,—by revealing its all-sufficiency,—by 'making known
to us the things that are freely given to us of God,'—and
disposing, and enabling, us to trust in Christ alone.

The question, 'How, and by whom, was salvation
procured for sinners?' should not supersede, but should
rather lead on, to that other question, 'How are we made
partakers of the redemption purchased by Christ?'   The
scriptural answer to this question is—By its being effectually applied to us by the Holy Spirit.   If it be asked
again, 'How does the Spirit apply Christ's redemption to
us?' the scriptural answer is—By working faith in us, and
uniting us to Christ.   And if it be still further asked,
'How does He work faith in us, and unite us to Christ?'
the scriptural answer is—that 'He persuades, and enables,
us to receive and rest on Christ alone for salvation as He
is freely offered to us in the Gospel.'   This is the grand
object of His whole work in conversion, to bring a sinner
to close with Christ, and to rely on Him as his own
Saviour.   This result may not be effected without a preparatory process, of longer or shorter duration, in different
cases ; for the sinner must be convinced of his sin, and
misery, and danger, before he can feel his need of a

[1] Eph. i. 17.   [2] 2 Cor. iv. 6.

Saviour, or have any serious desire for salvation,—he must be enlightened in the knowledge of Christ, in the glory of His person, and the nature of His redeeming work, before he can see in Him the very Saviour whom he needs,—and he must be made willing,—for naturally he is not willing to be saved, in the full scriptural sense of that expression, and still less to be saved in this way,—by the mere mercy of God through the righteousness of another; but then there comes a critical moment when he is effectually persuaded to receive and rest on Christ alone; and he is free to do so at once, for there is no barrier between him and Christ, except his own unbelief, or his own unwillingness. Receiving Christ by faith, he is united to Him; and being united to Him, 'he is complete in Him,'—Christ's righteousness becomes his for his Justification, and Christ's Spirit becomes his also for his Sanctification. (4)

If such be the nature of the Spirit's work, its necessity for our actual Justification cannot arise from any defect in the righteousness of Christ, for its great design is to lead the sinner to receive and rest on Christ alone; it must arise only from the depraved state of our own minds, which is such that, were we left to ourselves, we would never close with the gracious call of the Gospel,—partly because we are insensible of the evil and demerit of sin, —partly because we are spiritually blind,—and partly because we are unwilling to be saved in God's way, and on God's terms.   Hence arises the indispensable necessity of the Spirit's work, in applying the redemption, which was procured by Christ, for our Justification; while its necessity for other ends arises from the very nature of salvation itself, which *consists* in deliverance from the power and practice of sin, as well as from its guilt and punishment, and is designed, not only to give us a title to eternal life, but also to 'make us meet for the inheritance

of the saints in light.' For the doctrine of a free Justification, by grace through faith alone, is miserably misunderstood or perverted, if it be supposed to cancel that
unalterable law of Christ's kingdom—'This is the will of
God, even your Sanctification,' and 'Without holiness no
man shall see the Lord.'

Prop. XXXIV. Regeneration and Justification are
simultaneous ; and no man is justified who is not renewed, nor is any man renewed who is not also, and immediately, justified.

By the agency of the Holy Spirit, who works faith in
us, by enabling and persuading us to receive and rest upon
Christ alone for salvation, we are united to Christ ; and
by our union with Him, we are made partakers of all the
blessings which He died to purchase, and is exalted to
bestow. We are united to Him as our federal, or representative, Head, and are thus made partakers of His
justifying righteousness,—and we are united to Him, at
one and the same time, as our spiritual, or life-giving,
Head, and are thus made partakers of His sanctifying
grace. With reference to the former effect of our union
to Christ, it is said, that 'we are accepted *in* the Beloved,'—that 'we are made· the righteousness of God *in*
Him,'—that '*in* Him we have redemption through His
blood, the forgiveness of sins according to the riches of
His grace.' With reference to the latter effect of our
union to Christ, it is said, that 'we are sanctified *in* Christ
Jesus,'—that 'if any man be *in* Christ Jesus, he is a new
creature,'—and that from Him ' as the Head, all the body,
by joints and bands, having nourishment ministered, and
knit together, increaseth with the increase of God.'[1] And
with reference to both effects of our union to Christ, it is

[1] 1 Cor. i. 2 ; 2 Cor. v. 17 ; Col. ii. 19.

said, ' Ye are complete *in* Him,' and ' of God are ye *in*
Christ Jesus, who of God is made unto us wisdom, and
righteousness, and sanctification, and redemption.' It is
from ' the fulness that is in Christ,' that all saving blessings flow; for 'it pleased the Father that in Him should
all fulness dwell,' and ' of His fulness have all we received,
and grace for grace.'[1]   So intimate and endearing is the
union between Christ and His people, that they are said
to be in Him, and He in them.   ' Abide in me, and I in
you.   As the branch cannot bear fruit of itself, except it
abide in the vine, no more can ye, except ye abide in me.
I am the vine, ye are the branches : he that abideth in
me, and I in him, the same bringeth forth much fruit; for
without me,' or apart from me, ' ye can do nothing.'[2]   The
work of the Spirit produces, and maintains, this union
with Christ by faith; for 'we are strengthened with might
by His Spirit in the inner man ; that Christ may dwell in
our hearts by faith, . . . that we may be able to comprehend with all saints what is the breadth, and length, and
depth, and height, and to know the love of Christ, which
passeth knowledge, that we might be filled with all the
fulness of God.'[3]   The Holy Spirit, so far from withdraw-
ing our confidence from Christ, that it may rest on His
own work within, teaches us to rest on Him alone for all
the blessings of salvation, and to ' hold fast the beginning
of our confidence even to the end.'   So far from making
Christ less ' precious ' to us, the Spirit endears Him to us
the more, as at once ' the Author and the Finisher of our
faith,' and teaches us to ' rejoice in Him with joy unspeakable, and full of glory.'

If the work of the Spirit in us consists merely in the
effectual application of the work of Christ for us, and in
making us partakers of all the blessings of His redemption,

[1] Col. i. 19 ; John i. 16.   [2] John xv. 4.   [3] Eph. iii. 16, 17.

it follows that Regeneration and Justification are simultaneous, and that no man is justified who is not renewed,
nor is any man renewed who is not also justified.   This
is a most important truth, and one that is sufficient to
neutralize the two great errors, which have been maintained by opposite parties on this subject.   The one is the
error of the Antinomians, who have spoken of Justification
as being antecedent to, and independent of, Regeneration
by the Holy Spirit, and have identified it sometimes with
God's eternal election,—at other times with the redeeming
work of Christ,—as if there were no difference between an
eternal purpose to save, and the execution of that purpose
in time, or between the procuring of redemption, and the
actual application of it to the souls of men. (5) The other
is the error of Popish writers, and some of their followers
in the Protestant Church, who have spoken of Justification as dependent, not on the finished work of Christ alone,
but on our personal obedience and final perseverance ; and
have virtually postponed it till the judgment of the great
day, as if it were not the present privilege of believers,
and of every believer on the instant when he is united to
Christ,—or as if he did not receive Christ for his sanctification, and even for his perseverance, as well as for the
free pardon of all his sins, and the gracious acceptance of
his person and his services.   These two errors may be said
to lie at opposite extremes from each other ; but they are
equally false and dangerous.   Paul was ' a chosen vessel,'
and was redeemed by the blood of Christ ; but he was not
justified while he was ' a blasphemer and a persecutor ;' it
was not till he was convinced and converted, that he ' obtained mercy ;'[1]—but then immediately he could say, ' I
know whom I have believed, and am persuaded that He is
able to keep what I have committed to Him till the great

[1] 1 Tim. i. 16.

day;'—' I am crucified with Christ; nevertheless I live, yet not I, but Christ liveth in me; and the life which I now live in the flesh, I live by the faith of the Son of God, who loved ME, and gave Himself for ME.'[1] And so, invariably in the case of every true convert, there is a critical moment when he 'passes from death unto life,'—from a state of 'wrath' to a state of 'reconciliation,'—from being 'without Christ,' and therefore 'without hope, and without God in the world,' to being 'in Christ,'[2] as 'a fellow-citizen with the saints, and of the household of God;' and it is equally certain—that he was not justified before,—and that he is justified now.

It has sometimes been asked—Whether Regeneration or Justification has the precedency in the order of nature? This is a question of some speculative interest, but of little practical importance. It relates to the order of our conceptions, not to the order of time; for it is admitted on all hands that the two blessings are bestowed simultaneously. The difficulties which have suggested it are such as these, —How God can be supposed, on the one hand, to bestow the gift of His Spirit on any one who is still in a state of wrath and condemnation,—and how He can be supposed, on the other hand, to justify any sinner while he is not united to Christ by that living faith which is implanted only by the Spirit of God?   But such difficulties will be found to resolve themselves into a more general and profound question; and can only be effectually removed, by falling back on God's eternal purpose of mercy towards sinners, which included equally their redemption by Christ, and their regeneration by His Spirit. The grand mystery is how God, who hates sin, could ever love any class of sinners,—and so love them, as to give His own Son to die for them, and His Holy Spirit to dwell in them.   The

---

[1] Gal. ii. 20.   [2] Eph. ii. 12, 13.

relation which subsists, in respect of order, between Re-generation and Justification, is sufficiently determined, for all practical purposes, if neither is held to be prior or posterior to the other, in point of time,—and if it is clearly understood that they are simultaneous gifts of the same free grace ; for then it follows,—that no unrenewed sinner is justified,—and that every believer, as soon as he believes, is pardoned and accepted of God. (6)

CONCLUSION.

ON a review both of the History, and the Exposition, of the Doctrine of Justification, many reflections might be profitably suggested; but we can only indicate, without attempting to illustrate, a very few of these.

Any one who really understands the subject, can hardly fail to be impressed with the conviction, that the method of Justification which is revealed in Scripture,— considered simply in its intellectual aspect as a scheme of thought,—bears upon it the legible impress of profound wisdom. Were it only an invention of man, it must still be regarded as one of the most remarkable, and original, products of human reason. It is an attempt to solve the deepest problem, and to answer the most anxious question, which conscience continually prompts men to raise, but which their minds strive in vain to determine—'How shall man be just with God?' or, 'How can God be just,' and yet 'justify the ungodly?' That great problem may seldom occur to those that are habitually unmindful of God, and of their relation to Him; and should it be suggested to their minds, it will probably be lightly dismissed, as long as they cherish slight views of sin, and have little or no sense of their solemn responsibilities and prospects as subjects of the righteous government of God. Some vague opinion in regard to His general mercy, or some undefined purpose to propitiate His favour by future repentance and amendment of life, before they are brought face to face with the awful realities of death, and judgment, and eternity, may suffice, in the meantime, as an answer to the accusing voice of conscience, and as an opiate to allay its forebodings and fears. But minds in this state never grapple with any of the real difficulties of the problem, and can scarcely be said to have the slightest apprehension of its true meaning. They overlook all the most momentous conditions which are involved in it, and on which its right solution depends. The Gospel of Christ alone has presented that problem in all its magnitude, and in its just proportions ; and the Gospel of Christ alone has offered a solution of it, based on a full view of the Attributes of God,—of the unalterable requirements of His Law,—of the principles and ends of His Moral Government, —and of the state, character, and prospects of man, as a dying yet immortal being, chargeable with past guilt, and still depraved by inherent sin.

It lays a deep foundation for the doctrine of a sinner's pardon and acceptance with God, by revealing, in the first instance, the infinite holiness of God, His intense hatred of sin, His inflexible justice in punishing it,—the spiritual nature, the supreme authority, and unchangeable character of His law, as being, like Himself, 'holy, and just, and good,'—the principles and ends of His Moral Government, as a scheme which is designed and fitted to glorify His great Name, by manifesting, in their actual exercise, all the moral perfections of His nature, and making Himself known to His intelligent subjects as He really is,—the fallen, guilty, and depraved state of man, as a sinner, subject to condemnation, and utterly unable to save himself, while he is passing on, with the swiftness of time itself, to a state of strict and eternal retribution ; and it is not till after it has revealed these great truths, which might seem to render his salvation hopeless, that it reveals a method of Grace and Redemption by which God

Himself has solved the problem; and announces the stupendous fact, that He gave up His own Son,—to become incarnate, to assume the burden of our sins, to endure the punishment which these sins deserved, to shed His own precious blood for their expiation,—and all this that the Grace and the Justice of God might be made manifest, in their actual exercise, in the Cross of Christ;—and that thus,—His law having been 'magnified and made honourable,' and all the ends of His moral government effectually secured, — He might be more signally glorified by the pardon, than He could have been by the punishment, of the sinner,—and be revealed in the Gospel as 'the Just God and the Saviour,' as 'Just, and yet the Justifier of him that believeth in Jesus.'

The mere statement of such a problem, and of its indispensable conditions,—including the glory of God, the honour of His law, and the ends of His moral government, as well as the pardon of sin, and the salvation of sinners, —is peculiar to the Gospel of Christ, and may well be regarded as a proof of its superhuman origin : but the solution of it, by the Incarnation, Substitution, and Satisfaction of the Son of God Himself, is such a marvellous manifestation of divine wisdom as 'it could never have entered into the mind of man to conceive.' For none other than the infinite mind of God was capable of such a conception, either of Love, or of Justice, as that on which it is based; and far less of carrying it into effect in the stupendous work of Redemption. It may be esteemed as 'foolishness' by those who have never seriously considered, or sufficiently realised, the conditions of the great problem; but no sooner is any one brought, under the teaching of the Word and Spirit of God, to apprehend them aright, and to apply them in earnest to the case of his own soul, than that which hitherto seemed to be 'foolishness,' is seen to be the 'wisdom of God.' Hence, —while the very repugnance with which it is regarded by many affords ample evidence that it could never have been invented by men,—the best and most convincing evidence of its divine origin is discerned, when it is seen to be worthy of the infinite perfections of God, as well as adapted to the most urgent wants of man; and when 'He who commanded the light to shine out of darkness, shines into our hearts, to give us the light of the knowledge of the glory of God in the face of Jesus Christ.' (1)

But, if the method of Justification by faith in a divine Redeemer, when it is considered intellectually, as a scheme of thought, be so profound in itself and so peculiar to the Gospel of Christ, that method, when it is considered practically, as the only remedy for the evils of our condition as sinners, and the only means of obtaining pardon and acceptance with God, must be regarded as of supreme importance. For what can be more important, in any circumstances, than the relation in which we stand to God? and what can be more urgent, in our circumstances as sinners, than the question, how we may be delivered from a state of wrath and enmity, and brought into one of reconciliation and peace, with Him? Some may be disposed to say that the doctrine of Sanctification is more important, and more practical, than that of Justification: but have they duly considered, that God has revealed His own method of sanctifying, as well as of justifying sinners; and that there may be much danger in reversing that order of relation which He has established between the two? We are both 'sanctified and justified in the name of the Lord Jesus,' when we are united to Him by faith; but with this difference, that our Justification is immediate and complete, while our Sanctification is gradual and progressive, but never perfect, in the present life. So far from being founded on our Sanctification, our pardon and acceptance with God is simultaneous with its commencement,—precedes its subsequent stages,—and is largely conducive to its advancement. We are not sanctified by the law, any more than we are justified by the law; for the Apostle insists on its inefficacy in both respects, and shows that without the grace of Christ, the law, so far from subduing our corruptions, serves only to inflame and irritate them; while the same faith which justifies us 'worketh by love,' 'purifieth the heart,' and animates us in the path of cheerful and devoted obedience. For 'the end of the law is charity;' but it must be 'charity out of a pure heart, and a good conscience, and faith unfeigned.'

Another reflection, which is naturally suggested by a review both of the History, and the Exposition, of the Doctrine, is that, numerous and conflicting as have been the speculations of men on the subject, all the various shades of opinion in regard to it may be reduced, in their ultimate analysis, to one or other of these two opposite systems;—the system, which ascribes our Justification entirely to the grace of God, through the righteousness of Christ, by faith only,—and the system, which leaves it to depend, in whole or in part, on the personal holiness and obedience of man. The latter system includes many distinct grades of doctrinal belief,—from that of the mere moralist,—whether Atheistic, or Deistic, or Socinian,—who thinks that he may depend on his virtuous dispositions, and his integrity in the offices of common life, without considering, whether he discharges his duties in obedience to the will of God, or whether he is animated by the love of Christ,—up through that of the nominal Christian, who rests on his religious profession, and his regular observance of religious ordinances,—to the Evangelical Arminian, who trusts sincerely in Christ for the pardon of his past sins, but depends on his own inherent holiness, and his personal obedience, for his title to eternal life. These different grades of doctrinal belief are more or less dangerous in proportion as they recede more or less from the truth which is revealed in Scripture ; but while some of them are fatal, none of them can fail to be injurious, to those who cherish them. 'From an early period in the history of the Church,' says the venerable Dr. Hodge, of Princeton, 'there have been two great systems of doctrine in perpetual conflict. The one begins with God, the other with man. The one has for its object the vindication of the divine supremacy and sovereignty in the salvation of men ; the other has for its characteristic aim the assertion of the rights of human nature. It is specially solicitous that nothing should be held to be true, which cannot be philosophically reconciled with the liberty and ability of man. . . . Such directions as—receive Christ,—come to Him,—trust in Him,—commit the keeping of the soul to Him, naturally give place under this system to the exhortation—submit to God,—determine to keep His commands,—make choice of Him in preference to the world. The view which this system presents of the plan of salvation,—of the relation of the soul to Christ,—of the nature and office of faith,—modifies and determines the whole character of experimental religion. The system antagonistic to the one just described . . . regards the work of Christ as designed to satisfy justice, and to fulfil the demands of the law, by His perfect obedience to its precepts, and by enduring its penalty in the room and stead of sinners. His righteousness is so imputed to believers, that their Justification is not merely the act of a sovereign dispensing with law, but the act of a judge declaring the law to be satisfied.' (2)

Attempts have sometimes been made to show that there is no real, or at least no radical, difference between these two systems (3) ; and that neither the Popish, nor the Socinian, doctrine should be regarded as incompatible with the salvation of those who sincerely embrace them. It is not for us to sit in judgment on any class of men, or to determine, either their present relation to God, or their future prospects under His government. 'To their own Master, they stand or fall.' But if He has revealed the only method of pardon and acceptance with Him, we cannot regard it as a matter of indifference, whether they comply with it, or not. It is their duty to ascertain His mind and will on that subject, as it is revealed in His Word ; and if they fail in the discharge of that duty,— whether from carelessness, or prejudice, or hatred to the truth,—they are guilty of sin. The attempts which have been made to minimize the difference, on this subject, between the Popish and Protestant Churches, on the one hand, and between the different sections of Protestants, on the other, by those who have assumed the name of 'reconcilers,' have often resulted in the sacrifice of some portion of God's revealed truth, and have seldom, if ever, been conducive to the real peace, and spiritual edification, of His Church.

We conclude, in the brief, but clear and comprehensive, words of the Westminster Divines :

'JUSTIFICATION IS AN ACT OF GOD'S FREE GRACE,— WHEREIN HE PARDONETH ALL OUR SINS,—AND ACCEPTETH US AS RIGHTEOUS IN HIS SIGHT,—ONLY FOR THE RIGHTEOUSNESS OF CHRIST,—IMPUTED TO US,—AND RECEIVED BY FAITH ALONE.'

APPENDIX.

NOTES TO THE INTRODUCTION.

NOTE 1, p. 9.

THE personal experience of the Reformers throws much light on the origin, and causes, of the Reformation.

'The different phases of this work succeeded each other in the mind of him who was to be the instrument of it, before it was publicly accomplished in the world. The knowledge of the Reformation, as effected in the heart of Luther himself, is, in truth, the key to the Reformation of the Church. It is only by studying the work in the individual, that we can comprehend the general work.'—*D'Aubigné, History of the Reformation in Europe,* 5 vols., vol. i. p. 140.

'His conscience incessantly reminded him, that religion was the one thing needful, and that his first care should be the salvation of his soul. He had learned God's hatred of sin,—he remembered the penalties that His Word denounces against the sinner,—and he asked himself tremblingly, if he were sure that he possessed the favour of God. His conscience answered, No!' . . . 'One day, when he was overwhelmed with despair, an old monk entered his cell, and spoke kindly to him. Luther opened his heart to him, and acquainted him with the fears that disquieted him. The respectable old man was incapable of entering into all his doubts, as Staupitz had done; but he knew his " Credo," and he had found there something to comfort his own heart. He thought he would apply the same remedy to the young brother. Calling his attention, therefore, to the Apostles' Creed, which Luther had learnt in his early childhood at the school at Mansfeld, the old man uttered in simplicity this article,— " I believe in the forgiveness of sins." These simple words, ingenuously uttered by the pious brother at a critical moment, shed sweet consolation in the mind of Luther. " I believe," repeated he to himself on the bed of suffering, " in the remission of sins." '—*Ib.* pp. 159, 187.

'In these spiritual conflicts and inward wrestlings, how grievously he was encumbered, fighting against incredulity, error, and desperation, marvellous it is to consider, insomuch, that three days and three nights together, he lay on his bed, without meat, drink, or any sleep, labouring in soul and spirit on a certain place of St. Paul (Rom. iii. 25, 26) which was—"to show His justice,"—thinking Christ to be sent for no other end but to show forth God's justice as an executor of His law,—till at length, being answered and satisfied by the Lord touching the right meaning of these words—signifying the justice of God to be executed upon His Son, to save us from the stroke thereof,—he immediately upon the same started up from his bed, so confirmed in faith, as that nothing afterward could appal him.'—*Preface to English Version of Luther's Commentary on Galatians*, translated by ' certain godly learned,' 1575, p. v.

' His great terror was the thought of " the righteousness of God,"— by which he had been taught to understand, His inflexible severity in executing judgment against sinners. Dr. Staupitz and the confessor explained to him, that " the righteousness of God " is not *against* the sinner who believes in the Lord Jesus Christ, but *for* him,—not against us, to *condemn*, but for us, to *justify*. " I felt very angry," he said, " at the term —' the righteousness of God ;'—for, after the manner of all the teachers, I was taught to understand it in a philosophic sense—of that righteousness, by which God is just, and punisheth the guilty. . . . At last I came to apprehend it thus—Through the Gospel is revealed the righteousness which availeth with God,—a righteousness by which God, in His mercy and compassion, *justifieth* us, as it is written, ' The just shall live by faith.' Straightway I felt as if I were born anew ; it was as if I had found the door of paradise thrown wide open. The expression ' the righteousness of God,' which I so much hated before, became now dear and precious,— my darling and most comforting word. I see the Father—inflexible in justice, yet delighting in mercy—' just,' beyond all my terrified conscience could picture Him, He ' justifies ' me a sinner."—*Chronicles of the Schönberg-Cotta Family*, pp. 159, 160 ;—a graphic delineation of the state of feeling which prevailed at the time of Luther.

Many touching allusions to his personal experience occur in the writings of Luther. For example, on the subject of self-righteousness, he says, ' I have myself taught this doctrine (*i.e.* " of faith, by which embracing the merits of Christ, we stand accepted before the tribunal of God ") for twenty years both in my preaching and my writings ; and yet the old and tenacious mire clings to me, so that I find myself wanting to come to God, bringing something in my hand, for which He should bestow His grace upon me. I cannot attain to casting myself on pure and simple faith only, and yet this is highly necessary.' Again : ' He alludes to his former views when a monk, and the desire he then felt to converse with a saint, or holy person ; figuring to himself under that name a hermit, an ascetic, feeding on roots ; but he had since learned, that the saint was one, who, being justified in the righteousness of Christ, went on to serve God in his proper calling,—through the Spirit to mortify the deeds of the body, and to subdue his evil affections and desires.'—*Scott's Continuation of Milner's History*, i. pp. 233, 239.

' Luther became a Reformer, because, in his confessional, he had

learned to know the spiritual necessities of the people ; because he had
compassion on the poor people, even as the Saviour had compassion upon
them.   It was a hearty pity for the simple and ignorant, whom he, too,
saw given up to the Priests, and Pharisees, and Scribes, and cheated of
the highest blessings of life ; it was a deep manly sorrow over the mistaken road of salvation along which the poor misled multitude were
wandering, whereby Luther was inspirited to his first half-timid attempts ;
whereby, as he advanced, he was strengthened to stedfast perseverance,—
whereby, at length, he was raised and arrayed as the mighty champion
of evangelical freedom.   Luther had rushed deep into the gulf of moral
corruption, which was diffused among the lay commonalty, by the Romish
doctrine of Justification by works.   He knew from the liveliest experience
the miserable condition to which the sincerest souls, the devoutest spirits,
are reduced by this doctrine.   He had found an escape for himself out of
this tribulation—a path leading securely to the peace of the soul—in the
righteousness of faith.   Therefore he could not, and would not, keep
silence at that which was going on around him.   The princes and priests,
indeed, the learned and educated, did not need, for the most part, that he
should teach them the meaning of Indulgences, but the common unedu-
cated people urgently demanded his help.   This people Luther esteemed
as standing exactly on the same level—as requiring, just like all other
classes, to be led to the light of a purer knowledge of salvation ; he neither
deemed himself too high, or the multitude too low, to devote his services
to them.   In this state of mind, he boldly and powerfully tore down the
wall of separation, which had been built up in the course of centuries,
between the clergy and the laity.   The mass of the laity, who had hitherto
only been considered as a helpless body, to be moulded by the priests at
pleasure, and to be interceded for by the Church before God, he roused,
by the doctrine of Repentance and of Justification by faith, and gave them
a living principle of spiritual independence and personality, supplying
them with inexhaustible materials for contemplation, in the scriptural
ideas of Sin and Divine Grace ; and thus, out of the despised objects of
an arbitrary sway, he fashioned a living organized congregation of Christians, who had become free through their faith in their Redeemer.'—
Hemdeshagen, Treatise on German Protestantism.   See Archdeacon Hare,
' Vindication of Luther,' p. 296.
     ' His deep, irrepressible, unappeasable consciousness of sin was the
primary motive of his whole public life, and of all that he did for the
reformation of the Church.   It was on account of this deep feeling of the
inward disease in the conscience that he tore off the plasters and lenitives
with which the Romish quacks were wont to lull and skin over the
wounds at the surface.   It was on account of this that he set his foot on
the scandalous fraud of Indulgences.   It was by reason of this that he
saw through the utter vanity of the penances and so-called good works,
by which men were idly trying to purge their consciences.   He felt, as
St. Paul and Augustine felt, that the evil in man does not lie in the im-

perfection of his outward works, but in the corruption of his heart and will. Therefore did he insist so strongly on the frailty which clings to our very best works ; and therefore did he continually urge that, if we are to be justified, it must be wholly through grace, by the righteousness of our Divine Saviour, to be received and appropriated by faith, without any admixture of the works wrought by so frail and peccable a creature.' —*Archdeacon Hare, Vindication of Luther*, p. 135. See also *Pfizer's Life of Luther*.

The experience of Calvin was similar to that of Luther. 'The Reformation was not the fruit of abstract reasoning ; it proceeded from an inward labour,—a spiritual conflict,—a victory, which the Reformers won by the sweat of their brow, or rather, of their heart. . . . We have on a former occasion sought to discover the generative principle of the Reformation in the heart of Luther : we are now striving to discern it in the heart of Calvin.'—*D'Aubigné, History of the Reformation in the Time of Calvin*, vol. i. p. 20.

' His chamber became the theatre of struggles as fierce as those in the cell at Erfurth. Through the same tempests, both these great Reformers reached the same haven. Calvin arrived at faith by the same practical way which had led Farel and Augustine, Luther and Paul.'—*Ib.* i. p. 522.

' Calvin shut himself up in his room and examined himself. " I have been taught that Thy Son has ransomed me by His death ; but I have never felt in my heart the virtue of His redemption." His Popish professors spoke to him. " The highest wisdom of Christians," they said, " is to submit to the Church, and their highest dignity is the righteousness of their works." " Alas !" replied Calvin, " I am a miserable sinner." " That is true ; but there is a means of obtaining mercy. It is by satisfying the justice of God. Confess your sins to a priest, and ask humbly for absolution. Blot out the memory of your offences by good works." . . . Calvin went to church, fell on his knees, and confessed his sins to God's minister, asking for absolution, and humbly accepting every penance imposed upon him. . . . " O God," he said, " I desire by my good works to blot out the remembrance of my trespasses." He performed the satisfactions prescribed by the priest ; he even went beyond the task imposed upon him ; and hoped that after so much labour, he would be saved. But, alas ! his peace was not of long duration. . . . " Every time I descend into the depths of my heart—every time, O God, I lift up my soul to Thy throne, extreme terror comes over me." . . . His heart was troubled ; it seemed to him that every word of God he found in Scripture tore off the veil, and reproached him with his trespasses. " I begin to see," he said,—" thanks to the light that has been brought me,—in what a slough of error I have hitherto been wallowing,—with how many stains I am disfigured,—and, above all, what is the eternal death that threatens me." A great trembling came over him. He paced his room, as Luther had once paced his cell at Erfurth. He uttered, he tells us, deep groans, and shed floods of tears. Terrified at the divine holiness, like a man frightened by a violent thunder-storm, he exclaimed, " O God! Thou keepest me bowed down, as if Thy bolts were falling on my head."

' Then he fell down, exclaiming, " Poor and wretched, I throw myself on the mercy which Thou hast shown us in Christ Jesus ; I enter that only harbour of Salvation." He applied to the study of Scripture, and everywhere he found Christ. " O Father," he said, " His sacrifice has appeased Thy wrath ; His blood has washed away my impurities ; His Cross has borne my curse ; His death hath atoned for me. . . . Thou hast placed Thy Word before me like a torch, and Thou hast touched my heart, in order that I should hold in abomination all other merits save that of Jesus." Calvin's conversion had been long and slowly ripening ; and yet, in one sense, the change was instantaneous. " When I was the obstinate slave of the superstitions of Popery," he says, " and it seemed impossible to drag me out of the deep mire, God by a sudden conversion subdued me, and made my heart obedient to His Word." '—*Ib.* vol. i. pp. 525-530.

<h2 style="text-align:center">NOTE 2, p. 9.</h2>

Luther on the Epistle to the Galatians, English Translation (A.D. 1575), pp. 175, 176. Another testimony, equally clear and strong, may be quoted from the same work ; for although it abounds in bold, and sometimes unguarded, statements, and is neither a learned nor a critical exposition of the Epistle, yet as a popular statement of Gospel truth, delivered first in the pulpit, and designed for the instruction of his congregation at Wittemberg, it is one of the noblest and freshest utterances which ever proceeded from the heart of a Christian divine. Mr. Ward ventured to say of it in his ' Ideal of a Christian Church' (p. 172), that ' the Commentary, considered intellectually, as a theological effort, is perhaps one of the feeblest and most worthless productions ever written ;' but those who have considered Archdeacon Hare's estimate of Mr. Ward's competency to sit in judgment upon it, will probably attach more weight to the testimony of John Bunyan, who says of it, ' I do prefer this book of M. Luther on the Galatians, excepting the Holy Bible, before all the books that ever I have seen, as most fit for a wounded conscience.'—*Hare's Vindication of Luther,* 2d Ed. p. 155.

Luther sets the doctrine of Justification by the blood of Christ through faith, against all the inventions of men, in the following striking terms :—

' These words,—" the Son of God loved me, and gave Himself for me,"—are mighty thunderings and lightnings from heaven against the righteousness of the Law, and all the works thereof. . . . What wilt thou do, when thou hearest the Apostle say, that such an inestimable price was given for thee? Wilt thou bring thy cowl, thy shaven crown, thy chastity, thy obedience, thy poverty, thy works, thy merits? What shall all these do? Yea, what shall the law of Moses avail? What shall the works of all men, and all the sufferings of the martyrs, profit thee?

What is the obedience of all the holy angels, in comparison of the Son of God delivered, and that most shamefully, even to the death of the Cross, so that there was no drop of His most precious blood but it was shed, and that for thy sins? If thou couldst rightly consider this incomparable price, thou shouldst hold as accursed all these ceremonies, vows, works, and merits, before grace and after, and throw them down all to hell. For it is an horrible blasphemy to imagine, that there is any work whereby thou shouldst presume to pacify God, since thou seest that there is nothing which is able to pacify Him, but this inestimable price, even the death and blood of the Son of God, a drop whereof is more precious than the whole world. . . . If I through works or merits could have loved the Son of God, and so come unto Him, what needed He to deliver Himself for me? Hereby it appeareth how coldly the Papists handled, yea, how they utterly neglected, the Holy Scriptures, and the doctrine of Faith. For if they had considered but only these words, that it behoved the Son of God to be given for me, it had been impossible that so many monstrous sects should have sprung up amongst them. For Faith would by and bye have answered, Why dost thou choose this kind of life, this religion, this work? Dost thou this to please God, or to be justified thereby? Dost thou not hear, O wretched man, that the Son of God shed His blood for thee? Thus true faith in Christ would easily have withstood all manner of sects. Wherefore I say, as I have oftentimes said, that there is no remedy against sects, or power to resist them, but this only article of Christian Righteousness. If we lose this article, it is impossible for us to withstand any errors or sects. . . . What mean they to brag so much of works and merits? If I, being a wretched man and a damned sinner, could be redeemed by any other price, what needed the Son of God to be given for me?'—*Luther on the Galatians*, English Translation, p. 138.

'The Church had fallen because the great doctrine of Justification through faith in Christ had been lost. It was therefore necessary that this doctrine should be restored to her before she could arise. Whenever this fundamental truth should be restored, all the errors and devices which had usurped its place,—the train of saints, works, penances, masses, and indulgences,—would vanish. The moment the ONE Mediator, and His ONE Sacrifice, were acknowledged, all other mediators, and all other sacrifices, would disappear. "This article of Justification," says Luther to Brentius, "is that which forms the Church,—nourishes it,—builds it up,—preserves and defends it. It is the heel which crushes the serpent's head."'—*D'Aubigné, History of Reformation in Europe*, 5 vols., vol. i. p. 73.

'When the Gospel lifted up its voice in the days of the Reformation, the people listened. It spoke to them—of God, Sin, Condemnation, Pardon, Everlasting Life,—in a word, of Christ. The human soul discovered that this was what it wanted; and was touched, captivated, and finally renewed.'—*D'Aubigné, History of the Reformation in the Time of Calvin*, vol. ii. p. 399. See also p. 583.

Note 3, p. 14.

The titles of the works mentioned in the text, and the editions of them which will be referred to, are the following :—

'Remains of Alex. Knox, Esq.,' in 4 vols. 8vo, 1834.

'Thirty Years' Correspondence between Bishop Jebb and Mr. Knox,' 2 vols. 8vo, 1834.

Bishop O'Brien, 'Essays on the Nature and Effects of Faith,' 2d Edition, 1862.

Geo. Stanley Faber, 'The Primitive Doctrine of Justification,' 2d Edition, 1839.

Dr. J. H. Newman, 'Lectures on Justification,' 2d Edition, 1840.

Dr. James Bennett, 'Justification as Revealed in Scripture, in opposition to the Council of Trent, and Mr. Newman's Lectures,' 8vo, 1840. Dr. Bennett had previously published a volume entitled, 'The Theology of the Early Christian Church,' being the Eighth Series of the Congregational Lecture,—New edition, 1855,—which touches on the subject of Justification, pp. 118-132, and has a direct bearing on the question whether the Protestant doctrine is a novelty which arose in the sixteenth century.

Griffith's 'Reply to Dr. Newman's Lectures,' commended by Bishop Daniel Wilson, has not come into my hands. Bateman, 'Life of Bishop Wilson,' p. 357.

Dr. J. H. Newman, 'Apologia pro Vita Sua,' 1864.

Note 4, p. 15.

Robert Traill (of London), 'A Vindication of the Protestant Doctrine of Justification,' Works, vol. i. p. 321. Reprinted by the Free Church Committee on Cheap Publications.

NOTES TO LECTURE I.

Note 1, p. 17.

Many years ago, Bishop O'Brien announced his intention to prepare a History of the Doctrine of Justification ; but that intention has not yet been carried into effect, and there is scarcely any work in the English language which can be said to supply the want. It is in every respect desirable, that one so thoroughly competent for the task, in point both of ability and learning, should take up this comprehensive subject, which can only be treated cursorily in a series of Lectures like the present, and would require an entire volume for its illustration.

The sources of information on the subject are either general or special. Some works give the history of the doctrine,—or materials for construct-

ing its history,—in all ages, including the faith of the Church in regard
to it under the Old, as well as the New, Dispensation;—others give its
history, either in the Old Testament, or in post-apostolic times, only.

To the first class belong the Scriptures of the Old and New Testaments, which must ever have the first place assigned to them, as being
inspired records, both of the divine revelations which were vouchsafed
from time to time to the Church, and of the faith and worship which
were maintained in it from the beginning. A sound exposition of Scripture, which should follow the historical course of Revelation from its
commencement to its close in the sacred canon, would be the best history
of both.

The 'Magdeburg Centuriators,'—viz., M. Flacius Illyricus, Joannes
Wigandus, Matthæus Judex, Basilius Faber, and others who were associated with them,—were induced to write the History of the Church anew
by the conviction, that previous historians had not given due prominence
to the doctrinal truths of Scripture, especially to the doctrine of Justification; and they have collected valuable materials for its history, both
under the Old dispensation and the New. Two of their number,—
Joannes Wigandus and Matthæus Judex,—published separately from
their great work, in 1563, a thick quarto volume, entitled, ' SYNTAGMA,
seu *Corpus Doctrinæ* ex Veteri Testamento tantùm Collectum,' in which
they collect together, under distinct heads, the great truths which are
common to both Testaments; and treat ' De Evangelio,' p. 944, ' De
Justificatione Peccatoris coram Deo," p. 962, ' De Fide,' p. 1003, ' De
Bonis Operibus,' p. 1019, and other cognate topics. In their larger
work, the Centuriators give the history of the doctrine under the New
Testament dispensation, but not continuously; the passages which relate
to it must be collected from the account of each century. Century I.,
Book i. c. iv., includes the teaching of our Lord, pp. 9-111, and of the
Apostles, pp. 219-278, ' De Justificatione Hominis coram Deo;' and the
same topic is resumed in each successive century.

The two works of Buddeus,—' Historia Ecclesiastica Veteris Testamenti,' and 'Ecclesia Apostolica,'—embrace the teaching of both Testaments. Four admirable ' Exercitations,' by Witsius, give the history of
the opinions which prevailed among the Gentiles and the Jews; also the
doctrine which was taught by the Apostles: 'Miscell. Sacra,' vol. ii. pp.
668-752. They are entitled, respectively,—' De Theologia Gentilium
in Negotio Justificationis,' pp. 668-697,—' De Theologia Judæorum in
Negotio Justificationis,' pp. 698-721,—' De Controversiis quæ Apostolorum ætate in Ecclesia Christiana circa Justificationem ortæ sunt,' pp. 721-
731,—' De Mente Pauli in Negotio Justificationis,' pp. 732-752. These
dissertations were occasioned by Dr. Cave's ' Antiquitates Apostolicæ,' on
that work being translated and published on the Continent; and were
designed as an answer to it. Dr. Cave's opinion was, that the doctrine,
as taught by the Apostles, excluded Justification by ceremonial observances, and left it to depend entirely on Faith; but that this Faith,

which is the only condition of the New Covenant, is not any special grace, having an office or function distinct from that of other graces, but is rather comprehensive of them all ; and that, therefore, works of evangelical obedience are not excluded from the ground of our acceptance with God.   To this class of works may be added President Edwards' 'History of Redemption.'

The works which have been mentioned afford materials for constructing the history of the doctrine in the Church *both* of the Old and New Testaments.   Many other works give, more or less fully, the history of the doctrine either in the Old Testament, or in post-apostolic times.   Of works on the Old Testament, we may mention, Hengstenberg's 'Christology of the Old Testament,' 4 vols. (T. and T. Clark, Edinburgh), with the older 'Christology' of Robert Fleming, jun.; and that most instructive and edifying series of Lectures, in 4 vols., entitled, ' Christ as made known to the Ancient Church,' by my late venerable colleague, Dr. Gordon, of the High Church, Edinburgh.   Of works relating to the post-apostolic History of the Doctrine, we may mention, Dr. Hagenbach, of Basle, ' Compendium of the History of Doctrines,' vol. ii. pp. 267-274, and 447-460 ; Dr. Shedd, of America, ' History of Christian Doctrine,' Book v. 'History of Soteriology,' vol. ii. pp. 201-386 ; Dr. Muenschen, of Marpurg, ' Elements of Dogmatic History,' translated by Dr. James Murdoch, 1830, c. vii. pp. 72-80, and 184-190.

Petavius does not treat of Justification as a distinct topic in his 'Dogmata Theologica' (6 vols. fol., Antwerp, 1700), but frequent references occur to it ; as when he speaks of ' Preparations for Justification,' vol. i. lib. x. c. xxvii. s. 12,—of 'Justice,' or 'Righteousness,' vol. i. lib. vi. c. viii. s. 6; lib. x. c. ii. s. 4, c. xiv. s. 1,—of ' Justification and Adoption,' vol. ii. lib. viii. c. 4, 5, 10, 1 ; in vol. iii. 'De Pelagianis et Semipelagianis,' p. 336, and 'De Tridentini Concilii Interpretatione,' and ' De Sancti Augustini Doctrina,' p. 353, when he refers to the conflicting interpretations by *Soto* and *Vega* of the Canons and Decrees of the Council, c. xv. ; and in vol. v. vi. ' De Incarnatione Verbi,' in 16 books.

One of the most useful works on the subject is that of J. Forbes (of Corse), 'Instructiones Historico-Theologicæ.' See lib. viii. c. 2, 5-10, but especially c. 23, 24, pp. 423-429.

Chemnitz gives 'Veterum Testimonia de Justificatione' in the first part of his ' Examen Concilii Tridentini,' p. 141.

All the general histories of the Church may be consulted, such as Dr. Kurtz's ' History of the Old Covenant,' and Neander's, Weismann's, Mosheim's, and Milner's, Histories of the Christian Church.

The special sources of information, in regard to the state of the doctrine at particular eras, will be referred to in connection with each of the great controversies which have arisen in regard to it.   But full information cannot be obtained by merely reading an historical narative ; and recourse must be had to two or three of the best writers *on each side* of every discussion, as it passes under review.

Note 2, p. 21.

These various opinions are represented respectively by the following writers :—The *first* by Dr. Taylor of Norwich, in his ' Scripture Doctrine of Original Sin,' and his ' Key to the Apostolic Writings,' which are answered by President Edwards in his ' Great Christian Doctrine of Original Sin,' Works, vol. ii. pt. ii. sec. ii. The *second* by Henry Dodwell, in his ' Epistolary Discourse, proving that the Soul is naturally Mortal, but immortalized by its union with the Divine Baptismal Spirit, imparted only by the Bishops ;' which was answered by Dr. S. Clarke in his ' Letter to Mr. Dodwell.' It has been recently revived, in a different form, by Mr. Edward White, in his work entitled, ' Life in Christ' (1846) —which is directed to prove that ' Immortality is the peculiar privilege of the regenerate.' The *third* by many modern writers, who make spiritual death to consist entirely in sin, as a subjective moral evil, and overlook the wrath and curse of God on account of past transgressions. On this subject, see the profound treatise of Dr. Thomas Goodwin, ' An Unregenerate Man's Guiltiness before God in respect of Sin and Punishment,' Works, vol. x. pp. 1-56, Nichol's Edition.

Note 3, p. 22.

Professor M'Laggan's Lectures, pp. 307-367.

Note 4, p. 22.

Rom. iv. 4 : ' μισθὸς κατὰ χάριν,—μισθὸς κατὰ τὸ ὀφείλημα.' ' Meritum ex condigno' is distinguished, even by Popish writers, from ' Meritum ex pacto' or ' ex promissione ;' but in treating of the latter, in connection with the rewards which are promised to believers under the New Covenant, they overlook the fact that these are promised on account of the merits of Christ. There is still a wide difference between ' rewards of debt,' and ' rewards of grace ;' for while both were promised,—the one under the first, the other under the second, covenant,—yet the former were to be bestowed on the ground of personal obedience, while the latter are bestowed on account of the obedience of Him with whom the covenant was made on behalf of His people ; that is, on the ground of His vicarious and imputed righteousness. ' The whole tenor of Revelation shows, that there are but two methods whereby any of the human race can be justified : either by a perfect obedience to the law *in their own persons*, and then " the reward is of debt," *i.e.* pactional debt, founded on the obligation of the covenant, not springing from any worth in the obedience. Or else, because the Surety of a better covenant has satisfied all demands in their stead ; and then " the reward is of grace," Rom. iv. 4.'—*Hervey's Works*, vol. ii. p. 296.

Note 5, p. 24.

On the first covenant of life, see Witsius, ' De Œconomia Fœderum

Dei,' lib. i. c. ii.-viii. pp. 8-99 ; Burmann, 'Synopsis,' vol. i. lib. ii. c. ii.
pp. 389-475 ; Bishop Hopkins on 'The Two Covenants ;' Boston on
'The Covenant of Works ;' Dr. Russel (of Dundee) on 'The Adamic
and Mediatorial Dispensations ;' Dr. Meikle (of Beith) on 'The Edenic
Dispensation ;' Mr. Strong on 'The Covenants ;' Mr. Barrett on 'The
Covenants,' pp. 38-75 ; and many more. As some have denied the
literal truth of the Mosaic narrative on this subject, see also Holden's
' Dissertation on the Fall of Man, in which the literal sense of the Mosaic
Account of that event is Asserted and Vindicated,' 1823 ; also Jó. Witty,
' Vindication of the History of the Fall of Adam,' 1705.

'I begin with the *first* revelation which God made of Himself, and of
His will, to man in the beginning of time ; and from thence I would
descend to *later* revelations, both before, and in, Gospel times. The holy,
all-wise God, having created reasonable creatures, gave to them a Law,
the rule of that obedience and duty which is the natural result of the
relation between God the Creator, and *such* creatures. This Law required
perfect sinless obedience. No less could God call for ; no less was suited
to the state of innocence and perfection, wherein man was created. This
Law, given at first, was written on the heart, and needed not to be ex-
ternally proposed. That positive prohibition, *Not to eat of the tree of the
knowledge of good and evil*, was but for the trial of obedience ; and the
tree itself, a sacrament or symbol of *death*, in case of disobedience, as the
tree of life was a symbol or sacrament of *life*, in case of obedience. These
symbols clearly show that the Law was established into a covenant. And
a covenant it was, truly and properly ; for Adam had no right to deny
his consent to the terms which God proposed ; and, being yet sinless and
holy, he had no will thereto, but agreed both to the preceptive part, and
to the sanction, as "holy, just, and good." '—*Beart, Vindication of the
Eternal Law and Everlasting Gospel*, p. 2. London, 1753. This work
is recommended by Hervey ('Theron and Aspasio,' vol. ii. p. 20) as a
'most excellent treatise,' which has 'the very sinews of the argument,
and the very marrow of the doctrine.' It consists of two parts, and has
been frequently reprinted.

NOTE 6, p. 28.

The first promise, or primeval Gospel. 'De Evangelio ; Quid sit.
Evangelium est doctrina à Deo immediatè patefacta, de gratuita recon-
ciliatione hominum lapsorum, et remissione peccatorum per Messiam,
quæ fide accipienda est, adferens atque impertiens justitiam coram Deo,
Messiæ passione acquisitam, pacem conscientiæ, et vitam eternam. Hæc
definitio ex suavissimis dictis Scripturæ sacræ—Gen. iii. 22, et aliis
sumpta est.'—*Wigandus and Judex, Syntagma*, p. 944.

The effect of this revelation of God's purpose of mercy in changing
the whole state and experience of our first parents, is stated, with a grand
simplicity, by John Knox, when, speaking of the three cardinal points,—
our sin and misery,—God's promise of grace,—and the effect of faith in

it,—he says, ' All this plainly may be perceived in the life of our first parent Adam, who, by transgression of God's commandment, fell in great trouble and affliction,—from which he should never have been released, without the goodness of God had first called him. And, secondly, made unto him the promise of his salvation, the which Adam believing, before ever he wrought good works, was reputed just. After, during all his life, he continued in good works, striving contrary to Satan, the world, and his own flesh.'—*Knox's Works*, vol. iii. p. 439,—the admirable edition, for which the Church is indebted to David Laing, Esq., of the Library of the Writers to the Signet, Edinburgh.

' Had Adam felt,' says Zuingle, ' that he had anything remaining after his fall which might gain the favour of his Maker, he would not have fled " to hide himself;" but his case appeared to himself so desperate, that we do not read even of his having recourse to supplication. He dared not at all to appear before God. But here the mercy and kindness of the Most High are displayed, who recalls the fugitive, even when, with a traitor's mind, he is passing over to the camp of the enemy, and not even offering a prayer for pardon ; receives him to His mercy ; and, as far as His justice would permit, restores him to a happy state. Here the Almighty exhibited a splendid example of what He would do for the whole race of Adam, sparing them, and treating them with kindness, even when they deserved only punishment. Here, then, Religion took its rise, when God recalled despairing, fugitive man to Himself.'—*Zuingle, De Vera et Falsâ Religione*, p. 169.

' All the promises,' says Luther, ' are to be referred to that *first* promise concerning Christ, " The seed of the woman shall bruise the serpent's head," Gen. iii. 15. So did all the prophets both understand it, and teach it. By this we may see that the faith of our fathers in the Old Testament, and ours now in the New, is all one, although they differ as touching their outward object. Which thing Peter witnesseth in the Acts (xv. 11): " We believe that, through the grace of the Lord Jesus Christ, we shall be saved, *even as they*." . . . The faith of the fathers was grounded on Christ which was to come, as ours is on Christ which is now come. Abraham in his time was justified by faith in Christ to come; but if he lived at this day, he would be justified by faith in Christ now revealed and present. Like as I have said before of Cornelius, who at the first believed in Christ to come, but, being instructed by Peter, he believed that Christ was already come. Therefore *the diversity of times never changeth faith*, nor the Holy Ghost, nor the gifts thereof. For there hath been, is, and ever shall be, one mind, one judgment and understanding, concerning Christ, as well in the ancient fathers, as in the faithful which are at this day, and shall come hereafter. So we also have a Christ to come, and to believe in Him, as the fathers in the Old Testament had. For we look for Him to come again in the last day with glory, to judge both the quick and the dead, whom now we believe to be come already for our salvation.'—*On the Galatians*, pp. 187, 188.

'All the faithful have had alway one and the self-same Gospel from the beginning of the world, and by that they were saved.' . . . 'Christ came in spirit to the fathers of the Old Testament, before He came in the flesh. They had Christ in spirit. They believed in Christ which should be revealed, as we believe in Christ which is now revealed, and were saved by Him as we are, according to that saying, "Jesus Christ, the same yesterday, and to-day, and for ever." "Yesterday," before the time of His coming in the flesh; "to-day," when He was revealed "in the time before appointed." Now and "for ever" He is one and the same Christ: for even by Him only, and alone, all the faithful which either have been, be, or shall be, are delivered from the law, justified, and saved.'—*Ibid.* pp. 258, 295.

NOTE 7, p. 28.

In the question respecting the *Justification of Old Testament believers*, the principal points are these,—the *fact* that they were justified,—the *reason* or *ground* of their pardon and acceptance,—and the *means* by which they were made partakers of this privilege.

The *fact* that they were justified, in the full Gospel sense of that expression, can scarcely be questioned; since they are expressly declared to have been freely forgiven, and restored to the favour and friendship of God. The fact was even divinely attested: Abel 'obtained witness that he was righteous;' Enoch, 'before his translation, had this testimony, that he pleased God' (Heb. xi. 4, 5). They not only possessed, but they enjoyed, this Gospel privilege; for 'David describeth the blessedness of the man unto whom God imputeth righteousness without works, saying, Blessed are they whose iniquities *are* forgiven, and whose sins are covered; blessed is the man to whom the Lord will not impute sin' (Rom. iv. 6, 7; Ps. xxxii.). 'I acknowledged my sin unto Thee, and mine iniquity have I not hid. I said, I will confess my transgressions unto the Lord; *and Thou forgavest the iniquity of my sin*' (Ps. xxxii. 5). 'Bless the Lord, O my soul, and forget not all His benefits; *who forgiveth all thine iniquities*' (Ps. ciii. 2, 3). The *fact*, then, is undeniable that they were justified, in the full sense of that expression,—that they were freely forgiven, and graciously accepted as righteous, so as to be restored to the favour, friendship, and fellowship of God.

The *reason* or *ground* of their Justification was not their own personal righteousness,—for they were 'guilty,' 'ungodly,' unclean,' unable to 'stand in judgment,'—but the work of Christ, the promised Seed. For that work, although postponed till 'the fulness of times,' had a retrospective efficacy; it was accomplished for 'the redemption of the transgressions which were under the first testament' (Heb. ix. 15), and Old Testament believers could say, 'He was wounded for our transgressions, and bruised for our iniquities: the chastisement of our peace was laid upon Him, and by His stripes we are healed' (Isa. liii. 5). 'The covenant (of grace) was differently administered in the time of the Law, and the time of the Gospel: under the Law it was administered by promises, prophecies, sacrifices, circumcision, the paschal lamb, and other types and ordinances delivered to the people of the Jews, all fore-signifying Christ to come, which were, for that time, sufficient, and *efficacious*, through the operation of the Spirit, to instruct and build up the elect in faith in the promised Messiah, *by whom they had full remission of sins, and eternal salvation.'*—'Although the work of redemption was not actually wrought by Christ till after His incarnation, yet the virtue, efficacy, and benefits thereof, were communicated unto the elect in all ages successively from the beginning of the world, in and by those promises, types, and sacrifices, wherein He was revealed and signified to be "the Seed of the woman which should bruise the serpent's head,"—and "the Lamb slain from the beginning of the world," being "yesterday and to-day the same, and for ever."'—*Westminster Confession of Faith*, c. vii. s. 5, viii. s. 6.   See Bishop Barlow, 'Remains,' pp. 584-593 ; Bishop O'Brien, 'Nature and Effects of Faith,' p. 439 ; H. Witsius, 'Animadversiones Irenicæ,' Mis. Sac. ii. p. 780 ; Bishop Downham ' on Justification,' p. 180.

The *means* of their Justification was *faith*.   This follows necessarily from its being left to depend on the work of Christ, for that work was still future ; it was a matter of *promise*, and a promise can only be embraced by faith.   But it is expressly declared to have been by faith ; for it is written, 'The just shall live by faith' (Gal. iii. 11), and 'Abraham believed God, and it was counted to him for righteousness' (Rom. iv. 3 ; Gal. iii. 6).   Whether faith was itself their righteousness, and in what sense it was imputed to them, will be considered in the sequel.

NOTE 8, p. 31.

The question whether Sacrifice was a divine institution, or a human invention, has given rise to much discussion.   On the one side, see Davison, 'Inquiry into the Origin and Intent of Primitive Sacrifice,' also a note in his 'Discourses on Prophecy ;' 'Correspondence between Bishop Jebb and Mr. Knox,' vol. i. pp. 455-462 ; Dr. Sykes, 'Essay on Sacrifice.'   On the other, Archbishop M'Gee ' On the Atonement;' Shuckford's 'Connection of Sacred and Profane History,' vol. i. p. 177, i. 370-385, i. 439-495, iv. pp. 48-60,—American Edition in 4 vols.; James Richie, M.D., 'Criticism on Modern Notions of Sacrifice,' particularly recommended by Dr. M'Gee on the 'Origin of Sacrifice,' also his 'Peculiar Doctrines of Revelation,' p. 137 ; Dr. John Edwards, 'Survey of Divine Dispensations,' vol. i. 91-99 ; Dr. R. Gordon, 'Christ as made known to the Ancient Church,' vol. i. pp. 46-66 ; Dr. Outram on 'Sacrifices,' *passim*.

The moral meaning, and typical reference, of sacrifice, are well stated by Mr. Beart.   'The sacrifices of old were offered in the room of the offender, whose "laying his hand thereon" (Lev. i. 4, iii. 2) signified the transferring of his sin and guilt unto his victim.   As if he should say, "I freely own I have deserved to die for such and such sins ; but, Lord, by Thine appointment, I bring here a sacrifice, a poor animal, to die *for* me : accept it in my stead." It is true, these sacrifices could not do away sins (Heb. x. 1), but were referred, in their whole typical nature and use, to Christ's sacrifice, through which there is a real and eternal forgiveness, whereof that ceremonial forgiveness, which was by these sacrifices, was only a type.'—*Beart's Vindication*, p. 55. See Hervey's Works, ii. pp. 60, 88, 97-100, 264 ; P. Allinga, 'The Satisfaction of Christ,' translated by Rev. T. Bell, Glasgow, 1790, pp. 73-90 ; Dr. John Prideaux, 'Lectiones Decem,' pp. 138, 163.

NOTE 9, p. 34.

' The Divine Person who was so often *seen* by Abraham, when God was said to *appear* unto him, was our blessed Saviour, then in being ages before He " took upon Him the seed of Abraham." Abraham, therefore, literally speaking, saw Him ; and our Saviour might very justly conclude from Abraham's thus seeing Him, that He was really in being before Abraham. Abraham built his altars, not unto God, whom " no man hath seen at any time," but unto " the Lord who appeared unto him ;" and in all the accounts we have of his prayers, we find that they were offered up *in the name* of this Lord.'—*Dr. S. Shuckford's Connection*, vol. i. p. 177.

NOTE 10, p. 36.

On the Justification of Abraham, see Witsius, 'De Mente Pauli circa Justificationem,' Mis. Sac. vol. ii. p. 740 ; Bishop Downham, 'Treatise on Justification,' pp. 317-319, 432, 486 ; Brown (of Wamphray), 'The Life of Justification Opened,' pp. 116, 117 ; Dr. John Prideaux, 'Lectiones Decem,' p. 159 ; Buddeus, Misc. Sacr. vol. ii. p. 250.

NOTE 11, p. 37.

On the Theology of the Patriarchs, see J. H. Heidegger of Zurich, ' De Historia Sacra Patriarcharum, Exercitationes Selectæ,' 1667 ; Jurieu, ' Critical History of the Doctrines and Worship of the Church from Adam to our Saviour,' 2 vols. 8vo, translated and published at London in 1705, vol. i. c. 1 ; J. T. Biddulph, 'The Theology of the early Patriarchs,' 2 vols. 8vo, 1825 ; and Dr. Harris, ' Patriarchy,' a sequel to his ' Man Primeval.'

NOTE 12, p. 39.

On the external National Covenant of the Jews, see H. Venema, ' De Fœdere Externo Veteris Testamenti,' 1771, p. 250,—being Book ii. of his Dissertations ; Dr. John Erskine (of Edinburgh), Theological Dissertations, No. 1, 1765,—'The Nature of the Sinaitic Covenant,' pp. 1-66 ; Bishop Warburton's 'Divine Legation of Moses,' vol. ii. Book v. p. 235, Book vi. sec. vi. 329 ; Rev. T. Bell (of Glasgow, 1814), ' View of the Covenants of Works and Grace,' Part iv. 'The Covenant at Sinai,' p. 253 ; Adam Gib (of Edinburgh), ' Divine Contemplations,' c. i.

NOTE 13, p. 40.

On the Justification of Old Testament believers, see Bishop O'Brien's 'Sermons on the Nature and Effects of Faith,' p. 439, 2d Edition; Witsius, 'Mis. Sac.' ii. 744, 780; Bishop Downham, 'Treatise on Justification,' p. 412; Bishop Barlow, 'Genuine Remains,' pp. 583-593; Brown (of Wamphray), 'Life of Justification,' p. 247; Dr. John Prideaux, 'Lectiones Decem,' p. 162; Dickinson, 'Familiar Letters,' p. 191; and the precious work of Dr. Owen on the 130th Psalm, 'Works,' vol. xiv., Russell's Edition.

NOTE 14, p 42.

On the typical import of these rites, see Dr. Fairbairn's 'Typology of Scripture,' 2 vols. 8vo; J. Mather on the 'Types,' as recast in 'The Gospel of the Old Testament,' 2 vols. ; and Becanus, 'Analogia Veteris ac Novi Testamenti, in qua primum status Veteris, deinde Consensus, Proportio, et Conspiratio illius, cum Novo, explicatur.'

NOTES TO LECTURE II.

NOTE 1, p. 47.

'All, who allow of Revelation, own that the revelation of forgiveness, as well as the means of obtaining it, was twice universal,—in the days of Adam, and of Noah.'—*Professor Halyburton (of St. Andrew's), Works,* edited by Dr. R. Burns, p. 378. See also p. 395.

NOTE 2, p. 49.

For the universal prevalence of animal sacrifice, and the practice of offering human victims, see Archbishop M'Gee on 'The Atonement,' vol. i. pp. 96-128, and 251-286 ; Dr. J. P. Smith, 'Four Discourses on the Sacrifice and Priesthood of Christ,' Dis. i. pp. 1-19, and 219, 221-231 ; Benj. Constant, 'De la Religion,' vol. iv. livre xi. c. 1, 2, pp. 201-208.

NOTE 3, p. 50.

For the profound speculations of these Gentile thinkers, see Cicero, 'De Natura Deorum,' 'De Finibus,' 'De Senectute,' 'De Officiis,' 'De Fato,' and his 'Tusculan' and 'Academic' Questions, Foulis' Edition, Glasgow, 1748, vols. xi.-xv. ; The 'Enchiridion' of Epictetus; Senecæ 'Opera;' Lucretius, 'De Rerum Naturæ,' etc. An excellent selection from them is given in a recent French work, 1840, 'Moralistes Anciens,' including Socrates, Marcus Aurelius, Epictetus, Cebes, and others, pp. 566. The course of speculation on some of the deepest problems of human thought is traced in many histories of ancient philosophy, such as Brucker's 'Historia Critica Philosophiæ,' and is illustrated, in its relation to Theism, in Cudworth's ' Intellectual System of the Universe,' and Abbé Batteaux's ' Histoire des Causes Premières.'

NOTE 4, p. 51.

Dr. Owen's 'Theologoumena,' lib. i. c. 5, 6, 7, 8, 9, Dr. Goold's Edition; Witsius, 'De Theologia Gentilium circa Justificationem,' Misc. Sac. vol. ii. pp. 672-697 ; Leland, 'Necessity of Revelation,' c. v. p. 112.

The efficacy of repentance is strongly stated by Seneca : 'Quem pœnitet peccâsse, est innocens ;' and the Pelagian doctrine of Free-will, as opposed to Grace, is anticipated by Cicero : ' Virtutem nemo unquam Deo receptum retulit ; propter virtutem enim jure laudamur, et in virtute recte gloriamur : quod non contingerit, si *donum a Deo, non a nobis,* haberemus.'— *De Naturâ Deorum.*

On the Religion of the Gentiles, see Theophilus Gale, D.D., ' The Court of the Gentiles,' 2 vols., 1672. The two first parts of this work are designed to illustrate the influence exerted by the earlier Revelations of divine truth, on the Literature, Philosophy, and Religion of the ancient world. They are a rich storehouse of information on the traditions of primitive times, and their subsequent corruption, although the learned author may have occasionally pushed his favourite theory, of ' the traduction of Pagan Philosophy from the Jewish Church and the Sacred Oracles,' to an extreme. He takes occasion, also, to illustrate the reaction of Pagan Philosophy in corrupting the faith, first of the Jewish, and afterwards of the Christian, Church (vol. i. part ii. Pref. pp. v.-vii.). The evil influence which it exerted on both is ascribed to its character as a system of self-righteousness and self-dependence. ' That wherein the spirit of its malignity seems to consist is . . . its principal end and design, which is to reduce and advance lapsed man to a state of integrity and perfection, by the force and improvement of his own Free-will. The grand design of Ethnic Philosophy, in its original constitution, was to put men under a covenant of works, thereby to keep them from sin, and to merit life. Proud nature ever affects an independence as to God, and to procure a divine life by its own forces. What more pleasing to corrupt nature than to act from, and for, itself ! How fruitful is the root of the Old Covenant in corrupt nature ! How apt is every man by nature to run himself on a covenant of works, and deify some righteousness of his own, though never so unrighteous ! What latent veins of Pelagianism are there in the hearts of all by nature ! whence, according to Augustine,—*Pelagianism is the Heresy of Nature.*'—Vol. ii. part iii. Pref. pp. iii. iv. See also pp. 141, 143, 149.

Herbert (of Cherbury), in two of his works—' De Religione Laici,' and ' De Religione Gentilium,' published after his death in 1663—reduces what he calls the ' Catholic or Universal ' Religion to *five* points,—the fourth and fifth of which relate to the Justification of sinners : ' That we must repent of our sins, and if we do so, God will pardon them ;' and ' that there are rewards for good men, and punishments for bad men, in a future state.' He attempts to prove that these doctrines were generally believed by the Gentile nations, but admits that 'they seldom used the word Repentance in the sense which Christians attach to it,—that they did not look upon it to be an atonement for all crimes, but only for those of a less heinous nature,—and that they generally looked upon other things to be also necessary, and laid the principal stress upon lustrations and the rites of their religion, for purifying and absolving them from guilt.'

See in reply to Herbert, Dr. Leland, 'View of Deistical Writers,' vol. i. p. 12; Prof. Halyburton, 'Natural Religion Insufficient,' Works in 1 vol. (edited by Dr. R. Burns, 1835), c. x. pp. 344-398: 'Proving the light of Nature unable to discover the means of obtaining pardon of sin, or to show that it is attainable.'

Note 5, p. 54.

Dr. John Prideaux, 'Lectiones Decem,' pp. 135-139. See also Dr. Townley's translation of that part of the 'More Nevochim' ('Teacher of the Perplexed') of Maimonides (resembling the 'Ductor Dubitantium' of Jeremy Taylor) which assigns 'the Reasons of the Laws of Moses,'— Townley, Diss. vi. on 'The Typical Character of the Mosaic Institutions,' pp. 87-101,—in which some remarks are made on the question how far it was understood by the Jews, p. 93. See also Lightfoot, Works, vol. vii. p. 256.

Note 6, p. 59.

Witsius, 'De Theologia Judæorum in Negotio Justificationis,' Mis. Sac. vol. ii. pp. 698-720.

Note 7, p. 60.

Dr. Cunningham, 'Historical Theology,' vol. ii. 121.

Note 8, p. 64.

'Human inventiveness in things spiritual, or unspiritual, is very limited. It would be difficult, probably, to invent a new heresy. Objectors of old were as acute, or more acute, than those now.'—*Dr. E. B. Pusey, Daniel the Prophet*, 3d Ed., 1864, p. iii.

Note 9, p. 66.

Witsius, 'De Controversiis Ætate Apostolorum circa Justificationem,' Mis. Sac. vol. ii. pp. 668-751. Buddeus, 'Mis. Sacra,' Dissertatio Theologica de statu Ecclesiarum Apostolicarum, earum præcipue ad quas Paulus Epistolas suas scripsit, tom. ii. p. 215.

Note 10, p. 67.

Dr. Cave, 'Antiquitates Apostolicæ,' to which work that of Witsius is a reply.

NOTE 11, p. 73.

Witsius, 'De Mente Pauli circa Justificationem,' Mis. Sac. vol. ii. p. 734.

NOTE 12, p. 75.

G. S. Faber, 'The Primitive Doctrine of Justification,' pp. 238-243.

NOTES TO LECTURE III.

NOTE 1, p. 78.

Dr. Wordsworth's 'Letters to M. Gondon,' pp. 38-42.

NOTE 2, p. 78.

Isaac Taylor, ' Ancient Christianity,' *passim.*

NOTE 3, p. 79.

G. S. Faber, 'Primitive Doctrine of Justification,' Pref. pp. vii. xvii. xxxiv. xxxix.; pp. 52, 58, 140, 227, 238, 342, 346, 350, 447.

For an antidote, see Dr. Goode, ' Rule of Faith,' *passim.*

NOTE 4, p. 80.

Dr. Donaldson, Rector of the High School of Edinburgh, is far from denying the right of private judgment, and makes the freest use of it in his recent work, ' A Critical History of Christian Literature and Doctrine, from the Death of the Apostles to the Nicene Council' (vol. i. 1864, ii. and iii. 1866); but he argues on the erroneous principle, that the teaching of the earlier Fathers may be applied as a test,—if not of the truth of certain doctrines,—at least of their necessity and importance, as articles of faith. 'If the early writers were heterodox on the Trinity,—if they knew nothing of a satisfaction of divine justice, but spoke only in a vague way of the matter,—if they wavered in regard to Original Sin, some denying it entirely, and others expressing themselves with great uncertainty, —if their testimony to the Inspiration of the New Testament is unsatisfactory and inconclusive,—where was Christianity in those days? Did it really sleep for three long centuries? . . . Or may not the Evangelical School be wrong in asserting that it is necessary for a man to believe in Original Sin, the Trinity, the Atonement, and similar dogmas, before he can be a Christian?'—Vol. i. p. 64. Dr. Donaldson's work,—considered as a ' Critical History of Christian Literature' in the first three centuries,— is highly valuable, and exhibits the results of ripe scholarship, and extensive reading and research ; but considered as a ' Critical History of Christian Doctrine,' it is far from being a safe guide. His interpretation of many passages in the writings of the Fathers is, to say the least, highly questionable, and at direct variance with that of such writers as Bull, and Waterland, and Faber. But even were it more certain than it is, and did it afford proof that their writings were less in accordance with Scripture than we believe them to have been, we should still fall back on the cardinal principle, that they are to be tested by the only infallible standard —the inspired Word of God. 'To the law and to the testimony: if they speak not according to this Word, there is no light in them.' We should then be constrained to say of them, as the Prophet said of ancient Israel, ' They have forsaken the word of the Lord, and what wisdom is in them?' but we should have no difficulty in answering the question—Where was Christianity then? for it existed then, as it exists still, in 'the Word of God, the Gospel of our salvation ;' and it was neither dead nor asleep, but alive and active in the Church of the Catacombs. We shall have occasion afterwards to refer to his criticisms on some passages in the writings of the Fathers.

Note 5, p. 80.

Vincentius Lirinensis, ' Commonitorum.' His rule—' Quod semper, quod ubique, et quod ab omnibus '—is abandoned by Dr. Newman in his ' Essay on the Development of Christian Doctrine,' pp. 8, 24 ; Professor Butler, ' Letters on Development,' pp. 16, 18, 213 ; Wordsworth's 'Letters to M. Gondon,' pp. 23, 178, 259 ; Dr. Cunningham, 'N. British Review' for 1846, pp. 423, 429, 432, 436 ; 'Dublin Review,' No. xliv., pp. 271, 325, xlvi. p. 373. But while this rule is unsound and untenable, as a test of doctrine, both Vincent and Tertullian ('De Præscriptionibus Hæreticorum,' ' Opera Patrum Latinorum,' vol. ii. pp. 447-490) lay down the important principle, that the Post-Apostolic Church had no power to introduce new articles of faith.

Note 6, p. 81.

The writings of the Apostolical Fathers were collected and published by Cotelerius and Ittigius towards the close of the last century, and in the present by Jacobson, Oxford, 1847, and by Hefele, Tubingen, 1855. There have been many Commentaries upon them. They were translated into English by Archbishop Wake ; and a new edition of it was printed at Oxford in 1840.

Note 7, p. 82.

Isaac Taylor, ' Restoration of Belief,' pp. 48, 52, 79.
On the new life which then sprung up in the Roman world, Dr. Donaldson makes many striking and eloquent remarks, and pays a just and noble tribute to the ethical tone of the early Christian writers. ' Even to the most callous mind, Christianity must appear a movement of gigantic importance. The student of early Christian literature traces this great moral movement in the words of those who were influenced by it. He, as it were, speaks with those who felt the first waves of the

Spirit's influence ; and he examines their modes of thought that he may see how Christ's Gospel changed their whole being, and how, in consequence, they worked in, and on, the world.'—Vol. i. p. 4. ' The most striking feature of these writings is the deep living piety which pervades them. This piety is not of a morbid character. It consists in the warmest love to God, the deepest interest in man ; and it exhibits itself in a healthy, vigorous, manly morality. . . . This intense moral heat and fervour is all the more striking, that in contemporary writings, and writings shortly antecedent, the mind is sickened with the details of sin and vice, which were universally prevalent. The pages of Tacitus, Juvenal, Persius, and Martial, are full of the most fearful representations of universal licentiousness, and loss of all faith in God and man. And perhaps a student could not receive a more satisfactory impression of the truth, that God was working among the Christians in a most remarkable manner, than by turning from the fetid pages of stern Juvenal, or licentious Martial, to the pure, unselfish, loving words of Clemens Romanus, Polycarp, or Hermas. The simple reading of these writings by themselves does not strike us so much now, because what was loving, new, earnest morality to them, is now familiar to us, and often the words used by them are now used by men to cloak their deceit and worldliness. But let us not on this account hide from ourselves the marvellous phenomenon here presented,—of a morality that has nothing to do with selfish or worldly aims,—that seeks its source in God,—that fills the whole being,—that goes out to all men in love,—and that is to itself a boundless good.'— Vol. i. pp. 84, 85.

NOTE 8, p. 83.

Dr. Shedd, ' History of Christian Doctrine,' vol. ii. pp. 208-211.

NOTE 9, p. 84.

Clement, Epistle to Cor. i. c. vii. xxxii. Dr Donaldson says that ' Clement's answer to the question, how a man is saved, is various in form, but fundamentally the same. Salvation is, according to his idea, *dependent on good works*. . . . The most striking passage is in c. xxxii. " We," he says, " are declared and made righteous, not by means of ourselves, nor through our own wisdom, or understanding, or piety, or works which we did in holiness of heart, but through faith. Through which faith Almighty God has made and declared all men righteous from the beginning.'—P. 133. According to this rendering, ' to justify' means first to *make*, and then to *declare*, righteous,—that is, evidently, to make righteous subjectively, by the infusion of personal holiness ; and this is also the view of Mr. Knox, ' Remains,' i. 259, and of Dr. Newman, ' Lectures on Justification,' pp. 445-448. Both objected to the use which G. S. Faber had made of the passage ; but he vindicates it from their objections in the Appendix to the second edition of his ' Primitive Doctrine of Justification,' and insists specially on the clause which excludes ' works done in *holiness of heart*,' as sufficient to show that he meant to refer to works done after conversion, as well as before it.

NOTE 10, p. 85.

Ignat., Ep. ad Philadelph. sec. 8; Polycarp, Ep. ad Philip. sec. 2 ; Justin Martyr, Dial. cum Tryph., Opera, pp. 177, 250; Epistle to Diognetus, Opera Justini, p. 386. See Spanheim's 'Eccles. Annals,' p. 225 ; also, Le Clerc, 'Historia Ecclesiastica Duorum Primorum Sæculorum a Christo Nato,' Amsterdam 1716. The writings of the early Apologists, including Justin Martyr, Tertullian, and Minucius Felix, were translated by the Rev. Wm. Reeves, along with the ' Commonitorium' of Vincent of Lerins, 1709 ; and they throw much light on the doctrines and practices of the primitive Church, as well as on the objections which were urged against them, both by Jews and Gentiles.

NOTE 11, p. 88.

Mr. Knox, of Dublin, contends earnestly in his ' Remains' against a ' forensic,' and in favour of a ' moral,' Justification,—the latter consisting in a change of character and conduct, which is, substantially, nothing else than Sanctification, and God's acceptance of the sinner on that account. In support of his views, he adduces the testimony of Milner, as the concession of a reluctant witness,—to the effect, that the true doctrine of Justification had been all but lost to the Church for fourteen hundred years. ' Remains,' vol. i. pp. 257, 258. See also, vol. ii. pp. 55, 317 ; vol. iii. pp. 46-49. See Faber, ' Primitive Doctrine,' pp. vii. xvi. 2, 3, 4, 7, 8, 139.

Milner's statements, even were they admitted to be truly represented, are not sufficient to prove that, in his estimation, the doctrine of forensic Justification was ' a novelty,' introduced into the Church at the Reformation ; and, most certainly, they were not intended by him to convey that meaning.

Milner held, that the doctrine was taught by the Apostles, and is contained in the inspired writings of the New Testament ; and, in this respect, differs entirely from Mr. Knox.

Milner held, that the doctrine was taught by the Apostolical Fathers; a fact which is denied by Mr. Knox, but which Milner regards as ' an unequivocal proof of the faith of the primitive Church ;' for he says expressly, ' They all concurred in feeling conviction of sin, of helplessness, of a state of perdition ; in relying on the atoning blood, perfect righteousness, and prevalent intercession, of Jesus, as their only hope of heaven' (Milner's History, Nelson's edition, one vol., pp. 47, 51). Mr. Knox does not venture to deny that this was Milner's opinion; for he speaks only of what the historian says of the faith of the Church ' from the end of the first century.' But further,

Milner held, that the doctrine was taught, ' in substance,' by a series of writers from the Apostolic age till the Reformation, although it was stated less clearly, while it had not yet been made the subject of controversial discussion, than it afterwards was, when it had passed through that fiery ordeal, in the times of Luther and Calvin. He refers to, and quotes, the testimonies of Ignatius, Justin Martyr, Irenæus, Clemens Alexandrinus, Cyprian, Athanasius, Ambrose, Macarius, Optatus, Ephraim, Chrysostom, Augustine, Anselm, Bernard, and others, as all holding 'in substance' the doctrine of the primitive Church. (Milner's History, Nelson's edition, one vol., pp. 57, 61, 71, 97, 103, 117, 118, 122, 161-164, 251, 274-276, 279, 283, 282-284, 296.)

Milner does not say that the Fathers confounded Justification with Sanctification, as Mr. Knox unquestionably does, but merely that the *term* Justification was generally used by them in a comprehensive sense, so as to include the *whole of that change* which passes on the state of a sinner when he is ' turned from darkness to light'—*i.e.* both the change in his judicial relation to God, when he is pardoned and accepted, and also the change in his spiritual character, when he is ' renewed in the spirit of his mind.' It does not follow that these two things—distinct as they are in themselves—were confounded the one with the other, and still less, that the change in man's judicial relation to God was founded on, and resulted from, the change in his spiritual character, merely because they were both comprehended under the same term. If they held ' in substance' what was, in Milner's estimation, ' the true doctrine,' they could not have confounded two things so radically distinct as Justification and Sanctification unquestionably are ; but they might possibly include *both* blessings under one general *term*,—it might be Justification, —or Regeneration,—or Sanctification,—or Washing,—or Cleansing,—or Purging,—or Purification ; for all these terms admit of being applied to denote the *whole of that change* which passes on a sinner, in respect both to his judicial relation to God, and to his spiritual character, when he is ' reconciled to God,' and passes ' from death unto life.'—See William Pemble, of Magdalene Hall, Oxford, ' Vindiciæ Fidei,' or a Treatise on Justification, 1629, p. 13.

Milner's object throughout is to delineate the internal life of the Church, and to illustrate its necessary dependence on the knowledge and belief of the peculiar doctrines of the Gospel, in every succeeding age. He shows that it flourished in proportion as men were—impressed with a sense of sin,—enlightened with a knowledge of Christ,—and imbued with a spirit of simple reliance on His finished work ; and that it decayed as often as they became—ignorant of the spiritual meaning of the divine law, —or insensible of their absolute dependence on the grace of God, and the work of Christ, for their salvation. But he is careful also to show that, even in periods of prevailing declension and indifference, there was always a living Church on the earth, and of course a remnant who ' walked by faith,' and looked to Christ as ' the Lamb of God who taketh away the sin of the world.' How many such there were, or how few, at different times, and in different lands, none can say ; nor would it be safe to regard the writings which have come down to us, chiefly from the more learned and inquisitive office-bearers of the Church, as a gauge by which we may estimate the amount of living piety which existed within her pale ; but in Milner's view, all who were so convinced of sin as to rely simply on Christ for salvation, held the truth ' in substance,' although it might be associated with some errors, and obscured by some superstitious obser-vances. In any other view, his statements must be regarded as self-contradictory. Did he affirm, as Mr. Knox supposes, that the doctrine of Justification by grace, through faith in Christ, was lost to the Church for fourteen hundred years, how could he say of primitive Christians, that ' they all concurred . . . in relying on the atoning blood, perfect righteousness, and prevalent intercession, of Jesus, as their only hope of heaven ?' (p. 51.) How could he say of the second century, that ' it exhibited proofs of divine grace, as strong, or nearly so, as the first'— ' the same unshaken and simple faith of Jesus, the same love of God and of the brethren, the same heavenly spirit, and victory over the world ?' (p. 95.) How could he say of Irenæus, that ' notwithstanding some philosophical adulterations, he certainly maintained all the essentials of the Gospel ?' (p. 97.) Does he not say of Cyprian, that ' the essential doctrines of Justification and Regeneration by divine grace were not only believed, but experienced, by this zealous African' (p. 117) ;—that he was ' possessed of some rich portion of that effusion of the Holy Ghost, which, from the Apostles' days, still exhibited Christ Jesus, and fitted by experience to communicate to others the real Gospel, and to be an happy instrument of guiding souls to that rest which remains for the people of God' (p. 118) ;—that ' he felt the doctrines of the Gospel—namely, the grace of God, forgiveness of sins by Jesus Christ, and the influences of the Holy Ghost, powerful, exuberant, and victorious ;'—that ' his soul was brought into the love of God, and that of the purest kind, tempered ever with humility and godly fear ; and it is evident—that he always saw the work to be of God, and beheld nothing in himself as wise, holy, and glorious ; that a spirit of thankfulness for redeeming love—of simple dependence on the divine promises—and of steady charity to God and man, was the result ?' (p. 161.) Does he not say of Augustine, that ' the peculiar work, for which he was evidently raised by Providence, was to restore the doctrine of divine grace to the Church ;'—that ' the article of Justification must be involved in Augustine's divinity, and doubtless it savingly flourished in his heart, and in the hearts of many of his followers ?' And if he takes exception to Augustine's use of the *term* ' justify,' does he not add, ' Still he knew what faith in the Redeemer meant,—those parts of Scripture which speak of forgiveness of sins, he understands, he feels, he loves ;' . . . ' and I more admire that he was enabled to recover its constituent parts' (*i.e.* of ' this most important Christian doctrine') ' than that he did not arrange and adjust them perfectly ?' (pp. 354, 355.) Does he not say of Anselm, in a still darker age, ' That doctrine, which is " most wholesome, and very full of comfort," namely, the doctrine of " Justification before God, only for the merit of our Lord and Saviour

Jesus Christ, by faith, and not by our own works and deservings," is preached by a bishop of the eleventh century : so strong was the provision made by the God of all grace for the preservation of evangelical truth in the darkest times. . . . We have found the essential and leading doctrine of Christianity in the possession of Anselm. . . . He beautifully illustrates the all-important doctrine of Justification by faith in Christ ?' (pp. 491, 494, 495.) And does he not say of Bernard, the latest of the Fathers, that ' there is not an essential doctrine of the Gospel which he did not embrace with zeal, defend by argument, and adorn by life ;' and more particularly, that he taught the doctrine of Justification in such terms as these : ' If one died for all, then were all dead, that the satisfaction of One might be imputed to all, as He alone bore the sins of all ; and now he, who offended, and He, who satisfied divine justice, are found the same ; because the Head and the body is one Christ. The Head then satisfied for the members. . . . Why may not I have another's righteousness, since I have another's sin, imputed to me ? Is there sin in the seed of the sinner, and not righteousness in the blood of Christ ? . . . If the judgment was by one to condemnation, the free gift was of many offences to Justification. Nor do I fear, being thus freed from the powers of darkness, to be rejected by the Father of lights, since I am justified freely by the blood of His Son. He who pitied the sinner, will not condemn the just. I call myself just, but it is through His righteousness ; for " Christ is the end of the law for righteousness," and " He is made of God unto us righteousness." Thus is man made righteous by the blood of the Redeemer' (pp. 507, 508, 525).

On the whole, we conclude that Milner meant merely to show that the doctrine of a free Justification by grace, through faith in Christ, always existed in the Church from the time when it was first preached by our Lord and His Apostles,—but that it was obscured, as often as the Church exhibited tokens of declension, by the corruptions which infected both her faith and worship ; and that, even when it was revived and presented anew by some burning and shining lights, it was not so fully unfolded, or so correctly defined, as it was at the era of the Reformation, when it became, for the first time, a subject of controversy between the Romish and Protestant Churches. That doctrine was really involved in Augustine's great contest with the Pelagians ; for he contended for free, sovereign, and efficacious grace as the source of the whole salvation of sinners ; but the precise question of Justification did not then come out into distinct prominence, as it afterwards did in the times of Luther, simply because it was not formally questioned or denied by Pelagius, who professed to admit the free forgiveness of sins, while he contended for free-will, in opposition to free grace, in the application of the Gospel remedy. Augustine paved the way for the Reformation by establishing the doctrine of free grace in the regeneration of sinners, and Luther applied the same doctrine to their Justification.—Petavius, ' De Pelagianes¡', ' Dogm. Theolog.,' tom. iii. c. iii. s. ii. 14.

Note 12, p. 88.

Forbes (of Corse), 'Instructiones Historico-Theologicæ,' c. xxiii. p.
423. ' Admonitio de Justificatione; ubi ostenditur, statum controversiæ
inter Catholicos olim et Pelagianos diversum fuisse a statu controversiæ
quæ nunc inter Catholicos et Romanenses, de Justificatione agitatur.'
See also Petavius, ' Dogmata Theolog.,' lib. iii. c. xv. vol. iii. p. 353;
Bishop Downham, ' Treatise on Justification,' p. 122.

It is admitted that Augustine's doctrine of Justification is not so
distinctly defined as that of the Reformers, but its leading principle is
substantially the same. 'It appears to me,' says the late Dr. M'Crie,
' that the great difference between the ancient Anti-Pelagians and the
Reformers lies in this,—that, while both are advocates for grace, the
former considered it chiefly in relation to the change which it effects on
the heart, the latter in relation to the change which it produces on the
state, as divines express it, of the sinner. In the writings of Augustine,
for example, the great champion of grace among the Fathers, I have
found little about Justification; in the writings of Luther, again, this is
the grand point—" articulus stantis ac cadentis Ecclesiæ." This I look
upon as the glory of the Reformation,—the great advancement in evangelical light beyond what had been attained in the Pelagian or in the
Antichristian ages.'—*Dr. M'Crie's Life of Dr. T. M'Crie*, p. 329.

Augustine was honoured to do a great service to truth, by striking
at the fundamental error in regard to all the doctrines of grace—the
Pelagian heresy—which has been justly called 'the heresy of nature.'
There is reason to fear, that a latent Pelagianism lies at the root of many
false theories of Justification. 'Verendum est ne etiamnum serpat inter
Orthodoxos, plus quam par est, Pelagianismi cancer; ut penduli vacillent
inter gratiam et liberum arbitrium, nec cœlum attingentes, nec terram ;
sed statuentes potius de salute, juxta vocem illam meretricem (2 Kings
iii.). Nec Deo soli, nec libero arbitrio soli, *sed dividatur.*'—*Dr. John
Prideaux, Lectiones Decem*, p. 2. See Dr. Tully, ' Justificatio Paulina,'
p. 2.

Note 13, p. 90.

For the Patristic sense of the term Merit, see Bishop Downham ' On
Justification,' pp. 385, 503-506, 544, 550, 558, 583; Bishop Davenant,
' Disputation,' vol. ii. pp. 66-68, 75 ; Archbishop Usher, ' Answer to a
Jesuit's Challenge,' c. xii. pp. 472-506 ; G. S. Faber, ' Primitive Doctrine
of Justification,' pp. 126, 178, 195-197 ; Dr. Cunningham, ' Historical
Theology,' ii. p. 104.

The Augsburg Confession itself, which expressly excludes all ' merit,'
uses the words ' mereri præmia ' for obtaining rewards. ' It hesitates not
to say of repentance, " meretur remissionem peccatorum," and of good
works (those of the justified believer), " merentur præmia." " Mereri,"
however, though usually rendered " to deserve," lexicographers tell us,

means " to gain," whether by desert or otherwise; and such is evidently its sense in the writings of the Reformers. Luther himself, in his Lectures on the Sermon on the Mount, expressly admits the use of the word merit (*meritum*) in a qualified sense, namely, " if it be used for the *gracious* reward, or gratuitous recompense, which God has promised to piety and patience." ' But when it was used in another sense, ' Melancthon brands the term strongly enough—" Whence comes that profane word ' Merit,'—than which nothing could be devised more audacious or more impious?" '—*Scott, Continuation of Milner's History*, vol. i. pp. 44, 45.

Note 14, p. 91.

Forbes, ' Instruc. Historico-Theolog.' c. xxiii. p. 423. ' Justificatio . . . significat gratuitam donationem *justitiæ quâ justi constituimur*. Ea justitia duplex est. Una, per quam justitiæ Dei, peccatis nostris offensæ, plenaria sit sátisfactio, et remissio peccatorum, ac jus æternæ hæreditatis, ad eamque ducens gratia, sufficientissimi pretii solutione nobis acquiruntur. Hæc est illa Christi perfectissima obedientia, per quam " justi constituuntur multi." . . . . Hanc Christi justitiam nobis Deus donat *imputando*. . . . Altera justitia, nobis inhærens, et in moribus nostris elucens, per quam . . . habitualiter et actualiter justi sumus . . . est etiam gratuitum Dei donum; quod Deus nobis donat, *infundendo* habitus, et " operando in nobis et velle et perficere pro suo beneplacito." Hæc Justificatio, alia peculiari nomenclaturâ, appellatur Sanctificatio.' This definition of the terms is not in accordance with the ' usus loquendi ' of the sacred writers; but the passage clearly shows that he distinguished between imputed and infused righteousness, and ascribed both equally to the grace of God, and the merits of Christ. The same may be said of Augustine. ' Evangelical righteousness ' is described by James Hervey himself as including that of Justification, and that of Sanctification. ' To be *reconciled* to the omnipotent God,—to be interested in " the unsearchable riches of Christ,"—to be *renewed* in our hearts by the sanctifying operations of the Divine Spirit,—this is EVANGELICAL RIGHTEOUSNESS.' . . . ' All these blessings are centred *in* Christ,—were purchased *by* Christ,—are communicated *from* Christ.'—*Dedication to Theron and Aspasio, Works*, ii. pp. iv. v. See Pemble, ' Vindiciæ Fidei,' c. i. pp. 1-9.

Note 15, p. 92.

On Augustine's use of the term ' Justification,' see Bishop Downham's Treatise, p. 75; Bishop Davenant's ' Disp.,' vol. i. p. 194; Dr. John Prideaux, ' Lectiones,' p. 141; Dr. Cunningham, ' Hist. Theol.,' vol. ii. p. 41; Dr. Shedd, ' History of Christian Doctrine,' ii. pp. 255-257.

Note 16, p. 93.

Numerous testimonies have been collected from the Apostolic Fathers and their successors, by Archbishop Usher, ' Answer to a Jesuit's Challenge,' c. xii. pp. 472-505; G. S. Faber, ' Primitive Doctrine of Justification,' c. iv. pp. 96-200, 387-392. Faber gives Usher's and his own in a tabulated form, p. 392. Dr. James Bennett, 'Theology of the Early Christian Church,' Lec. iii. P. ii. iii. iv.; Gaspar Laurentius, 'Orthodoxus Consensus,' in Corpus et Syntagma Confessionum, Geneva, 1654. Those who have access to the writings of the Fathers will of course consult the originals: but common readers will find the leading testimonies on the subject of Justification profusely scattered through the works of the great divines of the seventeenth century, such as Downham, Davenant, Wake, Owen, and Jeremy Taylor.

NOTE 17, p. 96.

See his ' Cur Deus Homo ?' and Dr. Shedd's 'History of Christian Doctrine,' vol. ii. pp. 273-285.

NOTE 18, p. 97.

Irenæus, adv. Hær. lib. iii. c. 20, iv. c. 67 ; Cyprian, Op. ii. p. 140, Epis. lxxxiii.; Athanasius, Op. ii. 125, 270; Basil, Op. p. 550; Ambrose in Ep. ad Rom. iv. 5; Origen in Ep. ad Rom. lib. iii.; Jerome in Ep. ad Rom. c. iv., and in ii. Ep. ad Cor. c. v. 21 ; Chrysost. in Epis. ad Rom. Hom. vii., and in ii. Ep. ad Cor. Hom. xi. ; Augustine, Expos. in Johannem, Trac. iii. Opera, vol. ix. p. 7 ; 'De Fide et Operibus,' c. xiv., Opera, iv. p. 28; Enarratio in Ps. cx., Op. vol. viii. p. 464; Anselm, as quoted by Dr. Owen, Works, xi. p. 22; Bernard, Opera, pp. 285, 601, 630, 1556.

The writings of the Fathers are nòt always self-consistent ; e.g. those of Chrysostom : see Isaac Taylor's ' Ancient Christianity,' vol. i. p. 249. For the evangelical character of Anselm's Theology, see his ' Cur Deus Homo ?' which has recently (1858) been made accessible to the English reader ' by a Clergyman' (Parker, Oxford); and Dr. Shedd's ' History of Christian Doctrine,' vol. ii. pp. 273-285. For Luther and Melancthon's views of the Fathers, see Scott's ' Continuation of Milner's History,' vol. i. 527, 530, ii. 119, 254, 255. He states also the instructive fact, that Prince George of Anhalt, Provost of the Cathedral at Magdeburg, was convinced of the truth of Luther's doctrine by a careful study of the writings of the Fathers, and gives the Prince's striking testimony to that effect.—Vol. i. pp. 388-404.

Buddæus, 'Isagoge De Theologia Patristica,' lib. ii. c. iii. vol. i. pp. 478-544; Hoornbeek, Mis. Sac. lib. i. pp. 1-130, ' De Theologia Patrum usque ad Annum cclxxxv.;' Voetius, 'Disputationes Theologicæ,' vol. i. pp. 74-105, ' De Patribus, seu Antiquæ Ecclesiæ Doctoribus.'

NOTE 19, p. 98.

M. D'Aubigné, ' History of Reformation in the Time of Calvin,' vol. iii. 203. 'During four centuries, reckoning from the twelfth, minds of the highest order had formulated abstract systems, in which Scholastic Rationalism, and Ecclesiastical Authority, were habitually combined. . . . It was not a trifling matter to make Christian science pass from death to life, from darkness to light. It required an awakened conscience,—a heart thirsting for righteousness,—a high intelligence,—and a powerful will, to break through all the *chains* (Catenæ Patrum)—to scatter to the winds the *Sentences*, and the *Sums*, which the Schoolmen had painfully woven out of their brains, or out of traditions that were often impure, and to set up in their place the living rock of the heavenly Word on which the temple of God is to be built. CALVIN was the man called to this work. Until his time, Dogmatics, when passing from one period to another, had always advanced in the same direction, from abstraction to abstraction. But suddenly the course was changed; Calvin refused to tread the accustomed road. Instead of advancing in the way of the Schoolmen towards new developments of a more refined intellectualism, he turned eagerly backwards,—he heard the voice of conscience,—he felt the wants of the heart,—he ran whither alone they can be satisfied,—he traversed fifteen centuries. He went to the Gospel springs ; and there collecting in a golden cup the pure and living waters of Divine Revelation, presented them to the nations to quench their thirst.'

It has been objected to the Systematic Theology of the Protestant Churches, that it was derived from the scholastic writers, and that it bears upon it the impress of their influence. That their writings have exerted some influence on modern Theology, it would be folly to deny ; and Bishop Hampden has illustrated this point in his ' Bampton Lectures' for 1832,—' The Scholastic Philosophy considered in its relation to Christian Theology.' But the radical difference between the Popish and Protestant systems, consists in the one recognising several distinct sources of Theology, while the other recognises only the sole and supreme authority of Scripture: and the change which was effected by the Reformation, in this respect, resembled that which the Copernican doctrine effected in Astronomy ; for as this displaced the earth from being the centre of the planetary system, and substituted the sun in its stead, so the Reformation displaced the Church, or the authority of man, and brought in the Bible, or the authority of God, as the sole rule of faith. Authority remained, and therefore there was no anarchy; but it was that of God, and His Word. The Abbé Maret, in his ' Theodicée Chretienne,' p. 16, enumerates several different sources of Theology, and Melchior Canus speaks of ten,—viz., Scripture,—Tradition,—the Church,—Councils,—Rome,—Fathers,—Schoolmen,—Reason,—Philosophy,—History (*Loci Theologicæ*, p. 6) ; while Protestantism acknowledges one only, and regards all the others as helps merely, which are subordinate and subservient to that which alone is supreme. Markius has stated, in a few words, both the merits and defects of the Scholastic Theology :—' Hæc *placet* multis, (1) ob βραχυλογιαν, (2) philosophemata quædam acuta, (3) Veritatumque quarundam luculenta testimonia. . . . *Displicet* tamen omnibus, (1) ob principium suum, quod Patres magis et Philosophi Gentiles quam Prophetæ ; (2) ob argumentum, quod philosophicum sæpe, curiosum, inutile, vel falsum ; (3) ob modum tradendi, per terminos barbaros ac obscuras distinctiones ; (4) ob ejus finem et effectum, qui veræ ac Scriptuariæ Theologiæ obtenebratio, atque populi excæcatio fuit.'—*Marckii, Compendium ;* see De Moor's 'Commentary.' The Scholastic Method was defective and erroneous ; but it would be as absurd to reject Systematic Theology on that account, as to reject Astronomy, because it was once abused by astrologers, or Chemistry, because it was once mixed up with the dreams of alchemists. System in Theology arises from the same causes as system in Science ; namely, from the relations which subsist between different truths, and from the powers and laws of the human mind, which discerns these relations, and arranges the objects of its knowledge accordingly.—*The Princeton Theological Essays on ' Systems in Theology,'* Second Series, Essay iii. ; and *Professor Dunlop on Creeds and Confessions.*

NOTE 20, p. 99.

See Archbishop Usher, 'Answer to Jesuit's Challenge,' c. xii. of ' Merits ;' Dr. Shedd, 'History of Christian Doctrine,' ii. 31, 318; G. S. Faber, 'Primitive Doctrine of Justification,' pp. 335-341 ; Voetius, ' Disput.,' vol. i. 12-29, ' De Theologia Scholastica ;' Pemble, ' Vindiciæ Fidei,' on Bellarmine's doctrine of Merit, pp. 30, 31.

NOTES TO LECTURE IV.

NOTE 1, p. 106.

Some held the doctrine of Sinless Perfection in the present life. Bellarmine, tom. iv. lib. ii. c. vii. p. 915 : 'Adversarii dicunt imputationem (justitiæ Christi) propterea necessariam esse, non solùm quòd verè peccatum in nobis hæreat, sed etiam quòd justitia nostra inhærens non tam sit perfecta, ut simpliciter, et absolutè, justificet. At causam istam facile refutabimus. . . . Nam justitia inhærens, sive renovatio interior in fide, spe, et caritate, potissimum sita esse cognoscetur. . . . Quare si provabimus fidem, spem, et caritatem in hac vita posse esse perfectam, probatum quoque erit, non esse necessariam imputationem justitiæ Christi.' He then proceeds to prove the perfection of Faith, Hope, and Charity, in the present life.

Mr. Knox, who has recently reintroduced the Popish doctrine of a ' moral' Justification by infused and inherent righteousness, contends also for Christian perfection. 'Remains,' vol. i. pp. 1, 4, 6, 10, 24, 40, 94, 129, 317, 326, 343, 398 ; 'Correspondence with Bishop Jebb,' vol. i. pp. 113, 117, 140, 143, 209, 347, 352, 362, 365.

Osorio held that Faith includes all the graces, and is the principle or germ of Perfection: ' Hæc autem Fides cum viget, continet omnem religionem atque pietatem. Omnes enim virtutes ex illâ aptæ atque nexæ sunt; et cum illâ sanctissimo vinculo colligatæ et implicitæ.' . . . 'Hæc est illius præcipua notio—forma, nempe, et constans debiti muneris et officii perfunctio.'—*De Justitia,* lib. i. pp. 198, 200. He objects to Luther's doctrine of indwelling sin, and maintains that concupiscence in believers is not sin: lib. ii. 227, 230, 231. And he denies that Justification by obedience ascribes more than enough to human Merit: lib. ix. p. 408.

For a considerable time the doctrine of human Merit made progress under disguise: it was said that 'Christ merited for us that we might merit;' and further, that our inherent righteousness, being imperfect, was graciously accepted through His merits. But some of the scholastic writers threw off this disguise, and affirmed that our inherent righteousness was acceptable in itself, and was accepted simply on its own account, without reference to the merits of Christ. On the supposition of a perfect inherent righteousness, this was obviously the logical conclusion. Vasquez says: 'At vero, cum opera justi condigne mereantur vitam eternam, tanquam æqualem mercedem et præmium, non opus est interventu alterius meriti condigni, quale est meritum Christi, ut iis reddatur vita æterna; quinimo aliquid habet peculiare meritum cujuscumque justi, respectu ipsius hominis justi, quod non habet meritum Christi,— nempe reddere ipsum hominem justum et dignum vita æterna, ut eam dignè consequatur; meritum autem Christi, licet dignissimum sit quod obtineat a Deo gratiam pro nobis, tamen non habet hanc efficaciam et virtutem, ut reddat nos formaliter justos et dignos æterna vita, sed per virtutem, ab Ipso derivatam, hunc consequuntur effectum homines in se ipsis.' See Archbishop Wake's 'Exposition,' pp. 22, 23; 'Vindication of Bossuet,' p. 52; Wake's 'Defence,' pp. 29-31, 34. Also Archbishop Usher, 'Answer to a Jesuit,' c. xii., 'On Merits,' pp. 472-506.

NOTE 2, p. 108.

The origin of Indulgences, considered historically, is thus stated by ' le Pere Alexandre, D.D., dans son livre intitulé, "Selecta Hist. Eccles. Capita (1681)," ' as quoted by the editor of the French version of Baron Sekendorf's ' History of the Reformation in Germany : '—' Il fait voire de quelle manière les Indulgences se sont introduites successivement dans l'Eglise Romaine. D'abord, dit-il, on commença d'user d'indulgence envers ceux qui, coupables de grossier péchés, avoient été condamnes à une longue pénitence, et on les reçut plutôt dans la communion de l'Eglise ; surtout dans le temps de persecution, et lorsque ces penitens pouvoient produire une recommandation écrite de la main des Martirs qui étoient detenus dans les prisons. A la suite, les persécutions ayaint cessé, les Eveques s'arrogérent le pouvoir de mitiger, et d'abreger les peînes Ecclesiastiques, sans exiger acune recommandation de personne ; et ce droit fut accordé ensuite par le 1 Concile de Nicée. Dans le septieme siècle on commença *de racheter les pénitences par des aumones,* ou par des sommes d'argent, destinées à la construction, ou a la reparation, des Temples. Ce fut dans le onzième siecle que le Pape Urban II. promit des Indulgences a tous ceux qui s'engageroient dans les Croisades pour la conquéte de la Terre Sainte, ou qui fourniroient des sécours pour soutenir cette guerre contre les hérétiques, et les prétendus ennemies de l'Eglise,—fussent-ils d'ailleurs Chretiens. Au douziéme siècle les Indulgences furent accordées a ceux qui, par un motif de devotion, visitoient certains Temples ou certains Autels, ou qui observoient certaines ceremonies prescrites par l'Eglise.' ' C'est ainsi que cet Auteur prouve, que dans l'Eglise primitive, on ignoroit parfaitement ce que c'etoit que les Indulgences des Papes. En effet, ce que les anciens Auteurs appelloient indulgence n'étoit autre chose qu'un adoucissement de peine, ou une limitation de la durée, d'une pénitence imposée pour plusieurs années. . . . Mais par tout cela on ne croioet pas mériter la remission des péchés devant Dieu ; et il n'étoit point question de ce Trésor des Mérites de Jesus Christ, et des Saints, duquel les Evêques eussent la disposition ; bien moins attribuoit-on à cette indulgence une vertue qui s'étendit jusques sur le feu du Purgatoire.'— Hist. de la Reformation, par le Baron de Sekendorf, abregée par Messrs. Junius et Roos, tom. i. pp. 14, 15. Note par l'Editeur.

The history of Indulgences shows that they were far from being a casual corruption, such as had no vital connection with other parts of the system, and might have been lopped off without injury to the general doctrine of the Church. On the contrary, they were, in the words of Dr. Cunningham, the culminating point of ' a magnificent and well-compacted scheme, displaying great inventive genius, profound knowledge of human nature, and admirable skill in contrivance and adaptation. Each one of the principles or doctrines in the series, taken by itself, is fitted to obscure and pervert the scriptural account of the provision made for pardoning men's sins, and saving them from the punishment their sins deserve ; and all of them separately, and the whole conjointly, are necessary to be established, as the foundation of the doctrine of Indulgences, which may be regarded as constituting the climax of a long and intricate series of antiscriptural and most dangerous errors. If any one link in the series fail, the doctrine of Indulgences falls to the ground ; and, conversely, if the doctrine of Indulgences be thoroughly established, it will be able to afford support to all these positions, which are virtually involved in it. This illustrates how naturally the exposure of Indulgences led, in the hands of Luther, and under the guidance of God's Word and Spirit, to the full exposition of the doctrine of a free and complete Justification through faith in the righteousness of Christ. The doctrine of Indulgences, when analyzed and investigated, leads us back, step by step, through all the various questions which have been stated (of course in the inverse order to that which we have pursued), and thus brings us to the very threshold of the Scripture doctrine of Justification; while that great doctrine, on the other hand, once clearly seen, and steadily and faithfully applied, sweeps away at once all these errors, and all the practices and arrangements, all the fraud and imposture, which have been based upon them.'—*Dr. Cunningham, Hist. Theol.* ii. p. 95.

The late Cardinal Wiseman,—addressing an English, not a Spanish, or Austrian, or Italian, audience,—admitted that there had been some abuses in the *practice* of Indulgences, but attempted to defend the *doctrine* on which they rested ; and to show that it had been entirely misunderstood by Protestants. 'Many of you,' he says, 'have probably heard that this word signifies a licence to sin, given even beforehand for sins to be perpetrated ; at any rate, a free pardon for past sins. This is, in fact, the most lenient form in which our doctrine is popularly represented. And yet, mitigated as it is, it is far from correct. I fear many persons here present will be inclined to incredulity, when I tell them, that it is no pardon for sin of any sort, past, present, or future! What, then, is an indulgence ? It is no more than a remission by the Church . . . of a portion, or the entire, of the temporal punishment due to sin.'—*Cardinal Wiseman, Lectures on the Principal Doctrines and Practices of the Catholic Church,* vol. ii. pp. 69, 71. Be it so ; and suppose, moreover, that there is a real distinction between the temporal and the eternal punishment of sin,—was not its eternal punishment removed by baptism ? and, if it was, did any other punishment remain to be remitted, except the temporal, including the sufferings of Penance in this world, and of Purgatory in the world to come ? If that was the only punishment which men had any reason to fear, and if that was remitted, in part or in whole, by means of indulgences, might not the people reasonably regard the Pope's pardon as a plenary absolution from all the penal consequences of sin ? And that this was the light, in which it was not only regarded by the people, but represented also by the agents of the Pope in the sale of Indulgences, appears from some specimens of their eloquence which have been fortunately preserved. For example, at Berne, in 1518, Samson, one of these agents, proclaimed the following ' graces,'—that all persons who complied with his injunctions should ' receive absolution of all their sins, both guilt and punishment, and should be pure and clean from all sin, as they had been immediately after baptism,' and that ' they should deliver a soul, to be selected by themselves, out of purgatory.' When the multitude had fallen on their knees, he ended by crying out—' Now all the souls of the Bernese, in whatever place or manner they may have died, are altogether, and at the same moment, delivered, not only from the pains of purgatory, but from the torments of hell, and are raised to heaven.'—*Ruchat and Gerdes,* quoted by *Scott, Continuation of Milner's History,* ii. p. 361. This, it may be said, was a mere popular harangue, and cannot be regarded as a fair specimen of the teaching of the Church ; but we have also a copy of the ' Letters of Indulgence' which were issued by Tetzel in Germany, each being signed by his own hand. 'The Lord Jesus Christ have pity on thee, and absolve thee by the merits of His most holy passion! It is in His name, and on His authority, as also on that of the holy Apostles Peter and Paul, and of our most holy father the Pope, which has been entrusted to me for this end, that I absolve thee, first from all the ecclesiastical punishments which thou mayest have incurred, and *besides this*, from all the sins, crimes, and misdeeds, which thou mayest have committed, however great they may have been, even were they of a nature to be reserved for the Papal See.   And this I do, according to the whole extent of "the power of the keys," remitting to thee by a plenary indulgence all the punishments which thou shouldst have to endure in Purgatory.   At the same time, I restore thee to the use of the holy sacraments of the Church, to the communion of the faithful, and to the state of innocence and purity in which thou wast immediately after thy baptism; in such a manner, that at thy death, the gates of all punishments shall be closed for thee, and those of Paradise and the celestial joy shall be opened for thee.   As long as thou shalt live, this Indulgence shall have full force, even to the last breath of thy life : In the name of God the Father, the Son, and the Holy Spirit.   Amen!   Brother John Tetzel, Sub-Commissioner, has signed with his own hand.'—*Baron Sekendorf, Histoire de la Reformation en Allemagne*, abridged by MM. Junius and Roos, vol. i. pp. 19, 20.   With these historical documents in our possession, is it wonderful if we do listen with some 'incredulity,' even to a cardinal of the Romish Church, when he assures a Protestant audience, that an Indulgence is 'no pardon for sin of any sort, past, present, or future ?'

Archbishop Wake gives the 'Instructions pour gagne le Jubilée' at Paris, so late as 1683.   The Pope's Bull is in these terms : 'We give, and grant, by virtue of these presents, a plenary Indulgence, and *remission of all sins*.   And that the Confessors absolve them in the court of conscience of *all sins*, excesses, crimes, and faults, how grievous or enormous soever they have been.'   In publishing this Bull, the Archbishop of Paris promised the people that 'it will restore them to the same state they were first put into by Baptism.'—*Wake's Defence*, p. 35.   Bellarmine denies that Indulgences are mere relaxations of ecclesiastical penance, for they extend to souls in Purgatory, who are beyond Church discipline.—*Answer to Bossuet's Pastoral Letter*, p. 53.   Nor did they extend only to past sins, for they were expressly given for so many years, sometimes even till the hour of death.

Luther was a devout Monk, before he became a Reformer; and he bears witness to his personal experience when he first gives a form of monkish absolution, and then contrasts his own views as a Monk, and as a Reformer.   The form of absolution, as given by Luther, runs thus : ' Parcat tibi Deus, frater, Meritum passionis Domini nostri Jesu Christi, —et beatæ Mariæ semper Virginis,—et omnium Sanctorum : meritum Ordinis,—gravamen religionis,—humilitas confessionis,—contritio cordis, —bona opera, quæ fecisti et facies, pro amore Domini nostri Jesu Christi, cedant tibi in remissionem peccatorum tuorum,—in augmentum meriti et gratiæ,—et in præmium vitæ æternæ.   Amen !'   Luther's remark on this form of absolution is—' Si diligenter verba expenderis, intelliges Christum

planè òtiosum esse, et Ei detrahi gloriam et nomen Justificationis et Sal-
vatoris, et tribui monasticis operibus.' But the contrast between his
experience as a Monk and a Reformer, is still more striking. 'Ego in
eodem luto hæsitavi, putabam Christum esse Judicem (etsi ore fatebar
Eum passum et mortuum pro Redemptione generis humani), placamdum
observatione Regulæ meæ. Ideò cum orabam aut celebrabam Missam,
solitus eram semper adjicere in fine, " Domine Jesu, ad Te venio, et‿oro
ut gravamina Ordinis mei sint compensatio pro peccatis meis." Nunc
verò gratias ago Patri misericordiarum, qui me è tenebris vocavit ad
lucem Evangelii ; et donavit me uberrima cognitione Christi Jesu Domini
mei ; propter quem, una cum Paulo, " Omnia duco esse damna, putoque
esse σκύβαλα, ut Christum lucrifaciam, utque inveniar in Illo, non habens
meam Justitiam, ex regula Augustini, sed eam quæ est per fidem Christi ;
Cui sit laus, et gloria, una cum Patre et Spiritu Sancto, in sæcula
sæculorum. Amen !"'—*Archbishop Hare, Vindication of Luther*, pp. 143,
144.

On Indulgences, see Voetius, ' Disputations,' vol. ii. pp. 286-304 ;
Ullmann, ' Reformers before the Reformation,' vol. i. pp. 243, 276 ; Mr.
Lawson, ' Autobiography of Luther,' pp. 32-51,—mainly founded on the
second and third volumes of Michelet, ' Memoires de Luther, Ecrits par
Lui-Même,' 1835.

Note 3, p. 111.

Scott, ' Continuation of Milner's History,' vol. i. p. 220.

Luther refers to the terms in which one was admitted to the office of
the Priesthood : ' Accipe potestatem *sacrificandi* pro vivis et mortuis.'
Archbishop Whately did good service to the cause of truth, by maintaining and proving that there is no Priestly Caste in the Christian Church,
and no Priesthood except such as is common to all believers as ' a royal
priesthood, a holy nation, a peculiar people.' Whately, ' Essays on the
Peculiarities of the Christian Religion,' p. 382 ; ' Errors of Romanism,'
pp. 99-118; ' Cautions for the Times,' pp. 82, 383.

Note 4, p. 112.

Jo. Gerhard, ' Loc. Theolog.' vol. vii., Locus xvii. ' De Justifica-
tione,' pp. 1-317 ; Bishop Downham, ' Treatise on Justification,' *passim ;*
Bishop Davenant, ' Disput. de Habituali et Actuali Justitia,' translated
by Allport ; Brown (of Wamphray), ' The Life of Justification Opened ;'
Roborough (Scribe to the Westminster Assembly), ' The Doctrine of
Justification Cleared ;' Anthony Burgess, ' The True Doctrine of Justifi-
cation ;' Dr. Cunningham, ' Historical Theology,' ii. pp. 1-154 ; Dr.
Owen on ' Justification,' Works, vol. xi., Russel's edition.

Note 5, p. 112.

Fra-Paolo Sarpi, ' Histoire du Concile de Trente,' by Le Courayer,
2 vols. fol., vol. i. pp. 301-315.

'Quadriennio ferè ante Concilium Tridentinum, justo tractatu asseruit orthodoxam de Justificatione doctrinam Cardinalis CONTARENUS.'—*Dr. John Prideaux, Lects. Decem,* p. 143.

John Wesel, in 1489, had said, 'God *condemns,* yet God *justifies.* It is the greatest of wonders that the very same divine justice which is armed with an eternal law of threatening and condemnation towards the transgressor, should, in the day and hour of judgment, not only hold back the sword of vengeance, and absolve from the punishment threatened, but should raise the criminal to heights of glory and happiness. Who does not wonder to see the truthfulness of threatenings converted into the truthfulness of promises, so that strict truth is kept on both sides, and in both aspects? These two contradictions are reconciled in "the Lamb of God"—the infinite atonement of Christ.'—*Dr. Shedd, History of Christian Doctrine,* ii. p. 334. See for a full account of Wesel, Ullmann's 'Reformers before the Reformation,' vol. ii. b. iv. pp. 263-615; and for John Huss, and Jerome of Prague, Em. de Bonnechose, 'The Reformers before the Reformation,'—the Fifteenth Century, 'John Huss and the Council of Constance,' 2 vols. in one, Aberdeen, 1859.

NOTE 6, p. 113.

The post-Trentine bulls and decisions on points of doctrine are appended to some editions of the 'Canones et Decreta;' but they are given separately, in a convenient form, by a Louvaine divine, F. V. Ranst (1718), 'Veritas in Medio.' It contains—the 79 propositions of *Baius,* pp. 4-44,—at p. 30 the propositions 'De Justitia, seu Justificatione;' the five propositions of *Jansenius,* pp. 44-75; 110 propositions that were condemned by Alexander VII. and Innocent XI. in 1665, 1666, and 1679, pp. 78-165; additional propositions condemned by Alexander VIII. in 1690, pp. 166-202; 67 propositions of *Molino* by Innocent XI., pp. 203-207; 23 propositions condemned by Innocent XII. in 1699, p. 208; 101 propositions of *Quesnel* condemned by Clement XI., pp. 216-289. Besides these, many propositions were condemned by other recognised authorities; *e.g.* Lombard, in his 'Sententiarum, Libri 4,' gives a 'Collectio Errorum Parisiis Condemnatorum,' pp. 381-409. Mœhler, in the first edition of his 'Symbolism,' assumed that the Canons and Decrees of Trent were the only authority, but afterwards admitted that the bulls and decisions of the Papal See were equally binding. Dens appeals to the latter as well as the former; for he says that—the 'Bullam Clementis XI., cujus initium "Unigenitus Dei Filius,"—"esse legem dogmaticam Universalis Ecclesiæ, adeoque meritò vocari regulam Fidei, eique dissentientes esse hæreticos."' —*Theol.* vol. ii. p. 130. For the recent addition of the dogma of the 'Immaculate Conception,' see Dr. Pusey's 'Eirenicon'—the most valuable part of the work. This addition may have been made *informally;* but is there any limit to the process of development? May it not develop Protestantism itself, or even Pantheism? Or can it recognise any fixed creed? The *Dublin Review* affirmed that Rome has no symbolical books, and is not bound by the Decrees of Trent, vol. xliv. p. 277, vol. xlvi. p. 395.

Note 7, p. 121.

'Fides Formata.' See Luther on Ep. to Galatians, Eng. trans. 1575, pp. 67, 104, 112, 119, 125, 132.

'A true and stedfast faith,' says Luther, 'must lay hold upon nothing else but Christ alone. . . . This our adversaries understand not; and therefore they cast away this precious pearl—Christ, and, in His place, they set—Charity, which, they say, is their precious diamond.'—*On the Ep. to Gal.* p. 67.

Note 8, p. 126.

The two opposite systems are characterized by D'Aubigné, 'History of the Reformation in Europe,' i. 27, 277; Bishop Davenant, 'Disputations,' Pref. xvii. xix. ; Faber, 'Primitive Doctrine of Justification,' pp. xx. 209; Dr. Cunningham, 'The Reformers and Theology of the Reformation,' pp. 24, 64, 102; 'Historical Theology,' ii. 3, 10, 13, etc.

NOTES TO LECTURE V.

Note 1, p. 128.

Melancthon's 'Confession,' and 'Apology.' See 'Sylloge Confessionum,' and 'Harmony of Protestant Confessions,' Sekendorf, vol. ii. p. 205; Scott's 'Continuation of Milner,' vol. i. p. 89.

Note 2, p. 128.

The refutation of the Augsburg Confession, by Faber and Eck, 'divided the articles of the Confession into *three* classes; one of which, containing doctrines common to both parties, it wholly approved; another it wholly rejected; and the third it partly approved and partly condemned. Six doctrines were wholly rejected; and one of these was, "that men are not justified by the merit of good works, but by faith alone."'—*Du Pin*, quoted by Scott, 'Continuation of Milner's History,' i. 51.

Note 3, p. 129.

Melchior Adam, i. 69; Luther's 'Animadversions on the Edict of Augsburg' in 1531; Scott's 'Continuation of Milner's History,' i. p. 99.

Note 4, p. 130.

'It is enough for us to agree,' says Erasmus, 'that man can effect nothing of himself; that if he can do anything, it is entirely of divine grace; that very much indeed is to be ascribed to Faith, which is the peculiar gift of the Holy Spirit, *and is of much wider extent than is com-*

monly supposed, and is not possessed by all who say, " I believe that Christ
died for me." Let it be allowed that the hearts of believers are *justified,*—
that is, *purified,*—by faith; but only let us confess that the works of
charity are necessary to the attainment of salvation; for true faith cannot
be idle, being the fountain and source of all good works. God is not
properly any man's debtor, except He have made Himself such by free
promise; and even then, our performing the condition of the promise, is
itself the fruit of His bounty. Yet the word "reward," or "merit," is
not to be rejected, since God of His goodness is pleased to accept and
reward what He Himself works in us, or by us.'—*Scott, Continuation of
Milner's History,* i. 159, 160.

Note 5, p. 132.

The article is preserved by Du Pin. 'The first article about Justification, establishes these three principles beforehand :—1. That it is
certain that, since the fall of Adam, all men are born enemies of God,
and children of wrath by sin. 2. That they cannot be reconciled to God,
nor redeemed from the bondage of sin, but by Jesus Christ, our only
Mediator. 3. That persons of riper years cannot obtain these graces
unless they be prevented (first visited) by the motions of the Holy Spirit,
which inclines their mind and will to detest sin; that, after this first
motion, their mind is raised up to God, by faith in the promises made to
them that their sins are freely forgiven them, and that God will adopt
those for His children who believe in Jesus Christ. From these principles
it follows, that sinners are justified by a living and effectual faith, which
is a motion of the Holy Spirit, whereby, repenting of their lives past,
they are raised to God, and made real partakers of the mercy which Jesus
Christ hath promised, being satisfied that their sins are forgiven, and
that they are reconciled by the merits of Jesus Christ; which no man
attains, but at the same time love is shed abroad in his heart, and he
begins to fulfil the law. So that justifying faith "worketh by love,"—
though it justifies not but as it leads us to mercy and righteousness—
which (righteousness) is *imputed* to us through Jesus Christ and His
merits, and not by any perfection of righteousness which is *inherent* in us,
as communicated to us by Jesus Christ. So that we are not just, or
accepted by God, on account of our own works or righteousness, but we
are *reputed* just on account of the merits of Jesus Christ only. Yet this
is not to hinder us from exhorting the people to increase this faith, and
this charity, by outward and inward works; so that, though the people
be taught that *faith alone justifieth,* yet repentance, the fear of God and of
His judgments, the practice of good works, etc., ought to be preached to
them.'—See *Dr. Robertson, History of Charles V.,* vol. iii. p. 150; *Scott's
Continuation of Milner's History,* i. 277.

Note 6, p. 132.

Melancthon, ' Ad Gallos Consilium,' ' Opera,' i. p. 222.

NOTE 7, p. 134.

The dissatisfaction of both parties is strongly stated by Dr. Robertson:
—' All the zealous Catholics, particularly the ecclesiastics who had a seat
in the Diet, joined in condemning Gropper's treatise as too favourable to
the Lutheran opinion, the poison of which heresy it conveyed, as they
pretended, with greater danger, because it was in some degree disguised.
The rigid Protestants, especially Luther himself, and his patron the Elector
of Saxony, were for rejecting it as an impious compound of error and
truth, craftily prepared that it might impose on the weak, the timid, and
the unthinking.'—*History of Charles. V.* in 4 vols., vol. iii. p. 151.

On this, as on several other occasions, the sagacity and firmness of
the Elector frustrated the devices of the Romish party, and afforded
seasonable support and encouragement to the divines of Wittemberg.
He described the conciliatory article as a handle given to their adversaries to represent them as having departed from their original tenets.
He looked, it is said, ' with great jealousy on a sort of middle party
which he thought had risen up among the Protestants, and said that he
feared much more the caresses of Ratisbon, than the severity of Augsburg. He would have his representatives, therefore, adhere to the very
terms, as well as to the sense, of the " Confession," and reject all ambiguous language which might be twisted to opposite meanings. And he
declared that even if Luther himself should give way, which he trusted
would never be the case, it should not be with his countenance.' But
there was no reason to doubt the stedfastness of Luther. He entreated
the Elector, indeed, not to be severe on Philip, for ' it would break his
heart;' but characterized the article as ' botched and unsatisfactory.'
' It seemed to him, he said, that his friend had proposed an orthodox
formulary, asserting Justification by faith alone without works, according
to Rom. iii.; but that the collocutors on the contrary part had substituted another, taken from Gal. v., concerning " faith working by love;"
and that this having been rejected by Melancthon, one had been formed
out of the two, which seemed to sanction the opinions of both parties.'
Luther, commenting on the clause, that ' the repenting sinner is justified
by a living and efficacious faith,' says : ' Either Eckius must acknowledge
(which he will never do) that he and his friends have not before taught
this doctrine, and then the article may stand for a time; or he will boast
(and this is what he certainly will do) that they have always taught the
doctrine of an efficacious or operative faith, and then the article will
become a new patch upon the old garment, by which the rent will be
made worse.' He explains the expression, ' faith which worketh by love,'
by saying, that ' it does not treat of Justification, but of the life of the
justified. It is one thing to be made righteous, and another to act as
righteous ; one thing to *be*, and another to *do*. It is one question, How
a man is justified before God? another, How a justified man acts ? It
is one thing for a tree to be produced, another for it to bring forth fruit.'

And Melancthon himself strongly disclaimed all intention to relinquish any part of the Protestant doctrine, declaring that 'he would rather die than compromise the truth and wound his own conscience,' and expressing his regret 'for any undue facility in suffering himself to be employed in vain and foolish schemes of conciliation;—' Conciliationes fucosas,' 'fallaces,' 'plenas turpitudinis et periculi.' In a paper intended for his last will, he reiterates the same assurances,—exhorting his children 'to avoid connection with the Papists, who, on many points, taught a very corrupt doctrine, and were altogether without the true doctrine of Justification by faith, and of the remission of sins;' warning them 'against all hollow and insincere methods of reconciling the doctrines in dispute, by which old errors would be covertly introduced again, and the truth corrupted;' and protesting his own sincerity and singleness of purpose in these affecting terms: 'I can truly affirm that I have endeavoured soundly to explain the doctrine of our Church, that it might be rightly understood by younger students and handed down to posterity. I know, indeed, that it has at times been suspected that I attempted some things in favour of our adversaries; but I call God to witness that I had no wish to favour such persons, but aimed only at correct statements, excluding all ambiguities, though many are aware how difficult I found it to attain this. . . . Nor was it my design to introduce any new dogma, but perspicuously and correctly to explain the catholic doctrine as delivered in our Churches, which I judge to have been brought to light in these late years, by the singular goodness of God, through the instrumentality of Dr. Martin Luther, that thus the Church might be purified and restored, which must otherwise have utterly perished.'—See *Scott's Continuation of Milner's History*, vol. i. pp. 284, 289, 298.

NOTE 8, p. 135.

Scott's 'Continuation of Milner's History,' i. 453, ii. 93. In regard to Charles v., Thuanus, as quoted and translated by Dr. Owen (Works, vol. xi. p. 42), makes the following remarkable statement. He felt 'that in himself he was altogether unworthy to obtain the kingdom of heaven by his own works or merits,—but that his Lord God, who enjoyed it on a double right or title—by inheritance of the Father—and the merit of His own passion,—was contented with the one Himself, and freely granted unto him the other; on whose free grant he laid claim thereunto, and in confidence thereof he should not be confounded; for the oil of mercy is poured only into the vessel of faith, or trust;—that this is the trust of a man despairing in himself, and resting in his Lord; otherwise to trust in his own works or merits, is not faith, but perfidy;—that sins are blotted out by the mercy of God,—and therefore we ought to believe that our sins can be pardoned by Him alone against whom alone we have sinned, —with whom there is no sin, and by whom alone sins are forgiven.'

NOTE 9, p. 136.

Scott's ' Continuation of Milner's History,' vol. i. p. 285.

NOTE 10, p. 136.

' Satan can shape a trial,—he can put it to such ane frame,—he can draw it to a small point,—and set it like ane razor's edge, that, although there seem little between the two, the one side is a denying Christ, and the other a confessing of Him.'—*John Livingstone, Select Biographies of the Wodrow Society,* vol. i. p. 204.

NOTE 11, p. 139.

' Concilii Trident. Canones et Decreta,' Paris, 1832, Sessio vi., pp. 29-40, Decreta; pp. 40-46, Canones.

NOTE 12, p. 139.

Paoli Sarpi's words are : ' La doctrine *inouie* de la Justification par la Foi seule.'—*Histoire du Con. de Trent,* par Courayer, vol. i. pp. 298, 303. See also Scott's ' Continuation of Milner's History,' vol. ii. p. 270.

NOTE 13, p. 140.

See on Soto and Vega's Interpretations of the Trent Decrees, Petavius, ' Dogm. Theologica,' tom. iii. ' De Trident. Concilii Interpretatione,' c. xv. p. 353.   See also Bishop Stillingfleet's ' Reply to Gother,' edited by Dr. Cunningham, p. 26 ; and Dr. E. B. Pusey, ' Eirenicon,' pp. 98, 190, 209, 266, on the practical system of the Romish Church, as being worse even than her doctrinal creed.

NOTE 14, p. 141.

Calvin says : ' Sic quidem præfaritur, ut initio, nihil spirent præter Christum ; sed, cum ad rem ventum est, multum abest, quin illi relinquant, quod suum est.   Immo, nihil tandem aliud continet eorum definitio, quàm tritum illud scholarum dogma,—partim gratiâ Dei, partim operibus propriis, justificari homines.'—*Antidotum,* Tractatus, p. 277.

And Chemnitz, in like manner, says : ' Tridentini etiam dicunt, Justificationem esse translationem ab eo *statu,* in quo homo nascitur filius iræ, in *statum* gratiæ et adoptionis . . . in regnum filii delectionis suæ, in quo habemus redemptionem et remissiouem peccatorum.   Videt lector, ipsos ad veram significationem verbi " justificare," non obscurè alludere ; sed mox postea, ubi ad rem ipsam ventum est, ut explicetur, quid sit justificatio peccatoris, ibi justificare, ipsis nihil aliud significat, quam homini per Spiritum renovationis infundi habitum, vel qualitatem justitiæ inhærentem.'—*Examen,* p. 130.

The chief works on the Tridentine doctrine of Justification are these:

Calvin, ' Acta Synodi Tridentinæ, cum Antidoto,' Tractatus, Geneva, 1611, pp. 250-300, Sess. vi. pp. 272-292.

Chemnitz, 'Examen Concilii Tridentini,' in four parts, in reply to Andradius, Frankfort, 1585 ; 'De Justificatione,' Part i. pp. 126-173 ; 'De Bonis Operibus,' pp. 174-188.

Bellarmine, Op. vol. ii. ; 'De Justificatione,' in five books, pp. 811-1131.

Amesius, 'Bellarminus Enervatus; Scriptum Elencticum,' in four vols. ; tom. iv. lib. vi. 'De Justificatione,' pp. 113-178 ; 'De Meritis,' lib. vii. pp. 181-195.

Downham, Bishop of Derry, 'Treatise on Justification.'

Bishop Davenant, 'Disputatio de Justitia Habituali et Actuali,' translated by Allport, 2 vols. 8vo.

Lubbertus Sibrandus, in the Dedication of his able work in reply to Socinus, 'De Servatore,' intimates his intention to publish 'integram Bellarmini refutationem, quam penè ad finem perduxi,' which has not come into my hands.

Osorio, Opera, tom. ii. ; 'De Justitia,' lib. x. pp. 186-456, 1592.

John Foxe, the Martyrologist, answered Osorio in a Latin treatise, afterwards translated by his friend and fellow-labourer John Day, the printer, under the title, 'Of Free Justification by Christ.' It is given in an abridged form in the 'British Reformers,' vol. Fox and COVERDALE.

NOTE 15, p. 143.

Bishop Atterbury, 'Answer to some Considerations on the Spirit of M. Luther,' etc., 1687, p. 106.

NOTE 16, p. 143.

See Gother's 'Papist Misrepresented and Represented,' with Bishop Stillingfleet's Answer to it, edited by Dr. Cunningham; Dr. Thomas Butler, 'Truths of the Catholic Religion proved from Scripture alone,' 2 vols. ; Dr. Milner's 'End of Religious Controversy ;' Charles Butler, 'Book of the Roman Catholic Church,' answered in Bishop Philpotts' 'Letters,' and J. Blanco White's 'Internal Evidence against Catholicism;' Cardinal Wiseman's 'Lectures on the Doctrines and Practices of the Catholic Church ;' Berington and Kirk, 'Faith of Catholics confirmed by Scripture and attested by the Fathers,' etc., 3 vols. 8vo.

NOTE 17, p. 144.

Scott's 'Continuation of Milner's History,' vol. i. p. 508 ; Dr. Cunningham's Edition of 'Bishop Stillingfleet's Reply to Gother,' p. 46.

NOTE 18, p. 144.

Dezius, 'La Re-Union des Protestants de Strasburg à l'Eglise Romaine ;' 'Mosheim's History,' by M'Laine, vol. v. 127.

NOTE 19, p. 145.

Bossuet's 'Exposition of the Doctrine of the Catholic Church in

Matters of Controversy.' First printed in 1671 ; translated from the 9th French Edition, and published by His Majesty's command, 1686. It was answered, at first anonymously, in Archbishop Wake's ' Exposition of the Doctrine of the Church of England in the several Articles proposed by the Bishop of Meaux, with a Preface giving an account of his book,' 1686. This was met by ' A Vindication of Bossuet's Exposition, prepared by a Rev. Father, and published by His Majesty's Printer, 1686 ;' which called forth Archbishop Wake's ' Defence of the Exposition of the Doctrine of the Church of England.' Another, and a very able, ' Answer to Bossuet's Exposition' appeared in the same year. See a volume entitled, ' Sum of the Popish Controversy,' in the Library of the New College.

NOTE 20, p. 145.

Dr. Christopher Davenport, or Francis à Sancta Clara, published a work entitled, ' Paraphrastica Expositio Articulorum Confessionis Anglicanæ,' which has recently been reprinted in English from the Latin Edition of 1646, London, 1865. For some account of it, see Dr. Cunningham's Edition of ' Bishop Stillingfleet's Reply to Gother,' p. 29, and Dr. Goode's ' Rule of Faith,' vol. i. Pref. xiii.

NOTE 21, p. 147.

Dr. Mœhler's ' Symbolism ; An Exposition of the Doctrinal Differences between Catholics and Protestants, as evidenced by their Symbolical Writings ;' translated by J. Burton Robertson, Esq. For his high character as a theologian, see Dr. Cunningham, ' Histor. Theol.' vol. i. 485. For his views of the authority belonging to post-Trentine Bulls and decisions, as well as to the Decrees and Canons of that Council, see vol. i. pp. 21, 37 ; of Justification, vol. i. pp. 115-281 ; of Original Righteousness and Original Sin, vol. i. pp. 34, 37, 71.

Mœhler's attack on the Lutheran doctrine of Justification called forth several able replies in Germany, by Baur, Nitzsch, Hengstenberg, and Marheineke. Archdeacon Hare had not seen the two last, but speaks highly of the two former. ' Baur,' he says, ' when reprinting his masterly and triumphant refutation of Mœhler's attack on the Lutheran doctrine of Justification, remarks, p. 319, " It may be regarded as a cheering proof of the firmness and stability with which this fundamental doctrine of the Lutheran creed still maintains its central place in the minds of Protestants, that, among the Protestant theologians who have taken part in this controversy, there is no perceptible difference of any importance on this point." '—*Vindication of Luther*, p. 116. See also pp. 171, 172. Baur's peculiar opinions on other points,—such as the Atonement,—might not prevent him from vindicating, *on historical grounds*, Luther's real sentiments on Justification, when these were assailed or distorted ; but, *on doctrinal grounds*, Luther's doctrine cannot be understood or defended by any man, apart from the Atonement.

Note 22, p. 148.

Dr. Newman's 'Essay on the Development of Christian Doctrine,' 2d. Ed. 1846. The untenableness of the old defences, pp. 8, 24, 25; the Developing power of the Church, pp. 27, 37, 57, 63, 277, 337, 344.

It was vigorously assailed by Dr. Brownson, in America, and defended in the 'Dublin Review,' vol. xliv. p. 325, xlvi. p. 373. See also Dr. Wordsworth's 'Letters to M. Gondon,' p. 8, and Prof. Butler's 'Letters on Development,' *passim.*

Note 23, p. 148.

See Perrone, 'Prælectiones Theologicæ,' vol. vi. pt. ii. He treats of Justification under the title, 'De Gratia Sanctificante,' pp. 200-244; 'De Merito,' pt. iii. pp. 244-257; vol. viii. 'De Indulgentiis,' pp. 5-37. See Dens, 'Theologia Mor. et Dogm.' 8 vols.: on Justification, ii. p. 446; on Merit, ii. p. 458; on Guilt, i. 357, 363; on Prayer for Pardon, iv. 28, ii. 48.

Note 24, p. 148.

See Le Blanc, 'Theses Theologicæ,' pp. 191-304.

Note 25, p. 148.

See Mrs. Schimmelpennick's 'Memorials of Port Royal;' Pascal, 'Provincial Letters,' by Dr. M'Crie, p. 15; Gossner's 'Life of Martin Boos,' abridged by London Tract Society; 'Journal of M. de St. Amour, Doctor of the Sorbonne, containing a full account of the transactions both in France and at Rome, concerning the Five famous Propositions controverted between the Jansenists and the Molinists, till the Pope's Decision,' translated from the French, London, 1664;—a most instructive work, which throws much light on the views which then prevailed at Rome on the doctrine of grace, and on the manner in which such processes are managed there.

Note 26, p. 149.

Dr. Cunningham, 'Histor. Theology,' vol. ii. 113, 118; Archdeacon Hare, 'Vindication of Luther,' pp. 32, 33.

NOTES TO LECTURE VI.

Note 1, p. 152.

David Laing, Esq., the accomplished Editor of the Works of John Knox, quotes (vol. iii. p. 417) this striking testimony from Dr. M'Crie's 'Life of Knox' (vol. i. p. 390): 'In reading the writings of the first

Reformers, there are two things which must strike our minds. The first is, the exact conformity between the doctrine maintained by them respecting the Justification of sinners, and that of the Apostles. The second is, the surprising harmony which subsisted among them on this important doctrine. On some questions respecting the sacraments, and the external government and discipline of the Church, they differed ; but upon the article of FREE JUSTIFICATION, Luther and Zuinglius, Melancthon and Calvin, Cranmer and Knox, spoke the very same language. This was not owing to their having read each other's writings, but because they copied from the same divine original. The clearness with which they understood and explained this great truth, is also very observable. More able and learned defences of it have since appeared ; but I question if it has ever been stated in more scriptural, unequivocal, and decided language, than in the writings of the early Reformers. Some of their successors, by giving way to speculation, gradually lost sight of this distinguishing badge of the Reformation, and landed at last in Arminianism, *which is nothing else but the Popish doctrine in a Protestant dress.*' The Treatise on Justification by Henry Balnaves, 1584, is still one of the best in our language. It is given in Mr. Laing's Edition of Knox's Works, vol. iii. pp. 431-542, with Knox's recommendation and summary of it, iii. pp. 5-28. It is also reprinted from the Edition 1584 in the 'British Reformers,' London Tract Society, in the same volume, with the admirable 'Places' of Patrick Hamilton. Balnave's Treatise is the more valuable because 'Knox has informed us, that his design, in preparing it for the press, was to give, along with the Author, *his own* " Confession of the article of Justification therein contained." '

NOTE 2, p. 153.

Bishop O'Brien, 'Sermons on the Nature and Effects of Faith,' xx. 115, 129 ; 'Sylloge Confessionum ;' Hall, 'Harmony of Protestant Confessions ;' G. S. Faber, 'Primitive Doctrine of Justification,' pp. 3, 264-268 ; Dr. Cunningham, 'Histor. Theology,' ii. 21 ; 'The Reformers and Theology of Reformation,' p. 163.

NOTE 3, p. 155.

Dr. Newman, 'Lectures on Justification,' App. p. 436; Bishop Davenant, 'Disputatio, etc.,' by Allport, vol. i. pp. 161, 162; Scott's 'Continuation of Milner's History,' vol. i. 234, ii. 116.

'Since Osiander,' says Calvin, 'has introduced I know not what monstrous notion of *essential righteousness,* by which, though he had no intention to destroy Justification by grace, yet he has involved it in such obscurity as darkens pious minds, and deprives them of a weighty sense of the grace of Christ, it will be worth while to refute this idle notion. . . . Not being content with that righteousness which hath been procured for us by the obedience and sacrificial death of Christ, he imagines that we are substantially righteous in God, by the infusion of His essence as well as His character. . . . As this principle is like a cuttle-fish, which,

APPENDIX.

by the emission of black and turbid blood, conceals its many tails, there is a necessity for a vigorous opposition to it, unless we mean to submit to be openly robbed of that righteousness, which *alone* affords us any confidence concerning our salvation. For throughout this discussion, the terms *righteousness* and *justify* are extended by him to two things : first, he understands that to be *justified* denotes not only to be reconciled to God by a free pardon, but also to be *made righteous ;* and that *righteousness* is not a gratuitous imputation, but a sanctity and integrity inspired by the divine essence which resides in us : secondly, he resolutely denies that Christ is our righteousness, as having, in the character of a Priest, expiated our sins and appeased the Father on our behalf, but in being " the eternal God and everlasting life." To prove the assertion that God justifies, not only by pardoning, but also by regenerating, he inquires whether God leaves those whom He justifies in their natural state without any reformation of their manners. The answer is very easy : As Christ cannot be divided, so these two blessings, *which we receive together* in Him, are also inseparable. Whomsoever, therefore, God receives into His favour, He likewise gives them the Spirit of adoption, by whose power He renews them in His own image. But if the brightness of the sun be inseparable from his heat, shall we therefore say, that the earth is warmed by his light, and illuminated by his heat ?'—*Institutes*, translated by Allen, vol. i. pp. 579-592.

Melancthon was equally explicit in testifying against Osiander's doctrine. He conceived that it raised a question which was neither ' verbal nor trivial,' but vital and important,—Are we reckoned righteous ' from the indwelling of Christ *in* us, or by His obedience *for* us ?' and he gives his deliverance upon it. ' Osiander holds that we are righteous by the Divinity dwelling *in* us. . . . We also acknowledge that God dwells in the regenerate, so as to produce not only virtuous emotions, but even the commencement of eternal life, to make us "*partakers of a divine nature.*" But then there exists a question of another kind,—How may man receive remission of sins and reconciliation with God ? How may he have righteousness imputed, or reckoned, unto him ? Is this from the indwelling of Christ *in* us, or by His obedience *for* us ? Osiander in effect says, that we are justified by *our renovation to holiness.* We, on the other hand, while we admit the necessity of renovation, hold that the renewed man is justified, or accepted of God, for the sake of Christ's obedience.' He adds, 'I regard Osiander's dogma as no mere logomachy, or strife of words. He differs from our churches on a very essential point ; and obscures, or rather destroys, the only consolation provided for distressed consciences, seeing he leads us not to the promise of mercy, through the obedience of the Mediator, but directs us to another object.'—*Scott's Continuation of Milner's History*, vol. ii. p. 116.

Cranmer was married to a niece of A. Osiander. The latter must be distinguished from L. Osiander, who wrote the ' Enchiridion Controversiarum' of his age, published at Wittemberg in 1614.

Note 4, p. 156.

On Lauterwald's opinions, see Scott's 'Continuation of Milner's History,' ii. 118-121.

Note 5, p. 157.

On Stancari's opinions, see Calvin's 'Inst.' i. Book ii. c. xiv.; Turretine, vol. ii. p. 411, loc. xiv. ques. ii. I find some traces of the same opinion in the work of an able Scotch divine, Alex. Pitcairne of Dron, in Stratherne, 'The Spiritual Sacrifice' (pp. 831. London, 1664); see pp. 37-40. I am indebted to David Laing, Esq., of the Signet Library, for the use of this rare work.

Note 6, p. 158.

A letter by Luther against the Antinomians is given in Samuel Rutherford's 'Survey of Antinomianism and Familism,' pp. 69-74. Luther delivered also six public disputations against them at Wittemberg, and all his writings abound with indignant protests against their errors. Calvin was equally decided in his opposition to them. See his 'Instructio adversus Anabaptistas,' and his 'Instructio adversus Libertinos,' the former pp. 411-432, and the latter pp. 433-473, of his 'Tractatus,' folio, Geneva, 1611.

Note 7, p. 161.

Dickinson, 'Familiar Letters,' pp. 154-180 ; Beart, 'Vindication of the Eternal Law,' P. ii. pp. iv-vii.; Robert Traill, 'Vindication of the Protestant Doctrine of Justification from the charge of Antinomianism,' Works, vol. i. pp. 305-359 ; Witsius, 'Animadversiones Irenicæ,' Misc. Sac. ii. 771 ; Brown, 'Life of Justification,' p. 259 ; Dr. Burgess, 'True Doctrine of Justification,' pp. 18, 185.

Note 8, p. 164.

On the Socinian doctrine, see various treatises in the 'Fratres Poloni ;' L'Amy, 'History of Socinianism ;' F. Spanheim, 'Elenchus Controv.' pp. 137-144; Stapfer, 'Instit. Theolog. Polem.' pp. 350-383 ; Socinus, 'De Servatore,' with the answer of Sibrandus Lubbertus, 1611, especially lib. iii. and iv. pp. 309-630.

Socinus, 'Tractatus de Justificatione,' in his 'Opuscula,' Racoviæ (1611), pp. 1-143.

Also the 'Racovian Catechism,' with Bishop Stillingfleet's account of the important variations which it has undergone in successive editions, in the preface to his work on 'Christ's Satisfaction ;' Castellio, 'Dialogi' (1613), to which is appended 'Tractatus de Justificatione,' pp. 31-89. The great work of Hoornbeek, 'Socinianismus Confutatus' (1662), tom. ii. lib. iii. c. ii. 'De Justificatione,' pp. 671-721 ; also, his 'Compendium Disputationum Anti-Sociniarum,' Misc. Sac. lib. ii. c. xxv. pp. 233-261 (1672).

Maresius, 'Hydra Socinianismi Expuganata,' in reply to Volkelius and Crellius (1651), vol. ii. lib. iv. c. iii. 'De Fide, et de Justificatione,' pp. 449-479. Dr. Owen, 'Vindiciæ Evangelicæ,' in reply to Smalcius and Biddle, Works by Russell, vols. viii. ix., vol. ix. p. 206. He gives the doctrine of Socinians on Justification in their own words, vol. ix. p. 255. Dr. John Edwards, 'The Socinian Creed,' pp. 59-71, 201, 209. Andrew Fuller, 'Calvinistic and Socinian Systems Compared,' p. 148. Dr. Cunningham, 'Histor. Theology,' vol. ii. c. xxiii. sec. 3, 4, pp. 168-192.

NOTE 9, p. 165.

Dr. Channing, 'Works' and 'Memoirs;' Dr. Ellis, 'Half Century of Unitarianism in America;' Martineau, 'Rationale of Religious Inquiry,' with Blanco White's Letter. Also, B. White's 'Memoirs.'

NOTE 10, p. 167.

Dr. Hill, 'Lectures,' vol. ii. pp. 378-388 ; Balguy, 'Essay on Redemption ;' Rev. Henry Taylor, 'Apology of Ben Mordecai,' 2 vols., London, 1784 ; on 'Justification,' see Letter vi. p. 725.

NOTE 11, p. 170.

Robert Barclay, 'Theses Theologicæ,' and 'Apology for the True Christian Divinity ; an 'Explanation and Vindication of the Principles and Doctrines of the People called Quakers,' 8th Edition, London, 1780. The seventh Proposition relates to Justification, pp. 8, 196-241. John Brown (Wamphray), 'Quakerism the Pathway to Paganism,' an Examination of Robert Barclay's 'Theses' and 'Apology,' 4to, 1678. The doctrine of Justification is discussed, c. xiii. pp. 293-325. 'Journal of George Fox,' 7th Edition, in 2 vols., edited by W. Armistead (1852), and containing a preface by William Penn, vol. i. pp. 1-47. Dr. Wardlaw, 'Friendly Letters to the Society of Friends on some of their Distinguishing Principles' (1836); Letters v. and vi. on 'The Doctrine of Justification,' pp. 175-233. Dr. Wardlaw gives some pleasing extracts from the writings of Mr. Gurney, which show that his views approximated very nearly to those of the Reformers.

NOTE 12, p. 173.

The sentiments of Arminius on the doctrine of Justification may be collected from the following parts of his Works :—'Declaration of Sentiments,' art. 9, 'On Justification,' vol. i. 262 ; 'Public Disputations,' art. 19, 'On the Justification of Man before God,' vol. i. 595 ; 'Private Disputations,' art. 48, 'On Justification,' vol. ii. 116 ; 'Letter to Hippolytus,' art. 5, 'Justification,' vol. ii. 473 ; 'Certain Articles to be Diligently Examined and Weighed,' art. 23, 'On the Justification of Man as a Sinner, but yet a Believer, before God,' vol. ii. 504.

That his sentiments were, to a large extent, in accordance with those of the Reformers, will appear from the following extracts :—

Justification by the Moral Law is thus defined: 'It is that by which a man, having performed the duties of the Moral Law without transgression, and being placed before the tribunal of the severe justice of God, is accounted and declared by God to be righteous, and worthy of the reward of eternal life—in himself, of debt, according to the law, and without grace, to his own salvation' (welfare?), 'and to the glory both of divine, and human, righteousness.'—Vol. i. 597.

Justification by faith is thus defined : 'It is a Justification by which a man, who is a sinner, yet a believer, being placed before the throne of grace, which is erected in Christ Jesus the Propitiation, is accounted and pronounced by God, the just and merciful Judge, righteous and worthy of the reward of righteousness, not in himself, but in Christ,—of grace, according to the Gospel,—to the praise of the righteousness and grace of God, and to the salvation of the justified person himself.'—Vol. i. 598.

These two methods of Justification are thus contrasted : 'It belongs to these two forms of Justification . . . to be so adverse, as to render it impossible for both of them at once to meet together in one subject ; for he who is justified by the law, neither is capable, nor requires, to be justified by faith ; and it is evident that the man who is justified by faith, could not have been justified by the law. . . . They cannot be reconciled with each other, either by an unconfused union, or by admixture. For they are perfectly simple forms, and separated in an individual point, so that by the addition of a single atom, a transition is made from the one to the other. . . . A man must be justified by the one or the other of them, otherwise he will fall from righteousness, and therefore from life.'—Vol. i. 599.

From these premises his conclusion is, 'That Justification, when used for the act of a judge, is either—purely the imputation of righteousness, through mercy, from the throne of grace in Christ the Propitiation, made to a sinner, but who is a believer,—or that man is justified before God, of debt, according to the rigour of justice, without any forgiveness.'— Vol. i. 599.

He considers Justification as an act both of Justice and Mercy. 'Justification is a just and gracious act of God, by which, from the throne of His grace and mercy, He absolves from his sins, man, a sinner, but who is a believer, on account of Christ, and the obedience and righteousness of Christ, and considers him righteous, to the salvation of the justified person, and to the glory of divine righteousness and grace.'— Vol. ii. 116.

He considers it as an act of Justice, as well as of Grace, because it is founded on a Satisfaction. 'We say that it is the act of God as a Judge who . . . contained Himself within the bounds of justice, which He demonstrated by two methods,—first, because God would not justify, except as Justification was preceded by reconciliation and satisfaction, made through Christ in His blood ; secondly, because He would not justify any except those who acknowledged their sins and believed in

Christ. Yet it is "a gracious and merciful act"—not with respect to
Christ, as if the Father, through grace, as distinguished from strict and
legal justice, had accepted the obedience of Christ for righteousness,—
but with respect to us, both because God, through His gracious mercy
toward us, has made Christ to be sin for us, and righteousness to us, that
we might be the righteousness of God in Him; and because He has
placed communion with Christ in the faith of the Gospel, and has set
forth Christ as a propitiation through faith.'—Vol. ii. 117.

He describes Christ's righteousness as being both the meritorious and
the material cause of Justification. 'The meritorious cause of Justification is Christ through His obedience and righteousness, who may, therefore, be justly called the principal or outwardly moving cause. In His
obedience and righteousness, Christ is also the material cause of our
Justification, so far as God bestows Christ on us for righteousness, and
imputes His righteousness and obedience to us. In regard to this twofold cause, that is, the meritorious and the material, we are said to be
constituted righteous through the obedience of Christ.'—*Ibid.*

The imputation of faith for righteousness, in the sense in which he
held it, was not supposed to be incompatible with the imputation of
Christ's obedience, or proposed as a substitute for it. He includes both,
when he speaks of 'the gracious reckoning of God, by which He imputes to us the righteousness of Christ, and imputes faith to us for
righteousness,—that is, He remits our sins to us who are believers, on
account of Christ apprehended by faith, and accounts us righteous in
Him.'—Vol. ii. 118; also p. 474, quoted in the Lectures.

These extracts may suffice to show both what the doctrine of Arminius
was, and also how widely many who are called by his name have departed
from it in modern times.

See Arminius, 'Opera,' 4to, or in English, 2 vols. 8vo, translated by
James Nichols, and a third vol., translated by Rev. W. R. Bagnall, of the
Method. Episc. Church, American Edition, 1853. The passages quoted
occur vol. i. p. 263, vol. ii. p. 474. Episcopius, 'Opera Theol.,' two vols.
in one, containing his 'Institutiones' and 'Tractatus,' 1650. He was
prevented by death from completing his 'Institutiones,' and has no full
discussion of Justification, but refers to it in several places, vol. i. pp. 272,
437, ii. p. 412. Curcellæus, 'Quaternio,' a reply to Maresius, 1659,
art. iv. 'De hominis per Fidem et per Opera Justificatione,' pp. 403-
435. Limborch, 'System of Divinity,' 2 vols., London, 1713, vol. i.
pp. 226, 299, ii. p. 835. Amesius, 'Contra Remonstrantes,' Amsterdam,
1658 and 1661, 2 vols., containing 'Coronis ad Collationem Hagiensem,'
and 'Antisynodalia Scripta.' These contain a full discussion of the 'Five
Points,' which have an important, although indirect, bearing on the
question of Justification. 'Acta Synodi Nationalis Dordrechti Habitæ, '
Pref. pp. vii. xi. It appears that Arminius was supposed to differ more
from the Reformers on the subject of Justification, than appears from his
published writings. ' Gomarus probaturum se suscepit, de primario fidei

inostræ Articulo,—de Justificatione, scilicet, hominis coram Deo—sententiam eam docuisse, quæ cum verbo Divino atque Ecclesiarum Belgicarum confessione pugnaret. Ad cujus rei probationem, ipsissima ejus verba protulit, ex ejusdem Arminii autographo descripta, quibus asseruit, in hominis coram Deo justificatione, justitiam Christi, non imputare in justitiam, verùm ipsam fidem. Credere, per graciosam Dei *acceptationem*, esse justitiam illam nostram quâ coram Deo justificamur.'—P. vii. ' Quoniam verò is (articulus) qui erat de Justificatione, mâgis videretur necessarius, ab isto exordiendum, Gomarus putabat; quod et Illust. Ordinibus placuit. De hoc articulo eadem fuit controversia, quæ autem coram suprema Curia agitata fuerat; An, scilicet, fides, qua actus est, secundum gratiosam Dei æstimationem, sit ipsa justitia quâ coram Deo justificamur.'—P. xi. See also Vedelius, ' De Arcanis Arminianismi' (1631). Mr. Pemble (of Oxford) says, ' Arminius, as in other his opinions, so in the publishing of this, used much closeness, and cunning conveyance.'— *Vindiciæ Fidei*, p. 34.

Note 13, p. 175.

On the history and doctrines of the Protestant Church in France, see Quick's ' Synodicon,' and Smedley's ' History ;' Gale's ' Court of the Gentiles,' vol. ii. pp. 143-147 ; Scott's ' Continuation of Milner's History,' vol. ii. p. 471 ; Hickman's ' Animadversions on Heylyn's Quinquarticular Controversy,' pp. 383 ; Rev. James Young's ' Life of John Welsh, (1866), pp. 293-366 ; ' Miscellanies of the Wodrow Society,' vol. i. p. 559, where Welsh's Letter is given in the original French, and is more full than in the English translation. Tilenus was answered by P. Du Moulin, the author of ' Anatome Arminianismi,' in the ' Enodatio' of the Five Points, a ' Lettre contre Tilenus aux Ministres de France' in 1613 ; and in a larger work, not published, but still preserved at Geneva, entitled, ' Examen de la Doctrine de Tilenus.'—*Rev. J. Young's Life of John Welsh*, p. 365. Tilenus became so identified with Arminianism, that his name was used as the title to a controversial piece in England during the controversy there, ' The Examination of Tilenus before the Triers,' 1658.

Note 14, p. 177.

See Dr. Tobias Crisp's 'Christ Alone Exalted,' or 'Fifty-two Sermons,' edited with notes by Dr. Gill, 2 vols. 1755. On the combined influence of *Arminianism* and *New Methodism* on the Theology of England at this time, the late Dr. M'Crie gave the following opinion : ' I have thought I perceived a change in the tone and phraseology of the Reformed divines early in the seventeenth century, perhaps from the influence which the Arminian controversy exerted on the strain of Calvinistic writing. . . . I am inclined to think that an engrossing attention to the points controverted by Arminius and his followers was produced, and that preachers and practical writers became more shy than formerly in using the universal terms employed in Scripture, in proposing the Gospel remedy, and that they were more *hampered* (to use an expressive Scots word) than was necessary, either from the word of God, or their own declared principles concerning particular redemption, in proclaiming the glad tidings of salvation to sinners, and in calling on them to believe on the Saviour. . . .' ' The scheme of the New Methodists, as they were called, in France, who, about the middle of the seventeenth century, attempted a species of conciliation between Calvinists and Arminians on the head of election, and the extent of the death of Christ, added to the embarrassment,—which was still more increased by the Antinomianism of the Cromwellian period, to which you (the late Dr. Watson of Burntisland) justly refer as producing a partial revulsion from evangelical doctrine. This, as well as a passion for accommodating differences, led the excellent Baxter astray.'—*Life of Dr. M'Crie*, by his Son, pp. 329-331. See also *Dr. Cunningham, Hist. Theology*, ii. 47-49.

See Rev. Robert Traill's ' Vindication of the Protestant Doctrine of Justification from the unjust charge of Antinomianism,' Works, vol. i. pp. 304-359,—an admirable treatise.

Note 15, p. 178.

The Neonomian controversy was extremely voluminous on both sides. The following works may be consulted :—'Dr. Dan. Williams' Works' (1750),—vol. iii. ' Gospel Truth Stated,' a reply to Dr. Crisp ; vol. iv. contains various replies to objectors ; vol. v. ' An End to Discord ;' vol. vi. some of his pieces in Latin, entitled, ' Tractatus Selecti,'—viz. ' Veritas Evangelica,' in reply to Dr. Crisp, and 'De Justificatione per Christi Obedientiam.' John Goodwin, 'The Banner of Justification Displayed,' reprinted in 1835, by Thomas Jackson, in the same volume with Goodwin's ' Exposition of ix. c. Romans,' pp. 363-437. And a larger work, entitled, ' Imputatio Fidei ' (1642) ; ' A Treatise of Justification, wherein the Imputation of Faith for Righteousness is explained, etc.,' in 2 Parts, pp. 440 ; with a defence of it in reply to George Walker, pp. 161. Isaac Chauncy, ' Neonomianism Unmasked,' or ' The Antient Gospel pleaded against the New Law or Gospel,' in reply to Dr. D. Williams, ' Gospel Truth Stated ' (1692), and also his ' Alexipharmacon, a Fresh Antidote against Neonomian Bane,' in reply to Mr. Humphrey and Mr. Sam. Clark, 1700. Richard Baxter on ' Justifying Righteousness,' a volume in which five pieces on the subject are contained in reply to Dr. Tully and Mr. Cartwright. Dr. Tully, ' Justificatio Paulina, sine Operibus, ex mente Ecclesiæ Anglicanæ omniumque reliquarum Reform. contra nuperos Novatores,' Oxf. 1677. Mr. Brown (of Wamphray), ' Life of Justification Opened ;' this is peculiarly valuable, as containing several chapters devoted to the examination of the treatises of John Goodwin, c. vii-xii. pp. 57-181, and of Richard Baxter, c. xiii.-xvi. pp. 182-246.

Several other treatises might be mentioned, such as John Eaton, ' The Honeycombe of Free Justification by Christ alone ;' William Eyre, ' Vindiciæ Justificationis Gratuitæ,' or ' Justification without Conditions,'

1654, in reply to Woodbridge and Baxter; Benjamin Woodbridge, 'The Method of Grace in the Justification of Sinners,' in reply to W. Eyre, 1656; J. Crandon, Reply to R. Baxter's 'Aphorisms of Justification' (1654), in two parts, pp. 389 and 298. The author is indebted to Rev. John Laing, of the New College Library, for bringing under his notice the treatises of Woodbridge and Eyre.

An admirable review of the whole controversy will be found in Witsius, 'Miscel. Sac.' vol. ii. 'Animadversiones Irenicæ de Controversiis quæ, sub infaustis Nominibus Neonomorum et Antinomorum, nunc in Britannia agitantur,' pp. 753-849, and a shorter review of it in English, in Dickinson's 'Familiar Letters,' Lett. 13, pp. 206-237.

Note 16, p. 181.

See Wesley's 'Sermons,' and his 'Letter to Hervey,' Hervey's Works, vol. iv. pp. v. xviii. 52-71; Richard Watson's 'Theolog. Institutes,' c. xxiii. xxiv., Works, vol. xi. pp. 167-272; Rev. John Walker (Dublin), 'Expository Address to the Methodists,' 1802, and his 'Seven Letters to Alexander Knox, Esq.,' in defence of it; Southey, 'Life of John Wesley,' 2 vols., 1858, containing S. T. Coleridge's Notes on it, and Knox's 'Letter to Southey;' Fletcher (of Madeley), Works, 2 vols. (1834), containing his 'Five Checks to Antinomianism,' vol. i. pp. 115-444; 'An Equal Check to Pharisaism and Antinomianism,' vol. i. pp. 473-490; 'The Last Check to Antinomianism,' vol. ii. pp. 1-178; and many other pieces.

Note 17, p. 182.

For the early history of the Moravians, see 'Alregé de l'Histoire des Eglises Esclavonnes, etc.,' par le Baron de Sekendorf, 1794. For the tenets of the later Moravians, see Spangenberg, 'Exposition of Christian Doctrine' (1784), on Justification, p. 256; Southey, 'Life of J. Wesley,' vol. i. pp. 110, 117, 120, 125, 138, 166, etc.; Dickinson's 'Familiar Letters,' Lett. xi. pp. 154-180.

Some seem to have differed from others in the statement of their views. One of their number — Christian David — said at Herrnhutt, 'You must be humbled before God; you must have "a broken and a contrite heart:" but observe, this is not the foundation; it is not this by which you are justified. This is not the righteousness,—it is no part of the righteousness,—by which you are reconciled unto God. . . . The right foundation is not your contrition,—not your righteousness,—nothing of your own; nothing that is wrought *in* you by the Holy Ghost; but it is something *without you*,—the righteousness and the blood of Christ.' But another,—Peter Boehler,—taught, that when a man has a living faith in Christ, he is justified,—that this living faith is always given in a moment,—that in that moment he has peace with God,—that he cannot have this peace without knowing that he has it,—that being born of God, he sinneth not,—and that he cannot have this deliverance from sin without knowing it.' Zinzendorf, in his discourses on the 'Redemption of Man,' seems to teach the doctrine of universal pardon, and to regard faith as consisting in believing this, and applying it to ourselves; while he often speaks lightly of the obligations of duty, and rejects everything like self-denial. Spangenberg gives little prominence to the doctrine of Justification, and treats of it as if it were merely 'the forgiveness of sins, for the sake of the blood and death of Christ.'

NOTE 18, p. 188.

That we have given a correct account, in substance, of the nature of that assurance for which the 'Marrow' divines contended as being involved in the essence of faith, and that their doctrine was, in this respect, in harmony with that of the first Reformers, appears from their own explicit statement. They say that 'the Assembly had in effect excluded from faith that act by which a person *appropriates* to himself what before lay *in common in the Gospel offer*, and thereby turned it into "that general and doubtsome faith" abjured in our National Covenant;' and they state their belief, that 'receiving and resting upon Christ for salvation implies that assurance, by which it had been customary for divines to describe the fiducial act, or appropriating persuasion of faith; and that the Confession doth not exclude all assurance from the essence of faith, but speaks of that kind of assurance which is complex, and contains not only what is included in the direct act of faith, but also what arises from spiritual sensation and rational argumentation.'

The 'Marrow of Modern Divinity,' with notes by Boston. Dr. M'Crie's papers in the 'Christian Instructor,' 'Account of the Controversy respecting the Marrow of Modern Divinity,' (1831) vol. xxx. No. 253, pp. 539-551, 687-699, 811-826; (1832) vol. xxxi. pp. 73-94. It is to be regretted that this valuable series of papers has not been reprinted in his Miscellaneous Writings. See also 'Life of Dr. M'Crie,' pp. 330-334. Rev. Eben. Erskine, 'The Assurance of Faith;' reprinted in a volume entitled, 'Saving Faith, as Laid Down in the Word of God,' along with the 'Scripture Doctrine of the Appropriation which is in the Nature of Saving Faith,' by John Anderson, D.D., Pennsylvania, and 'Aphorisms concerning the Assurance of Faith,' by William Cudworth, of Norwich (Edinburgh, 1843). Rev. John Brown (Whitburn), 'Gospel Truth.' 'Memoirs of Thomas Boston,' pp. 291-298, 303-307. Fraser, 'Life of Ebenezer Erskine,' p. 528. Principal Hadow, 'Antinomianism of the Marrow of Modern Divinity Detected,' in a volume (1721) in the Advocates' Library, which came from the library of Wodrow, the historian; and which contains also 'The Politick Disputant,' the Act of Assembly 1720, the 'Representation by the Twelve Ministers,' and 'Dialogues' on the Controversy by James Hog of Carnock. For the use of this volume, and of several others, the author is indebted to the courtesy of Mr. Halkett and Mr. Dickson, of the Advocates' Library.

Note 19, p. 190.

See Sandeman's ' Letters on Theron and Aspasio,' 2 vols. 8vo, 4th Ed., Edin. 1803 ; Andrew Fuller's ' Strictures on Sandemanianism ;' Ecking's ' Essays ;' Archibald M'Lean (Edinb.), ' Works,' vol. i. pp. 359-418, ii. pp. 1-170, 313-388 ; Thomas Erskine (Linlathen), ' Essay on Faith,' and ' Unconditional Freeness of the Gospel ;' Richard Watson's ' Review of Erskine's Essay on Faith,' ' Works,' vol. vii. pp. 200-224 ; Joseph Bellamy, ' Letters and Dialogues between Theron, Paulinus, and Aspasio,' and ' True Religion Delineated ;' Dr. John Erskine (Edinb.), ' Theological Dissertations,' D. iii. pp. 139-199.

Note 20, p. 190.

See Dr. Hodge ' On the Epistle to the Romans ;' three valuable papers on the Doctrine of Imputation in the Princeton ' Theological Essays,' 1st Series, pp. 128-217, 285-307 ; Dr. E. Bennett Tyler, ' Letters on the Newhaven Theology ;' Crocker's ' Catastrophe of the Presbyterian Church in 1837 ;' ' Outlines of Theology,' by Rev. A. A. Hodge, edited by Dr. Goold (London, 1863),—On ' Justification,' pp. 388-404.

NOTES TO LECTURE VII.

Note 1, p. 193.

Dr. Cunningham, Preface to ' Bishop Stillingfleet's Reply to Gother,' p. 37. Bishop Gibson's ' Preservative ' has recently been reprinted in a more portable form, 9 vols. 8vo, edited by Dr. John Cumming of London.

Note 2, p. 194.

Alexander Knox, Esq., ' Remains,' vol. i. pp. 263-281, 347-355, iii. pp. 51, 55, 85 ; ' Correspondence with Bishop Jebb,' vol. i. p. 349 ; Dr. Newman, ' Tract No. xc.,' recently reprinted, with a commendatory preface by Dr. Pusey ; and ' Lectures on Justification.' See also G. S. Faber, ' Primitive Doctrine of Justification,' pp. 68, 71, 79.

Note 3, p. 195.

Dr. John Kaye (Bishop of Lincoln), ' Charges,' 1854, p. 247. See also Hickman's ' Animadversions on Heylyn,' p. 510. ' The whole question relates to a *matter of fact*. In this history we search, not what ought to be held, but what hath been held,—not of what mind our Reformers should have been, but of what they were. If Calvinism be truth, it will be truth, though it had never found entertainment in the Church

of England; if it be error, it will be error, though all the Church of
England be for it: for the Church cannot make truth, it can only declare
what is truth and falsehood.'

<h3 style="text-align:center">NOTE 4, p. 196.</h3>

See Augustus Toplady's 'Historical Calvinism of the Church of
England,' 2 vols. 8vo; The 'British Reformers,' 12 vols., London Tract
Society; The 'Parker Society's' publications, 55 vols., including the
'Zurich Letters,' which show how close was the connection between the
English and Swiss divines; William Prynne, 'Anti-Arminianism, or the
Church of England's Old Antithesis to New Arminianism,' small 4to, 2d
Ed. 1630; Dr. P. Heylyn's 'History of the Quinquarticular Controversy
in the Church of England,' Tracts, folio, 1673, pp. 501-639; Hick-
man's 'Animadversions' on Heylyn's History, 8vo, 1673. Hickman's
conclusion is thus stated: 'That is not the doctrine of the Church of
England, which, for above threescore years after her first establishment,
was not averred in any one licensed book, but confuted in many.'—P. 522.
See also 'Conferences of the Reformers and Divines of the Early English
Church on the Doctrines of the Oxford Tractarians,' held in the Province
of Canterbury in 1841; on Justification, pp. 185-224.

<h3 style="text-align:center">NOTE 5, p. 197.</h3>

See Lecture v. Note 7. Melancthon, 'In Epistolam ad Romanos,' 1532,
pp. 12-42; P. Martyr, 'Commentaries on Epistle to Romans,' in English,
folio, 1558, pp. 367-410, in black letter.

<h3 style="text-align:center">NOTE 6, p. 198.</h3>

Some use has been made of *two* facts in opposition to this view,—
first, the fact that the Lambeth Articles (1595) were not adopted by the
Church of England, although they were incorporated in the Articles of
the Church of Ireland by Archbishop Usher, 1615; and secondly, that
when the English Articles were submitted for revision to the Westminster Assembly, a proposal was made to render them more explicit
on some points. The Lambeth Articles are given in Ford's 'Ecclesiæ
Anglicanæ Articuli xxxix,' 1720, p. 411, and Neale's 'History of Puritans,' vol. iii. p. 520; and the reason of their non-adoption by the Church
of England is discussed in Heylyn's 'Quinquarticular History,' c. xxii.
p. 628, and Hickman's 'Animadversions on Heylyn's History,' p. 511.
The alterations on the Articles suggested by the Westminster Divines,
are given in the 'Harmony of Confessions,' by P. Hall, and in Neale's
'History of the Puritans,' vol. v. p. 519.

<h3 style="text-align:center">NOTE 7, p. 199.</h3>

John Fox, 'Of Free Justification by Christ, written against the
Osorian Righteousness, and other Patrons of the same doctrine of Inherent Righteousness,' 1583,—reprinted in an abridged form in the

'British Reformers,' 1831 ; Osorio, 'De Justitia,' Opera, tom. ii. pp. 186-456 ; Bishop Davenant, 'Disputatio de Justitia Habituali et Actuali,' translated by Allport; Downham (of Derry), 'Treatise of Justification ;' Bishop Barlow, 'Two Letters concerning Justification by Faith only,' reprinted by Rev. C. Bickersteth, 1828, Bishop Barlow's 'Genuine Remains,' p. 578; Wm. Pemble, M.A. of Magdalen Hall, Oxford, 'Vindiciæ Fidei,' or 'a Treatise of Justification by Faith,' 2d Edition, 1629 ; Bishop Andrewes, Sermon on the 'Lord our Righteousness,' Library of Anglo-Catholic Theology ; and Hooker's Sermon on 'Justification,' Works, vol. ii. pp. 601-653.

The 11th Article is entitled of 'the Justification of man ;' and this title, viewed in connection with the first sentence, shows clearly that the term Justification is used in a forensic, and not in a moral, sense. For 'the Justification of man' is described as consisting in this, that 'we are accounted righteous before God, only for the merit of our Lord and Saviour Jesus Christ, by faith, and not for our own works or deservings. Wherefore,' it is added, 'that we are justified by Faith only, is a most wholesome doctrine, and very full of comfort, as more largely is expressed in the Homily of Justification.' It is not said that we are made righteous inherently or by infusion, but that 'we are accounted righteous before God ;' and this 'only for the merit of Christ,'—His merit being the sole ground and reason of our being 'accounted righteous,' and 'faith' being merely the instrument by which we receive a saving interest in it. 'Our own works or deservings' are entirely excluded from the ground of our Justification : both our works done before Faith, and after Faith, for they are distinctly specified in the 12th and 13th Articles. Of the one it is said, 'Works done before the grace of Christ and the inspiration of His Spirit, are not pleasant to God, forasmuch as they spring not of faith in Jesus Christ, neither do they make men meet to receive grace, or (as the School authors say) deserve grace of congruity ; yea, rather, for that they are not done as God hath willed and commanded them to be done, we doubt not but they have the nature of sin.' Of the other, it is said, 'that Good Works which are the fruits of Faith, and follow after Justification, cannot put away our sins, and endure the severity of God's judgment ;' while the reason of this latter statement is given in the 9th Article, 'Although there is no condemnation for them that believe and are baptized, yet the Apostle doth confess, that concupiscence and lust hath of itself the nature of sin ;' and in the 15th, 'All we, although baptized, and born again in Christ, yet offend in many things ; and if we say we have no sin, we deceive ourselves, and the truth is not in us.'

In the 'Homily of Salvation' (Homilies, Oxford Edition, 1822, pp. 25-36) the same doctrine is more fully, and very clearly, stated. 'Because all men be sinners and offenders against God, and breakers of His law and commandments, therefore can no man, by his own acts, works, and deeds, (seem they never so good,) be justified, and made righteous before God ;

but every man of necessity is constrained to seek for another righteousness or justification, to be received at God's own hands, that is to say, the forgiveness of his sins and trespasses, in such things as he hath offended. And this justification or righteousness, which we so receive of God's mercy and Christ's merits, embraced by faith, is taken, accepted, and allowed of God, for our perfect and full justification.' . . . 'God sent His only Son our Saviour, Christ, into this world, to fulfil the law for us, and, by shedding of His most precious blood, to make a sacrifice and satisfaction, or (as it may be called) amends to His Father for our sins, to assuage His wrath and indignation conceived against us for the same.' . . . 'He provided a ransom for us, that was, the most precious body and blood of His own most dear and best beloved Son Jesu Christ, who, besides this ransom, fulfilled the law for us perfectly.' . . . 'The Apostle toucheth specially three things which must go together in our justification.—Upon God's part, His great mercy and grace ;—upon Christ's part, justice, that is, the satisfaction of God's justice, or the price of our redemption, by the offering of His body and shedding of His blood, with fulfilling of the law perfectly and throughly ;—and upon our part, true and lively faith in the merits of Jesus Christ.' . . . 'St. Paul declareth nothing upon the behalf of man concerning his justification, but only a true and lively faith, which nevertheless is the gift of God, and not man's only work, without God. And yet that faith doth not shut out repentance, hope, love, dread, and the fear of God, to be joined with faith in every man that is justified; but it shutteth them out from *the office of justifying.* So that, although they be all present together in him that is justified, yet they justify not altogether.' . . . 'Christ is now the righteousness of all them that truly do believe in Him. He for them paid their ransom by His death. He for them fulfilled the law in His life.' . . . 'The sum of all Paul's disputation is this : that if justice come of works, then it cometh not of grace ; and if it come of grace, then it cometh not of works.' . . . 'This saying—that we be justified by faith only, freely, and without works—is spoken to take away clearly all merit of our works, as being unable to deserve our justification at God's hands, . . . and therefore (or thereby, marginal reading) wholly to ascribe the merit and deserving of our justification unto Christ only, and His most precious blood-shedding. This faith the Holy Scripture teacheth us ; this is the strong rock and foundation of Christian religion ; this doctrine all old and ancient authors of Christ's Church do approve ; this doctrine advanceth and setteth forth the true glory of Christ, and beateth down the vain-glory of man ; this whosoever denieth, is not to be accounted for a Christian man, nor for a setter-forth of Christ's glory,—but for an adversary to Christ, and His Gospel, and for a setter-forth of men's vain-glory.' . . . 'Justification is not the office of man, but of God; for man cannot make himself righteous by his own works, neither in whole nor in part ; . . . but justification is the office of God only, and is not a thing which we render unto Him, but which we receive of Him,—not which we give to Him, but which we take of Him, by His free mercy, and by the only merits of His most dearly beloved Son, our only Redeemer, Saviour, and Justifier, Jesus Christ. So that the true understanding of this doctrine,—we be justified freely by faith, without works,—or, that we be justified by faith in Christ only,—is not, that this our own act to believe in Christ, or this our faith in Christ, which is within us, doth justify us, and deserve (or merit) our justification unto us, (for that were to count ourselves to be justified by some act or virtue that is within ourselves;) but the true understanding and meaning thereof is, that although we hear God's word and believe it; although we have faith, hope, charity, repentance, dread, and fear of God within us, and do never so many works thereunto,—yet we must renounce the merit of all our said virtues—of faith, hope, charity, and all other virtues and good deeds, which we either have done, shall do, or can do, as things that be far too weak and insufficient and imperfect, to deserve remission of our sins, and our justification ; and therefore we must trust only in God's mercy, and that sacrifice which our High Priest and Saviour Jesus Christ, the Son of God, once offered for us upon the cross.' . . . ' As St. John Baptist, although he were never so virtuous and godly a man, yet, in this matter of forgiving of sin, he did put the people from him, and appointed them unto Christ, saying, " Behold the Lamb of God which taketh away the sins of the world;' even so, as great and as godly a virtue as the lively Faith is, yet it putteth us from itself, and remitteth or appointeth us unto Christ, for to have only by Him remission of our sins, or justification. So that our faith in Christ (as it were) saith unto us— It is not I that take away your sins, but it is Christ only; and to Him only I send you for that purpose, forsaking therein all your good virtues, words, thoughts, and works, and only putting your trust in Christ.' . . . ' We be justified by faith in Christ only, (according to the meaning of the old ancient authors,) is this—We put our faith in Christ, that we be justified by Him only,—that we be justified by God's free mercy, and the merits of our Saviour Christ only,—and by no virtue, or good works of our own, which is in us, or that we can be able to have, or to do, for to deserve the same ; Christ Himself only being the cause meritorious thereof.'

Some stanch Churchmen oppose the doctrine of their own Articles from inadvertence. Wesley had said, ' I was fundamentally a Papist, and knew it not; but I do now testify to all . . . that *no good works can be done before Justification, none which have not in them the nature of sin.*' Southey says, ' This doctrine, however, was not preached in all the naked absurdity of its consequences ;' and Coleridge quietly appends this note,— ' Did Robert Southey remember that the words in italics are faithfully copied from the Articles of our Church ?'—*Southey's Life of Wesley*, vol. i. p. 175.

The leading divines of the Church of England were all but unanimous in teaching the same doctrine on the subject of Justification, for more than a hundred years after the Reformation. Thus Cranmer : ' What-

soever God hath commanded in the ten commandments, which we have
not fulfilled because we all are sinners, that Christ Himself hath fulfilled
for us; and whatsoever punishment we have deserved to suffer of God
for our sins and offences, that Christ hath taken upon Himself, and
suffered for us. . . . By our lively faith in Him, our sins are forgiven
us, and we are reconciled unto the favour of God, made holy and righteous.
For then God no more imputes to us our former sins; but He imputes
and gives unto us the justice and righteousness of His Son Jesus Christ,
who suffered for us.'   Bishop Andrewes, High Churchman as he was,
preached the same doctrine, in his celebrated sermon on 'This is the
name whereby He shall be called, Jehovah our Righteousness;' as did
many more of the ablest divines of the Church of England, who were
called, in their protracted controversy with Rome, to discuss the whole
question of Justification, in opposition to the arguments and evasions of
such writers as Bellarmine and Stapleton.   We give only two specimens
—the one from the writings of the 'judicious' Hooker, the other from
those of the saintly Bishop Beveridge.   That Hooker had a leaning
towards the sacramental doctrine of Justification is manifest from the
general scope of his 'Ecclesiastical Polity;' but, however this may affect
his personal consistency, it serves, in some respects, to make his testimony
all the more striking, when he speaks of 'the righteousness' by which
alone a sinner can be justified, in the following emphatic terms:—
'"Doubtless," saith the Apostle (Phil. iii. 8), "I have counted all things
loss, and I do judge them to be dung, that I may win Christ, and be
found in Him, not having mine own righteousness, but that which is
through the faith of Christ, the righteousness which is of God through
faith."   Whether they (the Romish divines) speak of the first or second
justification, they make the essence of it a divine quality inherent,—
they make it righteousness which is in us.   If it be in us, then it is
ours, as our souls are ours, though we have them from God, and can
hold them no longer than pleaseth Him.   But the righteousness
wherein we must be found, if we will be justified, is not our own;
therefore we cannot be justified by any inherent quality.   Christ hath
merited righteousness for as many as are found in Him.   In Him God
findeth us, if we be faithful; for by faith, we are incorporated into
Him.   Then, although in ourselves we be altogether sinful and unrighteous, yet even the man which in himself is impious, full of iniquity,
full of sin, him, being found in Christ through faith, and having his sin
in hatred through repentance, him God beholdeth with a gracious eye,
putteth away his sin by not imputing it, taketh quite away the punishment due thereunto, by pardoning it; and accepteth him in Jesus Christ,
as perfectly righteous, as if he had fulfilled all that is commanded him in
the law.   Shall I say more perfectly righteous than if himself had fulfilled the whole law?   I must take heed what I say; but the apostle
saith, 'God made Him which knew no sin, to be sin for us, that we might
be made the righteousness of God in Him.'   Such we are in the sight

of God the Father, as is the very Son of God Himself. Let it be counted folly, or phrensy, or fury, or whatsoever. It is our wisdom, and our comfort; we care for no knowledge in the world but this,—that man hath sinned, and God hath suffered; that God hath made Himself the sin of men, and that men are made " the righteousness of God."—*Hooker, Works*, Oxford Ed. 1845, vol. ii. p. 606. He says again in regard to our evangelical righteousness: 'There is a glorifying righteousness of men in the world to come, and there is a justifying and a sanctifying righteousness here. The righteousness wherewith we shall be clothed in the world to come is both perfect and inherent. That whereby here we are justified is perfect, but not inherent. That whereby we are sanctified, inherent, but not perfect.' . . . 'You see, therefore, that the Church of Rome, in teaching Justification by inherent grace, doth pervert the truth of Christ, and that by the hands of His Apostles we have received otherwise than she teacheth. . . . St. Paul doth plainly sever these two parts of Christian righteousness one from the other . . . "the righteousness of Justification," and "the righteousness of Sanctification."'—Vol. ii. pp. 603, 606, 607.

'I believe,' says Bishop Beveridge ('Private Thoughts,' Art. viii. pp. 69, 70, 73), 'that my person is only justified by the merit of Christ imputed to me. . . .'. It is a matter of admiration to me, how any one, that pretends to the use of his reason, can imagine, that he should be accepted before God for what comes from himself. For how is it possible that I should be justified by good works, when I can do no good works' at all before I be first justified? My works cannot be accepted as good, until my person be so; nor can my person be accepted by God, till first ingrafted into Christ. . . . I look upon " all my righteousness as filthy rags ; " and it is in the robes only of the righteousness of the Son of God that I dare appear before the Majesty of heaven. The Son, assuming our nature into His deity, becomes subject and obedient both to the moral and ceremonial laws of His Father, and at last to death itself, " even the death of the cross." In the one He paid an active, in the other a passive, obedience; and so did not only fulfil the will of His Father, in obeying what He had commanded, but satisfied His justice in suffering the punishment due to us for the transgressing of it. . . . This obedience, being more than Christ was bound to, and only performed upon the account of those whose nature He had assumed—as we, by faith, lay hold upon it,—so God, through grace, imputes it to us, as if it had been performed by us in our own persons. And hence it is that, as Christ is said to be "made sin for us," so we are said to be "made righteousness in Him" (1 Cor. v. 21). But what righteousness? Our own? No, "the righteousness of God,"—radically His, but imputatively ours: and this is the only way whereby we are said to be made "the righteousness of God,"—even by the righteousness of Christ being made ours, by which we are accounted and reputed as righteous before God.'

Note 8, p. 199.

There is a marked difference in spirit and tone between the ' Considerationes Modestæ et Pacificæ Controversiarum de Justificatione,' etc. etc., of Bishop William Forbes of Edinburgh, in reply to Bellarmine, and the ' Free Justification by Christ' of John Fox, in reply to Bishop Osorio. The ' Considerationes' have been reprinted in Latin and English in the ' Library of Anglo-Catholic Theology,' in 2 vols., Oxford, 1850 and 1856. The first volume is entirely on the subject of Justification, and is entitled in English, ' A Fair and Calm Consideration of the Modern Controversy concerning Justification, as it is explained in the Five Books of Cardinal Bellarmine.' It is an able and learned work, but, on several testing questions, indicates a greater leaning to the Popish, than the Protestant, doctrine. The volume extends to 500 pp., one half being occupied with the original Latin, the other with the English version, printed on alternate pages. The author gratefully acknowledges his obligation to Mr. Small, of the University Library, for the use of Bishop Forbes' work, and some treatises of Cardinal Cajetan. On Mœhler's work, see Lect. v. p. 145.

Note 9, p. 200.

See Lect. v. p. 145. Atterbury, writing against an ' Apologist' for Popery, strongly condemns what he calls ' the solifidian and fiduciary errors,' and seems to speak as if Rome had held, in substance, the same doctrine with the Reformers. ' Luther teaches that "faith alone" (fides sola justificat, sed non solitaria) justifies, but *not the faith that is alone ;* good works are inseparable attendants on this justifying faith, but they contribute nothing to the act of Justification ; they make not just, but are always with them that are made so. This is Luther's,—*was the Church of Rome's,*—and is now the Church of England's, doctrine.'—*Answer to some Considerations,* p. 17. Archbishop Wake, speaking of Bossuet's Exposition, says : ' Were these things clearly stated and distinguished the one from the other, the difference between us, considered only in idea, would not be very great : . . . if the doctrine of merit were understood as explained by Bossuet, there would be little to object to it ;'— and writing to Du Pin, he speaks as if there were little or no difference between the Anglican and Gallican Churches in point of doctrine, although Du Pin had put this interpretation on the eleventh Article—' We do not deny that we are justified by faith only in Christ, but by faith, charity, and good works conjoined, which are altogether necessary to salvation, as is acknowledged in the next Article.'—*Mosheim, History,* vol. vi. p. 94. Bishop Burnet, speaking of the difference between the statement of the Romish and Reformed doctrine, says : ' Yet, after all, it is but a question about words ; for if that which they call " remission" of sins be the same with that which we call " justification," and if that which they call " justification" be the same with that which we call " sanctification," then

there is only a strife of words.'—*Burnet's Exposition of Thirty-nine Articles,*
Art. xi. p. 151. Dr. Barrow goes so far as to say that, ' In the beginning
of the Reformation, . . . there did arise hot disputes about this point, and
the right stating thereof seemed a matter of great importance. . . .
Whereas yet, so far as I can discern, . . . there hardly doth appear any
material difference ; but all the questions depending, chiefly seem to consist about the manner of expressing things which all agree in. . . . Of
which questions, whatever the true resolution be, it cannot, methinks, be
of so great consequence—seeing all conspire in avowing the acts, whatever they be, meant by the word Justification, although in other terms ;
. . . whence those questions might well be waived as unnecessary grounds
of contention, and it might suffice to understand the points of doctrine
which it relateth to in other terms, laying that aside as ambiguous and
litigious.'—*Dr. Barrow, Sermons on the Creed,* Sermon v. ' Of Justification
by Faith,' *Works* in 8vo, edited by Hughes, 1831, vol. v. pp. 122, 124.
Archbishop Laurence, in his Bampton Lectures for 1820, made it his
object to show that the English Articles are not Calvinistic, and he tries
to obliterate the difference between the Romish and Lutheran doctrine of
Justification by affirming, that ' upon both sides, it is supposed entirely
to consist of the remission of sins' (p. 122). There is a double error
here ; for, in point of fact, it was not supposed on *either* side to consist
entirely in remission of sins. On the Popish side, it was held to consist
in remission and renovation ; on the Lutheran side, in remission and
acceptance as righteous in the sight of God ; and the very passages which
he quotes (p. 353) are sufficient to prove that Protestants contended for
Justification by *a righteousness imputed,* while Romanists contended for
Justification by *grace infused.* These extracts are sufficient to show that
the radical difference between the Romish and the Reformed doctrine on
the subject of Justification had come to be doubted or denied by many of
the leading divines of the Church of England.

NOTE 10, p. 201.

For an account of Barrett and Baro, see Prynne, 'Anti-Arminianism,'
p. 8 ; Heylyn, 'Quinquart. History,' pp. 614-624 ; Hickman's ' Animadversions on,' etc., pp. 502-508 ; Toplady's ' Historic Proof of the Doctrinal
Calvinism of the Church of England,' vol. ii. sec. xix. xx. pp. 213-380.

For an account of Bishop Montagu and his ' Appello Cæsarem,' see
the same authorities.

Bishop Carleton (of Chichester) published, in 1626, ' An Examination
of those things wherein the Author of the late " Appeal" holdeth the
Doctrines of the Pelagians and Arminians to be the Doctrines of the
Church of England ;' and in the second edition, ' revised and enlarged,'
there is annexed a ' joint Attestation, avowing that the discipline of the
Church of England was not impeached by the Synod of Dort,' which was
subscribed by Bishop Carleton, Bishop Davenant, Dr. Balcanqual, Dr.
Samuel Ward, Professor of Divinity at Cambridge, and Dr. Goad,—the

English deputies to that Synod. It relates chiefly to 'Discipline' or Church Government; but with reference to Doctrine they say, 'That whatsoever then was assented to, and subscribed by us, concerning the " Five Articles," either in the joint Synodical judgment, or in our particular collegiate suffrage (styled in the Acts of the Synod " Theolog. Mag. Britan. Sententia"), is not only warrantable by the Holy Scriptures, but also conformable to *the received doctrine of our* said venerable mother —the Church of England.' A very curious work appeared in 1626 at London, entitled, 'Parallelismus Novi-Antiqui Erroris Pelagi-Arminiani,' in which the old Pelagian and the new Arminian doctrines are exhibited in parallel columns. With a view to revive the old doctrines of the Church, Dr. John Edwards published in 1707 his work, entitled, 'Veritas Redux,' 'Evangelical Truths Restored,' pp. 558.

Note 11, p. 201.

Bishop Bull's 'Harmonia Apostolica,' and 'Examen Censuræ.' The first occasioned a keen controversy, by Gataker, Truman, Bishop Barlow, Tully, Tombes, Pitcairne, and others; see Nelson's 'Life of Bishop Bull,' pp. 89-265. Dr. Cave's 'Antiquitates Apostolicæ,' answered by Witsius, Misc. Sac. vol. ii. ; Bishop Hoadley's 'Terms of Acceptance.'

Bishop Bull represented faith, considered as a subjective grace, and the germ of holiness in heart and life, as the righteousness by which we are justified; which is in substance the Romish doctrine of Justification by grace infused and inherent, or by faith 'informed with charity,' and scarcely distinguishable from it even in form. As such, his work excited much opposition at the time of its publication; and his biographer says, 'There arose in the Church no small contention, whether this interpretation of Scripture were conformable to the Articles of Religion and the Homily of Justification therein referred to. Some maintained that it was; some doubted about it; and others downright denied it, and condemned it as heretical.' Bull himself tells us that 'tragical outcries' were raised against it, as if 'the very foundations both of Law and Gospel were hereby at once undermined and overturned;' and adds, 'but matters were come to that pass, that it was hardly safe for any one to interpret either the Articles of our Church, or even the Holy Scriptures themselves, otherwise than according to the standard of CALVIN'S INSTITUTIONS.' Yet so rapid and widespread was the dissemination of his views, that we find Dr. Samuel Clark affirming that 'the Bishop's explication of the doctrine of Justification is now as universally received as it was then contrary to the general opinion of divines,' and pleading this remarkable change as a reason why Arian subscription to the Articles should not be refused.— *Letter to Dr. Wells on Arian Subscription to the Articles*, pp. 76, 78.

Dr. Cave's work ('Antiquitates Apostolicæ,' answered by Witsius in four dissertations, 'De Controversiis ætate Apostolorum circa Justificationem,' Misc. Sac. ii. 668-751) is directed to show that the doctrine of Justification, as taught by the Apostles, excluded, under the name of works, only the ceremonial observances of the Mosaic law, from the ground of a sinner's pardon and acceptance with God; but did not exclude faith and its fruits,—or faith considered as the germ of all the Christian graces, and the spring of evangelical obedience; that this faith is the entire condition of the New Covenant, but not a special grace having a distinct and peculiar office or function, different from that of other graces, in our Justification, and that it is to be regarded as comprehensive of them all. This doctrine would have been accepted at Ratisbon and Trent.— Bishop Hoadley ('Terms of Acceptance with God,' 1727, p. 42; see also, pp. 180, 195, 200, 227, 252, 267, 316) represents the Gospel as a new law of works, differing from the first only in accepting sincere instead of perfect obedience, and in giving the assurance of pardon for all past sins on the fulfilment of the conditions which it prescribes. He speaks, as the Popish Church does, of a *first* justification which is bestowed on account of the merits of Christ, both on adults who had previously lived in heathenism, as soon as they professed faith in Him, and obedience to Him, as their Master; and also on all who are born within the Christian covenant, and educated in the Christian faith; and he speaks of a *final* justification at the last day, which will be founded entirely on the obedience which they have rendered to His law. The sins which were committed before baptism are pardoned through the sufferings and merits of Christ; and His people are further indebted to Him for having procured and promulgated a law which accepts sincere but imperfect obedience, while they must depend entirely on their own personal righteousness, and not on His finished work, as the ground of their ultimate salvation. In regard to post-baptismal sins,—or sins committed during their Christian profession, —no other provision seems to be made for their forgiveness except what may be found in their fulfilling the conditions of the new law. These conditions are, *first*, that they renounce and forsake their sins; *secondly*, that they practise. the contrary virtues; *thirdly*, that they forgive those who have injured them; and *fourthly*, that they make restitution, if they have been guilty of dishonesty and fraud: all of them duties of unquestionable obligation, but duties which belong to the life of sanctification, and which are here substituted in the place of Christ's atoning sacrifice and perfect righteousness, as the ground of their Justification.

NOTE 12, p. 203.

See Lect. vi. pp. 158, 176. Robert Traill's 'Vindication of the Protestant Doctrine;' Witsius, 'Animadversiones Irenicæ,' Misc. Sac. vol. ii.; M'Crie's 'Life of Dr. T. M'Crie,' p. 330; Dr. M'Crie in the 'Christian Instructor,' vol. xxxi. p. 541; Bishop Kaye's 'Charges,' pp. 244, 284.

NOTE 13, p. 204.

Scott's 'Continuation of Milner's History,' vol. i. pp. 42, 233.

Note 14, p. 204.

Archbishop Whately on 'The Errors of Romanism.' His own doctrine of Justification in his ' Essays on the Difficulties in the Writings of St. Paul,' Essay vi. pp. 170-198, affords only a fresh exemplification of the tendency of which he speaks. He wrote strongly against the doctrine of Imputed Righteousness: yet it is deeply interesting to learn from his daughter the state of his mind as he lay on his bed of sickness, expecting death. ' Now it was to be shown to all, how the same simple trust in Christ as the only Saviour, which had smoothed so many an humble deathbed, was to be the stay and staff of the mighty thinker and writer, while crossing the "valley of the shadow of death." He said, " Read me the 8th chapter of the Romans." When Dr. West had finished the chapter, he said, " Shall I read any more ? " " No, that is enough at a time ; there is a great deal for the mind to dwell on in that." He dwelt especially on the 32d verse, " He that spared not His own Son," etc. One of his friends had remarked, that " his great mind was supporting him ;" his answer,—most emphatically and earnestly given,—was, " No it is not that which supports me: it is FAITH IN CHRIST ; THE LIFE I LIVE, IS BY CHRIST ALONE." '—*Life of Archbishop Whately*, 2 vols., vol. ii, p. 414 (1866).

Note 15, p. 205.

Tract No. xc. was prepared by Dr. Newman, and directed to prove that the Articles are not distinctively Protestant, but might be subscribed by Catholics, perhaps by Roman Catholics. It treats of Justification under the 11th Art. p. 12 ; of Works before, and after, Justification, under the 12th and 13th, p. 14 ; of Purgatory, Pardons, etc., under the 22d, p. 23 ; of Masses, under the 31st, p. 59 ; of the Homilies, under the 35th, p. 66. It gave rise to a voluminous controversy ; and was strongly condemned by most of the Bishops,—see Bricknell, 'The Judgment of the Bishops upon Tractarian Theology,' extracted from Charges delivered from 1837 to 1842, Oxford, 1845, pp. 752. The charges of Bishop O'Brien are worthy of special notice.—This Tract has recently been reprinted, with a preface by Dr. Pusey ; and in his ' Eirenicon,'—a reply to Dr. Manning (1865),—he says, speaking of the Romish and English Churches, ' We both alike acknowledge our own unworthiness,—that His merits alone can stand between us and our sins ; both alike believe in the efficacy of His " most precious blood," wherewith He cleanseth us ; both in His perpetual intercession for us at the right hand of God. . . . I believe that we have the same doctrine of Grace, and of Justification. There is not one statement in the elaborate chapters on Justification in the Council of Trent which any of us could fail of receiving ; nor is there one of their anathemas on the subject, which in the least rejects any statement of the Church of England.'—P. 19.

Sancta Clara's ' Paraphrastica Expositio Articulorum Confessionis

Anglicanæ,' has been reprinted in Latin and English in 1865, and edited, in a handsome volume, by Rev. F. G. Lee, D.C.L. The doctrine of Justification is stated pp. 11-23, and pp. 39-43. There is prefixed the statement of 'The British Magazine,' that 'this remarkable treatise formed the basis of Mr. Newman's Tract No. xc.' It is reprinted avowedly to promote the 'high and holy object of Re-Union,' *i.e.* between the Anglican, Greek, and Romish, Churches; and in the advertisements which are appended, we find sufficient proofs of the earnestness and activity of an influential party with a view to that end, in the fact that a 'Union Review' has been established; that there is even a 'Union Review Almanack,'— that 'Prayers for the Re-Union of Christendom' have been compiled; —that a first, and second, 'Series of Sermons on the Re-Union of Christendom' have been published, and also 'Essays on the Re-Union of Christendom by Members of the Roman Catholic, Oriental, and Anglican Communions.' It may be hoped that this utopian project is not likely to be realised; but if it be frustrated, the result will be owing, not to any scruples on the part of its Anglo-Catholic promoters, so much as to the stedfastness with which the heads of the Romish and Greek Churches may adhere to their own distinctive principles. It has not hitherto been received favourably by either of these parties; and already Signor Gavazzi has raised his note of warning from Italy, under the title of 'No Union with Rome, being an answer to Dr. Pusey' (1866).

It has become fashionable, in some quarters, to laud the *comprehensiveness* of the Thirty-nine Articles, as if they had been framed on purpose to make the Church of England a huge ecclesiastical menagerie, that should afford accommodation to all sorts of men, whether their opinions be scriptural or unscriptural. But a creed may be *comprehensive* and *catholic* enough, in the sense of leaving some questions open and undetermined, without being *ambiguous*, with respect to those doctrines which it professes to define. The testimony of Dr. Heylyn, on this point, will be received as that of an unexceptionable witness. He refers to the statement of an opponent to the effect, that 'the intent of the Convocation in drawing up the Articles in so loose a manner was that men of different judgments might accommodate them to their own opinions,' and 'that the Articles of the English Protestant Church, in the infancy thereof, were drawn up in general terms, foreseeing, that posterity would grow up to fill the same,—meaning that these holy men did prudently discover, that differences of judgment would unavoidably happen in the Church, and were loth to unchurch any, and drive them off from ecclesiastical communion for petty differences,—which made them pen the Articles in comprehensive words, to take in all, who, *differing in the branches, meet in the root of the same Religion.* This hath formerly been observed to have been the artifice of those who had the managing of the Council of Trent, and is affirmed to have been used by such men also as had the drawing up of the Canons of the Synod of Dort.' 'But,' he adds, 'the composers of the Articles of the Church of

England had not so little in them of the "dove," nor so much of the "serpent," as to make the Articles of the Church *like an upright shoe, which may be worn on either foot,*—or like to Theramenes' shoe, as the adage hath it, *fit for the foot of every man that was pleased to wear it;* and, therefore, we may say of our first Reformers in reference to the book of Articles . . . that those reverend and learned men intended not to deceive any *by ambiguous terms.*' He proceeds to show that if, as had been alleged, our first Reformers did not so compose the Articles as to exclude ' any liberty to dissenting judgments,' or to ' bind men to the literal and grammatical sense,' ' they had not attained to the end aimed at, which was "*ad tollendam opinionum dissentionem, et consensum in vera religione firmandum,*" that is to say, to take away diversity of opinions, and to establish an agreement in the true Religion. Which end could never be effected, if men were left unto the liberty of dissenting, or might have leave to put their own sense on the Articles, as they list themselves; for where there is a purpose of permitting men to their own opinions, there is no need of definitions and determinations in a National Church, no more than there is of making laws to bind the subjects in an unsettled commonwealth, with an intent to leave them in their former liberty, either of keeping or not keeping them, as themselves best pleased.' —*Quinquarticular History,* Heylyn's ' Tracts,' pp. 553, 554.

NOTE 16, p. 208.

See Maurice, ' Unity of New Testament,' p. xxiv.; Brooke's ' Life and Letters of F. W. Robertson,' vol. ii. pp. 67, 69; see also vol. i. pp. 151, 155, 179, 333-337; Rigg, ' Anglo-Catholic Theology.'

NOTE 17, p. 211.

Coleridge's philosophy, as well as his application of it to Theology, is entirely based on his favourite distinction between the Reason and the Understanding, or the intuitive and the logical faculties. The former he held to be superior to the latter, and the ultimate test and judge of all truth, whether natural or revealed. He always connects this supreme faculty, and sometimes seems even to identify it, with the ' Logos.' It is not easy to determine whether he, and his disciples, mean to denote by that term a *faculty* or a *person;* but it is the less necessary to do so, because the faculty and the person, even if they be distinct, are held to be inseparable, and to coexist, invariably and universally, in the human mind. It may be that the personal ' Logos ' is there, to diffuse his light, and that Reason merely receives that light and reflects it: or that Reason itself is the ' Logos' in man, as ' the image of God ' in which he was created. It is enough to know that they are either one and the same, or inseparable from each other. Of this ' Logos ' or ' Reason ' we are told that ' there is a Light higher than all, even "the Word that was in the beginning "—the Light, of which light itself is but the schekinah and cloudy tabernacle;—the Word, that is Light for every man, and Life for as many as give heed to it.' We are further told that 'the universal Reason' is 'the image of God,' and is 'the same in all men:'—that 'the reason and conscience of man, interpreted by the Understanding, is the everlasting organ of the Spirit of truth,' and that the 'Reason' or the 'Logos' is 'the inward Light' which is not human, but divine. As this light exists in all men by nature, and needs only to be discerned to renew and save them, they are not absolutely dependent on any outward Revelation, although it may be useful in quickening the Reason, while Reason still continues to be the ultimate test and judge even of Revelation itself; and consequently it may be true, as some have thought, that 'what the best heathens called Reason,—and Solomon, Wisdom,—Paul, Grace in general,—John, Righteousness or Love,—Luther, Faith,—and Fenelon, Virtue,—may be only different expressions for one and the same blessing —the Light of Christ, shining in different degrees under different dispensations.'—*Confessions of an Inquiring Spirit*, xxxix. p. 12; *Aids to Reflection*, xviii. 4; *Biogr. Littera.* i. lviii.

Mr. Maurice tells us 'not to think that the world was created in Adam, or stood in his obedience,' but that 'it stood and stands in the obedience of God's well-beloved Son, the real "image" of the Father, the real bond of human society, and of the whole universe, who was to be manifested in the fulness of times, as that which *He had always been*, the original and archetype of human nature;'. . . that he looks 'upon Christ's death and resurrection as revelations of the Son of God, in whom all things had stood from the first,—in whom God had looked upon His creature man from the first:' that 'He actually is one with every man;' that 'in Him, whether circumcised or uncircumcised, they are one, *by the law of their creation;*' and that 'it is an accursed and godless scheme to drill men into certain notions about books, that they may be prepared to receive that which is an *eternal fact*, or *nothing*, namely, that Christ is the head of every man.' He speaks also of Paul's belief, that 'this Son of God, and not Adam, was the true root of humanity; and that from Him, and not from any ancestor, each man derived his life;' of Job's thought of '*a righteousness within him*, which is mightier than the evil,' and which is identified with 'his Redeemer;' and of the Baptist's message, 'Repent, for the kingdom of heaven is at hand,' as amounting to this— 'There is a Light within you, close to you.'. . . 'This light comes from a Person—from the King and Lord of your heart and spirit—from the Word,—the Son of God. When I say, "Repent," I say, Turn and confess His presence. You have always had it with you; you have been unmindful of it.'—*F. D. Maurice, On the Old Testament*, p. 41; *Unity of the New Testament*, pp. 220, 367, 536; *Claims of Revelation and Science*, p. 90, also pp. 47, 98, 116, 129; *What is Revelation?* pp. 40, 48, 54, 107, 110; *Essays*, pp. 57, 59, 117, 202.

'As I believe,' says Mr. Kingsley, 'one common "Logos"—Word— Reason,—reveals and unveils the same eternal truth to all who seek and hunger for it.'. . . 'In calling this person the "Logos," and making Him the source of all human reason, and knowledge of eternal laws, he (Philo) only translated from Hebrew into Greek the name which he found in his sacred books—"the Word of God."' But 'Proclus and his teachers despised the simpler, and yet far profounder, doctrine of the Christian schools,—That the "Logos," the Divine Teacher in whom both Christians and heathens believed, was the very archetype of men, and that He had proved that fact by being made flesh, and dwelling bodily among them, that they might behold His glory full of grace and truth, and see that it was at once the perfection of man and the perfection of God ; that that which was most divine was most human, and that which was most human, most divine.'—*Kingsley, Alexandria and her Schools*, pp. 98, 89, 123. The same views are infused into his lighter works—'Hypatia,' 'Alton Locke,' 'Yeast.'

We have already quoted a sentence from the writings of Mr. Robertson, which shows that, in the láter years of his ministry, he had adopted substantially the same doctrine. He affirms that all men are 'the children of God,' even when they are ignorant or forgetful of their relation to Him. He held the doctrine of Baptismal Regeneration to be partly right and partly wrong ; right, in affirming that Baptism *declares*, wrong in implying that it *creates*, the relation of sonship. And, speaking of one who had been removed by death, he said, 'We know of him—what is all that we can ever know of any one removed beyond the veil which shelters the unseen from the pryings of curiosity—that he is in the hands of the Wise and the Loving; Spirit has mingled with Spirit ; a child, more or less erring, has gone home. Unloved by his Father ? Believe it who may, that will not I.' He speaks, indeed, as if this child, 'more or less erring,' might be for a time, but surely not for ever, 'a child of wrath.' A heathen is God's child, if he only knew it. You send a missionary to him to tell him what he is, and to bid him realize his royal character ; but being God's child *de jure* avails him nothing unless he becomes such *in fact;* that is, changes his life and character, and becomes like his Father, pure and holy. Then he is regenerate. God's child before unconsciously, God's child now by a second birth consciously. Nay, in fact, till now he was 'a child of wrath,' in which I entirely take the Church's words—'by nature a child of wrath.'—*Brooke's Life and Letters of F. W. Robertson*, vol. i. pp. 126, 154, 176, 179, 333–337, vol. ii. p. 67.

It is unspeakably sad to read these lines from the pen of one, who in the earlier, and happier, years of his ministry, entertained very different views. 'It is strange,' he wrote at that time, 'into what ramifications the disbelief of *external Justification* will extend ; we *will* make it *internal*, whether it be by self-mortification, by works of evangelical obedience, or by the sacraments ; and that just at the time when we suppose most that we are magnifying the work of our Lord.' The Tractarian views 'amount to nothing less than a direct, or, as Hooker would call it, an indirect, denial of the foundation. Our motto must be, . . . "Stand fast, therefore, in the liberty wherewith Christ hath made you free, and be not

entangled again with the yoke of bondage." But how strangely that yoke
steals round our necks, even when we think we are most entirely free
from any idea of self-justification!' 'I believe there is at this time a
determined attack 'made by Satan and his instruments to subvert that
cardinal doctrine of our best hopes—Justification by faith alone; and how
far he has already succeeded, let many a college in Oxford testify. It is the
doctrine which, more than any other, we find our 'own hearts continually
turning aside from, and surrendering. Anything but Christ,—the Virgin,
the Church, the Sacraments, a new set of resolutions,—any or all of these
will the heart embrace, as a means to holiness or acceptance, rather than
God's way. . . . And the Apostle's resolution, in spite of all we say, is
one which we are again and again making, and yet for ever breaking—
"To know nothing but Jesus Christ, and Him crucified."' In conversation
with a Socinian, 'My chief point was to prove the death of Christ not
merely a demonstration of God's willingness to pardon on repentance and
obedience, but an actual substitution of suffering; and that salvation is a
thing *finished* for those who believe,—not a commencement of a state in
which salvation may be gained.'—*Brooke's Life and Letters,* vol. i. pp. 34,
38, 79, 82.

'The subtleties of Roman law,' says Dean Stanley, 'as applied to the
relations of God and man, which appear faintly in Augustine, more distinctly in Aquinas, more decisively still in Calvin and Luther, . . . are
almost unknown to the East. "Forensic justification," "merit," "demerit," "satisfaction," "imputed righteousness," "decrees," represent
ideas which in the Eastern Theology have no predominant influence,
hardly any words to represent them.' . . . 'Ecclesiastical history teaches
us that the most vital, the most comprehensive, the most fruitful (doctrine)
has been, and is still—not the supremacy of the Bible . . . not Justification, but the doctrine of the Incarnation. . . . It is the rare merit of
Athanasius, or his rare good fortune, that the centre of his Theology was
the doctrine of the Incarnation.'—*Dr. A. P. Stanley, Lectures on the History of the Eastern Church,* see pp. 27, 215, 294. One might be led by
this statement to suppose that the ideas of merit and demerit, justification
and condemnation, were peculiar to the 'subtleties of Roman Law,' as if they
were not involved in every code of law whatever, and familiarly known
in every community of civilised men; and that the Greek language,
copious as it was, had 'hardly any words to represent them,' while we
find it acknowledged that 'among the various figures which Athanasius
uses to express *his* view is that of 'Satisfaction,' and this too, as we
are assured, 'in entire subordination to the primary truth that the Redemption flowed from the indivisible love of the Father and the Son
alike.'

NOTE 18, p. 211.

See Lect. vi. p. 168; and Brown (of Wamphray), 'Quakerism the
Pathway to Paganism.'

Note 19, p. 211.

Athanasius, 'Four Orations against the Arians, and his Oration against the Gentiles,' by Sam. Parker, 2 vols. 8vo, 1713, Oxford, vol. i. pp. 20, 27, 28. See Bishop Bull, Mr. Treffrey, and Dr. Kidd, on the 'Eternal Sonship;' and, on the other side, Professor M. Stuart's 'Excursus,' i. in 'Commentary on Ep. to the Romans,' p. 557. See also R. Fleming (jun.), 'Christology,' Book ii. 'Of the Logos, or Christ as such;' Books ii. and iii. 'Of the Loganthropos, or as He is, the Word made Man.'

Note 20, p. 213.

Alexander Knox, Esq., 'Remains,' 4 vols.; 'Correspondence with Bishop Jebb,' 2 vols. On the 'Revelation of Wrath,' see Dr. T. Goodwin, 'Works,' vol. x., Nichol's Ed., 'An Unregenerate Man's Guiltiness before God in respect of Sin and Punishment.'

Note 21, p. 214.

'Propter incertitudinem propriæ justitiæ, et periculum inanis gloriæ, TUTISSIMUM EST FIDUCIAM TOTAM IN SOLA MISERICORDIA DEI et benignitate reponere.'—*Bellar. De Justif.* lib. v. c. 7, prop. 3, p. 1095, fol. (1619). He proceeds to explain his meaning: 'Hoc solùm dicimus, TUTIUS ESSE meritorum jam partorum quodammodo oblivisci, et *in solam misericordiam Dei* respicere, tum quia nemo *absque revelatione* certo scire potest, se habere vera merita, aut in eis in finem usque perseveraturum; tum quia nihil est facilius, in hoc loco tentationis, quàm superbiam ex consideratione bonorum operum gigni.' He then quotes Daniel ix. 18, and Luke xxii. 10; and refers to the public prayers of the Catholic Church, and to several quotations from the Fathers,—Chrysostom, Ambrose, Augustine, Gregory, and Bernard,—in confirmation of his statement.

Note 22, p. 216.

Dr. J. H. Newman, 'Lectures on Justification,' 2d Ed. 1840; Dr. James Bennett, 'Justification as revealed in Scripture, in opposition to the Council of Trent, and Mr. Newman's Lectures,' 8vo (1840), p. 363; Geo. Stanley Faber, 'Primitive Doctrine of Justification,' 2d Ed. (1839), p. 427. Mr. Griffith's 'Reply to Dr. Newman's Lectures' is commended by Bishop Daniel Wilson.

Note 23, p. 217.

A. G. Ryder, D.D. (Master of the Erasmus Smith Grammar School, Tipperary), 'The Scriptural Doctrine of Acceptance with God, considered with reference to the Neologian Hermeneutics.' The Donnellan Lectures for 1863. Dublin 1865. He describes his doctrine thus (p. 196): 'That theory of Acceptance with God which I have advocated throughout these Lectures—that the Christian covenant, namely, was made between God and the entire human family, but that its benefits shall finally apply,

without respect of persons, to those alone who have acted here according
to the light given them by God,—who have earnestly availed themselves
of such spiritual advantages as His providence had placed within their
reach.' Again (p. 311): 'While the mysterious sacrifice of Christ sufficiently, yea, more than sufficiently, atoned for all the sins, both actual
and original, of Adam and his posterity, and obtained for them the gift
of the Holy Spirit,—yet the benefit thereof, in the last great day of
account, shall be confined to those who, hearing the true nature of God
in the Gospel message, have obeyed from the heart the doctrine therein
delivered; and those who, not having heard that message, yet obeyed the
law of God, so far as it was otherwise known to them, and their natural
depravity allowed.' The strange statement in the last clause is probably
to be explained by p. 148: 'The decision in each case being made, not by
the standard of an impossible perfection, but in equitable and intelligible
conformity with all the circumstances and conditions, both external and
internal, of each individual.'

Note 24, p. 217.

A detailed analysis and examination of each of the works, which have
been mentioned, was prepared for these Lectures, but there is no room
for its insertion, either in the Text or Appendix, within the limits of a
single volume. Enough has been said, perhaps, to indicate their general
character and tendency.

These works have all been produced by Ministers or Members of the
United Church of England and Ireland. But it would be untrue and
unjust to represent all the recent attacks on the Protestant doctrine as
having proceeded from the Established Episcopal Church. Some lament-
able symptoms of departure from it have also appeared among Nonconformists. One remarkable example will be found in 'Orthodoxy,
Scripture, and Reason; An Examination of some of the principal Articles
of the Creed of Christendom,' by Rev. Wm. Kirkus, LL.B. (1865), pp.
416. He seems to belong to the school of Maurice and Kingsley, for he
speaks of the relation of the Logos to the human race, in these terms: 'A
race shall be created *in* the only-begotten Son, of which He should be
the Archetype and head, which should be His image, as He is the image
of the Father;' and adds, 'The race of man is to be seen, not in the first
Adam who fell, but in the second Adam, the Lord from Heaven,'—pp. 114,
115. His views of the Mediatorial work of Christ take shape from this
fundamental principle, pp. 137-177; and also his views of Justification,
pp. 181-230. As a Congregationalist, the author is not bound by the
Thirty-nine Articles, or the Westminster Confession; but he seems not
to be quite so free as he could wish; for he says: 'For all practical
purposes, every chapel with a doctrinal trust-deed, and the religious
belief of the people worshipping in it, is protected by the defences, and
bound by the fetters, which cannot fail, both for good and evil, to accompany the establishment of religion,'—p. 45. He seems to desiderate 'a

deed containing not even the faintest allusions to any Christian doctrine.'
This might suit some ministers, but would it be equally suitable to their
congregations, who are supposed to have some 'religious belief?'

Another recent writer, John Fuller, Esq., has published a work,
entitled 'Justification,' London, 1829, which is directed to disprove 'the
great error, that Justification takes place, either primarily or finally, in
this life,' and to show that 'it takes place only at the day of Judgment,'
pp. xiii. 14. But see Rom. v. 1, 2, viii. 1; Eph. i. 7, etc.

NOTE 25, p. 218.

'The Church of Christ in the Middle Ages,' by the author of 'Essays
on the Church,' Seeley, 1845, p. 12.

PART II.

NOTE TO INTRODUCTION.

NOTE 1, p. 225.

See Dr. Owen, 'Works,' vol. xi. pp. ii.-iv. 11, 17, 27, 30, etc.; Calvin,
'Institutes,' Book iii. c. xi. p. 575; Dr. Shedd, 'History of Christian
Doctrine,' vol. ii. 263-271, 285.

The late Lord John Scott, of the noble house of Buccleuch, carried
about with him continually an excellent tract, entitled 'Sin no Trifle.'
'His mind was deeply penetrated with a sense of the "majesty" of God,
and the "awfulness" of our relations to Him, in consequence of the sin
that has entered the world, and has infected the whole human race; and
therefore he vividly realized the indispensable necessity of Mediation and
Atonement, to give hope to sinful man in prospect of the grand account.
The origin of that earnestness, and attachment to spiritual religion, which
he manifested in his last years, was . . . the perusal of the tract entitled
"Sin no Trifle." Deep was the impression that tract had made. He read
it, and re-read it, and continually carried it about with him, till it was
entirely worn away. Under the impression springing from such views of
sin, he said, when in the enjoyment of health and vigour, "It is easy to
die the death of a gentleman, *but that will not do.*" His death was not
the death of a mere "gentleman;" it was evidently that of a "Christian."
. . . And in his painful illness, he manifested the supporting power of
faith, when faith has respect to "the truth as it is in Jesus," and appropriates Him as a personal, and Almighty, Saviour.'—*Rev. A. Hislop*
(*Arbroath*), *The Two Babylons*, p. xviii. Another short, but impressive,
tract 'On Sin,' by the Rev. Wm. Burns, now Missionary at Amoy, China,

cannot be too highly recommended to those who have no leisure for reading larger works. Of the latter, the following may be mentioned : ' The Christian Doctrine of Sin,' by Dr. Julius Müller, Clark, 1852, 2 vols. ; ' The Sinfulness of Sin,' by Bishop Reynolds, ' Works,' vol. i. pp. 101-353 ; ' On Indwelling Sin,' by Dr. Owen, ' Works,' vol. xiii. pp. 1-195 ; ' On Original Sin,' by President Edwards, ' Works,' vol. ii. p. 79 ; on ' The Unregenerate Man's Guiltiness,' by Thos. Goodwin, vol. x. Nichol's Series ; ' On Original Sin,' Princeton Theological Essays, First Series, Essay v. p. 109, and Melancthon's ' Doctrine of Sin,' Essay ix. p. 218.

NOTES TO LECTURE VIII.

Note 1, p. 227.

Dr. Donaldson offers the following criticism : ' The only great doctrinal difference which they (the Tubingen School) supposed to have existed between the Apostles disappears before a fair interpretation of the passages alleged. The doctrine is that of Justification by Faith. Paul is supposed to have preached a peculiar doctrine on this point. On all hands this peculiar doctrine is allowed to appear in a very modified manner in the subsequent ages ; and in the Epistle of James some have supposed that Paul's doctrine is flatly contradicted. The supposition of a difference arises mainly from *two* circumstances,—a false meaning attached to δικαιόω, and a forgetfulness that Paul speaks principally of trust in God, not in Christ. The word δικαιόω is not used in the New Testament in its classical sense. We have to fall back on its etymological meaning. This meaning is—either *to make a person who is sinful righteous*, or *to declare a person righteous who is righteous*. The meaning attributed to it is, to treat a person who is guilty as if he were really not guilty. Only the most concurring evidence of unquestionable examples of such a use of the word would justify a man in giving it this meaning. And no such examples can be found within the first three centuries at least. Now Paul's doctrine was this. He is arguing against Judaism. He maintains that if a man's righteousness is to depend on the performance of the law, then righteousness is an impossibility. No man can do, or ever has done, all that he ought to do. Can man, then, be righteous at all ? Unquestionably, says Paul ; there is a righteousness which consists in trusting in God. The person may have sinned, but his hope is in God ; and whatever he has to do, the motive is his confidence in God. . . . Now James's doctrine, instead of being opposed to this, is a representation of the *same* essential truth, in opposition to a different error. Paul struggled against dead works, James against dead belief.'— *Critical History*, vol. i. p. 77. The harmony between Paul and James is not the present question, but the meaning of δικαιόω according to the ' usus loquendi ' of the sacred writers. The great Popish controversy, which has now been waged for more than three hundred years, has always turned on this latter question; and all our British divines—such as Barlow, Davenant, Downham, Owen, Brown, Hooker—have agreed with the Reformers and foreign Theologians in contending for that sense of it which Dr. Donaldson rejects. See Bishop Barlow's 'Two Letters,' pp. 68-71; Bishop Davenant, 'Disputa,' vol. i. p. 157; Bishop Downham, 'Treatise,' pp. 51-55; Mr. Wm. Pemble, A.M., 'Vindiciæ Fidei,' or 'A Treatise on Justification by Faith,' delivered at Magdalen Hall, Oxford, Second Edition, 1629, Sec. i. c. 1, 2, 'Explication of the Terms Righteousness, and Justification,' p. 1; Dr. Owen, 'Works,' vol. xi. pp. 153-161; Hooker, 'Sermon on Justification,' vol. ii. p. 696; President Edwards, 'Works,' vi. 215; Calvin, 'Institutes,' Book iii. c. xi.; De Moori, 'Commentary,' iv. 535; Jo. Gerhard, tom. vii. lec. xvii. Sec. iii. 'Etymologia et Significatio Voca. Justific.;'—and more recently, Bishop O'Brien, 'Nature and Effects of Faith,' pp. 70-72, 387; G. S. Faber, 'Primitive Doctrine,' p. 393; Dr. Cunningham, 'Historical Theology,' vol. ii. pp. 34, 40. The importance which has all along been ascribed to this question shows that it was never regarded as a verbal one; as appears sufficiently from the strong statement of Chemnitz, 'De Vocabulo Justificationis:' 'Manifestum est . . . veram Scripturæ sententiam de Justificatione non posse commodius explicari, intelligi, et conservari, nec contrarias corruptelas rectius et illustrius posse refutari, quam *ex propria et genuina significatione verbi—justificare*. Neque ignorant hoc Pontificii; . . . ipsorum enim instituto accommodatius est, si *abutantur similitudine analogiæ Latinæ compositionis,* ut sicut *sanctificare* dicetur, ita etiam *justificare* intelligatur.'—*Examen. Conc. Trid. De Justif.* p. 130.

It is not wonderful, that those who have failed to see the Protestant doctrine of Justification in the Holy Scriptures, should have been unable to find it in the writings of the Fathers. If they attach an 'efficient, moral' sense to δικαιόω, and understand δικαιοσύνη as denoting an 'inherent, subjective' righteousness, as these terms are used in the one, they will naturally interpret the same expressions in the same way, when they occur in the other. It is equally true, that those who attach a 'forensic or judicial sense' to δικαιόω, and its cognates, in Scripture, will continue to understand them in the same sense, when they meet with them in the writings of the Fathers. In either case, it may be said that both parties interpret the Fathers, according to their respective views of the meaning of Scripture. But there is a wide difference between the two cases. Those who hold the Protestant sense of these terms, have adduced evidence from Scripture itself to prove, that justification is there opposed to condemnation, and does not denote a subjective moral change; and while they find that the word was used in this scriptural sense by *some* of the Fathers, they are not bound to show that it was never used by any of them to denote the infusion of personal holiness, any more than that it is not so used by some at the present day; for they are quite prepared to expect that its meaning would be obscured and perverted in the growing de-

generacy and corruption of the Church. Whereas those who hold the
Popish sense of these terms, can scarcely make out their case, unless they
are able to show, either that such expressions are incapable of bearing the
construction which Protestants have put upon them, or that, in point of
fact, they never convey that meaning, either in the Apostolic or Patristic
writings. A few clear examples of their being used in a purely ' forensic '
or 'judicial' sense, are fatal to the theory which insists on an exclusively
' moral ' Justification ; and the difference between the two interpretations
does not arise merely from verbal criticism, but has a much deeper root.

The difference between them,—and also its real cause,—may be illustrated by comparing what is said of Justification in Spanheim's 'Ecclesiastical Annals,' and Le Clerc's ' Historia Eccles. Duorum Primorum
Seculorum.' Spanheim had acquired a clear apprehension of the ' forensic '
or ' judicial ' sense of the term, as it is used in Scripture,—in other words,
he had found the Protestant doctrine there, (see ' Elenchus Controversiarum,' pp. 33, 49, 59, etc., and ' Dubia Evangelica,' pp. 126, 421, 525,
etc.) ; and accordingly he finds it also in the writings of some of the Fathers,
while he admits that it was gradually corrupted.—*Eccles. Annals*, pp. 227,
229, 293, 325, 355. Whereas Le Clerc, who had not acquired a clear
apprehension of the Apostolic doctrine, is equally at sea in regard to the
Patristic.—*Hist. Eccles.*, *Prolegomena*, p. 130, Sæc. i. p. 399.

NOTE 2, p. 227.

Bellarmine, ' Opera,' vol. iv. p. 814, ' De Nomine Justific. et Jus. ;'
Osorio, ' De Justitia,' lib. v. pp. 302, 425 ; Perrone, ' Prælec. Theolog.,'
' De Gratia Sanctificante,' vol. vi. p. 200, and under this title, ' De
Justificationis Essentia et Naturæ,' p. 204 ; Dens, ' Theologia,' ii. p. 446 ;
Bishop Downham's ' Treatise,' pp. 52, 62-69 ; Dr. Junkin, on ' Justi-
fication,' pp. 73-75.

' The question is—In what sense are the words Justification, and its
cognates, used in Scripture ? and more especially, *should any variety in its
meaning and application be discovered there*, in what sense is it employed in
those passages in which it is manifest, that the subject ordinarily expressed by it is most fully and formally explained ?' ' Popish writers do
not deny that the word is sometimes, nay often, taken in Scripture in
a forensic sense. . . . But they usually contend that this is not the *only*
meaning which the word bears in the Scriptures—that there are cases in
which it means to make righteous,—and that, consequently, they are entitled to regard this idea as contained in its full scriptural import. . . .
The position which Protestants maintain on this subject is not, that in
every passage where the word occurs there exists evidence by which it can
be proved from that passage alone, taken by itself, that the word there is
used in a forensic sense, and cannot admit of any other. They concede
that there are passages where the word occurs, in which there is nothing
in the passage itself, or in the context, to fix down its meaning to the
sense of *counting righteous*, in preference to *making righteous*. Their

position is this,—that there are many passages where it is plain that it *must* be taken in a forensic sense, and cannot admit of any other; and that there are *none*, or at least none in which the justification of a sinner before God is formally and explicitly spoken of, in which it can be proved that the forensic sense is inadmissible or necessarily excluded.'—*Dr. Cunningham, Historical Theology*, vol. ii. pp. 31, 34, 35.

NOTE 3, p. 230.

See Downham, 'Treatise,' pp. 9, 51-58; Dr. Burgess, 'The True Doctrine of Justification Asserted and Vindicated,' pp, 6-9; Dr. Junkin on 'Justification,' p. 77; Bishop Bull, 'Harmonia Apos.' Diss. i. c. i.; 'Magdeburg Centuriators,' Cent. i. B. i. c. iv. p. 94; Owen, 'Works,' vol. xi. p. 169; Rev. P. J. Gloag (of Dunning), 'Treatise on Justification' (1856), p. 36,—a sound and sensible work, which may be safely recommended to those who have little leisure to study larger treatises. The Centuriators say, '"Justificare" forensem habet significationem, pro absolvere, justitiam tribuere, ut Matt. xii. 37, Luke x. 29, xvi. 15, xviii. 14. . . . In hac significatione in presenti negotio, ubi de acceptione hominis coram Deo agitur, hæc vox propriè ac verè accipitur,—nempe quòd "justificare" in doctrina de remissione peccatorum coram Deo, Ebraica phrasi, significat absolvi ab accusatione legis,—attribui seu imputari legis obedientiam, seu justitiam per Christum partam, gratis omnibus credentibus, et sic justum in judicio Dei reputari ac pronunciari, ac consistere.'—P. 95.

NOTE 4, p. 232.

Downham, 'Treatise,' p. 57; Dr. Burgess, 'True Doctrine,' p. 15; Hervey, 'Theron and Aspasio,' vol. i. p. 57; Bishop Kaye, 'Charges,' p. 259.

NOTE 5, p. 238.

Bishop Bull, 'Harmonia Apos.' Diss. i. c. v.: 'Judicium Dei in futuro sæculo per omnia respondet Justificatione Divinæ in hac vita.' Dr. Sherlock, 'Practical Discourse on the Future Judgment,' c. vii. p. 334. John Fuller, Esq., 'Justification,' p. xiii. 4. See Bishop O'Brien's 'Sermons,' pp. 54, 149; Bishop Downham's 'Treatise,' pp. 55-58, 66, 70, 125, 137, 259, 379.

NOTE 6, p. 248.

The result is summed up *in two positions* by Dr. Cunningham :

1. 'That the Apostle James did not intend to discuss, and does not discuss, the subject of Justification in the sense in which it is so fully expounded in Paul's Epistles to the Romans and Galatians; that he does not state anything about the grounds or principles on which sinners are admitted to forgiveness and the favour of God; and that his great fundamental object is simply to set forth the real tendency and result of that

true living faith, which holds so important a place in everything connected with the salvation of sinners. . . .

2. 'That the Justification of which James speaks, and which he ascribes to works, refers to something in men's history *posterior* to that great era when their sins are forgiven, and they are admitted to the *enjoyment* of God's favour,—*i.e.* to the *proof or manifestation* of the reality and efficiency of their faith to themselves and their fellow-men.'

Note 7, p. 249.

On the harmony between Paul and James: Bishop Bull, 'Harmonia Apostol.;' Rev. A. Pitcairne, 'Harmonia Evangelica, Apostol. Pauli et Jacobi in Doctr. de Justific. (1685), adversus Socinianos, Pontificios, Arminianos, Curcellæum, Morum, Bullum, Sherlockum, et Alios Novaturientes;' Dr. Owen, vol. xi. c. xx. pp. 479-493; 'Dickinson, 'Familiar Letters,' Let. xv. p. 260; Witsius, 'De Mente Pauli circa Justif.,' Misc. Sac. vol. ii. p. 748; Bishop Downham, 'Treatise,' pp. 370, 408, 483, fully discussed pp. 484-497; Brown, 'Life of Justification,' pp. 486-506; Gossner, 'Life of Martin Boos,' pp. 67, 129, 152; W. Pemble, 'Vindiciæ Fidei,' pp. 187, 197; Young, 'Life of John Welsh,' pp. 125, 126; Hervey, 'Theron and Aspasio,' i. p. 261, iv. p. 109; G. S. Faber, 'Primitive Doctrine,' Augustine on Paul and James, pp. 165-175; Faber on the same, pp. 297-314; Bishop O'Brien, 'Sermons on Faith,' pp. 166-175, 357, 519; Dr. Cunningham, 'Historical Theology,' vol. ii. p. 67. Compare these with Dr. Newman, 'Lectures on Justification,' pp. 27, 134, 210, 211, 302, 312, 319, 328-333, and his 'Apologia,' p. 170; Brooke, 'Life and Letters of F. W. Robertson,' ii. p. 64.

NOTES TO LECTURE IX.

Note 1, p. 252.

Dr. Burgess, 'True Doctrine of Justification,' pp. 11, 12; Bishop Downham, 'Treatise,' pp. 61, 126; Dr. Owen, 'Works,' vol. xi. pp. 247, 253, 267; Brown, 'Life of Justification,' pp. 259, 262; Beart, 'Vindication of the Eternal Law and Gospel,' Part i. pp. iv-viii, 12; Dr. Heurtley, 'Bampton Lectures,' *passim;* but see pp. ix. 117; Halyburton, 'Works,' edited by Dr. Burns, p. 559; 'An Inquiry into the Nature of God's Act of Justification,' recently reprinted, with other pieces, by an esteemed Elder of the Free Church in Ayrshire, Essay iii. p. 119.

Note 2, p. 255.

Witsius, 'Misc. Sac.,' vol. ii. p. 671; Bishop Downham, 'Treatise, pp. 33, 38, 42, 48, 208; Brown, 'Life of Justification,' p. 28; Dickinson, 'Familiar Letters,' p. 182; Dr. Junkin on 'Justification,' p. 310; John Welsh in Young's 'Life,' p. 311; Beart's 'Vindication,' Part ii. pp. 24, 25; Hervey, 'Theron and Aspasio,' pp. 38, 44; Bishop O'Brien on 'Faith,' pp. 74, 98; Dr. Cunningham, 'Hist. Theol.' ii. p. 47.

NOTE 3, p. 255.

Dr. Burgess, 'True Doctrine,' pp. 50-57; Bishop Downham, 'Treatise,' pp. 82-88; Scott, 'Continuation of Milner,' ii. p. 281.

NOTE 4, p. 256.

See Part i. Lect. ii. p. 55. Witsius, 'De Theol. Judæorum,' Misc. Sac., vol. ii. p. 714.

NOTE 5, p. 256.

Bishop Downham, 'Treatise,' pp. 82, 83; Dr. Burgess, 'Lectures,' pp. 19-23; Dr. Newman, 'Lectures,' pp. 40, 47, 69; Faber, 'Primitive Doctrine,' p. 45.

NOTE 6, p. 257.

Knox, 'Remains,' vol. i. pp. 244-246, 461, vol. ii. pp. 23, 30, 44, 53, 56, 83, 316, vol. iii. pp. 101, 419, vol. iv. p. 260; Greg, 'Creed of Christendom,' pp. 262-297; Kirkus, 'Orthodoxy, Reason, and Scripture,' pp. 174-179.

NOTE 7, p. 258.

Bishop Downham, 'Treatise,' pp. 84, 90; Dr. Burgess, 'True Doctrine,' pp. 22, 139, 143, 235, 261; Dr. Junkin on 'Justification,' p. 77; Faber, 'Primitive Doctrine,' pp. 188, 192.

NOTE 8, p. 259.

Bellarmine, 'De Justificatione,' lib. ii. c. i. s. 1. See also Bishop Downham, 'Treatise,' p. 208; Roborough, 'Doctrine of Justification,' p. 77; Dr. Cunningham, 'Reformers and Theol. of Reformation,' Works, vol. i. p. 402; 'Historical Theology,' vol. iii. p. 14; Scott, 'Continuation of Milner's History,' vol. iii. p. 320; Calvin, 'Institutes,' Book iii. c. xi.-xviii.

NOTE 9, p. 261.

Southey's 'Life of Wesley,' vol. ii. p. 54; Dr. Cunningham, 'Hist. Theol.,' vol. ii. p. 54; Bishop O'Brien on 'Faith,' p. 418. It is to be regretted that Bishop O'Brien substitutes the term 'innocence' for the scriptural one, 'righteousness,' pp. 148, 151.

NOTE 10, p. 264.

Smith's 'Dictionary of the Bible,' art. 'Adoption;' Amesius, 'Medulla,' c. xxviii. pp. 127-132; Witsius, 'De Œconomia Fœderum,' lib. iii. c. ix. p. 315 ; Dan. Heinsius, 'Exercitationes Sacræ,' p. 138 ; Mastricht, 'Theol.,' lib. vi. c. vii. vol. ii. p. 723 ; Bishop Downham, 'Treatise,' p. 359 ; Dwight, 'Theology,' vol. iii. p. 167 ; Taylor, 'Establishment of the Law,' p. 48 ; Luther on Epistle to Galatians, p. 322 ; Hervey, 'Theron and Aspasio,' Works, vol. iv. p. 149 ; Ford, 'The Spirit of Bondage and Adoption' (1655).

Note 11, p. 264.

Dr. Shedd's 'History,' vol. ii. p. 321 ; Mr. Knox, 'Remains,' vol. i. pp. 256, 260 ; Dr. Newman, 'Lectures,' pp. 40, 44, 46, 69 ; Scott, 'Continuation of Milner's History,' vol. iii. p. 272 ; Archbishop Wake, 'Defence,' p. 25 ; Bishop Downham, 'Treatise,' pp. 49, 80 ; Dr. Burgess, 'True Doctrine,' p. 16.

Note 12, p. 265.

Principal Hadow, 'Antinomianism,' p. 24 ; Beart, 'Vindication,' Part ii. pp. 84, 86 ; N. Mather, 'The Righteousness of God,' p. 41.

Note 13, p. 265.

Bishop Downham, 'Treatise,' pp. 49, 76-81, in fifteen particulars ; Mr. Brown, 'Life of Justification,' p. 267, in ten particulars ; Dr. Burgess, 'True Doctrine,' p. 16 ; Hervey, 'Theron and Aspasio,' Works, vol. iii. pp. 348-351, vol. iv. p. 291 ; Westminster Larger Catechism, Q. 77.

NOTES TO LECTURE X.

Note 1, p. 270.

See Part i. Lect. i. p. 18 ; also Rawlin, 'Christ the Righteousness of His People,' Sermons at Pinners Hall (1797), p. 19. His propositions are extremely valuable. He shows : '(1.) That man is naturally and necessarily under a law to God. (2.) That man being under a law to God, some righteousness is absolutely necessary to his justification. (3.) That every righteousness is not sufficient for this purpose, but it must be such a righteousness as fully answers to the purity and perfection of that law under which man is placed, and which God hath given him as the rule of his obedience. (4.) That we have no such righteousness of our own, nor can any mere creature furnish us with it. (5.) That if ever we are justified, it must be by the righteousness of Christ, consisting in that complete and perfect obedience which He has performed to the law in our room and stead' (p. 19).

The Rev. John Beart, 'Vindication of the Eternal Law, and Everlasting Gospel,' in two parts, reprinted 1753. 'What is that righteousness, wherein a sinner may stand before God, pardoned and accepted unto eternal life? . . . That the righteousness of the Lord Jesus Christ, fulfilled by Himself here on earth, in our room and stead, is that alone righteousness, which answers all charges of all kinds whatsoever, on the behalf of the believer, is the true Gospel answer to this inquiry. . . . If Christ be owned in His office and works as a Saviour, there are but these two ways supposable, in which He can be so;—either, that making reparation for the breach of the first covenant, He hath procured a Remedial Law of lower terms, condescending to our weakness, that by obedience thereto we might work out a justifying righteousness ourselves, entitling to life and happiness; or, that coming into our place and stead, He hath fulfilled in our room, a justifying righteousness Himself, which, to all intents and purposes, is made ours, for Justification before God, from all condemnation. Here are the two ways; and how contrary these two are—that Christ hath procured by His death an abatement of the Law, that our obedience should justify,—and, on the other hand, that Christ hath altogether fulfilled the Law, and that His righteousness is imputed for Justification, let those believers judge, who have " their senses exercised to discern both good and evil." The bottom of the controversy, therefore, is about the justifying righteousness of a sinner—Whether it is Christ's, *or* his own ? or, at least, Whether it is Christ's alone, or Christ's *and* his own ?—the one, as answering the penalty of the law of works,—the other, as answering another law, that is supposed to have a charge against men, till they have fulfilled its conditions. All other arguings in this controversy are but incidental, and aimed to establish one of these two ways of righteousness.'—Part i. p. iv. He then proceeds to argue against the doctrine of the New Methodists, and Neonomians, as having a tendency to reintroduce Popery, and quotes the remarkable admission of Richard Baxter, as recorded in his Life by Sylvester : ' My censures of the Papists do much differ from what they were at first : I then thought, that their errors in the doctrines of Faith were their most dangerous mistakes,—as in the points of Merit, of Justification by works, of assurance of salvation, of the nature of Faith, etc. But now I am assured that their misexpressions, and their misunderstanding us, with our mistaking of them, and inconvenient expressing our own opinions, have made the difference in these points to appear much greater than it is, and that, in some of them, it is next to none at all' (Part i. p. ix.). The great value of Beart's ' Vindication' consists in his setting clearly forth the relation which Justification must bear to the Law and Justice of God. His leading positions are these : (1.) That the Law of God, which is the rule of duty and obedience, and which is perfect and unchangeable, is also the rule of righteousness for Justification, c. i. ii. (2.) That man, as fallen, even if renewed, is unable to fulfil it, c. iii. (3.) That Christ has fulfilled both its precept and penalty in our stead, c. iv. (4.) That Christ's righteousness is imputed to all believers, and is their justifying righteousness, c. v. (5.) That Faith justifies, not as a work, but as a means or instrument, c. vi. Part ii. is directed against the Antinomian doctrine of Justification.

See also Dutton, 'Treatise on Justification' (1778), Third Edition, pp. iv. viii. and *passim ;* Bragge, 'Lime Street Lectures,' pp. 246-295.

NOTE 2, p. 277.

On the first covenant of Life, see Bishop Hopkins on the 'Two Covenants ;' Samuel Petto, 'The Difference between the Old and New Covenant,' 1674 ; Witsius, 'De Œconomia Fœderum Dei ;' Burmann's ' Synopsis ;' Boston, Strong, Taylor, Russell (Dundee), Colquhoun (Leith), etc. etc.

The theory of Pre-existence is adopted in preference to the doctrine of the imputation of Adam's guilt to his posterity, by Dr. H. W. Beecher, 'The Conflict of Ages,' B. v. pp. 362-516.   It was mooted by Bishop Rust, 'Lux Orientalis,' an 'Inquiry into the Opinion of the Eastern Sages concerning the Pre-existence of Souls,—a Key to Unlock the Grand Mysteries of Providence ;' by Joseph Glanville, 'Essays,' p. 53 ; by Dr. H. More, 'Philosophical Works,' 'Immortality of the Soul,' pp. 111-114 ; 'The Cabbala,' pp. 86, 147 ; 'General Preface,' pp. xx. xxv.

On the new views which have sprung up in America on the Imputation of Adam's guilt, see Dr. Boardman, 'On Original Sin,' and three papers on ' Imputation' in the ' Princeton Theological Essays.'

NOTE 3, p. 286.

On the supposed Abrogation, or Relaxation, of the Law, see Beart, ' Vindication,' p. 9.   See also *supra,* Lect. vi. p. 176.

NOTE 4, p. 288.

Archdeacon Hare, ' Vindication of Luther,' p. 94.

NOTE 5, p. 291.

Dr. Owen, ' Treatise on Divine Justice,' Works, vol. ix. pp. 320-502 ; President Edwards, ' God's Chief End in all His Works,' vol. i. pp. 443-535 ; Dr. Shedd, ' History of Christian Doctrine,' vol. ii. pp. 246, 305, 306.

NOTES TO LECTURE XI.

NOTE 1, p. 293.

Dr. Bates, ' Harmony of the Divine Attributes in the Work of Man's Redemption.'

NOTE 2, p. 294.

Dr. Waterland, ' Importance of the Doctrine of the Trinity,' p. 66.

Note 3, p. 294.

Witsius, 'De Œconomia Fœderum Dei,' c. iii.; 'De Pacto Patris et Filii,' p. 110; Do., 'Misc. Sac.' vol. ii. pp. 820-823, 843; Dr. Junkin 'On Justification,' c. xiii. p. 192; Fraser's 'Life of Ebenezer Erskine,' pp. 235-238; Hervey's Works, ii. pp. 51, 54, 263, iv. pp. 162-165; Jones, 'The Mediation of Jesus Christ;' Buddeus, 'Misc. Sac.' tom. iii. c. x. 'Jesus Melioris Fœderis Sponsor,' pp. 361-402.

Note 4, p. 297.

M'Laurin, 'On Glorying in the Cross of Christ;' Sir Matthew Hale, 'Contemplations,' vol. i. p. 160; Owen, Works, vol. ix., 'On the Death and Satisfaction of Christ;' Rev. C. Jerram, 'Treatise on the Atonement,' pp. 27-45; Dr. Symington, 'On the Atonement,' pp. 56-65, 303-309, 328; Dr. Stevenson, 'Dissertation on the Atonement,' pp. 15-45; N. Mather, 'Righteousness of God,' p. 19; Dr. Janeway, 'Letters on the Atonement,' pp. 56, 167-200.

Note 5, p. 301.

Beart, 'Vindication of the Eternal Law,' etc., P. i. p. 41; N. Mather, 'The Righteousness of God,' p. 17. The question whether Christ suffered (*idem* or *tantundem*) the punishment of His people is discussed by Dr. Owen, 'Exercitation on Epistle to the Hebrews,' vol. ii. p. 130, vol. iii. p. 420; Brown, 'Life of Justification,' p. 443.

Note 6, p. 303.

Sir M. Hale's 'Knowledge of Christ Crucified,' Medit. vol. i. p. 162. Some divines in a former age doubted whether the Incarnation itself formed any part of the vicarious work of Christ. See Nath. Mather, 'The Righteousness of God,' pp. 11-14. On the general doctrine of the Incarnation, see Zanchius, 'De Incarnatione Filii Dei;' Dr. Owen, 'Christologia,' and 'Meditations on the Person of Christ,' vol. xii.; Rev. Marcus Dods, 'The Incarnation of the Eternal Word;' Archdeacon R. I. Wilberforce, 'The Doctrine of the Incarnation,' Second Edition, 1849; Petavius, 'De Incarnatione,' in 16 Books, Opera, vol. v. vi.; Peter Lombard, 'Sententiarum,' lib. ii.

Note 7, p. 307.

The Active and Passive Obedience of Christ. See Bishop O'Brien, 'Essays on Faith,' pp. 88-101, 432-440; Dr. Cunningham, 'Reformers,' Works, i. pp. 402-406; 'Historical Theology,' i. 54; Bishop Downham, 'Treatise,' pp. 18, 24-27, 151-159; Brown (of Wamphray), 'Life of Justification,' p. 431; Roborough, 'On Justification,' pp. vii. xiii. 24; Dr. Shedd, 'History,' ii. pp. 282, 348; Fraser, 'Life of Ebenezer Erskine,' pp. 97, 101; Young, 'Life of John Welsh,' pp. 293, 363; Dr. Tully, 'Justific. Paulina,' c. xi. p. 117; Beart, 'Vindication,' P. i. pp. 38, 40,

42, 49, 95, ii. pp. 46, 47; Hervey, Works, ii. pp. 64, 170-187, iii. 46, 47, 366.

NOTE 8, p. 308.

Robert Ferguson, 'Justification only upon a Satisfaction' (1668). Ferguson became a political partisan and intriguer in troublous times, and suffered in consequence both in his reputation and usefulness; but he was endowed with great ability, and well versed in theology, as appears from this work, and another on 'The Interest of Reason in Religion.' He is referred to both by Bishop Burnet and Lord Macaulay. See 'Essays and Reviews Examined,' p. 145. On Christ's Satisfaction, see the works mentioned in Note (8), Lect. vi. p. 459.

NOTES TO LECTURE XII.

NOTE 1, p. 317.

Wesley, 'Letter to Hervey,' Hervey's Works, vol. iv. 'Does "the righteousness of God" ever mean "the merits of Christ?" I believe not once in all the Scripture. It often means, and particularly in the Epistle to the Romans, "God's method of justifying sinners."'—P. xii. 'The "righteousness of God" signifies, the righteousness which God-man wrought out. No. It signifies "God's method of justifying sinners."'—P. xix. 'Therein is revealed "the righteousness of God,"—God's "method of justifying sinners."'—P. xx. Prof. Moses Stuart, 'Commentary on Epistle to the Romans:' 'Δικαιοσύνη Θεοῦ is the Justification which God bestows, or the Justification of which God is the Author, or . . . that state of pardon and acceptance which is the result of mercy proffered in the Gospel, and dispensed on account of the atonement made by Christ.'— P. 62. And he quotes with approbation J. A. Turretine's interpretation : 'Apostolus noster, ubi agit de justificatione et salute hominum, sæpe vocat "justitiam Dei" eam *justificationis rationem* quam Deus hominibus commonstrat;' or, 'Justitia Dei . . . est ipsamet hominis justificatio, seu *modus quo* potest justus haberi apud Deum.'—Pp. 69, 70. Dr. John Brown (Edinburgh), 'Analytical Exposition of Epistle to the Romans,' refers to Storr's 'Opuscula,' Voorst's 'Annotations' on Romans i. 17, to Zimmermann, 'De vi et sensu δικαιοσύνη Θεοῦ,' to Moses Stuart and Fritzsche ; and then gives his own view to this effect,—that δικαιοσύνη usually signifies Justification, either as a privilege bestowed by God, or as a benefit enjoyed by men—that when it is said, 'Christ is made of God unto us righteousness,' the meaning is, that we are justified. 'In the 3d chapter it exactly suits "the divine method of Justification," and it suits nothing else. I, therefore, consider "the righteousness of God" here, as meaning "God's way of treating a sinner," as if he were just in consistency with His own righteousness,—*the Divine Method of Justification.*'—Pp. 9, 10. This interpretation is far too vague to be satisfactory. The loose paraphrase of δικαιοσύνη Θεοῦ by 'the divine method of justifying sinners,' leaves the question open—What that method is? and whether it be by a personal and inherent, or by a vicarious and imputed, righteousness? whereas the Apostle specifies the righteousness by which we are justified, and contrasts it with another righteousness which is excluded. And then, when it is described as ' God's method of treating a sinner, as if he were righteous, in consistency with His own righteousness,' the statement is defective; *first*, because God's treatment of a sinner, as if he were just, must necessarily imply a righteousness which, in the case of a sinner, cannot be personal; *secondly*, because mere treatment is not all that is implied in Justification, for it presupposes a judgment by which the sinner is constituted and pronounced righteous, as the ground or reason of that treatment; and *thirdly*,.because the phrase, 'in consistency with His own righteousness,' is either altogether unmeaning, or it must refer to some provision, such as the satisfaction and vicarious obedience of Christ, by which God is 'declared to be just, and the justifier of him that believeth in Jesus.'

Note 2, p. 322.

Prof. M. Stuart, 'Commentary on Epistle to the Romans,' pp. 575, 581, 584.

Note 3, p. 326.

Dr. Owen, Works, xi. pp. 209-216 ; ' Princeton Theological Essays,' First Series, three excellent papers on ' Imputation,' Essays vi. vii. viii. pp. 128-217; Dr. Boardman (Philadelphia) on ' Original Sin,' p. 52.

Note 4, p. 327.

Antinomian misrepresentations of the Protestant doctrine have been made the ground of Popish, Socinian, and Neonomian objections against it. Bishop Downham, ' Treatise,' pp. 25-40, 245 ; Bishop Davenant, ' Disputations,' i. pp. 176-193; Brown, 'Life of Justification,' pp. 38-57, 188-214, 226, 242, 506 ; Roborough, ' The Doctrine of Justification,' P. i. p. 45, P. ii. pp. 1-50; Dr. Prideaux, ' Lecs. Decem,' pp. 162, 171 ; Dickinson, ' Fam. Letters,' pp. 185-200 ; Knox, ' Remains,' iii. 160 ; Beart, ' Vindication,' P. i. 66, 73; Luther on Epistle to the Galatians, p. 207 ; Hervey, Works, ii. 130, 240, iii. 53, 57.

Note 5, p. 329.

Placæus advocated the doctrine of a ' mediate ' imputation in the case of original sin ; and was followed by Stapfer. The doctrine of a 'mediate' imputation in the case of Christ's righteousness, is involved in the Popish and Neonomian scheme of Justification ; and in the former there is even a ' mediate ' imputation of Christ's *passive obedience* by means of our personal sufferings or penance. This is evidently implied in the statement of Vasquez, where he says that, God's grace being supposed, 'Nos re ipsa nunc satisfacere Deo pro nostro peccato et offensa.' And then, referring both to mortal and venial sins, he adds, 'Si contritio præcederet infusionem gratiæ habitualis ex parte efficientis, non solum *satisfaceret* pro maculâ peccati condignè, sed etiam condignè *mereretur* gratiæ habitualis infusionem. . . . Ita concedimus homini justo pro suo peccato veniali condignam et perfectam *satisfactionem*, ut ea *non indigeret favore Dei condonantis peccatum*, vel aliquid illius, aut acceptantis satisfactionem, sed talis sit, ut ex naturâ suâ deleat maculam et pœnam peccati venialis.'—*Archbishop Wake, Defence,* p. 34. It may be doubted whether this is so much as a doctrine of 'mediate' imputation; since the grace of God in the infusion of righteousness only is spoken of, and no mention is made of the satisfaction of Christ.

Note 6, p. 332.

On Imputed Righteousness, see a brief but clear and forcible statement of the doctrine by Dr. Chalmers, in his preface to Mr. Russell's (of Muthil) 'Sermons;' Rev. D. Wilson, 'The Doctrine of Justification through Imputed Righteousness a Divine Doctrine,' reprinted in 1845 by a respected elder of the Free Church in Edinburgh ; Nath. Mather, 'The Righteousness of God through Faith,' Second Edition, 1718 ; Rev. T. Cole, 'The Incomprehensibleness of Imputed Righteousness for Justification by Human Reason,' 1692; Bishop O'Brien, 'Essays on Faith,' pp. 88-97, 408-415, 424-440 ; Dr. Cunningham, Works, i. pp. 404, iii. 20, 45, 51, 116 ; Witsius, Misc. Sac. ii. pp. 735, 789-791 ; Ro. Traill, 'Vindication,' Works, i. p. 310 ; Bishop Downham, 'Treatise,' pp. 15-27, 39-42, 69, 125-138, 157-171, 371, etc.; Bishop Davenant, 'Disputation,' i. pp. 163, 176, 186, 230, 236-253 ; Brown, 'Life of Justification,' 22-25, 38-57, 58-97, 98-117, 118-179, 180-247, 431-446; Roborough, 'The Doctrine of Justification,' pp. 55-58, 139, 143-160; A. Burgess, 'The True Doctrine,' 17, 20 ; Dr. John Prideaux, 'Lec. Decem,' p. 163; Dickinson, 'Familiar Letters,' pp. 181-192; Dr. Junkin, 'Treatise,' pp. 109, 309; Faber, 'Primitive Doctrine,' pp. 17-26, 126, 178, 195-197; Bishop Kaye, 'Charges,' p. 259; Dr. Owen, Works, ix. 248-254 ; Bishop Andrewes, vol. v., on Jer. xxiii. 6, pp. 116, 123, etc. etc.

Note 7, p. 334.

Wesley's 'Letter to Hervey,' Hervey's Works, vol. iv. ; Richard Watson, 'Theol. Instit.,' vol. xi. c. xxiii. pp. 172, etc.

'It has been the general opinion of Christians,' says a profound writer, 'that Christ suffered instead of sinners, and that we have remission of sins through faith in His blood-shedding; but the opinion of an imputed righteousness is far from being general, though a substitution is every whit as intelligible, and perhaps as much wanted, in one case as the other; and the same reasons that hold for the rejecting one, will equally hold for the rejecting of both. . . . There is no more absurdity in trusting wholly to Christ, than there is in trusting to Him only in part; to His atonement and righteousness, or to His atonement only.'—*Adam, Private Thoughts,* pp. 152, 174. 'As Christ was "made sin for us,"' says another distinguished ornament of the Church of England, 'so we are "made the righteousness of God in Him." But what righteousness? Our own? No, "the righteousness of God,"—radically in Him, but imputatively ours; and this is the only way whereby we are said to be made "the righteousness of God," even by the righteousness of Christ being made ours; by which we are accounted and reputed as righteous before God. These things considered, I very much wonder how any man can presume to exclude the active obedience of Christ from our Justification before God; as if what Christ did in the flesh was only of duty, not all of merit; or as if it was for Himself, and not for us. Especially, when I consider, that suffering the penalty is not what the law primarily requireth, for the law of God requires perfect obedience.'— *Bishop Beveridge, Private Thoughts,* p. 74.

Many Wesleyan Methodists, following the example of their founder, have strenuously defended the doctrine of a free remission of sin through the atoning sacrifice of Christ, and have as keenly opposed that of His imputed righteousness. They have taught with great earnestness, that 'He who knew no sin was made sin for us,' but have not been equally clear and explicit in showing, that 'we are made the righteousness of God in Him.' Much of the success of their preaching has arisen from their bold proclamation of some of the peculiar doctrines of the Gospel, such as those of original sin, in so far as it consists in inherent hereditary depravity, of the imputation of our sins to Christ as our substitute, and of His atoning sufferings and death; for these great truths have commended themselves to the hearts and consciences of many anxious inquirers, even among the rudest classes of society; and no one will doubt, what even Southey and Coleridge have admitted, that we are largely indebted to them for the preservation of vital religion in many a neglected district of our land. All this may be granted, and yet we may still maintain the fundamental importance of the doctrine of Christ's imputed righteousness. For although they refuse to admit it, and often argue keenly enough against it, this arises, in many cases, either from some misconception of its meaning, or from some sincere but groundless apprehension of its moral tendency; and we cannot doubt that some earnest souls even in the Romish Church, and not a few amongst our Wesleyan brethren, really believe all that we mean by that doctrine, when, emptied of all self-righteousness, they cast themselves down at the foot of the Cross, and trust only in the 'merits of Christ.' It has been well said, that it is safer to judge of some men from their prayers, than from their professed opinions; for some will object in controversial discussion to the doctrine which affirms the irresistible efficacy of divine grace, and yet, when they fall down on their knees, they will make use of the Psalmist's prayer, 'Create in me a clean heart, renew in me a right spirit;' and others will object to the doctrine which affirms the imputation of Christ's righteousness, and yet, when they come into the divine presence, can find no language more suitable to their case, or more expressive of their feelings, than this: 'If Thou, Lord, shouldest mark iniquity, O Lord, who shall stand? Enter not into judgment with me, for in Thy sight shall no flesh living be justified.'[1]

For this reason we can cheerfully acquiesce, and cordially concur, in the truly catholic deliverance of Dr. Owen, when, speaking of the sentiments of Calvinistic divines on this point, he says: 'They do not think nor judge, that all those are excluded from salvation who cannot apprehend, or do deny, the doctrine of the imputation of righteousness, as by them declared. But they judge that they are so, *unto whom that righteousness is not really imputed;* nor can they do otherwise, whilst they make it the foundation of all their own acceptation with God and eternal salvation. These things greatly differ. To believe the doctrine of it, or not to believe it, as thus or thus explained, is one thing; and to enjoy the thing, or not enjoy it, is another. I no way doubt, but that many men do receive more grace from God than they understand or will own, and have a greater efficacy of it in them than they will believe. Men may be really saved by that' (irresistible, efficacious) 'grace which doctrinally they do deny; and they may be justified by the imputation of that righteousness which in opinion they deny to be imputed. For the faith of it is included in that general assent which they give unto the truths of the Gospel; and such an adherence to Christ may ensue thereon, as that their mistake of the way whereby they are saved by Him, shall not deprive them of a real interest therein. And for my part, I must say, that notwithstanding all the disputes that I see and read about Justification, I do not believe but that the authors of them (if they be not Socinians throughout, denying the whole merit and satisfaction of Christ) do really trust unto the Mediator of Christ for the pardon of their sins, and for acceptance with God, and not unto their own works or obedience. Nor will I believe the contrary, until they expressly declare it.'—*Dr. Owen, Works,* xi. p. 203.

Note 8, p. 336.

Archdeacon Hare, 'Contest with Rome,' p. 31; Dr. Junkin, 'Lectures on Justification,' pp. 50-64. G. S. Faber gives 'A Barrister's Opinion,' p. 428. A professional friend has kindly supplied the following note:— 'A "fictio juris" is something quite different from a presumption. Those things are presumed which are likely to be true; but a "fictio juris" is a supposition of law that a thing is true, which is either certainly not true, or at least is as probably false as true; and it is defined by some doctors, an assumption of falsehood for truth in a possible thing that it may have the effect of truth, in so far as is consistent with equity. Thus, in the Roman law, one was by adoption held for the son of him who

[1] Ps. cxxx. 2, cxliii. 2.

adopted, though he was not his son. . . . A "fictio juris" exists, where law, disregarding evidence and probability, holds as true what may be untrue, or what cannot possibly be true. Thus summonses narrate a complaint to the Sovereign by the real party, which might be true, but is always false; while the rules, that "the Sovereign cannot do wrong," —that "an heir is *eadem persona cum defuncto*," and that "the person of a wife is sunk in that of her husband," are examples of impossible fictions.' —*Erskine's Institutes*, B. iv. t. ii. sec. 38; *Principles*, B. iv. t. i. sec. 5, p. 178.

Note 9, p. 337.

Prof. M. Stuart, 'Commentary on the Epistle to the Romans,' and Albert Barnes, Introduction, p. xii. to 'Notes' on the same Epistle.

NOTES TO LECTURE XIII.

Note 1, p. 341.

The Socinian doctrine is referred to, Lecture VI., p. 161, and Notes.

Note 2, p. 343.

The Council of Trent rejects the meaning of the term GRACE which has been generally received by Protestants. Sess. vi. Canon xi. De Justificatione : 'Si quis dixerit, homines justificari, vel solâ imputatione Justitiæ Christi, vel solâ peccatorum remissione . . . aut etiam GRATIAM, quâ justificamur, esse tantum *favorem Dei*, anathema sit.'

Bellarmine treats of it at large, tom. iv. lib. i., 'De Gratia in genere, id est, de nomine, definitione, et partitione Gratiæ,' p. 470. Tourneley, 'Prælectiones Theol. De Gratia Christi,' 2 vols. (1725), vol. i. pp. 2, 3, 5, 7 : 'Proprie, nomine Gratiæ intelligimus *donum quod cunque*, seu beneficium supernaturale creaturæ rationale gratis concessum . . . Gratia vulgò definitur, donum supernaturale creaturæ rationali gratis à Deo concessum intuitu passionis et meritorum Christi, ordinatum ad vitam æternam,' p. 5. See Osorio, lib. v. p. 315 ; and Dens, Theologia, ii. 402, 'Quid est Gratia ? Est beneficiùm Divinum supernaturale creaturæ intellectuali gratis datum, in ordine ad salutem æternam.' See also iv. p. 39.

M. de Fontenay, 'De la Grace de Dieu,' 1787: 'La nature de la Grace consiste principalement dans l'amour de Dieu;' . . . 'l'amour, la Grace intérieure,' pp. iv. vi. Lombard treats 'De Gratia' ih lib. ii., and says, 'Gratia est duplex.'—*Dist.* 26 *a*. 'Gratia operans et co-operans. Gratia Dei prævenit voluntatem hominis.'—*Dist.* 26 *c, d.* 'Gratia præveniens voluntatem est FIDES CUM DELECTIONE.'—*Dist.* 26 *e, u.* 'Gratia principalis est bona voluntas,' etc. Petavius, 'Dogm. Theol.' tom. ii. lib. viii. c. 4, 5, 10, 11. 'Justificatio et Adoptio filiorum Dei per ipsam Spiritus Sancti substantiam communicatam nobis,' c. iv : ' Spiritus Sancti substantiam ipsam donum esse, illamque ad justos et adoptivos. Dei filios *efficiendos* divinatus effundi,' p. 457. ' Interior, sive spiritalis missio tum fit cum, . . . *Spiritualia dona,* quæ dicuntur *charismata,* tribuuntur. Præcipuum tamen, et quod *unum* propemodum communem appellationem sibi propriam facit, est *charitatis donum,*' p. 458. The χαρισματα seem to supersede the χαρις, from which alone they are derived. The subject is fully treated by M. Arnauld, in his ' Instructions sur la Grace, selon l'Ecriture, et les Peres ;' by M. Barcos, in his ' Exposition de la Foi de l'Eglise Romaine touchant la Grace ;' 'et plusieurs autres Pieces sur ce Sujet,' in a volume published at Cologne, A.D. 1700. The Jansenists held sounder views on this subject than were commonly received in the Romish Church.

Note 3, p. 349.

Archbishop Whately, ' Difficulties in the Writings of St. Paul,' Essay vi. pp. 182, 185.

Note 4, p. 351.

The proof of this point is much more fully stated by President Edwards, ' Works,' vol. vi. pp. 240-254,—an admirable specimen of moral proof.

Note 5, p. 357.

On the relation of Faith to Works, see Bishop O'Brien, ' Essays on Faith,' 140, 146, 186-194, 253-260 ; Dr. Cunningham, Works, iii. 79-84, 105, 108 ; Witsius, ' Misc. Sac.' ii. p. 824, 840 ; Bishop Downham, ' Treatise,' pp. 48, 351, 389-395, 502 ; Bishop Davenant, ' Disput.' i. 274-283, 294-302 ; Brown, ' Life of Justification,' pp. 24, 30, 254 ; Dickinson, ' Familiar Letters,' iii. pp. 229-333, 285-306 ; Dr. Junkin on ' Justification,' pp. 317, 321 ; Dr. Owen on ' True Gospel Holiness,' Works, iii. p. 75.

Note 6, p. 359.

Osorio, Bellarmine, Wesley, Whately, M. Stuart, and many others, have agreed in setting aside the latter part of Romans vii. 14-end, as a proof of remaining sin in believers. On this subject, see Bishop Downham, ' Treatise,' pp. 137-157, 249, 255, 454, 463 ; Bishop Davenant, ' Disput.' pp. 20, 50, 56, 83, 104-111, 286, 330-340, 373 ; ii. 7-28, 209-215 ; Brown, ' Life of Justification,' pp. 273 ; Dr. Burgess, ' The True Doctrine,' pp. 23, 58-79, 111, 139 ; Dickinson, ' Familiar Letters,' pp. 130, 142; Dr. Shedd, ' History,' ii. 69 ; G. S. Faber, ' Primitive Doctrine,' pp. 271-286 ; Bossuet, ' Exposition,' p. 13. See Dr. Owen's Treatises on ' Indwelling Sin,' and ' The Mortification of Sin in Believers,' Works, vol. xiii. ; Carmichael, ' The Believer's Mortification of Sin by the Spirit,' edited by the late Dr. W. K. Tweedie, Free Tolbooth Church, Edinburgh (1846); and Fraser (of Alness) on ' Sanctification.'

Those who have laboured to show that the passage in Rom. vii. 14-25 does not relate to the experience of Paul as a converted man, seem to have forgotten that the doctrine of indwelling sin does not rest on that passage alone, but is declared in general terms in Gal. v. 17 : ' The flesh lusteth against the Spirit, and the Spirit against the flesh ; and these are contrary the one to the other, so that ye cannot do the things that ye would.' The doctrine generally received among Protestants is, that the prevailing power of sin is broken, but its presence is not excluded, by the new birth of the soul : its dominion is taken away, but its influence is still felt, throughout the whole course of a believer's life on earth. This important practical truth is manifest from the Apostle's experience, as it is recorded in the latter part of the seventh chapter of his Epistle to the Romans, where he says,—as every true believer since his days has had occasion to say (Rom. vii. 14-25),—' That which I do I allow not : for what I would, that do I not ; but what I hate, that I do.' ' To will is present with me; but how to perform that which is good I find not. For the good that I would I do not : but the evil which I would not, that I do.' ' I find then a law, that, when I would do good, evil is present with me.' ' I see a law in my members warring against the law of my mind, and bringing me into captivity to the law of sin which is in my members.' Many strenuous attempts have been made to show that in this passage the Apostle is not speaking of his own experience as a believer, but is personating an unrenewed man, or a sinner awakened for the first time to a sense of the corruption of his nature. But the experience of a sinner under his first convictions is vividly delineated in the preceding verses, where he says, ' I was alive without the law once ; but when the commandment came, sin revived, and I died ;'[1] and the subsequent verses contain expressions which cannot be applied to the case of any unrenewed man, consistently with the doctrine of Scripture, that ' the carnal mind is enmity against God, for it is not subject to the law of God, neither indeed can be.' For how can any man whose carnal mind is ' enmity against God, and not subject to the law of God,' be supposed, without a great intervening change, to express himself thus : ' I consent to the law, that it is good,'—' I delight in the law of God after the inward man,'—it is ' the law of my mind,'—and, ' With my mind I serve the law of God ?' Is this the language of unrenewed nature, in which ' there dwelleth no good thing ;' and if it be, why was Pelagianism denounced by Augustine, and rejected by the Church, as an unscriptural and dangerous perversion of God's revealed truth ?

Note 7, p. 363.

The Christian community is much indebted to two elders of the Free Church—the late Mr. John Johnstone, for a new edition of Dr. Owen's Works, carefully edited by the Rev. Dr. Goold ; and to the late Mr. Nichol, for his excellent Series of the ' Puritan Divines,' published at a

[1] Rom. vii. 7-13.

price which makes them accessible to every Pastor and Preacher who is really interested in the study of divine truth.

NOTE 8, p. 364.

The *title* to eternal life depends entirely on the mediatorial work of Christ; the '*meetness* for the inheritance of the saints in light' is equally necessary, and depends on the renewal of our nature by the inward work of the Holy Spirit. See *infra*, Lec. xv.

NOTES TO LECTURE XIV.

NOTE 1, p. 367.

See *supra*, Lec. iv. Note (1), and *infra*, Lec. xv. John Foxe, 'Free Justification by Christ,' in reply to Osorio, 'De Justitia,' pp. 223-228.

NOTE 2, p. 370.

Dr. Tuckney (of Cambridge), 'Prælectiones Theologicæ,' p. 79; on Rom. i. 17, pp. 20-161; on Rom. iv. 1, pp. 177-196; on Rom. iv. 3, pp. 196-312. A solid and learned work, which,—like those of Dr. Owen, Dr. T. Goodwin, and Mr. Pemble,—shows what the Theology of the English Universities once was, and what it might yet become, were suitable men appointed to conduct a course of systematic study, and were candidates for the ministry required to give regular attendance on their Lectures and Examinations.

NOTE 3, p. 373.

Dickinson, 'Familiar Letters,' pp. 203-206; Bishop O'Brien, 'Essays on Faith,' pp. 445, 465-471.

NOTE 4, p. 376.

Works on Saving Faith are innumerable. The following may be mentioned:—Dr. T. Goodwin, 'The Object and Acts of Faith,' Works, vol. viii.; Dr. T. Jackson (of Oxford), 'Justifying Faith, or the Faith by which the Just do Live' (1631), 2d Edition; John Downe, B.D. (of Cambridge), 'Treatise of the True Nature and Definition of Justifying Faith,' Oxford, 1635; John Ball, 'A Treatise of Faith, in Two Parts—the Nature and the Life of Faith,' 1632; Polhill on 'Precious Faith;' James Fraser (of Brae), 'A Treatise on Justifying Faith,' 1749; Rutherford's 'Trial and Triumph of Faith;' Rev. Andrew Gray, 'The Mystery of Faith,' 1755; Dr. John Erskine, 'Dissertation on the Nature of Justification;' Rev. W. Romaine, 'Treatises on the Life, Walk, and Triumph of Faith,' 2 vols., 1824, with Essay by Dr. Chalmers; Henry Grove, 'A Discourse concerning Saving Faith,' 1736; 'Saving Faith: a Series of

Works by Dr. John Anderson, U.S., Rev. Ebenezer Erskine, and Rev. William Cudworth,' Edinburgh, 1843 ; Dr. James Carlile (of Dublin), 'The Old Doctrine of Faith,' 1823 ; Rev. William Burgh, 'Six Discourses on the Nature and Influence of Faith,' Dublin, 1835 ; Bishop O'Brien, 'Essays on the Nature and Effects of Faith,' 2d Edition ; Mr. T. Erskine (Linlathen), 'Essay on Faith ;' Rev. A. M'Lean, Works, i. 186, ii. 96-146, etc. etc.

Note 5, p. 379.

On the assurance which is involved in the direct act of Faith, see Lec. vi. p. 185, and the Note.

On the assurance which springs from the reflex exercise of Faith, see Boston's 'Marks of True Conversion,' appended to 'The Covenant of Grace ;' Guthrie's 'Trial of a Saving Interest in Christ.' 'Effectual calling,' says Archbishop Leighton, ' is inseparably tied to eternal *fore-knowledge* or *election* on the one side, and *salvation* on the other. These two links of the chain are up in heaven, in God's own hand ; but this middle one is let down to earth, into the hearts of His children ; and they, laying hold of it, have sure hold on the other two, for no power can sever them. If, therefore, they can read the characters of God's image in their own souls, those are the counterpart of the golden characters of His love, in which their names are written in the book of life. Their believing writes their names under the promises of the revealed book of life, the Scriptures; and so ascertains them, that the same names are in the secret book of life, that God hath by Himself from eternity. So, finding the stream of grace in their hearts, though they see not the fountain whence it flows, nor the ocean into which it returns, yet they know that it hath its source, and shall return to that ocean which ariseth from their eternal election, and shall empty itself into that eternity of happiness and salvation.'—*Commentary on First Epistle of Peter,* on c. i. v. 2d, p. 14.

Note 6, p. 379.

The Antinomian view of the function of faith as a mere evidence or manifestation, and not a means, of Justification, is refuted by Dr. Burgess, 'The True Doctrine,' pp. 189-215 ; Beart, 'Vindication,' P. ii. iv.-viii. Pref. ; Nath. Mather, 'The Righteousness of God,' p. 78 ; see Lec. vi., Antinomians, and Note.

Note 7, p. 380.

On the term ' Condition,' see Dr. Cunningham, 'Historical Theology,' ii. 74, 76 ; Dr. John Edwards' 'Survey of Dispensations,' i. pp. 368, 375; Barrett on 'The Covenants,' pp. 135-143, 183 ; Witsius, 'Misc. Sacra,' ii. pp. 742, 743, 801-804, 820, 821, 843 ; Bishop Downham, 'Treatise,' pp. 306, 307, 331, 372 ; Brown, 'Life of Justification,' pp. 20, 341-350; Dickinson, 'Fam. Letters,' p. 249 ; Fraser, 'Life of Ebenezer Erskine,' p. 235 ; M'Crie's 'Life of Dr. M'Crie,' pp. 333, 334; Dr. M'Crie on

'Marrow Controversy,' Christ. Instructor, xxx. pp. 542, 692 ; Faber, 'Primitive Doctrine,' pp. 72-80; Hickman, 'Animadversions,' pp. 355, 457 ; Walker (Dublin), 'Seven Letters to Alex. Knox, Esq.,' pp. 312, 313 ; Rev. J. Taylor, 'Establishment of the Law,' p. 37 ; Beart, 'Vindication,' Pref. xviii. xix. xxv.; Hervey, 'Works,' iv. pp. 124-128 ; Wesley's 'Letter to Hervey,' Hervey's Works, iv. x. xiv. xv., Hervey iv. pp. 63, 172-175.

NOTE 8, p. 381.

On the Reason and Warrant of Faith, see Owen, 'The Reason of Faith,' Works, iii. p. 233 ; Halyburton, 'Works,' edited by Dr. Burns, reprinted 1865 ; 'An Essay on the Ground and Formal Reason of Saving Faith,' pp. 3-87 ; Boston, 'Warrant of Faith,' appended to 'Covenant of Grace ;' 'Sum of Saving Knowledge,' appended to 'Westminster Confession of Faith,' p. 435.

NOTE 9, p. 385.

On the phrase 'by faith only,' see Bishop O'Brien, 'Essays on Faith,' pp. 99-105, 117-123, 138, 474 ; Dr. Cunningham, 'Works,' i. 146, iii. 23, 56, 61, 69, 72, 77; Bishop Downham, pp. 15, 179, 327-331, 366, 442, 494; Bishop Davenant's 'Disput.' i. pp. 313, 314 ; Bishop Barlow, 'Remains,' p. 601 ; Brown, 'Life of Justification,' pp. 417, 422; Dr. John Prideaux, 'Lectiones Decem,' pp. 155, 157, 168; Faber, 'Primitive Doctrine,' pp. 72-80, 228, 229 ; Scott, 'Continuation of Milner,' i. pp. 84, 98, 99, 238, 254, 264, ii. 235, 271, 272, 357; Bishop Kaye, 'Charges,' p. 263, etc. etc.

A recent work by the Rev. R. F. Collis, Rector of Kilconnel (Dublin 1856),—entitled 'The Three Tribunals, or the Vicarious Justification of Sinners in Christ,'—attacks the Lutheran doctrine of 'Justification by Faith only' as being unscriptural, and the last clause of the 11th Article of the Church of England, with the homily on salvation to which it refers, as containing that doctrine, pp. x. xi. 105, 109, 122, 124, 131, 169. It contains an elaborate and unfavourable criticism on Bishop O'Brien's 'Sermons on Faith' (1st Edition), pp. 110-168,—which evidently proceeds on the supposition that the Bishop substitutes faith for the righteousness of Christ, as the ground of our acceptance with God. But although one or two expressions in his 'Sermons' might possibly bear such an interpretation, the general tenor of his reasoning points to the satisfaction of Christ as the ground, and to Faith merely as the means or instrument, of Justification. Mr. Collis speaks of three Tribunals,—that of God's holiness and justice,—that of man's conscience and experience,—and that of the final judgment; and of three corresponding aspects of Justification,— that of our justification at the bar of God's holiness and justice, where neither faith nor repentance has any place, but only the vicarious righteousness of Christ; that of our justification *in foro conscientiæ*, where faith, but not faith only,—since it must be a living and not a dead faith, such as is associated with all other graces,—is the evidence of Justification ; and that of our Justification at the judgment of the great day, where neither faith nor repentance, but good works, will be the evidence. He does not speak of more than one Justification, but merely of its different aspects ; but his three distinctions may all be reduced to that between *actual* and *declarative* justification, unless his theory of the ' Vicarious Justification in Christ of believers,' should be intended to refer, not to their actual justification in time, but their justification merely on the eternal purpose of God, in which case faith can only be an evidence, and not in any sense a means, of their enjoying that privilege. The aged Rector promises another work, which may probably make his doctrine more complete ; at present, he seems to confound Election with Justification, and to make faith a mere manifestation, and not a means, of our acceptance with God.   See Note 5, Appendix, p. 509.

NOTES TO LECTURE XV.

Note 1, p. 389.

'Christianity,' says Bishop Butler, ' contains a revelation of a particular dispensation of Providence, carrying on by His Son and Spirit, for the recovery and salvation of mankind, who are represented in Scripture to be in a state of ruin.   And, in consequence of this revelation being made, we are commanded to be " baptized," not only " in the name of the Father," but also " of the Son, and of the Holy Ghost ;" and other obligations of duty, unknown before, to the Son and the Holy Ghost, are revealed. Now, the importance of these *duties* may be judged of, by observing that they arise, not from positive command merely, but also from the *offices* which appear from Scripture to belong to these Divine Persons in the Gospel dispensation, or from the *relations* which, we are there informed, they stand in to us.   By reason is revealed the relation which God stands in to us.   Hence arises the obligation of duty which we owe to Him.   In Scripture are revealed the relations which the Son and Holy Spirit stand in to us.   Hence arise the obligations of duty which we are under to them.'—*Analogy*, P. ii. c. i. p. 321.   See also Dr. Waterland, ' The Importance of the Doctrine of the Trinity,' *passim*.

Note 2, p. 392.

Dr. Thomas Goodwin has distinct treatises on the work of the Father, of the Son, and of the Holy Spirit, in the scheme of Redemption ; see vols. iv. v.

Note 3, p. 397.

Dr. Thomas Goodwin, ' The Work of the Holy Ghost in our Salvation,' Works, vol. v. ; Dr. Owen, 'Discourse concerning the Holy Spirit,' Works, vols. ii. iii. (Russell's edition); Dr. Jamieson, 'Reality of the Spirit's Influence ;' Howe, 'The Work of the Holy Spirit with reference to particular Persons ;' Archdeacon Hare, 'Mission of the Comforter ;' and M'Laurin's 'Essay on Divine Grace,' vol. ii., and 'Sermon,' vol. i.

NOTE 4, p. 399.

Dr Heurtley's 'Bampton Lectures,' *passim*, and his previous work on 'Union to Christ;' Dickinson, 'Familiar Letters,' pp. 311-334, 'The Nature and Necessity of our Union to Christ.'

NOTE 5, p. 402.

Dr. Samuel Çlarke, 'Discourse of the Being and Attributes of God,' p. 39. Dr. Clarke strikes at the root of the Antinomian error, when, speaking of 'the manner of our conceiving the eternity of God,' he says, 'The scholastic writers have generally described it to be, not a real perpetual duration, but *one point or instant comprehending eternity*, and wherein *all things are really co-existent at once*. But unintelligible ways of speaking have, I think, never done any service to religion. The true notion of the divine eternity does not consist in making past things to be still present, and things future to be already come (which is an express contradiction). But it consists in this, and in this it infinitely transcends the manner of existence of all created beings, even of those which shall continue for ever,—that, whereas their finite minds can by no means comprehend all that is past, or understand perfectly the things that are present, much less know, or have in their power, the things that are to come,—but their thoughts and knowledge and power must of necessity have degrees and periods, and be successive and transient as the things themselves,—the Eternal, Supreme Cause, on the contrary, has such a perfect, independent, and unchangeable comprehension of all things, that in every point or instant of *His* eternal duration, all things, past, present, and to come, must be,—not, indeed, themselves present at once (for that is a manifest contradiction); but they must be as entirely known and represented to Him in one single thought and view, and all things present and future be as absolutely under His power and direction, as if there was really no succession at all, and as if all things had been,—not that they really *are*,—actually present at once.'—*Ser.* i. p. 81.

NOTE 6, p. 404.

'A Modest Enquiry: Whether Regeneration or Justification has the precedency in order of Nature,' by Professor Halyburton, 'Works,' edited by Dr. Burns, pp. 547-558, reprinted in 1865, along with 'The Reason of Faith,' etc., pp. 9-118.

NOTES TO CONCLUSION.

NOTE 1, p. 408.

Reinhard published a striking work on this subject, from which copious extracts are given in the Appendix to the late Dr. Morren's 'Biblical Theology.' See also Brown, 'Life of Justification,' c. vi. p. 34 ; 'What Mysteries are in Justification ;' Dr. Shuttleworth, 'Consistency of Revelation with itself and Human Reason,' pp. 223-250.

NOTE 2, p. 410.

Charles Hodge, D.D., 'Essays and Reviews' (1857), pp. 575, 581.

NOTE 3, p. 411.

Le Blanc's 'Theses Theolog.,' pp. 248-316; Curcellæus, 'Quaternio,' Diss. iv. p. 463 ; Dr. Pusey, 'Eirenicon,' p. 19.

INDEX TO THE LECTURES ONLY.

For the Appendix, see the Numerals inserted in each Lecture, which refer to corresponding Notes.

2 K

OTHER RELATED SGCB TITLES

In addition to *The Doctrine of Justification* by Buchanan we are honored to offer the following related titles:

Notes on Galatians by J. Gresham Machen is a reprint that is long overdue, especially in light of the present-day battle of the doctrine articulated in Galatians.

Opening Scripture: A Hermeneutical Manual by Patrick Fairbairn is a favorite volume of Sinclair Ferguson. Once again you will find help in these long-buried pages to combat many errors in today's church.

Biblical and Theological Studies by the professors of Princeton Seminary in 1912, at the centenary celebration of the Seminary. Articles are by men like Allis, Vos, Warfield, Machen, Wilson and others.

Theology on Fire: Vols. 1 & 2 by Joseph A. Alexander is the two volumes of sermons by this brilliant scholar from Princeton Seminary.

A Shepherd's Heart by James W. Alexander is a volume of outstanding expository sermons from the pastoral ministry of one of the leading preachers of the 19th century.

Evangelical Truth by Archibald Alexander is a volume of practical sermons intended to be used for Family Worship.

The Lord of Glory by Benjamin B. Warfield is one of the best treatments of the doctrine of the Deity of Christ ever written. Warfield is simply masterful.

The Power of God unto Salvation by Benjamin B. Warfield is the first book of sermons ever published of this master-theologian. Several of these are found no where else.

Mourning a Beloved Shepherd by Charles Hodge and John Hall is a little volume containing the funeral addresses for James W. Alexander. Very informative and challenging.

Call us Toll Free at 1-877-666-9469
Send us an e-mail at sgcb@charter.net
Visit us on line at solid-ground-books.com

John Eadie Titles

Solid Ground is delighted to announce that we have republished several volumes by John Eadie, gifted Scottish minister. The following are in print:

Commentary on the Greek Text of Paul's Letter to the Galatians
Part of the classic five-volume set that brought world-wide renown to this humble man, Eadie expounds this letter with passion and precision. In the words of Spurgeon, "This is a most careful attempt to ascertain the meaning of the Apostle by painstaking analysis of his words."

Commentary on the Greek Text of Paul's Letter to the Ephesians
Spurgeon said, "This book is one of prodigious learning and research. The author seems to have read all, in every language, that has been written on the Epistle. It is also a work of independent criticism, and casts much new light upon many passages."

Commentary on the Greek Text of Paul's Letter to the Philippians
Robert Paul Martin wrote, "Everything that John Eadie wrote is pure gold. He was simply the best exegete of his generation. His commentaries on Paul's epistles are valued highly by careful expositors. Solid Ground Christian Books has done a great service by bringing Eadie's works back into print."

Commentary on the Greek Text of Paul's Letter to the Colossians
According to the New Schaff-Herzog Encyclopedia of Religious Knowledge, "These commentaries of John Eadie are marked by candor and clearness as well as by an evangelical unction not common in works of the kind." Spurgeon said, "Very full and reliable. A work of utmost value."

Commentary on the Greek Text of Paul's Letters to the Thessalonians
Published posthumously, this volume completes the series that has been highly acclaimed for more than a century. Invaluable.

Paul the Preacher: A Popular and Practical Exposition of His Discourses and Speeches as Recorded in the Acts of the Apostles
Very rare volume intended for a more popular audience, this volume begins with Saul's conversion and ends with Paul preaching the Gospel of the Kingdom in Rome. It perfectly fills in the gaps in the commentaries. Outstanding work!

DIVINE LOVE: A Series of Doctrinal, Practical and Experimental Discourses
Buried over a hundred years, this volume consists of a dozen complete sermons from Eadie's the pastoral ministry. "John Eadie, the respected nineteenth-century Scottish Secession minister-theologian, takes the reader on an edifying journey through this vital biblical theme." - Ligon Duncan

Lectures on the Bible to the Young for Their Instruction and Excitement
"Though written for the rising generation, these plain addresses are not meant for mere children. Simplicity has, indeed, been aimed at in their style and arrangement, in order to adapt them to a class of young readers whose minds have already enjoyed some previous training and discipline." – Author's Preface

Printed in the United States
74706LV00004B/12

9 781599 250731